THE EARLY EVANGELICALS:
A Religious and Social Study

THE
EARLY EVANGELICALS:
A RELIGIOUS AND SOCIAL STUDY

By
L. E. ELLIOTT-BINNS, D.D.

WIPF & STOCK · Eugene, Oregon

Wipf and Stock Publishers
199 W 8th Ave, Suite 3
Eugene, OR 97401

The Early Evangelicals
A Religious and Social Study
By Elliott-Binns, Leonard Elliott
Copyright©1953 James Clarke Lutterworth Press
ISBN 13: 978-1-5326-7708-3
Publication date 12/6/2018
Previously published by Lutterworth, 1953

PREFACE

A WRITER in *The Times Literary Supplement* for June 26, 1948, stated that "the history of the Evangelical revival in the Church of England has yet to be written". Although it is now more than two centuries since that movement arose, no account of it on any considerable scale has yet appeared. The present volume is an attempt, so far as the first half-century or so is concerned,[1] to supply this lack.

My task has been made lighter through the appearance, in recent years, of a number of sectional studies, such as Canon C. H. Smyth, *Simeon and Church Order*, and G. C. B. Davies, *The Early Cornish Evangelicals*. Furthermore, we are now able to see the eighteenth century in clearer perspective, thanks to the lapse of time and the work of historians such as Professor Norman Sykes and others.

I have described the volume as "a religious and social study" for two reasons. In the first place, because the revival was much more than is commonly realized the result of social conditions, and itself had an effect upon them; and, secondly, because the writings of those who took part in it throw an interesting light on such conditions and have not been greatly utilized by secular historians of the period, many of whom, indeed, are probably unaware of their existence.

As in the case of *Religion in the Victorian Era*, I have made an extensive use of contemporary biographies. But biographies of eighteenth-century ecclesiastics, if they are not to mislead us, must be used with great caution. Some of them reach a high standard of accuracy, but many are the work of pious admirers, lacking in critical ability and with no apparent desire to verify their statements. They are, in addition, often swayed by prejudices of one kind or another.

No bibliography has been provided, as a complete list, in view of the great variety of subjects and persons dealt with, would have swollen to vast proportions. References, however, will be found to the necessary literature in the footnotes.

I have to thank various incumbents, too numerous to mention by name, who have supplied me with information concerning their several parishes.

L. E. ELLIOTT-BINNS.

[1] In a number of cases I have strayed beyond the strict limits of my period (which ends at 1789), where light is thrown back on ideas and conditions then prevailing; especially have I availed myself of the very revealing journals of Henry Martyn

ABBREVIATIONS

In the eighteenth century, as in earlier days, it was customary to provide books with elaborate titles; some, indeed, almost perform the office of the modern "blurb". In my references I have not scrupled to condense these, for if the name of the author and a shortened title are given they are sufficient direction to the volume. References to the following works have been still further abbreviated (owing to my frequent citation of them), and they require amplification:

ABBEY AND OVERTON: C. J. Abbey and J. H. Overton, *The English Church in the Eighteenth Century* (1878);

COUNTESS OF HUNTINGDON: *The Life and Times of Selina, Countess of Huntingdon*, by a Member of the Houses of Shirley and Hastings (A. C. H. Seymour) (1839–40);

STEPHEN, *Ford Lectures*: Leslie Stephen, *English Literature and Society in the Eighteenth Century* (1904);

SYKES: Norman Sykes, *Church and State in England in the Eighteenth Century* (1934);

VENN FAMILY ANNALS: *Annals of a Clerical Family: being some account of the family and descendants of William Venn, Vicar of Otterton, Devon, 1600–1621*, by John Venn, Fellow and President of Gonville and Caius College, Cambridge (1904);

WESLEY: *Journal*, Edited by N. Curnock (1909–16);

WESLEY: *Letters*, Edited by J. Telford (1931).

CONTENTS

CHAP.		PAGE
	PREFACE	5
	ABBREVIATIONS	7
1	INTRODUCTION	11
2	POLITICAL CONDITIONS	23
3	SOCIAL AND ECONOMIC CONDITIONS	34
4	THE INTELLECTUAL AND EDUCATIONAL BACKGROUND	56
5	LITERATURE AND ART	72
6	RELIGION IN THE EARLY EIGHTEENTH CENTURY	85
7	REVIVAL MOVEMENTS: LADY HUNTINGDON	116
8	THE PIONEERS	143
9	DEVELOPMENT IN A CHANGING WORLD	170
10	THE GROWTH OF OPPOSITION	183
11	THE CALVINIST CONTROVERSY	196
12	THE SEPARATIONS	208
13	LOCAL EXPANSION: LONDON	234
14	THE SOUTH-EASTERN COUNTIES	248
15	THE EASTERN COUNTIES	268
16	THE MIDLANDS	290
17	THE NORTH	306
18	THE WEST	330
19	EVANGELICALISM IN THE UNIVERSITIES	353
20	EVANGELICAL METHODS	366
21	EVANGELICAL DOCTRINES	382
22	THE LITERATURE OF THE MOVEMENT	396
23	THE EVANGELICAL ACHIEVEMENT	418
24	THE POSITION AT 1789	446
	INDEX	458

CHAPTER I

INTRODUCTION

BARON VON HÜGEL has said that "Man's spirit [does not] live all aloof from man's body or from this physical body's physical environment."[1] Religion, in other words, is no isolated department of life, and as a consequence the various forms it assumes are profoundly affected by the surroundings in which they arise and have their development. This factor is seldom recognized, save by scholars, and even the gospel writers, with the significant exception of St. Luke, took no account of the political setting in which Christianity was first proclaimed. It is only in comparatively recent years that there has been any adequate conception of the effects upon the Church of the conditions amidst which it functions.[2]

Englishmen are by nature politically minded,[3] and the various forms which religion has assumed among them have been influenced by this circumstance, and that not least in the eighteenth century, when, as Professor Sykes has pointed out,

> The Georgian Church corresponded well with the unreformed parliament and with the régime of privilege and patronage in the civil administration.[4]

Nor is it altogether a fantastic notion to see in Deism a transference to the heavenly sphere of the current political conception of a limited monarchy. Even the revival movements of the century may have owed more to political considerations than has generally been suspected. The fact, for example, that the greater part of the population had no say in the conduct of mundane affairs and little influence on life around them, may have made them more responsive to a Gospel which was grounded on an other-worldly appeal.

[1] *Essays and Addresses on the Philosophy of Religion*, i, p. 58

[2] Cf. W. Temple in *Foundations*, p. 357: "It is the fact that we are members both of the Church and of our half-pagan nations which makes our Christianity and the Church's work so ineffective"

[3] "Elsewhere the defenders of a system may merely become a *school*. In England, because by constitution we are politicians and not systematizers, they must form a *party*. The moment we have adopted a peculiar theory, we begin to organize." F. D. Maurice, *The Kingdom of Christ*, ii, p. 317

[4] *Church and State in England*, etc., p. 330

This being so, any study of the Evangelical Movement must take account of the circumstances of the times, be they political, social, economic, or intellectual. Our inquiry must be firmly set in its environment. Even more important is the general condition of religion when the movement originated; nor must we neglect earlier events, such as the Restoration of 1660 and the Revolution of 1689, which had repercussions on the religious life of the nation; for the one led to the suppression of Puritan influences, and the other to the withdrawal of the Non-jurors. The controversies of the early eighteenth century also demand notice, for they helped to create an atmosphere, arid and rational, from which a recoil was bound to come.

Humanity, in spite of superficial differences, is much the same in all ages; for man's general disposition does not change. Moreover, his various attributes are but raw material which may become either vices or virtues in response to conditions around him and his attempts to adjust himself to them. The bodily and mental environment gives a framework to life and thought, exercising a control and restraint by innumerable conventions and traditions. In the eighteenth century even those who were genuinely religious submitted without any questioning to prevalent ideas. This has been well brought out by Ruskin, who contrasts the attitude of the Venetians, in the matter of portraits, with that of Englishmen.

> An English gentleman, desiring his portrait, gives probably to the painter a choice of several actions, in any of which he is willing to be represented. As for instance, riding his best horse, shooting with his favourite pointer, manifesting himself in his robes of state on some great public occasion, meditating in his study, playing with his children, or visiting his tenants; in any of these or other such circumstances, he will give the artist free leave to paint him. But in one important action he would shrink even from the suggestion of being drawn. He will assuredly not let himself be painted praying. Strangely, this is the action which, of all others, a Venetian desires to be painted in. If they want a noble and complete portrait, they nearly all choose to be painted on their knees.[1]

---

[1] *Modern Painters*, Pt. IX, chap. iii, § 15

INTRODUCTION

Now we may take it as certain that men like Wilberforce or Henry Thornton were as sincere in their religion and as entirely unashamed of it as any Venetian merchant prince; yet an attitude which revealed and reflected the deepest aspect of their lives was studiously avoided in such instances; simply because it was against the conventional habits of the day, and would have been regarded as a piece of ostentatious hypocrisy.

In considering a distant epoch, such as that of Greece and Rome, or even one nearer at hand, such as that of the Tudors, we are so fully aware of the differences between their manner of life and thought and our own, to allow for them. But this does not apply to the eighteenth century, which, on the surface, and apart from the immense effects of modern inventions, is not too unlike the age in which we are living. We seem to breathe the same air; the names of both places and persons are tolerably familiar; the clothes they wore are not too dissimilar; the houses in which they lived follow much the same plan, many of them, indeed, after being "improved", are still inhabited; we can read their writings with as great an ease as those of the Victorians or of our contemporaries. But these facts must not blind us to the presence of fundamental and most significant distinctions. In small matters as well as in great, many of the presuppositions of those who delivered the Evangelical message and those who heard it were very different from our own.

The revival movement of the eighteenth century made its primary appeal to the emotions, and in the early days its adherents were drawn mainly from the poorer classes; it was by slow stages only that it penetrated the higher ranges of society. One reason for its rapid spread among the common folk was that it brought a new interest into lives which were monotonous and shut off from rival interests. Not only had the common people no share in politics, but, owing to defective means of communication and the absence of such things as cinemas and the less noxious "wireless", they had few opportunities for amusement, even had they possessed the necessary leisure. There was, moreover, no national system of education, and few were able to read or write. Thus religion had an "entertainment" value with hardly any competitors.

To-day all that is changed, and the message of the Gospel has to make its appeal in the face of many rival attractions. Politics, for example, now provide a strong interest for the more thoughtful. Men who in the eighteenth century would have been impassioned lay-preachers now find a vent for their oratorical talents along more mundane channels, such as fervently haranguing groups of unofficial strikers. They often constitute, it may be remarked, as big a problem to responsible trade union leaders, as did their predecessors to the parochial clergy of their day, and even to Wesley himself. So, too, opportunities for amusement and pleasure are now so abundant as to be limited only by the ability to afford them. The spread of literacy enables many to occupy their minds, if they are of a serious disposition, and also lays them open to influences hostile to religion. The whole trend of modern development has been in a materialistic direction. There are, it is true, those, and their number is perhaps greater than is generally assumed, who long for some stable foundation for their lives and some clue to the meaning of things; there may even be a desire for "salvation", but that, as a rule, is not from "sin", but from insecurity and material evils such as war. Even among many higher and nobler spirits there is a tendency to reject the Christian explanation and to seek satisfaction in other quarters. Thus on the intellectual plane the Church's task is infinitely more arduous than in the eighteenth century, and Christian thinkers and writers endeavour to restate the faith in such a way as not merely to appeal to the emotions, though these are still, and must remain, fundamental as an approach to religion; but, by removing stumbling-blocks, real or imaginary, to commend it to the educated and to those who possess inadequate ideas of its meaning and content.

Another factor has also to be taken into consideration—the loss of clerical authority. In the eighteenth century the parson, in conjunction with the squire, was the centre of village life, and England then was overwhelmingly rural. He was often the only educated person with whom the people ever came into contact, and they naturally looked to him for guidance. Moreover, it was to the parson that they turned in times of need. Now all that is changed, and the centre of village life is often the schoolmaster, whilst other functions, once exercised by the clergy, have been taken over by a host of government and local officials.

But it is not the authority of the clergy alone which has diminished. In things intellectual and spiritual there has been a general revolt from all authority. In the eighteenth century the rebels and eccentrics were those who broke step and rejected the accepted conventions of the day; now it might almost seem that the eccentrics are those who still maintain their loyalty, though in a modified form, to ancient forms of belief and the ideals of their fathers.

In view of the immense differences in outlook between our own day and that of the eighteenth century, and of the vast complexities of modern life, it might seem that a study of the Evangelical Movement has a merely academic and antiquarian interest, and is devoid of practical value for religion to-day. But this is far from the case. The differences are only superficial, and, underneath the surface, men and women have the same needs and longings. As Christians we believe that in one way only can they be satisfied.

Apart, however, from any lessons which we may learn from a journey into the past, to breathe for the moment the air of an age other than our own has a renewing quality (even if it arouses regret); for it provides a challenge to our way of life, and may even be a corrective of our ways of thought. The eighteenth century, without any doubt, furnishes us with warnings and examples. It reveals, perhaps more than the present, the depths to which men can sink who repudiate the claims of religion and morality, and at the same time it throws a vivid light on our failure to profit by the hardships and misfortunes which come upon us. Then England was raised from a shameful and dissolute condition by the sobering effect of a great war and by the sense of national danger. We ourselves have behind us two great wars, and we have to confess that any chastening effect they have had on the nation at large has been but temporary, and their impact upon religion, apart from haphazard recognitions, far from beneficial.

For those upon whom God has placed the heavy burden of leadership in His Church in these disquieting days there are profound and salutary lessons to be learned from our study. Canon Smyth has stated that "the history of the Evangelical Revival is essentially a history of personalities rather than of opinions".[1] This is well said, and it is from a consideration of the lives of these personalities that we shall glean the greatest harvest. They were men for whom life and existence had a seriousness and significance which seems lacking to-day. They saw all things in the light of eternity, with man's destiny ever at stake. We, with our materialistic and limited outlook, are in danger of ignoring the "supernatural" element in our faith, and of degrading Christianity into a kind of religious philosophy

[1] *Simeon and Church Order*, p. 6

lacking in vital inspiration and power. Their consequent insistence on man's need for redemption and definite conversion again needs emphasizing. Such was the opinion of Dr. Figgis, who, in 1917, made the noteworthy admission that "The Tractarian Movement went too far in its reaction from the crude language and excited appeals 'to be saved' of the Evangelicals".[1] To-day we have lost the sense of "sin", and even the most respectable of men are more likely to be ashamed, not by the recollection of their sins, but of their follies. The remembrance of a foolish or unseemly action or utterance is a recurring sting; a sin is often passed over as something regrettable no doubt, but hardly to be avoided.

Another characteristic which calls forth our admiration and demands our imitation is that note of utter reliance on the divine aid which vitalized all their endeavours. There was nothing of "defeatism" about them, and they were ever on the offensive. The Church to-day is too prone to "dig itself in", and to feel that if it is still the *Civitas Dei*, it is a city in a state of siege. The Evangelical leaders had no such doubts or hesitations, and were willing to commit themselves and all that they had, in bold attempts to carry the war into the enemy's country. They were, indeed, heroes of the faith, who "out of weakness were made strong, waxed valiant in fight, turned to flight the armies of the aliens" (Heb. 11: 34).

But if, as Canon Smyth has rightly said, the movement was a history of "personalities" rather than of "opinions", it was the opinions which made the personalities. That is our difficulty; for we are compelled to recognize that many of the beliefs which gave force and coherence to their lives and filled them with fervent zeal, can no longer be held, at least in the form in which they held them, by educated men and women. The great problem of the Church to-day is to recapture their spirit and to combine with it our own much more adequate theology, to link an enlightened faith with converting power. Unfortunately, heat and light seem seldom to be generated at one and the same time, and the frequent accompaniment of the spread of liberal ideas is a diminution of fervency and zeal. It is "intuition" and not reasoning which seems to stir the soul and persuade the will.

A strange, yet constantly recurring, phenomenon revealed by the study of history is the habit of one age to despise its immediate predecessor and then in turn itself to be displaced

[1] *Hopes for English Religion*, p. 22

by that predecessor. It would seem that distance is required to see an age in true perspective, and that close proximity leads to hasty judgments and condemnations from which reaction is inevitable. So it has been with the eighteenth century. The writers of the nineteenth century could hardly find words strong enough to express their contempt; according to Carlyle, "it lies massed in our minds as a disastrous wrecked inanity, not useful to dwell upon", and Edward Jenks turned with a sense of relief to "see it disappear before the whirlwind of the French Revolution, in a cloud of full-bottomed wigs, hoops, patches and powders, sedan chairs, preposterous family coaches, and heavy theological quartos."[1] Now a literary critic of brilliant insight can affirm that "To-day the eighteenth century is in fashion."[2] This change of opinion, however, had been long maturing; for when in 1878 Abbey and Overton wrote their admirable history of *The English Church in the Eighteenth Century*, they could, even then, state that the claim which the intellectual and religious life of England in the eighteenth century has upon our interest has been much more generally acknowledged of late years than was the case heretofore.[3] A generation later Leslie Stephen, in his Ford Lectures for 1903, said that though its enemies described it as "the century . . . of coarse utilitarian aims, of religious indifference and political corruption", he himself preferred to call it "the century of cold common sense and growing toleration, and of steady social and industrial development."[4] The contrast between these two estimates discloses one reason for the change; there is a difference of emphasis and a new standard of valuation. The conventional depreciation of the century had been the result of giving too great importance to certain elements only in a very complex era. By isolating its admitted weaknesses and ignoring its finer qualities, condemnation is certainly easy. Possibly we ourselves are in danger of too great a reversal of the process; at any rate Lord David Cecil can say that "people like the eighteenth century because they see it as a Golden Age of the qualities they value; and so they conceive it as possessing these qualities and no others."[5]

No age has a uniform texture, and the immense variety of the eighteenth century, a variety which verges on the paradoxical, is one of its attractions. Even individual men were

[1] I owe both these quotations to W. F. Reddaway, *A History of Europe from 1715 to 1814*
[2] Lord David Cecil, *The Stricken Deer*, p. 3   [3] *Op. cit.*, I, p. 1
[4] *Ford Lectures*, p. 97   [5] *Op. cit.*, p. 3

B

strangely inconsistent when judged by present-day standards. They were in many ways what we now call "tough", yet they slept in beds shut in by curtains for fear of the night air, and avoided sea-bathing except under medical orders. The literary characters alone furnish a whole gallery of contrasts. That Pope, with his elusive and complex nature, was ever taken as typical of this supposed age of sanity and common sense should be enough to guard us against hasty generalizations; then we have such diverse characters as Swift and Addison, Lord Chesterfield and Sir Joshua Reynolds, Dr. Johnson and Horace Walpole, to name but a few.

Another reason for the popular misconception, also due to selectivity, was the narrow social basis on which it was founded. The tone of the century is taken as that which was characteristic of a clique of aristocrats who formed London society.[1] But they were but a very small minority, and to regard them as in any way representative shows a lack of proportion. There were other circles of equal importance, such as the friends of Dr. Johnson, whose ideals and conventions were very different. There were, too, the country squires whose rough and "knockabout" manners provoked the derision of the refined gentlemen of metropolitan society. Behind them all were the vast multitudes of the common people. But their views and outlook, since they were inarticulate, and unrepresented save when portrayed in contemporary fiction, are in danger of being forgotten.

The eighteenth century is often called a classical age, meaning by the term an age which takes things for granted, and tests its life and achievements by fixed and universally accepted standards; an age, too, which looks back to the past with a consciousness of its own falling short of those who have gone before it. But there was no such sense of shortcoming in the men of the eighteenth century; for it was a time of self-complacency and self-satisfaction, which, if it calls forth a kindly amusement, also evokes a feeling of envy. Without unduly depreciating the past, it stood confidently by its own ideas and standards; Hooker's observation that "the world will not endure to hear that we are wiser than any which went before",[2] would certainly not apply to it.

Since progress is generally the result of discontent and

[1] A similar misjudgment of conditions under the Roman Empire is due to exactly the same causes: see my *Beginnings of Western Christendom*, pp. 41 ff.
[2] *Ecclesiastical Polity*, Bk. V, ch. vii, 3

dissatisfaction, a classical age is apt to lack incentives. It is so serene and secure, so complete in itself, that to strive for improvement, even if it were possible, seems scarcely worth the necessary effort.[1] C. F. G. Masterman once said of the period between Augustus and Marcus Aurelius:

> The only sorrow which disturbed such an age was the sometimes transient regret that all the great things had been accomplished; that humanity, in a completely rational society, had nothing to contemplate in the future but a continuous repetition of the present.[2]

But such a society, because it is immune from the vanity of progress, may provide a quiet and unhurried atmosphere in which the seeds of future development are slowly maturing. Thus it was with the eighteenth century; it was a kind of boundary period whose significance is only realized in retrospect. Because it was satisfied with things as they were it preserved and nurtured institutions in both Church and State for resuscitation in due season. There was never a century in English history which was less destructive.

The idea that the whole of the eighteenth century was a dull and stagnant epoch, an idea which can still be found in text-books, is the outcome of a failure to distinguish between its different periods, of an undiscriminating selection. The early part of the century may provide some justification for such a view, but the later part was one of the most exciting and momentous in the whole of our history. An age which saw the victories of Clive in India and Wolfe in Canada; the loss of the American colonies and their compensation by the acquirement of a new empire; can hardly be called dull. At home, too, there was much political excitement in the latter years of the century with the careers of the two Pitts, of Charles James Fox, and of Burke. In addition, there were the beginnings of considerable social and economic changes. If in the realm of thought there was for long little progress, yet Kant published his

---

[1] The prevalent idea seems to have been that progress would come about of itself. Gibbon in 1781 concluded the first part of *The Decline and Fall of the Roman Empire* with the following revealing passage: "We may therefore acquiesce in the pleasing conclusion that every age of the world has increased, and still increases, the real wealth, the happiness, the knowledge, and perhaps the virtue of the human race" (Ed. Bury, iv, p. 169)

[2] *The Condition of England*, p. 301

Critique of Pure Reason in 1781, and in the field of natural science important discoveries were being made by Priestley and Cavendish. In literature, we notice the rise of the novel, and the first blossoming of the Romantic school. In religion, there was a very distinct stirring of the waters in the Methodist and Evangelical Movements which are our primary concern. That much in these developments was later to achieve enhanced momentum must not blind us to their origin in the eighteenth century.

The spirit of self-complacency which was a characteristic of Englishmen in the eighteenth century was almost solely a beverage for home consumption. If they had exceedingly high notions of their own achievements, resources and opinions, these did not extend to the race as a whole nor to the qualities of foreign peoples. It was no accident that the name of John Bull was then first applied to the collective Englishman.

But if there was undue conceit on the part of Englishmen in this period it had much to justify it. For the century, especially in its closing decades, was a period of many ambitious projects. Large estates were being accumulated, and farming was being conducted on an ever-increasing scale; in the industrial world, capitalism was providing the means for fresh advances; and already the twin revolutions in Industry and Agriculture were well on their way, and this before other nations had made similar ventures. In spite of a number of distressing wars, the country was able to meet the most stringent economic trials. Prosperity, indeed, went back as far as the arrival of the Hanoverians, and Hallam judged that the generation between 1714 and 1744, with its slow but uniform progress, was the most thriving period in all our history.[1] There is much truth in this, for the more rapid advances in the later part of the century tended to benefit only the wealthy, and to leave the less fortunate worse off by comparison than they were before.

One source of the new self-confidence, and it was something novel in Western Europe, was a belief in the ability of reason to solve all the problems with which mankind is confronted. Even in religion, traces of the same idea might be found. Here it took the form of an emphatic conviction that "the Creator was not only wise, but beneficent".[2] A trust in reason and a "roundabout common sense", as Locke had called it, were the hallmarks of the period; and, as a necessary consequence, there was an intense distrust of extremes, and above all of anything

[1] *Constitutional History*, ii, p. 464   [2] Sykes, p. 343

"enthusiastical" or emotional. This restriction, however, was reserved for matters of high importance; enthusiasm was allowed considerable scope in lesser things. It was not thought objectionable if exhibited in the collection of objects of art, or the erection of "Gothic" monstrosities; in controversy, too, some feeling was shown, though this moderated considerably after the days of Swift.

But even in their most ambitious building projects and in the use of their ever-increasing wealth, "measure" was the supreme test, for it was "a prime moral truth of the eighteenth century that grandeur of life consists in wealth subdued to decorum."[1] This truth, however, did not apply universally—there was little moderation in gambling, for instance, and in matters of dress the fashionable world failed badly in its observance. Here, alongside much striving after real elegance, there was much that was sheer foppery. The female head-dress seems to have been particularly extravagant. Hannah More said of a company of fashionable ladies that they had among them: "an acre and a half of shrubbery, besides slopes, grass-plots, tulip-beds, clumps of peonies, kitchen-gardens, and green-houses." This fashion was eventually "scotched" by Garrick, who appeared in female attire with an even more extravagant head-dress which included hanging carrots.[2]

Such exuberance was perhaps a degenerate expression of that genuine love for beautiful things which was one of the more admirable characteristics of the age, a characteristic which would later sink into mere competitive elegance of which, indeed, such eccentricity may have been a forewarning. This love of beautiful things seemed to spring up spontaneously and almost universally; there has never been an age, it may be said, in our land when there was so wide a diffusion of artistic excellence, for even the articles in daily use by the poorest had considerable merit. Art was unconsciously part of every-day life, and fine handicraft was appreciated as it has never been appreciated since. The rich who travelled the Continent might bring back samples of foreign workmanship and æsthetic achievement, but these were matched, and supplemented, by native manufacture and skill. "There is nothing more typical of the English eighteenth century than an eighteenth-century chinoiserie chair, with all the flowing grace of Pekin, tamed into the delicate regularity of Bath."[3]

[1] Michael Innes, *Hamlet Revenge*, p. 10   [2] *Memoirs*, i, p. 100
[3] Lord David Cecil, *The Stricken Deer*, p. 2

An age which made reason and common sense the test of all things, and distrusted enthusiasm and extremes, might from its very qualities have become banal and tedious. From this it was saved by its wit. That this wit should have taken a somewhat cynical form is doubtless due to its being an outlet and safety-valve for the pressure of too comprehensive a suppression of the emotions. It was also very frank and outspoken, at least when compared with that current in the following century.

The whole tone of society was in fact much more akin to the age of Elizabeth than to that of Victoria, and if it was not quite so blatant as it had been in the later part of the seventeenth century, yet, as Saintsbury has remarked: "the prudery which was supposed to have succeeded Restoration licence was a very odd prudery".[1]

Such, in general terms, was the age in which the Evangelical Movement had its origins and infancy. It was a time of great material advancement, but of moral and spiritual decline, pervaded by an atmosphere so calm and cold that in it ideals withered as a flower withers at the touch of an early frost. Religion, so far as it was accepted, was as conventional as the age itself and as careful to avoid what was strange or outlandish. But in this as in other spheres of life, the eighteenth century was a period of preparation; for the very strictness and stringency of the conventions which it imposed could not be endured for ever and inevitably provoked a recoil. The spirit of man resents all attempts to confine it within narrow limitations, and sooner or later it will rebel against them.

[1] *The Peace of the Augustans*, p. 39

CHAPTER 2

POLITICAL CONDITIONS

To deal with the political background of the movement in any elaborate or comprehensive manner is obviously beyond the scope of our inquiry, and all that will here be attempted is to give a brief outline of political events with special attention to those which affected religion and morals and the life of the people.[1]

The eighteenth century opened with all the promise of a summer dawn. Upon the throne there sat a prudent sovereign who held the willing allegiance of her subjects and encouraged them in the exhibition of their powers. In both Church and State there was much commendable activity. The union of England and Scotland in 1707 marked an epoch for both countries, for it promoted freer intercourse, and, as a consequence, the growth of commerce. If old rivalries were not entirely removed they would gradually be mollified with the passage of time. The presence of Scots in England and their employment by the British government was an immense advantage; in fact, it would scarcely be an exaggeration to say that without them the development of English commerce, and indeed the establishment of the colonial Empire, would hardly have been possible. If the closing years of Anne's reign had their disquiets and violent party feuds they were a sign of life and energy. No one could accuse Englishmen of that generation of torpor or apathy.

The coming of the Hanoverians brought about a drastic change, for the policy of the Whigs, who then obtained a long lease of power, was averse to all manifestations of unusual activity. Peace both at home and abroad was the maxim of Walpole and his lesser associates and successors; and peace, for the most part, they obtained, and with it much outward prosperity.

As the Whig acquisition of power had been due to royal and not popular favour (the Tories had opposed the accession of George I), their "let sleeping dogs lie" policy was really inevitable. For though the Tories were divided among themselves

[1] For a useful account (with a full bibliography) see J. H. Plumb, *England in the Eighteenth Century*

they had a strong backing in the country, and there were many who were of Jacobite sympathies. This fostered an unquiet spirit and created a general air of suspicion which persisted until after the fiasco of 1745. This suspicion was so widespread that it often assumed grotesque forms. John Wesley, for example, was thought to be a recruiting agent for the Young Pretender; and even more odd was the charge brought before the Wakefield magistrates against Charles Wesley of showing Jacobite leanings, since he had prayed that God would bring home His "banished ones". Fortunately, one of the bench was a clergyman who was able to support his statement that the words were Biblical and had a spiritual and not a political connotation.

This general unsettlement was naturally prejudicial to the progress of religion, for the Church itself was equally divided, and a spirit of rancour began to emerge as the traditional parties were transformed into rival factions, for the High Churchmen were predominantly Jacobite.

The Whig rise to power was a recovery from the rebuff received under Anne, for their ascendancy went back to the Revolution, when Parliament became no longer an intrusive body but "the great driving-wheel of the political machinery."[1] More and more political power was to be in the hands of those who controlled Parliament, the life of which had been prolonged by the Septennial Act of 1716. During the course of the century this development continued through the emergence of the cabinet system with its dependence on a parliamentary majority.[2]

George I was unable to speak the language of his new subjects, and was much more interested in Hanover than in the country over which he had been called to rule. This, however, saved England from any attempt at royal interference in its religious or political liberty, and if George brought over a crowd of German favourites and hangers-on, who were not slow to use the good things which Providence and their royal master had put in their way, they were doubtless more restrained than would have been the entourage of the Old Pretender had the Stuart dynasty been restored. The Hanoverians, in spite of many disadvantages, were certainly cheaper and less dangerous.

[1] Leslie Stephen, *Ford Lectures*, p. 33

[2] Cf. Plumb, *op. cit.*, pp. 49 f. "Walpole and George III encouraged the development of a small inner cabinet . . . the true ancestor of the modern cabinet, but still a remote one, and it is extremely misleading to try to impose modern . . . constitutional ideas on the eighteenth century"

POLITICAL CONDITIONS

The dominant figure in English politics from 1721 to 1742 was Sir Robert Walpole, who came into power after the panic aroused by the South Sea Bubble, and was one of the greatest finance ministers this country has ever had. His policy of peace and retrenchment suited the country's needs and was in line with his own temperament. Walpole's chief failing was an inability to work with others and a too marked fondness for his own ideas. He is frequently accused of bolstering his position by jobbery and bribery; but this was no innovation, and when his accusers themselves came into power they soon forgot their virtuous indignation and made use of the same methods. Corruption was, indeed, unavoidable in the conditions of the time.

The death of George I in 1727 seemed for the moment to threaten Walpole's supremacy, but George II was unable to dispense with his services, and the new queen, Caroline of Anspach, was his sincere friend. Twelve years later Walpole was compelled by a national outburst to enter upon a war which neither his judgment nor his desires approved; it might have been well had he resigned rather than consent to carry it on, for until his retirement in 1742 he was in constant difficulties; there was even the possibility that he might be impeached—it was a case of Downing Street or the Tower, as Horace Walpole put it. Finally he sought refuge in the House of Lords, with the title of Earl of Orford, but by that time his course was nearly run, for he died in 1745. His death "was more than the defeat of a man, it made the passing of an age . . . he believed England existed for the sake of men of substance, who gained from security and low taxation, and not for the sake of rash commercial adventurers."[1]

The policy adopted by Walpole was advantageous and even necessary for the country as he found it, but only as a temporary measure; for a "rest-cure" if unduly prolonged must lead to depression and loss of energy. To discourage originality and genius and to promote only "safe" men does not make for national progress or vitality. The Church, too, suffered as well as the nation from the same treatment; it may even be surmised that Walpole was anxious that it, above all else, should remain dormant, for he had been closely connected with the impeachment of Sacheverell in 1710 and the experience had taught him the dangers that might arise from ecclesiastical excitements.

[1] Plumb, *op. cit.*, pp. 72 f.

The period between the fall of Walpole and the rise of the elder Pitt was an inglorious one for England, even if the last Stuart attempt to recover the throne was successfully overcome. The outbreak of the Seven Years' War in 1756 found the country, as so often, quite unprepared, and the government went from one muddle to another. But as always in moments of grave crisis, England had an uncanny ability for discovering great men to come to her rescue. The nation might be on the verge of panic, but Pitt believed firmly in its power to recover, and in his own part in that recovery; "I know that I can save this nation and that nobody else can", was his proud declaration. But he soon justified it. Alongside him there rose the necessary agents to carry out his plans; military leaders like Clive and Wolfe, and the admirals, Rodney, Boscawen, and Hawke, who kept the land free from invasion. So great was the change in the aspect of affairs that it has been stated that the Seven Years' War was "the most profitable and the most glorious that this country has ever waged".[1] Amongst its other results was the founding, under widely separated skies, of the first British Empire.

When the war came to an end in 1763 a new king was on the throne, for George II had died suddenly in October, 1760, after a reign of thirty-three years; and John Wesley, apparently without the slightest irony, could comment, "King George was gathered to his fathers. When will England have a better Prince?"[2] George II was no worse as a sovereign than his contemporaries—and no better. He had the physical courage of his family which he proved on more than one field of battle—a striking contrast to his pusillanimous rival, the Old Pretender—none the less he merited the condemnation of Thackeray as being "one who had neither dignity, learning, morals, nor wit —who tainted a great society by a bad example; who in youth, manhood and age, was gross, low, and sensual."[3] As an offset to these personal vices he possessed that supremely valuable gift in a monarch—he knew when he had efficient ministers; and, if he had no affection for them, he allowed them to go their own way and gave them his unwavering support.

The successor to George II was his grandson, of whom Horace Walpole has written:

[1] G. O. Trevelyan, *The Early History of Chas. Jas. Fox*, p. 32
[2] *Journal*, iv, p. 417. Bishop Butler also regarded him as an excellent constitutional monarch, and severely denounced exaggerated or unfounded charges against him
[3] *The Four Georges*, p. 80

No British monarch has ascended the throne with so many advantages as George the Third. Being the first of his line born in England, the prejudices against his family as foreigners had ceased. . . . In the flower and bloom of youth, George had a handsome, open and honest countenance; and with the favour that attends the outward accomplishments of his age, he had none of the vices.

In addition, he had the benefit of the removal of any threat from the Stuarts, who were now definitely discredited, with "Bonny Prince Charlie" sinking into a premature and dissolute old age. Well might Gray write in 1769: "The star of Brunswick smiles serene."

The early years of the new reign present a confused spectacle; but the legendary picture of George III as endeavouring to resume something like despotic power must be abandoned. Until some cohesion was attained under Lord North he was "forced to use one makeshift ministry after another."[1] Meanwhile he had formed his own party, known as "the King's friends."

The King's friends were a dissolute lot; but George III, although pious himself and respectable in his private life, did not allow moral considerations to interfere with politics. He even refused to dismiss the Duke of Grafton, who had introduced a common prostitute into a royal assembly—an achievement which shocked even the low opinion of the times—because he feared that the alternative would be submission to the Whigs or to Pitt. The latter he had dismissed on his accession in favour of Lord Bute. But in the end he was forced to recall him. By this time, however, Pitt, who went to the House of Lords as Earl of Chatham, was in failing health and often unable to carry out his responsibilities. No longer in a position to sway the House of Commons by his eloquence, he adopted a despotic attitude towards his bewildered colleagues in the government, who were often left in complete ignorance of what was being done. The acceptance of a peerage also robbed him of his reputation for disinterestedness with the populace. To everyone's relief he resigned late in 1768.

The removal of the Jacobite threat had weakened the position of the Whigs, and with the accession of George III their

[1] Plumb, *op. cit.*, p. 118. Cf. further R. Pares, *King Geo. III and the Politicians*

monopoly came to an end. Like the Tories earlier in the century, they were now divided amongst themselves, and had indeed no definite policy. On the whole they had used their power wisely and without ostentation or tyranny. To liken them, as Disraeli did in *Coningsby*, to a Venetian oligarchy is absurd; for the only "tyranny" which England then knew was that of the local squires and J.P.s, and they were predominantly Tory —a fact which prevented any such tendencies on the part of the Whigs. Since the latter controlled the House of Commons they strove to increase its powers; but as it was so much a single party concern it was largely out of touch with public opinion, and interest in politics steadily declined in the country; a tendency which was reinforced by the absence of any alternative claimant to power, for the Tories, for the time being, were moribund.

But public interest could on occasion be aroused, and then in opposition to the power of Parliament. This was the case in the famous Wilkes affair. John Wilkes had attracted some attention by his violent attacks on the ministry of Bute in *The North Briton*, and when he was elected for Middlesex in 1763 the House of Commons refused to allow him to take his seat. Immediately there was a popular outcry, and a worthless agitator was exalted into a symbol of popular liberties and became a public hero.[1] Wilkes, however, in spite of his dissipated and unwholesome habits, had a better side. In later life he became quite respectable and was even elected an alderman of the city of London.

Parliament's effort to preserve its supremacy in the case of Wilkes was followed by an even more disastrous struggle—that with the American colonies. It was this rather than any supposed attempt on the part of George III to assert the rights of the crown which was the cause of the dispute.

British opinion tended to regard colonies as founded for the benefit of the mother country and to exploit them accordingly. But as the colonies increased in population, that of America rose from 200,000 in 1700 to some 2,000,000 by 1770, they began to resent this attitude. The matter came to a head with the imposition of the Stamp Duty in 1765. This was resisted

---

[1] Wesley, who was an ingrained Tory, in his *Free Thoughts on the Present State of Public Affairs* (1768), expressed his scorn of Wilkes and his like: "Cobblers, tinkers, porters, and hackney-coachmen think themselves wise enough to instruct both king and council." Gladstone, however, who must have disapproved strongly of Wilkes's private life, could say, looking back, that his name would be enrolled among the greatest champions of English freedom

by the colonists, who claimed the right to tax themselves. The measure proved unworkable and was almost immediately withdrawn; but by an act of extreme folly Charles Townsend then taxed American merchandise. In retaliation America refused to purchase British goods. The whole policy was disapproved of by Pitt and the wiser statesmen, as well as by the mercantile community, and so political leadership fell into the hands of the weak though well-meaning Lord North. He abolished the duties on American imports, apart from that on tea, which was retained as a symbol of Parliament's right to impose taxes. This action, incidentally, met with the approval of the king, who wrote: "I am clear that there must always be one tax to keep up the right", but it was a most unwise procedure, for, as Junius commented: "In the repeal of those acts which were most offensive to the Americans, the Parliament had done everything but remove the offence. They had relinquished the revenue, but judiciously preserved the contention." The colonies refused to pay the tax and broke out into open revolt. Though many Englishmen were opposed to coercion, the measure to apply it passed the House of Commons by 305 votes to 105, and the House of Lords by 104 to 29.

Warfare continued from 1773 to 1783. In 1778 the French intervened on the side of the rebels, and Spain in the year following, thus transforming the whole nature of the conflict and making an English defeat almost inevitable. The defeat when it came was largely due to the neglected state of the navy,[1] for it was England's inability to maintain the control of the seas which enabled the French to land an army in North America and thus to force Cornwallis to surrender in 1781. Even more serious consequences might have followed, for a fleet of nearly seventy French and Spanish ships surprised Plymouth, which was defended by only a small garrison with two cannon. Fortunately, they were ignorant of this, and after cruising up and down at length withdrew without attempting a landing. Soon afterwards they were crippled by a sudden outbreak of fever.[2] Wesley attributed both these events to divine Providence.[3] Earlier he had written:

[1] When the *Royal George* was being repaired at Portsmouth in August, 1782, she was so rotten that part of the bottom fell out, and Admiral Kempenfelt with over 500 officers and men were drowned. The tragedy called forth one of the best known of Cowper's poems

[2] Rodney regained the command of the sea in 1782, but too late to affect the American War

[3] *Letters*, vi, p. 358

It is the judgment of many that, since the time of the Invincible Armada, Great Britain and Ireland were never in such danger from foreign enemies as they are at this day. Humanly speaking we are not able to contend with them, either by sea or land.[1]

Well might the younger Pitt, in that hour of humiliation, exclaim: "The sun of England's glory is set." But such was far from the case; another empire would quickly arise to replace the lost American colonies, and after years of grievous endurance the sun of England's glory would shine out once again, and with added lustre. Within a few years the first British settlement in Australia, which Captain Cook had "picked out of the sea" in 1770, was established, whilst a new and vaster Britain in America "took embryo shape amid the snows of Canada, where 140,000 defeated French, 60,000 immigrant loyalists from the United States, and a few thousand rough Scottish emigrants contrived to live together under King George's writ."[2]

Little did the "embattled farmers", who fired the first shots at Lexington on April 19, 1775, imagine that would bring to an end, not only British rule in part of North America, but the entire European colonial system as then understood, and inaugurate an era of revolution and warfare which ended only with the downfall of Napoleon. But so it was, and England was quick to learn the lesson and to adopt a new attitude to oversea dominions, for she gradually devised a completely novel idea of Empire, an idea in which a sense of mission was preeminent over the desire for exploitation.

Meanwhile affairs at home had been far from happy. A succession of bad harvests had reduced a large portion of the nation to the verge of starvation. The contemporary press is full of descriptions of the hard lot of the poor, nor did it refrain from criticisms of the extravagances of the wealthy. The threat of invasion, coupled with troubles in Ireland, seriously embarrassed the administration of Lord North, who was then in power.[3] Further embarrassment came in 1780 with the extraordinary outbreaks known as the Lord George Gordon riots, when for four days the mob was in complete control of the

---

[1] *Works*, xiii, p. 117   [2] Bryant, *The Years of Endurance*, p. 19

[3] For a detailed study of this important epoch see H. Butterfield, *George III, Lord North and the People*, 1779–80.

capital, burning down houses and other buildings.[1] Among others who have left a description of the scene was the poet Crabbe, then on his first visit to London. He witnessed the burning of the governor's house at Newgate and the release of the prisoners; and described Lord George Gordon, whom he saw in his coach drawn by the mob and bowing to the crowd, as a "lively-looking young man". Lord George Gordon was tried for high treason, but acquitted; and thanksgiving services were held to commemorate his release in a number of London churches.[2] Later he became a Jew, and in 1788 was sent to prison for libelling Marie Antoinette. There he died five years later, by which time his mind had completely collapsed.

This surprising outbreak was only possible owing to the absence of any police force capable of coping with such an emergency. Each parish had its constable, but they were unused to acting as a body and quite without experience in dealing with large crowds. The only resource was to call out the military, which was eventually done by the orders of the king, who showed great firmness in the crisis.

One effect of the outbreak was greatly to alarm the middle classes and to prejudice them against all forms of radicalism (an attitude which would later be strengthened by the French Revolution); as Gibbon put it: "The flames of London, which were kindled by a mischievous madman, admonished all thinking men of the danger of an appeal to the people."[3]

In spite of the support of Fox, Lord North was compelled to resign in March, 1782, and George III entrusted Pitt with the formation of a ministry. Pitt, like Walpole, was a great finance minister; and his administration, again like that of Walpole, gave England a breathing space for recovery after the vicissitudes through which she had passed, whilst his budgets of 1784 to 1787 did much to reorganize the finances of the country. Pitt's accession to power marked the revival of the Tory party, and, indeed, of the party system as a whole. But though the old names of Whig and Tory were retained they had acquired a different significance. Pitt was strong in the support of the king and of the city of London, but his position was threatened by the madness of George III in November, 1787. The Whigs, indeed, were preparing to take office when the king recovered in the following March.

[1] Among them that of Lord Mansfield with its fine library and collection of pictures. As in the time of Jack Cade the mob had a special animus against lawyers
[2] *Memoirs of Hannah More*, i, p. 200   [3] *Memoirs*, p. 208

From this brief sketch of political conditions up to 1789 it will be seen that the period in which the Evangelical Movement had its beginnings was one of varying fortunes for the country. There had been the threat of the Jacobite rising in 1745; the disastrous commencement of the Seven Years' War, followed by a glorious recovery; then, once again, England had seemed to go down into the trough of the wave with the loss of the American colonies, only to recover and exhibit renewed energy and power.

What effects, it may be asked, had all this on the religious life of the country? As so often, times of stress and danger made many turn belatedly to the God whom they commonly neglected; or at least to throng His courts. Such hasty and superstitious seeking after God, for that is all that it amounts to, has, save with a very few, no permanent influence; it may, indeed, cause a reaction. So, too, with the thanksgiving services after victory. There may, for the moment, have been a sense of gratitude, but here again the effects were only transitory.

What, it may next be asked, was the attitude of politicians to religion, and how did they affect it? Politicians in all ages have realized that religion, if properly controlled, may be a ready instrument for their purposes. Gibbon, in the well-known tag, affirmed that: "The various modes of worship which prevailed in the Roman world were all considered by the people as equally true; by the philosopher as equally false; and by the magistrate as equally useful";[1] and Hooker had said much the same thing two centuries before: "For a politic use of religion they see there is, and by it they would also gather that religion itself is a mere politic device, forged purposely to serve that use."[2]

In the eighteenth century politicians used religion, or rather the established Church, as a means for furthering their influence and rewarding their supporters. Even those who had no belief in the truths of Christianity were fearful of anything which might undermine its influence with the multitude, an attitude shared by all who were concerned over the stability of the country, and, in order to bolster up the Church, were not averse to giving it the occasional support of their presence at divine worship.

One political event, however, had very definite ecclesiastical repercussions—the loss of the American colonies. When America

[1] *Decline and Fall of the Roman Empire*, i, p. 28
[2] *Ecclesiastical Polity*, Book V, chap. ii, § 3

acquired its independence, many loyalists migrated to Canada, and most of these would be members of the Church of England. Those Anglicans who remained would be regarded with suspicion, and Methodism was much in favour. The growth of Methodism led to the appointment by Wesley of Methodist "bishops", which in turn was a step towards the breach with the Church at home.[1]

A comprehensive survey of the political conditions of the country suggests that their effect upon the movement was almost entirely indirect. On the one hand, the policy of the government served to discourage any unwonted activity on the part of the established Church and its leaders; on the other, the shutting out of the common people made them more open to an appeal, such as that of the revival, which would provide an outlet for their energies and compensation for their exclusion.

[1] It is worth noting that the situation that made it necessary to provide bishops was itself due to political causes, for it was the detestation of the colonists for Laud and his methods (many of them had emigrated to avoid them) which had made them oppose the appointment of bishops

CHAPTER 3

SOCIAL AND ECONOMIC CONDITIONS

THE England in which the Evangelical Movement arose was very different from England to-day, and if we are to understand its history this must constantly be borne in mind. For the social and economic conditions and tendencies of the time were more than a mere background against which the movement developed; they were a not unimportant factor in determining its course.

Perhaps the most striking difference was in the matter of population. Until about 1750 it was little more than an eighth of the present total, and for some time it had been stationary. Then it began to increase, slowly at first, but more rapidly after 1781; but when the first census was taken in 1801 it had not reached 9,000,000. This smaller population, moreover, was widely distributed. London was the only large town, and of the rest probably Bristol alone exceeded 50,000 in 1740. Many of the new towns still ranked as villages,[1] and their administration was parochial. Local government was a very tardy growth in England.[2]

Another important factor which requires notice is the poorness of the means of communication. The roads were quite inadequate and their upkeep neglected. Towards the end of the century there was a much needed improvement, but even this was confined to the main roads. In 1754 it took four and a half days to travel from London to Manchester; but the new roads enabled the journey to be accomplished by stage coach in twenty-eight hours. As late as October, 1787, Wesley records travelling from Hinxworth to Wrestlingworth "through such roads as no chaise could pass. So we had the pleasure of riding on a farmer's cart."[3]

Until the last quarter of the century it was transport by

---

[1] At the beginning of the century Defoe had described Manchester as "one of the greatest, if not the greatest, mere village in England . . . including the suburbs of that part of the town on the other side of the bridge [Salford], it is said to contain 50,000 people"

[2] The ways in which the towns gradually sought wider powers is a social phenomenon whose significance is not always recognized: see Plumb, *England in the Eighteenth Century*, p. 86

[3] *Journal*, vii, p. 338

water which showed the greatest improvement. The Duke of Bridgewater, with the aid of Brinkley, constructed the first canal in 1761, and others quickly followed. This lack of efficient transport was a handicap to industrial and commercial development; but its effects on the social life of the country must have been even greater. It meant that each community was in large measure isolated from its neighbours, and as a result its interests were confined to things near at hand. Villages were much more self-contained, and produced not only their own food, but almost everything else, apart from a few luxuries, which they required. Town and country were largely cut off from one another and had different tastes and preoccupations. The rustic squires who occasionally came up to London were objects of ridicule, and their amazing powers of eating and drinking aroused amused wonder. Horace Walpole, in his facetious way, said that he could hardly distinguish between a country gentleman and a sirloin. They retained their local dialect, and most of them were only too glad to avoid the metropolis and to remain in spheres where they were persons of consequence.[1]

Conditions in rural England, however, did not stand still during the eighteenth century. On the contrary, they experienced a revolution whose importance is apt to be forgotten owing to the even more spectacular changes in the industrial world with which it was contemporary. The agricultural revolution began as early as 1740, and though enclosing made steady progress half the country still retained the open-field system up to 1760. Enclosure was beneficial to the country as a whole (had it not taken place, it is doubtful whether England would have been able to maintain itself during the Napoleonic blockade), but individuals suffered in the process. Farming was conducted on more scientific lines, and large landowners gave themselves up to the cultivation of their estates with equal skill and enthusiasm; but the smaller men were squeezed out, and the labourers deprived of their holdings and of that stake in the soil which had been traditional. Before enclosure, many cottagers had worked half the time on their own strips and half for an employer: thus preserving a certain spirit of independence, the great characteristic of the English freeman. After enclosure, they were reduced to landless labourers. In consequence there was a flight from the land, and large numbers migrated into the growing towns where industry was ever demanding fresh labour.

[1] Earlier still, Congreve, in *The Way of the World*, had depicted the contrast

Poets, from the days of Theocritus and Virgil, have made it their business to idealize rural life, and those who read their works in the eighteenth century fondly imagined that they gave a true picture of their own times and country. False notions as to rustic happiness were further popularized by Goldsmith in *The Deserted Village*, but the realistic pen of Crabbe in *The Village* and *The Parish Register* revealed the actual conditions. Wesley, it may be noted, had a poor opinion of rural life, and affirmed that:

> Our eyes and our ears may convince us that there is not a less happy body of men in all England than the country farmers. In general, their life is supremely dull; and it is usually unhappy too; for, of all people in the kingdom, they are the most discontented, seldom satisfied either with God or man.[1]

The revolution in industry which so fundamentally changed the face of England and so deeply affected its social and economic life is conventionally dated from 1760. In reality, it goes back much further and had long been coming to birth; even when it reached more rapid and noticeable stages its development was still gradual. The new methods, for one thing, were not immediately profitable, and much prejudice had to be overcome. It took two decades for the power loom to displace the hand loom;[2] the steam engine was not used in the cotton trade until 1785. Even the rural character of industry was maintained for a time, and village "slums" sprang up round mills and mines and factories. Towns only developed with the realization of the greater convenience of large centres.[3]

But if the industrial movement was slow in developing, it merits the title of a revolution, so drastic were the changes it wrought; and the flame and smoke of the ironworks were, for those who had eyes to see, beacons proclaiming the arrival of a new era and the collapse of the old. It was certainly a momentous achievement, and Disraeli could aver that "rightly understood Manchester is as great a human exploit as Athens";[4] but many of its effects were disastrous.

[1] Quoted Southey, *Life of Wesley*, ii, p. 67
[2] Macgregor, *The Evolution of Industry*, p. 39
[3] Cf. John Morley, *Recollections*, i, pp. 3 f. "It took three quarters of a century or more before the factory system with all its opulent triumphs and all its strange new social perplexities had definitely established itself in the Lancashire cotton towns"
[4] *Coningsby*, Book IV, chap. i

SOCIAL AND ECONOMIC CONDITIONS 37

The evils which would follow for the individual were clearly foreseen by Wordsworth when he wrote:

> Our life is turned
> Out of her course, wherever man is made
> An offering, or a sacrifice, a tool
> Or implement, a passive thing employed
> As a brute mean, without acknowledgment
> Of common right or interest in the end;
> Used or abused, as selfishness may prompt.
> Say, what can follow for a rational soul
> Perverted thus, but weakness in all good,
> And strength in evil.[1]

As the factory system developed and crowds were drawn in from the countryside, the older towns began rapidly to expand, and new towns arose. To provide for the additional inhabitants houses had to be built. These were invariably cheap and ugly, and many of them were deficient in even the most elementary sanitary conveniences. The whole atmosphere, with its reeking thoroughfares, darkened by the perpetual drift of smoke from the factory chimneys, must have been intensely depressing. Whilst the houses, huddled together in long unlovely streets, added to the general squalor. To those whose younger days had been spent in the country they must have seemed a veritable inferno. Even when the country was still near at hand, as was the case at first, the dwellers in the towns can have had but little heart and but scanty leisure to return to it.

The social consequences were enormous. In their village homes the new-comers had been members of a community with a definite position in their own small society. Now they were but driftwood, with no centre of interest or unity, save the mill or factory which employed them. There thus grew up a kind of debased and novel feudalism; but the new "lords" had nothing of the kindly feelings of the old. Many had been artisans, who, by good fortune or superior energy, had raised themselves to be employers of labour. Such had no tradition of responsibility behind them and no care for the welfare of their dependants.

If individuals had thus to suffer, the country as a whole was reaping an abundant harvest. In spite of foreign wars, after

---

[1] *Excursion*, ix, 113 ff. A modern poet has exposed, in the spirit of Blake, the evils of the system; see Gordon Bottomley, *To Iron-Founders and Others*

the rising of 1745 the country was at peace at home, and this security gave the opportunity for great advance. Trade grew enormously, for whereas in 1720 imports amounted to a little over £6,000,000, by 1789 they had passed £37,000,000, and this in spite of the temporary setback when the command of the sea was lost during the American War. British ships, carrying their merchandise, sailed the seven seas, and British merchants gained concessions and planted factories in all quarters of the globe. Commerce was becoming the chief preoccupation of the country, and politics would more and more be dominated by the interests of trade.

The increase in trade and in the wealth of the nation naturally had important social effects. The standard of living was raised immensely—for those who were lucky enough to have their share of the increase. But for others conditions really deteriorated. Luxury and gross extravagance at one end of the ladder was accompanied by greater stringency at the other. As commercial and industrial operations were conducted on an ever growing scale the gap between masters and men was also widened. Even on the land this was noticeable, for though some better-class farmers still lived with their servants in the kitchen and only opened their parlours when entertaining a guest of higher quality, many of them, or at least many of their wives and daughters, were consumed with social ambitions and despised their dependants and servants.

Social and class distinctions were exceedingly rigid and were taken for granted as part of the natural order of things. This can be seen in the attitude of great artists such as Reynolds and Gainsborough; both had been bred in the country, and to the end of their days they painted the squire and the squire's lady as if they were the centre of the universe. Unless we grasp firmly the way in which the whole social structure was permeated by this notion, we shall be apt to condemn unduly the subservience of the various Evangelical leaders to Lady Huntingdon and other noble persons who took part in the movement. This subservience, however, was tempered by a high conception of their rights as ministers of the Gospel; none the less it was there. John Newton after speaking his mind very freely to Lord Dartmouth ended up: "I dropt the consideration of whom I was addressing from the first paragraph: but now I return, and subscribe myself with the greatest deference," etc.[1]

[1] *Cardiphonia*, p. 18

SOCIAL AND ECONOMIC CONDITIONS

The spirit of subordination extended to all ranks of society, and was perhaps strictest in the servants' hall. But there was nothing servile about it; if privilege was not resented, any approach to injustice or tyranny might cause trouble. The acceptance of a settled social status certainly made life easier and more natural; for where there is instability an atmosphere of strain is apt to be produced, and even of conflict. Dr. Johnson once gave it as his opinion that "subordination is very necessary for society, and contentions for superiority very dangerous. . . . Subordination tends to human happiness".[1]

One important change in social status was due to a growing prejudice against those engaged in trade. At the beginning of the century, trade was never despised, and Addison could write:

> It is the happiness of a trading nation like ours that the younger sons . . . may be placed in such a way of life as may perhaps enable them to vie with the best of their family; accordingly, we find several citizens that were launched into the world with narrow fortunes rising, by an honest industry, to greater estates than those of their elder brothers.[2]

Such successful merchants, having rural tastes, followed a natural impulse and acquired country estates to which they devoted their ample wealth. Thus the land was being fed from the town. But as the scope of trade increased they tended to use their wealth in financing fresh ventures, and enterprising young men felt that business held out better prospects than agriculture. So a new type of merchant arose who had no interest in the land. This cut them off from the country gentry from whom originally they had come. The disappearance, too, of the smaller squires, as large estates became more common, also cut off a source of supply. But trade on a sufficiently large scale was still open to the landowner and even to the aristocrat. No one, one imagines, looked down on the Duke of Bridgewater because he possessed coal mines and canals.

One outward mark of class differentiation in the eighteenth century was the difference in dress, a distinction which persisted until quite recent times when mass production and other more economical methods have enabled the poorer classes to wear clothes which in style and general appearance are not

[1] Boswell, *Life of Samuel Johnson* (ed. G. B. Hill), i, p. 442
[2] *The Spectator*, No. 108

very dissimilar from those of their betters. As we have already noticed, a devotion to dress and fashion was typical of the aristocrat, and it was by no means confined to the gentler sex; men and women vied with one another in forms of senseless ostentation.

The years before the French Revolution were a golden age for English aristocracy. Just as mankind, until the Copernican era, had thought the earth was the centre of the universe, and sun, moon, and stars merely a means of illumination, so did they regard their own position. All things had been created for their benefit and enjoyment. As the chosen of the earth they held in contempt the plebeian herd of those who had to work for their living and to spend their lives in monotonous occupations. They gazed out loftily from their self-created paradise upon a world outside which blindly accepted their superior status. Gray, in the solitude of some rustic glade, might sing:

> How vain the ardour of the crowd,
> How low, how little are the proud,
> How indigent the great!

but he would have found few to agree with his estimate.

The typical "fine gentleman" was not without his admirable qualities—he was, as a rule, witty, intelligent, a patron of art and letters—but these were offset by levity and a conceit which reached the verge of insolence. The rights and wishes of those who did not belong to his class were beneath his notice, nor was he afraid of public opinion, save that of his fellows. In him selfishness seemed to reach the pitch of perfection. Such was his outward aspect, though one may hope that Hannah More's young man of fashion had some counterparts in real life.[1]

Society was narrow and select, but it was also cosmopolitan. London and Paris were so closely linked that even the outbreak of the Seven Years' War did not interrupt their intercourse. (That was before war became "total".) The hero of Sterne's *Sentimental Journey* ignored it, and only found difficulties when he arrived in France because he had forgotten his passport. So, too, Suzanne Necker could invite Gibbon, then a member of Parliament, to visit her and her husband in Paris during the American War.

The habit of the English aristocracy of making the grand

---

[1] He "studied to be cold and rude
Tho' native feeling would intrude"
Florio, I, 47 f.

tour of the Continent, so well described in *Dunciad*, Bk. iv, led to the formation of friendships with foreigners, though the welcome extended to Englishmen was sometimes only a preliminary to fleecing them at the card tables. These connexions introduced many new ideas and fashions; but they also did much to lower the standard of English morals and to corrupt English society. And so France gained the reputation of being the home of forbidden sins, and men could suggest that the inscription over the gate of Hell was not, as Dante had supposed: "Abandon hope all ye who enter here", but "Ici on parle Français". This influence, however, was strictly limited to the aristocracy and those who took them for models. To the solid mass of Englishmen everything alien was contemptible; and even Dr. Johnson could declare that all foreigners were fools.

Such was English society in the eighteenth century, "a society so agreeable that posterity is tempted to forget how little else it had to recommend it".[1] But if it was amusing and attractive, and free from the bondage of hampering restrictions, it still had its own conventions. To us these seem strangely inconsistent. If it scoffed at religion, it was careful about church attendance—doubtless to set a good example to the lower classes; if its moral tone was low, certain proprieties must be observed and vice masked behind a decorative screen; if the affectation of republican views was not thought amiss, at least until the French Revolutionaries ventured on regicide, these must not undermine the position of the aristocrat. Its fundamental weakness was a concern for mere externals, and a witty tongue and polished manners more than outweighed a weak or dissolute character.

The life of the ruling classes in the country was very different from that of London or Bath. There the great landowners were absolutely supreme, petty monarchs whose slightest wish had the force of law; and even the voice of public opinion weighed little with men who lived amid their own dependants. Often enough those who suffered most from their immunity were the members of their families to whom they acted as domestic tyrants. Those who chose to oppose them, or to adopt views of which they disapproved, had to suffer the consequences; there were cases of men being evicted from their farms because they became Methodists. As local justice and administration was entirely in their hands, there was no redress; a single magistrate could hold a court in his own house and administer

[1] G. O. Trevelyan, *The Early History of Chas. Jas. Fox*, p. 348

summary justice. Pamela said to her master: "You are a justice of the peace, and may send me to gaol, if you please, and may bring me to trial for my life. If you can prove that I have robbed you, I am sure I ought to die" (Letter XXIV). But though abuses may have been more common than they are to-day it would be an error to suppose that the landed aristocracy habitually regarded themselves as above all law, or that squires bullied or defrauded their tenants. On the contrary, they had a very high sense of responsibility towards those who depended upon them and made it their business to enforce standards of decency and to check vice and brutality. They and their ladies were ever most solicitous in caring for the sick and poverty-stricken. Landowners might even extend their feeling of responsibility to towns in their neighbourhood. Hartlepool, for example, rose "from obscurity to eminence . . . through the bounty of the neighbouring nobility and gentry, whose custom it has been to accept by turns the office of mayor, and to subscribe upon that occasion one hundred pounds towards the improvement of the town."[1]

The spaciousness and dignity of the age, a spaciousness and dignity which these islands will never again behold, is reflected in the great houses they built—many of them in the eighteenth century—and adorned so lavishly and magnificently. The stately homes of England had then real meaning. All this has gone, but the remembrance of it may do something to console us in the aridity and meanness of much in contemporary life, even if we have no wish that it should return. The price paid for such magnificence was indeed too high, and those who enjoyed it were far too few. It could only be achieved and maintained at an immense cost in human misery and subjection, and modern ideas, quite rightly, do not desire that so much sacrifice on the part of the multitude should be made for the selfish enjoyment of a small minority. But even then the process of decay had already begun, and here and there landowners (often through the gambling habits of their predecessors, or their taste for extravagant overbuilding) were finding it hard to maintain their position. Hannah More has described some of them as full of apprehension and as making the best of things:

> Before our tottering castles fall
> And swarming nabobs seize on all.[2]

[1] Cadogan, *Life of Romaine*, p. 1   [2] *Works*, i, p. 61

SOCIAL AND ECONOMIC CONDITIONS 43

A new type of landowner was thus arising who lacked that feeling of responsibility which had characterized the older families; though he might, more so than in the present day, often be shamed into emulating them.

In one aspect polite society differed from that of later times; the enjoyment of it was largely a masculine privilege; for women, apart from a few strong characters who refused to accept the common valuation of their sex, were in general despised. If the feudal system was in decay, the age of chivalry had disappeared. This attitude is to be seen in Chesterfield's *Letters to His Son*, who is told to flatter women and even to make use of them, but never to take them seriously. The only writer, in the early part of the century, who is really chivalrous in his attitude was Steele. Chivalry had been discouraged by the Puritans as savouring of Catholicism, and in its place they had revived the Old Testament idea that women were to be subject to men. This can be seen in Milton's treatment of his daughters, and in his declaration that:

> Nothing lovelier can be found
> In woman, than to study household good.[1]

Women, however, were not always entirely submissive to their menfolk, and an incident which occurred in the House of Lords in May 1738 reads like a suffragette exploit of the twentieth century. The House decided to exclude all outsiders from a certain debate. This excited the protests of a number of ladies of high rank, including two duchesses and the youthful Countess of Huntingdon. Lady Mary Wortley Montagu in her vivid account of what took place tells how they attended the House, and on being refused admittance, banged on the doors from nine in the morning until five in the afternoon. They then suddenly became silent, and it was thought that they had gone away, and so the doors were opened. Upon this they rushed into the House and occupied the front rows of the galleries, from which they refused to be dislodged, and remained until the House rose at eleven, making their presence felt by various interruptions.

There was little formal education for women in the eighteenth century, which produced but few learned ladies apart from the famous "blue stockings" whose merits and attainments are celebrated in Hannah More's *The Bas Bleu*. The object of such

[1] *Paradise Lost*, ix, 233

education as they received was to fit them for the management of a household. In the later part of the century, however, there was a considerable extension of the curriculum, and French, Italian, music and painting, were added, when the necessary instructors were available, a matter of some difficulty in country districts. It was, of course, always possible for a woman to educate herself, for which process abundant leisure and the comprehensive libraries of most country houses provided ample opportunity.

The women of the upper classes had much leisure by reason of the immense number of servants who were employed. Richardson, in *Pamela*, gives for the comparatively small establishment of Mr. B——, a housekeeper, five maids, a gardener, a coachman, three footmen, besides grooms and other helpers. The high proportion of men servants should be noted. Both Richardson and Fielding speak of the servants as part of the "family", retaining the old Roman meaning of the term as including all the members of the household.

As we have already seen, the conventional view of English society in the eighteenth century is largely disproportionate because based on too restricted a foundation. That it should be so is natural, since information about the upper classes is so much more available; though it must be observed that the highly conventional life which they led forms a screen which it is not always easy to penetrate. For our purposes the condition of the middle and lower classes is of much greater importance since it was principally among them that the movement spread.

The growth of trade which was so marked a feature of the later part of the century had a profound effect on the social life of the nation, for it gave added power to the commercial and manufacturing classes. Commerce was dominated by the wealthy merchant princes who had their headquarters in the city of London. Their wealth also gave them great political influence, for the government of the day often depended on their support, and in return they expected that their privileges would be respected and fresh opportunities for expansion would be provided. Thus a new upper class, a kind of plutocracy, began to emerge. Its members built spacious mansions or bought up old estates; they enabled their women folk to dress lavishly and to drive about in their own coaches. The wiser and more sober did not allow their heads to be turned by this access of consequence; but many found it irresistible, with unfortunate results. The "nabob, the contractor, and others, by a sudden influx of unaccustomed wealth, become voluptuous, extravagant, and insolent".[1] The new industrialists were also pressing upwards in the rest of the country, in spite of the efforts of the landowners to "keep them in their places", and often found scope for the exercise of their influence in the new and growing towns.[2] Typical of this class was Josiah Wedgwood (1730–95), whose pottery had a world-wide sale. Although he was immensely successful and developed his business on a vast scale, he still remained in personal touch with his workmen; he had, moreover, like many of his kind, a genuine love of art and literature.[3] Wilberforce has left an interesting account of a visit he paid to the family on November 16, 1791: "Dined at Etruria—three sons and three daughters, and Miss W.—a fine, sensible, spirited family, intelligent and manly in behaviour—situation good—house rather grand, and all conveniences."[4] Stubbs's painting of this family reveals their character and attitude towards life, which was, indeed, typical of the class to which they belonged. They look very comfortable, very complacent and very self-assured; but not in the least aggressive. Their position and achievements made it unnecessary for them to assert themselves, as lesser men might have done.

Below the merchant princes and the new industrialists was the growing class of tradesmen and shopkeepers to whom town life was bringing fresh, if limited, wealth and opportunity. They, on the whole, are a less admirable class, for they had no idea what to do with their newly acquired riches, having few interests outside their business; and were apt to waste their substance in vulgar and unmeaning display, and their sons to plunge into dissipation in a foolish desire to ape their betters.

When Voltaire visited England he compared society to the ale of the country; there was a good deal of froth at the top, and of sediment at the bottom, but the middle on the whole was good. In this he confirmed the judgment of Bishop Butler, who welcomed the growth of trade and commerce as leading

---

[1] Hannah More, *The Manners of the Great* (*Works*, vi, p. 30)

[2] The election of Wilberforce as member for the county of York in 1784 in face of the whole force of Whig control and influence was "an intimation of that power, with which intelligence and property had now armed the middle ranks of society" (*Life of Wilberforce*, i, p. 64)

[3] Trevelyan, *English Social History*, p. 392, points out that "many of them took an active part in the best cultural and artistic life of the period. 'Captains of industry' were not necessarily 'Philistines' "

[4] *Life of Wilberforce*, i, p. 318

to the progress of the middle classes, "many of whom are, in good measure, free from the vices of the highest and lowest part of mankind". The middle classes, however, were far from "angels of light"—they shared, for instance, in the common failing of drunkenness and indulgence in doubtful forms of amusement—but, taking them all in all, they formed the backbone of the country, and restored to England many of the characteristics which had made it great: characteristics which had come to be despised by the aristocracy, such as integrity and honesty, stern independence, and a respect for moral standards and for hard work. Among them family life was more highly valued than in other classes, and family life has always been the great strength of English life and character. The aristocrat might have his family pride, but it was too often based on position and privilege rather than on character; the family pride of the middle classes and of the yeomen had more worthy and enduring foundations. Every family set great store by its reputation among its neighbours, and the most precious legacy a man could leave to his children was a good name. Any failure on the part of one member was considered a family disgrace, and though such an attitude might lead to a harsh and cruel treatment of the unfortunate, it undoubtedly served to maintain the highest standards of conduct and character.

Of conditions among the lower classes we have not so much information,[1] but it may be assumed that their moral state was much higher in the country, where they had the guidance and control of squire and parson, than in the towns. In the latter, indeed, the example of their betters often had a degrading effect, and the taverns and ale houses echoed the scoffs and jeers against religion and morality which found utterance in the salons of the great and the coffee houses of the literary. In an attempt to ape the manners and dress of the upper classes many of them were only too ready to descend to dishonourable and even criminal practices. In London, above all, there were numbers who got their living by their wits and by pandering to the vices of the wealthy. As very few could read or write they were apt to be ignorant and brutal, and conditions seemed to be deteriorating; at least, such was the opinion of Horace Walpole, who asserted that their vices were "increased to a degree of robbery and murder beyond example".

The working class suffered grievously from economic causes.

[1] See J. L. and Barbara Hammond, *The Town Labourer*, *The Skilled Labourer* and *The Village Labourer*.

SOCIAL AND ECONOMIC CONDITIONS   47

There was frequent unemployment, and no adequate means of dealing with it; nor did employers in many instances feel any sense of responsibility for those whose labours they exploited. A collier might slave for sixteen hours a day in return for a wage of about a shilling, and when he was no longer fit for work, be turned off to fend for himself as best he could.

In such conditions it is not surprising that outbreaks of violence occurred when things became intolerable. One frequent cause was the suspicion, often justified, that the price of food was being artificially kept up or even raised. In 1740 there were serious riots, especially in the North,[1] when corn reached a very high level owing to much of it being exported. In June, 1740, after the Newcastle merchants had failed to keep their promise to reduce the price of bread, the mob rose in protest. In the disturbance one of them was killed, and they proceeded to sack the Guildhall by way of reprisal. At Blyth in the following spring the granaries were plundered. But violence was only a last resort. The people, if their complaints received sympathetic hearing, would always refrain from exercising it. In Hartlepool the father of William Romaine, meeting an excited throng, inquired as to their grievance. On being told that it was the price of wheat, he promised to let them have it at five shillings a bushel. Although the other merchants refused to co-operate he kept his promise, and the mob went quietly away.[2] Some of the outbreaks reached such a dangerous level that troops had to be called out, and at Hexham in 1761 they opened fire on the crowd, killing or wounding about a hundred of them before order was restored.[3]

Turning our attention to more pleasant topics, we come now to sport. Our glance at it can be brief only, since it has no great significance for our inquiry.[4] None the less, some notice is necessary since sport, then as ever, was a favourite interest of all classes of Englishmen, and without it we can get no complete idea of their lives. It will also reveal some characteristics. For the country gentleman its most prominent form was hunting, though now the fox had displaced the deer as the object of the chase. Hares, too, were hunted, and as this took place on foot it was a more democratic form.

Just as the hunting of the fox was displacing that of the deer, so too the ancient art of hawking was giving way to

---

[1] There were also outbreaks in Cornwall in 1727, 1729, 1748 and 1757
[2] *Life of Romaine* (*Works*, p. 2)   [3] *London Chronicle*, March 5, 1761
[4] For a full treatment see Trevelyan, *English Social History*, pp. 406 ff.

shooting. The sport was still in a very primitive form, and the old-fashioned muzzle-loading gun was both slow and dangerous. There was no driving of the birds, nor were beaters employed; but game was preserved, which led to the introduction of severe laws, and many encounters with poachers.

Horse racing, which goes back to very early days, was being put on an organized basis. The Jockey Club, established at Newmarket in the middle of the century, provided a controlling body. In 1740 an Act of Parliament had made a number of regulations for the conduct of racing, down to the weights which horses were to carry. In 1752, about the time of the formation of the Jockey Club, racing was held at some seventy places, ten of them in Yorkshire. But even in 1789 the number of horses taking part in flat races was only a thousand, which is about a seventh of the number to-day.

The typically English game of cricket had become widely popular and served to draw the different classes together, since all had a share in it. Trevelyan shrewdly remarks that "if the French *noblesse* had been capable of playing cricket with their peasants, their chateaux would never have been burnt".

Prize-fighting was a very popular sport, which is natural in view of the English habit of settling disputes with the fists. Boxing was then carried on with the bare hands, and the contestants suffered much damage; but the victors were held in such veneration that it seemed worth it. There was a famous fight in April, 1787, when, in the presence of the Prince of Wales, the Jew Mendoza defeated Martin. After the fight he was conducted to London by a torchlight procession, and a band playing Handel's "See the conquering hero comes". Soon after this, boxing got into bad odour owing to the entry of corruption, and it was some time before it was restored to favour.

The brutality of the age comes out in its sports. A favourite village pastime was the baiting of bears and bulls. Lecky quotes an advertisement of 1730: "A mad bull to be dressed up with fireworks; a dog to be dressed up with fireworks over him; a bear to be let loose at the same time, and a cat to be tied to the bull's tail".[1]

Another popular sport which caused much cruelty was cock-fighting. Even the clergy indulged in it, and some enthusiastic votaries recorded their successes in the parish registers. The men of the eighteenth century were a hard lot, and thought

[1] *History of England in the Eighteenth Century*, i, p. 552

little of the sufferings of others, especially of animals. The fear of hydrophobia, for instance, could lead to the indiscriminate slaughter of harmless dogs. But under the surface there was much kindliness, and such cruel practices were simply accepted as customary. A more refined spirit and the recognition of the evils of suffering of any kind (to the spread of which the revival of religion undoubtedly contributed) gradually led to the abandonment of some of the more outrageous forms of sport.

Nowadays a trip to the seaside, of longer or shorter duration, is part of the routine of most families. In the eighteenth century the poorer classes had no holidays, save for a few odd days, and such expeditions were out of the question for them. The upper classes paid visits to one another in their country houses and went up to London or some provincial capital or to an inland watering-place for the "season". Trips to the seaside came but slowly into vogue, for bathing was as a rule only indulged in on medical advice;[1] but by 1720 it was sufficiently in demand to make Margate a fashionable resort. An engraving reproduced in *Johnson's England* shows bathing at Scarborough in 1735, with bathing machines,[2] and, what is most surprising in view of later prudery, some of the bathers are practically naked.

It is generally supposed that England in the eighteenth century had recovered somewhat from the very loose morality which followed the Restoration and the reaction against Puritanism. There was certainly a revolt against the wild licence of dramatists such as Wycherly, Etheridge, Congreve and their fellows, and even against Dryden. But the reaction was only limited; Congreve's plays were still in demand, and to some observers conditions had not improved; they might even be considered worse, for Dr. Moss in 1708 speaks of the decay of virtue in "this degenerate people" of England. It is always difficult to assess the state of morals at any given epoch, for the witnesses are often prejudiced, and their memories not too reliable. Probably loose living and a low moral tone were taking on different forms. Dr. John Brown, who wrote his *Estimate of the Manners and Principles of the Times*, under George II, considered that "vain, luxurious, and selfish effeminacy" were characteristic of the times rather than "abandoned wickedness

---

[1] Smollett, before going on his travels, "proposed to bathe in the sea, with a view to strengthen and prepare my body for the fatigue of such a long journey" (*Travels through France and Italy*, § 5)

[2] Charles Wesley saw them at Margate about this time: see *Journal*, ii, p. 186

and profligacy". By the later part of the century, if the descriptions of Hannah More are at all accurate, conditions were much better.

Whether morals were as low as in the closing years of the seventeenth century or not, they were certainly very bad. Society even in the early years of George III, in spite of its outward refinement, was very corrupt;[1] a not unusual consequence of idleness and irresponsibility. Its vices, indeed, were open and notorious, for hypocrisy was not among them, and were almost a necessary qualification for entry into fashionable life. Excessive drinking and gambling could hardly be avoided, and sexual immorality was taken as a matter of course. Charles James Fox was taken away from Eton by his father, the first Lord Holland, for a trip on the continent that he might be initiated into habits which would make him a man of the world. Such vices had behind them the example of the previous generation, for both George I and II were notoriously immoral, and Sir Robert Walpole was an unashamed adulterer. Even quite "good women", if *Pamela* and Sophia in *Tom Jones* give a true picture, thought little of pre-marital irregularities, and many had to condone them after marriage. That a higher standard was expected in women was not a genuine tribute to the superior morals of the sex, for Bishop Warburton, commenting on Pope, could suggest that "every woman is at heart a rake".

Card-playing was almost a universal occupation, and it filled so many hours of the day that one wonders how people found the necessary time, especially those who held office. One effect, to the indignation of Hannah More and her "blue-stocking" friends, was to kill polite conversation:

> Long was society o'er-run
> By Whist, that desolating Hun.[2]

The amounts staked were excessive, and many were ruined at the card-table, or by other forms of gambling. "The gaming is worthy of the decline of our Empire. The young men lose five, ten, fifteen thousand pounds in an evening", wrote Horace Walpole in 1770.

Another evil was duelling. Every fine gentleman cherished so nice a regard for his honour as to be prepared on the smallest

[1] For a vivid and detailed account of society in the early years of George III, see G. O. Trevelyan, *The Early Hist. of Chas. Jas. Fox*, chap. ii
[2] *Works*, i, p. 15

provocation to risk his life and endanger that of another in its defence. There were few who ventured to protest against so senseless a custom, though among them had been Addison and Steele.

Drunkenness was a vice from which no class was exempt, and was found in town and country alike. In 1775 Crabbe wrote a satire on *Inebriety* in which he described the effects of intemperance on various classes from the squire to the labourer, not omitting the parish priest. In a later poem he speaks of "girls who heed not dress for gin". In the towns things were perhaps even worse, for if the ale of the countryside was exceedingly harmful, its effects were nothing when compared with those of spirit-drinking. Spirits are said to have been first imported from Holland early in the reign of George I, and in London and the large towns led to degrading and repulsive scenes, making the common people "what they never were before, cruel and inhuman".[1]

Opportunities for indulgence in drunkenness and even worse evils were provided for the Londoner in the popular resorts of Vauxhall and Ranelagh, where the commoner and the aristocrat might be found rubbing shoulders. Sadler's Wells also offered less fashionable delights. Vauxhall was at its prime between 1750 and 1790. As there was no bridge until the end of the century, those who did not go round by the new bridge at Westminster went there by river from the stairs at Whitehall. As the working and middle classes were only free on Sunday, that was the great day for amusements. But even the upper classes chose it for their most elaborate entertainments.

In view of the low state of morals it is not surprising that crime was rampant, or that there was not much public feeling against it. Often enough, indeed, it was the result of need and destitution. Bishop Dawes of Chester in 1713 referred to the increase of "whippings, pilloryings and executions" as due to the increase of unemployment and the threat of starvation. Highwaymen, who were often old soldiers for whom no provision was made, infested the roads and even penetrated into the towns. Horace Walpole was robbed and nearly shot in Hyde Park in 1749, and a post-chaise was actually stopped in Piccadilly, the assailant riding down the watch and making good

[1] A contemporary writer quoted by Lecky, *op. cit.*, i, p. 481. He comments: "It was not till about the year 1724 that the passion for gin-drinking appears to have affected the masses of the population, and it spread with the rapidity and violence of an epidemic. . . . The fatal passion for drink was at once and irrevocably implanted in the nation"

his escape. There was much admiration for the daring and resource of the highwaymen and many became popular heroes. The streets of London were also made dangerous for innocent passers-by through the exploits of the "Mohacks", fashionable young men who took a delight in attacking respectable citizens, both men and women, not for gain, but out of sheer devilment.

Smuggling, a less vicious practice, was common around the coasts, being countenanced by the gentry and winked at by the clergy, who in many parts had their share of the proceeds or were willing to buy cheap liquor without inquiring where it had come from.

There was as yet no organized police force to restrain or arrest the criminal, and the night watchmen were often old and feeble, and quite incapable of doing more than raise an alarm. The Bow Street runners, organized by the Fielding brothers, were efficient, but too few in numbers to have any appreciable effect.

Those criminals who were so unfortunate as to be caught were subjected to barbarous and quite excessive punishment. But this only made them more desperate to escape arrest, and also had the effect of making jurymen unwilling to convict. There were over 250 offences for which the death penalty could be inflicted, ranging from the picking of pockets to the damaging of bridges, and no consideration was given to age or temptation. In 1785, an exceptionally bad year, there were 500 hangings; in fact, they became so numerous that Dr. Johnson could suggest in irony that the navy would soon run short of ropes:

> Scarce can our fields, such crowds at Tyburn die,
> With hemp the gallows and the fleet supply.

Hanging, before the invention of the drop, meant at least half-an-hour's slow torture before suffocation brought an end to the sufferings of the victim. Thus the onlookers had plenty of diversion, and thousands flocked to the weekly hangings at Tyburn, where special seats were provided for the fashionable world. For other crimes the penalty was transportation, and whole shiploads of men and women of varied character, some comparatively innocent, some ingrained in vice, were sent to the criminal establishments in Australia, from which few ever returned.

The chorus of lament over the low moral state of the country, in which good men of all shades of opinion had their part, was,

I would suggest, not so much the result of continued deterioration (this was probably not the case), but evidence of a keener perception and a more sensitive conscience. Evils were no longer being taken as a matter of course.

No society is entirely corrupt; if it were, it could not long survive; and it must not be forgotten that the England of the mid-eighteenth century gave birth to the men who in the face of immense odds saved the liberties of Europe, and at the same time gave a notable impetus to commerce, science and art. Leslie Stephen has pointed out that the paintings of Sir Joshua Reynolds "suggest the existence of a really dignified and pure domestic life in a class too often remembered by the reckless gambling and loose morality of the gilded youth of the day".[1] There were beyond all question numerous homes of a modest character, especially among the professional and middle classes, where a refined culture and a quiet religious spirit prevailed. They might seem a little ultra-respectable, but they had true dignity, and were an admirable training ground, with their high sense of duty and responsibility, for those who were brought up in them. It was there that the true strength of England really lay. In the villages, too, the country folk worked industriously in the fields and farms, and on Sunday they went regularly to church.

Attempts to improve the moral state of the nation were frequent. One of the objects of Addison and Steele had been "to recover virtue and discretion out of that desperate state of vice and folly into which the age is fallen".[2]

In 1692 a Society for the Reformation of Manners had been established, but interest in it declined, and by 1730 it had ceased to exist. It was, however, revived a generation later and received support from Wesley and the Methodists. One of its objects was to see that the law was enforced, and in five years about 10,000 successful prosecutions were undertaken.[3] It came to an end in 1766 owing to damages of £300 being awarded against it through the perjury of one of its witnesses. The society was unable to recover its costs, and had to be wound up. On which Wesley commented: "Lord, how long shall the ungodly triumph?"[4]

If the eighteenth century as a whole was a cruel and callous age, there was a growing sensitiveness on the part of a few to the evils and sufferings around them. The century, especially

[1] *Ford Lectures*, p. 191
[2] *The Spectator*, No. 10
[3] *Works*, vi, p. 145
[4] *Journal*, v, p. 154

towards its close, abounded in philanthropists.[1] The motives which inspired these men and women were many and diverse. Some were moved by the desire to preserve the social structure from possible dangers[2]—there were even those who thought it wasteful to let children die when so many were needed to work in the factories; some were moved by tenderness of heart; many by the promptings of religion.

It has been remarked that the philanthropists of the eighteenth century did their good works with a high hand. But such a temptation besets philanthropy in all ages, and acts of charity ever tend, for the human heart is deceptive above all things, to engender and foster a comfortable feeling of power and even of patronage.

Everyone has heard of the efforts to abolish slavery; but not everyone knows that there were, during the period, many other enterprises undertaken to check or mitigate similar evils. As early as 1729 General Oglethorpe persuaded Parliament to hold an inquiry into conditions in the Fleet and Marshalsea debtors' prisons. These prisons were run by private persons for their own profit and fees exacted from the wretched inmates. Then in 1773 John Howard began his crusade to improve conditions in prisons of every description. It was in the eighteenth century, too, that hospitals began to be established; the Westminster in 1719, Guy's in 1723, followed by St. George's, the London and the Middlesex. Captain Thomas Coram's famous Foundling Hospital was started in 1742, and from 1749 various lying-in hospitals were founded. In the country there was similar if more limited activity—Addenbrooke's Hospital at Cambridge and the Radcliffe Hospital at Oxford belong to the same era. These enterprises received strong support from Christian people, and sermons in their support became a regular feature. Some, however, were opposed to them on the ground that they interfered with natural penalties for certain sins, and also discouraged thrift, since the poor ought to make their own provision for such emergencies as sickness.[3]

The subject of hospitals naturally leads on to the wider one

[1] See Betsy Rodgers, *Cloak of Charity: Studies in Eighteenth Century Philanthropy*

[2] Cf. M. G. Jones, *The Charity School Movement*, p. 4: "The political and religious unrest of the eighteenth century contributed in no small degree to the desire of the upper and middle classes to establish social discipline among the poor, who in contemporary opinion were peculiarly susceptible to the poison of rebellion and infidelity"

[3] Bishop Butler answered such objections in the last of his *Six Sermons preached on Public Occasions*

of health and disease. In the eighteenth century the expectation of life was but short, and in its early years deaths actually exceeded births. This was in part due to excessive gin-drinking, which was mainly prevalent in London. Many members of the upper classes shortened their lives by hard drinking, and their indulgence in any case undermined their constitutions and sowed the seeds of future evils, which might be reaped in succeeding generations, as by the innocent inheritors of the fearful legacy of gout. Consumption was rife, and carried off several of the leaders of the Evangelical Movement, whilst Wesley made an almost miraculous recovery from it in middle life.

Mortality among children seems to have been particularly excessive. Richardson the novelist, who was twice married, lost all his six sons, and two out of an equal number of daughters; Gibbon had five brothers and a sister, all of whom died in infancy; only three of Edmund Burke's fourteen brothers and sisters survived childhood; whilst Sir Walter Scott had six brothers and sisters who all died in infancy. The majority of children, it has been stated, never reached the age of nine.[1]

Other causes, in addition to the consequences of evil living, were at work to shorten life; such as defective medical knowledge and skill, and an unbalanced and inadequate diet. After 1730 conditions began to improve, especially in the field of medical practice. Surgery was no longer left to the barber-surgeon, but became a learned profession, and more attention was paid to the art of midwifery. There was also a great improvement in diet. The keeping of animals alive through the winter, instead of slaughtering them and salting their carcases, made possible a more abundant supply of fresh meat. This reduced and almost stamped out scurvy and other forms of skin diseases which had afflicted all classes.

The prevalence of disease encouraged the manufacture of "patent medicines," one of the most popular being Dr. James's Fever Powders, the proprietor of which was John Newby, a well-known bookseller. These powders were understood to have royal patronage; and lesser lights, including Horace Walpole and Oliver Goldsmith, had a firm belief in their efficacy.

[1] G. B. Hill, in *Memoirs of Gibbon*, p. 29

CHAPTER 4

THE INTELLECTUAL AND EDUCATIONAL BACKGROUND

Since the Evangelical Movement (and still more the Methodist) made its primary appeal to the emotions, and spread, at least in its early stages, chiefly among the common folk, it might seem that the intellectual and cultural background of the period would not have any great significance. But this was far from being the case. The over-intellectualization of religion had robbed it of life, not only for the uneducated, but even for those who had some learning. They were thus ready to welcome a more emotional presentation. Again, it must not be forgotten that the leaders, with few exceptions, were university men, and some of them had more than a superficial acquaintance with the philosophical ideas of the times and were deeply influenced by them. This was eminently true of Wesley; and here Principal Shairp has made a revealing comment:

> It is a striking proof of how entirely the mechanical philosophy had saturated the age, that Wesley . . . in the opening of his sermon on Faith, indorses the sensational theory, and declares that to man in his natural condition sense is the only inlet of knowledge.[1]

To this I would add the suggestion that Wesley's insistence on "degrees" of faith, one cause of dispute between him and other leaders, was due to Locke's theory that assent of every kind must have its degrees. Moreover, philosophy in England at this epoch was no purely academic pursuit, such as it afterwards became in Germany, and for that matter in England itself. Philosophic questions were discussed in every coffee-house and other places where men gathered together. Even a popular novel such as *Tristram Shandy* is full of expositions of Locke's philosophy, as indeed were Sterne's other writings.[2] Philosophers wrote, not for students, but for the average cultivated man,

[1] *Studies in Poetry and Philosophy*, p. 106
[2] Sterne believed that Locke's influence could be seen "in all his pages, in all his lines, in all his expressions": quoted by Laird, *Philosophical Incursions into English Literature*, p. 84

and, since they refrained from wrapping up their ideas in technical terms, the average man was able to follow and appreciate their arguments.[1]

Because this was the case with philosophy in England, it developed along practical lines and was largely interested in ethical problems. Moreover, thought in England had at last broken with the old Scholasticism, and, as a consequence, was becoming isolated and insular; it was also indifferent to theology, which seemed to have little practical value. This practical bent can be seen even in political thought which abandoned alike "the theocratic dreams of the Puritans, or the divine right of High-Churchmen, or the historic traditions of feudalism [for] the more prosaic, but not less unreal, phantasy of an original contract".[2] The disparagement of theology, as traditionally expounded, was also intensified by reason of its failure, for the time at least, to meet the changing situation brought about by the influx of new ideas and the growth of knowledge of the world of nature. A situation which has its parallels in times more recent.

There was certainly much stirring of thought, and the problems that were being discussed went far deeper, in both their speculative and practical implications, than they had in the immediate past. Not a few, perhaps half unconsciously, were so dazzled by the immense achievements of human reason as to rely upon it for the solution of all problems and the satisfaction of all needs. But those who were mainly responsible for this point of view did not deny the truths of Christianity; both Locke, in philosophy, and Newton, in natural science, had been religious men, as were Boyle and Halley among their successors.

The most profound changes were those taking place in natural science, where there was an increasing awareness of the problems to be solved and a keen anxiety to find solutions. Compared with scientists of more recent times, the men of the eighteenth century were only amateurs with little training and no very comprehensive range of knowledge;[3] as a consequence, some of

[1] Locke and Hume "wrote as citizens of the world, anxious (in no bad sense) for effect; and even if their conclusions were remote from popular belief, still presented them in the flesh and blood of current terms used in the current sense" (T. H. Green, *Works*, i, p. 4). This had also been true of Hobbes and Berkeley still earlier

[2] Shairp, *op. cit.*, p. 105: see also J. N. Figgis, *The Divine Right of Kings*

[3] Prominent among them was Henry Cavendish, a man of immense wealth and grandson of the second Duke of Devonshire. He spent some time at Peterhouse, Cambridge, but never took his degree

them were apt to be led astray by strange will-o'-the-wisps, such as Stahl (1660–1734), with his theory of phlogiston. This theory was eagerly accepted, and when Priestley discovered oxygen in 1774 he called it "dephlogisticated air". Even after Lavoisier had shown its falsity in 1787, and his exposure had been made known in this country by James Black, a number of scientists refused to give it up.

In the seventeenth century, scientists had concentrated on physics and mechanics. They now began to turn their attention to chemistry and biology. This led to a greater interest in individual specimens in both plants and animals, and was in line with the philosophical thought of the age which was coming more and more to take account of the individual man. This was something entirely novel, for even Descartes, in spite of his *Cogito ergo sum*, had concentrated on mathematical and mechanical problems in which the individual is of little account. Spinoza with his notion that the individual hardly existed apart from God and Nature tended in the same direction. Reaction came with Leibniz, and still more with Locke, whose appeal to experience was to the experience of the individual. This was in reality the basis of his doctrine of toleration, for he insisted that every man had the right to select that form of religion which he felt the most useful for his own salvation. This growing emphasis on the value of the individual, in both science and philosophy, found religious expression in the Evangelical insistence on the necessity for personal acceptance of the benefits of redemption.

Confidence in the power of reason, to which reference has just been made, was characteristic of eighteenth-century thought above all else, though it had its origin in the previous century, being a heritage from Descartes. But the position of Descartes had already been attacked by Locke, and this onslaught was pressed home by Bishop Berkeley, and finally by Hume, whose position was one of absolute scepticism. Hume, however, had his usefulness, for he showed, unintentionally, that the unassisted reason was helpless to solve ultimate problems. He was an outstanding example of those thinkers who are so enamoured of logic as almost to make it an end in itself, rather than an instrument of thought. They recall the fishermen of Habakkuk 1: 16 who offered sacrifices to their nets.

Those who were willing to go all lengths with Hume were but few; none the less, rationalism was the accepted method, not only of philosophers, but also of Churchmen. Butler had

INTELLECTUAL, EDUCATIONAL BACKGROUND

affirmed that reason was "the only faculty we have wherewith to judge concerning anything, even revelation itself".[1] Wesley held much the same position, saying: "I am ready to give up any opinion which I cannot by calm, clear reason defend"; and, again: "I would just as soon put out my eyes to secure my faith, as lay aside reason."[2]

The trust in reason which characterized the eighteenth century, and to which it remained so faithful, was ultimately based on a pathetic belief in the fundamental goodness and rationality of man. If only the truth could be made known to him he would surely respond to it. But such an attitude ignores those deeper passions and instincts which may render the truth unacceptable, may pervert it, and may blind the eyes so that they cannot perceive it.

One effect of the appeal to reason was a diminution of authority, especially in theology and religion. In the previous century the great divines were accepted as experts in their own special science, and their utterances were received as final. But once the appeal to reason and the free judgment of the individual was allowed, this state of affairs came to an end, even though the individual's own knowledge of theology might be but scanty, and his ability to handle the mysteries of the faith quite inadequate.

The phrase "appeal to reason" is a deceptive one; for though ideally there may be such a thing as pure reason, it has never acquired a habitation in the minds of men; and, as Mark Pattison observed with his accustomed cynicism, reason is in reality only another name for the philosophy in vogue at any particular time. In the eighteenth century that philosophy beyond all question was that of Locke. We have already observed how it affected the mind of Wesley and found expression in the novels of Sterne. These are but examples of its widespread influence, an influence which also affected some Evangelicals; one of the very few personal references in the works of Romaine is to Locke.[3] The writing of his which was most studied was the treatise *On the Understanding* (Wesley printed extracts from it in the *Arminian Magazine* for 1781), which found a good deal of favour among Evangelicals of a thoughtful turn of mind—Dr. Hey recommended it to John Jowett—but they were not unanimous in their attitude to his writings as a whole. Before he became an Evangelical, Thomas Scott had

[1] *Analogy*, Part II, chap. iii, § 3   [2] *Works*, ix, p. 105; x, p. 267
[3] *Works*, p. 555

valued *The Reasonableness of Christianity*, which later he condemned, though he never ceased to admire Locke's *Letters concerning Toleration*.[1] Locke's influence outlived the eighteenth century, and in 1804 *On the Understanding* was a set book on which Henry Martyn examined the young men at Cambridge.

The predominance of Locke is not difficult to account for. It lay in the fact that, as Leslie Stephen has said: "he interpreted so completely the fundamental beliefs which had been worked out in his time".[2] In addition, his temper and outlook exactly suited the men of the age. He was shrewd and practical, and, ignoring matters which seemed to promise little hope of solution and led only to confusion and perplexity, he based his system on the evidence of the senses, and his ethics "on the selfish instincts of pleasure and pain".[3]

"Sensationalism", when pressed to its legitimate conclusions, as by Hume, might lead to absolute scepticism; but Locke had exercised the Englishman's privilege of being logically inconsistent, or rather, of combining views which were apparently incompatible. He had, it would seem, two sides to his mind; the one critical and rationalizing, the other reverent and devout. And so he could remain a sincere and not merely a professing Christian, and go so far as to affirm: "I read the revelation of Holy Scripture with a full assurance that all it delivers is true."[4]

But if Locke himself had this devotional side to his mind, it was the other, critical and rational, side which most influenced thought, tending to weaken more spiritual forms of philosophy and being mainly responsible for the "dry, hard, unpoetical tone of eighteenth-century religion".

The thought of the first half of the century had suffered from one serious weakness: it lacked any sense of continuity and development, and was, moreover, so greatly impressed by the present that it forgot its debt to the past. This failing was gradually corrected with the emergence of a new interest in history.[5] It was in 1754 that the first volume of Hume's *History of England* appeared, to be followed five years later by Robertson's *History of Scotland*. Then between 1776 and 1788 Gibbon published his epoch-making *Decline and Fall of the*

---

[1] *The Force of Truth* (*Works*, i, p. 32 n.)   [2] *Ford Lectures*, p. 47
[3] Shairp, *op. cit.*, p. 105   [4] *Works*, iv, p. 341
[5] Clarendon's *History of the Great Rebellion* had been published in 1702–04; and Rollin's *Histoire Ancienne* (1730–38) found many readers in England

Roman Empire. Perhaps even more significant, though less often noticed, was the printing, from 1783 onwards, of Domesday Book.

A recognition of the value of history, however, was slow in gaining ground. Dr. Johnson, it will be remembered, had but little appreciation of it, partly because there was so much that was uncertain about the past, and partly because of the impossibility of getting at the motives of the actors. He rather despised the writer of history, for if he wrote what was true little room was left for any display of ability. But, if thought in England was slow to appreciate the lessons of the past as depicted by the historian, it did not decry them as was the case with the contemporary *philosophes* in France. D'Alembert, one of the most sober of them, once expressed the wish that all record of the past events might be blotted out.[1]

The revived interest in history naturally exercised a considerable influence upon religious thought and method. In fact, it revolutionized Christian apologetics. In the early part of the century it had been the internal evidences of Christianity that had been in question, and Christian apologists tried to show that revelation and reason were not inconsistent; in the later half, the field of discussion shifted, and it was the external evidences which came into prominence and the question of the reliability of the records.

We now turn from philosophy to what might have been expected to be the natural centres for its study in the two universities of the land. But in neither Oxford nor Cambridge was any great interest shown in the subject. For this they have been condemned by Mark Pattison, who wrote: "instead of taking students through a laborious course of philosophy, natural and moral, [they] turned out accomplished gentlemen upon 'the classics' and a scantling of logic".[2] Having no rivals, for between them they monopolized higher education, they were content to stand in the old ways and to carry on their inherited traditions.[3] The universities were, indeed, typical English institutions and had no real parallels elsewhere; admission was still limited to members of the Church of England, and their whole outlook was predominantly clerical. At the same time, it must not be forgotten that they constituted societies which were not only cultivated, at least in ideal, but

[1] See J. S. Mill, *Dissertations*, i, p. 426   [2] *Essays*, ii, p. 25

[3] Cf. G. M. Trevelyan, *English Social History*, p. 365: "the spirit of chartered monopoly was seen at its worst on the banks of the Isis and Cam"

also polite. The education, however, which they provided was both expensive and inadequate, and it was left to the Dissenting Academies to give fuller attention to the study of modern languages and natural science. Such studies, however, if they were not encouraged, were not entirely neglected. In 1724 Regius Professorships had been founded at both universities in Modern History and Modern Languages. The main object of these foundations was to train the young men for diplomatic and political service. In actual practice they enabled youthful graduates to fit themselves for acting as tutors for Englishmen going on the grand tour, and so to break the monopoly hitherto enjoyed by French Huguenots and Scottish graduates. Nor was natural science without its students. Bishop Watson's lectures on Chemistry in 1766–69 drew crowded audiences from both undergraduates and seniors at Cambridge,[1] as did those of Isaac Milner.[2] Whilst at Oxford Dr. Thomas Beddoes had a very large class in the same subject.

The older professors seldom felt it incumbent upon them to lecture; indeed, during the latter part of the century the government definitely discouraged them, fearing that they might arouse dangerous political tendencies. Nor was much account taken of the qualifications requisite for the posts to which they were appointed.

The future Bishop Watson was a notorious case. When he was elected to the Professorship of Chemistry (to which, incidentally, no stipend was attached) he had never read a syllable on the subject, nor seen a single experiment. Seven years later he became Regius Professor of Divinity, for which his qualifications were not much better. Another example is the poet Gray, who, having failed to secure the Professorship of Modern Languages at Cambridge, for which he may have had some qualifications, was compensated by being presented to that of Regius Professor of Modern History, for which he had none.

As most of the fellows of colleges were merely hanging on until a suitable living came vacant, it was not strange that they should take but a perfunctory interest in their duties. The really able men were drawn away by openings elsewhere. But if many tutors neglected their duties, there were a number who were doing their best under discouraging circumstances. When Dr. Johnson went up to Oxford in 1731, Mr. Bateman at Christ Church had a high reputation, and it is said that he "accepted the mild but judicious expostulations" of the

[1] *Life of Bishop Watson*, i, pp. 46 and 53   [2] *Life of Dean Milner*, p. 32

Rev. W. Adams, D.D., at Pembroke, a "worthy man, whose virtues awed him, and whose learning he revered".

Conditions at Oxford during the first half of the century were more backward than at Cambridge. Though fewer residents became Non-jurors, Jacobitism was much more prevalent; it even survived the fiasco of 1745, and, as in Scotland, lingered on as a harmless sentiment. But its continued prevalence was harmful to the reputation of the university and to the studies which were supposed to be conducted there. Few, however, seem to have been interested in study. Between 1730 and 1740 the Bodleian on many days had no readers, and it was most unusual for more than a couple of books to be consulted on a single day. But things were never so bad as is generally supposed. "Degenerate as it was, and far inferior to Cambridge in the performance of its highest functions, the University was not so utterly effete as is sometimes represented."[1]

Speaking of Oxford as he had known it in his youth, Lord Westbury likened it to "a great ship, left high and dry upon the shore, which marked the place where the waters of knowledge had once flowed".[2] Such a comparison would have been still more apt a hundred years before the period which the noble lord was describing.

The appointment of Lowth to the Professorship of Poetry in 1741 (it had been established in 1708) promised an awakening from the torpor and subservience of the previous age. But here again that age may have been unduly disparaged, for Lowth claimed that he had rekindled the study of Hebrew which had almost fallen out of use.[3] There is, however, some evidence that Hebrew had been studied before his appointment. The Hutchinsonians, for example, were much given to it, and John Wesley had been taught Hebrew by his elder brother, and in turn instructed Hervey and others.

Gibbon went up to Magdalen in 1752, just after Lowth had resigned his professorship, and his derogatory comments on the condition of the university are so well known as not to require repetition.[4] They have, however, been given too much significance. When Gibbon went into residence he was not yet fifteen, had never been to a public school (apart from a short time at

---

[1] Brodrick, *Hist. of the Univ. of Oxford*, p. 183
[2] Nash, *Life of Lord Westbury*, ii, p. 288
[3] His lectures, *De Sacra Poesi Hebræorum*, were published in 1753
[4] See *Memoirs* (ed. G. B. Hill), pp. 47 ff.

Westminster), and his education had been most irregular. It would therefore have been difficult for him to have fitted into any kind of academic institution.

At Cambridge conditions were much more alive and active. The scientific traditions of Barrow and Newton were still maintained; and Richard Bentley, Master of Trinity from 1700 to 1742, was not one to encourage quiet and apathy. The opening of the new Senate House in 1730 was celebrated by the holding of public examinations and by the novelty of grading the candidates. Three years earlier the foundation of the Woodwardian Professorship of Geology had revealed an awareness of the importance of physical science. But Cambridge suffered from too great an obsession with mathematics, and Gray could look forward to a time when, having taken his degree, he might be "at full liberty to give myself up to my friends and classical companions, who, poor souls! though I see them fallen into great contempt with most people here, yet I cannot help sticking to."

Gray went up to Peterhouse in 1734, where his experiences, until he found a more congenial home across the street at Pembroke, were far from happy. His opinion of the condition of the university in his day may therefore have been prejudiced. It was certainly not flattering, as can be seen in his unfinished *Hymn to Ignorance*, and in his letters. One of the latter contains this scathing exposure:

> The masters of colleges are twelve grey-haired gentlefolks who are all mad with pride; the fellows are sleepy, drunken, dull, illiterate things; the fellow-commoners are imitators of the fellows, or else beaux, or else nothing; the pensioners grave, formal sots, who would be thought old, or else drink ale and sing songs against the excise. The sizars are graziers' eldest sons who come to get good learning that they may all be archbishops of Canterbury.

Elsewhere, he compares Cambridge to the Babylon spoken of in Isaiah 13: 21 f., adding, "here is a pretty collection of desolate animals".

If little help was given to those who wished to acquire learning, the opportunity, for men who were determined to study, was present. Residence, it must be remembered, was almost continuous for poor students, especially if they came from a distance and could not afford the expense of long journeys to and from their homes.[1] They thus had to fend for themselves, and perhaps this system had advantages over the spoon-fed training of modern universities; certainly, as G. M. Trevelyan has pointed out:

> the intellectual life of the country was never more brilliant, and the proportion of men of genius per head of the population in the irregularly educated England of George III was immensely higher than in our own day.[2]

The moral condition of the universities, however, was much that of society in general. Howell Harris went up to Oxford with a view to ordination, but was so appalled by the immoralities he found there that he left after only one term.[3]

If opportunities for learning and competent instruction were hard to come by, the universities were still places for acquiring those social advantages which were highly valued in their day. Social distinctions were very strong, and there was a wide gap between servitors or sizars and other undergraduates for whom they performed menial services. This was resented by the more independent spirits, and Dr. Johnson has voiced their reaction: "The difference, Sir, between us Servitors and Gentlemen Commoners is this, that we are men of wit and no fortune, and they are men of fortune and no wit."

When Isaac Milner was a sizar at Queens' he made the resolution that if ever he came into power he would abolish the menial services attached to sizarships. When he became President of Queens' he nobly carried out his early resolution.[4] Many poor and humble students had no similar force of character, and their one aim was to obtain the patronage and notice of those who had influence. Hence the spirit of subservience which pervaded their class. It was mainly from them that the future clergy were drawn; men who had come, with rough manners and uncouth ways, from humble homes and hoped by way of the university to attain to some eminence.

Thus the universities had a direct and significant effect on the Church, for not only were the fellows of colleges in orders, but it was in them that ordinands received the only training

[1] Adam Smith never left Balliol between July, 1740, and August, 1746: *Wealth of Nations* (ed. Thorold Rogers), i, pref., p. 7
[2] *English Social History*, p. 367   [3] Wesley, *Journal*, ii, p. 223
[4] *Life of Dean Milner*, pp. 6 f.

which was open to them. After their brief sojourn they would be scattered over the length and breadth of the land, carrying with them the impressions, both good and evil, they had there acquired.

In view of the influence of the universities on the ideas of the clergy of the future, a number of private benefactors attempted to improve the teaching they there received, and to provide them with weapons for meeting the unbelief and criticism to which Christianity was being subjected. In 1770 the Norrisian Professorship "of revealed religion" was established at Cambridge, where seven years later the Hulsean Lectures were established through the benefactions of John Hulse. The similar foundation at Oxford went back to the legacy of John Bampton, who died in 1751, though the first series of lectures was not delivered until 1780.

As Nonconformists were not received at Oxford and Cambridge, those of them who wished to obtain higher education had to go to universities outside England, or to find a place in the academies which were established by various Dissenting ministers up and down the land. The most famous of these was that of Doddridge at Northampton. As these institutions were untrammelled by past traditions they could develop on their own lines and teach what subjects they chose. Hence great attention was paid to science, modern languages, and philosophy. Thus they were real pioneers, and from the point of view of useful knowledge, superior to the universities themselves, if they lacked the prestige which the latter could give. It has been said of Doddridge: In his day, to mention Northampton Academy was not merely to speak of the best educational centre in the country, it was also to speak of a new education.[1] From them that philosophical radicalism which was to reach such a significant level of influence largely proceeded.

Before going up to the university the youth of the upper classes sought education at that other peculiarly English institution, the misnamed public school. Public schools, however, were not entirely monopolized by the wealthy; there were scholarships at Eton, one of which was gained by a boy from a village school in Norfolk, the famous Porson. Even without such aids boys went to Eton from comparatively humble homes. Gray went there on the earnings of his mother, who kept a milliner's shop in Cornhill, and among his contemporaries was

[1] Irene Parker, *Dissenting Academies in England*, p. 101

Thomas Ashton, the son of an usher in a Lancashire school; nor did a difference of social background prevent his forming an intimate friendship with Horace Walpole. Gray seems to have been happy at school, so his *Ode on a Distant Prospect of Eton College* suggests; and even Cowper looked back with pleasure to the scenes of his youthful studies and games.

> The pleasing spectacle at once excites
> Such recollections of our own delights,
> That viewing it, we seem almost to obtain
> Our innocent sweet simple years again.

Life in a public school was hard and rough, a "simple alternation of classics and cuffs", as Bagehot has somewhere described it. Its object was to produce a strong and manly type, modelled on the old Romans whose literature formed so large a part of the curriculum. All classes were treated alike, and Gibbon wrote: "there is not, in the course of life, a more remarkable change than the removal of a child from the luxury and freedom of a wealthy house to the frugal diet and strict subordination of a school".[1] Title or rank might indeed, be a definite handicap, and a certain duke habitually received double punishment; once for the offence, and once for being a duke.

In the first half of the century public schools had a bad reputation. Fielding represents them as places where boys learned all manner of evil, and makes Parson Adams call them "the nurseries of all vice and immorality"; and Squire Allworthy have his nephew and Tom Jones educated at home in order to avoid the temptations which they offered.[2] Southey, who entered Westminster in 1788, nine years after some of the boys had been convicted of stabbing a man in Dean's Yard, held a like opinion, and envied the advantages of a day boy over a boarder:

> He suffers nothing from tyranny, which is carried to excess in schools. . . . Above all, his religious habits, which it is almost impossible to retain at school, are safe. I would gladly send a son to a good school by day; but rather than board him at the best I would, at whatever inconvenience, educate him myself.[3]

[1] *Memoirs*, p. 34
[2] *Joseph Andrews*, Bk. III, chap. v; *Tom Jones*, Bk. III, chap. v
[3] *Life and Corr.*, i, p. 80

On the other hand, Dr. Johnson, who had never been to a public school, spoke strongly in their favour and considered that their advantages far outweighed their drawbacks. On his advice, the faithful Boswell sent one of his sons to Westminster and the other to Eton, and was able to declare with "high satisfaction", that his boys had "derived from them a good deal of good, and no evil". No doubt one school differed from another, and any school was liable to strike a bad patch.

Next in standing to the public schools were the old endowed grammar schools. Between 1660 and 1730 they were flourishing, 172 new ones being established and the endowments of 51 old ones being supplemented. They were especially strong in the North, where Lady Elizabeth Hastings (1682–1739) was a great benefactor. During the century many of them were allowed to decay, to the great loss of the nation. In that age of vested interests some of the headmasters seem to have looked upon them as their private property, and cases were not unknown when the school was actually closed, though its revenues were still being enjoyed. Under a conscientious headmaster, however, they performed very useful services. It was Dr. Moore, headmaster of Leeds, who sent Joseph Milner to Cambridge.

Wilberforce as a boy of seven went to Hull Grammar School and remained there for two years, going daily from his father's house with his satchel on his shoulder. Later he went to Pocklington Grammar School, where he had a very easy time, being often allowed to pay visits to neighbouring gentry.[1] It is worth noticing that many of the early Evangelicals came from these schools. Adam, like the two Milners, was at Leeds, Walker at Exeter, Romaine at Houghton-le-Spring (founded by Bernard Gilpin when rector there), Hervey at Northampton, and Henry Venn for a time at Bristol.

In addition to the public and grammar schools there were numerous private schools whose quality differed even more, depending as it did on the ideas of education and duty held by the proprietors. Henry Venn found one master so lenient that he asked to be moved to a school where the discipline was more severe and incentives to learning more compelling;[2] but Henry Venn must have been a very exceptional schoolboy. In many schools supervision was lax and there was much bullying. Cowper, that sensitive soul, was permanently injured by what he had to endure at Dr. Pitman's Academy in Hertford-

---

[1] *Life of Wilberforce*, i, pp. 4, 9   [2] *Venn Family Annals*, p. 67

INTELLECTUAL, EDUCATIONAL BACKGROUND 69

shire. Henry Venn went to this school in 1741, the year that Cowper left for Westminster, but his hardy spirit was doubtless well able to look after itself. Wilberforce was at a private school near London from 1768 to 1770 which was frequented mainly by the sons of merchants. The teaching and conditions were far from satisfactory, and to the end of his life he remembered "the nauseous food" he had to eat.[1]

Girls seldom left home, but even then there were a number of girls' boarding schools, which called forth the severe criticism of Wesley, who, indeed, regarded all boarding schools with disfavour.[2] He noticed in his journal for April 6, 1772, the change for the bad in girls who were sent to such institutions:

> The children who used to cling about me, and drink in every word, had been at a boarding school. There they had unlearned all religion, and even seriousness, and had learned pride, vanity, affectation, and whatever could guard them against the knowledge and love of God. Methodist parents, who would send your girls headlong to hell, send them to a fashionable boarding-school![3]

Such establishments were mainly patronized by tradesmen and farmers whose newly-acquired wealth had infected them with the bug of gentility. They wanted their daughters to be brought up as "ladies" and were not without hope that they might thus be able to marry into a higher social rank. The education provided was certainly not of a nature to fit them to be the wives of middle-class husbands, or to settle down happily in their homes. The disastrous effects which might follow such a policy have been vividly portrayed by Hannah More in her story *The Two Wealthy Farmers*.[4]

What, it may be asked, were the subjects taught in the schools of the eighteenth century? In its early part, all alike seem to have concentrated on the teaching of classics, including Greek.[5] This applies not only to the great public schools but to the grammar schools as well; even in remote Westmorland and Cumberland there were nearly thirty schools where Greek

---

[1] *Life of Wilberforce*, i, pp. 4 f. Erasmus similarly never forgot the rotten eggs and bad wine which he had to endure at the college of Montagu in Paris
[2] *Works*, xiii, p. 276 [3] *Journal*, v, p. 452 [4] *Works*, iv, pp. 65–287
[5] See M. L. Clarke, *Greek Studies in England, 1700–1830*

was taught. But later there came a reaction in schools other than public. Parents wanted something more practical, and the growing middle-class morality objected to the tone of many of the classical writings. When Wilberforce was at a private school the subjects taught were writing, French, arithmetic, Latin, and a little Greek; for, as he himself put it, in order to meet the needs of the sons of merchants who formed the bulk of the pupils, "they taught everything and nothing".[1]

In the absence of regular inspection and outside supervision the tone and influence of schools depended, even more than to-day, on the headmaster. He was often a law unto himself and, in consequence, his powers for good or for evil were immense. Fielding speaks of "the voice of the schoolmaster, or, what is often much the same, of a tyrant".[2] When Hervey was at Northampton Grammar School he was deliberately kept back by the headmaster, who would never allow any boy to advance more quickly than his own son. Many headmasters exercised a great influence for good, such as Thomas Barnard (St. John's, Cambridge), headmaster of Leeds Grammar School from 1712 to 1750, and author of the *Life of Lady Elizabeth Hastings*; and Dr. Conon of Truro. Though most proprietors of private schools regarded them merely as money-making concerns, there were not lacking some who had a real keenness for education. Such was the Rev. William Gilpin of Cheam, who had many original ideas which he put into practice.[3]

The level of scholarship in the grammar schools was often high; in 1759 Manchester Grammar School secured the first, third, and fifth wranglers at Cambridge,[4] and Isaac Milner, the *incomparabilis*, came from Leeds Grammar School. Many distinguished men held at some time in their careers the office of headmaster in these schools, including Richard Dawes at Newcastle (1738–49)[5] and Dr. Samuel Parr (Colchester and then Norwich); both of these were graduates of Emmanuel College, Cambridge.

The education of the lower classes was greatly neglected. In many towns and villages there were, indeed, Dames' Schools. But these taught little beyond the alphabet and the numbers, and perhaps a little reading. As soon as children could be useful

---

[1] *Life*, i, p. 4   [2] *Tom Jones*, Bk. XI, chap. vii

[3] See W. E. M. Brown, *The Polished Shaft*, pp. 93 ff.

[4] A. A. Mumford, *Manchester Grammar School*, p. 193

[5] His *Miscellanea Critica*, published in 1745, gained a great reputation, not only in England, but also on the Continent

they were taken away. More adequate provision was made by the charity schools established by the S.P.C.K. and private patrons in many places. By 1740 these numbered some 2,000. Their object was primarily religious, but they served a useful purpose when there was no national system of education.[1] Later they would be supplemented by the Sunday schools.

[1] See M. G. Jones, *The Charity School Movement*

CHAPTER 5

LITERATURE AND ART

CONTEMPORARY literature and art have, for the historian, an untold value, and together and by way of supplementing one another, they illuminate and illustrate the manners and the thought of the times. Of our own period Ruskin has said: "Hogarth . . . and Fielding pull so splendidly together, stroke and bow."[1] But their office is not limited to illumination and illustration; in their day they were a most telling influence on individuals and on society as a whole. For the eighteenth century each of these aspects has considerable significance; though they are less revealing in the case of religious conditions than elsewhere. For this there are two reasons. In the first place, convention was strong, and few writers or artists, whatever their personal ideas, dared to defy public opinion. Secondly, when religion or piety is introduced it is only to subserve artistic or literary ends, such as the development of the plot of a novel, and therefore they cannot be taken as evidence of the standpoint of the author or that of the world in general. Even when regarded in its totality, the literature of the period is robbed of much of its evidential value by its extremely artificial character; for it was mainly concerned with perfection of form, and though it may give a clue to manners, it merely floated over the surface of life and can tell us little of its depths.

In the early part of the century literature made no wide appeal. A library might be a necessary adjunct to a country house, but the reading public formed only a small section of the nation. As the century advanced, however, a change took place. The rise of the bookselling industry made authors less dependent on private patrons; though it might reduce some of them to bookseller's hacks. The growing middle classes were feeling their way towards culture, and so provided a new field in which literature could thrive. It was their taste which helped to popularize the novel, which became, it might almost be said, the typical middle-class form of reading, as poetry and the drama were for the aristocracy.[2] Richardson, with his portrayal

[1] Letter to F. S. Ellis, January 21, 1875 (*Collected Works*, xxxvii, p. 154)

[2] Fiction, as such, since its main object was entertainment, was despised by the "high-brows". Lord Shaftesbury even condemned *The Arabian Nights* as frivolous and idle reading (*Letters to His Son*, ii, p. 335).

of the "triumph of puritanical virtue over the feudal vices", especially appealed to them, and they were not unduly put off by the rather morbid sentimentality of *Pamela*.

A new era of periodical literature began with the appearance of *The Gentleman's Magazine* in 1731, to which Dr. Johnson contributed. Up till then the century had been the great age of pamphleteers and essayists—the latter form would be revived at its close by Charles Lamb and William Hazlitt. The writings of Swift, and of Addison and Steele, had immense vogue; as many as 20,000 copies of *The Spectator* were sold in a single day, and this by no means represents its full circulation, for copies were handed on. Both Addison and Steele were authors with high ideals, though of a limited nature; Wesley even regarded the national weakness for *The Spectator* as harmful to the spread of the Gospel, since it advocated morality and religion "unvivified by the spirit of Christianity". This is a narrow judgment, and it was not shared by other religious leaders, who welcomed their advocacy of Christian doctrine and Christian practice in an age when both were being depreciated.

The revival of the study of history was noted in the previous chapter; the related form of biography was also popular, and in Boswell's *Life of Samuel Johnson* the century produced a supreme example of the art. There were also numerous volumes of Memoirs, amongst which those of Lady Mary Wortley Montagu (who died in 1760) and of Horace Walpole (who nearly spanned the century) may be mentioned. Letter writing, too, was still an art and universally practised. This was natural at a time when newspapers had no wide circulation and people had to depend largely on correspondence for descriptions or news of the events of the day. The habit of writing long and detailed letters was shared in by the Evangelical leaders, a valuable source for our inquiry. Some of the best letters were produced by poets; those of Gray are most attractive, and Lord David Cecil placed Cowper's letters above his poems.[1] The practice slowly decayed until the introduction of the penny post reduced it from a literary exercise to a mere means of communication. Volumes of letters were frequently published, and the form was adapted to political ends as in the notorious *Letters of Junius* (1767-72). Of other political writings those of Burke stand out supreme. Meanwhile, the flow of pamphlets had continued with only occasional abatement. The habit of

[1] *The Stricken Deer*, p. 180

writing pamphlets, as Augustine Birrell once said in reference to Milton, "is one seldom thrown off. It is much easier to throw off the pamphlets". Pamphlets were especially suited to an age when preoccupation with pleasure made the reading of longer works rather tedious, an age when an epigram was rated above an argument, and brilliant wit above solid thought.

For the obtaining of news, in addition to private correspondents, men had relied on special sheets published for the purpose. By the middle of the century these were giving place to something much more like the modern newspaper. The journals, in addition to giving the news of the day (after 1771 they published accounts of debates in Parliament), contained articles, poems, correspondence, social items, government announcements, and that most useful source of revenue, advertisements. But they received only meagre support, and few had circulations of more than two thousand.

The outstanding achievement of the eighteenth century, however, was the invention of the modern novel,[1] which was then set on lines which it would pursue until well into the next century, when George Meredith took it in hand and revealed fresh possibilities of development. Some critics look upon Defoe as the pioneer, but his works of fiction which began with *Robinson Crusoe* (1719), though they point the way, do little more. Leslie Stephen assessed *Robinson Crusoe* as "a simple application of journalistic methods, not a conscious attempt to create a new variety of novel".[2] The emergence of the novel really came later, and then gradually and tentatively entered on a period of development. Some of the experiments were definitely dull, and some disreputable.

The true pioneer was Samuel Richardson, whose *Pamela*, in the not very attractive form of a series of letters, was published in 1730. His novels give "a slow-motion picture of human life on its purely sentimental side",[3] and as his sentimentalism was of a rather "namby-pamby" type, it laid him open to attacks from more robust and manly writers. But in spite of this and other defects his novels became immensely popular. Lady Mary Wortley Montagu, though she scoffed at his attempts to depict life in high society, could not resist them; "I heartily despise him, and eagerly read him, nay sob over his works in the most scandalous manner"; and even Henry Venn, so sober and so cultivated, when by chance he picked

---

[1] See Sir Walter Raleigh, *The English Novel*   [2] *Ford Lectures*, p. 134
[3] J. B. Priestley, *The English Novel*, p. 23

up the first volume of *Clarissa Harlowe* did not put it down until he had finished it.[1]

Among those who attacked Richardson was Fielding, at first by way of a caricature of *Pamela*. It was Fielding who brought the novel out of its hothouse atmosphere into the open air by his more realistic attitude towards life and deep common sense. By many critics he is regarded as having had a more decisive influence on the development of the novel than Richardson. Some have claimed him as the discoverer of a new province in the kingdom of letters.[2] But most of his characters are "stock" types, already existing in the dramatists, rather than new creations, and he lacked Richardson's acute understanding of human nature; as Richardson was the first in time, so has he the right to the title of pioneer. None the less, Fielding will always rank very high amongst the masters of the art.

Smollett resembled Fielding in his realism, so much so that when *Roderick Random* (published anonymously in 1748) was translated into French, it was attributed to the latter. Actually there was considerable difference between them, for Smollett's boisterous licence and farcical inventiveness were only saved from being intolerable by his superb powers of narration. Smollett inspired many imitators, and his *Ferdinand, Count Fathom* (1753) gave a lead to the "thriller" school which became so popular towards the close of the century. After this, Smollett devoted himself to journalism and vague and grandiose literary schemes, but shortly before his death in 1771 he returned to fiction and wrote *Humphrey Clinker*, the best and most mature of all his novels.

Sterne, from whatever angle one looks at him, was an extraordinary person and had an extraordinary career. When the first volume of *Tristram Shandy* appeared in 1759 he was an obscure Yorkshire parson of forty-six; but at once he became famous. The book, by exaggerating the absurdities of men, left them puzzled; whilst his sniggering innuendoes, though only saved from vulgarity by the genius of the author, suited the taste of the age. His quaint and at times unsavoury humour seemed little in keeping with the clerical calling, yet it did not stand in the way of offers of preferment. There was, however, another side to the man; and his sermons were considered by

[1] *Venn Family Annals*, p. 101. The taste seems to have persisted in the family, for his grandson, John, afterwards vicar of St. Peter's, Hereford, used to say that he lost a place or two in the tripos through spending a whole night reading it (*op. cit.*, p. 204)

[2] See M. P. Willcocks, *A True-Born Englishman*

Gray to exhibit a style "most proper for the pulpit, and [to] show a very strong imagination and a sensible heart". When the opportunities which fame afforded came to Sterne he was already threatened by disease, and the remaining ten years of his life were spent mainly abroad in search of health, and, it must be confessed, also of pleasure. The ninth and last volume of *Tristram Shandy* was published in 1767, to be followed in the next year by two volumes of *A Sentimental Journey*. Before he could add to them death had stepped in to end his career.

Goldsmith's solitary novel, *The Vicar of Wakefield* (1766), which greatly impressed Goethe,[1] opened up another vein, a vein which would later be worked with such admirable skill by Jane Austen. If it is defective in plot it introduces us to a number of simple, but amiable characters.

By this time the great lights which had illuminated the first age of the English novel had nearly all gone; to be succeeded by a plethora of inferior luminaries, many of them of the gentler sex. In 1763 Dr. Johnson had commended Mrs. Sheridan's novel, *Memoirs of Miss Sydney Biddulph*, as containing "an excellent moral, while it inculcates a future state of retribution"; but the majority of feminine productions were poor stuff. Macaulay said of the period which saw the publication of Fanny Burney's *Evelina* (1778), "works of that sort were then almost always silly, and very frequently wicked".

The so-called "Gothic" movement began in 1765 with Horace Walpole's *Castle of Otranto*. The volume had not been intended as a serious effort, but it provoked an innumerable swarm of imitators. The movement, by awakening interest in the Middle Ages, prepared the way for Sir Walter Scott; though it need hardly be pointed out that his representations were based, not on fantasies, but on actual events.[2] Although there was much that was morbid and unwholesome in this type of literature, with its sinister and eerie atmosphere, its combination of romance and vague terror, those who produced it were careful to see that truth and virtue should always triumph. Most of the writers of fiction in this period, with the exception of Sterne, professed to be inspired by the desire to promote morality and high ideals. But it may be doubted whether they had this effect.

---

[1] See *Dichtung und Wahrheit*, Pt. II, Bk. x

[2] Sir Walter and Horace Walpole were alike in their love of erecting pseudo-Gothic buildings—there is an undoubted resemblance between Strawberry Hill and Abbotsford

Richardson, whose professions were the most fervid, was possibly more harmful than others whose works are often condemned. He seems to have had an unpleasant mind, and in describing vice enters into the most intimate details.[1] Fielding, who spares us detailed descriptions, is more open in referring to vicious habits and their acceptance as something normal, but he does not conceal their evil consequences.[2] The influence of Sterne was perhaps the most noxious on account of its insinuating character. That such writings should have come from a beneficed clergyman was not calculated to commend the Church in the eyes of the growing number who were disposed to take religion seriously.

In looking to the fiction of the period for light on social conditions and customs we must exercise caution; Richardson, especially, may lead us astray, for his writings have the nature of "tracts", and tend to idealize conditions. Moreover, like other and lesser writers, emboldened by success, he ventured to describe sections of society of which he had no first-hand knowledge. When he submitted a volume of *Sir Charles Grandison* to one of his lady admirers who was not unacquainted with the life of the aristocracy, she pointed out so many errors that in chagrin he said that he would throw the book on the fire. Fielding, with his realistic approach to life, is a much safer guide.

The writings of the English novelists had immense popularity on the Continent, which raises the interesting question as to how far they were thought to represent English life.[3] One wonders what sort of impression was created, for example, by the eccentric productions of Smollett? This question finds a parallel in our own day in view of the wide circulation of the works of Mr. P. G. Wodehouse. Did the Germans really believe that Bertie Wooster was typical of the young men of the leisured classes in England?

Poetry for the greater part of the eighteenth century was

---

[1] Yet he was praised by Dr. Johnson in *The Rambler*, No. 97; whilst Pope recommended *Pamela* as capable of doing "more moral good than many volumes of sermons", an opinion which was decisively rejected by Sir Walter Scott in his introduction to the 1824 edition of Richardson's works (p. xxi)

[2] The only occasion upon which Dr. Johnson was really angry with Hannah More was when he discovered that she had read *Tom Jones*—"a confession which no modest lady should ever make. I scarcely know a more corrupt work" (*Memoirs of Hannah More*, i, p. 169)

[3] Taine, the eminent nineteenth-century French critic, regarded Fielding and Smollett as giving accurate accounts of contemporary life

dominated by the influence of Pope, which lay like a shadow across the landscape, obscuring its human and emotional aspects. So persistent was his example that even Crabbe never wholly threw it off. The art of Pope and his imitators is often called classical; but it would be more accurate to call it conventional and formal, as it lacked that imaginative freedom without which there can be no true classical poetry. But even in the early years of the century the coming revolt was being heralded by Gray and Collins. The former, in such a passage as—

> The meanest floweret of the vale,
> The simplest note that swells the gale,
> The common sun, the air, the skies,
> To him are opening Paradise

seems already to anticipate Wordsworth. Poetry in the eighteenth century was, indeed, like "a clear canal", broadening itself here and there into "as clear a lake",[1] in contrast with the oncoming rapids and waterfalls of the nineteenth. In a narrower sense it was classical, however, for it was designed for a public familiar with Greek and Latin literature and able to appreciate allusions to it. It was also marked by clarity and restraint, and by a dislike of eccentricity which was a reflection of the tone of the period.

But though it might reflect the tone of the period, poetry, from its conventional form and impersonal nature, could do little more; at least, until we come to the intense realism of Crabbe. It was not, however, entirely free from sentimentalism, sometimes of a religious character, as can be seen in Young's *Night Thoughts*. When it was published in 1742 it immediately enjoyed much favour and continued to be widely read. Wesley prepared an edition (with judicious omissions) in 1770, and among its admirers was the youthful Burke. Boswell went so far as to declare that "No book whatever can be recommended to young persons with better hopes of seasoning their minds with *vital religion*". Young's style was marred by pretentiousness and over-elegance; in many ways it resembles the prose of Hervey, whom we shall consider, together with Cowper and other Evangelical literary figures, in Chapter 22.

The history of the theatre in England reveals the many vicissitudes through which it has passed. In the days of Elizabeth it had great popular support; then came the Puritan eclipse,

[1] Saintsbury, *The Peace of the Augustans*, p. 105

followed by a revival at the Restoration. But this revival was only limited, for the drama then became: "simply the melancholy dependent of the court of Charles II and faithfully reflected the peculiar morality of the small circle over which it presided".[1] The Restoration dramatists certainly did the theatre grave injury with their disgusting scenes and characters, their ridicule of virtue, and their excessive licence; and it was long before it recovered from the prejudice against it which they aroused, for it was not only the Puritans who denounced and avoided it, but most decent-minded people. Tillotson had called the playhouse "the devil's chapel", a term which became almost a cliché, and William Law later maintained that "the Stage never has one innocent play". Although conditions undoubtedly improved during the eighteenth century, they were still so bad that in 1737 a Bill was introduced into Parliament to put all actors under the control of the Lord Chamberlain. Lord Hervey, by no means a Puritan, said of this measure: "The present great licentiousness of the stage did call for some restraint and regulation."[2]

There were those who called for the abolition of the theatre—but this was an impossible step; a wiser policy was to attempt to purify and elevate it. Addison wished to see it occupy the place that it had had with the Greeks and Romans;[3] whilst Steele, though he denounced immoral plays such as Wycherley's *Country Wife*, declared that: "so noble an entertainment as the stage should be ambitious of pleasing people of the best understanding, and leave others, who show nothing of the human species but risibility, to bear-gardens, etc."[4]

A better state of affairs came in with the plays of Goldsmith, whose *Good Natured Man* was produced in 1768, and *She Stoops to Conquer* five years later. Sheridan also did much to improve the stage, and in putting on the comedies of Congreve and Vanbrugh, for which there was still a popular demand, did not scruple to prune them of their worst features. His own *The Rivals* (1775), *The School for Scandal* (1777) and *The Critic* (1779) not only helped to improve the tone of the theatre, but also aroused fresh interest in the drama. But Sheridan had to take account of what is now known as the "box-office", nor was he above poking fun at the new strictness, and in the preface to *The Critic* he remarks that the Comic Muse:

[1] Leslie Stephen, *Ford Lectures*, pp. 30 f.
[2] *Memoirs of the Reign of George II*, ii, p. 341
[3] *The Spectator*, No. 446   [4] *Op. cit.*, No. 141

Once so ill behav'd and rude,
Reform'd, is now become an arrant Prude,
Retailing nightly to a yawning pit,
The purest morals undefil'd by wit.

David Garrick also did much to raise the standard and produced some of Hannah More's plays, of which she herself was afterwards a little ashamed.

If, however, the theatre was improving, it was still hampered by the old, bad tradition. Thomas Scott, before he became an Evangelical, attended a performance in London in April, 1773, but found "so much folly and wickedness, and heard so much profaneness and ribaldry, both from the stage and in the audience", that he never went again. George III, it may be remarked, was a frequent attender at the theatre, and his example was followed by bishops and clergy; though one may be permitted to suppose that they hardly shared his preference (which would have aroused the contempt of Steele) for farces and pantomimes.

The technique of the theatre had greatly altered since the days of Elizabeth, for performances were now given in buildings, and with an illuminated stage, instead of in the open air, and the women's parts were no longer taken by boys. Productions were almost entirely confined to London, though there were some touring companies; Parson Woodforde tells of regular visits to the small Somerset town of Castle Cary. Such companies had often to perform in any building they could find, and Hogarth's *Strolling Actresses dressing in a Barn* reveals some of the difficulties they had to encounter. The standard of acting can hardly have been very high, but this did not prevent the inclusion in their repertoire of Shakespearian plays and classical dramas. In course of time theatres were opened in some provincial towns.

In estimating the effect of the drama, it must not be forgotten that it was not restricted to actual performances; the drama was, indeed, a favourite form of literature, and it would be no exaggeration to say that during the century plays were more frequently read than witnessed.

The eighteenth century was, in England, a great age of music, and above all of sacred music; one need but mention the names of Handel, Boyce,[1] Greene, Croft, John Blow, Thomas Norris,

---

[1] Boyce was the organist of the Chapel Royal and taught Charles Wesley, Junior. John Wesley presented his nephew with three volumes of Boyce's cathedral music (*Letters*, v, p. 329)

Samuel Attwood, and William Crotch. This development had a varied reception by Methodists and Evangelicals. Wesley himself approved, on the whole, and records a visit to Bristol Cathedral on August 17, 1758, when Handel's *Messiah* was performed: "I doubt if that congregation was ever so serious at a sermon, as they were during the performance."[1] Henry Venn, when blamed for attending a sacred concert, defended himself by saying: "I was never more serious and devout in my thoughts than there." He had been taken to it by Madan, whose productions of oratorios at the Lock Chapel were famous; Madan's cousin, Cowper, however, was greatly shocked by the growing habit of holding sacred concerts in churches on Sunday:

> I believe that wine itself, though a man may be guilty of habitual intoxication, does not more to debauch or befool the natural understanding than music, always music; music, in season and out of season, weakens and destroys the spiritual discernment, if it is not done in an unfeigned reverence to the worship of God and with a design to assist the soul in the performance of it, which cannot be when it is the only occupation.[2]

The music in the average parish church, especially in the villages, was restricted to the singing of versified psalms, accompanied by a variety of instruments played by minstrels who sat in the west gallery.[3] Although a long-established custom, it failed to meet the desire for musical expression on the part of the congregation, and many were drawn away by the novel Methodist custom of hymn-singing,[4] until the Church, too, was compelled to adopt it. Dr. Vincent in 1787 considered that "for one who has been drawn away from the Established Church by Preaching, ten have been induced by Music".[5]

We come now to the subject of art, and here again the

---

[1] *Journal*, iv, p. 282

[2] This dislike of sacred music long persisted with those who had had an Evangelical upbringing. Ruskin once wrote: "There is excuse, among our uneducated classes, for the Christmas pantomime, but none, among our educated classes, for the Easter Oratorio", Preface to *Sir Philip Sidney's Psalter* (*Collected Works*, xxxi, p. 107)

[3] See K. H. MacDermott, *The Old Church Gallery Minstrels*

[4] The Methodists did not approve of music in which the congregation took no part, and the Conference of 1787 forbade the use of anthems (*Journal*, vii, p. 307, n. 1)

[5] *Considerations on Parochial Music*, p. 14

eighteenth century had a definite contribution to make, especially in painting in water-colours, where English artists were supreme. It had begun with Paul Sandy in the middle of the century, and in such masters as Crome and Cotman would attain a rich maturity. Mention must also be made of Richard Wilson, the great landscape painter. The development of landscape painting is very noteworthy, for it revealed a new interest in nature, which now came to be valued for itself and not as a mere background to historical subjects or human drama. Not that the individual was being neglected; wealthy society demanded portraits, and so there arose Sir Joshua Reynolds, Thomas Gainsborough and George Romney. There were also the famous miniatures of Cosway. The formation of the Royal Academy in 1768 marked an epoch in English art.

For the student of religious and social history, however, the outstanding artist was William Hogarth, a stern moralist who deliberately set himself to expose the worst features of the times, in the hope that such exposure might lead to remedial measures. Hogarth did not spare the Church, and his *Sleeping Congregation* recorded the effect of dull sermons and was no doubt typical. If Hogarth's works are somewhat brutal (they stand in striking contrast with the mild and pleasant canvases of his Venetian contemporary, Longhi), and are admittedly caricatures, his moral fervour is sufficient to excuse him, and it may be that his examples are not so far from reality as we might be disposed to imagine.

Of all the arts, architecture, if it is spontaneous, and not a mere following of conventional styles, is the most revealing. The houses which men choose to erect for their habitation disclose, even more clearly than painting, the ideals which possessed them.

England by the eighteenth century had evolved a style of its own, which, going back well into the previous century, continued to develop harmoniously until nearly the end of our period, when French influences began to come in. Architecture, moreover, was a subject which aroused great public interest and frequent discussion, more so perhaps than at any other epoch of our history. There was much activity in erecting government buildings, such as Somerset House and some of those in Whitehall, and also in municipal circles. Here the Mansion House and town halls in Liverpool and other towns may be cited. Ecclesiastical architecture[1] continued in the clas-

---

[1] See further Marcus Whiffen, *The Architecture of the Church of England, 1603–1837*.

sical style favoured by Wren and his pupils, as can be seen in St. Martin-in-the-Fields, St. Leonard's, Shoreditch, with its famous steeple, and in St. Philip's, Birmingham.

For our purpose, however, domestic architecture is the most revealing and important branch of the art. Georgian houses, with their air of solid comfort, are significant of an age of contentment and security, not ungraced by elements of beauty. Their outstanding merits are proportion and simplicity. So strong was the tradition that even the wealthy who brought back new ideas from their travels never fundamentally departed from it. There were, it is true, a number of colossal palaces erected in the period, in which display and splendour rather than comfort and simplicity were the dominant notes; but they are no evidence of the general taste and well deserve the comment of Pope on Woodstock, "'tis a house, but not a dwelling". Equally untypical were the eccentricities of the pseudo-Gothic enthusiasts, a tendency which showed itself in architecture before blossoming in literature. Such fondness for artificial ruins and imaginary reconstructions of antiquity could never have been anything more than the possession of a few whimsical characters. Gray in 1766 exposed their foolish affectation:

> Here mouldering fanes and battlements arise,
>   Turrets and arches nodding to their fall,
> Unpeopled monasteries delude our eyes,
>   And mimic desolation covers all.

The interiors of the houses were equally admirable, and had the same dignity and charm as had the furniture with which they were filled. English craftsmanship in the eighteenth century was probably the finest that the world has ever seen.

In the country districts the owners of large estates were turning their thoughts, not only to architecture, but to the arrangement of their parks and gardens. Taste at the beginning of the century had been guided by the Dutch idea of a garden as regular and controlled, with walks adorned by statuettes and clipped yew hedges; but now a new conception was arising, and a desire for something more akin to natural scenery. So there arose England's only pioneer contribution to art, that of landscape gardening. The great name in this connexion is "Capability" Brown, who, incidentally, was no mean architect;[1] but others should not be forgotten, such as William Kent and

[1] See Dorothy Stroud, *Capability Brown*

Humphrey Repton. Between them they changed the face of the country so far as it surrounded great houses, and the results of much of their work have survived to our own time. As in all innovating movements there was loss as well as gain, but the latter far outweighed the former, though Brown and his fellows were a little dictatorial in their methods, and modern taste would doubtless have insisted on a greater variety in design.

CHAPTER 6

RELIGION IN THE EARLY EIGHTEENTH CENTURY

(A) GENERAL CONDITION

THE atmosphere in England after the coming of the Hanoverians was distinctly unfavourable to the growth of religion, and there are not a few witnesses to a positive decay of some magnitude. But too much credit must not be given to them. Many of the complaints came from High Church clergymen, who were not at all averse to discovering evidence of a general deterioration, which they attributed to the neglect of their own principles. So, too, there were Roman Catholic witnesses inspired by similar motives. The cynical comment of Montesquieu that "In England there is no religion, and the subject, if mentioned in society, excites nothing but laughter" is often quoted. But his opinion merely reflects that current in the circles in which he moved, and by no means applies to the people in general. More impressive is the lament of Bishop Butler, in the advertisement prefixed to *The Analogy*, that most men had ceased to look on Christianity even as a subject of inquiry, its fictitious nature being so obvious. This was in 1736. Fifteen years later, on his primary visitation of the diocese of Durham, he took up the matter at greater length, avowing that the decay of religion was "now observed by every one", and that it had been "for some time the complaint of all serious persons" (§ 1); and he deplored "an avowed scorn of religion in some and a growing disregard of it in the generality" (§ 2).

That much vague scepticism was to be found in fashionable circles cannot be denied, but it hardly extended further; the great bulk of the people were certainly not unbelievers, and it was ignorance and carelessness, rather than infidelity, which prevailed among the lower classes before the days of Tom Paine. This was, indeed, recognized by Butler, who attributed their lack of religion not "to a speculative unbelief or denial of it, but chiefly to thoughtlessness and the common temptations of life" (§ 12). Certainly the revival preachers took it for granted that those whom they addressed had a belief in God, though they might neglect His service; they never anticipated, nor did they encounter, save from an occasional Deist, opposition on intellectual grounds. So, too, in the writings of Richardson, which reflected the tone of the middle classes for whom they were mainly intended, even the most degraded characters never go so far as to be sceptical in religion. Religion, according to his accounts, was common among domestic servants—the butler in *Pamela* says that he will pray for Pamela and her lord, and she herself found the maids on their knees praising God for her good fortune. But *Pamela* represents an ideal rather than reality. Fielding's *Joseph Andrews* gives the picture of a pious footman, but it was definitely intended as a skit on *Pamela*, and it would probably have been difficult to find such a footman in real life. Servants, no doubt, supported the established religion; but, like their masters, on political or social grounds. Their partisanship sometimes took the form of harrying the Methodists; on August 29, 1751, Wesley says that at Tiverton "a rabble of gentlemen's servants . . . endeavoured to make a disturbance", and at Cheltenham on August 4, 1774, he reports that "Some of the footmen, at first made a little disturbance; but I turned to them, and they stood reproved".[1]

Outward profession of Christianity was often accompanied by the greatest hypocrisy. A striking illustration was the so-called Christian Club formed at Shoreham in 1764. In spite of the title and the oath sworn on the Gospels by its members on admission, the real purpose of the club was to sell their votes to the highest bidder. As a lump sum was paid, they could still affirm that their individual votes had been freely cast. The plot was revealed in a public inquiry after a notoriously corrupt election, and they were all disfranchised.

The scepticism which prevailed among the upper classes arose from two main causes: impatience with the restraints of Christian moral standards, and a desire to be thought enlightened. In both cases the attitude was very often a mere pose, "the foppery of men who wanted new excuses for old sins", as T. H. Green has said of a later period. The combination of libertinism and scepticism was a legacy from the Restoration court, and in some sections was coupled with the open mockery of the rites and beliefs of Christianity—as by the so-called Franciscans (named after Sir Francis Dashwood) at Medmenham Abbey.

Those who took a cynical pride in holding sceptical views were by no means eager to propagate their opinions, being well content that the vulgar multitude, and even their own women folk, should conform to the traditional religion. But many who

[1] *Journal*, iii, p. 356; vi, p. 34

wished to take their place in fashionable society indulged in these "tapeyard infidelities", as Swinburne (not himself a very orthodox person) once called them. Steele describes a young gentleman who was: "so ambitious to be thought worse than he is, that in his degree of understanding he sets up for a freethinker, and talks atheistically in coffee-houses all day, though every morning and evening it can be proved upon him, he regularly at home says his prayers".[1]

This suggests that there was little in this talk of unbelief; but, on the other hand, it was taken very seriously by Bishop Watson, who stated that:

> The age in which we live has been called the age of philosophy—the age of reason: if by reason and philosophy, irreligion be understood, it undoubtedly merits the appellation; for there never was an age since the death of Christ, never once since the commencement of the history of the world, in which atheism and infidelity have been more generally professed.[2]

Even if we discount the good bishop's rhetoric, his denunciation is certainly exaggerated; for many who rejected Christianity by no means denied the existence of God—among them Gibbon and Voltaire. They may have been Deists, but they were certainly not Atheists.

The position is very confused, for even "freethinkers" in their writings might profess a belief in Christianity. Shaftesbury, for example, declared that he submitted unreservedly "to the truly Christian and Catholic doctrines of our Holy Church as by law established", and that he held "the mysteries of our religion even in the minutest particulars";[3] whilst Bolingbroke could affirm that "Man is a religious as well as a social creature, made to know and adore his Creator, to discover and obey His will."[4]

For this dissimulation, for such it undoubtedly was, two explanations may be offered: the legal position, and the desire not to undermine religion among the common people.

By the law of the land, anyone who had been brought up as a Christian was liable to three years' imprisonment if he denied its truth in writing. "Christianity", as Blackstone said,

---

[1] *The Tatler*, Letter lxxvii [2] *Sermons and Charges*, p. 1
[3] *Characteristics*, iii, p. 315 [4] *Works*, v, p. 470

"is part of the laws of England." This law was seldom enforced, though Toland fled to Dublin, and Collins took refuge in Holland, to avoid the possible consequences of their writings. It was not, however, a completely dead letter. Thomas Woolston, Fellow of Sidney Sussex College, Cambridge, was sentenced to a year's imprisonment and fined £100 for his *Six Discourses on the Miracles of Christ* (1727-29). As he was unable to pay the fine, he was kept in the King's Bench Prison until his death in 1733. There was some reason for the application of the law in his case, for he had indulged in blasphemous language so outspoken that a general outcry was aroused.

Often enough those who administered the law did not themselves believe in the doctrines of Christianity, though they avoided any written denial of them. The fact was notorious, and one effect was to undermine the Church's influence with serious men, and also to arouse resentment against it as a mere instrument of the State.[1]

The second reason was that some religion, even a false one, was necessary for the preservation of order. Hence the scrupulousness with which many whose religion was at best lukewarm kept up the convention of church-going. A foreign visitor once remarked that the only sign of Christianity in England was the observance of Sunday. Even those who advocated scepticism had no desire to upset the popular beliefs. Hume himself was a Tory in politics, and recognized the value of Christianity for keeping quiet the vulgar. The men of that age were wiser in their generation than those of more recent times, for they saw clearly that Christian ethics depend on Christian beliefs, and that to discredit the one is to weaken the other. This was the case with Shaftesbury;[2] whilst Collins, when asked why he made his servants go to church, is reported to have replied: "That they may neither rob nor murder me." Horace Walpole, at least in old age, deplored the habit of French *philosophes* who criticized religion in the presence of the servants.[3] But if religion was valued as an incentive to virtue and a deterrent to vice, it must be a decent and respectable religion, devoid of excitements and enthusiasms. Men had no desire to see the spread of Methodism or anything resembling it. Thus,

---

[1] There was nothing new about this attitude, for Leslie, in 1700, saw in it (but seemingly without much positive evidence) a cause of the growth of Dissent

[2] *Characteristics*, ii, p. 66

[3] So Butler had deplored the habit of "sceptical and profane men of bringing up objections to religion on social occasions" (*Durham Charge*, § 4)

outward conformity and caution in attacking Christianity were inspired merely by the recognition of the service it rendered in binding together the social structure. Even some defenders of orthodoxy could take a similar line. Archdeacon Balguy of Winchester (who refused the Bishopric of Gloucester) wrote in 1772: "The crime of Atheism consists in this, that it subverts morality." Such a statement ignores the dishonour done to God by the denial of His existence, and by its emphasis on the practical utility of religion exposes the weakness of much that passed for orthodoxy in the eighteenth century. In addition, it reveals an acceptance of the current notion that humanity has a native capacity for virtue and that mankind will respond to its attractions when once these have been brought to its notice. There was no realization that something more was needed if sin and frailty were to be overcome. Though it had some admirable qualities and was effective up to a point, judged as a whole, orthodox religion was pitifully inadequate for the task with which it was confronted, and neglectful of much that was of the essence of the Gospel.[1]

If the common people neglected religion, or observed it largely in a conventional manner, there were occasions when they were suddenly stirred to deeper earnestness—such as a national emergency. Wesley records that on the National Fast Day (December 18, 1745) the places of worship were thronged, "such a solemnity and seriousness everywhere appeared as had not been lately seen in England."[2] Such impressions were only transient, and indicated no genuine desire to turn to God but partook rather of the nature of superstition. It was, indeed, an age of superstition—the not infrequent accompaniment of loss of faith. Even a highly critical thinker such as Whiston was given to it, and in 1746 gave out that the Millennium would begin twenty years later.[3] But Whiston, as Macaulay has somewhere remarked, could believe anything except the doctrine of the Trinity. Superstition, however, was not confined to the unorthodox and unbelieving. When forecasts of the end of the world were made, they inevitably aroused widespread terror. Wesley pointed out the absurdity of this at Spitalfields on February 28, 1763; but in spite of his efforts many feared to go to bed, and some wandered about in the fields.[4] The same

[1] Cf. the comment of Wilberforce (*Life*, iv, p. 52) on *The Vicar of Wakefield*: "What an utter ignorance does it indicate of true Christianity! Morality is its main vital principle"
[2] *Journal*, iii, p. 228 [3] *Memoirs of His Own Life*, i, p. 398
[4] *Journal*, v, p. 9

thing occurred in connexion with the London earthquakes. Again, the abolition of the death penalty for witches in 1736 aroused general indignation. Wesley himself was a firm believer in witchcraft, holding that to give it up was to give up the Bible and the testimony "of all history, sacred and profane".[1]

Just as philosophy during most of the eighteenth century was dominated by the influence of Locke, so orthodox theology was equally dominated by the seventeenth-century divine, Archbishop Tillotson. Three characteristics of his teaching seem to stand out: (*a*) in all matters of religion there must be an appeal to reason; (*b*) claims to spiritual intuition are to be distrusted; (*c*) man's knowledge of truth must always be imperfect. Such views were bound to arouse fierce criticism, and in his lifetime he was bitterly attacked, especially by the Non-jurors, though here Robert Nelson was an exception. Nelson remained his close friend, and it was in his arms that the archbishop died in 1694, his death having been hastened by the unscrupulous attacks of his enemies.[2]

Tillotson's writings had an immense vogue, and above all his published sermons. His works were translated into German by the father of Lessing, and the latter took no small pride in his parent's achievement; whilst his sermons were read by all sorts and conditions of men; the surgeon in *Joseph Andrews*, for example, is represented as having come across them when a child.

It was not only the Non-jurors, however, who found fault with Tillotson's views; they were equally unacceptable to some Evangelicals. Whitefield was especially bitter, though later he modified his criticisms, condemning him as one "who sold his Lord". Wesley, from his different standpoint, commended him for his insistence on virtuous conduct, and admired his sermons.[3] But by most Evangelicals he was regarded as defective, if not harmful, in his teaching. Wilberforce described his mother in her early days as "what I should call an Archbishop Tillotson Christian".[4]

The Orthodox, as upholders of the Reformation, recognized

[1] *Op. cit.*, v, p. 215; vi, p. 109

[2] One of the worst scandals they spread was that he had never been baptized—they called him "undipped Jack"—as his parents had been Anabaptists. Yet the entry of his baptism could be seen in the parish registers

[3] *Works*, x, p. 299

[4] *Life*, i, p. 5. For the persistence of Tillotson's influence, cf. Dean Lake's statement, quoted in Davidson, *Life of A. C. Tait*, i, p. 139: "His special hero in the English Church was for long, perhaps always, Archbishop Tillotson"

the right of private judgment, but were careful to bear in mind its definite limitations. This could hardly be affirmed of those who rather comprehensively were dubbed Latitudinarians. They were very numerous in the Church, and not a few Dissenters held similar views, emphasizing the value of freedom of thought. This had also been upheld by Tillotson, who had even been called a "free-thinker", in an obnoxious sense, by his enemies. The advocacy of freedom in religious opinions led to strenuous controversies and disclosed fundamental differences of opinion among professing Christians. Some, cherishing the notion that man was quite capable eventually of solving all problems by the application of reason and common sense, held that a divine revelation was unnecessary. This raised the question of the relation between natural and revealed religion, and led to the famous Deist controversy.

Although the Deistic Controversy[1] was a thing of the past when the Evangelical Movement arose, it is important for our inquiry, as it affected the whole atmosphere of religious thought, and traces of it persisted in various parts of the country. Wesley on a number of occasions came across those who professed it. On April 2, 1753, he found "a whole clan of infidel peasants" at Davyhulme near Manchester, and "an innkeeper who drinks and laughs, and argues into Deism all the ploughmen and dairymen he can light on. But no mob rises against him; and reason good: Satan is not divided against himself."[2] About eight years later he wrote when in the Lake District: "Who would imagine that Deism would find its way into the heart of these enormous mountains! Yet so it is. Yea, and one who once knew the love of God is a strenuous advocate of it."[3]

The apparent triumph gained by orthodoxy over Deism was in reality a Pyrrhic victory in which severe losses had been sustained. It took long for this to be realized, for casualty lists are not issued after such warfare. Although there had been an almost universal outcry against Deism, it caused much unsettlement; and some of its ideas, gained vaguely at second-hand (as men to-day gain imperfect notions of psycho-analysis), were an excuse for throwing off Christianity and even the restraints of morality, though the accusation that the Deists in general held low moral views cannot be sustained. The controversy, furthermore, had diverted the energies of some of the clergy,

---

[1] See, further, Abbey and Overton, chap. iv   [2] *Journal*, iv, p. 59

[3] *Op. cit.*, iv, p. 448; cf. also his letter (quoted, pp. 141 f.), and his encounter at Matlock Bath (pp. 473 f.).

and especially of some of the bishops, from their true business; for when truth and error are at war there is often "a kind of truce, which virtue on both sides doth make with vice", as Hooker had observed.[1] In the bitterness of the long-drawn-out contest many of the characteristic graces of Christianity slowly evaporated.

To give an exact account of the views held by the Deists is a difficult, if not an impossible, task; for Deism, like Gnosticism in the early Church, was rather a tendency of thought than a consistent body of opinions. Two points, however, stand out: an emphasis on the transcendence of God so great that after recognizing Him as Creator the Deists politely dismissed Him from the scene; and a reliance on natural religion which made them look upon a divine revelation as superfluous. Deists also questioned the need for any kind of authority in matters of faith.

The difficulty of defining Deism is made greater by a habit on the part of the Orthodox of lumping together all opponents as Deists; those who were thus confounded ranged from sceptics, like Hume,[2] to the advocates of various shades of Socinianism. Some who were classed as Deists claimed to be orthodox Christians who merely wished for discussions of the matters involved and even professed to accept revelation. Many of them, before accepting Deism, had held a variety of religious opinions. Tindal began as a High Churchman, was then a Roman Catholic, returned to the Church as a Low Churchman, and finally adopted Deist views. Behind such changes, and this perhaps explains the attractions of Deism for certain types of mind, there probably lay a desire to get away from unprofitable controversies and to adopt an all-inclusive and all-tolerant system which would ignore them as unimportant and irrelevant.

Butler dealt the Deists a decisive blow by demonstrating that "natural religion" was open to the same objections as "revealed", and was far removed from being that clear and universal thing which its advocates imagined. Others took a different line and endeavoured to justify revelation. Warburton, in *The Divine Legation of Moses*, argued that since Moses had a divine commission the doctrines of the old covenant ought to be accepted; others adopted the same argument in support of the teaching of Christ, the author of the new covenant. In combating Deism, the Orthodox for the most part tried to meet

[1] *Ecclesiastical Polity*, Bk. V, Dedication, § 7
[2] Leslie Stephen, *Ford Lectures*, p. 105, thinks that Hume's *Treatise on Human Nature* (1739) destroyed the foundations of the Deist position, which rested on the optimistic formula that whatever is is right

it on its own ground, and though in this they were successful, the after-effects were not entirely happy. Law took a line of his own, claiming that "natural religion" and nature itself, far from being in conflict with the Bible, could only be understood in the light of the revelation which it contained when mystically interpreted.[1]

Although Locke had written before the controversy reached its peak, he had, by anticipation, already controverted some of the ideas set forth by the Deists. At the same time, Deism was in part a development of his principles, though not in a way of which he would have approved. Such developments are, of course, frequently encountered in the history of thought—both philosophical and theological.

By separating natural religion from revealed, a distinction which has the sanction of the Schoolmen, the Deists laid themselves open to the onslaughts of scepticism. In any case such a distinction, though useful for speculation, is not without its hazards for Christian faith, leading as it may to inadequate conceptions of the divine nature and activity.

At length the controversy died down, not so much through any spectacular victory, as by a kind of process of attrition. It had never attracted very wide interest, and such interest as it had aroused gradually diminished. Men had grown tired of it, and in any case it seemed a sort of halfway house between Orthodoxy and Socinianism, or even scepticism. As an angry sea slowly recovers its calm, so the controversy lapsed. But, unlike many such disputes, it did not "leave wrecks on every shore", though some ships, to continue the figure, were left high and dry, and there they would remain.

It had been a thoroughly unsatisfactory dispute which really settled nothing, for both sides lacked any sufficient equipment for dealing with the problems which it raised. In fact, it may be said that the extent of such problems was but imperfectly comprehended; there was, for example, no clear understanding of the issues raised by the antithesis between natural and supernatural, and furthermore neither side had any adequate sense of history. The Deists, for the most part, were thinkers of much smaller intellectual stature than their opponents, and though the latter might claim the victory, opinion to-day on many points (e.g. on questions of Biblical criticism) would be against them. The collapse of the controversy, however, served to demonstrate the limitations of reason alone as a basis for religion.

[1] See Stephen Hobhouse, *William Law: Selected Mystical Writings*, pp. 251 ff.

But if the conflict died down in England, it was to be renewed on a different terrain and with sharper weapons. In France, it would greatly influence men like Voltaire, Diderot, and Rousseau; and when Goethe left Leipzig in 1768 he described Germany as wavering between historical Christianity and Deism.[1] It is curious that in Germany the course of development should have been so different from that in England; in the former country, Deism had been preceded by Pietism, whereas over here it had come first. But Pietism in Germany had soon lost influence through its over-emphasis on the emotions, and, in spite of the great name of Bengel, its lack of learning.

One beneficial effect of the Deist Controversy was to call forth on the Orthodox side a number of theological treatises of considerable merit, and above all, Butler's *Analogy of Religion*. Its popularity in its own day was hindered by its closely reasoned arguments and rather involved style. Wesley, on January 1, 1746, described it as "a strong and well wrote treatise; but I am afraid far too deep for their full understanding to whom it is primarily addressed". This opinion he repeated on May 20, 1768, calling it "that fine book", but adding: "Freethinkers, so called, are seldom close thinkers. They will not be at pains of reading such a book as this."[2] Evangelicals of a later generation, ignoring the circumstances which had called forth *The Analogy*, deplored its lack of true Christianity. This view was set out by Daniel Wilson in the preface to a new edition in 1825, whereupon Bishop Copleston wrote to him:

> I have no doubt . . . that you are right in thinking that Butler has fallen short of that view of Christianity which is most effectual in subduing the heart of man and training him for heaven. But allowance may surely be made for the nature of his argument, which was principally to refute the infidel, and to bring men as willing disciples to the Gospel.[3]

As an answer to Deism it was admirable; both James Mill and his better-known son admitted that "no Deist could answer Butler: any such, any beginning with belief in God, he compels to be a Christian".[4] But for those who read the treatise

[1] *Dichtung und Wahrheit*, Pt. II, Bk. viii
[2] *Journal*, iii, p. 232; v, p. 264
[3] Quoted Bateman, *Life of Daniel Wilson*, i, p. 161
[4] Quoted W. E. Gladstone, *Corr. on Church and State*, ii, p. 101

for other purposes it was apt, as the younger Pitt remarked to Wilberforce, "to raise more doubts than it solved".[1] This is true of "apologies" in general, for many who were previously ignorant of objections to revealed religion may come across them, with unhappy results, in works composed to defend it.[2] There are arguments—
> that prove
> God's being so definitely, that man's doubt
> Grows self-defined the other side of the line,
> Made atheist by suggestion.[3]

The circumstances of the times, however, demanded that apologies for Christianity should be written, and that there should be an attempt to restate it in terms which would place it in the most favourable light in view of contemporary developments of thought. In so doing much was lost, for there was a tendency to minimize the element of mystery, and to rationalize the Gospel. In spite of Tillotson, men failed to comprehend that ultimate reality cannot be expressed in human language. The apologists, in admitting that revelation must be tested by reason, failed to realize that though religious truth is capable of verification, it can never be proved, as a mathematical proposition can be proved. This led to another fundamental defect in eighteenth-century apologetical literature; it was much more anxious to show that Christianity was true than to apply it. "The mind never advanced as far as the stage of belief, for it was unceasingly engaged in reasoning up to it."[4] Furthermore, this desire on the part of the apologists to establish the truth of Christianity was inspired, not by speculative needs, but by the urgency of preserving religion and morality; "they wrote less in the interests of truth than in that of virtue".[5]

As one ponders over the course of religion in the eighteenth century one lesson seems to stand out prominently: that a faith which never gets beyond preaching up reason and morality is powerless to reform society or to meet the spiritual longings of the individual. "Good men saw with alarm, almost with despair, that . . . the more they demonstrated, the less people believed. As the proof of morality was elaborated and

[1] *Life of Wilberforce*, i, p. 95

[2] Gibbon acquired sceptical views through reading Grotius, *De Veritate Relig. Christ* (*Memoirs*, p. 249)

[3] E. B. Browning, *Aurora Leigh*   [4] Mark Pattison, *Essays*, ii, p. 6

[5] *Op. cit.*, ii, p. 57

strengthened, the more it was disregarded, the more ungodliness and profaneness flourished."[1] The revival of religion when it came was based on a very different appeal, and clearly demonstrated that burning conviction is a more potent force than the keenest logic.

(B) THE CHURCH OF ENGLAND

At the beginning of the century the Church of England was in a strong and hopeful position, and continued progress seemed to be assured. Abroad, it was in close touch with other Reformed bodies; whilst at home Dissent was so feeble that it seemed about to disappear. Even the presence of different parties within the Church and some indulgence in controversy were signs of life and expansive power. Many new forms of activity were manifest, such as the starting of religious societies, and of charity schools for the children of the poor. New churches were being built, and the services, on week-days as well as on Sunday, were well attended both in town and country.[2] The Church also stood in high favour with the nation, and the cry "The Church in danger" was a potent political weapon.

With such prospects of ever-growing usefulness before it, why did the Church enter upon a period of decline? Before discussing the possible causes, two preliminary remarks must be made. In the first place, the decline was not nearly so great as later ages imagined; for the Church in the eighteenth century has shared in the general depreciation to which the whole century was subjected,[3] and too much credit has been allowed to the criticisms of prejudiced witnesses, such as the Non-jurors, the Deists, and, later, the Methodists. Secondly, the state of the Church under Queen Anne was not so promising as it appeared to be. It suffered from many abuses, such as pluralism, nonresidence, and a too great distinction between the higher and the lower clergy. As long as the Church was full of energy and life the effect of such abuses was inconsiderable, but once it began to show signs of weakness they became more potent. In the same way, a human being in perfect health may suffer

[1] *Op. cit.*, ii, p. 61

[2] The Rev. Lord Willoughby de Broke said of London in 1712: "Never were our churches so well filled; never our Communions so frequented; never more holy zeal, more humble devotion; never larger charities, than what are constantly offered up at the Holy Table in every church of this great city" (quoted Lowther Clarke, *Eighteenth-century Piety*, p. 70). Addison gives some charming descriptions of religion in rural areas

[3] Cf. the account in Sykes, *Church and State*, etc.

no evil consequences from disorders which will overwhelm him in time of sickness. One piece of evidence that even in the country districts all was not well may be found in the inscription ordered for his tomb by a rector of Crowle, near Epworth, who died in 1711:

> Here lies the body of Solomon Ashburn
> Forty years rector of this parish.
>
> All the day long have I stretched out my hands
> Unto a disobedient and gainsaying people.
> So I gave them up to their own heart's lusts,
> And let them follow their own imaginations.[1]

We now turn to a consideration of the causes which may be adduced to explain the debility of the Church of England; and as religion in England during the greater part of the century was mainly confined to the Church, they are largely identical with those already noticed as accounting for the more general decay. The whole atmosphere not only prevented expansion, but made it difficult for any institution even to maintain its position. The Church, it cannot be denied, ought to have shown greater powers of resistance to the spirit of the age; but political circumstances, and the bad example set by the first two Georges, were against it.

> The low tone, the worldliness, the spiritual drowsiness, the want of elasticity, which characterized the Church of the Hanoverian period may be traced in no slight degree to her peculiar position under those foreign potentates. Instead of rising to the high level of the grand old Church of their adoption, they seem to have dragged her down to their own level.[2]

Queen Caroline, during her lifetime, exercised a more salutary influence, especially through her use of the royal patronage. She was deeply interested in religious and philosophical questions, and every night from seven to nine was in the habit of assembling distinguished men to discuss them, including the future Bishop Butler. Her death on November 20, 1737, was a grave disaster for the Church.

[1] See *Journal*, v, pp. 377 f.; vi, p. 244. Wesley, however, seems not to have given an exact quotation of the inscription itself
[2] Abbey and Overton, i, p. 105

The rise of the Deist controversy, with its diversion of the energies of the leaders of the Church, may have prevented their dealing with some of the more obvious abuses. Bishop Watson, a somewhat maligned figure, had suggested various means to this end, but nothing was done. The Church also suffered from the weakness of Dissent, since it deprived it of any serious rival; and, even in religion, competition has its uses.

Had the Church retained within its ranks the Puritans excluded at the Restoration it would have been stronger to resist the debilitating atmosphere of the times. Puritanism is an ancient strain in the English people and goes back long before the Reformation; as Trevelyan has pointed out, the two "dreamers", Piers the Plowman and John Bunyan the tinker, resemble one another more than any two other writers divided by three centuries.[1] Before the Restoration, Puritanism had not been confined to any one class; after that event, it became the mark of the lower orders, as Anglicanism was of the higher. Puritanism, if it has obvious drawbacks and is open to grave exaggerations, has a noble and healthful side; and it would have been well for the nation, as well as for the Church, if its stern and robust influence had prevailed more widely in the eighteenth century. Rather strangely, Puritan ideas and a fondness for Puritan literature was to be found more frequently in the Church than among the Dissenting sects, and played no small part in the Evangelical Movement. One of the greatest services which that movement performed was to revive the spirit of Puritanism.

A more recent, and perhaps more serious, loss had befallen the Church in the withdrawal of the Non-jurors on the accession of William and Mary. This robbed it of a number of high-minded bishops and lesser clergy, men such as Archbishop Sancroft and Bishop Ken. Their withdrawal lowered the Church's prestige, especially in the matter of learning, for many of them were distinguished historical scholars and carried on the great tradition of the previous century. After about 1730 this came to an end. The story of the Non-jurors has been told by Mr. Lathbury, and must not detain us here; but we may note that after an internal schism, following on which some returned to the Church, they continued in separation until the end of the century, gradually diminishing in numbers and influence. The example of their lives, however, persisted, and

[1] *English Social History*, p. 2

even some sympathy with their views. When Dr. Pusey expressed a depreciatory opinion of them, Keble replied: "I cannot think that the Non-juror's position was so bad or so useless a one. I seem to trace our present life in good measure to them."[1] Though the Church was weakened by the schism, it is possible that in the long run it worked for good, as the Non-jurors were very rigid and impractical folk, and their continued presence might have led to much disputing and strife.

Something of the tradition represented by the Non-jurors was retained by the High Church party. But this party was apt to take on a political cast and became identified with a narrow Toryism. It had, however, an admirable exemplar in Martin Routh, President of Magdalen (1756–1855), whom Newman described in the dedication to his *Via Media* as one "who has been reserved to report to a forgetful generation what was the theology of their fathers".

One cause which is often advanced to explain the decline of the Church in the eighteenth century is the suppression, or rather the silencing, of Convocation.[2] It had become a sort of cockpit in which the lesser clergy baited the bishops, and, after various previous suspensions, was silenced in 1717 owing to its attack on Hoadly's notorious Bangor Sermon. There was a session in 1741, but as it was marked by similar disorders, suspension again followed. Thus Convocation was a perpetual scene of strife, and brought no little discredit to the clerical order. It is true that its suspension prevented any considered or concerted action in regard to the Methodists; but had the question been raised in Convocation, as it undoubtedly would sooner or later, it might have led to hasty and unconsidered action, and would probably have been but another occasion of party strife and disorder.

If the condition of the Church in the eighteenth century was not so bad as is generally supposed, it cannot be denied that it was far from adequate to meet the demands which were being made upon it. It shared too much in the characteristics of the times and was self-complacent and satisfied with things as they were. The very abuses which called for remedy were valued as part of the traditional system. Respectability seemed to be the end and aim of religion, and the spirit of adventure and romance was entirely lacking. Thus it was incapable of making any appeal to those who lived sordid lives in the growing towns

---

[1] Quoted by W. Lock, *John Keble*, p. 4
[2] For a history of Convocation at this time, see Sykes, pp. 297 ff.

and who could only be roused from their brutality and squalor by some vigorous and emotional call.

The failure of the Church to cope with the new conditions, due to the shift of population and the growth of new towns, was exceedingly grave in its consequences, and was, indeed, a turning-point for the worse, for religion in England. The Church took little account of the appalling conditions that were growing up, nor did it realize the strain they would place on its organization. But too much blame must not be placed on the Church. The government was equally at fault, and like other constituted bodies it was taken completely out of its stride and unable at the time to adapt itself, or even to comprehend that adaptation was necessary. The changes came about so gradually, by a species of infiltration, that it was long before their effects became manifest, and then it was too late. The old parochial divisions were obsolete,[1] but to create new parishes required an Act of Parliament, a slow and expensive process which raised all kinds of problems, such as the apportionment of revenues.

The effectiveness or otherwise of any institution depends almost entirely on the personality of those who direct and control it. This is certainly true of the Church, and so our next step will be to inquire into the condition of the bishops and clergy.

At the Restoration, the episcopate stood very high in men's esteem on account both of its learning and its devotion;[2] the loss of the Non-jurors, however, robbed it of some of its prestige. The Revolution also sapped its influence in another way, for after the coming of the Hanoverians the Whigs had a virtual monopoly of the episcopate. The effect was not immediately apparent, for many bishops appointed under Queen Anne still held their sees, but as these died the standard of the episcopate sensibly declined. The Whig bishops were a well-meaning body of men, but not anxious to encourage undue activity; they might even try to check it. In 1775 Bishop Peploe of Chester, when visiting the Collegiate Church at Manchester, found fault with

[1] Newman, in an article in *The British Magazine* for 1836 entitled "Home Thoughts from Abroad", wrote: "Great towns will never be evangelized by the parochial system. They are beyond the sphere of the parish priest, burdened as he is with the endearments and anxieties of a family, and the secular restraints and engagements of the Establishment. The unstable multitude cannot be influenced and ruled except by uncommon means"

[2] Cf. Gwatkin, *Church and State in England*, p. 381: "The Bench has never been more fully adorned with examples of learning, of courage, of princely munificence, of true devotion"

the holding of a weekly Communion as "a great and grievous innovation and a heavy charge upon the parishioners".[1]

As the new bishops were appointed for their political views, they were expected to support the government by their votes in the House of Lords—they saved Walpole in 1733—and by exercising local influence. Attendance at the House of Lords involved residence in London for a great part of the year, and the consequent neglect of their dioceses. Whiston records that a Durham friend told him in 1730 that not a single bishop had been seen in the North for two years.[2]

Just as the bishops received their promotion in return for services, past and future, to the government, so were they apt, as Butler observed, to regard their own patronage as a means of enriching friends and relatives, rather than as an opportunity for promoting those who were worthy of the various offices in their gift.[3] They might even accept government suggestions as to its disposal.[4]

From a social point of view the bench became more aristocratic, for among the new bishops were the younger sons and brothers of peers, and even baronets in their own right. When Durham was vacant on the death of Bishop Butler in 1752, Warburton wrote to Hurd: "Reckon upon it that Durham goes to some noble ecclesiastic. 'Tis a morsel only for them. Our grandees have at last found their way back into the church. I only wonder they have been so long about it."[5] The appointment went to Richard Trevor, Bishop of St. David's, a protégé of the all-powerful Duke of Newcastle, in spite of the objections of George II, who considered that Trevor was "a high-church fellow, a stiff, formal fellow, and nothing else".[6]

As the bishops were Whig in politics so were they Latitudinarian in doctrine. Many of them were men of considerable learning, but they were apt to neglect divinity for more profitable studies, and even to employ their literary ability in the composition of pamphlets in support of the government.[7]

Criticisms of the clergy are very easy to formulate, for any body of men who are in touch with so many people and at so many points in their lives must inevitably fail to please some. And it is these who are most vocal. Hence we shall not be surprised to find them frequent in the eighteenth century. But

[1] John Byrom, *Journal*, II, Pt. ii, p. 357 [2] *Memoirs*, p. 337
[3] See Bartlett, *Memoir of Bishop Butler*, p. 116 [4] Sykes, pp. 179 f.
[5] *Letters of a Late Eminent Prelate*, p. 118 [6] Sykes, p. 39
[7] For the state of the bishops, see further, Sykes, chaps. ii, iii, iv, and pp. 411 ff.

complaints of the state of the Anglican clergy were no new thing. Bishop Burnet in *The History of His Own Times* compared them, much to their disadvantage, with those of other lands whom he had encountered in his travels. "I must own", he said, "that the main body of our clergy has always appeared dead and lifeless to me."

In the eighteenth century the Church as established was held in honour, even by some who attacked Christianity itself; but its ministers were openly disliked and derided. Archbishop Secker testified that "Christianity is ridiculed and railed at with very little reserve; and the teachers of it without any at all". Part of the dislike for the clergy was due to the haughtiness of those of higher rank; but as some of them were learned, and most of them possessed power and influence, men were chary of offending them. They worked out their spleen on the lower clergy, and it was the average country parson who was their target. Many country parsons were indeed likely, from their illiteracy and sycophantic spirit, to arouse contempt and derision. A writer in 1756, who was not entirely unsympathetic, after deploring the bad state of many church buildings, went on to say that in others "nothing unseemly or ruinous is to be found except in the clergyman". The feeling that the laity were unfriendly led the clergy to keep much to themselves, and this in turn helped to increase the gap between them. For this they had been criticized by Dean Swift in his *Project for the Advancement of Religion*: "The clergy prevent themselves from doing service to religion by affecting so much converse with each other, and caring so little to mingle with the laity." At the same time, those of the clergy who seriously tried to carry out the duties of their high office did not go without honour. Fielding, in the preface to *Joseph Andrews*, met possible criticism for his introduction of Parson Adams by disclaiming any wish to depreciate the clergy, "for whom, while they are worthy of their sacred order, no man can possibly have a greater respect".

The clergy were drawn from very different strata of society, and, both in their virtues and in their failings, reflected the classes from which they originated. Some of the higher clergy were of gentle birth, and even among the lower grades there were to be found the sons of the clergy and of others who thus hoped to preserve a foothold on the social ladder; but most of the clergy came from less cultivated circles, and in rural districts differed little from the more respectable of their parishioners. Many of them were men of strong physique, and able, if the necessity arose, to take their own part in fisticuffs.[1] They were also capable of immense feats of endurance such as were demanded in long walks across their large parishes, and still longer rides for those who itinerated, often over very rough tracks and in severe weather.

Although criticism of the clergy and sarcasm at their expense was common, much of it may be discounted as inspired by anti-clerical bias or aroused by particular instances. Probably the great majority were carrying out their duties well and faithfully according to the not very exacting standards of clerical conduct in their day.[2] Smollett in his *Continuation of Hume*, v, p. 375, said that in the reign of George II "the clergy were generally pious and exemplary". The real trouble, however, was that few of them had any genuine vocation for holy orders; they entered them as a matter of course because no other opening was provided, or because there was a family living waiting for them; or, if of lowly origin, because they hoped to improve their position in life. Orthodox in views, and blameless in life, they were content with a minimum of service, and, having no deep religious convictions, their ministry was inevitably lacking in inspiration and zeal. The ideal of clerical life set up by William Law, if they came across his writings, would have seemed to them quite impracticable, for it demanded prayers twice daily, constant visiting of the sick and poor, and an entire devotion to the care of souls. Law even found fault with those who in college livings gave themselves over to the continuance of their studies to the neglect of other duties. There cannot have been many who imitated Parson Adams in combining a fondness for learning (he carried about a volume of Æschylus in his pocket to read at odd moments) with a high sense of pastoral responsibility.

In considering the state of the country clergy, one must bear in mind the isolation in which they lived. This led many of them to become a kind of law unto themselves, for there was little outside guidance or interference, save an occasional visitation by the archdeacon. There was thus nothing to encourage them to adopt lofty standards in their various ministries; nor was there anything, either by word or example, in many of

[1] Cf. Parson Adams, and Mr. Thwackum and Mr. Supple in *Tom Jones*

[2] Cf. Ollard and Walker, *The Visitation Returns of Archbishop Herring*, i, p. xviii, where it is stated that the Diocese of York in 1743 had "a body of dutiful and conscientious men, trying to do their work according to the standards of their day"

those who were their leaders, to inspire them to strive after better things.

One feature, however, must not be passed over. Though the clergy were accused of many failings, especially of neglect, there are, save in a few very exceptional cases, no suggestions of immorality. This is very notable in an age when moral standards were so lax; in an age, moreover, when critics were not unduly handicapped by an exact regard for truth. The value of such lives must have been immense, and we must not forget them.

The relations between parson and flock were in many ways very different from those which now prevail. The parson usually remained for a long period, perhaps for his whole life, in a single parish. This enabled him to gain an intimate knowledge of his people and all the varied circumstances of their lives. The people, too, were much more stationary then they are in these days of easy communication. For generations the same families had lived in the village, and this gave them deep roots in the soil and a pride in their church and its traditions which are notably lacking in modern villages where there are many newcomers. In the absence of medical men and of an educated class of school teachers, the inhabitants were very dependent on the clergy for the care of their bodies as well as of their souls, though in this the incumbent might be helped by the squire and his ladies where good traditions of such services had been maintained.

If many of the clergy remained in one parish it was seldom by their own wish, but was due to the absence of opportunities for promotion. The majority of the lower clergy had little expectation beyond a curacy or the charge of a parish for some fortunate pluralist. Their remuneration seldom exceeded £50 a year, which seems a poor return financially for the long and expensive education they had received. Moreover, unless they were actual incumbents, they had no security of tenure; some even, in order to avoid the payment of the necessary fees, did not obtain a licence from the bishop which would have given them a little protection.

In such circumstances it is hardly a matter for wonder that many of the clergy were obsessed by the need for gaining preferment, or of adding to preferments already held. Bishop Hurd considered that "The general body of the clergy have been, and I am afraid always will be, very intent upon pushing their temporal fortunes." Many young men of ability adopted the clerical profession in the hope of gaining some prize—but, as Bentley once remarked, the whole thing had very much the nature of a lottery; few black-robed parsons could ever hope to become "lawny bishops", and even the more fortunate might have to be content with the status of what Sterne has called "a lousy prebendary". Everything depended on influence, and, as Cowper said, "The parson knows enough who knows a duke".[1] Without influence, merit and the faithful performance of his duties were of little avail in obtaining promotion. A passage in one of Samuel Richardson's *Familiar Letters* well illustrates this:

> Parson Matthews goes on preaching and living excellently, and has still as many admirers as hearers, but no preferment: while old clumsy Parson Dromedary is made a Dean, and has hopes, by his sister's means, who is a favourite of a certain great man, to be a bishop.

Young men at the university might, if they were lucky, make the acquaintance of some noble or squire, and from him obtain a post which would provide the first step in the ladder of advancement. Some, in expectation of a living, served as domestic chaplains. These often had a hard road to tread, for domestic chaplains were usually treated with little consideration by their employers; and even if this were not the case, they had to endure the dislike of the servants of the household, as Crabbe was to discover.[2]

Preferment hunting was no new thing, for Hooker had joined it with notable ignorance and non-residence as forming the threefold blot or blemish of the clergy of his day. He also noted that those who already held preferments were the most eager to add to their number.[3] Pluralism and non-residence were indeed long-standing evils; they had been notorious in the Middle Ages, and are closely connected, for the holder of more than one benefice cannot be permanently resident in them all.

As the abuses which follow pluralism and non-residence are so obvious, it is surprising that they did not arouse more comment. They were, however, so widespread that they were taken for granted. Aggrieved parishioners might complain that the

[1] *Tirocinium*, 403
[2] On the condition of the lower clergy, see, further, Sykes, chap. v
[3] *Eccles. Polity*, Bk. V, chap. lxxxi, § 1

only time they saw the incumbent was when he came down to receive his tithes, and a few pious reformers might press for a remedy; but nothing was done, and even men of real religion accepted the system. Pluralism was, indeed, so much a matter of course that an additional living was regarded merely as a new source of income, and not as involving, save in a very modified degree, any fresh responsibility. The result was that in many parishes there was not even a resident curate, and the services were confined to Sunday and then perhaps cut down to one. The times of holding services were often uncertain, for they would be conducted by a curate who might combine a number of them and ride from one church to the next. The sexton would keep a look-out, and when he saw the parson in the distance would begin to ring the bell, and so the congregation assembled for what might be their only act of public worship in the week. Even this scanty allowance was often interrupted by bad weather.

Celebrations of Holy Communion under these conditions must have been very rare; but the custom of frequent communions had not yet come in. George Herbert, in the previous century, considered that there should be a minimum of five or six yearly —at Easter, Christmas, Whitsuntide, and "afore and after harvest".[1] This seems to have been the rule in the country in the eighteenth century, though a single celebration at harvest time seems to have been more usual.[2] As harvest came about Michaelmas, it was a convenient distance between Whitsuntide and Christmas. In the towns there were more frequent celebrations, though the ideal of one a month was seldom attained. Since opportunities for communicating were rare, the attendance when they were available was sometimes very great, going into thousands at times, and the service might last for several hours. The consequent hurry and waiting about may have led to some irreverence, but the comparative rarity of communicating made many regard the act with greater awe and respect than is the case now that it has become so very frequent. There was no little anxiety lest unworthy communicating should bring not a blessing but a curse.

The manner in which public worship is conducted is of supreme importance. This had been emphasized by Steele, in *The Spectator*, who complained of the carelessness of many of

---

[1] *A Priest to the Temple*, xxii

[2] The notion that harvest festivals are a modern innovation is quite fallacious

the clergy; though by contrast he was greatly impressed on hearing the service read at St. James's, Garlick Hill: "I heard the service read so distinctly, so emphatically, and so fervently, that it was next to an impossibility to be unattentive."

He attributed "indifferency" to the desire "to avoid the imputation of Cant". There are, indeed, faults in two opposite directions—the "preaching of the prayers" of which the Puritan was so fond, and a dull formality. It was the latter evil which was the more prevalent in the Church of the eighteenth century. When the service was conducted by hireling curates, whose one object was to get it through as quickly as possible, it must have been robbed of all impressiveness and reverence; but even when there was a resident parson the opportunity was often lost and the offices read in a perfunctory manner. Such services must in any case have been very dull, as the responses would often be left to the clerk, whilst the congregation simply drowsed. There was little music save the singing of the psalms, and in some churches a barrel-organ or a few musicians. The great majority of services were lifeless formalities with no power to arouse the religious sense or to elevate it if already present.

This was also true of much of the preaching of the day. It was not of a kind to stir either zeal or interest, and its defects had already brought complaints from both Addison and Steele. They speak of "people lulled asleep with solid and elaborate discourses of piety, who would be warmed and transported out of themselves by the bellowings and distortions of enthusiasm".[1]

The clergy, in conformity to the spirit of the age, so well expressed in Pope's familiar lines:

> For modes of faith let graceless bigots fight;
> He can't be wrong whose life is in the right;
> In faith and hope the world will disagree,
> But all mankind's concern is charity.[2]

had a distaste for the more mysterious aspects of Christianity, and wished to avoid in the pulpit subjects that were matters of dispute, and to confine themselves, as Dr. Bliss had said in 1716, to "good, plain, practical morality". The result was that sermons were dull and drab, with little in them to stimulate true piety or touch the heart. Those of the hearers who were able or willing to follow the argument may have received sustenance for their minds, but their souls were starved. But even

[1] *The Spectator*, No. 407; cf. No. 408 and *The Tatler*, No. 66
[2] *Essay on Man*, iii, 305–308

as moral essays such sermons did not escape criticism, and Blackstone, the eminent lawyer, contrasted them, to their disadvantage, with the moral discourses of Plato and Cicero.[1]

Taste in preaching, as in other matters, differs with the individual. Goldsmith condemned English preachers when compared with those of France, considering their sermons as "generally dry, methodical and unaffecting; delivered with the most insipid calmness".[2] Wesley, however, had a very different opinion. In his journal for June 24, 1750, after visiting a French Church in Dublin, he wrote: "I have sometimes thought Mr. Whitefield's action was violent, but he is a mere post to Mr. Caillard."[3] In old age he still retained the same views: "I cannot admire French oratory; I despise it from my heart."[4] By this time he had come to the conclusion that sermons on practical morality did more permanent good than "what are vulgarly called gospel sermons".[5]

> Let but a pert self sufficient animal, that has neither sense nor grace, bawl out something about Christ, or His blood, or justification by faith, and his hearers cry out, "What a fine gospel sermon!" Surely the Methodists have not so learned Christ! We know no gospel without salvation from sin.[6]

In spite of the attempts of the clergy to avoid subjects which might cause disputes or contradiction and to confine themselves to practical advice, the idea that they were by no means sincere in their utterances became prevalent. As Squire Weston said to the clergyman in *Tom Jones*: "Art not in the pulpit now! When art got up there, I never mind what dost say."

Long before the rise of the industrial revolution and the consequent shift of population it had been realized that additional churches were necessary. In 1709 Swift in his *Project for the Advancement of Religion* complained of the lack of provision in London where one incumbent, with the help of curates, had the oversight of 20,000 souls. In the city itself there were abundant churches, but some of the new suburbs were practically destitute of "religion", so *The Spectator* said in May,

---

[1] J. C. Colquhoun, *William Wilberforce*, p. 110. The Wesleys, because they insisted on good works, were accused of not preaching the Gospel, but "Heathen morality; Tully's *Offices* and no more": see *Journal*, iii, p. 39

[2] *Essays*, iv [3] *Op. cit.*, iii, p. 479 [4] Tyerman, *Oxford Methodists*, p. 284

[5] He himself uses the phrase in a favourable sense on occasion: see *Journal*, iv, p. 338 (July 18, 1759)

[6] *Works*, xiii, p. 33

1711, when commending the scheme for building fifty new churches in London and Westminster. Though this project was never carried out in full, a number of churches were erected including St. Martin-in-the-Fields and St. Mary-le-Strand in 1722–23.[1]

At the beginning of the century existing church fabrics were being well cared for. William Law, a critical observer, speaks of churches in 1726 as in good order and characterized by stateliness and beauty. But not all incumbents realized their responsibility in the matter, and those who were non-resident may be presumed to have been uninterested in it. The result was that many churches came to be neglected and some even fell into ruin. The laity, apparently, in spite of their rapidly increasing wealth and extravagance, were not disposed to contribute towards church building or maintenance; and Bishop Butler, lamenting the fact in his Durham charge in 1751, urged the clergy to give especial attention to the preservation of church fabrics.

(c) DISSENT

When the Evangelical Revival began, Dissent in England was at a very low ebb, and was steadily declining. There were, indeed, those who considered that within a generation it would probably die out altogether. Evidence for this decline is ample, though often casual. Grimshaw, when he went to Haworth in 1742, found four disused Presbyterian chapels and a Quaker meeting-house which was only used once in the year. One result of his labours, rather to his concern, was to revive Dissent; for although on friendly terms with all sincere Christians, he much preferred that they should belong to the Church. Another testimony to the low state of Dissent may be found in Wesley's comment when one of his preachers became an Independent minister in 1753: "Did God design that this light should be hidden under a bushel in a little obscure dissenting meeting-house?"[2]

One cause of the decline was the cessation of persecution and the granting of liberty to follow their own way. This led

[1] There was some activity in church-building in the provinces. St. Ann's, Manchester, was erected in 1712; and in the country districts I have noted the following: Wolverton (Hants), in 1717; Gayhurst (Bucks), in 1728; and Blandford (Dorset), in 1732. For church-building during the period, see below, p. 172

[2] *Journal*, iii, p. 403, n. 1

to carelessness and complacency. Forgetting the great principles for which their fathers had suffered and striven, Dissenters were content to enjoy their newly-won privileges and to leave it at that. A foreign observer wrote in 1740:

> Those who are best acquainted with the state of the English nation, tell us that the Dissenting interest declines from day to day, and that the cause of Nonconformity owes this gradual decay in a great measure to the lenity and moderation that are practised by the rulers of the Established Church.[1]

Another explanation of the decline was the constant tendency of Dissent to break up into still more sects, and the quarrels which such dissidence provoked. This seems to have influenced both Bishop Butler and his friend, the future Archbishop Secker, who were fellow students at the Dissenting Academy at Tewkesbury, in their decision to conform to the Church.[2]

The decay of Dissent had not come about suddenly, and for more than a generation vital religion had been at a low ebb among Nonconformists. The change might be said to coincide with the life of Isaac Watts, who was born in 1674, the year of Milton's death, and lived until 1748. He himself has testified to a lack of fervour "in the hearts and lives of men", doubtless having primarily in view Dissenters like himself. One cause of the decay was a tendency, even among those who did not become Unitarians, to water down the Gospel message, and a consequent abandonment on the part of many ministers of pastoral work in favour of teaching. Watts himself, by his scholarship and literary connexions, did something to redeem Nonconformity from the reputation of narrowness; but less notable Dissenting authors tended to form small coteries which were given up to mutual admiration. Even Watts did not entirely escape from this vagary, for he could speak of some of his fellow ministers who dabbled in literature as "awful Mead" (using the term in the contemporary, not the modern, sense), "charming Bates", and "great Goudge".[3]

The change in the attitude of the leaders of the Church had

[1] Mosheim, *Ecclesiastical History* (E.T.), v, p. 95

[2] Priestley declared in 1771 that "in the present state of Christianity I am for increasing the number of sects, rather than diminishing them"

[3] Southey took a malicious delight in unearthing and publicizing these complimentary notices

also another effect—it led many Dissenters to an appreciation of its advantages. They realized the greater freedom enjoyed by Churchmen and the less restricted atmosphere when compared with their own sects;[1] they began also to attach more significance to the points they had in common. The preaching typical of the Church, with its emphasis on the practical duties of the Christian and its absence of emotional appeal, was also attractive to many. The great figure among Dissenters in the early part of the century was Philip Doddridge (1702–51).[2] He believed in an establishment, and was anxious that there should be an arrangement by which Nonconformist ministers should be allowed to return to it; but he discouraged any piecemeal action, and though offered preferment in the Church refused to abandon his fellow Dissenters. His commentaries were widely read by the clergy and even recommended by some of the bishops. Among the latter was Bishop Warburton, who wrote to express his approbation; adding, with unconscious humour, that "he read the notes himself, and his wife read the practical observations".

The more friendly relations between the Church and Dissent led naturally to the increase of occasional conformity and attendance at Church services, and to a considerable drift back to full membership. The famous Dissenting Academy of Samuel Jones (first at Gloucester and then at Tewkesbury) not only gave Butler and Secker to the Church, but also Maddox, who became Bishop of Worcester. Among Butler's contemporaries was Samuel Chandler, who, though he did not follow the example of some of his fellow students, retained a strong friendship for them. Lardner, it may be noted, was also a student at the same academy, though at a later date. He followed what was perhaps a more normal course among English Presbyterians by becoming a Unitarian.

Among the Dissenting sects there was one which had an influence far beyond the mere number of its adherents—that was the Quakers. They had long since abandoned the fanaticism which had marked their first days, and had settled down to trade and respectability, but without losing that spirit of love and philanthropy which was, and would remain, one of their chief characteristics. The prosperity which soon attended

[1] Henry Venn (*Life*, p. 449) cites the case of an elderly clergyman who was dissuaded from leaving the Church by a Dissenting minister who emphasized the superior advantages of the Church

[2] See further the volume of centenary essays edited by G. F. Nuttall under the title of *Philip Doddridge (1702–1751)*

on their honesty and quiet industry was already being noted and taken as a justification for their peculiar notions—as Matthew Green (d. 1737) wrote:

> They who have lands, and safe bank stock,
> With faith so founded on a rock,
> May give a rich invention ease
> And construe scripture how they please.[1]

Some of them became bankers, and their trustworthiness helped to establish the tradition of English commercial stability and honesty.

Although the Hutchinsonians are now forgotten, they demand notice on account of the effect they had on certain of the Evangelical leaders and as contributing to the revived study of Hebrew. Their founder, John Hutchinson (b. 1674), was an inventor of mechanical devices, and the ingenuity of his mind led him to devise a whole system of philosophy and theology based on the mystical interpretation of Hebrew roots. His efforts naturally aroused opposition, for his notions were "such as give pain to those who believe the Bible, and diversion to those who do not".[2] In spite of his eccentricities he attracted many admirers, including some promising young men at Oxford who were impressed by his earnestness and by his criticism of some of the prevailing theological tendencies. Among them were Hervey,[3] Romaine, Bishop Horne, and later, and of a very different theological complexion, Jones of Nayland. Hutchinson died in 1737, and eleven years later his works were published in twelve volumes which helped to establish his influence in many quarters. He had also a number of disciples who wrote in explanation and defence of his system. The restless curiosity of Wesley led him to study the writings of Hutchinson, but in a highly critical spirit.[4]

We come now to consider what is loosely called Unitarianism,

---

[1] Quoted by G. M. Trevelyan, *English Social History*, p. 363. Wesley, although on friendly terms with a number of Quakers, disapproved of their notions and methods, especially their depreciation of the sacraments. He once wrote to Archbishop Secker: "I should as soon commence deist as Quaker" (*Works*, xii, p. 74)

[2] So Wesley, *Journal*, vi, p. 6 (November 9, 1773)

[3] He thought that Hodges's *Elihu* published in 1750 brought out some of the grand peculiarities of the Gospel (Letter of October 2, 1750)

[4] See *Journal*, iv, pp. 147, 190, 261; v, p. 353; *Letters*, vii, pp. 250 ff. He was even dubious of Hutchinson's knowledge of Hebrew (*Letters*, iii, p. 207)

a term which covers a variety of theological opinions. Unitarianism spread rapidly, in part as a result of the Deist controversy and in part as a reaction to a too narrow orthodoxy; it was also helped by the Arian views which had a certain vogue during the period. From Arianism to Unitarianism was an easy step, and not a few took it. The case of Thomas Scott, who reversed the process, must have been almost unique.

The Socinians, to whom Unitarianism can be traced back, had been willing to worship Christ, and many Unitarians in the eighteenth century differed but little from the orthodox, though critical of the orthodox idea of the personality of the Godhead. In addition they disliked the Puritan notion of setting up the Church against the world, and the claim of individuals to special enlightenment. They were also critical of crude ideas of the Atonement.

Unitarian views naturally flourished most among Dissenters though a few of the clergy adopted them, and some even gave up their livings. Southey tells us that Susanna Wesley, herself the daughter of a well-known Dissenting minister, had adopted Socinianism, but was reclaimed from it by her husband. The reclamation must have been very thorough, if the epitaph which she is supposed to have composed for him is actually her work. It runs as follows:

> Here lieth all that could die of Samuel Wesley, A.M., thirty-nine years rector of this parish. As he lived, so he died, in the true Catholic faith of the Holy Trinity in Unity, and that Jesus Christ was God Incarnate, and the only Saviour of mankind.

At the beginning of the eighteenth century, though Unitarian views were not uncommon, Unitarianism had not become a definite sect. This came to pass as a result of the Salters' Hall Conference held in 1719. A number of Baptists, Presbyterians, and Independents there met to discuss the question of the necessity of a definite creed. In the end, by a narrow majority of 57 to 53, it was decided that such was not to be imposed, not even a simple expression of belief in the Trinity.[1] The majority included most of the Presbyterians, and about half the Baptists; but the Independents to a man opposed the motion. The

[1] The main argument against insisting on acceptance of the doctrine of the Trinity was that it is not definitely stated in the Scriptures. Hence it was said, after the result of the voting became known, that "the Bible won by a majority of four"

new sect became a continuation of Presbyterianism as it had existed in England for many generations, but it rapidly drew in other Nonconformists; by 1756 all but two of the Independent meeting-houses in the large towns of the North had gone over to it.[1]

Another Christian body which stood outside the Established Church in England requires notice: the Roman Catholic communion, or, as people then preferred to call it, Popery. It has some importance for our study, since the early Methodist preachers, if not the Evangelicals, were frequently denounced as papal agents. In the Calvinist controversy, Lady Huntingdon accused Wesley of being a Papist, though only in the sense that he encouraged papal practices such as fasting on Friday and the insistence on good works.

This aspect of Roman Catholicism has but a fanciful interest; more serious was the undoubted fact that it was steadily gaining adherents. Wesley records on August 14, 1741, that he "called on a person near Grosvenor Square" and found that—

> there was but too much reason here for crying out of the increase of Popery; many converts to it were being continually made, by the gentleman who preaches in Swallow-street, three days in every week. Now, why do not the champions who are continually crying out "Popery, Popery!" in Moorfields, come hither?[2]

Nine years later Bishop Sherlock of London wrote that unbelievers on their deathbeds, in fear of coming judgment, became "an easy prey to popish priests, and greedily swallowed their absolution cordials".[3] In 1757 Romaine published *A Seasonable Antidote against Popery* in which he declared that:

> The Papists have their emissaries everywhere; and they are vastly busy at present. They have more interest in this kingdom, and their doctrines have more advocates, than people imagine. Some of their pretended enemies are their best friends, and do them great service.[4]

In the early part of the eighteenth century anti-papal feeling was very rife. Protestantism had been accentuated by the

[1] R. W. Dale, *Congregationalism*, p. 560   [2] *Journal*, ii, p. 286
[3] *London Magazine*, 1750, p. 139   [4] *Works*, p. 954

change of dynasty in 1689, and the suspicions aroused under James II had not died down. The presence of numerous Jacobites helped to keep the sentiment alive, for many felt that the return of the Stuarts would mean the establishment of Popery. In 1735 Sir Michael Foster, chief justice of the King's Bench, described the Roman Catholic Church as "the most impious and oppressive tyranny that ever exercised the patience of God or man; an Empire founded in craft and supported by blood and rapine, breach of faith, and every other engine of fraud and oppression". So general was the suspicion of Popery that quite innocent practices might lead to denunciation; it was not the Methodists alone who aroused it, for when Bishop Butler placed a cross in his chapel some accused him of being a secret Papist, and the idea persisted long after his death. The failure of the 1745 invasion allowed matters to die down, but it was easy for anti-papal feeling to flare up again on the slightest provocation. This happened in 1751, when the Gregorian Calendar was introduced, and, even more absurdly, when Italian opera singers were imported.

If some alarm was aroused by the spread of Roman Catholicism, its claims were not taken seriously by an age which prided itself on the appeal to reason and common sense, and Bishop Warburton could dismiss it as "rather an impious and impudent combination against the sense and rights of mankind than as a species of religion".[1]

[1] *Chatham Correspondence*, ii, p. 189

CHAPTER 7

REVIVAL MOVEMENTS: LADY HUNTINGDON

THE type of Christianity current in the early years of the eighteenth century, owing to its savourless conception of religion, its intellectual and rational outlook, its prudential system of ethics, and its suspicion of anything which aroused the emotions and affections, could provide no sufficient satisfaction for the needs of the human soul. That such needs are fundamental the experience of the race seems to demonstrate, and the now rather trite saying of St. Augustine, "Thou O God hast made us for Thyself, and our heart is restless until it find its rest in Thee", has permanent validity. The need for God may be driven under and suppressed, as pain by the action of a powerful drug, or attention may be diverted by some passing substitute, but it still persists.

The weaknesses of the prevalent religion did not go without comment, however, and as early as 1700 Benjamin Jenks of Harley in Shropshire wrote his *Submission to the Righteousness of God* (it was later to receive the commendation of Whitefield and of Wesley),[1] which he followed up by his *Evangelical Meditations* (1701 and 1704). Then in 1715 Dr. Richard Smallbroke, Prebendary of Hereford, preached a sermon that attracted some notice, in which he lamented the lack of true faith, in spite of the intellectual victories of the defenders of Christianity, and the general prevalence of profligacy. These he put down to the failure to win men's hearts, a task which God alone could accomplish. At a still higher level Bishop Gibson in 1724 urged the clergy of his diocese of London to pay greater regard in their preaching to the doctrines peculiar to Christianity as "a new way of obtaining forgiveness of sins and reconciliation with God"; morality alone was not enough.

Such satisfaction as eighteenth-century religion provided could appeal only to the educated and serious; for it made faith an intellectual rather than a moral virtue, and probability the guide of life. For the unlettered and ignorant who formed the vast bulk of the nation it could bring little comfort. They had neither the time nor the ability to weigh evidences or assess

[1] *Journal*, ii, p. 146 (March 27, 1739)

probabilities; yet they needed something outside themselves to sustain them in the conflict with the hardships of life and the devastating power of sin. Many, no doubt, had vague spiritual longings which they did not perhaps recognize as such until their nature was revealed to them by hearing the Gospel message. This being so, it is not surprising that it was among the poorer classes that the revival of religion had its beginnings. The same had been true of the rise of Christianity itself, and it seems to be a general rule that religious movements, and, indeed, revolutionary movements of every kind, first arise among the populace.[1]

The origins of all great movements in history are shrouded in darkness, and religious revivals in particular have a habit of breaking out suddenly and almost unaccountably. But invariably they have been preceded by a sense of dissatisfaction and of need. Thus the revival of the eighteenth century, which came as a breath from the Spirit of God into a hopeless and fainting world, can only be accounted for, from a human point of view, by that instinct for God which never quite dies away in the hearts of men. It certainly owed nothing to human organization, and when it came, it came almost without observation or expectation. As in the case of the revivals in the latter part of the following century,[2] there were spontaneous and apparently unconnected outbreaks in widely separated quarters. In recent times, and indeed in the middle of the nineteenth century, the report of revivals, through the wide circulation of newspapers, might stimulate similar movements; but this cannot account for their rise in the eighteenth century.

In the course of the history of the race it would seem probable that when a certain stage of development has been reached there comes the realization of new needs, and with it quite independent attempts to meet them. Hence the rise of novel institutions and the discovery of fresh inventions. Perhaps the most serviceable invention of primitive man was the wheel; but it is improbable that it was the discovery of a single individual or community, from which it was handed on to others. Similar conditions originated it without any direct borrowing. There is in humanity an innate creative power, and the recollection of this should prevent us from postulating influences

---

[1] That other classes were also conscious of spiritual needs can be inferred from the early correspondence of Lady Huntingdon. Among them, also, the movement would spread, though not so readily or so extensively

[2] See *Religion in the Victorian Era*, pp. 215 ff., and J. Edwin Orr, *The Second Evangelical Awakening in Britain*

and connexions which may never have existed. "What march of opinions can be traced from mind to mind? They are one and all in their degree the organs of One Sentiment, which has risen up simultaneously in many places very mysteriously."[1]

In England, one of the first harbingers of the coming revival was an awakening among the villagers of Lakenheath in Suffolk in 1718,[2] but it soon died out, and for the first real signs of the coming of the movement we must look to Wales, that breeding-ground of revivals. There the start was even earlier, for it goes back to the work of Griffith Jones in 1709. Later it was taken up by Howell Harris, who began to itinerate long before any of the Methodists. Amongst those whom he influenced was the celebrated Daniel Rowlands. In America, the revival broke out in 1729 under Jonathan Edwardes. It was not until 1740 that Scotland was affected, and among those who were there converted was probably William Darney, who later founded many societies in East Lancashire and the West Riding of Yorkshire and exercised great influence over William Grimshaw.

On the Continent, there were also noteworthy revival movements, such as the Camisards in France. Though a number of French Protestants sought refuge in England during the early part of the century, including the fathers of Romaine and Roquet, they do not seem to have had any effect on the revival. There were several French congregations in Spitalfields, and some French Protestants may have joined religious societies; in a few instances they shared buildings with the Methodists or even handed them over when they could no longer maintain them. The French church at Spitalfields became a great Methodist centre, and it was there that the first "covenant" services were held on September 11, 1755, when 1,800 people were present.[3]

At an even earlier date a wave of Pietism had swept over Germany, bringing fresh life to Protestantism. It was led by Spener and centred round the university of Halle. Amongst others who were revivified by it were the Moravians. As the Moravians exercised so much influence over the Wesleys and the Methodist side of the revival, they require fuller notice. The outstanding leader was Count Zinzendorf, who established a settlement at Herrnhut which endeavoured to reproduce the life of the primitive Church. To this community all Christians

---

[1] Newman, *Essays*, i, p. 274   [2] See Wesley, *Journal*, iv, p. 295
[3] *Op. cit.*, iv, pp. 3, 126; *Letters*, v, p. 100

were welcomed, and there was no demand that they should surrender their special denominational beliefs. The Moravians appeared first in England in 1728, but their strictness of life prevented their gaining many adherents, though William Whiston, ever ready to try some new thing, was drawn to them for a time.[1] They hoped to bring fresh life into the Church of England, and to this end strove to work closely with it, and even elected the saintly Bishop Wilson of Sodor and Man to their synod. In 1737 Archbishop Potter carried on a correspondence with Count Zinzendorf.

Unfortunately, the count proved a most eccentric leader, and under his guidance the Moravians became infected with antinomianism, and also developed a very elaborate ritual of their own; by 1751 they had become "to a great extent, a luscious morsel of antinomian poison".[2] Zinzendorf seems to have been carried away by a belief in his own inspiration; he even produced a translation of the New Testament from which the Epistle of St. James was excluded, thus going further than Luther. By some means or other he obtained special privileges for his sect from the British Parliament, and embarked on ambitious schemes involving immense financial outlay which he was quite unable to meet.[3] In 1753 Whitefield published a pamphlet exposing Moravian practices and teaching which caused an immense sensation,[4] and others who had left them also gave their testimony. When the count was in London, Lady Huntingdon took the occasion to give him a piece of her mind and remonstrated with him "on the farrago of superstitious fopperies and shocking offences introduced by the leading brethren in London and other places, whereby hundreds of honest-hearted Christians were deluded and involved in unspeakable distress and anguish of mind".[5] After the death of Zinzendorf, whose sanity towards the end of his career seems to have been doubtful, the Moravians entered on a more respectable, if less spectacular, stage.[6]

The influence which the Moravians, and especially Peter Böhler, exercised upon John Wesley is too well known to require description. Later he reacted from them most violently,

[1] *Memoirs*, p. 575   [2] Tyerman, *Life, etc., of John Wesley*, ii, p. 96

[3] He had a house in Chelsea which Wesley described as "a palace for a prince" (*Letters*, v, p. 156).

[4] *Works*, iv, p. 253   [5] *Countess of Huntingdon*, i, p. 454

[6] Such excesses were no part of Moravian beliefs: see Spangenberg, *Christian Doctrine as taught in the Protestant Church of the United Brethren*

though he still maintained his friendship with Peter Böhler, who was himself critical of many things done by Count Zinzendorf. What Wesley disliked above everything else was their teaching that until faith had been received as a gift from God all the means of grace, including prayer and the reading of the Bible, were to be abandoned. In his account of the dispute between them he has not been entirely candid, for he passes over attempts by the German Moravians to heal the breach.[1] Count Zinzendorf instructed the Moravians in England to seek Wesley's forgiveness, and himself saw Wesley when over here. But his intervention only made matters worse, for Wesley could not stomach Zinzendorf's lofty airs of superiority; a sentiment in which his brother Charles also shared, for he wrote:

> What my soul does as hell-fire reject,
> A Pope—a Count—a leader of a sect.[2]

The Moravians certainly proved very attractive to some of the early Methodists, including members of the Holy Club; even Whitefield was deserted by some who had looked to him as their spiritual father.[3] Charles Wesley himself had been tempted to break with his brother and join them. From this course Lady Huntingdon claimed that she had managed to keep him back.[4] With Cennick she was less successful, and his secession brought great confusion to the London Methodists.

John Wesley's initial admiration for the Moravians may have been due to a Puritan strain derived from his maternal grandfather. He was not, however, so consistent a lover of Puritanism as Whitefield. The latter wrote to him on September 25, 1740: "If you think so meanly of Bunyan, and the Puritan writers, I do not wonder that you think me wrong"; and on February 26, 1741, he affirmed: "I am more and more in love with the good old Puritans."[5]

There were, it is scarcely necessary to point out, many resemblances between the Puritans and the Methodists, and it was natural for Bishop Warburton to speak of the "old Puritan fanaticism revived under the new name of Methodism";[6] and

---

[1] Southey, *Life of Wesley*, i, p. 353
[2] *Poetical Works of J. and C. Wesley*, vi, p. 62
[3] *Works*, ii, pp. 204, 215
[4] *Countess of Huntingdon*, i, pp. 41 f.
[5] *Letters*, i, pp. 212, 255
[6] *The Doctrine of Grace*, p. 326

REVIVAL MOVEMENTS: LADY HUNTINGDON 121

for Horace Walpole to write in 1748: "The nonsensical New Light is extremely in fashion, and I shall not be surprised if we see all the cant and folly of the last age." It was, however, among the Evangelical leaders that Puritan influences were strongest. Romaine, who came of Huguenot stock, was especially open to them, and, indeed, both in his character and in his writings he was a kind of successor to the Puritanism of the seventeenth century. In any case there was much in the Thirty-nine Articles and the Homilies which had a Puritan savour, even if this element had been obscured and forgotten; Tillotson, however, was deeply read in the Puritan divines; and the tradition of Baxter, Bunyan, and their fellows was more alive among Churchmen than among Dissenters. The Puritan element was, indeed, part of the heritage of the Church: for it went back, behind the sects which arose in the sixteenth century, to the exiles in Geneva in the reign of Mary.

There was another influence at work on the first Methodists, an influence which also affected the Evangelical leaders, that of William Law;[1] Bishop Warburton, indeed, could affirm of Methodism that "William Law was its father, and Count Zinzendorf rocked the cradle".[2] This influence was admitted by the first generation of Methodist historians; Coke and Moore wrote that "by his excellent pen" Law was "the great forerunner of the revival which followed, and did more to promote it . . . perhaps than the rest of the nation collectively taken".[3]

Law's *Serious Call* was published in 1729, the year in which the "Holy Club" began its meetings in Oxford, and its members looked to him for guidance. Wesley himself used to go to see him at Putney, walking the whole way in order to save money for his charitable activities. Later he turned against Law (as he turned against the Moravians; as also against

[1] William Law probably exercised a deeper and more persistent influence on religion than any writer of the century. The effect of the *Serious Call* on Dr. Johnson is well known; but there were many others, apart from the Methodists and Evangelicals, who would respond to its appeal. When R. H. Froude remarked to John Keble that he thought it a clever book, the latter replied that he might just as well have said "that the Day of Judgment would be a pretty sight" (Isaac Williams, *Autobiography*, p. 28). Even his mystical writings, which many preferred to ignore, had their influence. Principal Shairp said that Coleridge found in them, and other similar writings, a message which "helped to keep alive the heart within the head", and in his time of doubt and darkness were a pillar of fire by night, enabling him "to skirt, without crossing, the sandy desert of utter unbelief" (*Studies in Poetry and Philosophy*, p. 191)

[2] *Works*, iv, p. 623   [3] *Life of Wesley*, p. 7

Luther),[1] though even in September, 1760, he could write: "Mr. Law, whom I love and reverence now, was once a kind of oracle to me."[2] In the controversy between them, Law had much the best of the matter; he was, indeed, of far higher mental calibre than Wesley and a very skilled, if restrained, disputer.[3] Charles Wesley was far from happy about the affair, and notes on October 21, 1756, when on a visit to Manchester: "I drank tea with Dr. Byrom, and was hard put to it to defend my brother's book against Mr. Law. We got at last to a better subject."[4]

Law's main contribution in preparing for the revival was that he set before men a forgotten ideal of the Christian life, and when they tried to attain to it they found that their unaided efforts were but vain. As Henry Venn said, the pun was perhaps unintentional, "Law came before the Gospel."[5]

That Law fell out of favour with his one-time admirers may be accounted for by his later books. *The Spirit of Love* and *The Spirit of Prayer* seemed to Henry Venn to belittle the Atonement, and after being an ardent disciple he ceased to follow him.[6] A similar judgment had been expressed by Wesley on July 27, 1749: "I read Mr. Law on the Spirit of Prayer . . . it is another Gospel: for if God were never angry (as this Tract asserts), He could never be reconciled; and consequently, the whole Christian doctrine of Reconciliation in Christ falls to the ground."[7]

Whitefield, who had been deeply stirred by *The Serious Call*, regretted Wesley's attack, and still retained his early admiration. He could even say a good word for *The Spirit of Prayer*, excusing its blemishes on the ground that "the sun hath its spots, and so have the best of men".

In spite of criticisms of his other works, Law's *Serious Call* continued to be read by Evangelicals. Thomas Scott, though feeling that it contained as little Gospel as any religious book

---

[1] He wrote on June 15, 1741: "Read Commentary on Galatians. I was utterly ashamed. How I have esteemed this book, only because I heard it commended by others! Or, at best, because I had read some excellent sentences occasionally quoted from it." He then goes on: "the author makes nothing out, clears up not one considerable difficulty; that he is quite shallow in his remarks on many passages, and muddy and confused almost on all" (*Journal*, ii, p. 467).

[2] *Op. cit.*, iv, p. 410. As late as March 8, 1787, he recommended: "next to the Bible . . . Mr. Law's works" (*Letters*, vii, p. 374).

[3] See further J. B. Green, *John Wesley and William Law*; and Stephen Hobhouse, *William Law and Eighteenth Century Quakerism*.

[4] *Journal*, ii, p. 129   [5] *Venn Family Annals*, p. 72

[6] *Op. cit.*, p. 74   [7] *Journal*, iii, p. 422

he knew, was moved to greater earnestness by it.[1] This cautious attitude continued, and in the next century Henry Martyn, while recognizing its limitations from an Evangelical point of view, yet found help in it. On November 11, 1803, he wrote to his friend Sargent: "As you have read Law tell me your opinion of him. He is rather a favourite of mine, though not without his faults."

In considering the revival of the eighteenth century it is very tempting, in view of later developments, to look upon it as following from the first a definite plan and programme. This was certainly not the case, as it was with the Oxford Movement of a century later. The movement developed as its leaders were led by circumstances and the gradual realization of the needs they had to meet; by the closing of some doors and the opening of others (cf. Acts 16: 6 ff.). When Whitefield stood up and preached to the colliers of Kingswood, and Wesley began to itinerate, they had no thought of starting a new denomination. The various features which would distinguish Methodism—such as lay preaching, the class system, and separate organizations—arose spontaneously to meet actual requirements.

The promoters of the revival were firmly united "in their central and dominating conviction, that the only hope for fallen humanity is the Propitiary Sacrifice of Christ on the Cross", but on many secondary matters they held different views. The progress of the movement has been compared by G. W. E. Russell, from whom I have just quoted, to the effect of a sudden cloudburst on a mountain lake. This may cause it to overflow its banks and release a number of separate streams down the hillside, which for a time will cross and recross one another, until they find definite channels of their own. At first all three sections, Methodists, Calvinist Methodists, and Evangelicals, were contained within the Church, but after a time the more turbulent waters flowed off in different directions, though not without leaving permanent effects on the parent stream.[2]

It has been customary to begin accounts of the Evangelical Movement with a reference to the Holy Club and its meetings in 1729. But such a procedure is not fully justified, and that for two reasons: the Evangelical Movement was parallel to the Methodist, and not derived from it; and the Methodist Movement did not really originate with the little group at Oxford. On this point more may be said.

[1] *Works*, i, p. 42   [2] See *A Short History of the Evangelical Movement*, pp. 2 ff.

Wesley himself is partly to blame for the confusion, for he began his *Short History of Methodism* by recording that: "In November 1729 four young gentlemen of Oxford, Mr. John Wesley, Fellow of Lincoln, Mr. Charles Wesley, Student of Christ Church, Mr. Morgan, Commoner of Christ Church, and Mr. Kirkham of Merton College, began to spend some evenings in a week together in reading chiefly the Greek Testament." But these meetings, which soon attracted other members, have no connexion, beyond a personal one, with the later Methodist Movement. The members had their faces to the past, rather than to the future, and are akin to other similar societies whose activities have already been noticed. It is significant that the Methodists themselves date the movement from the beginning of field-preaching in 1739, holding their world-wide centenary in 1839.

That Wesley should thus commence, however, is natural in view of his dominance of the earlier movement—when he left Oxford for a short time in 1733 it nearly collapsed. But he was aware that its ethos was different, having too much of the faith of the servant rather than that of the son; though it should not be forgotten that by 1772 this view had been modified. "I often cry, *Vitae me redde priori!* Let me be again an Oxford Methodist. I am often in doubt whether it would not be best for me to resume all my Oxford rules, great and small. I did then walk closely with God, and redeem the time. But what have I been doing these thirty years?"[1]

The Oxford Methodists, indeed, are a kind of epitome of what was to come, for the different members later followed very diverse courses—Wesleyan, Calvinist Methodist, Moravian, High Church and Evangelical. Only a few took any part in the Methodist Movement as such—the two Wesleys, George Whitefield (as a Calvinist) and Hervey (as an Evangelical). After many vicissitudes, Ingham ended as an eccentric evangelist, after being a Moravian, as was Gambold. Several retained the original spirit of the group, which was fundamentally High Church, and continued to be definite Churchmen. Clayton, indeed, pressed their principles still further, and in a way anticipated the Tractarians.

In view of these divergences and the way in which they illustrate and help to explain subsequent developments, it will not

---

[1] *Letters*, vi, p. 6. Against the entry February 1, 1738 (*Journal*, i, p. 422), "I, who went to America to convert others, was never myself converted to God", he later wrote, "I am not so sure of this"

be amiss to trace out the careers of some of the members of the Holy Club. Of John Wesley nothing need here be said; we shall consider his relations to the Evangelical Movement at a later stage; but his brother Charles calls for notice. He is popularly known as the hymn-writer of the movement, but in its early days his activities were as great as those of his brother or of Whitefield. That they are often overlooked is due in part to the circumstance that he did not publish his journals (they did not appear until 1849) as did the other two; and also to his abandonment of itinerating after his marriage. It should be noted that John always coupled their names together and continually used the phrase "my brother and I". Charles was a more consistent Churchman than John, and was much more far-sighted as to the consequences of "irregularities", and quite scathing in his denunciation of the "ordinations". But he was not himself quite consistent, for when he and his followers had been refused Holy Communion at Temple Church, Bristol, he administered it in the schoolroom at Kingswood.[1] One great service he performed in the early days of the movement was as a kind of liaison officer between John and Whitefield. For this he was well fitted as he had certain virtues which they held in separation, being a man of culture and refinement with an acute and logical mind like his brother, but nearer to Whitefield in being more impulsive and demonstrative.

Of Whitefield himself it is more difficult to write, for though his individual success was spectacular, and though he gave the movement its initial impetus by field-preaching, his real contribution was but meagre. He had many faults and made many mistakes, as he himself was the first to admit, but he must have been a man of a pure and disinterested outlook not to have been overwhelmed by the sudden fame which his preaching brought to him. He never became a mere "windbag, blown large by popular art". His mistakes were almost entirely due to his lack of experience, and were often the aberrations of an impulsive and generous nature. For Whitefield had no "background". Brought up in the vulgar bustle of an inn, his status was little improved when he "exchanged the drawer's apron for the degrading badge of a servitor at Pembroke College, Oxford".[2] No wonder his head was a little turned by the great people who took notice of him. Philip has said that his "self-complacency in the patronage of the countess and his 'elect ladies', his many and fulsome compliments to them admit of

[1] *Journal*, i, p. 267   [2] Abbey and Overton, ii, p. 93

no excuse".[1] But this is too harsh a judgment, and makes no allowance for the sentiments of the day. Then, a countess *was* a countess, and no one forgot it.

The great crisis in Whitefield's religious life occurred in the spring of 1735. Under the influence of Castanza's *Spiritual Combat*, he indulged in such excessive austerities that he became ill. Then he saw the need for another way if he were to receive pardon. All that he had by way of guidance was his Greek Testament and Hall's *Contemplations*, lent to him by his tutor, and by their aid he realized the atoning power of the death of Christ as the foundation of any genuine religion, and thus came to a knowledge of the "truth" long before Wesley himself. It is to be noted that he received no help from his fellow "Methodists"; Wesley, indeed, had by this time left Oxford.

After his ordination as deacon, Whitefield's preaching in London led to the offer of a well-paid curacy, but he refused this in order to follow the example of Wesley and go to Georgia. He did not receive priest's orders until his return. On going to Bristol he found that most of the churches were closed to him, and thereupon he began preaching, as he had done in Georgia, in the open air, and thus inaugurated the most effective and most typical of the methods of the revival. Before arriving at this truly momentous decision he went through much mental conflict. The date was Saturday, February 17, 1739, and the place Rose Green in Kingswood. His life henceforth was one of perpetual movement, not only in the British Isles but between England and America. It was in the latter region that he died on August 30, 1770. His health had been uncertain for some time, but only a week before his death he wrote that it had been improved by riding fifty miles in order to preach.[2]

Benjamin Ingham was born at Ossett in the parish of Dewsbery and educated at Batley Grammar School. After leaving Oxford he did much for Methodism in his native county, and also made an unexpected marriage with the Lady Margaret Hastings. Ingham is said to have been exceedingly handsome, "too handsome for a man", and the lady, who was deeply religious, was twelve years his senior. However, their twenty-seven years of married life were very happy. In 1742, the year after his marriage, Ingham became a Moravian, and later formed a sect of his own which aroused the admiration of Romaine. But many of his followers were drawn away to the

[1] *Life of Whitefield*, p. 365 [2] *Letters*, iii, p. 427

Sandemanians, "that horrid blast from the North", as Romaine called it, which plunged him into deep depression. He died in 1772.[1] The Inghams had one son, Ignatius by name, and like the children of not a few Methodists, he by no means followed in the footsteps of his parents.

Among those who worked with Ingham was John Simpson. His career was even more devious, and he is a good example of the vagaries which marked the less stable minds who came under the influence of the revival. Wesley looked upon him as a sincere but eccentric enthusiast who depended on "inward impressions".[2] Soon after his ordination he was presented to a valuable living in Leicestershire, but gave it up to join the Moravians. Although he drew many away from the Church, he himself later wished to rejoin it. Lady Huntingdon wrote to Wesley on January 9, 1742: "Mr. Simpson . . . has left the Moravians, as he tells me, and is not quite at rest now."[3] Wesley records an interview with him on November 27, 1747:

> Poor Mr. Simpson spent an hour with me, distressed on every side: drawn up to London by fair and specious promises, and then left to perish, unless he would promise "Never more to preach out of a church"—Alas! what a method of conversion is this? I love the Church too: but I would no more starve men into the Church than burn them into it.[4]

The last notice of "poor Simpson" occurs on August 1, 1757, when he was still unsettled.[5]

Charles Kinchin, Fellow of Corpus, became rector of Dummer in Hampshire, but as he lived only until 1742 he had little time in which to exercise his influence. Wesley described him as "one of the humblest, truest, most faithful of the Methodist brotherhood at Oxford".[6]

Of all the members of the Holy Club, Hervey alone can be classed as an Evangelical in the strict sense of the term, and as such he will be reserved for more detailed treatment. Others, however, retained their strict Churchmanship, and prominent among them were Thomas Broughton and John Clayton.

[1] For fuller details see Tyerman, *Oxford Methodists*, pp. 57–154
[2] *Journal*, iii, p. 26
[3] *Countess of Huntingdon*, i, p. 46
[4] *Journal*, iii, pp. 322 f.
[5] *Op. cit.*, iv, pp. 231 f.
[6] *Op. cit.*, i, p. 443

Broughton, who was a native of Oxford, after being at University College, became fellow of Exeter. He held a lectureship at St. Helen's, Bishopsgate, but lost it through allowing too free a use of the pulpit to Whitefield. After this he seems to have drifted away from the Methodists objecting strongly to their insistence on "sudden" conversions. He was also a bitter foe to the Moravians. In 1741 he became lecturer at All Hallows, Lombard Street, and twelve years later, through the influence of Henry Venn, rector of Wotton in Surrey. But as he had been appointed secretary of the Society for Promoting Christian Knowledge in 1743, he committed the care of it to a curate. He held both offices until his death on December 22, 1777. Broughton was a convinced Churchman, but in spite of his friendship for Venn can hardly count as an Evangelical.

The career of Clayton was in some ways the most consistent of all the members of the Holy Club, for he developed their High Church ideas more fully. He had been educated at Manchester Grammar School and went up to Brasenose College, Oxford, where he became tutor. In 1733 he went to the Collegiate Church in Manchester (the present cathedral) as chaplain; later he would become a fellow. At first he kept in touch with his old associates, and in 1738 allowed Whitefield to preach and help in the administration of the sacraments in the chapel of ease which was in his charge. The same privileges were accorded to John Wesley. Later he came under the influence of Dr. Deacon, the non-juring bishop, and from him acquired very advanced ideas of Churchmanship as well as Jacobite sympathies. When the Young Pretender reached Manchester in 1745, Clayton knelt in the streets and offered up prayers for his success. In this he was at one with the chapter of the Collegiate Church, where the Young Pretender attended service. The result was a number of suspensions, and Clayton gave himself up to teaching. He lived in Greengate, Salford, where he had a very successful "classical academy". By this time he had completely broken with the Methodists, and when Charles Wesley daily attended the services in 1756 he took no notice of him. Clayton was an intimate of John Byrom, from whose journals we learn a good deal about him. He died on May 25, 1773, and a memorial tablet was placed in the church.

These rather detailed accounts of the lives of some of the original members of the Holy Club may not seem at first sight very germane to our inquiry; but they are necessary for two reasons. In the first place they show how little the Evangelical

Movement, as indeed the Methodist Movement, owes to the gatherings in Oxford; and in the second they should help us to understand some of the reasons why the authorities and the parochial clergy took up so unsympathetic an attitude. Unless we realize the vagaries and eccentricities of those who, rightly or wrongly, were lumped together as "Methodists", their excessive suspicions seem unwarranted. Moreover, there were other wandering exponents of the Gospel who were far worse. With a people hungry for spiritual food and quite ignorant in matters of religion, it is not surprising to find that they were willing to respond to any who promised to meet their needs, especially if they were possessed by the self-assurance of some of the fanatics who preached their own unbalanced and often dangerous notions of Scripture truth. The same thing had occurred in the primitive Church when many wrested the Scriptures to their own destruction (2 Pet. 3: 16).

So far, in considering the influences which affected the revival movements, we have taken note of those outside the Church of England. It must not, however, be forgotten that in both wings of the movement the writings of some of the older Anglican theologians were highly valued. John Wesley said that they had saved him from the "well-meaning wrong-headed Germans",[1] whilst Whitefield commended Bishops Hopkins and Beveridge, "and indeed almost all the writers a century ago".[2] This was in November, 1748, and in August of the same year he had written: "I would recommend Bishop Beveridge's sermons more, but they are too voluminous for the common people, and I have not read them all."[3]

Charles Wesley seems to have held Beveridge in especial esteem and made much use of his sermons, and when attempts were made to move Susanna Wesley from her allegiance to the Church he commented: "Bishop Beveridge would as soon have given up the ordinances."[4] Richard Hill owed his conversion to Beveridge's *Private Thoughts*,[5] and through the same medium brought about that of his brother Rowland to whom he read one of Beveridge's sermons.[6] Some of the less known figures

[1] *Journal*, i, p. 419. He also read Beveridge's *Pandectae Canonum Conciliorum* (*op. cit.*, i, p. 274)
[2] *Letters*, ii, p. 206 [3] *Op. cit.*, ii, p. 166
[4] *Journal*, i, pp. 116, 144, 207 [5] Sidney, *Life of Sir Richard Hill*, p. 17
[6] See William Jay, *Funeral Sermon on Rowland Hill* (*Works*, vii, p. 425) Richard Hill was also interested in the writings of Archbishop Leighton

I

among the Methodists also knew and treasured Beveridge, for when James Field, an early lay preacher, wrote to his sons on the subject of "unequal marriages", he drew their attention to "the resolutions of Bishop Beveridge".[1]

The Evangelical wing were no less appreciative of the earlier Anglican divines, and included in Erasmus Middleton's *Biographia Evangelica* are lives of Archbishop Leighton and Bishops Beveridge and Hopkins. The last was styled by Hervey "a fervent and affectionate preacher".[2] Romaine, in the preface to his commentary on Psalm 107, speaks of "My good Bishop Beveridge . . . whom I admire so much, because he was as great an enthusiast as myself". He also quotes from *The Sinfulness of Sin* by Bishop Reynolds.[3]

Beveridge was attractive to the Evangelicals on account of his supposed Calvinism, but even more because of his devoted life. His work as rector of St. Peter's, Cornhill, to which he was appointed in 1662, earned for him the title of "The great reviver and restorer of primitive piety".[4] Beveridge's popularity seems to have continued, for Walter Mayers, the Calvinist clergyman who influenced Newman during his schooldays, gave him a copy of the *Private Thoughts*.[5]

Before discussing the distinction between Methodists and Evangelicals, it will be well to notice the terms themselves. "Methodist" had been applied to the Holy Club in reprobation;[6] but later it came to be attached indiscriminately to anyone who showed signs of taking religion at all seriously. It was apparently well known in this sense as early as 1749, being so used in *Tom Jones*, Bk. I, chap. x; and even earlier Samuel Richardson's not very reputable friend, Mrs. Pilkington, complained of the harshness of "her saint-like, Methodist landlady". Wesley in his tract "The Character of a Methodist" (1739), although pointing out that the name had been applied as a reproach by others, accepts it, and in an address to the king five years later he speaks of "societies in derision called Methodist".

[1] L. F. Church, *Early Methodist People*, p. 233
[2] *Theron and Aspasio*, ii, 319   [3] *Works*, pp. 376 f.
[4] Erasmus Middleton, *op. cit.*, iv, p. 144
[5] Newman retained his interest in Beveridge and in his *Lectures on the Prophetic Office of the Church* made use of him, whilst the pamphlet "On Frequent Communions" was reprinted in the Tracts for the Times: see further, *Correspondence of J. H. Newman with John Keble*, pp. 114 ff., and Anne Mozley, *Letters and Correspondence of J. H. Newman*, i, p. 24

[6] It was easy for opponents to point out that the only two occurrences of the word in the Greek New Testament (Eph. 4: 14, 6: 11) refer to cunning and deceitful craftiness

In April, 1761, he declared that "those who are connected with me do not call themselves Methodists. Others call them by that in derision, and they cannot help it".[1] Yet with his customary inconsistency in things indifferent, in that very year he issued *Select Hymns designed chiefly for the Use of the People called Methodists*.

Archbishop Secker deplored the application of the term to the followers of Wesley, since it did the sectaries "the honour of miscalling other persons of more than ordinary seriousness by their *name*".[2] The term, indeed, was soon extended to Evangelicals by those who were not at pains to distinguish them from the Methodists,[3] and could even be used by Evangelicals themselves. As examples of the former extension there may be cited Mr. Mitchell, rector of Brighton, who humorously defended himself for allowing Henry Venn to use his pulpit by saying: "Who would have thought that such a cheerful, open countenance could have any connexion with Methodism?"; and the remark of a sceptical man of the world: "Talk of Methodists! Why, this Mr. Venn is one of the most agreeable men I was ever in company with."[4] Examples of the use of the term by Evangelicals themselves are rare, but one clear instance may be found in the dying injunctions of Grimshaw in 1763 that his funeral oration should be delivered by a Methodist preacher; the condition was fulfilled by Henry Venn. Another apparent example is not so clear, since it merely reports the opinion of others; that is a letter of Berridge to John Thornton on November 24, 1781, in which he writes that there was a prejudice in Cambridge against John Venn because he was the son of a Methodist clergyman.[5]

Although they might preach the same doctrines as the Methodists, the great majority of Evangelicals strongly insisted on their distinction from them. Thomas Adam wrote to Walker on November 21, 1756:

[1] *Letters*, iv, p. 144   [2] Charge in Bishop Watson's *Tracts*, vi, p. 77

[3] Thomas Scott, *The Force of Truth* (*Works*, i, p. 19 n.), states that the term Methodists as a stigma of reproach "was first applied to Mr. Wesley, Mr. Whitefield and their followers; to those who, professing an attachment to our established church, were not conformists in point of parochial order but had separate seasons, places and assemblies for worship. The term has since been extended by many to all persons, whether clergy or laity, who preach or profess the doctrines of the reformation, as expressed in the articles and liturgy of our Church. For this fault they must all submit to bear the reproachful name, especially the ministers; nor will the most regular and peaceful compliance with the injunctions of the rubric exempt them from it"

[4] *Venn Family Annals*, pp. 104, 106   [5] *Venn Family Annals*, p. 102

Methodism, as to its external form, is such a deviation from the rule and constitution of the Church of England, that all attempts to render them consistent must be in vain. . . . The truth is, either they set out wrong and must return wholly to the order of the Establishment, so long as they assume to be out of it; or they have acted hitherto by superior direction of the Spirit and must not flinch from their leader. The latter may pretend to have gone all along upon that supposition, and if I mistake not it is that they will abide by.[1]

Walker himself wrote that though Talbot was "cried out against as a Methodist by most of the clergy [he] is quite sound from all leaning that way".[2] Dr. Stonhouse, after his ordination, had a distinct fear of being called a Methodist, for which he was reproved by Lady Huntingdon.[3]

The term "Evangelical" has a long history behind it, for it was used of Wycliffe and his followers. As in the case of "Methodist", it may originally have been applied by opponents, or it may have been adopted by those who felt that they stood in a great succession, though there "is not the slightest evidence . . . that the early Evangelicals claimed the title as their own in any spirit of self-glorification".[4] An early example of its use occurs in a letter from Haweis to Walker in which he says: "Talbot took his living with a view to do good, before he could be at all called evangelical."[5] The use here, however, may not be anything more than a recognition that he was acting in conformity with the Gospel, a sense which it seems to have in Sterne's *Sentimental Journey* (1768), where Yorick attributes his supposed respect for the fair sex to his "evangelical views".[6] By 1770, however, the application to a definite

---

[1] Sidney, *Life of Walker*, p. 224   [2] *Op. cit.*, p. 480

[3] *Countess of Huntingdon*, i, p. 138

[4] Abbey and Overton, ii, pp. 60 f. At a later date the Evangelicals were accused of arrogance for using the title: see *The Anti-Jacobin Review*, April, 1799, p. 362; Ludlam, *Essays*; and Daubeny, *A Guide to the Church*. John Overton retaliated by pointing out the similar "arrogance" of those who claimed to be "Rational Divines" (*The True Church*, p. 11)

[5] *Life of Walker*, p. 479

[6] Gibbon, *Decline and Fall of the Roman Empire*, chap. xxxvii (ed. Bury, iv, p. 68), speaks of the "evangelical poverty" of the monks

party seems to have been established, for Toplady refers to Wesley's complaint that "the Evangelical clergy are leaving no stone unturned to raise John Calvin's ghost".

Thus it will be seen that the terms Methodist and Evangelical are used in a distinctive manner.[1] How far back, it may now be asked, does the distinction go? It is often taken for granted that the Evangelical Movement was merely one of the offshoots of the Methodist Revival; but such an opinion requires considerable modification: "The two movements were far from being identical. They were often warmly opposed. . . . Evangelicalism, or something nearly akin to it, would certainly have arisen about the same period, even if Methodism had never existed."[2] Both were manifestations of that peculiar activity of the Spirit of God in the early and middle years of the eighteenth century to which reference has already been made. Furthermore, the majority of those who are recognized as leaders of the Evangelical Movement arrived at their opinions quite apart from Wesley or even from Whitefield. Of the pioneers, Thomson of St. Gennys was converted in 1733 following on a dream and the reading of Romans 3 (this was before Wesley himself was converted); Grimshaw arrived at his views quite independently; Walker was indebted to a Presbyterian layman, George Conon, headmaster of Truro Grammar School; Adam, after being roused by Law's *Serious Call*, found peace through the study of the Scriptures; whilst Romaine during his time of spiritual stress found the Methodists a hindrance rather than a help. The experience of Henry Venn was very similar to that of Adam, though he later received valuable guidance from Lady Huntingdon; whilst Joseph Milner was awakened through Hooker's "Sermon on Justification".[3] On the other side, we find that Toplady was converted through hearing a Methodist lay preacher in a barn in Ireland; Madan directly by a sermon of Wesley; whilst Fletcher was drawn into the movement through hearing a description of the life and activities of the Methodists. One of the most striking acknowledgments of Wesley's influence came from Thomas

---

[1] There is a tendency on the part of some Methodists to appropriate the term. In the standard editions of both the *Journal* and the *Letters* of Wesley the phrase "Evangelical Revival" is used when it is clear that the Methodist Movement is intended

[2] Abbey and Overton, i, p. 417

[3] It has been claimed that Milner was converted through students from Trevecca: see below, pp. 312 f.

Vivian, a less well-known though not unimportant early Evangelical, who wrote that to his writings he owed "the blessing wrought on my soul".[1]

But if the Evangelical Movement was not directly derived from the Methodists, it certainly owed much to them.[2] In the second generation there was a strong tendency to repudiate this,[3] and to emphasize the entire independence of the two movements. This is to go too far, and Sir James Stephen quite rightly upholds the justice of the complaints of Philip in his *Life of Whitefield* against those who thus sought to disavow their connexion with his hero: "The consanguinity is attested by historical records, and by the strongest family resemblance. The quarterings of Whitfield (*sic*) are entitled to a conspicuous place in the Evangelical scutcheon; and they who bear it are not wise in being ashamed of the blazonry."[4]

In view of their similarity of outlook it was but natural that Evangelicals and Methodists should have reacted upon one another, and that awakened Churchmen should have been drawn into a co-operation which if limited was quite definite; but it must not be forgotten that the link was much less close with Wesley and his followers than with Whitefield and his patron Lady Huntingdon.

Lady Huntingdon[5] holds so prominent a place in the revival of the eighteenth century that it is high time that we turned to a consideration of her achievements, and it will be an advantage to deal here with her life as a whole, leaving, however, her part in the Calvinist controversy and in the events which led up to the separation of her followers from the Church for consideration later.

The wind bloweth where it listeth, and the Spirit of God chooses for its instruments and agents some who in the eyes of men might seem to be the most unlikely subjects. This is perhaps especially marked in the choice of women. In the fourteenth century Caterina Benincasa, the daughter of a poor dyer,

---

[1] Letter of "T.V." to Wesley (October 10, 1748), printed in *The Arminian Magazine*, 1778, pp. 586 ff.

[2] The debt was not all on one side, and the Methodists owed much in the beginning of their movement to Evangelical help. Meeting-houses were built by Grimshaw and Venn, and Evangelical preaching often resulted in converts to Methodism, as did changes in incumbencies

[3] See below, pp. 447 ff.   [4] *Essays in Ecclesiastical Biography*, ii, pp. 64 f.

[5] See, further, *The Life and Times of Selina, Countess of Huntingdon*, and Sarah Tyler, *The Countess of Huntingdon and Her Circle*. The former work must be used with caution as it contains many errors in details

can be transformed into St. Catherine of Siena, the adviser and reprover of popes; and, in the century which followed, a peasant girl from the countryside of Domrémy is raised up to become, as St. Joan of Arc, the saviour of her country. By recalling such examples of the Spirit's working we shall find the career of Lady Huntingdon less inexplicable than otherwise it might seem. That one of the most active and influential leaders of the revival should have been a woman, and a woman of quality, was something that mere human foresight could never have anticipated, for women in the eighteenth century were expected to keep in the background and to submit to the guidance and control of their fathers and husbands.

Selina Shirley was born on June 3, 1728, being the second daughter of Washington, Earl Ferrers, and married the ninth Earl of Huntingdon in 1756, being left a widow in 1774. From a child she had had a deep seriousness of mind and a religious outlook, reading the Bible and being active in works of benevolence among her father's dependants. Although she attended court from time to time and engaged in other social activities, this was done from a sense of duty rather than as a source of pleasure. Her serious outlook on life was intensified by a dangerous illness, but her conversion to Evangelical views was due to a remark from her sister-in-law, Lady Margaret Hastings (later the wife of Benjamin Ingham), to the effect that since she had known the Lord Jesus Christ for life and salvation she had been as happy as an angel. From 1738 onwards Lady Huntingdon and her husband attended the Fetter Lane meetings, as did other persons of rank; but it was not until ten years later that Calvinist doctrines began to make an appeal to her. Although she had met Whitefield in 1736 and had attended the Moorfields Tabernacle, it was only in 1748 that she made him her chaplain and gave him unique opportunities for exercising his powers of preaching.

The influence of Lady Huntingdon affected the revival movement in all its various phases and forms, but its main outlet was undoubtedly in connexion with the work of Whitefield. He himself, unlike Wesley, was no organizer or administrator, and avoided any responsibilities which might hamper his evangelistic activities. Accordingly he was only too glad to hand over to Lady Huntingdon such societies as looked to him for direction. He wrote to her in 1749: "A leader is wanting. This honour hath been put upon your Ladyship by the Great Head of the Church."

Although a strict churchwoman according to her own ideas, and on several occasions using her influence to keep her followers true to the Church, she was wide-minded and eager to co-operate with and support all whom she regarded as preaching the Gospel, having friendships with ministers of all denominations. The lax views of many Dissenters caused her especial anxiety, and she did all in her power to spread more Evangelical views among them. Her relations with Wesley and his followers were not so happy, and a number of disagreements and controversies arose between them. This may partly be explained on personal grounds, for Wesley was as little disposed to submit to her as to Count Zinzendorf, and he was perhaps ironical about her claims. It is not therefore remarkable that her feelings towards him were never really cordial, and that it was only her Christian spirit which held her back from actual dislike. Her followers, however, had no scruples in drawing away men and women from the Methodist societies. Wesley notes, on December 4, 1771, that at Ashford her preachers had "gleaned up most of those whom we had discarded. They call them 'My Lady's Society' and have my free leave to do them all the good they can".[1]

With those of the clergy who adopted Evangelical views Lady Huntingdon had very close relations, choosing her chaplains from among them and making every endeavour to open up ways for their advancement to positions which would give them fuller opportunities. Romaine, who was her senior chaplain, owed to her his appointment to St. Anne's, Blackfriars, and she chose Fletcher to be the first superintendent of the college at Trevecca. Nor did she confine her efforts to finding posts for Evangelical clergymen; she also took an interest in their actual preaching, and in his early days Henry Venn owed much to her outspoken criticism. She wrote to him:

> O my friend, we can make no atonement to a violated law; we have no inward holiness of our own. . . . No longer let false doctrine disgrace your pulpit. Preach Christ crucified as the only foundation of the sinner's hope. Preach Him as the Author and Finisher as well as the sole object of faith, that faith which is the gift of God.

The admonitions of the august lady seem to have been effective,

[1] *Journal*, v, p. 438

for his son records that after 1756 Venn no longer made use of his old sermons, and in the year following Whitefield wrote to his patroness: "Your exertions in bringing him [Venn] to a clearer knowledge of the everlasting gospel have indeed been blessed." Venn continued to be a close ally, and helped to draw up the rules for Trevecca, though apparently he was never one of her chaplains.[1] When he left Huddersfield in 1771 he wrote: "I shall still be your ladyship's willing servant in the service of the Gospel."[2]

But if the Evangelical clergy had a high regard for Lady Huntingdon and were willing to accept her help, they were not so subservient as her special preachers, and on occasion took their own line and refused to obey her "commands". Berridge, with his customary crudity, told her that his instructions "must come from the Lamb, not from the Lamb's wife, though she is a tight woman"; and, with better taste, on another occasion he wrote, referring to her "Vatican Bull": "You threaten me, madam, like a pope, not like a mother in Israel, when you declare roundly that God will scourge me if I do not come." Romaine, also, in spite of all he owed to her influence and support, was by no means at her beck and call. In spite of two summonses to attend the opening of her chapel at Bath in the autumn of 1765, he refused to leave the work he was doing at Oathill and Brighton.[3]

When Lady Huntingdon was compelled to register her chapels as Dissenting places of worship all her chaplains resigned, and thenceforward her direct contacts with Evangelical clergymen practically ceased. As time went on the relations of her followers and the Church became very strained, and open opposition was not wanting. Five years after her death Henry Venn wrote to his son: "I am not displeased with the opposition of the Huntingdonians to your preaching. Their hatred is much to be preferred to their praise."[4]

Lady Huntingdon's most conspicuous work, however, was done among people of her own class; and it was a work which she alone could do. It is true that some were affected by the Methodist preachers—an example is the Duchess of Queensberry, who often went to hear Charles Wesley and Ingham, though the great world in which she was so conspicuous a figure

[1] *Venn Family Annals*, p. 94

[2] On November 5, 1769, he wrote: "In Lady Huntingdon I see a star of the first magnitude in the firmament of the Church" (*Life*, p. 159)

[3] *Countess of Huntingdon*, i, p. 467   [4] *Venn Family Annals*, p. 95

obliterated these early impressions—but they counted for little among the upper classes. Wesley himself rejoiced over this, writing on November 17, 1759: "It is well a few of the rich and noble are called. Oh that God would increase their number! But I should rejoice . . . if it were done by the ministry of others. If I might choose, I should still (as I have done hitherto) 'preach the gospel to the poor'."[1] He had, indeed, no great opinion of the wealthy who claimed to be religious. "In most genteel religious people there is so strange a mixture that I have seldom much confidence in them. But I love the poor; in many of them I find pure, genuine grace, unmixed with paint, folly, and affectation."[2]

There were among the upper classes many more than is generally supposed who were conscious of their religious needs; but it was difficult for them to obtain real help in an age when the domestic chaplain was regarded as a kind of upper servant, and the social position of the parochial clergy, unless as sometimes happened they were of good birth, was so low. At all times it is difficult to reach the upper classes, and less is done for them, or can be done in normal circumstances, than for other classes.

The meetings which Lady Huntingdon arranged for her friends and acquaintances were held in her drawing-room at Chelsea and in her various houses elsewhere. She built a chapel on to her Brighton house, selling her jewels to pay for it. She also bought a house at Bath, and added a chapel with its famous "Nicodemus corner" where those who did not wish their presence to be known might hear the preacher. She had also a house, provided with a chapel, at Tunbridge Wells. Those who took advantage of the opportunities she provided surprise us, alike by their numbers and by their high station; for they included statesmen, society ladies, and even members of the royal family, not to mention the suspected attendance of occasional bishops. By means of these gatherings she enabled Whitefield to display his extraordinary gifts and helped to establish his reputation as a preacher.

But though large numbers came to her meetings, the results were only meagre. Those who attended were moved by no realization of their spiritual needs, though some, even Chesterfield and Bolingbroke, not only listened to Whitefield but had private talks with him. Bolingbroke had indeed a genuine admiration for Whitefield, and wrote to Lady

[1] *Journal*, iv, p. 358   [2] Quoted Abbey and Overton, ii, p. 88

Huntingdon: "He is the most extraordinary man in our times. He has the most commanding eloquence I ever heard in any person—his abilities are very considerable—his zeal unquenchable, and his piety and excellence genuine, unquestionable." Yet Bolingbroke remained a Deist, and on his death-bed gave orders that he was not to be disturbed by the presence of any of the clergy. Can we wonder that the effect on other, less serious minds, was at best only fleeting. Whitefield was merely the latest sensation, and everybody flocked to hear him, as they would to the latest actor. It became "the thing to do". Horace Walpole wrote in March, 1749: "Methodism in the metropolis is more fashionable than anything but brag; the women play very deep at both; as deep, it is much suspected, as the matrons of Rome did at the mysteries of the *Bona Dea*."[1]

Some of those who were persuaded to attend went away deeply offended. The Duchess of Buckingham, who claimed to be a natural daughter of James II, found their doctrines "most repulsive, and strongly tinctured with impertinence and disrespect towards their superiors. . . . It is monstrous to be told that you have a heart as sinful as the common wretches that crawl on the earth." She expressed her amazement that Lady Huntingdon should "relish sentiments so much at variance with high rank and good breeding". The pride of the good duchess may have been extreme, but her letter is of value as throwing light on both the religious and social aspects of the times. There were some, however, whose skins were not quite so thick; but the effect was only to kindle a deeper resentment. The notorious beauty, Lady Suffolk, the mistress of George II, once went to hear Whitefield who, entirely ignorant of her presence, preached words which were a damaging condemnation of her character. So enraged was she that she openly accused Lady Huntingdon of having plotted the whole thing, and grew so abusive that she was at last compelled by those present to apologize.[2]

But if only a few received permanent impressions through Lady Huntingdon's noble efforts, those few included men who exercised considerable influence for good in their day. Perhaps the most outstanding was Lord Dartmouth, of whom Cowper

[1] *Letters*, ii, p. 149
[2] Lady Suffolk, as Mrs. Howard, had been the subject of Pope's panegyric, and was a patron of the poet Gay. Thackeray, in his *Four Georges*, thought her the only one in the court of George II, save Queen Caroline, "with whom it seems pleasant and kindly to hold converse". At the end of her long life she was the friend of Horace Walpole

wrote "he wears a coronet and prays", and who was the recipient of Newton's "Letters to a Nobleman" in *Cardiphonia*. Lord Dartmouth was born in 1725, and succeeded to his title in 1750, six years before his conversion. He held various high posts, amongst others the Secretaryship for American Affairs and Steward of the Royal Household. He was also President of the Royal Society. He had immense wealth, which he used lavishly for the furtherance of good works and in aiding needy clergymen. He had also a number of livings in his gift which he bestowed on Evangelicals, and he also obtained preferment for them from others.[1] Another convert of Lady Huntingdon's was David Stewart, who became Earl of Buchan in 1767, and immediately appointed Venn, Berridge, and Fletcher to be his chaplains. His conversion created something of a sensation in the fashionable world.

In summing up the character of Lady Huntingdon, her biographer claims that she was "neither the gloomy fanatic, the weak visionary, nor the abstracted devotee which different parties have delighted to paint her".[2] This is certainly true, for she undoubtedly possessed great organizing ability, and, but for her, the effects of Whitefield's preaching would have been very much less. In spite of continual bodily suffering, and occasional severe illnesses which caused much anxiety to her friends and disciples, she displayed extraordinary energy and was constantly on the move from place to place accompanied by her bevy of chaplains and preachers. The one object of her life was to proclaim the Gospel, and in whatever company she found herself this was the sole topic of conversation. Those who did not share her enthusiasm might well be pardoned if they regarded her as a "gloomy fanatic". But if all her powers and resources were dedicated to the service of Christ, this, as with other servants of His, did not mean that the process of sanctification had been completed. How can it be in this life? The very virtues, indeed, which adorned her character were the source of what cannot be otherwise described than faults and failings.

As with many others possessed by intense religious convictions, the very intensity of her opinions convinced her that in similar experiences alone lay the way to salvation. Men must be saved—but unless they were saved along the lines that she

[1] Richardson is supposed to have said that had he not been a Methodist he would have realized the ideal set up in Sir Charles Grandison

[2] *Countess of Huntingdon*, i, p. 76

REVIVAL MOVEMENTS: LADY HUNTINGDON 141

laid down something was still lacking. Again, she was not always judicious in her decisions, or in the means by which she tried to implement her plans, being prone to be misled by hasty impressions. But, as such decisions and methods had been the subject of earnest prayer, she could not doubt that they had the divine approval. One notorious example of this hastiness was her sudden condemnation of the minutes of the Conference at Bristol during the Calvinist controversy, and the demand for recantation. In this step she found small support even among her closest followers, who were not a little embarrassed by her action. Lady Huntingdon had the ways of a spiritual dictator, and was impatient of either criticism or opposition. Had she been in the habit of consulting others more than she did, especially her chaplains, things might have been different. Their withdrawal, after the separation of her Connexion, was a grave disaster, for it left her with few who dared to offer advice or advance criticism. She was, moreover, no very good judge of character, and preferred to have around her those who would defer to her wishes and readily carry out her orders. But even so, sooner or later, she had quarrels with some of her most faithful associates, such as Thomas Wills. The truth of the matter seems to have been that, though she sincerely imagined that she had renounced all earthly advantages for the sake of her Saviour, much of them still clung to her—she was still the daughter of one earl and the widow of another. She might call herself "a poor worm", but, as Canon Smyth has remarked, "few worms have ever turned more fiercely or more often".[1] The wives of those of the clergy who co-operated with her were not all of them able to stand her imperious and overbearing manner; but those who submitted were heavily patronized—Mrs. Pentycross was even given a silver teapot as a token of her regard.[2]

Lady Huntingdon certainly retained a very proper idea of her dignity, and when Rowland Hill dared to poke fun at her, although he might receive Christian forgiveness, yet he was deprived of the opportunity of ministering in her chapels.[3] This is perhaps no very pleasing aspect of her character, and it must not be emphasized, for it is to be explained largely by the ideas

---

[1] *Cambridge Hist. Journal*, vii, p. 183   [2] *Countess of Huntingdon*, ii, p. 77

[3] Cf. Sidney, *Life of Rowland Hill*: "Though he always treated her memory with respect, and vindicated her character against aspersions during the Wesleyan controversy, I think he was not one of her ladyship's most cordial admirers. The mode in which she exercised her authority was not suited to a mind impatient of restraint"

of the times and by the deference to which she had been accustomed from childhood. She certainly had made great sacrifices in worldly things for the sake of her faith; more, it may be said, than any other who was associated with the early days of the revival, for she exposed herself to the contempt and ridicule of her equals, and that is sometimes harder to bear than actual persecution. In later life she was made happy by the interest and admiration of George III and his queen. The good king had a profound respect for her and recognized the value of what she was doing. On one occasion he replied to a bishop who complained of her activities: "I wish there was a Lady Huntingdon in every diocese in the Kingdom."[1] In spite of the defects which are so obvious, because they lie so much on the surface, Lady Huntingdon was greatly used by God for the extension of His Kingdom, and on the long and shining roll of godly women who have given themselves to the furtherance of the Gospel her name must stand high—and deservedly so, for it had no equal in her day and generation.

[1] *Christian Observer*, 1857, p. 707

CHAPTER 8

THE PIONEERS

So far, we have discussed in general terms the various manifestations of the revival of religion which, in the providence of God, took place in the first half of the eighteenth century. We come now to a more detailed consideration of the lives of those who in a definite sense may be called Evangelicals, the founders of what would later become a distinct party within the Church of England.

The first name which suggests itself is that of James Hervey, and it does so, not because Hervey had the greatest influence, but because he was the first in time, and had also been a member of the Holy Club.[1]

Hervey was born on February 26, 1714, at Hardingstone, near Northampton, and was the son of the rector of the parishes of Weston Favell and Collingtree. Of his family and early surroundings we have but scanty knowledge, though we know that he was at Northampton Grammar School, where he made good progress in Greek and Latin. In 1731 he went up to Lincoln College, Oxford, where at first he was careless about spiritual things and rather idle, though moral and upright in conduct. A great change followed his becoming acquainted with the Wesleys in 1733. He began to take an interest in his work, and among other books read Ray's *Wisdom of God in Creation*, and, under the direction of John Wesley, started Hebrew. Wesley also "cared for his soul"[2] and brought him into the little group of Oxford Methodists. Hervey went down in 1736, and was ordained by Bishop Potter of Oxford on the title of a curacy to his father; this he exchanged in 1738 for one with another Oxford Methodist, Charles Kinchin, at Dummer.

Then came a break through that ill-health which dogged him to the end of his days, and he retired to the home of his friend Mr. Orchard at Stoke (Hartland) Abbey in North Devon. At this time he was much perplexed over religious matters, finding it hard to reconcile justification by faith with James 2: 24,

---

[1] See further John Brown, *Life of Hervey*; and the full account in Tyerman, *The Oxford Methodists*, pp. 201–333. Tyerman considered that previous biographies were far from satisfactory. The literary side is dealt with by W. E. M. Brown, *The Polished Shaft*, pp. 3 ff.

[2] Letter of December 30, 1747

which "I dare not blot from my Bible", though it seemed to hold that a man was justified by a conjunction of faith and works. He carried on a long correspondence with Whitefield, who on November 10, 1739, wrote from America: "Let me advise dear Mr. Hervey, laying aside all prejudices, to read and pray over St. Paul's Epistles to the Romans and Galatians, and then to tell me what he thinks of this doctrine." He also found help from Jenks's *Submission to the Righteousness of God*, and from Marshall, *The Gospel Mystery of Sanctification*. The latter work showed him that "we must partake of the comforts of the Gospel, before we can practise the duties of the law".[1] In 1739 he returned to clerical work, taking a curacy at Bideford; but it was not until 1741 that he was able to embrace the whole system of Evangelical doctrine, writing to Whitefield: "Was I possest of all the righteous acts that have made saints and martyrs famous in all generations . . . I would renounce them all that I might win Christ."

Whilst at Bideford, Hervey got into touch with Thomson of St. Gennys and other Cornish Evangelicals; he also established a society which survived for forty years. His own time in the parish, however, was comparatively short, for a new rector, disapproving of his teaching, dismissed him from his curacy. He then returned to help his father at Weston Favell, where he took up his duties in October, 1743, after an interval spent at Bath. Whilst there he addressed a searching letter to a clergyman whose preaching at the Abbey had stirred his indignation owing to its flattery of the rich. He also wrote to Beau Nash, who kept his letter, which was found among his papers after his death.

From Weston Favell Hervey was destined never again to depart, save for a visit to London for the sake of his health. He went there in June, 1750, on the advice of Lady Huntingdon and Whitefield, and remained until recalled by the death of his father in May, 1752. In London he was able to do a little preaching, but was mainly engaged on *Theron and Aspasio*. On his return to Weston he wrote to Lady Fanny Shirley: "My house is quite retired; so that we hear none of the tumultuous

[1] In 1756 Hervey wrote a "recommendatory letter" for a new edition of this work. It was a great favourite with Cowper, who thought Marshall "one of the best of writers, and the most spiritual expositor of the Scriptures I ever read". This view was not shared by his physician, Dr. Cotton, who condemned Marshall's work as inconsistent with Scripture and repugnant to reason. Wesley approved of the work as a whole, but thought that some passages tended towards antinomianism (*Letters*, vii, pp. 101 f.)

din of the world, and see nothing but the wonderful and charming works of the Creator." Weston Favell was indeed a quiet place, and as the population was small, between three and four hundred, the duties were light and allowed time for meditation, study and writing. Hervey's weak health and his disposition fully justified the manner of life which he adopted, for his gentle nature and physical limitations quite unfitted him for the rigorous life of an itinerant. He was a faithful pastor to the souls committed to his care, and, in addition to his literary work, carried on an immense correspondence, and thus fulfilled his ministry.

Hervey never married, although he seems to have been on the verge of falling in love on one occasion, for he wrote on May 23, 1745:

> I believe it will be my most prudent course not to visit a certain lady. If I debar myself that pleasure, it will be entirely owing to an apprehension of wounding my own ease and tranquillity. Who knows what impressions may be made by an amiable person and engaging behaviour, heightened by the exercise of good sense, and completed by an apparent regard for religion and eternity? Indeed . . . my heart is not proof against such charms.[1]

The need for feminine sympathy and companionship was in part supplied by the patronage and friendship of Lady Fanny Shirley, whose cultivated mind had been attracted by his style, as well as by his views on religion. With her he carried on a regular correspondence.

When Hervey returned to the quiet of Weston Favell he had but six more years in which to enjoy it, for he died of consumption on Christmas Day, 1758. A few hours before his passing he said: "How thankful I am now for death. It is the passage through which I pass to the Lord and giver of eternal life. It frees me from all the misery which I now endure, and which I am willing to endure, as long as God sees fit." He was buried beneath the altar of the parish church, and at his funeral many of the congregation were in tears; some, indeed, so gave way to their grief as to lose their self-control. Among those who preached memorial sermons were Romaine, at St. Dunstan's-

[1] The fact that Hervey dedicated his *Meditations* to a daughter of Thomson of St. Gennys has led some to suspect an earlier romance. But as Thomson did not marry until 1740, his daughter can only have been a small child at the time

in-the-West, and William Cudworth at his chapel in Margaret Street, London. A hymn by Charles Wesley supplied an additional and more enduring memorial.

Hervey was by nature quiet, devoted and humble, and, although a good classical scholar with some knowledge of Hebrew, never regarded himself as possessing more than ordinary powers. Even when his literary labours had brought him fame his self-effacing spirit was in no way puffed up, and he valued his reputation principally as a means for increasing his religious influence. The money which came to him from this source he spent in charity, not lavishly or indiscriminately, but as the steward of God. The patience with which he endured his constant ill-health was admirable, even though it was not for him the handicap it would have been for one of more active ways and ambitions. Henry Venn well summed up the effect of his life on those who knew him when he wrote: "Mr. Hervey was the most extraordinary man I ever saw in my life, as much beyond most of the excellent as the swan for whiteness and stately figure is beyond the common fowl."

In his conduct of worship Hervey adopted what were then novel methods. He preached extempore, and for only about thirty minutes; but he was so clear and simple that such crowds flocked to hear him that at times the windows were removed so that those outside could listen. He also introduced hymn-singing. One of Lady Huntingdon's preachers after a visit to Collingtree wrote: "To my great surprise as well as satisfaction, having never seen such a thing before in prayer-time, instead of singing psalms, they sung two of Dr. Watts' hymns, the clerk giving them out line by line."[1]

Hervey corresponded with Dr. Watts, and was also on intimate terms with Doddridge at Northampton. Although a convinced churchman, he had many friends among the Dissenters. These tended to increase towards the end of his life, and among his intimates was John Ryland, the famous Baptist who afterwards wrote his life. Another Dissenting friend was William Cudworth, to whom he was drawn by his Calvinism. Cudworth was a bitter enemy of Wesley, and he seems to have supplanted him entirely in Hervey's affections.[2] Before his death he was

[1] *Countess of Huntingdon*, i, p. 192

[2] Wesley in the last letter which Hervey received from him wrote: "How you can converse with a man of his spirit I cannot comprehend. O leave not your old well tried friends! The new is not comparable to them. I speak not this because I am *afraid* of what any one can say or do to *me*; but I am really concerned for *you*" (*Letters*, iv, p. 47)

almost completely estranged from Wesley, mainly owing to the latter's criticisms of *Theron and Aspasio*.

When *Theron and Aspasio* appeared in 1755 its views aroused a small war of pamphlets, and it was ardently defended by Cudworth. But Wesley disliked much in it, and especially the over-emphasis on the "imputed righteousness of Christ", a phrase which he felt was unscriptural and liable to encourage antinomianism.[1] Two years later he included these criticisms in his *Preservatives against unsettled Notions in Religion*, much to Hervey's indignation. Hervey began a considered reply, but death stepped in to prevent his completing it. In 1764, however, *Eleven Letters against John Wesley* by Hervey were published by an anonymous editor who styled himself Philoalethes. Cudworth had died in the previous year, but he was probably behind the matter.[2] The letters, as then published, contain many bitter passages which are quite out of keeping with Hervey's gentle spirit, though mild when compared with much that was then considered allowable in such disputes. As Hervey, on his death-bed, had forbidden their publication, since they were incomplete and unrevised, their appearance was a distinct outrage. Wesley was greatly hurt and annoyed, especially as the *Letters* had a very wide circulation. In 1765 Hervey's brother put forth an authentic edition of the *Letters* explaining what had happened. Whatever may be said of the principals in the controversy, nothing can excuse the bad faith of those who allowed Hervey's letters to become public; to publish anonymously the unfinished writings of one who had definitely forbidden their appearance, for purposes of controversy, was "a base, treacherous, nefarious deed".[3] Unfortunately, those who engage in controversy, and not least in religious controversy, often forget common notions of decency and fair play, and stoop to devices which the better type of man of the world would utterly scorn.

Before leaving Hervey something must be said of his writings: not as literature, that will be considered later, but from the point of view of their effectiveness. Charles Wesley once referred to him as the Isocrates of the movement,[4] and the

---

[1] See *Letters*, iii, pp. 371–88. Simeon held the same opinion: (see Carus, pp. 14 ff.)

[2] He had been lent the letters and is reported to have said that he had "full power to put out or put in" what he pleased

[3] Tyerman, *Oxford Methodists*, p. 331. He adds: "No wonder the name of the editor was never authoritatively announced"

[4] *Journal*, ii, p. 393

parallel was an apt one, for Isocrates was no orator and owed his influence to his writings.

His first publication was *Meditations among the Tombs*, a subject which occurred to him as he rode between Bideford and Kilkhampton. It appeared in 1746, and its object was to remind the readers "to set, not their houses only, but, which is inexpressibly more needful, their souls in order". Included in it was "Reflections in a Flower Garden", which pointed to the Redeemer as all-sufficient for "the grand and gracious purposes of our everlasting salvation". It was printed by Samuel Richardson, the author of *Pamela*, and was an immediate success. This encouraged him to write *Theron and Aspasio*, which, after being submitted for criticism to various friends, finally appeared in 1755 with a dedication to Lady Fanny Shirley, Lady Huntingdon having declined the honour. A copy was presented to H.R.H. the Princess of Wales, who duly sent her thanks to the author. The first edition of 6,000 copies sold out at once, and was followed by two further editions within the year. Hervey's writings, which were translated into almost every modern language, were immensely popular with Evangelicals, and with some they displaced Law's *Serious Call*. That this should have been so is rather surprising, in view of their elaborate and stilted style and of their somewhat unhealthy tone. Thomas Scott, who owed much to them in his early years and never lost his esteem for Hervey himself, could write: "I always thought his writings in the point of religious experience *narcotic* to those *within*, and calculated to excite prejudices and give plausibility to those *without*."[1] But not all were of the robust spirit of the great Evangelical commentator, though modern taste would be decidedly in agreement with his judgment.

Next in order of time we come to William Grimshaw,[2] a man whose career and character, save in devotion to their common Lord, were as unlike as can be imagined from those of the quiet, studious, refined and delicate Hervey.

Grimshaw was born on September 3, 1708, at Brindle, an agricultural parish in the low land between the estuary of the Ribble and the Lancashire moors. We know little of his early life, and even his family and circumstances remain obscure. Like Hervey, he attended a local grammar school, and then in

---

[1] *Life of Scott*, p. 598

[2] See the account in Wesley's *Journal*, iv, 493–98 (from which quotations are made); and G. G. Cragg, *Grimshaw of Haworth*

1726 went up to Christ's College, Cambridge. There the bad examples of his fellow undergraduates so led him away that "he seemed utterly to have lost all sense of seriousness".

In spite of his carelessness in spiritual matters, Grimshaw was ordained deacon in 1731 to a curacy at Rochdale, then a quiet old market town. His ordination did indeed have a sobering effect, but it was quickly forgotten, and when he was put in charge of Todmorden, some ten miles from Rochdale though in that parish, he was quite content to limit his activities to the Sunday services and not to give much thought to those in his care during the week. His time was largely spent out of doors, for he had a great fondness for sport of every kind. However, he had some sense of the fitness of things, for it is said that: "he refrained as much as possible from gross swearing, unless in suitable company, and, when he got drunk, would take care to sleep it out before he came home."[1]

In 1734 two events combined to produce in him a more serious frame of mind; he lost his first wife, and one of his parishioners committed suicide. So great indeed was his depression that he even thought of taking his own life; there seemed nothing left to make it worth while. However, his religion, although dormant, was real, and he made up his mind to try and live in a more worthy manner. Among other things, he set apart four periods every day for private prayer and began a systematic visitation of his flock. But he found no peace for his soul. This time of darkness persisted for several years, and Grimshaw struggled on, keeping his own secret. Perhaps he had none whom he cared to consult, though his vicar lent him two Puritan works, Brooks's *Precious Remedies against Satan's Devices*, and Owen, *On Justification*. It was to the latter and to the regular study of the Bible that he was to owe his deliverance.

This came suddenly in 1742, when it is related that he was found on a Sunday morning at five o'clock by his servant still praying. During the day he fainted several times, but gave every spare moment to prayer. After his second fainting fit he seemed to be in a state of rapture, and his first words on regaining consciousness were: "I have had a glorious vision of the third heaven". On going to church he continued the afternoon service from two until seven. Grimshaw's position was identical with that of the Methodists, but he had reached it quite independently; as Wesley himself emphasized, "All this

[1] Middleton, *Biographia Evangelica*, iv, p. 398

time he was an entire stranger to the people called Methodists. ... He was an entire stranger also to their writings."[1]

In May, 1742, Grimshaw was put in charge of Haworth, part of the great parish of Halifax, though apparently administered as a separate district. Haworth was then a long straggling village on the road to Keighley, from which it rises sharply. It was an isolated spot (the houses between it and Keighley had not yet been built) and stood amid cold, bleak moors. In 1839 it was described as "one of those obscure places which, like the fishing towns of Galilee favoured with our Lord's presence, owe all their celebrity to the Gospel. The name of Haworth would scarcely be known at a distance, were it not connected with the name of Grimshaw."[2] The writer little foresaw that to-day few, outside some restricted circles of pious Christians, would have heard of Grimshaw himself but for the introductory chapter of Mrs. Gaskell's *Life of Charlotte Brontë*.[3]

A clerical scandal, following on a long period of neglect, had allowed the village to relapse into a state of almost complete paganism; even the dead were hurried to their graves without any religious ceremony. Strange superstitions flourished and weird rites were performed to propitiate a phantom dog—a kind of hound of the Baskervilles—which was supposed to haunt the moors. The observance of Sunday was quite unknown; some of the villagers went to the market at Bradford, about nine miles away; the rest made it a holiday, the young men playing football. A more unlikely locality for the outbreak of a revival can hardly be imagined, nor a more difficult sphere for a parson. Yet Grimshaw proved equal to the task. Like Charles Kingsley at Eversley, he could meet his parishioners on level terms in any pursuit where strength of body and athletic skill were demanded, and so he earned their respect.

Grimshaw began by stopping the Sunday football; but, finding that the young people still frequented the moors for all kinds of rough and objectionable horse-play, he determined to surprise them at it. To do this it is said that he disguised himself as an old woman. When he suddenly arrived among them he took down their names and ordered them to come to

---

[1] A little later he was much influenced by William Darney, an eccentric Methodist preacher who caused a good deal of embarrassment to John Wesley (see *Letters*, iv, pp. 275, 278, 288). The people of Haworth scoffingly called their parson "mad Grimshaw, Scotch Will's disciple" (*Journal*, iii, p. 293)

[2] *Countess of Huntingdon*, i, p. 252

[3] At the time the Brontës were actually at Haworth, having gone there in 1820, but their first writings were not published until 1846

him, which they did "as punctually as if they had been served with a warrant". He made them kneel down, and prayed earnestly for a long time with them, and then gave them "a close and affecting lecture". This friendly discipline was completely effective, and he never had to repeat it.

More difficult was the task of stopping the race meetings, which brought many undesirable elements into the village and gave occasion for disgraceful scenes. But here at length he was also successful. Grimshaw's care for Sunday was not confined to negative measures, however; he also insisted on regular attendance at church. His methods of enforcing this were probably as unique as they were effective; he would sally forth immediately before the sermon with a riding-crop in his hand, and round up all absentees. John Newton, in one of those letters to which we are indebted for much detailed knowledge of Grimshaw's ministry, describes how the process struck a visitor:

> A friend of mine passing a public-house on a Lord's Day saw several persons jumping out of the windows and over the wall. He feared the house was on fire, but upon inquiring what was the cause of the commotion he was told that they saw the parson coming. They were more afraid of the parson than of a Justice of the Peace. His reproof was so authoritative, and yet so mild and friendly, that the stoutest sinner could not stand before him.[1]

Grimshaw's manner of preaching and of reading the prayers was characterized by a deep earnestness. So much so that the Prayer Book seemed to take on new meaning. He also explained the lessons as he read them, sometimes turning a difficult passage into broad Yorkshire. Before he began the service he looked round to see that all were ready and in an attitude of devotion, and any carelessness or want of attention was immediately rebuked. He preached twice every Sunday, or else expounded the Thirty-nine Articles, or read a Homily. His sermons sometimes lasted two hours, a practice which he held to be necessary, as the slowness and ignorance of his hearers demanded much repetition. He also held a service in the evening for those who were too poor to come to church in daylight "for want of better clothes". The effectiveness of his message cannot be measured in terms of converts alone; for many who did not accept the

[1] *Letters to H. Foster,* v

Gospel, no doubt had the fear of God, or perhaps of Hell, so deeply implanted in them that even if they did not turn to God, they were restrained from sin.

Grimshaw's preaching inevitably attracted hundreds of hearers from the surrounding parishes, and as they were receiving no spiritual sustenance from their own clergy they begged him to hold occasional services for them and also for those who were unable to get to Haworth. Thus the deplorable and neglected condition of the countryside compelled him to become an itinerant; he felt that such openings ought not to be set aside. This added immensely to his labours, for he covered long distances in the adjoining counties; in fact, he deserves the title of "the apostle of the North" given in Reformation times to Bernard Gilpin. So great were the demands upon him that he seldom preached less than twenty times a week, and in his journeys had often to be content with very humble fare and rough accommodation. Yet in spite of it all he kept his health. Wesley testifies that: "In sixteen years he was only once suspended from his labour by sickness, though he dared all weathers, upon the bleak mountains, and used his body with less compassion than a merciful man would use his beast." When friends urged him to greater moderation he would reply: "Let me labour now; I shall have rest enough by and by. I cannot do enough for Christ, who has done so much for me."

Grimshaw limited his work to the Northern folk, and never visited London or the well-known centres of Evangelical preaching. He did, however, preach at Bristol in 1749, but probably because he was on a visit to his small daughter who was at school at Kingswood.

Grimshaw's intrusion into other men's parishes did not go unresented, and many attacks were made upon him. The ringleader was the Rev. George White, curate of Colne, who did not scruple to raise the mob to acts of violence. He also preached a sermon against him which he published with a dedication to the Archbishop of Canterbury. In return, Grimshaw made a devastating reply; an easy task, for his assailant was far from a reputable character, and would have been well advised to avoid too much prominence. White had originally been a Roman Catholic priest, but was no very worthy convert to Anglicanism, for he neglected his charge and lived mostly in London, where his manner of conducting himself was very questionable. He eventually died in April, 1751, during an imprisonment for debt in Chester gaol.

THE PIONEERS 153

Grimshaw's long and arduous labours went on for another ten years; he died of a fever on April 7, 1763. On his deathbed he was visited by both Ingham and Henry Venn, who risked the considerable danger of infection in order to be with him. When Venn asked him how he was feeling, he replied: "As happy as I can be on earth and as sure of glory as if I was in it." Yet his last words were "here goes an unprofitable servant". He was buried at Haworth "with what is more ennobling than all the pomp of a royal funeral: for he was followed to the grave by a great multitude, with affectionate sighs and many tears, who cannot still hear his much-loved name without weeping for the guide of their souls, to whom each was dear as children to their father".

The relations of Grimshaw with the Methodists were exceedingly close; in fact, he acted as an "assistant" to Wesley, who speaks of Mr. Grimshaw's circuit,[1] visiting classes, giving out tickets, and holding love-feasts. He also made his parsonage a headquarters for Methodist preachers, training and encouraging them. Fearing that his successor might be unsympathetic with Evangelical views, he built a meeting-house at Haworth in 1759. None the less, he was a most decided Churchman, and only willing to co-operate with the Methodists so long as they remained loyal to the Church. In 1750 Charles Wesley wrote: "Mr. Grimshaw, whom the separatists claimed for their own, designed coming to the Conference, only to take leave of us, if we did the Church."[2] Ten years later Grimshaw wrote to Charles Wesley:

> This licensing of preachers, and preaching houses, is a matter I never expected to have seen or heard of among the Methodists. If I had, I dare say I had never entered into connexion with them. . . . The Methodists are no longer members of the Church of England. They are as real a body of Dissenters from her as the presbyterians, baptists, quakers, or any body of independents. I hereby assure you, that I disclaim all further and future connexion with the Methodists. I will quietly recede, without noise or tumult.[3]

Our third study is of one who was unlike either Hervey or

---
[1] *Works*, xii, p. 255   [2] Jackson, *Life of Charles Wesley*, ii, p. 78
[3] *Op. cit.*, ii, p. 191

Grimshaw, a circumstance which illustrates the very different agents used by the Spirit in the beginning of the movement. Walker is perhaps a more usual type than the others, for he restricted himself to the care of his own people, and that with exemplary diligence.[1]

Samuel Walker was born at Exeter on December 16, 1714, being the fourth son of Robert Walker of that city and Margaret, daughter of the Rev. Richard Hall, a descendant of the famous bishop of that name. Walker was educated at Exeter Grammar School, from which he went up to Exeter College, Oxford. He worked hard during his time there, and thus laid up a store of knowledge which served him in later life; it is said that he hoped for a fellowship.[2] At this period of his life, although he had undergone no deep experience, he was moral and upright in conduct. As Exeter is a neighbouring college to Lincoln it is strange that he was unaffected by the Methodist group; they cannot have escaped his notice in view of the stir they created in the university, and he must have seen the Wesleys from time to time.

Walker was ordained in 1737 to the curacy of Doddiscombleigh, not far from his native city. The week before he had spent with the other candidates "in a very light, indecent manner; dining, supping, and laughing together, when God knows we should have been all on our knees, and warning each other to fear for our souls in the view of what we were about to put our hands to".[3] His stay in Devon was not a long one, for from 1737 to 1739 he travelled on the Continent as tutor to the younger brother of Lord Rolle. On his return he became curate of Lanlivery, near Lostwithiel, and was appointed vicar to hold the living for the nephew of the patron who was then under age. He gave up Lanlivery in 1746, and his former patron then presented him to Talland. He did not reside there, as in the same year he had accepted the curacy-in-charge of Truro. Although he received a licence of non-residence from the bishop, his scruples were later aroused, and in 1752 he resigned the living.

Walker did not become an Evangelical until he had been more than a year at Truro, and then in a rather curious way.

---

[1] See, further, James Stillingfleet, in preface to *Walker's Sermons*; Sidney, *Life of Walker of Truro* (revised ed. 1838); F. W. B. Bullock, *Hist. of St. Mary's, Truro*, pp. 67 ff.; H. M. Brown, *Methodism and the Church of England in Cornwall* (MS. in Phillpotts' Library, Truro), pp. 40 ff., 295 ff.; and G. C. B. Davies, *The Early Cornish Evangelicals*

[2] Sidney, *op. cit.*, p. 310   [3] Sidney, *op. cit.*, p. 4

George Conon, the headmaster of Truro Grammar School, had been ordered wine by his medical attendant, and suspecting that the wine he obtained had never paid duty, he sent the amount as a kind of "conscience money" to Walker, asking him to see that it reached the proper quarter. This led to a close friendship which ended only with the death of Walker. The latter said of Conon that he was "the first person I ever met possessed with the mind of Christ".[1]

Before continuing the story of Walker's life it will be well to glance at the state of religion in Cornwall in his day, for it is a subject which has been grievously misrepresented, mainly because the witnesses are usually Methodists, who naturally judge it by their own standards and ideas. Soon after he went to Truro as its first bishop, Benson wrote in his diary:

> It would be a great mistake to suppose that when he [John Wesley] first began to preach in Cornwall, he found empty churches and godless parishes. Mr. Kinsman of Tintagel told me of an aged parishioner of higher rank, who died many years ago, that she used to tell him, how before Wesley came, the church had been always crowded, how the monthly celebration of the Sacrament was most largely attended, and the children catechized every Sunday afternoon. So too a parishioner of Dr. Martin's at St. Breward, who died at an advanced age, remembered her father's expression that "when he was young you might have walked a mile to church on the heads of the people in the lanes".[2]

These opinions have been confirmed by the researches of Charles Henderson, the well-known historian of Cornwall, and more recently by G. C. B. Davies on the basis of the returns in the Exeter registers. He testifies that they "compare more than favourably with conditions in other parts of England at this time".[3] No doubt there were parishes in Cornwall as elsewhere that were suffering from neglect; but the standard seems to have been high on the whole.

Walker's reason for accepting the curacy at Truro was that the town had great social amenities, being the centre of fashion for the county, and, like more famous resorts, it had its season. Many county families had houses there, some of which still

---
[1] Sidney, *op. cit.*, p. 8   [2] Quoted Donaldson, *Bishopric of Truro*, pp. 13 f.
[3] *Early Cornish Evangelicals*, pp. 22 ff.

survive, though turned to other uses. Walker had an intense delight in cards and dancing, and Truro gave him every opportunity for indulging his taste. But his growing friendship with Conon gradually revealed to him the unworthiness of the life he was leading; though it was only after a severe and lengthy struggle that he changed it. The result may easily be imagined. He felt in duty bound to proclaim his altered views, and from the pulpit he began to condemn practices in which he himself had habitually indulged. So his former friends, instead of being shamed by his example, turned against him. He was scoffed at as a "kill-joy", and it was even suggested that he was not quite sane. Upon most of his parishioners, however, his new devotion and obvious sincerity made a deep impression, and St. Mary's was crowded by those wishing to hear him. It was said that during service time "you might fire a cannon down every street in Truro without the chance of killing a single human being".[1]

Some of the leading people in the town went so far as to report him to the bishop, and to request the non-resident rector to dismiss his over-zealous curate. This he promised to do, but on entering Walker's apartment he was received with an elegance and dignity of manner which were natural to one who had long been the charm of society, and became so embarrassed as to be perfectly unable to advert to his errand. Urged on by Walker's opponents, he made a second attempt, with a like result. When pressed to make a third effort, he replied: "Do you go and dismiss him, if you can. I cannot. I feel in his presence as if he were a being of a superior order, and I am so abashed that I am uneasy till I can retire."

The chief means by which Walker made his influence felt was by his preaching. In their printed form his sermons are certainly much more attractive than those of his contemporaries, and having read many of them I fully agree with Bishop Ryle's judgment: "For simplicity, directness, vivacity, and home appeals to the heart and conscience, I am disposed to assign them a very high rank among the sermons of a hundred years ago. It is my deliberate impression, that if he had been an itinerant like Whitefield, and had not confined himself to his pulpit at Truro, he would probably have been reckoned one of the best preachers of his day."[2] Simeon went even

[1] Sidney, *op. cit.*, p. 17
[2] *The Christian Leaders of the Last Century*, p. 324. His sermons were much used by Hannah More and her sister for reading to simple folk in the Mendips (*Memoirs*, i, p. 247)

farther, and he was no mean judge of sermons, and ranked them as "the best in the English language".[1]

Two other methods were also much used for promoting and deepening the religious life of his people, both young and old. He made a great point of catechizing the children in the presence of the congregation, and he established societies. These last were modelled on those already in existence, and Walker made use of their rules, adapting them to local circumstances where necessary. One good point about these societies was that they kept his people "in the generality clear from the peculiarities of Methodism".[2]

So he went on his arduous way, bearing on his shoulders the whole burden of the parish for fourteen years. Unfortunately, he had not the robust health of Grimshaw; like Hervey, he was threatened by pulmonary consumption. At last this gained such a hold upon him, aggravated by his ceaseless labours,[3] that he was compelled to retire to Hot Wells and then to the house of Lord Dartmouth at Blackheath. He died there on July 19, 1761, at the comparatively early age of forty-six.[4] A few days before his death he wrote to Dr. Conon: "Well, my dear friend, I am but stepping a little before you. You will soon also get your release, and then we shall triumph for ever in the name, love, and power of the Lamb. Adieu! Yours in the Lord Jesus Christ for ever. Amen."

Although he avoided itineration, Walker's influence spread to other parishes. Wesley speaks, on September 21, 1757, of preaching to a large congregation at St. Ewe, "many of whom were in Mr. Walker's societies".[5] He also had a remarkable influence over some of the neighbouring clergy, and in 1750 formed a Clerical Club which used to meet monthly on the Tuesday after the full moon to discuss religious questions.[6] Though its numbers never seem to have exceeded eleven, it performed a very useful office in drawing Evangelicals together. Among his lay friends and converts were William

[1] A. W. Brown, *Recollections of Simeon's Conversation Parties*, p. 320

[2] Sidney, *op. cit.*, p. 156

[3] One of his few recreations was bell-ringing, for which he often went out to Kenwyn where the peal is one of the best in Cornwall. It had been placed there mainly owing to the efforts of William Lemon, Mayor of Truro, 1737–50

[4] Among those who visited Walker during his illness was Wesley, who on November 1, 1760, speaks of spending time with "that venerable man, Mr. Walker" (*Journal*, iv, p. 418)

[5] *Op. cit.*, iv, p. 238

[6] See Davies, pp. 74 ff. He thinks that the real date of the foundation of the club was 1750, not 1755, as Sidney states

Rawlings of St. Columb (later of Padstow),[1] and a daughter of Stephen Tippet who married Mr. Henshaw, a lawyer very active in Shropshire on behalf of Lady Huntingdon,[2] and the father of Henry Martyn.[3]

Walker's death, and the succession about the same time of a new rector who chose to reside, brought much confusion to his flock, as will be narrated later.

Walker's relations with the Methodists are interesting and enlightening.[4] Wesley's first direct contact with the work that Walker was doing seems to have been on August 30, 1755, when he had happy relations with members of his society when passing through Truro.[5] He had a great admiration for Walker's achievements, and once wrote: "We know several regular clergymen who do preach the genuine gospel, but to no effect at all. There is one exception in England—Mr. Walker of Truro."[6] But Walker, disliking some of the practices of the Methodists and doubtful of their loyalty to the Church, was careful to keep his flock apart from them. Wesley once remarked that the Methodists did not need him, but that he needed the Methodists.[7] After his death, even those who left St. Mary's still kept aloof; as Wesley laments: "I was in hopes that when Mr. Walker died, the enmity of those who were called his people would have died also: but it is not so."[8] Thus Walker, on account of his strict Churchmanship, was unable to co-operate fully with Wesley and the other Methodist leaders, much as he appreciated the work that they were doing. But he could not approve of any deviation from the Church, and one of the last counsels which he gave to a clerical follower was: "Whatever good you design to do, do it in the Church."[9] Truro, under his ministry, wrote Sidney: "presented a delightful example of the happy effects which may be produced on a Christian community by our Church's discipline and doctrines wisely enforced and spiritually explained."[10]

---

[1] Sometimes confused (as by *Countess of Huntingdon*, i, p. 276) with his son, who was vicar of Padstow, 1790–1836

[2] *Countess of Huntingdon*, ii, p. 40

[3] When Dean Milner examined him for the Smith's prize he found out that he came from Truro and asked him about Walker. He replied that he and his relatives had reason to bless God for him (*Life of Dean Milner*, p. 229). This was some forty years after the death of Walker

[4] See Davies, pp. 71 ff., 88 ff. [5] *Journal*, iv, p. 130

[6] *Letters*, iii, p. 151. "Regular clergymen" were those who respected the Church's discipline and did not itinerate, etc.

[7] *Journal*, v, p. 279   [8] *Op. cit.*, v, p. 185   [9] Sidney, *op. cit.*, p. 562

[10] Davies, p. 221, thinks that Sidney rather over-emphasized Walker's Churchmanship

Among Walker's closest friends and allies, at least in his later years, was Thomas Adam.[1] Adam was born at Leeds, where his father was later town-clerk, in 1701. He began his education at the local grammar school, and afterwards moved to that at Wakefield. In due course he went up to Christ's College, Cambridge, where his tutor was Matthew Hutton, the future archbishop of both York and Canterbury. After two years he migrated to Hart Hall, Oxford, of which Dr. Richard Newton, a stern critic of pluralism, was principal.

Adam took his B.A. degree in 1723, and in the following year was offered the living of Winteringham, but as he was not yet of sufficient age he had to wait a further two years before he could hold it. There he was to remain for the rest of his life, and that a long one, for he reached the advanced age of eighty-three. At the time of his ordination he speaks of himself as "a youth of levity and frolic"; but this must not be taken too seriously, representing as it does a judgment by later standards. He was certainly fond of society, and social amusements such as card playing, but that in itself was no evil. Nor can we take literally his writing to Walker that he took orders "more for the sake of worldly advantage than anything else".

Winteringham lies at the end of the long ridge which runs from Lincoln, some thirty-four miles away, and looks across the broad estuary of the Humber, with delightful views of the opposite Yorkshire coast. The parish, when Adam went there, was in a very low state; as at Haworth, Sunday was ignored, and there was much disorder and unseemly conduct. Adam himself had had as yet no deep spiritual experience; but in 1736 a reading of Law's *Serious Call* had a profound effect upon him. He realized the wide gulf between his own life and the ideal which Law set forth. For some ten years he continued in a state of uncertainty, almost of bewilderment, which grew so strong that he trembled and wept when taking the services, and even refrained from preaching. At last the dawn came, and the long darkness fled away. The means by which he came to see fresh light was St. Paul's Epistle to the Romans 1–6.

Adam now had a message to preach to his people, and we may be sure that he delivered it with confidence and assurance. Hervey wrote to a friend about this time concerning "the amazing reformation amongst the people in his neighbourhood and of the large congregations which he drew, not only from

---

[1] See Stillingfleet's memoir prefixed to *Posthumous Works*; and Charles Hole, *Memoir of the Rev. T. Adam*.

his own parish but from round about".¹ But though the people might flock to hear him, little seems to have resulted. The great part of his parishioners retained their rough ways, though a few were helped by a school which Adam started. Wesley held that the reason for his failure, in spite of his excellent preaching and character, and his unwearied labours, was that he opposed the Methodists and insisted on narrow Church views. Wesley was annoyed because it had been reported to him that Adam had said that "no sensible and well-meaning man could hear and much less join the Methodists; because they *all acted under a lie*, professing themselves members of the Church of England while they licensed themselves as Dissenters". Wesley pointed out that most preachers had no licence, and those who had were not licensed as Dissenters.² This was on July 19, 1768. Four years later he found another cause for his failure, after reading Adam's paraphrase of Romans 1: 11: "How are the mighty fallen! It is the very quintessence of antinomianism. I did wonder much, but I do not wonder now, that his rod does not blossom."³ These views may be prejudiced, as coming from one who was opposed to Calvinism in all its forms; but such could not have been the case with Henry Venn, who both shared Adam's views and held him in special reverence; yet after his death he could comment on the "exceeding small success" which followed his preaching of the Gospel for thirty years.⁴

The reason for Adam's comparative failure probably lies in a certain lack of vigour and driving force; he was no Grimshaw to bring the fear of God (and of himself) to the disorderly elements in his parish, and perhaps his preaching was above the heads of the more pious. From 1759 he suffered from constant ill-health, and even felt that he had not long to live.⁵ Yet he survived until 1784. From 1768 he had the help of a succession of curates; John Lawson, Robert Storry (who later went to Colchester) and Samuel Knight, who would acquire local fame as vicar of Halifax.⁶

If, however, Adam was not too successful in his own parish he exercised a wide influence on the Evangelical Movement as

---

[1] *Letters*, No. 112   [2] *Letters*, v, pp. 97 ff.
[3] *Journal*, v, p. 480   [4] *Life*, p. 387

[5] He lost his wife, a daughter of the vicar of Roxby, in 1760. They had been married thirty years, and her death may have affected his health and work

[6] Knight, who was a fellow of Magdalene, was born at Halifax on March 9, 1759, the son of an Independent minister, for whom see *Countess of Huntingdon*, ii, pp. 285 ff.

THE PIONEERS 161

a whole, especially after the appearance of his *Lectures on the Church Catechism*. It was through them that he became acquainted with Walker, who began a correspondence in October, 1754, and three years later paid a visit to Winteringham. Adam was also much respected by Lord Dartmouth, to whom he gave advice as to how to live a Christian life and yet take part in affairs and society. Another layman who sought his advice was John Thornton, who went to Winteringham to consult him. Adam also did the Evangelical cause another service by his encouragement of Henry Venn when the latter was engaged on his *Complete Duty of Man*. Venn wrote in 1760: "If it had not been for dear Mr. Adam's encouraging approbation, I should faint in my book."[1]

Adam in some respects was not unlike John Keble, for he kept to his parish and there received visitors who came to ask for his counsel; he was also like him in his avoidance of preferment. This spirit of retirement vexed some of his friends who wished to see him in a sphere of greater influence. He certainly had the opportunity of gaining preferment when his old tutor became archbishop; but he refused absolutely to apply to him. So Adam stayed on at Winteringham, persisting in his not very rewarding labours among his flock, but ever ready to give advice and guidance to men who had greater opportunities of exercising influence.[2] He died on March 31, 1784, and was buried in his own churchyard. By his express wish, his body was carried to its last resting place by six of his poor neighbours.

Of his writings more will be said later. In addition to his catechism lectures, a selection from his diaries was published after his death under the title of *Private Thoughts on Religion*, which had an immense and deserved popularity. A new edition with a preface by Daniel Wilson was published in 1823.

The early leaders whom we have so far considered, with the exception of Adam, died after comparatively short ministries, and even in the case of Adam his ministry followed a very even course. With Romaine,[3] to whom we now come, things were very different, for his ministerial life covered nearly sixty years, and was attended by many vicissitudes. He also differed from his fellow pioneers in character, methods, and background.

[1] *Life*, p. 85
[2] Romaine wrote in 1876: "I owe more to this man (saving the honour of grace) than to all the world. May you read, as I did, to my first comfort, his lectures on the church catechism" (*Works*, p. 629).
[3] See memoir by Cadogan prefixed to his collected works, and Haweis, *Life of Romaine*

L

With Grimshaw the contrast is especially striking; the one laboured in the wilds of the North, the other in the civilized metropolis; the one was willing, by his eccentricities, to be thought a fool for Christ's sake, the other behaved with such circumspection that he gained the reputation of being aloof.

William Romaine was born on September 25, 1714, at Hartlepool, where his father, a refugee from the revocation of the Edict of Nantes, carried on the trade of a corn merchant. The home in which he was brought up was a pious one, and seems to have left permanent traces upon him. This probably has led to the mistaken notion that he never endured those spiritual "growing pains" which were the lot of most Evangelical leaders. Bishop Ryle states that: "There never seems to have been a period, from the time of his ordination, when he did not preach clear, distinct, and unmistakable evangelical doctrines. The truths of the gospel appear to have been applied to his heart by the Holy Spirit from the days of his childhood."[1] In a similar vein Overton has written that in view of his upbringing, "it is not surprising that Romaine should have identified himself with the movement without having passed through any of those changes which are found in the career of most of the Evangelical leaders."[2] Both these eminent authorities, however, are mistaken; for Romaine himself speaks of a very profound and definite spiritual crisis in his life. He wrote to a friend that he went up to London: "a very, very vain young man who knew almost everything but himself, and met with many disappointments to his pride, till the Lord was pleased to let him see the plague of his own heart". During this crisis he found no human helper, for his Saviour "would not let him learn of man". Although he went everywhere to hear preachers, he found none that "touched his case". The Methodists, in particular, proved a hindrance rather than a help.

> [They] flocked about me, and courted my acquaintance, they became a great snare to me. By their means I was brought into a difficulty which distressed me for years. I was made to believe that part of my title to salvation was to be inherent—something called holiness in myself, which the grace of God was to help me to. And I was to get it by watchfulness, prayer, fasting, hearing, reading, sacraments, etc., so that after

[1] *Christian Leaders*, pp. 153 f.   [2] *The Evangelical Revival*, pp. 64 f.

much and long attendance on these means I might be able to look inward and be pleased with my own improvement, finding I was grown in grace, and a great deal holier, and more deserving of heaven than I had been. I do not wonder now that I received this doctrine; it was sweet food to a proud heart.

He failed, however, to make any progress in the spiritual life, and came to the conclusion that he was on entirely wrong lines. At once the Bible became a new book to him, and his self-conceit was abased.[1]

After this digression we now return to Romaine's career. He received his education at the grammar school at Houghton-le-Spring, and at Oxford, where he entered Hertford in 1731, afterwards going on to Christ Church. Although he was at the university during the period when the Holy Club was active, he had no contacts with its members. His one aim and object seems to have been to pursue his studies, though he had some association with the Hutchinsonians, probably through his interest in Hebrew.[2] So great was his absorption in his work that he neglected his dress. Goode, who was his curate, told of a visitor to Oxford who asked the head of a college with whom he was walking: "Who is that slovenly person with his stockings down?" and received the reply: "That slovenly person ... is one of the greatest geniuses of the age, and is likely to become one of the greatest men in the kingdom."

Romaine received deacon's orders at Hereford in 1736, and was made a priest by Hoadly of Winchester, famous for his part in the Bangorian controversy. The early years of his ministry are a little obscure. He held a curacy at Lewtrenchard in Devon, and then went to Banstead, near Epsom. Here he remained for ten years during which he studied intensely, and published his criticism of Warburton's *Divine Legation of Moses* as well as a new edition of the *Hebrew Concordance and Lexicon* of de Calasio.

Among the inhabitants of Banstead was Sir Daniel Lambert,

[1] *Works*, pp. 716 f.

[2] Romaine was never ashamed of being called a Hutchinsonian. In the preface to a sermon preached on May 19, 1755, he wrote: "It will give me no concern to be reckoned an enthusiast, while the Scripture is on my side, or an Hutchinsonian, while the Church of England supports me; and if men will call the plain doctrines of the Scripture enthusiasm, and will treat the articles, and homilies, and liturgy of our church as Hutchinsonianism, I hope I shall live and die a Church of England-Hutchinsonian-Enthusiast" (*Works*, p. 931)

who on being made Lord Mayor of London in 1741 appointed Romaine as his chaplain. As chaplain he had to preach in St. Paul's, and his sermon attracted much attention. But nothing came of it for the moment, and he made up his mind to go back to his native North country. That he did not do so was due to one of those seemingly trivial and chance occurrences which have so often determined a whole career. He had already made his preparations when he happened to meet an acquaintance of his father's who told him that he ought to apply for a lectureship at St. Botolph's, Billingsgate, which was then vacant. He did so, and was elected in October, 1748. In the following year he obtained that at St. Dunstan's-in-the-West, a post he was to retain to the end of his days. The position was one of great importance owing to the nearness of the church to the Law Courts, for it is situated in Fleet Street almost opposite the entrance to Salisbury Square, where the Church Missionary Society would have its modest beginnings, and where already Samuel Richardson had his printing works. One wonders if he ever heard the new lecturer, and if so what opinion he formed of him. Another who must often have passed the church was Dr. Samuel Johnson.

Lectureships went back to Puritan times, and as the holder was often appointed by the parishioners, he was quite independent of the incumbent of the parish. Such posts in London churches were eagerly sought after by ambitious young clerics, and a number of famous churchmen thus began their careers.[1] Romaine seems to have had similar views, for he took the office "looking for honours and promotion".

As St. Dunstan's was closed during the Law Court vacations he had considerable liberty to preach elsewhere, and frequently travelled about on behalf of Lady Huntingdon, whose patronage he soon acquired. Romaine had an aversion to preaching in the open air, though he once did so for Grimshaw at Haworth, and restricted himself to such pulpits as were granted to him. As his scrupulous observance of the Church's rules became generally known, he was often allowed to use pulpits which were closed to Wesley, Whitefield and other leaders of the movement. At St. Dunstan's his preaching quickly attracted notice, and the church became so crowded that the parishioners were excluded from their pews. This aroused the enmity of the churchwardens, and in conjunction with the vicar they suddenly changed the hour of the lecture to 7 p.m., at the same

[1] See Sykes, pp. 254 f.

time refusing to light the church or allow it to be opened before the commencement of the service. An appeal against their action in the King's Bench was a failure, so it came about that the only Evangelical service in the city was illuminated by a single taper held in the hand of the preacher, with his hearers sitting or standing around him. This disgraceful state of affairs was ended at last by the intervention of the bishop, who insisted that the churchwardens should make proper arrangements for the lectures.

An additional opportunity for delivering his message came to Romaine in 1750 when he was appointed assistant morning preacher at St. George's, Hanover Square. The church was situated in the heart of the West end, and its pulpit was the most important he ever occupied regularly. As at St. Dunstan's, his sermons began to draw crowds of outsiders, and also to arouse the resentment of the regular worshippers who found their pews filled up. Their objections met with a shrewd remark from the Earl of Northampton, who observed: "If the power to attract be imputed as a matter of admiration to Garrick, why should it be urged as a crime against Romaine? Shall excellence be considered exceptionable only in divine things?" However, when Dr. Andrew Trebeck succeeded to the living in 1755 he dismissed the morning preacher. This had an important sequel, for many of his hearers still wished to have the benefit of Romaine's guidance and meetings were arranged in private houses. This irregularity was brought to the notice of the authorities, who threatened prosecution. Lady Huntingdon thereupon stepped in and appointed Romaine as one of her chaplains, and so he was free to make use of her house.

During his time at St. George's, Romaine held the post of Professor of Astronomy at Gresham College. This was an odd appointment, and he can scarcely have been an efficient professor since one of the principal tasks of the office was to promote the study of his special subject. This Romaine can hardly have done, for he asked: "Were dying sinners ever converted by the spots on the moon? Was ever miser reclaimed from avarice by Jupiter's belt?" One wonders why he ever undertook such uncongenial duties, or why, having undertaken them, he did not attempt to fulfil them in a more satisfactory manner. The whole incident is typical of the outlook of the times, in which even a convinced Evangelical might share.

After being dismissed from St. George's, Romaine accepted a curacy at St. Olave's, Southwark, and went to live in Walnut

Tree Walk, Lambeth, which he describes as a delightful rural retreat giving him quiet for his studies. Here he remained until 1759. As this was about the time that the attacks upon him at St. Dunstan's were coming to a head and his dismissal from his lectureship seemed possible, he seriously doubted whether employment in the Church might not become impossible for him. Some of his admirers offered to build a chapel where he might carry on as an independent preacher. At this crisis he went down to Truro to consult Walker, who was able to reassure him and persuade him to remain loyal to the Church.[1] Although Romaine was a convinced Churchman, he did not withhold his admiration, and even his co-operation, from what he regarded as effective work done by those outside. He was, for example, on intimate terms with Ingham and his wife, and he said of their connexion: "If ever there was a Church of Christ upon earth that was one. I paid them a visit, and had a great mind to join them."

Another very important pulpit was also lost to Romaine at this time, that of the university church at Oxford. Two sermons of his in 1757 on "The Lord our Righteousness" were so unacceptable that he was never again asked to preach there.[2] There had been for some time a growing feeling against him in Oxford, and Whitefield wrote in 1755: "The greatest venom is spit out against Mr. R., who, having been reputed a great scholar, is now looked upon and treated as a great fool, because made wise himself, and earnestly desirous that others should be made wise to eternal salvation."

Romaine's career in the Church continued to be hazardous; his lectureship at St. Dunstan's he was able to retain, but during the next five years he had little other employment. He was morning preacher at St. Bartholomew's the Great from 1759 to 1761, and had a brief tenure of the preachership of Westminster Chapel, being speedily dismissed by the Dean and Chapter. Lord Dartmouth offered him the living of West Bromwich, but he was unwilling to leave London. Then at length came the offer of the much more congenial parish of St. Andrew-by-the-Wardrobe with St. Anne, Blackfriars.

The appointment to this important parish lay with the Lord Chancellor and the parishioners alternately. On this occasion it was the turn of the parishioners. When the vacancy occurred

[1] Sidney, *Life of Walker*, pp. 488 f.

[2] He published the sermons with a dedication to the Vice-Chancellor: see *Works*, p. 14

Romaine was in Yorkshire, and hearing that his friends were moving to get him nominated he gave a grudging consent, feeling that he could not reject the chance of such an opening. He agreed to preach a probationary sermon, but refused to canvass for votes. His sermon, preached on September 30, 1764, was on the text 2 Corinthians 4: 5, and is contained in his printed works.[1] In it he explained why he had not canvassed the parishioners; it was not pride, but another motive: "I could not see how this could promote the glory of God." But his friends, including Lady Huntingdon, Mr. Thornton, and Mr. Madan, were very active on his behalf. The poll went in Romaine's favour, but it was followed by an appeal to the Court of Chancery, which did not announce its verdict for more than a year. Again it was favourable to Romaine, and he was instituted in February, 1766. When he heard of this decision, Romaine wrote to his sister (January 7, 1766): "I have retired and been alone this afternoon to abase myself."[2] On February 4 he wrote:

> My friends are rejoicing around me, and wishing me that joy which I cannot take. It is my Master's will, and I submit. I can see nothing before me, so long as the breath is in my body, but war—and that with unreasonable men—a divided parish, an angry clergy, a wicked Sodom, and a wicked world.[3]

One of the most vigorous of Romaine's supporters had been a certain publican, and the reason for his advocacy had been a mystery. Romaine on thanking him received the reply: "Indeed, sir, I am more indebted to you than you to me; for you have made my wife, who was one of the worst, the best woman in the world."

Romaine held St. Anne's, and also his lectureship at St. Dunstan's, to the end of his life, which stretched beyond our period, for he reached the advanced age of eighty-one, dying in 1795. Among his curates was Henry Foster, and, from 1786, William Goode, who succeeded to the living.

Romaine has been described as "all in all . . . the strongest man connected with the Evangelical branch of the Movement".[4] With this judgment I am not disposed to quarrel, so long as it does not lead to the inference that his influence was greater

[1] *Op. cit.*, pp. 785 ff. [2] *Op. cit.*, p. 679
[3] *Op. cit.*, p. 711 [4] Overton, *The Evangelical Revival*, p. 68

than that of some other leaders. Undoubtedly he exercised a considerable influence on the movement and its adherents, but it would have been immeasurably greater but for certain defects of temperament. Romaine had an affectionate nature and a deep anxiety to promote the spiritual welfare of those under his care; but he was shy and reserved, severe in manner and difficult to approach, so that those who did not know him well might easily regard him as pedantic and morose. One gets the impression that he lived under considerable strain—the frequent opposition which he encountered may have helped this —which probably accounts for his occasional outbursts of irritability. Thus it came about that Romaine chiefly told on others through his preaching and writing rather than by personal dealings.

His sermons were certainly effective, and drew numerous hearers. Among those who attended them when in London was Richard Hill; and his younger brother, Rowland, had such an admiration for Romaine that he had his portrait in his rooms at St. John's, Cambridge.[1] His writings, which will receive fuller consideration later, were marked by a stronger Calvinistic tone than the milder outpourings of other Evangelical leaders, save Toplady, a circumstance which aroused the indignation of Wesley, who wrote on January 20, 1765: "I looked over Mr. Romaine's strange book on the 'Life of Faith'. I thought nothing could exceed Mr. Ingham's, but really this does; although they differ not a hair's breadth from each other, any more than from Mr. Sandeman."[2] Romaine was a very careful and laborious writer, and those who read his works, unless they are capable of a similar attention, may easily misunderstand them. When *The Life of Faith* appeared, although it keeps closely to the Homily "On Salvation", a reviewer condemned it as "the death of all reason, all piety, all humility, all meekness". But such an opinion ignores the safeguards which the book itself contains. Romaine speaks of the glory of Christ being "to save His people from the dominion of their sins"; he also makes a great point of progress in the Christian life, and strongly insists on the use of the means of grace—prayer, public worship, and the Lord's supper.[3]

A survey of the lives of these pioneers brings out very strikingly their variety in type and in location. Hervey worked in

[1] Sidney, *Life of Sir Richard Hill*, pp. 71 f.
[2] *Journal*, v, p. 105   [3] *Works*, pp. 254, 261 f.

Northampton; Grimshaw in the North; Walker in far-off Cornwall; Adam in North Lincolnshire; and Romaine in London. They were thus cut off geographically from one another, though some amount of communication existed between them; and here tribute must be paid to the work of Walker. His importance for the early days of the movement can scarcely be exaggerated, though it is often overlooked,[1] and if during this period there was a leader it was he who occupied the position. To him they went in their difficulties (after his death Adam filled the position to some extent) and on his judgment they largely relied. Had he not been cut off in early life the movement might have found unity and coherence much sooner than it did. As it was, the work was carried on largely in isolation and without sufficient co-ordination.

Another fact which must be admitted by any candid reader is their distinction from the Methodists. None of them owed much to Methodist influence, and they soon became suspicious of the way in which the wider movement was developing. This is true even of Grimshaw, who was most closely associated with it. The others, from the first, viewed its developments with distrust, foreseeing, as Wesley himself failed to do, their inevitable outcome. For them, the Church was the only legitimate body through which to exercise their ministry, and nothing could shake their resolve to be loyal to its teaching and discipline. Their principles might be much the same as those held by the followers of Wesley, but they exhibited them actively at work within the framework of the Church and in full submission to its authority. This was a very important achievement, and bore fruit in the coming era. Sidney wrote his *Life and Ministry of Walker* "to prove that the spirit of wisdom and zeal which now animates such numbers of the ministers of our Establishment, is the fruit, not of the ardour of the *irregulars* of the last century, but of the gradual influence of that example which was set by Mr. Walker and his contemporary *regulars*".

[1] Abbey and Overton give him but scanty attention

CHAPTER 9

DEVELOPMENT IN A CHANGING WORLD

IN a previous chapter I sketched out the development of thought up to the middle of the eighteenth century, and also the condition of religion. I now propose to continue the survey in the later part of the century when the revival was developing and expanding.

An age of enlightenment, in which reason is ruthlessly applied to accepted traditions and inherited beliefs, may well turn in upon itself, as in ancient Greece, and scepticism as to man's ability to gain any reliable knowledge of the universe be the result. This, indirectly has a further consequence, for it restores interest in man as an individual; cosmology and metaphysics are displaced by psychology and moral philosophy. So it was for the greater part of the latter eighteenth century; Hume had exposed the flaws in the predominant philosophy of Locke, and sheer scepticism seemed the only alternative; a bleak prospect, indeed, for it offered nothing but a bare negation. From this it was rescued by the teaching of Kant.

The threat of scepticism had little effect on the Evangelicals; they were too intent on the practical matter of saving souls to take much interest in the deeper questions of philosophy and theology. Their scheme was based on the Bible, and human speculations could not affect it. But if the Evangelicals were unconcerned by philosophical developments, others were not so immune. There were those who wished to take orders but found that intellectual difficulties stood in their way—especially the acceptance of the Thirty-nine Articles. This was not entirely novel, for Edward Venn, the elder brother of Henry, after taking his degree in 1740, abandoned the idea of ordination and turned to medicine instead. He still retained his membership of the Church of England, however.[1] Brian Hill, the younger brother of Rowland, after being ordained and still ardently attached to the Church, refused to accept any benefice through conscientious scruples.[2] Difficulties over the Articles often arose in connexion with the retention of fellowships. Tyrwhitt, the son of a canon of St. Paul's and a grandson of Bishop Gibson, resigned a fellowship at Cambridge as he was

[1] *Venn Family Annals*, p. 62   [2] *Life of Rowland Hill*, p. 7

DEVELOPMENT IN A CHANGING WORLD 171

unable to accept the Articles, and Porson took a similar course in 1788. In the majority of these cases the refusal did not imply the rejection of the fundamental doctrines of Christianity. Porson himself once declared that "If the New Testament is to determine the question, and words have any meaning, the Socinians are wrong."[1]

In 1772 there was a determined attempt to persuade Parliament to abolish subscription to the Articles. This was known as the Feathers' Tavern case, from the meeting place of the promoters of the agitation. The prime mover, Archdeacon Blackburne, was strictly orthodox, but he objected to the imposition of such exact and detailed definitions as those contained in the Articles. Others, however, who took part were far from orthodox, as is shown by the number who seceded after the failure of the petition. Its supporters were distinguished by academic distinction, rather than by numbers (in Cambridge the master and fellows of Peterhouse signed in a body) and it had little general backing in the country. The promoters, indeed, had difficulty in finding a member of Parliament to present it, in view of unfavourable public opinion.

Meanwhile, the opponents of the petition were exceedingly active; Lady Huntingdon canvassed many M.Ps., including Lord North. Among those who opposed was Edmund Burke, who quite correctly insisted that there was not sufficient demand for the relaxation, though conceding that the Church should have liberty to alter, within limits, its confessional forms and liturgy. Others saw in the movement a first step towards the subversion of all dogmatic religion. This was the view of Newton, who declared that the promoters "would not (if they had their wish) stop there, but would go on with their projected reform till they had overturned the Liturgy also".[2]

When the petition came before Parliament there was an animated debate, but the cause of relaxation was hopeless from the start. Only seventy-one voted in its favour, perhaps more than might have been expected, and 217 against.[3]

The fears of the orthodox may have been stimulated by the continuance of infidelity, though it is difficult to assess its extent or influence, for, as we saw earlier, it was often merely a pose. Its prevalence was lamented by Dr. Johnson in 1769, who was, however, a little reassured when six years later he was informed by a Deist, who had abandoned Quakerism, that

[1] Quoted Smyth, *Simeon*, p. 109   [2] *Cardiphonia*, p. 110
[3] See, further, G. O. Trevelyan, *The Early Hist. of C. J. Fox*, pp. 460 ff.

there were not above 200 likeminded in the whole of England. In the same year he noted that Good Friday was strictly kept in the country towns, though in London some shops remained open. This does not suggest that there had been any serious decline in religion. The very fact that Dr. Johnson and those who formed his circle were at least nominal Christians is significant, even if not all possessed the sturdy and reasoned faith of their leader.

There seems to have been among the upper classes a certain amount of sincere, if largely conventional, religion. Lady Spencer wrote to her daughter Harriet in 1780, just before her marriage to Lord Duncannon, a man of religious upbringing: "Christianity as taught in the Gospel has nothing formidable in it; the end and design of it is not to sour but to sweeten life."[1] But the revival doctrines, in spite of Lady Huntingdon's exertions, had as yet made little permanent impression outside the lower and middle classes. It was not until the close of the century, when a deeper seriousness began to emerge and men like Wilberforce and his friends adopted Evangelical views, that the higher strata of the nation were much affected.

Methodism had certainly made considerable progress, as the following figures show:

Year	Circuits	Preachers	Members
1767[2]	41	104	25,911
1780	64	171	43,380
1790	118	294	71,568

It was well that this was so, for the Church was doing little to meet the demands of the growing towns. Very few new churches were built, though in 1755 St. George's, Kingswood, Bristol, had been erected for the neglected colliers; in 1774 St. Mary's, Birmingham; and Christ Church, Macclesfield, in the year following; whilst in Manchester St. John's was built in 1769 and St. James's in 1788.

The religious provision of the towns was certainly inadequate. In Manchester, with a population of 70,000, all the places of worship combined had room for 20,000 only, and even such provision as existed was gravely neglected.[3] Henry Venn, after a preaching tour, reported that: "in the churches, at all the

---

[1] Bessborough, *Lady Bessborough and Her Family Circle*, pp. 35 f.
[2] This was the first year for which statistics are available
[3] *Life of Wilberforce*, ii, p. 163

DEVELOPMENT IN A CHANGING WORLD 173

great towns we came to, there are no worshippers scarce of any sort to be found. Absolute profaneness begins visibly to reign. Formality and pharisaism is and has been of late so much besieged and battered down, that a crisis seems approaching."[1]

The effects of town life on religion were disastrous, even apart from the lack of provision. The first generations of those who came in from the country brought with them some knowledge of Christianity, and might hand on to their children vague memories of the religious influences amidst which their own childhood had been spent; but in succeeding generations this quickly faded away. In the country, the green landscape and open skies might draw men's thoughts to higher things than the drab struggle for existence; but in the dreary, smoke-laden air of the towns, God seemed shut out.[2] Even the Bible lost much of its meaning, for it had been written for pastoral peoples in the main, and its words would come strangely to the ears of an essentially urban and industrial population. How could they find consolation in "The Lord is my Shepherd", when the only sheep they ever saw were being driven through the streets to market, harried by barking dogs? Even to-day, existence in cities, where there is provision for worship for those who desire it, tends to deaden all awareness of spiritual things. How much worse must it have been in the neglected towns at the beginning of the industrial revolution?

Turning to the state of the clergy, we find the evidence somewhat conflicting, especially as regards the bishops. Some of them were certainly very active, for records show that between 1768 and 1771 nearly 42,000 candidates were confirmed in the diocese of York; and at the other end of the country about the same number is given for that of Exeter, but in a shorter period. When the state of the roads and the long distances to be covered is recalled, this was no mean achievement, and is evidence that not all bishops were seriously neglecting their dioceses.

One criticism which is often brought against the bishops at this period, and a just one in general, was that they were exceedingly careless over ordinations. Here again there were exceptions, for when James Glazebrook was ordained priest by Bishop Hurd in 1777 he commented:

[1] *Countess of Huntingdon*, i, p. 486

[2] Cf. Farnell, *The Attributes of God*, pp. 117 f.: "In overlaying the beauty and healthful purity of our world of nature with ugliness, noise, and dirt, it had destroyed two deep springs of religious feeling. In the great centres of industrialism the emotions evoked by the kind of life led there seem for the most part anti-religious, and the æsthetic nature-sense is atrophied"

Never can I forget the serious manner with which the worthy Bishop of Worcester addressed himself to the candidates. . . . His warning and exhortations were such as well became a governor of the Church, and were truly expressive of that anxious concern which every godly prelate must feel when sending forth persons to undertake the pastoral office.[1]

That is the favourable side of the picture; but it was hardly representative of the majority of the bishops. Hannah More, for example, thought that a bishop who preached was as rare as a peer who paid.[2] Dr. Johnson attributed the low state of the bench to the method of selection and appointment, saying in 1775 that no one "can now be made a Bishop for his learning or piety; his only chance for promotion is his being connected with somebody who has parliamentary influence".[3]

A notable feature of the later eighteenth century was the improving social status of the clergy. The country parson[4] was ceasing to be a sort of peasant farmer working his own glebe, and was often taking his place alongside the gentry, letting his land or employing labour. This was largely due to the contempt for trade which arose in the Hanoverian period, for many younger sons qualified for the family living as an alternative. The clergy as a body were still poor, but higher yields from tithe and glebe which came from more skilled farming increased the value of many livings. The "gentleman" cleric had seldom any real keenness for religion, and was content to take the Sunday services; but he was often resident and in close touch with his flock, to many of whom he had been known from childhood. This made the parsonage a centre for a certain amount of refining and educative influence, and "it might be discerned whether or no there was a clergyman resident in a parish by the civil or savage manner of the people".[5]

Non-residence and its twin evil pluralism were still rampant, and still so much a matter of course that few complained. Even

---

[1] *Countess of Huntingdon*, ii, p. 87   [2] *The Bas Bleu* (*Works*, i, p. 23)

[3] Boswell, *Life of Samuel Johnson* (Everyman's Library ed.), i, p. 551

[4] Much light has been thrown on the life of the country clergy by the publication in recent years of a number of their journals, of which Woodforde's *Diary of a Country Parson* is a good specimen

[5] The opinion of Dr. Percy, Dean of Carlisle and later Bishop of Dromore, quoted by Dr. Johnson in a letter to a young clergyman on August 30, 1780

the poet Crabbe, a man of some conscience, had a bad record. From 1783 to 1793 he held two small livings in Dorset, but lived as chaplain to the Duke of Rutland at Belvoir Castle, and even took a curacy in the neighbourhood. He was then presented to the living of Muston and Allington, which he held until his appointment to Trowbridge in 1814. For three years he resided at Muston, and then went to Parham, where his wife had inherited a small property, moving later to Great Glenham. The Bishop of Lincoln then ordered him to reside, but so far relented as to give him four years in which to obey. Crabbe duly returned in October, 1805, after an absence of sixteen years.

In *The Vicar of Wakefield* Goldsmith has given us an attractive picture of the life of a country clergyman, and in *The Deserted Village* he has transferred Chaucer's "poor parson" to his own day. But it is to be feared that his account is as highly idealized as the village in which he located it. Crabbe, in *The Village*, rejected such descriptions in favour of:

> a shepherd of a different stock
> . . . . .
> A jovial youth, who thinks his Sunday's task
> As much as God or man can fairly ask.

Cowper, whose *Table-Talk* appeared in May, 1782, shortly before Crabbe's poem, is full of condemnations of the clergy and their shortcomings, and "a varied gallery of the existing types of clerical inefficiency may be formed from his pages". But Cowper judged the clergy by the standards of his own Evangelical outlook, and by that they were certainly defective.

The spread of Evangelical views was, however, by this time beginning to have its effects on the state of the clergy, some of whom were shamed by the example of their more conscientious fellows. Others resented the zeal and devotion which they showed, and a clergyman who adopted Evangelical views and practices might find himself regarded with distrust or even active dislike by men who had been his intimate friends.

If only a few of the clergy were moved to emulation or to appreciation by the example of the Evangelicals, there were still many who were quietly carrying out their duties, often in dull and depressing surroundings. Dr. Johnson was once offered a valuable living by the father of a young friend if he would take orders. This he refused, as he felt himself unfitted temperamentally for the life of a country parson. Some years later he went to stay with his would-be patron, and had the opportunity of meeting "a respectable clergyman". The meeting confirmed his earlier impressions. "This man, Sir," he said, "fills up the duties of his life well. I approve of him, but could not imitate him."[1]

A good sample of a country parson of this period was Gilbert White of Selborne, who went about his little Hampshire parish keeping a kindly eye on his people and observing with loving eyes the world of nature around him. So content was he with his life that in spite of straitened means he refused all offers of preferment. In his way he was a kind of "regular" itinerant, for on his numerous travels on horseback over the south of England he made a point of preaching wherever he went, always, of course, with the consent of the incumbent. The *Natural History of Selborne* appeared in 1789, four years before his death.

One reason for the comparative inefficiency of the average cleric was that he had never received any special training for his job, in either its practical or intellectual aspects. This lack of suitable preparation made the more conscientious clergy spend much time in study in order to overcome their defects. Jones of Creaton "fagged" so hard that it brought about a nervous disorder.[2] The learning which most of them possessed was not fitted to make them understood by their people. The sermons they prepared, often with much labour, especially if the squire and his family and friends were likely to be present, passed over the heads of the rest of the congregation, at least in country churches. In the town churches the prominence of the pulpit is a testimony to the value which was attached to preaching; but even there it was the better educated for whom provision was made, and the subjects dealt with were often of little practical value. Wilberforce records on October 5, 1788, that he heard a sermon on "the Nature of Angels", and dismissed it as "most unprofitable".[3] Sermons, however, were not delivered at all services, and Dr. Johnson, in this, rather modern in his opinions, preferred a service in which there were prayers only.

The requirements for ordination were not excessive, and, on occasion, very meagre. Again to take Crabbe as an instance, we find that he had no scholastic qualifications at all, though

[1] Boswell, *Life of Johnson*, i, p. 297
[2] Owen, *Memoir of Jones of Creaton*, pp. 77 f.   [3] *Life*, i, p. 185

DEVELOPMENT IN A CHANGING WORLD 177

he was sincerely religious, and he was ordained on the advice and through the influence of Edmund Burke, who wished to find some remunerative employment for his protégé.[1] Similar entries into holy orders were by no means infrequent.

One of the great problems which faced both Methodists and Evangelicals alike was the providing and training of suitable ministers. The expulsion of the students from St. Edmund Hall, Oxford, led Lady Huntingdon, who had subsidized some of them, to open a college of her own. Accordingly, she leased a country house from Howell Harris at Trevecca, in the parish of Talgarth,[2] and opened it on her birthday, August 24, 1768, and for a time she made it her principal place of residence. The college was designed to train men for the ministry irrespective of the denomination to which they belonged, and at first the Wesleyans took a large share in the enterprise. John Wesley, writing to Charles on May 14, 1768, speaks of it as "our college",[3] and the first headmaster, Easterbrook, was a Wesleyan; as was Joseph Benson,[4] the second master; whilst Fletcher was one of the visitors and took a very active part in the starting of the institution. Such co-operation, however, was brought to a sudden end by the rise of the Calvinist controversy. Benson was dismissed and Fletcher resigned.

Lady Huntingdon hoped that some of her students would be ordained in the Church; but the bishops regarded them with suspicion. Berridge, with his customary bluntness, told her that: "The bishops look on your students as the worst kind of Dissenters; manifest this by refusing that ordination to your preachers which would be readily granted to other teachers among the Dissenters."[5]

The Trevecca students, indeed, became an embarrassment to those who did not see eye to eye with their patroness, for not only did they itinerate in the neighbourhood of the college, but went all over the country. Wesley accused them of neglecting places where "Christ has not been named", in order to draw away his own converts. He referred to them as "those striplings, who call themselves Lady Huntingdon's preachers", and in his sermon at the laying of the foundation stone of the City Road Chapel in May, 1777, he denounced "a school set

[1] The Archbishop of Canterbury granted him the degree of LL.B. in 1783
[2] It was moved to Cheshunt in 1792   [3] *Works*, xii, p. 135
[4] Benson when appointed was only twenty-one and classical master at Kingswood; he had, moreover, entered at St. Edmund Hall, Oxford. It was only after much hesitation that Wesley released him
[5] Quoted Gledstone, *Life of Whitefield*, p. 465

M

up at Trevecka" (sic) and its students, who "as they disclaimed all connections with the Methodists, so they disclaimed the Church also; nay, they spoke of it upon all occasions with exquisite bitterness and contempt".

Wesley, no doubt, exaggerated; but it seems clear that these youths, as many of them were, had more zeal than knowledge. Even Howell Harris, a convinced Calvinist, was disgusted by them, and said to Wesley: "I have borne with these pert, ignorant young men, vulgarly called students, till I cannot, in conscience, bear any longer. They preach barefaced Reprobation, and so broad Antinomianism, that I have been constrained to oppose them to the face, even in the public congregation." Wesley commented: "What better can be expected from raw lads of little understanding, little learning, and no experience."[1]

Meanwhile, the Evangelicals had been devising their own plans for the training of suitable ordinands. These took the form, not of setting up a college of their own, but of subsidizing approved students, or even providing for their whole education. This scheme originated with the Elland Clerical Society.[2]

Henry Venn when at Huddersfield had founded in 1767 a clerical society and later it was continued by Burnett at Elland, where he was rector. At a meeting in 1777 the question of finding curates came up for discussion, and it was suggested that a fund should be started for the training of Evangelical candidates for orders. This duly came to pass, and among its early supporters, in addition to clergymen such as Romaine, Miles Atkinson, and Simeon, were prominent laymen, including Lord Dartmouth, Richard Hill, William Hey and William Wilberforce. The latter took a keen interest in the project, writing to Hey in December, 1789:

> I wish to know what state are the funds of your West Riding Charity for catching the colts running wild on Halifax Moor, cutting their manes and tails, and sending them to college. If a contributor would be acceptable, I would most cheerfully give something towards an institution I so highly approve, but my name must not be mentioned.[3]

---

[1] *Journal*, v, p. 482

[2] See, further, Hulbert, *A Review of the Origin and Hist. of the Elland Clerical Society*. It was not until 1795 that the Bristol Clerical Education Society was established to perform a like function in the South and West

[3] *Life*, i, p. 252

DEVELOPMENT IN A CHANGING WORLD 179

Among the first to receive a grant was Samuel Marsden, the future apostle of New Zealand.

The revival movement and the quickening of spiritual religion which followed in its train were not confined to the Church. The Dissenters also reaped a harvest from its sowing. It is true that many joined the Methodist movement, but numbers of these afterwards returned to their former denominations, finding Methodism not quite to their liking. There were also other defections. In 1756 a Mr. Edwards left to form an Independent chapel at Leeds, and another Methodist preacher, Charles Skelton, set himself up at Southwark.[1] The Dissenters, or some of them, also tried to draw away Methodist converts; the Baptists seem to have been especially active in this matter; as in Manchester.[2] In 1770 Dan Taylor, a Yorkshireman who had been affected by the movement, founded the Baptist New Connexion; whilst a body of seceders started the Baptist chapel at Bingley.[3] Some preachers who set up for themselves afterwards regretted the change, as Charles Wesley, not without a touch of irony, records in one such case: "I talked kindly to poor J. Whitford, who seemed quite sick of his separate congregation. So headstrong and untractable; so like their humble slave and teacher!"[4]

Thus, new life was coming to stimulate the various Dissenting bodies, and even to add to their number; none the less, the drift to Unitarianism still persisted, especially among the Presbyterians. This aroused the regret and anxiety of George III, who wrote to Lord North in 1772: "I am sorry to say the present Presbyterians seem so much more resembling Socinians than Christians that, I think, the test was never so necessary as at present for obliging them to prove themselves Christians."[5]

One of the outstanding figures in Unitarianism was Joseph Priestley, a product of the Dissenting Academies which did so much to foster radical ideas in both religion and politics during the later eighteenth century. He began as a strict Calvinist, then drifted into Arianism, and finally, under the influence of the writings of Lardner, became an avowed Socinian. In 1782 he published his *History of the Corruptions of Christianity*, in which he claimed that the original Gospel had been overlaid with needless and false doctrines. This aroused a controversy

[1] Charles Wesley, *Journal*, ii, pp. 121 n., 124   [2] *Op. cit.*, ii, p. 129
[3] John Wesley, *Journal*, v, p. 180   [4] *Journal*, ii, p. 128
[5] *Correspondence of George III with Lord North* (ed. W. Bodham Donne), i, p. 89

with Bishop Horsley which, if it did nothing else, served to define the issues at stake. Priestley found a generous patron in the Earl of Shelburne, who appointed him as his librarian, and also provided a house at Calne, where he had the means and the leisure to carry on his scientific experiments.

Unitarianism is often regarded as an almost purely intellectual movement of a rather negative character. But this was not true of all who embraced it. A striking example of a very different convert is the elder William Hazlitt, who became a Unitarian minister in 1764. It was said of him by his more famous namesake and son that he flamed with enthusiasm for God and His Christ, and showed in his conduct a high standard of living and a scorn of all worldly advantage. He, and others like him—

> set up an image in their own minds—it was truth; they worshipped an idol—it was justice. They looked on man as their brother, and only bowed the knee to the Highest. Separate from the world, they walked humbly with their God, and lived in thought with those who had borne testimony of a good conscience, with the spirit of just men in all ages.[1]

It was not, however, from Dissent alone that adherents were drawn. Unitarianism had attractions for not a few of the clergy. Berridge had been affected, and only drew back when he realized that it must lead to pure scepticism; and so had Thomas Scott. In the universities it was supposed to have many sympathizers, including Dr. Hey, the Norrisian Professor of Divinity at Cambridge, and brother of William Hey. The failure of the Feathers' Tavern petition led to a number of secessions, including Dr. Jebb, Fellow of Peterhouse. His lectures on the New Testament had aroused much adverse criticism, and in 1775 he resigned his living and became an avowed Unitarian. A notorious case was that of William Friend, Fellow of Jesus College, Cambridge, and vicar of Madingley. He took a similar course in 1787, and some years later was expelled from the university.[2] Another Cambridge graduate who took the same course was Edward Evanson, vicar of Tewkesbury, who resigned in 1778. Some years later he published *The Dissonance of the Four generally received Evangelists*, which brought forth replies from

---
[1] "On Court Influence", in *Political Essays*
[2] The case is fully reported in *The Life of Dean Milner*, pp. 84 ff.

Priestley in *Letters to a Young Man* (1792), and T. Falconer in the Bampton Lectures for 1810.

The most famous of all the cases of secession, however, was that of Theophilus Lindsay. He and his relatives had received many kindnesses from the Hastings family (Theophilus was so named after the Earl of Huntingdon, who was his godfather), and it was they who had paid for his education and presented him to the living of Puddletown in Dorset, which he later exchanged for Catterick. This he resigned in 1773, and in the following year established a chapel in Essex Street, Strand. Among his hearers were the Duke of Grafton, a man of dubious character, both morally and politically,[1] and William Wilberforce. The latter attended, as he explained after ceasing to hear Lindsay, "not for any preference for his peculiar doctrines, for in this, except on some great festivals, his preaching differed little from that which was then common among the London clergy, but because he seemed more in earnest and practical than others".[2] Wilberforce never lost his respect for Lindsay, recognizing that he had acted from conscientious motives, and contrasting him with others, who held the same views, yet still clung to their livings.[3]

Lady Huntingdon, who had vainly endeavoured to dissuade Lindsay from resigning, did not lose her interest in him, and in 1786 he paid a visit to Trevecca. She was greatly impressed by his suggestion, made in reference to her dead son, who in his lifetime had been a source of bitter disappointment to her, that there might be some kind of purgatory in the future state and a hope of final salvation.

Those few of the clergy who gave up their livings for conscience sake, as in the case of Lindsay, were respected even by those who regretted their action. But such an attitude was impossible for Cowper, who could not restrain his disgust.

> They now are deem'd the faithful, and are prais'd
> Who, constant only in rejecting Thee,
> Deny Thy Godhead with a martyr's zeal,
> And quit their office for their error's sake;
> Blind, and in love with darkness!

These secessions, and the not unfounded suspicion that there were many others holding similar views who had not the courage to come out openly, naturally aroused much alarm among

---
[1] He was among those attacked in the *Letters of Junius*
[2] *Life*, i, p. 76   [3] *Op. cit.*, i, p. 129

orthodox Christians. Newton wrote in 1775: "I fear Socinianism spreads rapidly amongst us, and bids fair to be the prevailing scheme in this land, especially with those who profess to be the thinking part."[1]

If Unitarianism was on the increase, so also was Roman Catholicism. In 1779 Erasmus Middleton complained of the great strides being made by "Popery and other heretical tenets".[2] The fear of Rome, so constant until the failure of the 1745 Rising, had been revived among the populace by the passing of the Catholic Relief Act in 1778, a measure which incidentally went through both Houses of Parliament without a division. Opposition first became manifest when the attempt was made to apply it in Scotland, and fierce riots broke out in Edinburgh in 1779. Wesley himself shared in the alarm, and wrote on January 18, 1780: "Receiving more and more accounts of the increase of Popery, I believed it my duty to write a letter concerning it, which was afterwards inserted in the public papers. Many were grievously offended; but I cannot help it; I must follow my conscience."[3] In England, a Protestant Association was formed early in 1780 to counteract Popery, with Lord George Gordon at its head. This led to the violent and fanatical riots of the following June.

The bishops, to their credit, refused to join in the general outcry, thereby exposing themselves to much abuse. Wesley also was opposed to extreme measures, and in November, 1780, preached a sermon against the persecution of "Papists"; all that should be done was "barely to prevent their doing hurt".[4] Newton showed a genuine Christian spirit, writing to a friend in Scotland: "If you know a Papist who sincerely loves Jesus, and trusts to Him for salvation, give my love to him."

[1] *Cardiphonia*, p. 120
[2] *Biographia Evangelica*, I, p. i
[3] *Journal*, vi, p. 267
[4] *Op. cit.*, vi, pp. 299 f.

CHAPTER 10

THE GROWTH OF OPPOSITION

THE revival movement had not got far on its way before it began to meet criticism, and then definite opposition. That this should have been so in an age such as the eighteenth century need occasion no surprise, for what first attracted attention to it was the fanatical and "enthusiastic" character of its proceedings. Men had not then studied the question of mob psychology and the tendency of crowds to develop emotions of a quite irrational kind. This tendency is especially prone to show itself in connexion with religion, and it cannot be denied that revival meetings often degenerate into exhibitions of mass hysteria, a wallowing in emotion for its own sake which has nothing religious about it save the terminology. This is admitted by so sympathetic an observer as Bishop Ryle, who wrote: "Nothing perhaps, is so infectious as a kind of sham, sensational Christianity, and particularly among the unlearned and ignorant."[1]

What was particularly abhorrent to contemporaries was the occurrence of violent seizures which, especially in the early days, were a not infrequent accompaniment of Methodist, and even of Evangelical,[2] preaching. To understand these manifestations we must consider the circumstances of the times and the outlook of the hearers. Many of them had led evil lives, and when their consciences or fears had been aroused by the earnestness of the preachers to the doom which they merited, it is not to be wondered at that they should be thrown into a state of terror which might easily express itself in distressing and extravagant physical forms. To make the matter worse, not all such seizures were genuine. Charles Wesley wrote on August 5, 1740: "I talked sharply to . . . a girl of twelve years old; who now confessed that her fits and cryings (above thirty of them) were all feigned that Mr. Wesley might take notice of them."[3]

The leaders themselves were conscious of the dangers involved in emotional outbreaks, and aware of the defects of "enthusiasm" in the sense in which it was then generally understood. Wesley wrote on November 1, 1762:

[1] *Christian Leaders*, p. 187
[2] Especially in the case of Berridge: see below, pp. 276 ff.   [3] *Journal*, i, p. 247

> I dislike something that has the appearance of enthusiasm; over-valuing feelings and inward impressions; mistaking the mere work of imagination for the voice of the Spirit; expecting the end without the means; and undervaluing reason, knowledge, and wisdom in general.[1]

Even those who were not habitually subject to outbursts could use language which was revolting in its lack of restraint. On September 6, 1742, Wesley had reproved certain of his followers who claimed that they felt "the blood of Christ running up their arms, or going down their throat, or poured like warm water upon their breast or heart".[2] A similar condemnation was expressed by Thomas Scott when he wrote:

> What revivals of religion were ever free from scandals? Where the Lord sows His good seed, there the enemy will be sure to scatter his tares. It must be confessed, that some of the most eminent instruments in this work . . . have, by the greatness of their zeal, through human frailty, been betrayed into sentiments, expressions, and deportment, in some instances, justly to be censured as enthusiastical.[3]

The dislike of "enthusiasm"[4] is usually regarded as being typical of the eighteenth century, but it had had its birth even earlier. The Cambridge Platonists had been alive to its evils, and Henry More, in his *Enthusiasmus Triumphatus* (1656), had written against what he defined as "a full but false persuasion in a man that he is inspired".[5] So far, indeed, had the condemnation of enthusiasm gone that there was grave danger that in it might be included any kind of zeal for religion. Bishop Butler on more than one occasion made a protest against this, and in the preface to his *Sermons at the Rolls Chapel* (1733) he wrote: "The Love of God will everywhere, by the generality of the world . . . be called Enthusiasm." Dean Church has said of him:

---

[1] *Journal*, iv, pp. 536 f. Cf. v, p. 162: "O what power less than almighty can convince a thorough-paced enthusiast!"
[2] *Op. cit.*, iii, p. 44   [3] *The Force of Truth* (*Works*, i, pp. 112 f.)
[4] See, further, R. A. Knox, *Enthusiasm*
[5] Cf. Walker, *Fifty-two Sermons*, i, p. 89: "God's testimony is not made out by any new revelation to the soul (that being merely an enthusiastical fancy, and a very dangerous opinion)"

THE GROWTH OF OPPOSITION 185

In that age of cold decorum in the pulpit, himself the example and champion of calm reason, he was deterred by no fashionable sneers at fanatics and enthusiasts from anticipating, before Wesley, all that was deepest and truest in the Methodist appeal to the heart. He threw back a sarcasm on the fashionable preaching of his age which had its sting in truth. "We are got," he says, "into the contrary extreme to enthusiasm under the notion of a reasonable religion; so very reasonable as to have nothing to do with the heart and affections if these words signify anything but the faculty by which we discern speculative truth (*Works*, ii, p. 194)."[1]

Another cause for suspicion, of a very different nature, was that the advocates of the movement were in reality secret Papists. When this accusation was brought to the notice of Whitefield he replied: "If I am a Roman Catholic the Pope must have given me a large dispensation."[2] It was, however, the Wesleys who were chiefly accused of Popery; John was denounced as being a Jesuit in disguise and a recruiting agent for the exiled Stuarts, and we have already seen that Charles found himself in difficulties through a supposedly Jacobite utterance. These were but vulgar errors. The insistence, however, by the Wesleys on such things as weekly fasts and good works undoubtedly laid them open to the accusation by some who perversely misrepresented them. Cennick and others at Bristol said in February, 1741, that they had often heard both the Wesleys preach Popery; and a dissenting minister at Newcastle affirmed publicly, so Wesley reported on March 28, 1743, that "We were all Papists and our doctrine was mere Popery".[3] Even Bishop Lavington was not above making use of the same argument, and in his *Enthusiasm of Methodists and Papists Considered* he gave it as his opinion that Rome was the obvious end towards which the activities of the Methodists were tending.[4]

Lavington was the fiercest and most bitter of all the episcopal opponents of Methodism, and that, owing to an unfortunate incident. Soon after his appointment to Exeter in 1747 an incorrect version of his primary charge was published, and

[1] *Pascal and Other Sermons*, p. 42   [2] Philip, *Life of Whitefield*, p. 357
[3] *Journal*, ii, p. 431; iii, p. 73
[4] During the Calvinist controversy Lady Huntingdon made use of the same denunciation

he accused the Methodist leaders of being privy to it. His volume *Enthusiasm of Methodists and Papists Considered* appeared in 1749, but without the name of any author, and led to a prolonged controversy; but it was not until 1753 that the bishop came out into the open.[1]

As Convocation had been suspended, each bishop dealt with the Methodists as he thought best. Some were definitely alarmed by it as making for disorder. In 1746 Bishop Smallbrooke of Lichfield told his clergy that "if the false doctrines of the Methodists prevail, they must unavoidably create a general disorder in our Constitution, and, if so, favour the return of popery itself". Some disapproved of the doctrines that were being taught. Conyers was told by Archbishop Drummond of York that "he would be better employed preaching the morality of Socrates than canting about the New Birth"; but the great majority were estranged by the defiance of the Church's discipline, as well as by the disorders and excitements which accompanied some of the meetings. One of the earliest to take action was Bishop Gibson (London, 1723–48). At first he had been friendly towards the Methodists,[2] and he always treated them personally "with great tenderness and moderation";[3] but he came to see the dangers arising from the movement, and so ordered the clergy in his diocese to refuse to allow them the use of their pulpits. Hume (Oxford, 1758–66) withdrew Haweis's licence; whilst Warburton (Gloucester, 1760–79) insisted that one of his clergy whom he suspected of Methodism should never preach outside his parish, "not so much from the good you are likely to do there, as to prevent the mischief you may do by rambling about to other places". Warburton, like Lavington, carried on a controversy with Wesley,[4] during the course of which the latter came to question his scholarship, writing to Charles on January 5, 1763: "notwithstanding all his parade of learning, I believe he is no critic of Greek".[5] Warburton, and his disciple Hurd (Lichfield, 1774–81), refused to take the movement seriously, looking upon it as a passing phenomenon which would soon work itself out. Others, wiser and more far-seeing, saw in it a challenge to mend their ways. Archbishop

[1] See Wesley's answers to him in *Letters*, iii, 259–71, 295–331
[2] Sykes, *Edmund Gibson*, p. 321   [3] *Countess of Huntingdon*, i, p. 197
[4] See a long answer of November, 1762, in *Letters*, iv, pp. 338 ff.
[5] *Op. cit.*, iv, p. 199. An abler critic than Wesley held much the same opinion of Warburton's scholarship, for Bentley said of him that he had a voracious appetite for knowledge but was doubtful whether he had a good digestion (see Monk, *Life of Bentley*, ii, p. 410)

THE GROWTH OF OPPOSITION 187

Secker held that the best method of preventing secessions was to adopt a more vigorous and vital style of preaching, and told his clergy:

> You must be assiduous in teaching the principles not only of virtue and natural religion, but of the Gospel ... you must set forth the original corruption of our nature; our redemption according to God's eternal purpose in Christ, by the sacrifice of the cross; our sanctification by the influence of the Divine Spirit; the insufficiency of good works, and the efficacy of faith to salvation.[1]

What more could any Evangelical demand?

A few of the bishops were consistently friendly, even if they did not fully approve all that was being done. Benson of Oxford (1735-52) showed great kindness to Whitefield, though he warned him against irregularities and advised him to minister "to the congregation to which he was lawfully appointed". This advice, however, Whitefield could by no means swallow, and exclaimed: "my blood runs chill at the very thought of it. If you and the rest of the bishops cast us out, our great and common Master will take us up."[2] Here one cannot withhold sympathy from the kindly old prelate whose warnings were thus summarily rejected, but the interview throws a strong light on the clash between constituted authority and the ardent confidence of the revival preachers. Late in life Benson once said to Lady Huntingdon that he regretted that he had ordained Whitefield, and received the reply: "My Lord ... when you are on your dying bed, that will be one of the few ordinations you will reflect upon with complacence." Unlike many similar predictions this was almost literally fulfilled, for just before he died the bishop sent ten guineas to Whitefield as a token of his regard, and at the same time entreated his prayers.[3]

Lady Huntingdon in some cases succeeded in getting the bishops to take a more kindly view of the movement. Archbishop Potter, who as Bishop of Oxford (1715-37) had ordained several of the Holy Club, was critical of their irregularities, though admitting that they had done good, and even praying for God's blessing on their labours. His tolerant attitude was

---

[1] In Bishop Watson's *Tracts*, vi, p. 79
[2] Gledstone, *Life of Whitefield*, p. 154   [3] *Countess of Huntingdon*, i, p. 18

largely due to his close friendship with Lady Huntingdon, and it was to her that he wrote his last letter on October 10, 1747:

> Dear Madam,—I have been very ill since last I saw you. I hope soon to hear from you, that your health is better for your being at Bath. Continue to pray for me until we meet in that place where our joy shall be complete. I am, as ever, your affectionate friend, John Cantuar.[1]

Towards the end of his life Wesley received cordial treatment from some of the bishops. In 1777 he was a fellow guest with Bishop Lowth (then in the last year of his Oxford episcopate), and described the latter's conduct as "worthy of a Christian bishop; easy, affable, and courteous", and with "a dignity . . . suitable to his character". The bishop refused to sit above him, saying: "Mr. Wesley, may I be found at your feet in another world." When Wesley demurred, the bishop told him that he was deaf on one side and did not wish to lose anything which Wesley said.[2] In 1782 he dined at Exeter with Bishop Ross (1778–92), together with five other clergymen, and four of the city fathers.[3] One wonders what the shade of Bishop Lavington thought of the occasion.

The Evangelical clergy, so far as they adopted the irregularities of the Methodists, shared also in their condemnation. They also suffered from the disapprobation of their fellow clergy. If they invaded their parishes this was not surprising; but even those who refrained from itinerating attracted hearers from neighbouring parishes, which must have caused annoyance to the incumbents. In any case the unwonted zeal of the Evangelical clergy could hardly fail to displease their neighbours whose own neglect was thereby shown up. Jones of Creaton may be taken as a typical case. During his curacies at Oswestry he was frowned upon by other clergymen and at last dismissed. The result was that forty people left the Church to join the Methodists, and others joined different Dissenting bodies. The same thing occurred in his next curacy at Loppington, where after his dismissal a Dissenting chapel was opened. Here some twenty of the richer members of the congregation had made a

---

[1] After completing it he rose from his desk, collapsed, and died, still clutching the letter in his hand (*Countess of Huntingdon*, i, p. 447)

[2] *Journal*, vi, pp. 165 f.; Tyerman, *Life of Wesley*, ii, p. 352

[3] *Journal*, vi, p. 365

point of walking out before the sermon.¹ It was quite a common thing for Evangelical curates to be dismissed; sometimes, as in the case of Romaine at St. George's, Hanover Square, because their preaching overcrowded the churches and interfered with the comfort of the regular congregation. It may be surmised that some of these dismissals were caused, at least in part, by the jealousy of the incumbent.

Opposition on the part of the parochial clergy to the Methodists and all who seemed "fellow-travellers" with them, arose from the nature of things. Often enough, however, it came from the best among them—as the careless and non-resident did not worry about such matters. Sometimes it was the result of ignorance of the doctrines which were being set forth. The Rev. Josiah Tucker of All Saints, Bristol, the friend of Hannah More, and later Dean of Gloucester, wrote to Wesley towards the end of 1739: "I think too many clergymen are culpable, in that they do not inform themselves better of Mr. Whitefield, yourself, and your doctrines from your own mouths."² Sometimes it took rather quaint forms, as when Dr. Trapp, a city incumbent and chaplain to Bolingbroke, published a sermon against the Methodists entitled "The Great Folly and Danger of being Righteous Over-much". This drew from the Countess of Hertford the cynical comment: "a doctrine which does not seem absolutely necessary to be preached to the people of the present age".³

One reason for clerical opposition was that many bitter attacks were made upon them and the Church by the less informed Methodist preachers, and even by Whitefield, who dubbed the clergy "letter-learned"; whilst others declared that "the scarlet whore of Babylon is not more corrupt either in principle or practice than the Church of England".⁴ Wesley, and those associated with him, though they might on occasion criticize the clergy, for the most part never descended to abuse. Wesley himself made a careful statement of the case between the Methodists and the clergy,⁵ and also gave orders that there was to be no railing against them, a proceeding which never did any good and frequently did harm.⁶

The Calvinist section of the movement were also guilty of unscrupulous methods of obtaining possession of pulpits. Richard Venn, the father of Henry, and rector of St. Antholin's,

---

¹ Owen, *Memoir of Jones of Creaton*, pp. 53, 58 f.   ² *Journal*, ii, p. 305
³ *Countess of Huntingdon*, i, p. 197   ⁴ Seward, *Journal*, p. 45
⁵ *Journal*, iii, pp. 166–69   ⁶ *Op. cit.*, v, 316

says that they would obtain permission for some acceptable clergyman to preach in a church, and then Whitefield or some other would take his place.[1] In February, 1739, Whitefield intruded into the pulpit of St. Margaret's, Westminster, in spite of the efforts of the rector and churchwardens to prevent him; whilst it is said that even Charles Wesley, after having been refused permission to preach in a church in Bloomsbury, suddenly rushed into the pulpit at the conclusion of the prayers.[2] Whitefield was also accused of obtaining permission to preach for his work in Georgia, and having got into the pulpit, of using the opportunity to proclaim his peculiar ideas.

Moreover, it is very necessary for us to remember that when they first began to preach Wesley and Whitefield were not the well-known characters which later they became, and that all kinds of fantastic rumours were current about them and others who sympathized with them. Even Hervey when he was in Devonshire wrote to Kinchin on April 17, 1739, that he had heard that the latter was about "to throw off his gown, renounce the Church of England, relinquish his fellowship and living, and become an itinerant preacher". There were also at the time many wandering fanatics, some of them really insane, who went about propagating opinions that were subversive of society and morals. We must not therefore be surprised that incumbents should be suspicious and cautious when an unknown clergyman suddenly asked for permission to use their pulpits.

When the Methodists established their own preaching houses, even if their services did not clash with those of the Church, men and women were drawn away to hear them. The fervid utterances of the preachers were much more exciting and attractive than the dull sermons of the average parish priest. The doctrines of the Methodists were also more calculated to stir the emotions, and even their insistence on "conversion" found favour. Thus, the position of the parish priest was made difficult; for, if he denounced the Methodists he helped to advertise them; and, if he carried on along the traditional lines of a sober and dignified piety he proved unattractive. An Evangelical clergyman could, of course, preach to his people on similar lines and so hold their attention and interest; but others were unwilling to follow such a course. Crabbe says of one such:

[1] *Venn Family Annals*, p. 51

[2] *Weekly Miscellany* for February 10, 1739. Tyerman, *Life of Wesley*, i, p. 226, neither rejects nor accepts these accounts

He either did not, or he would not see,
That if he meant a favourite priest to be,
He must not show, but learn of them, the way
To truth—he must not dictate, but obey;
They wished him not to bring them further light,
But to convince them that they now were right.[1]

Some of the clergy objected to the Methodists on the ground that they were adding to their work by increasing the number of communicants! On October 13, 1739, Charles Wesley received such a complaint from a Bristol incumbent who said: "There were a hundred of new communicants last Sunday; and I am credibly informed, some of them came out of spite to me." He refused Charles's offer to help in the administration. The latter commented: "We bless God for this cause of offence, and pray it may continue."[2]

The itinerating lay preacher was in a different category, for he made no claim to occupy a pulpit. None the less, he could be equally objectionable. The clergy were not accustomed to having their parishes invaded by loud-voiced and vociferous orators, and resented their presence just as their predecessors in the Middle Ages had resented the equally unwelcome intrusion of the wandering friars.

In the few parishes where there was an Evangelical incumbent conditions were not always happy, for they were by no means exempt from such invasions, a circumstance which led to disagreement between Evangelicals and Methodists and to no little tension. The same was true where a Methodist Society was established in an Evangelical parish. Walker of Truro suggested to Wesley in 1757 that in such cases it should be handed over to the clergyman. Wesley replied with a variety of objections to such a course, declaring that not every one who preached the truth had wisdom and experience to guide and govern the flock, and that in any case he had neither the right nor the power to compel any society to give up its independence.[3]

A notorious clash between an Evangelical vicar and a society in his parish took place at Huddersfield in the days of Henry Venn. The latter wished the society, which had been started before his arrival, to be placed under his control. The members,

[1] *The Tales of the Hall*, Bk. iii   [2] *Journal*, i, p. 189
[3] *Letters*, iii, pp. 221 ff.

however, insisted on having their own preachers. This was not, as Wesley reported, "in opposition to Mr. Venn (whom they love, esteem, and constantly attend), but to supply what they do not find in his preaching. It is a tender point. Where there is a gospel ministry already we do not desire to preach; but whether we can leave off preaching because such an one comes in after, is another question; especially, when those, awakened and convinced by us, beg and require the continuance of our assistance".[1]

Wesley met Venn at Bradford in July, 1761, and in the following month a compromise was reached by which the visit of the preachers should be limited to one a month. Later Wesley agreed to withdraw them for a year; but this did not meet with local approval, and in 1765 they again appeared, though without Wesley's permission. Venn's curate went from house to house warning the people not to attend their meetings, but without effect.[2]

The matter became sufficiently urgent for it to be discussed at the Conference of August, 1764, when the twelve clergymen present asked that Methodist preachers should be withdrawn from every parish where there was an Evangelical incumbent. Charles Wesley openly said that if he had a parish he would not allow Methodist preachers to enter it. This brought the reply from one of them that he would do so with or without permission if he felt called to it. The withdrawal of the preachers was really impossible, and the disagreement continued. As late as 1790 the Rev. Robert Storry of St. Peter's, Colchester, was accused not only of insisting that the societies in his parish should be handed over to him, but of offering gifts and bribes to attract their members. Thus he was guilty of stealing "both sheep and lambs from his neighbour's fold".[3]

The Methodists had much on their side; for, as Wesley said, not all awakened ministers were truly effective, and the handing over of a society would greatly hamper the freedom of those who were already running it. The great argument, however, was the lack of any guarantee of continuity of Evangelical teaching in a particular parish. If the societies were handed over, a new incumbent might utterly disapprove of the views for which the Methodists stood, as happened in the case

---

[1] *Op. cit.*, iv, p. 160   [2] *Op. cit.*, iv, pp. 214 ff.

[3] Occasionally an Evangelical clergyman took a different line. Joseph Easterbrook, at the Temple Church, Bristol, for example, made a rule of attaching his converts to Methodist classes .

THE GROWTH OF OPPOSITION

of Huddersfield after Venn's departure, and in not a few other places.

Although the Dissenters were to owe a new stage of life and influence to the revival, in the early days of the movement they were often found opposing it. Rather strangely, the main animus was directed not against the Wesleys, who were highly critical of Dissent, but against Whitefield, whose attitude was much more friendly. Doddridge was especially critical of Whitefield, and considered that his utterances and conduct came little short of "an assumption of inspiration and infallibility". At the same time he recognized the sincerity of the Methodists, and hoped that "some may be reformed, instructed, and made serious by their means".[1] Later he became intimate with Whitefield, thereby exposing himself to criticism from other Dissenters, and he himself was not exactly proud of the connexion.[2] Wesley paid a visit to Doddridge on September 9, 1745,[3] and later asked for his advice as to books suitable for Methodist preachers.[4]

One reason for the opposition of the Dissenters, as with the clergy, was the fear of losing their congregations. The ministers took very drastic steps to overcome this, and in some cases at least excluded from Holy Communion all who even went to hear Methodist preachers.[5] This threat was often successful, for Wesley found on March 12, 1743, that one society alone had lost fourteen members because of it.[6] Denunciations, as in the case of the clergy, were usually futile, or even helped the cause they condemned. A certain Dr. Clegg at Chinley was very active in such measures, with the result that some of his congregation felt that they must find out for themselves what Methodism really was, and ended by joining it.[7]

Opposition from the mob does not greatly concern us, as few Evangelicals had to encounter it.[8] But the Methodists, and, above all, the lay preachers, suffered grievously. Mobs are always glad of an excuse for a riot, particularly if countenanced by authority. And authority had no keen desire to protect the Methodists, especially in the country districts where the clergy and magistrates might even provoke attacks upon them. In the towns the necessity of preserving public order, rather than

---

[1] *Correspondence*, iii, p. 381 [2] *Countess of Huntingdon*, i, pp. 137, 139, 200
[3] *Journal*, ii, p. 206   [4] Tyerman, *Wesley*, i, p. 516
[5] Wesley, *Journal*, iii, pp. 73 f.   [6] *Op. cit.*, iii, p. 70
[7] *Countess of Huntingdon*, i, p. 44
[8] They were, however, not entirely exempt (cf. Fletcher)

a desire to save the Methodists from brutal attacks, made the magistrates more strict. In London, Sir John Gunson, the chairman of the Middlesex bench, protected Wesley and checked further outrages.[1] In Manchester, the courage and activity of a single constable brought about a cessation of violence.[2] At Sheffield, the mob burnt down the meeting-house in 1742, and on the matter coming into court were ordered by the magistrates to rebuild it.[3]

One device for harrying the Methodists was to have them seized by press gangs for service in the army or navy. Tenants too might be turned out of their houses or farms for adopting the unpopular religion. At Hawnby near Richmond in Yorkshire over forty thus suffered. They thereupon built small houses for themselves on the outskirts of the town and formed a settlement.[4]

Persecution was met by fortitude, and even humour. Wesley speaks of a mob at Plymouth Dock (Devonport) "fighting valiantly with the door and windows".[5] Sometimes the avenging hand of Providence was seen in the misfortunes which came upon persecutors. On one occasion a gang of young men hired a boat at Richmond intending to waylay Rowland Hill and duck him in the river. The boat met with an accident, and all were drowned.[6]

In literary and artistic circles the Methodists, and even the Evangelicals, were often held up to ridicule. Smollett seems to have been especially hostile, for, having sneered at them in *Humphrey Clinker*, in his *Continuation of Hume* he dismissed the whole movement with a scathing reference: "Many thousands in the lower ranks of life were infected with this enthusiasm by the unwearied exertions of a few obscure preachers, such as Whitefield and the two Wesleys."[7] Hume himself had written to Gibbon in 1776: "among many marks of decline, the prevalence of superstition in England prognosticates the fall of philosophy and the decay of taste".[8]

Some of the clergy made use of literature to aim sarcasms at the Methodists. The best known of such attempts was *The Spiritual Quixote: or, the Summer's Ramble of Mr. Geoffrey*

---

[1] *Journal*, ii, p. 425; and Charles Wesley, *Journal*, May 31, 1740
[2] Wesley, *Journal*, iv, p. 185; cf. p. 310   [3] *Op. cit.*, iv, p. 18
[4] *Op. cit.*, iv, p. 223   [5] *Op. cit.*, iii, p. 304
[6] Sidney, *Life of Rowland Hill*, p. 98   [7] *Op. cit.*, v, p. 375
[8] Gibbon, *Memoir*, p. 197

Wildgoose. A Comic Romance[1] by Graves rector of Claverton, near Bath, who had held a fellowship at All Souls. He had been a contemporary of George Whitefield at Pembroke, and there can be but little doubt that the reference is to the latter. Apart from anything else, the identity of the initials seems to be conclusive.[2]

For artists, the Methodists did not provide so ready a target, and for the most part they ignored them. It is, however, surprising that Hogarth, in view of the strong moral purpose which inspired his art, should have been an exception. He was apparently bitterly opposed to the Methodists, whom he "exposed" in his cartoon, "Credulity, Superstition, and Fanaticism".

The stage also took a hand in attacks, some of them highly scurrilous, on the Methodist leaders. In 1743 a farce called *Trick upon Trick, or Methodism Displayed* appeared. When the Edinburgh Company of Comedians attempted to produce it at Newcastle so great was the audience that the floor began to sink, and even the stage. A panic followed, and the performance had to be abandoned. But it was produced a week later.[3] Samuel Foote's *The Minor*, in which Whitefield was caricatured as Dr. Squintem, ran at the Haymarket for ten years.

As in the case of denunciations from the pulpit, all these onslaughts probably helped the movement in the long run, for they must have aroused popular curiosity and stimulated a desire to find out whether Methodism was as bad or as foolish as it had been represented to be.

[1] It was originally published in 1773, but a new edition with a preface by Charles Whibley appeared in 1926

[2] Tyerman, *Wesley*, iii, p. 339, says that it was aimed at Sir Harry Trelawney, the eccentric Cornishman who, after various experiments in "hot-gospelling", ended up as a Roman Catholic

[3] Wesley, *Journal*, iii, p. 111

CHAPTER II

THE CALVINIST CONTROVERSY

To enter into the Calvinist controversy[1] in minute detail is outside the scope of our inquiry; it belongs to the domestic history of Methodism. None the less, it requires notice at some length, since a number of Evangelicals were drawn into the contest. It is also important to remember that the great majority of Evangelicals were definitely on the Calvinist side; a circumstance which stood in the way of that co-operation with Wesley which he so strongly desired. But Calvinism as understood by the majority of Evangelicals was of a very moderate type. Hervey, in spite of his controversy with Wesley, "never taught or held, the doctrine of unconditional election and reprobation".[2] So too Venn wrote on July 8, 1775: "Though the doctrines of Grace are clear to me, I am still no friend to High Calvinism. . . . Predestination cancels the necessity of any change, and dispenses at once with all duty." Thomas Scott held firmly to the belief that love and good works are the evidence of genuine religion, and equated faith with "fruitfulness".[3] The wisest of the Evangelicals deprecated any attempt to define doctrines which the Bible had left vague, and in the New Testament, as Cecil insisted, "justification by the imputed righteousness of Christ is declared, not explained. Let us not, therefore, darken a subject which is held forth in a prominent light by our idle endeavours to make it better understood".[4] Dean Milner, who abandoned Arminianism in 1780, could yet say: "Calvin is much too systematical for me: though, perhaps, the hardest things he says may have some foundation; but I am sure it is not the system of Scripture to speak as he speaks in many instances."[5]

By thus holding Calvinism in a moderate form, the Evangelicals avoided that emphasis on the separation "between the temper and purposes of the Father and the Son" which, especially in America, where Calvinism was generally held in an

[1] See, further, Tyerman, *Wesley's Designated Successor: the Life, etc., of the Rev. J. W. Fletcher*; *Countess of Huntingdon*, ii, pp. 232 ff.; and Abbey and Overton, ii, pp. 144–66

[2] Tyerman, *Oxford Methodists*, p. 305

[3] *The Growth of Grace* (*Works*, i, pp. 251 ff.)

[4] Quoted Abbey and Overton, ii, p. 208   [5] *Life*, p. 660

THE CALVINIST CONTROVERSY 197

undiluted form, "produced repulsion against the idea of such a divided Godhead".[1]

Although the controversy is associated with the name of Calvin, not many of those who engaged in it had any adequate knowledge of his system; Toplady, on the one side, and Fletcher, on the other, being notable exceptions. The former had acquired his knowledge by intense study; the latter had been brought up as a Calvinist in Switzerland. Up to August, 1740, at least, Whitefield was completely ignorant of Calvinism as such; he had "derived his doctrines from Christ and His apostles and had never read a line of Calvin".[2] The same was true of the laymen who took a prominent, if restricted, part in the dispute. Thomas Scott, a Calvinist himself, was amazed and disgusted when he discovered that they knew practically nothing of his teaching and were incapable either of explaining or defending it.[3] The controversy, in short, was of the kind described by Hooker, "wherein they that are most fervent to dispute be not always the most able to determine".[4]

The Methodist Movement from its inception had been accompanied by numerous and bitter disputes, as even a slight perusal of the *Journals* of Wesley makes clear. Some were occasioned by the Moravians and their quietist doctrines, but others by questions of predestination and election. And so it continued, as ignorant and zealous men insisted on the truth of their own ideas and denied the right of others to differ from them. Romaine wrote in March, 1763, of conditions in London: "We have precious souls, but we really want LOVE. The *Foundry*, the *Tabernacle*, the *Lock*, the *Meeting*, yea, *St. Dunstan's*, has each its party, and brotherly love is almost lost in our disputes. Thank God, I am out of them. I wish them all well, and love them all; and where we differ, there is exercise for my charity." It would have been well for Methodism, as also for Evangelicalism, if this spirit had prevailed more widely. Wesley himself was, on the whole, conciliatory, though he had spoken of driving John Calvin out of Bristol,[5] and he and Charles agreed so far as possible not to preach on the disputed doctrines. He even made concessions, which later he felt to have been wrong, for he had "leaned too much to Calvinism".

Wesley was anxious to avoid controversy among brethren, knowing that it could only lead to weakness and the dissipation

---
[1] F. D. Maurice, *The Kingdom of Christ*, i, p. 4   [2] *Letters*, i, p. 205
[3] *Life*, p. 235   [4] *Ecclesiastical Polity*, Bk. IV, chap. xiv, § 6
[5] Whitefield, *Letters*, i, p. 205

of energy. When he tried to unite the "awakened" clergy under his leadership he mentioned as fundamental doctrines—original sin, and justification by faith, producing inward and outward holiness—but deliberately omitted questions in dispute, such as the predestination of the Calvinists and the Christian perfection of his own followers. His anxiety to avoid disputing can also be seen in his relations with Whitefield. At first these had been decidedly strained. In January, 1741, the Bristol Calvinists had begged Whitefield to go there, as the Wesleys were preaching against predestination; and, in the following March, Wesley and Whitefield had an interview which ended by the latter saying that they preached different gospels. He also announced his intention no longer to refrain from preaching against Wesley, and confessed that his promise not to do so had been due to human weakness. Whitefield was far inferior to Wesley in mental ability and learning, and although he was firmly convinced of the truth of the doctrines which he preached, may have felt that he had been overmatched in argument. After a time, the Christian spirit of both men, and the mediating efforts of Charles Wesley, lessened the acrimony between them, and no lasting estrangement ensued. A witty writer has summed up the correspondence between them as follows:

> Dear George,—I have read what you have written on the subject of predestination, and God has taught me that you are wrong, and that I am right. Yours affectionately, J. Wesley. And the reply: Dear John, —I have read what you have written on the subject of predestination, and God has taught me that I am right and you are wrong. Yours affectionately, G. Whitefield.[1]

For a time the disputes sank into the background, though Wesley's pamphlets, *Serious Thoughts upon the Perseverance of the Saints*, and *Predestination Considered*, published in 1751 and 1752, aroused the opposition of Hervey.

Wesley's failure to organize the Evangelical clergy under his leadership seems to have made him desirous of drawing nearer to Whitefield and his patroness, Lady Huntingdon. There was certainly closer co-operation after 1766, and in September of that year Lady Huntingdon wrote: "I do trust that this union,

[1] Quoted Abbey and Overton, ii, pp. 149 f.

which is commenced, will be for the furtherance of our faith, and mutual love to each other."¹

Those who opposed Calvinism did so mainly on two grounds. In the first place, Calvinism, strictly interpreted, took away all urgency from the proclamation of the Gospel, for if certain souls were elect they would in any case be saved. Here it may be said that, in practice, the Calvinist Methodists were quite inconsistent; Whitefield, although he held the doctrine of election, offered "Jesus freely to every individual soul".² The other ground of objection was that Calvinism might easily lead to antinomianism. This was no mere debating point which those who opposed Calvinism were in the habit of making in their disputes.³ It was a real danger manifested in a number of instances. That weaker souls, convinced that they were "saved eternally", should relax their efforts to lead a holy life and even to suspect such efforts as having the nature of "works" was not unnatural. Some unfortunately went even further and fell into actual and notorious sins. This was the chief ground of Wesley's own opposition. He wrote to a friend on May 14, 1765, that he and his brother had for thirty years opposed predestination with all their might: "not as an opinion, but as a dangerous mistake, which appears to be subversive of the very foundation of Christian experience, and which has in fact given occasion to the most grievous offences".⁴ Wesley had come across an extreme case in Birmingham as early as March 23, 1746;⁵ but what must most deeply have aroused the antagonism of him and his brother was the career of Westley Hall, who married their sister Martha.

Hall was a man of prepossessing manners and a very fervent preacher, but fundamentally fickle and weak in character. Repudiating the moral law, he seduced a domestic in his house at Salisbury, and finally fled to the West Indies with one of his mistresses. After a time he returned in great distress and professing penitence was received back by his long-suffering wife. He died at Bristol on January 3, 1776, and Wesley took a charitable view of his end.⁶ A further cause of alarm was Madan's advocacy of polygamy.

It was never suggested that the leaders of the Calvinist

---

¹ Letter in *Methodist Magazine*, 1797, p. 304
² *Letters*, i, p. 331 (October 10, 1741)
³ Fletcher entitled several of his writings *Checks to Antinomianism*
⁴ *Journal*, v, p. 116   ⁵ *Op. cit.*, iii, pp. 237 f.
⁶ See Southey, *Life of Wesley*, ii, pp. 4 ff.

Methodists and the Evangelicals, who mostly agreed with them, had a lower standard of holiness of life, yet their teaching, in the case of unstable hearers, might lead to dangerous consequences. Newton once admitted that even the saintly Romaine had made many Antinomians.[1]

Although the controversy seemed to have lapsed, Wesley never lost his disquietude, and on March 20, 1768, he wrote to Fletcher:

> Do they gather [any real holiness] from that *amorous* way of praying to Christ, or that luscious way of preaching His righteousness? I never found it so. On the contrary, I have found that even the precious doctrine of Salvation by Faith has need to be guarded with the utmost care, or those who hear it will slight both inward and outward holiness.[2]

The matter was so much on his mind that he laid a number of propositions dealing with it before the Conference held in London on August 7, 1770. After referring to resolutions adopted in 1744, he goes over the whole of the questions in dispute and exposes the dangers inherent in Calvinism and in teaching of a similar nature.[3] This was the beginning of the real controversy, for it aroused an immense volume of protest from the Calvinist camp. Lady Huntingdon described the propositions as "popery unmasked", and denounced all who did not at once disown them. She seems to have thought that Charles Wesley was not in full sympathy with his brother, and tried to detach him: "as an honest man I pity you, as you must suffer equal disgrace and universal distrust from the supposed union with him." Charles did not even deign to reply, and endorsed the letter, "Lady Huntingdon's last: unanswered by John Wesley's brother."[4] She also insisted that all those connected with her college at Trevecca should disavow the propositions, and in consequence lost the services of Benson, and, more grievous still, the assistance of Fletcher.

Calvinists in general felt that the propositions struck a serious blow "at the fundamental truths of the Gospel", and in view of Wesley's wide influence did all they could to counteract the effect which they might have. The Rev. Walter Shirley, Lady

---

[1] *Life of Wilberforce*, ii, p. 137   [2] *Letters*, v, p. 83
[3] Printed by Tyerman, *Wesley*, iii, pp. 70 ff.
[4] Jackson, *Life of Charles Wesley*, ii, p. 256

Huntingdon's kinsman, was especially prominent in the opposition, and stated publicly that he "deemed peace in such a case a shameful indolence, and silence no less than treachery".

After the death of Whitefield in November, 1770, Wesley preached a memorial sermon in which he sought to make peace between the warring sections of the movement; but it was in vain, for in the following January he was made the object of a violent attack in *The Gospel Magazine*, a leading Calvinist organ, of which Romaine was the editor. To this he in turn replied.[1]

Fletcher's defence of Wesley seems to have made a deep impression on Lady Huntingdon, and checked her impulsive measures. She wrote to Wesley early in 1771 asking for fuller explanations of the propositions. But Wesley felt that the time was not yet come for such approaches, and that further explanations might only give her additional cause for condemning him. So he made no reply. After receiving a second letter, however, he determined to defend himself, and the minutes of the Conference, and so wrote a long letter on June 19, 1771.[2] Amongst other things he pointed out that there was no new development in his teaching, and referred to his sermon on "Salvation by Faith", published in 1738. The closing passage of his letter is a noble plea for understanding and tolerance:

> Such as I am I love you well. You have one of the first places in my esteem and affection; and you once had some regard for me. But it cannot continue if it depends on my seeing with your eyes, or my being in no mistake. . . . My dear friend, you seem not well to have learned yet the meaning of those words, which I desire to have continually written upon my heart, "Whosoever doeth the will of my Father which is in heaven, the same is my brother and sister and mother."

The next step determined upon by the Calvinists was to attend the Conference to be held at Bristol in the following August and to compel the Methodists "to revoke their heresies; or to sign a formal protest against them".[3] Little support, however, was forthcoming for the protest, and even the trustees of Whitefield's chapels in London refused to take part in the proposed agitation.

---

[1] *Letters*, v, pp. 223 ff.   [2] *Letters*, v, pp. 259 f.
[3] *Countess of Huntingdon*, ii, p. 239

When the Conference met, some dozen representatives of Lady Huntingdon were admitted, and a letter from her was allowed to be read.[1] The discussion was marked by an unexpectedly conciliatory spirit. Wesley then drew up a declaration which met, in part at least, some of the objections of the Calvinists, and they on their side admitted that they had been a little hasty in their condemnation of the propositions. The declaration ran as follows:

> Whereas the doctrinal points in the minutes of a conference held in London, August 7th, 1770, have been misunderstood to favour justification by works—Now, we, the Rev. John Wesley and others assembled in conference, do declare that we had no such meaning, and that we abhor the doctrine of justification by works as a most perilous and abominable doctrine. And as the said minutes are not sufficiently guarded in the way they are expressed, we hereby solemnly declare, in the sight of God, that we have no trust or confidence but in the alone merits of our Lord and Saviour, Jesus Christ, for justification or salvation, either in life, death, or the day of judgment, and though no one is a real Christian believer (and consequently cannot be saved) who doth not good works when there is time and opportunity, yet our works have no part in meriting or purchasing our justification, from first to last, either in whole or in part.

This seemed a reasonable compromise and explanation, and ought to have brought peace. But not all those who signed the declaration were in full agreement with it, and many of them were still angered at Lady Huntingdon's crude attacks. The consequence was that instead of bringing hostilities to an end, it gave the signal for six years of bitter and futile strife, during which many unwise and many unchristian utterances were brought to birth. The pulpits and the press rang with noisy defamations. In the meantime numerous attempts were made to reconcile the combatants, by John Thornton amongst others, and for a time the warfare slackened owing to the excitement over political events in America on which both Wesley and Fletcher wrote pamphlets.

Before the Conference of 1770 a literary squabble had already

[1] Wesley's reply is to be found in *Letters*, v, pp. 274 f.

arisen in connexion with the expulsion of the students from St. Edmund Hall in 1768, for one of their supposed offences had been the belief in predestination. In his pamphlet *Pietas Oxoniensis* Richard Hill had claimed that Calvinism was the true doctrine of the Church of England. This was denied by Dr. Nowell in his reply to Hill. Then Toplady stepped in with his *Church of England Vindicated from the Charge of Arminianism*, to which he added a translation of parts of Zanchius' *Doctrine of Absolute Predestination*. This provoked a reply on the Arminian side from Walter Sellon, who now came forward as Wesley's lieutenant. He and Fletcher would henceforth bear the chief brunt of the literary side of the conflict, as Wesley himself refrained, being engaged in more profitable activities.

After Lady Huntingdon's attack on the propositions of 1770 Fletcher wrote five letters in their defence, but, in view of the compromise, held them back. As the contest still continued, he published them under the title of *A Check to Antinomianism*. A reply was then made by Walter Shirley, on which Fletcher issued *A Second Check to Antinomianism*, following it up with a *Third* when in 1772 Richard Hill wrote five letters to him. Hill in his turn then wrote six more letters, and Fletcher once more replied with *Logica Genevensis; or A Fourth Check to Antinomianism*. Then Hill in 1773 delivered what he called *The Finishing Stroke*, and Berridge joined in with *The Christian World Unmasked*. But Hill's *Finishing Stroke*, in spite of its title, was no "knock-out" blow, and the contest pursued its unhappy way, reaching a new depth of bitterness when Toplady re-entered the arena with *More Work for John Wesley*, and, in 1775, *Historic Proof of the Calvinism of the Church of England*.[1]

The combatants were really going round in circles, and merely repeated well-worn arguments without bringing in anything fresh on the one side or the other. All they added were fresh terms of invective and satire which only served to increase their mutual hostility. The Calvinists were called "devil factors", "Satan's synagogue", "advocates for sin" and "Satan-sent preachers". They in return showed equal if not greater

[1] Bishop Ryle, *Christian Leaders*, p. 380, considered that this treatise was unanswerable. It is certainly true that a form of Calvinism had been held by most leading Anglicans before the days of Laud; but, as John Overton, *The True Churchman Ascertained*, pp. 93 f., pointed out, there are striking differences between the Articles and the teaching of Calvin. They "unquestionably built upon *the same foundations* ... but they have not carried the *superstructure to the same height*".

powers of invention,[1] and amongst other things made personal attacks on Wesley, who was referred to as "An old Fox tarred and feathered", and accused of "low, serpentine cunning" and "dirty subterfuges [which] sink a divine to the level of an oyster woman". Rowland Hill, whose pen had been as venomous as that of others, confessed afterwards that "a softer style and spirit would better have become me".

Even apart from the intemperate and vindictive feelings which it called forth, the Calvinist controversy was a most unfortunate affair; for not only were energies dissipated which might have been used for the furtherance of the Gospel, but rivalries led to actual interference with work already going on. Wesley's journals are full of complaints of Calvinist efforts to draw away his converts; efforts which had, indeed, long antedated the crisis of the conflict. On April 1, 1751, he wrote of Wednesbury: "What a work would have been done in all these parts, if it had not been for doubtful disputations! if the Predestinarians had not thrown back those who had begun to run well, partly into the world, partly to the Baptists, and partly into endless disputes concerning the secret counsels of God!"[2] On April 17, 1764, he exclaims: "O that our brethren were as zealous to make *Christians* as they are to make *Calvinists*."[3] Things were made even worse by the open warfare which the controversy aroused. On November 1, 1773, Wesley records of Lynn: "Here was once a prospect of doing much good, but it was almost vanished away. Calvinism, breaking in upon them, had torn the infant society to pieces."[4] As late as March 28, 1782, the same thing was still going on. "Coming to Congleton, I found the Calvinists were just breaking in, and striving to make havoc of the flock. Is this brotherly love? Is this doing as we would be done to? No more than robbing on the highway. But if it is *decreed* they cannot help it; so we cannot blame them."[5]

The controversy made no addition to theological knowledge, and left the matters in dispute exactly where they were before it arose. But very real harm was done by each side pressing its doctrines, in the face of attacks upon them, to doubtful extremes. Seymour said that "real Antinomians became the pest

---

[1] Seymour admits that "The Calvinists were the more guilty; for Mr. Toplady bore away the palm for contempt and bitterness" (*Countess of Huntingdon*, ii, p. 249).

[2] *Journal*, iii, p. 519   [3] *Op. cit.*, v, p. 59
[4] *Op. cit.*, vi, p. 5   [5] *Op. cit.*, vi, pp. 345 f.

of many churches", while some Arminians "almost rushed into the arms of a mystical deism".[1] This was true also on the intellectual side; for there was an insistence on a too narrow orthodoxy and an application and expansion of the Scriptures which was unjustified. Bishop Ryle, in spite of his own Calvinism, said of Toplady: "his statements are often extreme, and . . . he is frequently more systematic and narrow than the Bible. He often seems . . . to go further than Scripture, and to draw conclusions which Scripture has not drawn, and to settle points which for some wise reason Scripture has not settled."[2]

Of the Evangelicals who took part in the controversy, Toplady alone showed a lack of Christian spirit. The rest were much more moderate, and Fletcher, it need hardly be said, never forgot what was seemly to his profession, keenly though he might press home his arguments. Most of the leaders stood aside, at least for a time, if not entirely. Soon after the Bristol Conference of 1771 Berridge wrote to Rowland Hill: "The late contest at Bristol seems to turn upon this hinge, whether it shall be *Pope John* or *Pope Joan*. My dear friend, keep out of all controversy, and wage no war but with the devil."[3] His advice, however, was not taken, and Berridge himself took a minor part with his *Christian World Unmasked*.[4] Romaine, though perhaps more of a Calvinist than the rest, took no open part in the dispute. Henry Venn deprecated the whole matter, and especially the attempt to apply tests. When he was once asked whether a certain young clergyman was a Calvinist or an Arminian, he replied: "I really do not know; he is a sincere disciple of the Lord Jesus Christ, and that is of infinitely more importance." Newton also abstained, and wrote: "I cannot, I must not, I dare not contend; only as a witness for God. I am ready to bear my simple testimony to what I have known of His truth, whenever I am properly called to it."[5]

One reason why the bulk of the Evangelical leaders preferred to stand aside was perhaps the moderate form in which their Calvinism consisted. It was Toplady, the extremist, who rushed into the conflict. This prevented disputes among their own congregations, though there were those who objected to even the slightest tinge. Henry Jowett, the great-grandfather of

---

[1] *Countess of Huntingdon*, ii, p. 250   [2] *Christian Leaders*, p. 379
[3] Sidney, *Life of Rowland Hill*, p. 430
[4] Berridge later regretted certain passages "in an unpleasant manner", and these were omitted in the edition which appeared after his death
[5] *Cardiphonia*, p. 231

Benjamin, preferred to attend the Wesleyan chapel, rather than listen to his Calvinist vicar.[1]

Among Evangelicals themselves the disputes over Calvinistic doctrines produced no controversy, and did not interfere with co-operation even with Arminians. Thus a note of toleration and of hope was sounded. It came out strongly in the interview on October 30, 1787, between Wesley and Charles Simeon; the one nearing the end of his long life of great achievements; the other, with a long life, also of great achievements, still before him. The following record of the conversation between them has been preserved.[2]

> "Sir," said Simeon, "I understand you are called an Arminian; now I am sometimes called a Calvinist, and therefore, I suppose, we are to draw daggers. But, before I begin to combat, with your permission, I will ask you a few questions, not from impertinent curiosity, but for real instruction. Pray, sir, do you feel yourself a depraved creature, so depraved that you would never have thought of turning to God, if God had not put it into your heart?"
>
> "Yes," said Wesley, "I do indeed."
>
> "And do you utterly despair of recommending yourself to God by anything that you can do; and look for salvation solely through the blood and righteousness of Christ?"
>
> "Yes, solely through Christ."
>
> "But, sir, supposing you were *first* saved by Christ, are you not somehow or other to save yourself afterwards, by your good works?"
>
> "No; I must be saved by Christ, from first to last."
>
> "Allowing, then, that you were first turned by the grace of God, are you not in some way or other to keep yourself by your own power?"
>
> "No."
>
> "What, then, are you to be upheld every hour and moment by God, as much as an infant in its mother's arms?"
>
> "Yes, altogether."
>
> "And is all your hope in the grace and mercy of God, to preserve you unto His heavenly kingdom?"
>
> "Yes, I have no hope but in Him."

[1] Abbott and Campbell, *Life of Benjamin Jowett*, i, p. 3
[2] See Carus, *Memoirs of Simeon*, pp. 182 f.

"Then, sir, with your leave, I will put up my dagger again: for this is all my Calvinism; this is my election, my justification, my final perseverence. It is in substance all that I hold, and as I hold it; and therefore, if you please, instead of searching out terms and phrases to be the ground of contention between us, we will cordially unite in those things wherein we agree."

The interview took place at Hinxworth in Hertfordshire, and in noting it Wesley described Simeon as one "who breathed the very spirit of Mr. Fletcher".[1] Had all Calvinists and Methodists been able to discuss their differences as did these two saints of God the revival movement would have been spared much unnecessary tension, and a serious setback to the cause of Christ in this land would have been avoided. In fact one might even venture to say, that, in spite of fundamental differences, there would have been no Calvinist controversy at all.

[1] *Journal*, vii, p. 738

CHAPTER 12

THE SEPARATIONS

THE Calvinist Controversy made a deep rift in the ranks of those who supported the revival, and even Evangelicals were divided. A more permanent and more serious breach was soon to follow when the adherents of Lady Huntingdon, and then those of Wesley, separated themselves from the Church.

These separations, though in the end they came about almost suddenly, had long been maturing, for as the movement developed certain differences gradually became manifest. All parties alike had set before them the task of quickening and revivifying the Church and in this they had quite notable success; but the Methodists set up, alongside the Church, not by way of rivalry but of supplement, what was in effect a new organization. This organization was not the outcome of any premeditated design, but, as in the Primitive Church, the gradual response to the challenge of novel conditions and the disclosure of fresh needs. Quite apart from this, however, there had been from the initiation of the revival certain features which distinguished the Evangelicals from the Methodists. These may be considered under five heads: (*a*) the Evangelical Movement was more clerical; (*b*) it was stricter in its Churchmanship; (*c*) it disliked certain Methodist practices; (*d*) it appealed to the middle classes rather than the poor; and, finally, (*e*) it held different views on a number of questions.

(*a*) THE CLERICALISM OF THE EVANGELICAL MOVEMENT

As it progressed, Methodism became more and more a lay movement using lay preachers as its chief agents. The main reason why it followed this course was the failure of even the "awakened" clergy to co-operate. Had Wesley been able to enlist them under his banner the whole future of Methodism and of religion in England might have been very different; for at his death the movement was left in the control of the lay preachers, who had not the same anxiety to keep up the link with the Church—and who were, moreover, jealous of the clergy.

In the early days of the movement Wesley had the close support of a number of the clergy, such as Grimshaw and

Berridge, and later of Fletcher; but this did not continue when it became evident that Methodism was adopting measures which suggested that it was not entirely at one with the Church. Thereafter those of the clergy who co-operated or definitely helped Wesley were but small fry and few in number; men like B. B. Collins and Peard Dickenson cannot have carried much weight either within Methodism or outside it.

Wesley from the first had made it a definite policy to get into touch with any of the clergy who were reported to be "awakened", and in general his approaches were well received. In some cases the first step was taken by the clergymen themselves. Henry Venn, for example, wrote to Wesley in 1754, thanking him for his writings and the inspiration of his example, though not concealing certain differences from him. Wesley's friendship with Fletcher arose in a similar manner, for the latter had consulted him in a letter of November 24, 1756, as to whether he ought to take orders. This Wesley had strongly advised, and when Fletcher was ordained he went the same evening to help Wesley at West Street chapel. This was the almost casual beginning of an amazingly fruitful co-operation and friendship. To Wesley the sudden offer of help "from the mountains of Switzerland" was a sign of providential guiding.

But Wesley desired something more than merely friendly contacts between those who were like-minded. He had an urge to organize everything. It was this "urge" which, humanly speaking, accounts for the success of Methodism. So now he wished to forge some outward bond. The matter was discussed with various people, and in a letter to Samuel Furly on May 21, 1762, he expressed his anxiety that none "who preach the essential gospel truths should stand aloof from one another".[1] Then in April, 1764, he sent out a circular (composed two years earlier) to some fifty of the clergy suggesting a definite association.[2] The response filled him with disappointment, and even indignation, for only three made any reply, though doubtless others had already expressed their opinion by word of mouth. Further efforts met with similar lack of success, and at the Conference of 1769 Wesley expressed his chagrin in a paper which included a phrase which was to become almost proverbial. "So I give up. I can do no more. They are a rope of sand, and such they will continue." Wesley believed, as he told Venn on June 22, 1763, that the refusal to unite was deliberate; and complained that "when one and another sincere minister

[1] *Letters*, iv, p. 182   [2] Printed in *Journal*, v, pp. 60 ff.

of Christ has been inclined to come nearer me, others have diligently kept him off."[1] His complaint seems to have been justified. In September, 1761, he had written to Samuel Furly complaining that Henry Venn was trying to separate them.[2] In the letter to Venn just quoted, Wesley had given as reasons why efforts were being made to prevent union under his leadership, that the clergy "talked largely of my dogmaticalness, love of power, and irregularities". Here, no doubt, is the explanation of the aloofness of the Evangelical clergy. They had no desire to place themselves under any authority beyond that provided in the Church's system, and many of them were increasingly afraid of being linked in any way with those who were committing breaches of the Church's discipline.

Another factor which prevented more cordial relations with the Wesleyan branch of the movement was the predominance of Calvinist sympathies among Evangelicals. During the early years of the movement there is no doubt that their connexions were much closer with the followers of Lady Huntingdon. None the less, their abstention moved Fletcher, who evidently realized what it might involve, to express his opinion that it was "shameful that no clergyman should join John Wesley to keep in the Church the work which God had enabled him to carry on therein".

(b) THE STRICT CHURCHMANSHIP OF THE EVANGELICALS

Those of the clergy who adopted Evangelical views were for the most part intensely loyal to the Church; some from the first suspected Methodism and foresaw the subsequent separation. Even Grimshaw, who was guilty of many irregularities and even had a place in the Methodist organization, was a strict Churchman. Richardson of York probably spoke for many of them when he said of the Methodists: "I think of them as I do of other Protestants who differ from myself in opinion *with charity*. As far as I think their opinions agree with the Word of God and the doctrines of the Church of England I follow them, without regarding common prejudices."[3]

As strict Churchmen the Evangelical clergy were chary of any co-operation with Dissenters (here they were at one with Wesley), though some were not so strict as others. Newton worked with them when he was at Olney, though later, though he wished well to the efforts of Dissenting ministers, he felt that

---
[1] *Letters*, iv, p. 215   [2] *Op. cit.*, iv, p. 163
[3] Quoted Overton, *The Evangelical Revival*, p. 48

he could not act with them in public. "They called him a bigot, and he in return prayed that they might not be really such".[1] Berridge, too, encouraged Cambridge undergraduates to work with Robinson, the Baptist. But these were exceptions, and most Evangelicals were more strict in their attitude. On one occasion a nonconformist minister called on Romaine to protest against his attacks on Dissent. Romaine refused to have anything to do with him, and the unfortunate man then took his departure. Later on, it is well to learn, Romaine apologized to him for his rudeness, though at the same time he reaffirmed his attitude.[2] Leading Evangelical laymen took the same line. In 1789 Wilberforce wrote to a relative who was thinking of attending a meeting-house as she was getting little help from her parish priest: "Its individual benefits are no compensation for the general evils of dissent. The increase of dissenters, which always follows from the institution of unsteepled places of worship, is highly injurious to the interests of religion in the long run."[3] Wilberforce also opposed the relaxation of the laws against Dissenters, although some of his Yorkshire constituents were in favour of them.

The position of the Methodists, before separation definitely placed them in the category of Dissenters, was equivocal. By some they were already classed as such, though with uncertainty. In answer to the Bishop of Exeter's inquiries one Cornish incumbent said there were no Dissenters in his parish "unless they be called dissenters who go by the name of Methodist".[4]

(c) DISLIKE OF METHODIST PRACTICES

From the first, many of the Evangelical clergy had been suspicious of some of the devices adopted by the Methodists, not on the ground that they were innovations or necessarily objectionable in themselves, but because they were attended by possible dangers. This was true for example of prayer meetings. Walker took stringent measures to regulate them and to limit the part taken in them by laymen. At Olney, Thomas Scott found that they were apt to make people dissatisfied with the quieter and more dignified offices of the Church, and in some cases to draw them over to Dissent. He also noticed that those who were

---

[1] Cecil, *Memoirs of Newton*, pp. 68 f.
[2] Haweis, *Life of William Romaine*, pp. 129 f. In old age Romaine became less rigid, and when in Southampton attended the chapel of Mr. Kingsbury (p. 133)
[3] *Life*, i, p. 248   [4] Davies, *Early Cornish Evangelicals*, p. 26

most prominent in prayer were by no means the most consistent in their lives.[1] When the clergy themselves took part in them they must often have been annoyed by "the endless and senseless effusions of undigested prayers" such as Hooker had condemned in the Puritans.[2]

Prayer meetings were naturally associated with lay preaching. This was an especial bugbear to the clergy. Many realized that if persisted in it would lead to disorders and eventual separation from the Church. Adam wrote to Walker that "lay preaching is a manifest irregularity, and would not be endured in any Christian society."[3] Their dislike was, of course, intensified when their parishes were invaded by such agents.

In the early days of the revival a number of Evangelicals had itinerated, and even Simeon "amidst the general ignorance and indifference that prevailed" took advantage of any opportunity that came his way to preach the Gospel,[4] but as the movement developed this ceased to be the case, and itinerancy came to be one of the great distinctions between Methodists and Evangelicals. To the former, it was the very breath of their spiritual lives, and Whitefield once wrote: "When thou seest me in danger of *nestling*—in pity—in tender pity—put a *thorn* in my nest to prevent me from it."[5]

There was a good deal to be said in favour of itinerating in days when there was little exchange of pulpits, for the clergy had to address the same congregation Sunday by Sunday, and the people seldom heard any other voice. Wesley made much of this in a letter to Walker in 1756:

> Be their talents ever so good, they will ere long grow dead themselves, and so will most of them that hear them. I know, were I myself to preach one whole year in one place, I should preach both myself and most of my congregation asleep. . . . No one whom I yet know has all the talents for beginning, continuing, and perfecting the work of grace in one whole congregation.[6]

There is a great deal of truth in this; but what aroused the resentment of the clergy was the practice of Wesley and others

---

[1] *Life*, pp. 502 ff.   [2] *Ecclesiastical Polity*, Bk. V, chap. xxv, § 5
[3] *Life of Walker*, p. 224
[4] He was a little ashamed of his irregularity in later life: see Carus, pp. 277 f.
[5] Philip, *Life of Whitefield*, p. 366   [6] *Letters*, ii, p. 195

of intruding into parishes against the wish of the incumbent. Wesley might claim that having been ordained as a fellow of a college he had a general commission,[1] but that did not excuse his preaching in other men's parishes against their wish.

Rather oddly, the practice had been condemned in advance by Samuel Wesley, the older brother of John and Charles, in a poem (written in 1736) which describes their father as:

> A parish priest, not of the pilgrim kind,
> But fixed and faithful to the post assigned;
> Through various scenes with equal vigour trod,
> True to his oath, his order, and his God.

Cowper, with full knowledge of the effects of itinerancy, and complete sympathy with the doctrines taught by those who undertook it, could condemn it utterly.

> Ye clergy, while your orbit is your place,
> Lights of the world, and stars of human race;
> But if, eccentric, ye forsake your sphere,
> Prodigies ominous, and view'd with fear;
> The comet's baneful influence is a dream;
> Your's real, and pernicious in th' extreme.

Some Evangelicals, without definitely disapproving of the practice, held it in low esteem. Newton once wrote to a clergyman:

> I wish well to irregulars and itinerants who love to preach the Gospel. I am content that they should labour that way, who have not the talents, not the fund to support the character of a parochial minister; but I think you are qualified for more important service. I wish there were more itinerant preachers. If a man has grace and zeal but little fund, let him go and diffuse the substance of a dozen sermons over as many counties.[2]

The great number of Evangelicals felt that their duty was to the congregation committed to their care, and they refused to neglect it in order to run about the country seeking to arouse

---

[1] *Works*, xiii, p. 470 [2] *Cardiphonia*, p. 359

others. This was the attitude of Fletcher, who, in spite of repeated urging by Wesley, "insisted upon wasting his sweetness on the desert air of Madeley". Fletcher's collier convert, James Glazebrook, whom he sent to Trevecca, after being used as an itinerant, deliberately sought orders, so as to be able to settle down in one place.

The avoidance of itinerating did not, of course, mean that Evangelicals never preached outside their own parishes. It was their constant habit, where circumstances allowed, to help one another in this manner, and they took every opportunity which came their way for delivering their message. But travel was difficult, and conscientious incumbents who had no curates did not like to leave their parishes to the casual attention of the average *locum* whom they might engage.

(*d*) APPEAL TO DIFFERENT CLASSES

The strict observance of the Church's system by the Evangelical clergy had, in the circumstances of the times, some disadvantages and limited the range of their operations. The ordinary parochial machinery and the conventions of the day tended to the neglect of the very poor. This was especially true of the growing population of the towns. The use of lay preachers by the Methodists was a means of approaching the lower orders of which the Church did not avail itself. These preachers were often drawn from this class themselves, and though their effusions, owing to their lack of education, might be repellent to many churchgoers, they were well suited to more homely folk, who were thus able better to understand them. The fact, too, that Methodist meetings were held in "rooms", and not in church, meant that they could be attended by those who possessed no "Sunday clothes". Thus it came about that Methodism spread mainly among the very poor, and to a lesser extent at first among the lower middle-classes, whilst Evangelicalism affected a slightly higher class of society.[1]

(*e*) DIFFERENCE OF OUTLOOK

Although the teaching and outlook of the Evangelicals had much in common with those of the Methodists, there were also a number of differences. The most obvious and important was, as we have seen, their attitude to Calvinism. The Evangelical

[1] This does not mean that none from the higher classes were drawn to Methodism; there were a number of exceptions, such as R. C. Brackenbury of Raithby Hall. See, further, L. F. Church, *The Early Methodist People*, p. viii, and *More about the Early Methodist People*, p. xii

clergy did not in general share in the "sheep-stealing" methods of the Calvinists; for the most part, they were on the defensive against Methodist intrusions, but those of them who acted as agents for Lady Huntingdon might occasionally be guilty of the practice. In 1767, Wesley complained bitterly of the activities of Joseph Townsend, rector of Pewsey, who had been preaching in Edinburgh, at the invitation of Lady Huntingdon. Although he had been on friendly terms with Wesley and the Methodists, on going there he declined to have anything to do with them and attacked their Arminian views.[1]

Another difference was over Christian perfection, which the Evangelicals regarded as unscriptural. Yet another was their attitude to what they regarded as the over-exaltation of the emotions by the Methodists. Walker accused them of thinking that believing was feeling, and elsewhere wrote "faith and feeling appear to me direct opposites, and feeling alone cannot be the witness of the Spirit".[2] The same charge was made by Henry Venn in 1763, who wrote: "It is much to be lamented that our Christian brethren the Methodists made the ground of their Assurance an inward feeling instead of the faithfulness of Jehovah, the sensation of a fluctuating heart instead of the unchangeable promises of God."[3]

There was one striking difference in general outlook which has often been overlooked. Wesley had a great regard for the Primitive Church (many of his supposed innovations were derived from it);[4] the Evangelicals, especially as the movement developed and gained an ethos of its own, looked to the Church of the Reformation and to the Puritan tradition which had then arisen. The Methodists, of course, valued the Puritans, but not, I think, to the same degree. Typical of the Evangelical attitude was the practice of Hervey, who constantly read their writings and commended them to others: "Be not ashamed of the name Puritan. The Puritans were the soundest preachers, and, I believe, the truest followers of Christ in their day." This strain of Puritan influence long persisted. Henry Martyn, for example, thought highly of Flavel's *Saint Indeed*, and in his journal for December 28, 1803, he wrote: "That blessed man

[1] *Letters*, v, pp. 57 f. The effects were still visible in 1770 (*Journal*, v, p. 366)

[2] *Life*, pp. 154, 214

[3] Quoted Cragg, *Grimshaw of Haworth*, p. 71, from an unpublished letter

[4] In 1777, during the octave of Easter, he administered the Lord's supper every morning "after the example of the Primitive Church" (*Journal*, vi, p. 142)

Baxter, in his 'Saint's Rest', was enabled to kindle a degree of devotion and love, as I have long been a stranger to."

It must not be forgotten, however, that admiration for the Puritans was limited to their devotional and practical life, though even as to the latter some Evangelicals were critical. The Puritans had attacked the Prayer Book, the bishops, and the ceremonies of the Church; the Evangelicals keenly appreciated them. The Puritans had also intervened in politics; this was far from the mind of both Evangelicals and Methodists, who were intensely loyal to the monarchy.

The first body of Methodists to break away from the Church were the followers of Lady Huntingdon. Her "connexion" had arisen in part from the unwillingness of Whitefield to organize a party of his own. Lady Huntingdon, after becoming his patroness, began to set up an organization similar to that already instituted by Wesley, founding societies, building chapels, and appointing ministers. At first, in order to avoid difficulties with the ecclesiastical authorities, Lady Huntingdon had made use of private chapels[1] attached to her own residences where her "chaplains" could minister without requiring any licence. Whitefield tried to get the Tottenham Court chapel placed under her wing; but it was obviously not a private chapel, and so had to be licensed as other chapels had already been. The licensing of this chapel was perhaps a sign that separation would eventually become inevitable, though in 1760 Shirley had written to Wesley:

> I have hitherto learnt to consider the Methodists, not as any sect, but as the purer part of the Church of England; but, if any of them grow so wantonly fond of division as to form a schism, I foresee that they will lose much of the gospel meekness, humility and love; and a party zeal will take place, instead of a zeal according to knowledge.[2]

As with the followers of Wesley, the separation when it came was not due to any definite policy or even intention, but was the result of outward circumstances. Both drifted into separation rather than steered for it; and both set a high value on being loyal to the Church, as came out during the Calvinist

---

[1] Such chapels were not to have doors opening on the street, so as to admit the general public: see Whitefield, *Letters*, iii, p. 82

[2] Printed in *The Methodist Magazine*, 1780, p. 334

Controversy when each accused the other of wishing to become a sect. Wesley, when laying the foundation-stone of the City Road chapel in 1777, vindicated his followers from the charge, and retorted that his own reason for separating from Whitefield was the too great friendship of the latter for Dissenters. He also denounced the college at Trevecca as a training place for Dissenting ministers. The Calvinists retorted in *The Gospel Magazine* that Lady Huntingdon had separated from Wesley because he was a schismatic: "Mr. Wesley's apostasy from the Church is a chief reason why her ladyship has justly discarded him; and her disavowal of him, of his Dissenting principles, and of his sectarian conduct, is the true reason why he has the insolence to spit his venom against one of the most respectable characters that ever existed." It adds that "Mr. Whitefield was *too much* a Churchman for Mr. Wesley's fanaticism to digest."

Whitefield certainly professed to be loyal to the Church, and told the Bishop of Bangor that he would never willingly leave it, and if he were driven out would still adhere to its teaching.[1] Lady Huntingdon also professed to be a loyal churchwoman, and believed in a ministry of the word and sacraments. Whitefield describes a conference at her house in October, 1750, when five of the clergy were present, and the sacrament was administered every morning and sermons were delivered every evening.

The occasion of the schism of Lady Huntingdon's followers was casual and regrettable. There was in Clerkenwell a large theatre, the Pantheon, surrounded by gardens known as Spa Fields, and here on Sundays entertainments were given. In order to stop the practice a number of religious men acquired the building, and it was opened as a chapel on July 5, 1777, with the Rev. H. Jones, chaplain of the Misericordia Hospital, and the Rev. William Taylor, fellow of Magdalene College, Cambridge, in charge. The vicar of St. James's, Clerkenwell, in whose parish the theatre was situated, then objected, and as a result the preachers were suspended and the chapel temporarily closed. Lady Huntingdon then stepped in, and with the help of Lord Dartmouth and John Thornton bought the place, which was reopened on March 28, 1779, when Dr. Haweis preached the sermon. She had hoped that it might be regarded as her private chapel; but the vicar again intervened, claiming to exercise supervision over the chapel and to receive all fees,

[1] *Works*, iii, p. 160

and on the matter being brought before the ecclesiastical authorities the case went in his favour.

Lady Huntingdon refused to allow her plans to be disturbed by this rebuff, and the chapel was registered as a Dissenting meeting-place. At the same time Wills and Taylor decided to secede from the Church so as to be free to minister there. A further step on the way to schism was the ordaining by Wills and Taylor of six students from Trevecca. In spite of this breach of the Church's discipline, Lady Huntingdon considered that the fault lay with the Church:

> I am to be cast out of the Church now, only for what I have been doing these forty years—speaking and living for Jesus Christ; and if the days of my captivity are now to be accomplished, those that turn me out, and so set me at liberty, may soon feel what it is, by sore distress themselves for those hard services they have caused me.[1]

In her chapels the Prayer Book services were still largely used, and when an independent chapel was established at Reading, by seceders from St. Giles's, which looked to her for a supply of ministers, she criticized the managers for wishing to run it as "a mere Dissenting church".[2] The way of schism is indeed a hard one; when those who instigate it desire still to enjoy the benefits of conformity.

In spite of this final tragedy, for such it may well be called, Lady Huntingdon had been a sincere and most useful friend to the Evangelical movement, for she had provided a valuable centre of union such as Wesley, owing to his different views, could never have afforded. Her chapels, too, gave to the Evangelicals opportunities of preaching when such were all too few. But her separation from the Church brought this to an end; and her chaplains, to a man, sent in their resignations.

Lady Huntingdon's Connexion, as the new denomination came to be called, eventually passed from Methodism, and her followers became Independents or Congregationalists. By the end of the century, though the Prayer Book was still in use at Tottenham Court Road chapel, it had fallen out of favour in most of the other chapels. Dr. Haweis, surely in an optimistic frame of mind, states that at this time the Connexion had

---

[1] *Countess of Huntingdon*, ii, p. 315   [2] *Op. cit.*, ii, p. 404

almost as many adherents as the Wesleyans, though it was "not so compact or united".[1]

The separation of the followers of Lady Huntingdon, grievous as it was, cannot be compared, for the hurt it inflicted, with that of the followers of Wesley. This separation was delayed by the influence of Wesley himself, but sooner or later it was inevitable.

Lord Macaulay in his famous essay on Ranke's *History of the Popes* (in which he foretold the survival of the Papacy, when some traveller from New Zealand shall, in the midst of a vast solitude, take his stand on a broken arch of London Bridge to sketch the ruins of St. Paul's) criticized the Church for its treatment of enthusiasts, which he compared unfavourably with the policy of Rome. "At Rome", he declared, "the countess of Huntingdon would have a place in the calendar as St. Selina", and the Methodists, he inferred, would have been turned into an order similar to that of the Jesuits. To pass such judgments, which in the nature of things can neither be proved nor disproved, is an easy task, especially if they are based on a merely superficial study; deeper consideration, however, would suggest that in this at least, Macaulay was mistaken. There was no possible place, given the conditions of the Church in the eighteenth century, for the Methodists within it. It was no mere obscurantism or lack of statesmanship on the part of the Church's leaders which led to the breach, but a real appreciation of the situation as they found it.

As in the days when Christianity was first preached the new wine demanded new wine-skins. Furthermore, it must be recognized that from the first the Methodists were definitely a "sect"; that is, they wished "to combine in one exclusive society all men of a special kind of temperament in religion".[2] This alone made it impossible for the Church to fit them in, and had the Methodists been granted full recognition as an organization within the Church, they would have accepted it only on their own terms. Macaulay, in his comparison of the Methodists with the Jesuits, furnished a parallel more apt than he realized, for a time came when the Jesuits attempted to gain complete control of the Roman Church, and had to be temporarily suppressed.

It is, of course, easy to say that many of the "irregularities" for which the Methodists were condemned, such as preaching by

[1] *Impartial and Succinct Hist. of the Rise, Decline, and Revival of the Church of Christ*, iii, pp. 259 ff.
[2] J. N. Figgis, *Hopes for English Religion*, p. 120, so defines a sect

the laity, extempore prayer, the holding of parochial missions, and open air services, are now commonplace in the Church's system. But that is not the crux of the situation. Had an "order" of Methodists been recognized within the Church of England it would have proved as disruptive as the Jesuits in that of Rome.

The breach came about by gradual and almost imperceptible stages. We have seen that even men like Grimshaw who took a part in the Methodist organization were prepared to sever their connexion if it involved any disloyalty to the Church, and the rift between Evangelicals and Methodists was widened when Wesley failed to unite them under his leadership. Although Wesley refrained from attacking the clergy, he had but a poor idea of their effectiveness in gaining converts, though he recognized that the Evangelical clergy might do good work, up to a point. As for the rest he could write: "Soul-damning clergymen lay me under more difficulties than soul-saving laymen."[1] His general attitude must have been well known to his own followers and could not have increased their respect for the Church.

The various Methodist organizations, even in parishes where there was an Evangelical incumbent, must inevitably have led to distinctions being made between them and the ordinary Churchman, whom they regarded as little more than a nominal Christian. (Such distinctions are not unknown in our own day where the Oxford Groups have established themselves in a parish.) They might even feel that those outside were a drag on the progress of true religion, an attitude found in similar circumstances in America, on which Jonathan Edwardes had written: "We may pray concerning all these saints that are not lively Christians, that they may either be enlightened, or taken away; if that be true which is often said, that these cold, dead saints do more hurt than natural men, and lead more souls to hell, and that it would be well for mankind if they were all dead."

The Methodist societies (again like the Oxford Groups) welcomed any who were willing to join them without any kind of denominational test. The result was that numbers who were not Churchmen were admitted, and this no doubt introduced a leaven of ill-will against the Church and fostered the spirit of division.

Since open-air preaching is only possible in the English

[1] *Letters*, iii, pp. 149 ff. (October 31, 1755)

climate at certain seasons of the year, and, in any case, is at the mercy of our very fickle weather, meeting-houses were soon established. These in themselves were not necessarily a sign of any wish for separation, they were needed for specifically Methodist activities; but they naturally tended in that direction. When public services were held in them some kind of "staff" was needed, and as no clergy were normally available lay-preachers had to be employed. It was this innovation which was perhaps the most direct cause of the final breach, as Walker, Adam, and even Charles Wesley had foreseen. John Wesley himself did not altogether like the growing power of the lay-preachers and did his best to control it. But he could not do more; writing in 1755, that if "he could not stop a separation without stopping lay preachers, the case was clear—he could not stop it at all."[1]

Many of the lay preachers were ignorant and uninstructed men, but possessed of the gift of a ready and persuasive tongue, and their ministrations were often more acceptable than those of the clergy. Their superficial success easily led them into pride and arrogance, and even to the denial of any such thing as orders at all. The two Perronets, who as educated men ought to have known better, actually began to administer the sacraments. The matter came before the Conference in 1755, when it was condemned, and, for the moment, suppressed. But in 1760 three preachers at Norwich, ever a troublesome place, again began the practice; and Charles Wesley, whose rigid views on the matter robbed him of influence with the lay preachers, implored his brother to take stern measures. But in spite of all John Wesley's efforts to keep the lay preachers in their place they continued to press for fuller rights. A quarrel broke out at Bath in November, 1779, after Wesley had appointed the Rev. Edward Smyth to preach at all Sunday evening services. The lay preachers opposed this, and, turning on Wesley, told him that they were appointed by the Conference and not by him, and that they "would not suffer the clergy to ride over their heads".[2] Some lay preachers finding the Methodist discipline as obnoxious as that of the Church set up as independents.

A further complication was introduced when women began to preach.[3] This, strangely enough, had been done frequently in the Fakenham district of Norfolk by members of the Church

[1] *Letters*, iii, p. 144   [2] *Journal*, vi, pp. 262 f.
[3] On the whole subject see L. F. Church, *More about the Early Methodist People*, chap. iv

before ever the Methodists arose.[1] In 1761 Sarah Crosby,[2] expecting to meet a class of thirty people at Derby, found a congregation of three hundred and felt impelled to address them. In reporting the incident she wrote: "My soul was much comforted in speaking to the people, as my Lord has removed all scruples respecting my acting thus publicly." Wesley in reply advised her to go on calmly and steadily, but to tell the people that women preachers were not recognized by the Methodists, and that she did not claim to be such, but was only telling them what was in her heart.[3] This was the beginning of a practice which, though never formally sanctioned, continued to grow as other women felt that they were called to the office.[4] This was a little shocking to the ideas of the times (except among the Quakers), for though Lady Huntingdon might be accepted as a kind of "pope" ruling her Connexion and employing others to preach for her (she herself never undertook the task), the sudden appearance of simple and less educated women as preachers was a very different matter. Thomas Scott even held that for a woman to offer prayer in the presence of males was not only unscriptural, but "inconsistent with all the subordination of domestic life".[5]

In order to regularize the position of the preachers Walker had suggested to Wesley that such of them as were qualified should be ordained. But this did not suit Wesley, for when ordained they would be stationed in parishes, and so no longer available for itinerancy. Some of the lay preachers were anxious for orders, and in 1765 a great scandal arose when six of them paid five guineas a head to a certain Erasmus, who styled himself Bishop of Arcadia, in return for ordination. At a meeting held at the Foundery they were expelled from the society, but, on renouncing their supposed orders, were eventually restored,[6] except Thomas Bryant, who set up as an independent at Sheffield.

Then came a much more serious development following the withdrawal of clergy from America after the War of Independence. In 1779 some of the preachers in the South began to ordain one another, but they were for the time persuaded not

---

[1] Wesley, *Journal*, vi, p. 338

[2] Said to have been the original of Sarah Williamson in *Adam Bede*

[3] *Letters*, iv, p. 133

[4] Among them was Elizabeth Hurrell, a convert of Berridge, who itinerated in Yorkshire, Lancashire and Derbyshire (*Letters*, v, p. 184)

[5] *Life*, p. 505   [6] *Letters*, iv, pp. 290 f.

to administer the sacraments. Wesley tried to get clergy sent out specially to America, but his efforts were unsuccessful.[1] By 1784 the position had become desperate and Wesley determined on a very serious proceeding. He had been convinced, after reading Stillingfleet's *Irenicon* in 1756, that there was no distinction between a bishop and a presbyter,[2] and in 1780 had written to Charles: "I verily believe that I have as good a right to ordain, as to administer the Lord's Supper."[3] He now determined to exercise his supposed right, and that in an extreme form, for not only did he ordain two preachers for work in America,[4] but he went further and set apart Dr. Coke as "superintendent."[5] Coke, on arriving in America, himself ordained Asbury to be his joint superintendent. Both Coke and Wesley were a little uneasy over their doings, and this uneasiness must have been increased when only two months later Segrave was consecrated by the Scottish bishops for work in America.

Coke was a man of outstanding abilities, and his ambitions seem to have been as great as his abilities. In May, 1789, he and Asbury presented an address to President Washington in which they described themselves as bishops of the Methodist Episcopal Church. In the same year at a Conference in America, Wesley, entirely without his knowledge or consent, was described as bishop over Europe.

When the ordinations became public property, there was naturally a great outcry, and this extended even to Methodist circles. One preacher wrote: "I wish they had been asleep when they began this business of ordination: it is neither *episcopal* nor *presbyterian*; but a mere hodge-podge of inconsistencies."

Wesley, however, was not to be deterred, and having, so to speak, tasted blood over America,[6] he next ordained men for

[1] See his letter of August 8, 1780, to Bishop Lowth of London, in whose jurisdiction America was included (*Letters*, vii, 30 ff.)

[2] In this he was right, up to a point, for the Medieval Church (as the Church of Rome to-day) does not recognize a separate order of bishops; the episcopate is only a "grade" within the priesthood. What he failed to realize was that the Church had committed special functions to the bishops, and, above all, the right to ordain. These could not be usurped by an individual

[3] *Letters*, vii, p. 21   [4] Tyerman, *Wesley*, iii, pp. 432 ff.

[5] It was a most extraordinary proceeding even from Wesley's own point of view, for Coke was already a priest; and, as has been pointed out: "Dr. Coke had the same right to 'ordain' Mr. Wesley, that Mr. Wesley had to ordain Dr. Coke"

[6] Charles wrote to him: "When once you began ordaining in America, I knew, and you knew, that your preachers would never rest till you ordained them" (Jackson, *Life of Charles Wesley*, ii, p. 394)

work in Scotland. He wrote on August 1, 1785: "Having, with a few select friends, weighed the matter thoroughly, I yielded to their judgment, and set apart three of our well-tried preachers, John Pawson, Thomas Hanby, and Joseph Taylor, to minister to Scotland; and I trust God will bless their ministrations, and show that He has sent them."[1]

Wesley's subsequent treatment of these three men is typical of his dictatorial ways and defiance of principles where any practical step was involved. Having "ordained" Pawson he addressed him as "reverend" and allowed him to wear gown and bands. But when, only four years later, he transferred him to work in England, he stripped him of his canonicals and thereafter simply called him "Mr.". Pawson, in spite of much natural soreness, loyally submitted, though he wrote rather pathetically to a friend, "We are to be just what we were before we came to Scotland—no Sacraments, no gowns, no nothing at all of any kind whatsoever." He felt that it was unjust "that men, approved of God and their brethren, and that for many years, should be regularly ordained in the capacity of ministers, and yet should be deposed by one single man, and that without any crime committed, great or small, real or pretended. Even the pope himself never acted such a part as this. . . . However, I am satisfied, and have nothing but love in my heart towards the good old man. But really it will not bear the light at all."[2]

When Joseph Taylor was moved to Newark in 1788 he received the same treatment and duly submitted.[3] But with Thomas Hanby there was more difficulty, for he determined to continue, being persuaded "by the earnest request of the people, who had not communicated for years, and would not communicate with drinking, whoring, swearing, and fighting parsons". In the end, however, he gave way when he was threatened with expulsion, and lived to preside over the fourth Conference after Wesley's death.[4]

I have dealt with these incidents in detail as illustrating the despotic powers which Wesley exercised over his followers, and also the extent to which they were accepted, or at least acquiesced in, by them. Three worthy ministers were "unfrocked" simply because he judged it expedient to do so. No doubt he felt that he ought not to "ordain" men for work in England; but surely he was sufficient of a theologian to realize

[1] *Journal*, vii, p. 101   [2] Tyerman, *Wesley*, iii, pp. 497 f.
[3] *Letters*, viii, p. 105   [4] Tyerman, *Wesley*, iii, pp. 574 ff.

that "orders", once given, are effective in the absence of moral failings. His knowledge of the primitive Church should also have taught him that such changes of status were characteristic of heresy and not of the Church.¹

The matter of the ordinations also reveals the immense difficulties which might have arisen had Methodism been incorporated into the Church. It may, of course, be argued that had such a step been taken Wesley would not have been forced to adopt his irregular practices; but that is an uncertain conclusion. In any event, his masterful and restless spirit would have found it hard to endure any kind of restraint. As things were, the ecclesiastical authorities simply ignored his actions. Many of the bishops had a respect for him personally, and recognized the value of the work which God had given him to do in England, a work which they themselves had failed fully to undertake; and by this time they must have realized that he was quite beyond their control. So they made it their policy quietly to ignore him. There was thus never any expulsion of either Wesley or his followers from the Church. The breach, when it came, was entirely on their initiative.

The Methodist Movement had not been long under way when the desire to sever all connexion with the Church began to appear in some quarters. When meeting-houses were erected, in order to avoid prosecution for unlawful assembly, they had to be registered; this made the whole position extremely anomalous. An early attempt to check the tendency to break away was an agreement signed on March 16, 1752, by John and Charles Wesley, William Shent, John Jones and John Nelson, which contained a clause "never to leave the communion of the Church of England without the consent of all whose names are subjoined". In spite of this agreement, which kept Charles Wesley in the movement,² a crisis arose in 1755 when three days were devoted to the question. It was finally decided that separation was inexpedient, but no decision was reached as to whether it was lawful.

Under the surface, however, there was much discontent, especially over the rule that meetings were not to coincide with Church services. Some wished that the lay preachers should be allowed to celebrate the Lord's Supper, since it might be refused to known Methodists. The lay preachers themselves had

---

¹ Cf. Tertullian, *De Praes. Haereticorum*, xli

² He wrote in 1756: "I should have broken off from the Methodists and my brother in 1752 but for the agreement" (*Life of Walker*, p. 201)

P

special grievances, quite apart from the refusal to allow them to celebrate the sacraments, though it is by no means certain that as a body they desired to break away; the pressure came from below.[1] But many of them considered that the clergy were not true ministers, because not sent by God; they also wished to be free from "forms", for though they thought the Prayer Book excellent in its way, they disliked being bound to a merely human composition. The more extreme considered that the doctrines of the Church still retained "the very dregs of popery".

From time to time the matter cropped up at the Conferences. In 1778 the question was debated: "Is it not our duty to separate from the Church, considering the wickedness both of the clergy and people?" The answer was in the negative, in view of the similar state of the Jewish Church! The Leeds Conference of 1781 witnessed an acrimonious dispute. Dr. William Hey, who had been connected with the movement for twenty-seven years, got leave to address the assembly, and then complained of the growth of Dissenting ideas. He specified intrusion in parishes where there were pious clergymen; the breach of the rule not to hold meetings during times of divine service; and even declared that some societies never went to church. A clamour arose, and on the excuse of pressure of other business Wesley ruled that he should finish his paper on another occasion. Dr. Hey thereupon severed his connexion with the Methodists.

The really decisive year was 1784, which saw the ordinations for America, as well as Wesley's Deed of Declaration giving the Conference legal standing, and, in effect, setting up a new form of church government. The Conference of 1786 relaxed the rule about not holding services during church hours, making it permissible if the minister was notoriously wicked, or preached Arian or other pernicious doctrines; if the churches in a town were not sufficient to contain half the people; and if there was no church within two or three miles. These loopholes really meant that the rule would become a dead letter; but Wesley himself was still insistent that it should be kept, and when the Methodists at Deptford agreed to break it, he warned them that if they did so they would see his face no more.[2] The Conference of 1786 was the last which Charles Wesley attended, and at its close he preached a sermon in which

---

[1] See L. F. Church, *More about the Early Methodist People*, pp. 261 ff.
[2] *Journal*, vii, pp. 217, 232

he foretold that not more than one in three of the Methodists would remain in the Church when he and his brother were dead, but that those who did so would receive a special outpouring of God's Spirit and that His work would prosper in their hands.

Wesley at this time was very urgent that separation should be avoided, and wrote on March 25, 1787, to Samuel Bardsley: "I still think, when the Methodists leave the Church of England, God will leave them. Every year more and more of the clergy are convinced of the truth and grow well-affected towards us. It would be contrary to all common sense as well as to good conscience to make a separation now."[1] At the Conference that year Pawson noted that: "Mr. Wesley seems more determined to abide in the Church than ever. He talked about it again and again ... and in such a hot, fiery spirit, as I did not like to see." But it was in that year that Wesley decided that all chapels and all itinerant preachers should be licensed, not, indeed, as Dissenters, but simply as "preachers of the gospel". This was a mere evasion, for the Conventicle Act was designed for Dissenters. Next year meeting-houses were allowed to hold services during church hours, except on Sacrament Sunday. It was then also that Wesley issued his "revised" prayer book, originally intended for America, but now for the use of societies in England. It made some drastic omissions.

The breach became absolute in 1791, when the circuit system was set up to cover the United Kingdom in lieu of the ancient parishes. After that it was no concern of the Church that four years later tardy permission was given to the preachers to celebrate the Holy Communion.

How far, it must now be asked, was Wesley, in spite of his protestations, really responsible for the schism? That he was a sincere Churchman according to his lights there can be no shadow of doubt. This being so, it is difficult not to be impatient with him and to wonder that he was so oblivious to the consequences of his own actions. So practical was his mind and so great his ability to compromise that he seldom foresaw what these consequences would be. In this, Charles was much wiser and more far-seeing. Wesley had an amazing power of "wishful thinking", to use the modern and rather horrible phrase, and of deceiving his own self. Even his allegiance to the Church was based on expediency rather than on principle; for he had admitted in 1755 that "his conclusion (which he

[1] *Letters*, vii, p. 377

could not give up), that it was lawful to continue in the Church, stood, he knew not how, almost without any premises that were able to bear its weight".[1]

It would probably be true to find the basis of his Churchmanship in an innate conservatism, and in a dislike of Dissent. In his father's parish there had been neither Papists nor Dissenters. So his Churchmanship expressed itself negatively in an almost intolerant and contemptuous attitude which is remarkable in so broad-minded a Christian. This attitude is always coming out in his journals. On June 2, 1777, when in the Isle of Man, he notes: "A more loving, simple-hearted people than this I never saw. And no wonder: for they have but six Papists and no Dissenters in the island."[2] In October, 1778, he wrote: "Few of the Methodists are now in danger of imbibing error from the Church ministers; but they are in great danger of imbibing that grand error—Calvinism—from the Dissenting ministers. . . . I myself find more life in the Church prayers, than in any formal extempore prayers of Dissenters."[3] Earlier he had written (on July 19, 1768) to Thomas Adam: "I dare not, like Mr. Venn, leave the parish church where I am, to go to an Independent meeting. I dare not advise others to go thither rather than to church."[4] Yet it was to be Wesley's fate, not merely to found a new body of Dissenters, but also, quite inadvertently, to revive the old Dissenting bodies which were in a process of decay.

There was, however, a more positive side, for Wesley had a deep affection for the Church of England, as can be seen in words which he wrote in August, 1780: "I am fully convinced that our own Church, with all her blemishes, is nearer the scriptural plan than any other in Europe."[5] This love for the Church was especially concentrated on its liturgy (we saw above his preference for set prayers over extemporare), and he was shocked by those who "made a mere jest of going to church, or to the sacrament".[6] On June 27, 1740, he records that he preached on the Sacrament, reminding his hearers that for many of them the beginning of their conversion to God "was wrought at the Lord's Supper".[7] From his own experience Wesley knew the value of sacramental grace: writing on November 13, 1763,

---

[1] *Letters*, iii, p. 146

[2] *Journal*, vi, p. 152: cf. p. 294 (of Trowbridge), "as most of the hearers were Dissenters, I did not expect to do much good"

[3] *Letters*, vi, p. 326   [4] *Op. cit.*, v, p. 98   [5] *Letters*, vii, p. 28

[6] *Journal*, ii, p. 327   [7] *Op. cit.*, ii, p. 361

"I found much of the power of God in preaching, but far more at the Lord's table."[1]

How then did it come about that after his death the followers of Wesley, in spite of his warnings, separated from the Church? One reason is, of course, that they were compelled by circumstances to do so. But their action is, in part, explained by Wesley's own peculiar temperament. He was by nature despotic; made too much of personal allegiance to himself; did not train his followers in real loyalty to the Church; and, by setting up a supplementary organization he prepared the way for the schism. The institution of lay preachers, the gradual extension of their functions, the unfortunate "ordinations",[2] the licensing of the meeting-houses, and the "new" prayer book were all incitements to this end. He did, indeed, urge them to be regular in church attendance; but this was to be a matter of duty, and he did little to make them realize its value. Their real religion was centred in the society, not in the parish church. Moreover, his depreciation of the clergy, mild as it was, undermined their prestige and authority. At the same time he had high notions of the position of the minister in face of the congregation. One reason why he insisted that the trust deeds of all chapels should be in his name was his fear of that bane of Dissent, the control of the minister by the congregation.

Wesley never fully comprehended the extent to which the desire for separation had spread among his followers. He was, no doubt, aware of occasional murmurings and some secessions by individuals, but his iron rule awed the majority into silence and drove their grievances underground. So it had been from the beginning, as can be seen from his treatment of Cennick and other malcontents at Bristol.[3] Wesley was by nature and by training an autocrat, and his superior education and social standing—though he might not realize it—carried great weight with the type of men and women whom he drew to him.

Dean Inge has declared that the secession of the Methodists from the Church of England was a blow comparable to that inflicted on the Papacy by the loss of Northern Europe.[4] This is a sound piece of judgment; and a further parallel may be

[1] *Op. cit.*, v, p. 40

[2] On August 19, 1785, he wrote to Charles that his "ordaining" did not mean that he had the least idea of separating from the Church (*Letters*, vii, pp. 284 f.)

[3] *Journal*, ii, pp. 428 ff.   [4] *Outspoken Essays*, i, p. 108

found in the gradual manner in which its consequences came to be felt. Even when the Methodist preachers began to celebrate the sacrament, many Methodists still retained the habit of attending their parish churches on Sacrament Sunday. Some did so because they were unwilling entirely to forsake the Church; others, probably because they hoped by preserving this link to avoid being confounded with Dissenters.

The various separations were practically confined to the laity. In the early days of the revival a few clergymen had abandoned the Church to become Moravians or undenominationalists, and Wills[1] and Taylor had followed Lady Huntingdon. Those of the clergy who held livings would not be at all anxious to take a step which would involve resignation, unless strongly urged to it by their consciences. Some contemplated secession owing to the treatment which they received from their fellow clergy; as was the case with Crosse of Bradford, who actually offered himself to the Conference for duty at the City Road chapel.[2] A number of the clergy also helped Wesley at various times, but that was before the separation. After the death of Wesley, and the ensuing schism, co-operation was no longer to be thought of.

The refusal of the Evangelical clergy to co-operate with Methodists, however, had an interesting exception; they were still willing to preach for Rowland Hill at Surrey Chapel. The only occasions when Thomas Scott acted in an "irregular" manner were his annual exchanges of pulpits with Hill, who delivered a charity sermon at the Lock whilst Scott appeared at Surrey Chapel.[3] Henry Venn was another habitual "offender". In 1785 he wrote: "When I go to London I shall chiefly preach at Surrey Chapel. He [Hill] writes me word that the people for the much greater part prefer the clergy, but if none will officiate there it must be supplied by Dissenters."[4] He also records preaching there in May and June, 1786, to crowded congregations, among whom were a number of clergy, including the sub-dean of the Chapel Royal.

Rowland Hill is so interesting and important a character that he demands some notice.[5] He was the sixth son of Sir Rowland Hill of Hawkstone in Shropshire, and was born on July 23, 1745. By his family and intimates, including Berridge, he was

[1] Wills afterwards returned to the Church: see below, p. 351
[2] Wesley, *Journal*, vii, p. 157   [3] *Life*, p. 169
[4] *Venn Family Annals*, p. 103
[5] See Sidney, *Life of Rowland Hill*, for fuller details

always called "Rowley", though Whitefield usually addressed him as "My dear Professor". When at Cambridge he engaged in itinerating and other activities which brought him into conflict with the authorities, who threatened to withhold him testimonials and even a degree. He was, however, more fortunate than Benson at Oxford, and the threat was never carried out. This was perhaps due to family influence, for the Hills had six valuable livings in Norfolk to which they always appointed fellows of St. John's.[1] His parents, too, highly disapproved of his conduct. Lady Huntingdon, however, to whom he was introduced at Bath in 1767, received him "with open arms", and began to take an almost maternal interest in him, at the same time endeavouring to reconcile him with his parents. In May, 1771, Berridge wrote to her: "I find you have got honest Rowley down at Bath: he is a pretty young spaniel, fit for land or water, and has a wonderful yelp. He forsakes father, mother, and brethren, and gives up all for Jesus; and I believe he will prove a useful labourer, if he keeps clear of petticoat snares."[2] Berridge's hope proved vain, so far as "petticoat snares" were concerned, for Hill married a Miss Tudney in May, 1773: but she proved a worthy help to him and was often his companion on his preaching tours and shared all his difficulties and privations.

In 1772, although still unordained, Hill by his forceful and simple preaching did much to revive Lady Huntingdon's chapels in London (she called him a "second Whitefield"). Then on June 6, 1774, just after his marriage, he was ordained by the Bishop of Bath and Wells to a curacy at Kingston in Somerset. But he found he could not settle down there and was soon back again in London, as well as itinerating elsewhere. It is not therefore surprising that he found no bishop willing to ordain him priest (the Bishop of Carlisle promised to do so, but withdrew on further reflection). Hill's friends tried to bring him to a better mind; Berridge called him a "comet", and Toplady remonstrated in vain.[3] He felt that at all costs he must pursue what he regarded as his peculiar work. In 1780 the riots in London and the crowds who were drawn by them gave him a great opportunity, and he addressed vast congregations in St. George's Fields.

By this time his relations with Lady Huntingdon were becoming strained, for he found her much too masterful, and

[1] *Op. cit.*, pp. 19, 27 [2] *Countess of Huntingdon*, ii, p. 49
[3] *Life*, pp. 90 f.

was never one of her most cordial admirers. Being more her equal in birth he was not overcome by her lofty rank, and, what displeased her most, was quite capable of making fun of her, and that in the pulpit. This conduct caused deep offence, as she wrote to a friend: "All this, though not fair or upright, I should have so far despised, as for peace' sake to have passed over; but the worm that still lies at the bottom of the gourd, is his taking us all up into the pulpit, as his merry andrews, and, through his evil jokes, leaving a bitter sting behind." So Rowland Hill was no longer allowed to appear in any of her chapels from 1781 onwards. Nothing could make her lift the ban, and, being then in her seventy-fifth year, she wrote: "Without reserve to you, my kind friend, and with every best wish to dear Mr. Venn, Mr. Hill CANNOT *preach* for me."[1] But she still wished him well and made a generous contribution towards setting him up in Surrey Chapel.

Surrey Chapel was planned by a number of Hill's admirers, some of whom were people of wealth. As he could no longer make use of Lady Huntingdon's chapels they wished to provide him with a pulpit of his own. At a meeting in February, 1782, they decided to build a chapel in a neglected district of Southwark. The chief trustee was his brother, Sir Richard Hill, and among those who contributed was Lord George Gordon, who gave £50. The foundation-stone of the building, which was octagonal in shape and perhaps copied from the Octagon Chapel in Bath, was laid in the following June.[2]

The trustees kept a hold on the chapel, but agreed that Hill should have complete freedom in the choice of ministers so long as they refrained from preaching anything contrary to the doctrinal articles of the Church of England.[3] Hill himself always refused to be called a Dissenter and when in his later days he visited Cambridge would never preach in Dissenting places of worship, so as not to seem to disagree with Simeon.[4] He made his position quite plain in 1799, when he wrote: "I had much rather be under the Right Reverend Fathers in God with us, than under the jurisdiction of the Most Reverend Mothers in God among the stricter Independents."[5]

So the services at Surrey Chapel were those of the Church of

---

[1] *Countess of Huntingdon*, ii, p. 318

[2] After Surrey Chapel ceased to be used for religious services, it became a centre for pugilism and was known as "the Ring". Like many other notable buildings in Southwark, it was destroyed in the air raids

[3] *Life*, p. 139   [4] *Life*, p. 162

[5] *Journal, through the North of England*, p. 108

England. But, as Hill held no bishop's licence and his chapel was not recognized by the Church, he was perfectly free, within the limits laid down by the trust deeds, to open his pulpit to all and sundry, whether Dissenters or Churchmen. His ministry proved very successful and formed what was a unique link among those who adhered to the revival doctrines. He continued there until his death on April 11, 1833.

CHAPTER 13

LOCAL EXPANSION: LONDON

In the early days of the revival movement Evangelical clergymen were but few in number, and, save for a small group in Cornwall, widely separated from one another; but after the middle of the century Evangelicalism began to spread to nearly all parts of the kingdom. Our next step will therefore be to examine this local development.

Information as to the spread of Evangelical views, however, is not easy to come by. If incumbents here and there allowed Evangelicals or even Methodists to use their pulpits this may not mean more than a general sympathy, and, by itself, does not imply a willingness to join the movement. On the other hand a refusal to allow such use was not necessarily a sign of disapprobation, unless it concerned the regular Sunday services. Preaching was not usual during the week. An instance of this is recorded by Wesley in his journal for July 17, 1739. Mr. Rogers, the minister of Bradford-on-Avon, had given him a standing invitation to preach for him whenever he was in the neighbourhood. He went on a Tuesday, and was informed that no special service could be arranged, but that the invitation still held good for the Sunday. As this did not fit Wesley's plans he held a meeting in the open air.[1]

In tracing the growth of Evangelical influences, apart from the few parishes where the incumbent was a definite Evangelical, I have had to rely mainly on casual references, chiefly in the letters and journals of the leaders; use has also been made of local and parochial histories, but any comprehensive survey of such numerous productions was out of the question; the information which they might have furnished is, as Macaulay would have said, "scanty and dispersed", and a detailed search would have involved an expenditure of time and energy out of all proportion to its possible results.

In pursuing our study, an arrangement based on counties will be adopted, though this is obviously not entirely satisfactory, as there was some overlapping, as for example, between Yorkshire and Lincolnshire in the case of the group of clergy centred on Hotham. We begin, however, with London.

[1] *Journal*, iii, p. 243

LOCAL EXPANSION: LONDON 235

London in the second half of the eighteenth century was very different from the London of to-day.¹ Although it far exceeded in population any other town in England, the area it covered was only small.² To the west, it hardly extended beyond Bond Street and Westminster; and milk warm from the cow could still be bought in St. James's Park, as Pastor Moritz noticed in 1782.³ There was, however, a new, aristocratic suburb growing up round Cavendish Square, and Hannah More in that same year described a mansion in Portman Square as adding "the scenery of a country retirement" to "all the magnificence of a very superb London house."⁴ To the north, it went little beyond Oxford Street and Bloomsbury; Marylebone and St. Pancras were still undeveloped, as was Islington. To the east, it included Spitalfields and Whitechapel.

Though London was not much affected by the industrial revolution it already had slums, not only in the heart of the city, but even in outlying parts. Spitalfields, originally a pleasant village with houses and gardens containing mulberry trees, had already become squalid, and its crowded tenements, once the homes of Huguenot silk-weavers, were now the haunt of vicious and abandoned characters. It was from such slums that the mobs emerged on occasion, as in the Lord George Gordon riots, and the iron railings which stood outside the better-class houses were intended for protection as well as ornament. The metropolis was, indeed, already beginning to merit Shelley's description in 1819:

> Hell is a city much like London—
> A populous and smoky city;
> There are all sorts of people undone,
> And there is little or no fun done;
>   Small justice done, and still less pity.⁵

The advocates of the revival had been very active in London, and it provided a convenient centre for the followers of Wesley and of those who looked to Lady Huntingdon for guidance. Wesley, after severing his connexion with the Moravians in

¹ See M. Dorothy George, *London Life in the Eighteenth Century*

² Maps showing its boundaries at different epochs are to be found at the end of Trevelyan, *English Social History*

³ Some of the lands which brought large fortunes to the Portmans and others were originally farms intended to supply them with fresh milk and vegetables during the season

⁴ *Memoirs*, i, p. 241   ⁵ *Peter Bell the Third*, III, i

Fetter Lane, moved in 1740 to a large building in Moorfields, called the Foundery.[1] Until the opening of the City Road chapel opposite to Bunhill Fields in 1778 this was the headquarters of Wesleyan Methodism in the capital. In addition there were a number of other chapels, including the French Protestant chapel in West Street, Seven Dials, which Wesley took over in 1743. Whitefield and the Huntingdonians had the Tabernacle (so named to denote its merely temporal nature) in Moorfields, and the chapel in Tottenham Court Road established after the troubles in Long Acre chapel.[2] Evangelicalism, however, was at first represented only by Romaine at St. Dunstan's, and that solitary candle was in constant danger of being extinguished. Things became less precarious when he was appointed to St. Andrew and St. Anne in February, 1766; and by this time other figures were arising to share the burden and the privilege of proclaiming the revived teaching of the Gospel.

Religion in London was greatly stimulated, though by no means in a permanent or healthy manner, by the earthquakes of 1750. The first shock was felt on February 8 in the neighbourhood of Southwark, from which it travelled across London;[3] the second, a month later, was much more violent, and many houses were shaken, though beyond the fall of chimneys little real damage was done.[4] George Selwyn, the well-known wit, said that the earthquake was "so gentle you could have stroked it". None the less, there was widespread panic. The reactions, indeed, were not dissimilar to those occasioned by air raids in our own day. People deserted their houses and slept in the open fields; whilst Horace Walpole tells us that women made themselves "earthquake gowns" in case shocks occurred during the night. Many left London for the country, and the Westminster end of the town was full of coaches and flying crowds. London, so Charles Wesley said, "looked like a sacked city". Matters were made worse by the forecasts of a fanatical soldier who proclaimed that London and Westminster would both be destroyed.

The fears aroused by the outbreak gave an opportunity to the advocates of religion to address the assembled crowds, and sermons on the subject were also preached to the overflowing

---

[1] So named from its former use going back to the casting of cannon during the Civil War

[2] See *Letters*, iii, pp. 176, 180, 191   [3] Wesley, *Journal*, iii, p. 453

[4] The Foundery was shaken as Charles Wesley was giving out his text, and many thought the building would collapse (*Journal*, ii, p. 70)

congregations which swarmed into the places of worship. Charles Wesley delivered an oration on "The Cause and Cure of Earthquakes", and also issued a collection of nineteen hymns for the occasion. One verse, which has a distinctly modern application, ran as follows:

> How happy then are we,
> Who build, O Lord, on Thee!
> What can our foundation shock?
> Though the shattered earth remove,
> Stands our city on a rock,
> On the rock of heavenly love.

The alarm soon subsided; but it was again aroused by the news of the disastrous earthquake at Lisbon in 1755, when 60,000 people are said to have lost their lives.[1] On this occasion John Wesley, in response to many requests, wrote a popular pamphlet entitled "Serious Thoughts on the Earthquake at Lisbon"; whilst Horne, later to be Dean of Canterbury and Bishop of Norwich, preached a sermon before the University of Oxford in which he described the disaster as a judgment on the profligate manners and licentiousness of the nation. Bishop Sherlock also urged the clergy to take advantage of the terror aroused by the earthquake to move their people to a sense of their shortcomings; whilst at St. Dunstan's Romaine preached sermons on "Alarm to a Careless World" and "The Duty of Watchfulness Enforced".[2] Archbishop Herring, however, took a wiser line, and, whilst realizing the value of such "awakening instances of Divine power", commended those who were more impressed by the regular course of nature, "the stability, not the shaking of the earth".[3]

The feebleness of the Evangelical representation until just before the end of our period is the more surprising, as there had been promise of better things. This was made of none effect as the divergence of the Methodists became manifest. Thomas Broughton, for example, a member of the Holy Club, after encouraging Whitefield, drew back owing to the preaching up of instantaneous conversion. Whitefield was also allowed to use the pulpit of St. Bartholomew the Great, where R. T. Bateman

---

[1] Goethe has told us that this event was the cause of the first disturbance of his boyish peace of mind, and made him doubt the beneficence of the Creator (*Dichtung und Wahrheit*, Pt. I, Bk. i).

[2] *Works*, pp. 872 ff.   [3] Quoted Sykes, p. 420

was rector. Bateman was a man of good birth and considerable natural talents, and had come under the influence of Howell Davies, rector of Prengast, in Wales.[1] He had known John Wesley at Oxford, and he too preached in St. Bartholomew's from time to time. Bateman attended the Fourth Conference.[2]

Many other pulpits in London were open to the Wesleys and Whitefield before the Methodists had become notorious, especially in the matter of field-preaching. The journals of both John and Charles contain numerous records of their preaching in London. Charles was at Westminster Abbey on September 3, 1738, and at St. Margaret's, where he also took the service on October 1 of the same year.[3] At St. Botolph's, Bishopsgate, the incumbent, Dr. Crowe, was especially friendly. At St. Clement Danes, Dr. Johnson's parish church, John preached on November 5, 1738, but did not again occupy the pulpit until more than forty-four years later, when John Burrows was the incumbent.[4] The rector of St. Antholin's[5] from 1725 to 1738 was Richard Venn, the father of Henry, who allowed the Methodists to use his pulpit until the eccentric conduct of Whitefield caused him to change his mind. John Wesley preached there on December 15, 1738, but not again until November 15, 1778, when the Hon. Jerome de Salis was rector.[6] When Charles occupied the pulpit on October 20, 1738, the smallness of the congregation induced him to make the experiment of preaching extempore. On going there on the following December 21 the clerk interposed and told him that Dr. Venn had vetoed the use of the pulpit to Methodists. He asked: "Do you call yourself a Methodist?" Charles replied, "I do not: the world may call me what they please." As the congregation was expecting him to preach, the clerk allowed him to do so.[7]

John records that on October 22, 1738, he took prayers and preached in the morning for the Rev. Edward Vernon, rector of St. George's, Bloomsbury, and in the afternoon at St. Paul's, Shadwell, for the Rev. J. Nash.[8] At Spitalfields a chapel for the use of his tenants was built by Sir George Wheeler, who

[1] Whitefield, *Letters*, i, pp. 30, 150, 164, 176
[2] *Journal*, ii, p. 117; iii, pp. 300, 302 n.
[3] *Journal*, i, pp. 129, 131   [4] *Journal*, ii, p. 99; vi, p. 377
[5] Later the parish was united with St. Mary, Aldermary, when the church was taken down and another St. Antholin's built at Peckham Rye from the proceeds of the sale of the site
[6] *Journal*, ii, p. 115: vi, p. 217   [7] *Journal*, i, pp. 133, 138 f.
[8] *Journal*, ii, p. 95

had married Lady Catherine Hastings. Here there were opportunities for proclaiming the Gospel for Huntingdonians.

The parish of Islington, afterwards to fill so splendid a place in the annals of Evangelicalism, had early, though chequered, connexions with the movement. The incumbent, and also the patron, was the Rev. George Stonehouse, who gave both Whitefield and John Wesley a cordial welcome. With Charles his relations were even closer, for the latter gave him regular help and eventually acted as his curate.[1] But the course of his ministry did not run smoothly, and in the end the churchwardens, defying the vicar, stood guard over the pulpit steps and refused to allow him to preach.[2] Stonehouse, "through fear of man",[3] failed to take a strong line; but already he was being drawn away by the Moravians, which may account for his conduct. Eventually he joined them openly, and his wife became the adopted daughter of Count Zinzendorf. Stonehouse resigned his living in July, 1740, and retired to the neighbourhood of Woodstock, near Oxford, where the rest of his life was spent in "inglorious stillness".[4] Charles Wesley wrote a poem on his "fall".[5]

A much-needed reinforcement to the Evangelical cause came with the appointment of Thomas Jones as junior chaplain of St. Saviour's, Southwark, in 1753. Jones was a graduate of Queens' College, Cambridge, and having been aroused to a sense of spiritual need, got into touch with Romaine. He was a devoted worker, but greatly handicapped by ill-health. His activities were innumerable, ranging from the distribution of literature to catechizing the children in his house. So great were his labours that he found but little time for the preparation of his sermons, which were criticized for their want of polish. His teaching met with but little sympathy from his superiors, who more than once thwarted efforts he made to find new opportunities, including the holding of a weekly lecture in the church. But others became aware of his faithful labours, and in March, 1759, John Wesley wrote offering his friendship, an offer which Jones gratefully accepted.[6] However, he was not destined to

---

[1] *Journal*, i, p. 123. A writer in the *Transactions of the Wesleyan Historical Society* (v, pp. 238 f.), after consulting the vestry records, denied this. But in view of the express statement of Charles himself, his objection can hardly be sustained. Probably Charles was never licensed.

[2] *Journal*, i, pp. 148 f.   [3] *Op. cit.*, i, pp. 154 f.

[4] Jackson, *Life of Charles Wesley*, i, p. 279

[5] Printed in his *Journal*, ii, pp. 215 f.   [6] *Methodist Magazine*, 1780, p. 165

enjoy it for long, as his weak frame proved unable to endure the burdens he laid upon it, and on June 6, 1762, his short life of only thirty-three years came to an end.[1]

The year after Jones came to Southwark, Henry Venn was appointed curate of Clapham, a post which he held until his move to Huddersfield in 1759, combining with it lectureships in various city churches. That same year, 1754, saw also the conversion of John Thornton, the layman who was to do so much for the Evangelical cause in London and elsewhere. It was he who in 1769 presented Roger Bentley to St. Giles, Camberwell, and thus provided London with one of its first Evangelical incumbents. Two years earlier he had appointed his brother-in-law, Conyers of Helmsley, to the living of Deptford, which he held until 1787. But Conyers had already done his best work and made but little impression, though Wesley spoke well of him on February 17, 1783: "I had an opportunity of attending the lecture of that excellent man, Dr. Conyers. He was quite an original: his matter was very good, his manner very bad. But it is enough that God owned him, both in the conviction and conversion of sinners."[2]

At Chelsea parish church, Cadogan, who had been appointed there in 1775, became an Evangelical in 1780, and preached the Gospel; though not with the same success as at St. Giles's, Reading, which living he also held. At first, Cadogan divided his time equally between the two parishes, but, finding the burden too great, handed over most of the work at Chelsea to Erasmus Middleton, whom, on his death in 1797, the parishioners unsuccessfully wished to succeed him. When Middleton published his *Biographia Evangelica* in 1779, he obtained among the subscribers the Rev. Stephen Addington, D.D., of Mile End Green, the Rev. Stephen Eaton, rector of St. Anne's, Westminster, and the Rev. William Haggie, vicar of Bromley, who presumably held views of an Evangelical tinge.

It was in 1779 also that John Newton came from Olney to St. Mary Woolnoth, where he was to exercise a most telling influence. For a time he lived in Charles Square, Hoxton, but later removed to Coleman Street Buildings.[3] Newton depended for his power, not on his preaching, but on the affectionate terms which he established with his congregation, entering into

---

[1] Romaine preached a memorial sermon (*Works*, pp. 817 ff.). To it and the memoir prefixed to his own works we are mainly indebted for details of his career. Jones had vainly applied to Lady Huntingdon to get him a country living (*Life and Remains of R. Housman*, p. li)

[2] *Journal*, vi, p. 391   [3] See Cecil, *Memoirs of John Newton*, p. 68

all their trials and sympathizing with all their interests.¹

Another parish where Evangelical views were proclaimed was St. John's, Horsley Downs, Southwark. William Abdy, who had been at Magdalen Hall, Oxford, became curate in charge in 1782, but did not succeed to the living as rector until 1805.

If Evangelical clergymen had difficulties in obtaining livings, and even curacies, in London, for some of them provision was made by means of what were known as proprietory chapels. These chapels had no districts attached to them, and were managed by those responsible for maintaining them. Many were erected in the suburbs to meet the needs of the expanding population; but as they were intended for those who could afford to pay pew rents, they made no provision for the less affluent classes. Most of them, indeed, were little better than financial speculations. A property owner might erect a chapel as an inducement to those who were in search of new houses to acquire them on his estate, and at the same time with the hope of some profit to himself. The proprietors of these chapels, in order to attract congregations and fill the pews, were ever on the look out for some rising popular preacher, to whom a fixed stipend would be paid.² Sometimes a cleric who fancied himself as a preacher would open such a chapel on his own account; a type which was depicted in scathing terms by Thackeray in *The Newcomes*. The system was a bad one and open to obvious abuses; but for a time it was often the only way by which an Evangelical preacher could obtain a hearing.

The most famous of these chapels in the early years of the movement was that attached to the Lock Hospital at the corner of Chapel Street, near Hyde Park, the site of which is now 18-20 Grosvenor Place. Its founder was Martin Madan, who became himself the first chaplain.

This remarkable man was a brother of Spencer Madan, Bishop of Peterborough, and a cousin of Cowper, the poet, whom he influenced in early days. Madan was born in 1726, and after being at Westminster and Christ Church, Oxford, was called to the bar in 1748. He lived a somewhat gay life, and his conversion came about owing to an apparently trivial incident. He and some companions went as a diversion to hear Wesley preach. They entered the building just as the text was being

---

¹ Newton lost his beloved wife, whom he was tempted "to make almost an idol", on December 15, 1790. Her niece, who had been brought up by them as a daughter, looked after him for the remaining years of his life

² Some proprietors were more generous. A Mr. Southwell, who had a chapel in Spring Gardens, divided the pew rents between the officiating ministers

given out. It was *Prepare to meet thy God*, and the solemn tones in which it was announced immediately struck home to Madan's heart and conscience. Madan was a skilled mimic, and when the party returned to their coffee house the others begged him to "take off the old Methodist". He made the totally unexpected reply: "No, gentlemen, he has taken me off." There followed a complete change of life and associates.

Madan took orders, apparently on the suggestion of Lady Huntingdon, but with the encouragement of Romaine and other leaders. As a man of means and also of some learning—he knew the Scriptures in the original—Madan was a most important convert to the movement. In appearance he was tall and well-built, with a dignified and impressive manner; this in combination with a musical voice made him a very attractive preacher. He delivered his first sermon at All Hallows, Lombard Street, and it aroused much comment. It was a decided novelty for a barrister to become a preacher, but Madan found nothing strange in it. On one occasion he said: "I have long been accustomed to plead at the bar the cause of man; I stand here to plead the cause of God, and to beseech sinners to be reconciled to Him." His legal training was, indeed, a great asset, and his discourses were always well thought out and well arranged.

Madan's musical gifts were far beyond the ordinary, and in 1760 he published a collection of Psalms and Hymns for the Lock Chapel which not only reached a high literary standard, but were also characterized by a bright and joyous spirit. Not a few Evangelical churches subsequently adopted them. Another musical innovation was the annual production of an oratorio in the chapel. This aroused some criticism, but Wesley attended the performance from time to time. He heard *Judith* on February 29, 1764, and was annoyed by the constant repetitions of the same words, and by different words being sung at the same time(!); none the less, he went to hear *Ruth* a year later. This he considered might impress "rich and honourable sinners".[1]

Madan was undoubtedly a kind of genius, but as with others of his type, genius might spill over into eccentricity. This came out when in 1780 he published his notorious volume *Thèlyphthora, or a Treatise on Female Ruin*, in which polygamy was advocated as a remedy for prostitution, the evils of which he had abundant opportunities of studying among the victims

[1] *Journal*, v, pp. 47, 106

treated at the Lock Hospital. When the book was in the press Lady Huntingdon entreated him not to allow it to appear, as did his friend Richard Hill. But Madan was obdurate. The work was of immense length and one of its chief arguments was an appeal to the Old Testament where polygamy was allowed; Christians were in error in thinking that Christ was superior to Moses in this respect.

The publication of the treatise aroused something like horror among Evangelicals. Hannah More has told us of her reactions to it,[1] and Henry Venn, to whom Madan sent a copy, was equally shocked. Venn's former curate, Riland of Birmingham, however, was for a time carried away by its arguments, until he was convinced of their unsoundness by Powley.[2] One consequence of Madan's venture was that he had to retire "into deserved oblivion".[3] He found a retreat at Epsom, where he occupied himself over a *New and Literal Translation of Juvenal and Perseus*. Another consequence, and that inevitable, was the appearance of a host of pamphlets attacking his conclusions. The first, composed by Thomas Wills under the title of *Remarks on Polygamy*, was produced on the orders of the ever-watchful Lady Huntingdon. Richard Hill, also, in spite of his friendship for Madan, could not restrain his busy pen, and issued a pamphlet with the ironical title of *The Blessings of Polygamy, displayed in an affectionate address to the Rev. Mr. Madan*.

For many years the Lock Chapel was served by two chaplains appointed by the Governors of the Hospital, who seem to have regarded it mainly as a source of revenue. It sometimes happened that the two chaplains, one of whom officiated in the morning, the other in the afternoon, were by no means agreed in their presentation of the Gospel message, as well as differing in character and sentiments.[4] Among them were many whose names became well known in the Evangelical world, such as Thomas Haweis, De Coetlogon, and Thomas Scott. De Coetlogon had a great reputation for his extempore preaching, though there were differences of opinion as to the merits of his sermons. Henry Venn, after hearing him in February, 1775, wrote: "His discourses are all I wish to hear—judicious, doctrinal in a proper degree, very experimental, and faithfully applied."[5] Wilberforce, on the other hand, who attended

---
[1] *Memoirs*, i, p. 198   [2] *Venn Family Annals*, p. 107
[3] *Countess of Huntingdon*, ii, p. 464
[4] Much information as to its administration will be found in *Life of Thomas Scott*, pp. 218 ff., 365 ff.
[5] *Life*, p. 224

regularly at the Lock, was not so appreciative, and on the evening of Christmas Day, 1790, records that he "much disliked De Coetlogon".[1] More to his taste was the less popular Thomas Scott, for whose preaching he frequently expressed his admiration, an admiration which was shared by his friend Eliot, later Lord St. Germans.[2]

Scott came to the Lock in 1785 and remained until 1803, so that his ministry there lies mainly outside our period. It was no very happy time for him, as he was far from popular, and the congregations went down, to the disgust of the Governors, who even suggested that he should change his mode of preaching. But he had a number of loyal and ardent supporters, including Wilberforce and Henry Thornton, both of whom often went on to hear his evening lecture at Bread Street church.[3] Scott had immense intellectual energy which revealed itself in his youth and continued into old age. When he was over sixty he undertook the study of Arabic in order to help candidates of the Church Missionary Society. In spite of much ill-health, he never allowed himself to be idle and in general took up a robust and manly attitude to life. Dr. Claudius Buchanan regarded him as the greatest divine in the English Church.[4]

If the Lock was famous in the early days of the movement it later found a serious rival in Bedford Chapel.[5] To it in 1780 came Richard Cecil, a man of refined and scholarly tastes, who quickly drew round him a notable following. Cecil differed in many ways from the other Evangelical leaders, and though he wrote little,[6] exercised a considerable influence on the development of the movement. Since his career is not so well known as it deserves to be, it will be well to describe it in some detail.

Cecil was born on November 8, 1748, in Chiswell Street, London, where his father, who claimed to be descended from Lord Burleigh, carried on the family business of dyers to the East India Company. In his youth he adopted infidel views which he propagated amongst his friends. He had also an intense dislike for trade, and wished to become an artist; so

---

[1] *Life*, i, p. 286   [2] *Op. cit.*, i, pp. 203 f., 253
[3] *Life of Scott*, p. 617   [4] *Op. cit.*, p. 587
[5] This was the chapel where Stopford Brooke carried on his ministry, at first as an Anglican, and then, after his secession in 1870, on independent lines. The Evangelicals would have been horrified by the views that were propounded by him
[6] A small volume of *Remains*, with a memoir, was published after his death by Josiah Pratt

passionate, indeed, was his love of art that on one occasion he paid a secret visit to France to see the works of the great painters and only came back when his funds were exhausted.

His return to Christianity was the result of the calm and sincere faith of his mother, which gradually overcame his youthful aberrations; but to the alarm of his father he was drawn into Dissenting circles. By this time it was agreed that he was quite unfit to enter the family business, and so he was promised that if he would go to the university and take orders his expenses would be paid, and in due course, a living purchased for him. To this course he at length agreed and went up to Queen's College, Oxford, in May, 1773. He was ordained on September 22, 1776, to the curacy of Rauceby in Lincolnshire, and later took charge of three small parishes in the neighbouring county of Leicestershire. He was then presented to two livings near Lewes, but the damp situation brought on a rheumatic disorder from which he long suffered; so in 1777 he became lecturer at Christ Church, Spitalfields, and also at Long Acre chapel.

His taking over Bedford Chapel in 1780 was a serious matter, as he himself undertook all financial responsibility and repairs were badly needed. But friends came to his rescue and advanced money for his immediate requirements, and also gave guarantees of future support. As the chapel proved a very successful enterprise, no call was made upon them. There Cecil continued to minister until long after our period; a great source of strength to the Evangelical cause in London, not only on account of his preaching, but even more on account of his pure and lofty character.

Long Acre, where Cecil had a lectureship for a short time, was another well-known chapel. It had been originally a Dissenting place of worship, and for a time Whitefield had preached there, but he encountered so much opposition, and even threats to his life, that he moved elsewhere. Its fame as an Evangelical centre goes back to 1780 with the coming of Henry Foster. Foster was a Yorkshireman, having been born at Halifax in 1745, and, like Cecil, a graduate of Queen's College, Oxford. He had already held a number of lectureships in London and had also been curate to Romaine. It was to Foster that Newton wrote the letters from which we derive much information about some of the early Evangelicals. Wilberforce heard him preach in November, 1785, but though he felt much devotion, that did not prevent his falling asleep during the sermon. He heard him again a month later and found him "very good".[1] Foster's greatest admirer, however, was John Thornton, and in his will he left instructions that Clapham, the most valuable of the livings in his gift, when it came vacant was first to be offered to him, and, if he refused, then to John Venn. When the vacancy occurred Foster was unwilling to leave Long Acre and so John Venn became rector of Clapham.

These were the most noteworthy of the proprietary chapels in the hands of Evangelicals. In addition, there were Ram's Chapel at Homerton; Broadway Chapel, now Christ Church, Westminster; and the Bentinck Chapel off the Edgware Road where Basil Woodd ministered from 1785.[2]

Another means by which Evangelicals managed to secure pulpits for themselves, apart from those who were incumbents or curates, was by means of lectureships. These, as we have already seen in the case of Romaine at St. Dunstan's, were in the gift of the parishioners, and, within limits, uncontrolled by the incumbents. They could be held in conjunction with livings, as in the case of Romaine; or with curacies or other appointments, as with Venn and Thomas Scott. It was quite possible and even customary for a clergyman to hold several such appointments if the times of service did not clash. Lectureships were held by Evangelicals at the following churches, among others: St. Dunstan's; St. Bride's; St. Alban's, Wood Street; St. Swithin's, London Stone; St. Mary Somerset; St. Margaret's, Lothbury; St. Bartholomew-the-Great; St. Mary Aldermary;[3] Bow Church; All Hallows; St. Peter's, Cornhill; St. Lawrence Jewry; and Spitalfields.

Another lecturer was George Dyer at St. George the Martyr. He once took charge of Everton during Berridge's absence, and the latter on his return wrote to Lady Huntingdon in February, 1766, that his people were "in a mighty ferment, occasioned by the sounding brass of a Welsh DYER . . .'Tis a pity he should have charge of anything but wasps."

One of the most effective of all the Evangelical lecturers was George Pattrick at St. Leonard's, Shoreditch, who deserves mention although a little beyond our period. Pattrick had previously been chaplain at Morden College, from which he was

[1] *Life*, i, pp. 90, 101

[2] He had been a pupil of Clarke at Chesham Bois. He then went to Trinity College, Oxford, and after ordination was lecturer at St. Peter's, Cornhill

[3] Here Watts Wilkinson was lecturer from 1779. He had been a violent Dissenter, but was won over by Foster. He was a graduate of Worcester College, Oxford

dismissed because he constantly preached about "faith and grace and such like controversial points". Like Romaine in regard to the living of St. Andrew, Blackfriars, when the post was vacant he refused to canvass. In spite of this and of the opposition of the vicar and churchwardens he was elected by the parishioners, receiving 947 votes to his opponent's 357.

St. Leonard's, it may be remarked, had only been built in 1740, and the vicar, John Blake, invited Wesley to preach a charity sermon there on November 15, 1789,[1] so the atmosphere must have been decidedly sympathetic to Evangelicalism. Wesley's preaching at Shoreditch was no isolated event, for from about 1776 onwards he was in great demand, especially for charity sermons. He wrote on January 19, 1783: "The tide is now turned, so that I have more invitations to preach in churches than I can accept."[2] This is a definite testimony to the spread of Evangelical views, or at least to the breakdown of opposition to them. Amongst other incumbents who invited Wesley to preach for them in the last years of his life were T. L. Barbault, of St. Vedast, Foster Lane; John Thomas, of St. Peter's, Cornhill; and Joseph Butler, of St. Paul's, Shadwell.

[1] *Journal*, viii, p. 23   [2] *Op. cit.*, vi, p. 387

CHAPTER 14

THE SOUTH-EASTERN COUNTIES[1]

THE spread of Evangelical views in this area was slow, and largely confined to a few favoured centres; in Surrey they seem not to have penetrated at all. Beginning with Middlesex, we have Charles Manning, vicar of Hayes, as an early adherent of the movement and one of Wesley's most faithful friends. Manning, who attended the Conferences of 1747 and 1748, suffered much from the neighbouring clergy. He also encountered ill-feeling from his own people (on one November 5 the bells were suddenly rung when he was preaching), and especially from the choir, who showed their disapproval during the services. Some of the opposition arose through Manning's connexion with Wesley, who was suspected as a crypto-Jesuit. Wesley, however, in spite of fears of trouble, took the services at Hayes on February 5, 1749, when the vicar was ill, and there was no interruption either then or on the following Sunday.[2] Manning's sincere and devoted labours gradually bore fruit, so much so that a year later Wesley could write: "What a change here within a year or two! Instead of the parishioners going out of church, the people now come from many miles round. The church was filled in the afternoon likewise, and all behaved well but the singers; whom I therefore reproved before the congregation; and some of them were ashamed."[3] Wesley continued to preach at Hayes at regular intervals, and his brother Charles preached there morning and evening on January 13, 1751, when he records that the people "were very patient, at least, of the truth".[4]

Manning's influence and example began slowly to extend to the nearby parishes, as is shown by the following account, not without its humorous side, of a visit paid by Wesley to Uxbridge on February 12, 1758:

[1] For convenience the block of counties from Hampshire to Oxfordshire are included in this chapter
[2] *Journal*, iii, p. 390   [3] *Op. cit.*, iii, p. 453   [4] *Journal*, ii, p. 77

At the request of the Vicar, Mr. J——,¹ ... I preached
... both morning and afternoon, to a large and serious
congregation. How uncommon a providence is this!
The gospel was preached in the church at Hayes. Several
of the parishioners ran from it and took pews at
Hillingdon. It followed them into Hillingdon church,
where I preached twice in one day. Some of them went
to Uxbridge. And now it is come to torment them at
Uxbridge also.²

In Kent there was more Evangelical activity. Henry Piers, who had been converted by Charles Wesley in June, 1738,³ became vicar of Bexley shortly afterwards. Piers was the son of Sir Henry Piers, the first baronet; and until, in 1759, he suffered financial loss, through the dishonesty of his agent in the West Indies, a man of means. He was an original member of a small society which met in Fetter Lane, and a close friend of the Wesley family. Keziah lived for a time in his vicarage. Piers shared Wesley's views on the Millennium, and also attended the first Methodist Conference in 1744. He was not, however, a very strong character, for he refused to let Charles Wesley preach in his church on November 11, 1738, "through fear of man; pretending tenderness to his flock". There was perhaps some excuse, as he must have been feeling his way in his new parish. At any rate, he was bolder a few months later, as he allowed Charles to preach on January 26 and February 25; on both of which occasions some of the congregation walked out during the sermon.⁴ Piers died on January 27, 1770, at the age of sixty-five.

The revival made but a tardy entry into Tunbridge Wells, which, like other inland watering-places, would later be a strong centre of Evangelicalism. Lady Huntingdon went there, in company with Madan and Venn, in 1763, when it is described as "celebrated for its waters [but] remarkable for little else than the ignorance and profaneness of its inhabitants".⁵ The use of the church was forbidden to Madan and Venn, so they preached in the Presbyterian chapel (which on an earlier occasion had been granted to John Wesley) and in the open air. Five years later Lady Huntingdon bought a house in the Mount

---

[1] There seems to be some mistake here, for the vicar was the Rev. R. Mills; perhaps a confusion with the churchwarden, whose name was Jennings
[2] *Journal*, iv, pp. 248 f.   [3] *Journal*, i, pp. 101 ff.
[4] *Op. cit.*, i, pp. 135, 141, 144   [5] *Countess of Huntingdon*, ii, p. 124

Ephraim district, and so provided a more certain basis for her activities.

Towards the end of his life Wesley was able to make some impression on Sheerness, preaching in the church on November 11, 1783, and December 12, 1784. The Methodists built a meeting-house there shortly before October, 1786.[1]

We come now to the most noted centre of Methodist and Evangelical propaganda in Kent. This was Shoreham, where Vincent Perronet was vicar from 1728 to 1785. Perronet, who came of Huguenot stock, was born in 1693, and received his education in the North of England and at Oxford. He was a man of private means, and had a small estate near Canterbury. At first he was prejudiced against the Methodists, and never became an itinerant, but Wesley, when he met him, through Henry Piers on August 14, 1744, at once recognized their kinship of soul, and wrote: "I hope to have cause of blessing God for ever, for the acquaintance begun this day."[2] Wesley often consulted Perronet in the early days of the movement, and by some he has been dubbed the archbishop of Methodism.

After Perronet threw in his lot with the Methodists, progress was extraordinarily slow, and he met with much opposition. Charles Wesley had an unpleasant experience at Shoreham on September 16, 1746: "As soon as I began preaching, the wild beasts began roaring, stamping, blaspheming, ringing the bells, and turning the church into a bear-garden. . . . The rioters followed us to Mr. Perronet's house, raging, threatening, and throwing stones."[3] John also preached there on the following October 5, and though he seems to have encountered no violence he was disappointed with his hearers, who "seemed to understand just nothing of the matter, but God can give them understanding in time".[4] His hopes, thus expressed, received but little fulfilment, for later he wrote that Perronet laboured, "and that with all his might", for some thirty years before he saw any fruit of his efforts.[5]

Perronet laboured on to an advanced age, retaining his faculties almost to the end. When Wesley visited him in his ninetieth year he wrote: "I do not know so venerable a man. His understanding is little if at all impaired, and his heart seems to be all love."[6] This was on January 10, 1783, two years before the death of Perronet. For the last three years of his ministry he

---

[1] *Journal*, vi, p. 462; vii, pp. 38, 213   [2] *Op. cit.*, iii, p. 145
[3] *Journal*, i, p. 428   [4] *Journal*, iii, pp. 265 f.   [5] *Letters*, vii, p. 154
[6] *Journal*, vi, p. 386

had the assistance of Peard Dickinson as curate, and many of the parishioners thought that he would be appointed to the vacant living. But this was not to be, and as the new vicar did not require his services he joined Wesley at the City Road chapel in August, 1786. Two years later he married Betsy Briggs, the grand-daughter of his late vicar.[1]

Perronet had two sons who became Methodist preachers; and, though they took no direct part in the Evangelical movement, they demand some notice. Both were men of considerable literary powers, but also of much eccentricity. Charles itinerated with his Wesley namesake at various times, and was a trustee of his marriage settlement. John thought highly of his poetry, though he considered that the author's lack of education had handicapped him. His opinion of the man himself was not so favourable, for he wrote to Samuel Furly on August 12, 1757, concerning him: "I never knew one so altered for the worse . . . in so short a time."[2] Edward, the other brother, became notorious for his satirical attack on the establishment, to which he gave the title *The Mitre*. It was so unfair in the eyes of Wesley that he persuaded him to suppress it. But much can be forgiven to the author of "All hail the power of Jesu's name." Both brothers worked for Lady Huntingdon at Canterbury; but Edward was dismissed after his attack on the Church and ended his days in 1792 as minister of a small Dissenting congregation. He was buried in the cathedral cloisters. Charles had died in 1767, pre-deceasing his father by many years. The latter must have been a little saddened by the antics of his sons; but such aberrations were not uncommon in the offspring of Methodist leaders.

In Sussex, little apparently was being done, except in Brighton. Whitefield had preached there in 1759, and it was in North Street that Lady Huntingdon opened the first of her chapels. This was a piece of wise strategy, for Brighthelmstone, as it was then called, was becoming a seaside resort.[3] The royal connexion, however, did not begin until 1765, when the Duke of Gloucester, brother of George III, took the cure there. Its most famous royal patron, the Prince of Wales (later George IV), did not pay his first visit until 1783. Lady Huntingdon made good use of her chapel, and Romaine records working

---
[1] Wesley, *Letters*, vii, p. 272   [2] *Letters*, iii, p. 220
[3] Brighton had been brought to the notice of the public by Dr. Richard Russell, who in 1750 advocated the use of sea water for diseases of the glands. The population was then about 2,000; by the end of the century it exceeded 7,000.

there in 1765 "among a sweet people, with whom I am exceedingly happy".[1] Toplady, also, paid a most fruitful visit ten years later.

At Lewes, as we have already seen, Richard Cecil had two small livings in 1780; but he was there too short a time to make his influence felt. The Rev. John Eyre, who became minister of Ram's Chapel, acted as his curate.[2]

In Hampshire, Methodism made but slow progress. It was introduced into Winchester in 1765, and John Wesley paid routine visits to that city, as well as to Romsey, Portsmouth, and Southampton. He does not seem to have been admitted to the pulpits in any of these towns—though on October 10, 1783, he was offered the use of a church in Winchester, but when the time for the service arrived the key could not be found, so he was forced to preach in the street.[3]

The only definitely Evangelical parish, so far as I have been able to discover, was Dummer, near Basingstoke, where Charles Kinchin, a member of the Holy Club, was rector. Whitefield worked in the parish for two months in the autumn of 1736, and Hervey was curate there two years afterwards. As Kinchin died in 1742 the influence was of but short duration. During Kinchin's lifetime Wesley paid frequent visits to the family, and also preached in the neighbouring church of Popham.[4] Kinchin's widow, Esther, became a prominent Moravian, marrying one of the leaders as her second husband.

Going north, we can discern much more activity in Berkshire. In 1768 the Lord Chancellor presented the important living of Reading to the Rev. William Talbot, LL.D., who was then vicar of Kineton in Warwickshire.[5] Henry Venn paid a visit to Reading in 1771, when he "was received with unfeigned love by Mr. and Mrs. Talbot".[6] But Talbot had but a short ministry there, for he died in March, 1774, of a fever caught when visiting. His successor was the Rev. (and later the Hon.) W. B. Cadogan.[7] As Mr. Cadogan was not yet in orders the duties devolved on the curate, the Rev. John Hallward. The parishioners hoped that he would be allowed to continue under the new vicar, but in this they were disappointed, as Cadogan on being instituted, at once dismissed him. This action had

---

[1] *Works*, p. 707   [2] Bateman, *Life of Daniel Wilson*, i, p. 3
[3] *Journal*, vi, p. 453   [4] *Op. cit.*, i, pp. 449 ff., 481; ii, pp. 150, 166
[5] For Talbot's early life, see p. 292   [6] *Venn Family Annals*, p. 90
[7] For a good account of Cadogan, see Smyth, *Simeon and Church Order*, pp. 202 ff., and Cecil's *Memoir* prefixed to Cadogan's *Discourses*

been anticipated by Lady Huntingdon, with her customary alertness, and she had already visited the parish to consult with Mrs. Talbot and Hallward. Hallward himself was soon provided for, being presented to Shawbury in Shropshire; but the congregation was a different matter, and they quickly scattered—some joined Dissenting chapels, but others, wishing to preserve at least the outward forms of the Church, opened a chapel of their own, where they could still enjoy the Prayer Book service, and looked to Lady Huntingdon to supply them with preachers.[1] The scanty remnant who remained faithful to St. Giles's were naturally critical of their new vicar, who had also been appointed to the parish of Chelsea, and in consequence was with them for only half the year. Cadogan was a man of sincere religion, but not at all in sympathy, during his early years in orders, with Evangelical views. Then in 1780 there came a new experience, and for the remaining seventeen years of his life he definitely identified himself with the movement. One of his first acts after this change of views was to invite Hallward to return to Reading. This, however, he was unable to do permanently, though he consented to help for six months.

Although there was still much prejudice against Cadogan, and in spite of his preaching being impeded by a poor delivery, he soon collected a large congregation to St. Giles'; so great, indeed, did it become that a new gallery had to be constructed. He remained at Reading until his death in January, 1797.

During Talbot's incumbency the congregation at St. Giles' had often had the opportunity of hearing sermons from the Rev. Philip Gurdon, curate of nearby Cookham. Gurdon, who had an estate in Suffolk, was a fellow of Magdalen College, Oxford, from 1770 to 1780, but chose to spend his energies in proclaiming the Gospel. His fervent preaching drew large crowds to hear him, and he made many converts.

The great Evangelical light in Berkshire, however, and that for the longest period, was Thomas Pentycross, vicar of Wallingford from 1774 to 1808. Born in 1748 he had been educated at Christ's Hospital and Pembroke College, Cambridge, where he was a contemporary of De Coetlogon. He was also a close friend and ally of Rowland Hill in the various enterprises promoted by the latter. At this time he became very unsettled in his views, and even contemplated leaving the university, and all prospects of orders, and going to Trevecca. Berridge, with

[1] *Countess of Huntingdon*, ii, pp. 401 f.

whom he was a great favourite, wrote to Whitefield: "He came to my house about three weeks ago, and brought two pockets full of doubts and scruples relating to the Articles and Liturgy. I would fain have had the scruples left at Everton, but he took them all back with him to college, and seemed determined not to part with them. . . . When he left he talked of going to the Welsh College."

At length, however, he managed to overcome his objections to taking orders, but it was some time before he found a bishop willing to ordain him. After his ordination he occasionally helped Romaine, who was very good to him. Then in 1774 he was appointed to Wallingford, a living worth only £12 a year; but Lady Huntingdon gave him generous assistance, including £25 to enable him to settle there. He found many difficulties in his parish, but faced them with energy and courage, and in the end not only attracted his own parishioners, but also drew many from the surrounding villages. At one time he was reported to the bishop for over-crowding his church and for the introduction of hymn-singing. But the latter, after going into the matter, very wisely told him to continue along his own lines. Henry Venn paid him a visit soon after his arrival and commented: "He is in a most useful sphere indeed, and has much favour with the people."[1] Pentycross's success seems to have a little turned his head and revived his eccentric ways. At any rate, a number of his congregation broke away and built a chapel of their own, which was opened in 1791 by the Rev. Thomas Wills, the henchman of Lady Huntingdon. But even before it was built the seceders had already quarrelled among themselves over the question of baptism. At first Pentycross was hurt by their desertion, but on reflection he decided that perhaps it was all for the best, as his own successor might not preach the Gospel. He died in 1808, when the funeral sermon was preached by Thomas Scott.[2]

In the early days of the movement there seemed some prospect that there might be an opening at Abingdon, for Wesley, although he was not allowed to preach in the church, attended prayers at the rectory on July 22, 1741. But nothing seems to have come of it.[3]

Crossing the Thames, we come to the neighbouring county of

---

[1] *Life*, p. 223 (February, 1775).

[2] It was published under the title of *The Duty and Advantage of remembering Deceased Ministers*

[3] *Journal*, ii, p. 477

Buckinghamshire where there was much activity, especially at the famous village of Olney. But before considering Olney it will be well to deal with other, less well-known centres. At Aston Sandford, to which Thomas Scott would retire from more strenuous labours in 1803, the rector G. C. Brodbelt was an Evangelical, as was the Rev. Jeremiah Newell at Great Missenden. High Wycombe and its neighbourhood had for a season the doubtful advantage of hearing the sermons of the Rev. Thomas Williams, a very popular preacher, especially with the young of the opposite sex, but a man of a headstrong and conceited disposition. He had originally been a Methodist, but after spreading scandals about the Wesleys he was expelled, though received back on December 2, 1744, after retracting them. In the following year he had the honour of introducing Methodism into Ireland. But he was again expelled in 1755, and was later ordained through the good offices of Lady Huntingdon. The Rev. J. Harmer preached at High Wycombe in the summer of 1774, though it is not certain that it was in the church.[1] At Clifton Reynes, near Olney, the incumbent for a short time was the Rev. Thomas Jones, one of the students expelled from St. Edmund Hall. Jones was among the first to follow the example of Raikes in opening a Sunday School. It was whilst visiting his widow that Cowper first met her sister, Lady Austen.

Among the minor figures of the movement one of the most effective was Thomas Clarke, rector of Chesham Bois from 1766 to 1793. He was a man of scholarly tastes and considerable learning—Romaine once described him as the "Solomon of the age". Clarke had been of a religious turn of mind from his youth, and after taking his degree at Oxford, where he was at Brasenose, was ordained to a curacy at Amersham. He did not remain there very long, as his views met with the disapprobation of his rector; the congregation, also, were confused by hearing very different teaching from the same pulpit. He then took a curacy in Yorkshire, where he attracted the notice of Venn, who mentioned him to Lady Huntingdon. Through her influence he was appointed to the living of Chesham Bois, then a small village of a couple of dozen houses. As Chesham Bois is only three miles from Amersham the appointment must have caused some annoyance to his former rector. One great service rendered by Clarke to the movement was the training of young men for Holy orders. After the establishment of the Elland Society he

[1] Wesley, *Letters*, vi, p. 105

accepted candidates recommended by them without payment beyond the cost of their board.

We come now to the parish of Olney, whose fame rested more upon its connexion with a number of leading names than upon any striking religious achievements. One and all they found it a difficult and disappointing sphere of labour, and seem to have been only too glad to move elsewhere when the opportunity came their way. The situation was depressing, with mists creeping up from the sluggish Ouse. The one redeeming feature was the church with its tower and pinnacled broach spire, more typical of Northampton than Buckinghamshire, standing near the river. The town was squalid and shabby, and the inhabitants, who gained a precarious livelihood by lace-making, were often on the verge of starvation. In one crisis Cowper wrote to a rich Nottingham banker who sent £50 to meet their needs. But to Cowper they seemed contented enough, for he speaks of:—

> Yon cottager, who weaves at her own door,
> Pillow and bobbins all her store;
> Content though mean, and cheerful if not gay,
> Shuffling her threads about the live-long day,
> Just earns a scanty pittance, and at night
> Lies down secure, her heart and pocket light.

Even to-day Olney has few attractions, and has been described as having "a long straggling High Street and an avenue down the middle of it, a bow-windowed inn, and a roomy . . . church. But it lacks the cheerful charm associated with such places: its streets are stagnant, but not peaceful." It was at the end of the High Street that Cowper had his home, in a house with a "tall façade of dingy brick, faced with dingier stone, and crowned by a row of false Gothic battlements . . . it abutted on Silver End, the worst district of the place, whose sordid jollities were a constant offence to Cowper's simple but fastidious taste."[1] This combination of ceaseless labour, broken only by "sordid jollities", could hardly provide a soil in which the Gospel seed would readily take root and flourish.

Whitefield had paid occasional visits to Olney in his early days, and large crowds had come to hear him; but the first Evangelical vicar was Moses Browne, who went there in 1754

---

[1] Lord David Cecil, *The Stricken Deer*, pp. 110 f. The house, known as Orchard Side, is now the Cowper Museum.

and held the living until 1785, though from 1764 he was non-resident. Browne is an interesting figure. Originally a pen-cutter he developed mild literary gifts;[1] and his verses attracted the attention of Dr. Watts, who introduced him to Lady Huntingdon. Browne wished to be ordained, but it was some time before he found a bishop who would accept him. At last, through the efforts of Lady Huntingdon and James Hervey, he succeeded; and it was as curate to the latter that he began his clerical life. After that he was domestic chaplain to the Duke of Somerset. When he had been vicar of Olney for ten years he received the offer of the chaplaincy of Morden College, and having a family of thirteen, he gladly accepted this addition to his income. Richard Cecil described Browne as "an evangelical and a good man",[2] but he was hardly suited to the task of coping with the people of Olney. None the less, Newton, whom he appointed as curate in charge of the parish,[3] reported on his arrival that he had "a pleasant lot, where the Gospel has been many years known, and is highly valued by many. We have a large Church and congregation. . . . I meet with less opposition from the world than is usual where the Gospel is preached. This burden was borne by Mr. B—— for ten years, and in that course of time some of the fiercest opposers were removed, some wearied, some softened."[4]

Newton himself was one of the most remarkable of the Evangelical leaders, one of the most remarkable men, indeed, in the whole history of the Church of England.[5] Readers of his *Authentic Narrative*, unless they are entirely devoid of imagination, cannot fail to be amazed, not to say bewildered, by the experiences there recorded. Well might he paint up over the mantelpiece of his study at Olney the words of Deuteronomy 15: 15: "But thou shalt remember that thou wast a bondman in the land of Egypt, and the Lord thy God redeemed thee." Few men have managed to crowd into their lives so much of sin and doubtful adventure and still to retain something that was noble and admirable.

Newton was born in London in 1725 and received in childhood a too intensive religious training from a Puritan mother. Unfortunately she died when he was only seven, and a reaction

---

[1] See pp. 412 f.   [2] *Memoirs of John Newton*, p. 41

[3] He had previously approached Haweis, who had just been driven out of Oxford. It was the latter who suggested Newton

[4] *Cardiphonia*, pp. 302 f.

[5] The latest study is Bernard Martin, *John Newton, a Biography*

R

followed. At the age of twelve he went to sea in a merchant ship of which his father was captain. Four years later, through reading the works of Lord Shaftesbury, he became an infidel. His very unsettled disposition made him lose one post after another, until suddenly there came a new influence into his life which was to prove the one fixed point in a wild career. Having been appointed to a ship sailing for Jamaica, he paid a visit, on his way to joining it, to some friends of his father named Catlett. At once he fell in love with Mary, the thirteen-year-old daughter of the house, and abandoning his voyage, gave himself up to romantic dreams of a speedy union. But much suffering and much sinning were to fill up the seven years which passed before his dreams could be realized. During the interval, in spite of the depths of evil and unbelief into which he plunged, his love never wavered; it was, in fact, the only restraint that he knew, as he himself has said, "though I neither feared God nor regarded man, I could not bear that *she* should think meanly of me when I was dead."

In 1744 his career took a new turn for he was seized by a press-gang of H.M.S. *Harwich* and taken to the Nore. His own talents and the influence of his father soon gained him promotion to the rank of midshipman; but, longing again to see his lady, he deserted, was captured, and after being publicly flogged, reduced to the ranks. By some means unknown he managed to escape and join a trader bound for the coast of Africa. Arriving there he felt a spirit of exultation; for now he could be as abandoned as he liked, and, in his own words, "from this time I was exceedingly vile indeed. I not only sinned with a high hand myself, but made it my study to tempt and seduce others upon every occasion".[1] Those who turn to God are often apt to exaggerate the plight of sin and wickedness from which they have been delivered; but in Newton's case his statements are so detailed and circumstantial that we must accept them. Few men can ever have sinned more deeply and more deliberately than he did—and yet the boundless mercy of God was able to pardon and restore him.

A deeper degradation than even he could have anticipated, however, was to be his lot; for he became practically the slave of the negro mistress of a white trader. At her hands he suffered every imaginable act of tyranny, and his only solace seems to have been to work out the problems in Barrow's Euclid, a copy of which came into his hands. As he had no means of writing he

[1] Cecil, *Memoirs of Newton*, p. 13

carried out his studies in the sand. A change of masters, however, brought a change of fortune, and even a share in a slave factory. Meanwhile for more than two years he had been cut off from news from England; then he received a letter from his father and obtained a post in a ship sailing for home. During the voyage his blasphemy was such as even to provoke rebukes from the hardened captain of the vessel. But another of those sudden changes which marked his life was about to take place. The ship ran into a storm off the coast of Newfoundland and all hope of safety seemed to be lost. In an instant the whole of his past life seemed to pass before him, and he recognized, as by the revelation of a flash of lightning, that his misfortunes and sufferings all dated from his abandonment of religion. Then and there he resolved that if God would spare his life he would devote it to His service.

When he reached England he found that his father was away on a voyage, but that he had procured for him the post of mate on a slave ship. In this capacity, and later as captain, he had a further series of wild adventures; among natives in African forests, among mutinous crews, and in quelling revolts of slaves who tried to seize his ship. But at last he had an established position, and it was not long before he was united to his beloved Mary Catlett. Although he never forgot his vow to serve God and made every effort to lead a more worthy life, the depths of his soul had not been really touched. Then in 1754 he met at St. Christopher's a Captain Clunie and from him learned of Evangelical religion. At once he recognized that this was the answer to all his needs, and a message that he could commend to others with all his heart. None the less, he continued for the time to engage in the slave trade, finding nothing inconsistent between it and his quite genuine religious professions. Day by day he conducted prayers for the crew on the deck, below which all the horrors inseparable from a slaver were to be found. He himself has assured us that on what was to prove his last voyage he experienced "sweeter and more frequent hours of divine communion" than he had known before.

Further voyages were stopped through an illness, and he was given a lucrative post as tide surveyor at Liverpool. Now his thoughts began to turn in the direction of taking orders; a truly strange ambition, in view of his past life and lack of the necessary qualifications. The latter defect, however, he gradually overcame. He had always had a profound love of reading, and even on board ship had pursued the study of Latin, of which he had acquired the elements during his brief days at school. Now, by intense exertions, he learned not only to read the New Testament in the original Greek, but also acquired some knowledge of Hebrew and even of Syriac. At the same time he made it his business to get into touch with various Methodist leaders such as Wesley and Whitefield, and Evangelicals like Berridge, Grimshaw, Venn, and Romaine. But the fact that he had no university degree was still held to be a bar. This, to Wesley, was an absurd position, as he wrote on March 20, 1760:

> His case is very peculiar. Our Church requires that clergymen should be men of learning, and, to this end, have a university education. But how many have a university education, and yet no learning at all? Yet these men are ordained! Meanwhile, one of eminent learning, as well as unblamable behaviour, cannot be ordained *because he was not at the University*! What a mere farce is this![1]

Newton had an interview with the Archbishop of York, but found that his close association with the Methodists and other Dissenters was an additional barrier to his being ordained. At last, however, through the influence of Lord Dartmouth, he was accepted by Bishop Green of Lincoln, and ordained to the curacy of Olney.

By this time Newton was not far short of forty years of age, and the contrast between his former life and that upon which he now entered must have been profound, even if account is taken of the interlude at Liverpool. The excitements of a career at sea were exchanged for a dull countryside; the swelling waves of the Atlantic for the sluggish waters of the Ouse; fierce struggles with mutinous sailors and rebellious slaves for others, no less arduous, though in a different sphere, to bring a sense of sin to the apathetic dwellers of a decaying town. Even after ordination he still wore his old sea-captain's jacket on all possible occasions while at Olney. But it may be that the contrast lies mostly on the surface. There was a strain in Newton, perhaps his interest in books was one manifestation of it, which loved the countryside, and no doubt he would have agreed with his friend Cowper that:

---

[1] *Journal*, iv, pp. 372 f.

> Nor rural sights alone, but rural sounds,
> Exhilarate the spirit, and restore
> The tone of languid nature.

Though his own "nature" can never have been "languid", he himself has testified to the benefits of the country: "I always find these rural scenes have some tendency both to refresh and to compose my spirits",[1] and it was a strong sense of duty alone which urged him to exchange them for the noise and dirt of London.[2]

Lord Dartmouth proved to be a most helpful friend and patron, and some time after Newton's going to Olney built a new parsonage house. Cowper speaks of it in a letter to Lady Hesketh on April 17, 1786: "The vicarage ... was not finished till some time after we arrived at Olney.... It is a smart stone building by much too good for the living."

Although Newton laboured diligently and devotedly, he made but little progress at Olney; indeed, he apparently lost ground, for the "large congregations" which he found on his arrival seem to have diminished, that is, if Venn's experience was typical, for on a visit there in March, 1769, he contrasted the tiny congregation with those at "favoured, dear Huddersfield".[3] Perhaps his methods were too forceful and too direct for the slow-minded country folk, and he may have lacked patience in dealing with them. Undoubtedly he managed to arouse a good deal of hostility, and it must have been with no little relief when in 1779 he received the offer of the important city living of St. Mary Woolnoth in Lombard Street. Perhaps this comes out in the humorous manner in which he announces the offer to a friend. "I am about to form a connexion for life with one Mary Woolnoth, a reputed London saint in Lombard Street." And a life connexion it proved to be.

If Newton's work at Olney had been a comparative failure, it was whilst there that he began to reveal those qualities which made him so outstanding a director of souls. The varied experiences of his own life had given him an insight into the temptations of others and an abiding sympathy with them in their struggles. He had also a natural bent for psychology, likening himself to a physician who is mainly interested in anatomy.

---

[1] *Authentic Narrative*, p. 90

[2] See his letter to Hannah More in 1787, printed in her *Memoirs*, ii, p. 89

[3] *Life*, p. 148

Certainly he was profoundly skilled in "the study of the human heart, with its workings and counterworkings, as it is differently affected in a state of nature or of grace".[1] Many came to Olney for the benefit of his advice, and, in addition, he carried on an immense correspondence with all sorts and conditions of men and women. The move to London merely gave him the opportunity still further to develop gifts which were first disclosed at Olney.

Newton's time at Olney was fruitful in another way, for it was there that he produced, in conjunction with Cowper, the hymns that take their name from the parish. Cowper, after his early mental breakdown, had found a refuge with the Unwins at Huntingdon, but the death of the father by a fall from his horse in 1767 made them wish to find another home. It was at Newton's suggestion that they and Cowper came to Olney.

On the surface, the close friendship between Newton and Cowper is hard to explain. What could they have in common, the virile ex-sea-captain and the delicate, nervous ex-lawyer, the self-taught curate and the refined scholar and man of exquisite taste? In actual fact they had many things in common, and not least that enduring bond, a strong sense of humour. That Cowper should lean on a man of Newton's immense strength of character, when once he had given him his confidence, seems natural enough; but the relationship between them was by no means one-sided, for Cowper's mind when unclouded by disease was strong and vigorous. Newton, for his part, though seemingly rough and uncouth, was tender and sympathetic at heart; he had, too, an intense love of classical literature, which though it was self-acquired, went deeper than that of many professed scholars. But the closest link between them was their similar outlook in religion.

There have been those who look upon Cowper's connexion with Newton as accounting for his fits of madness; but this can scarcely be maintained, and is looked upon by most recent students of the poet as unfounded.[2] Cowper had had a severe mental breakdown before coming to Olney, and if future attacks took a religious form, that was only to be expected, since religion was Cowper's greatest interest in life. If the remainder of his existence was tinged with melancholy, his sufferings had at least taught him to seek comfort outside himself, and "the stricken deer", to use his own expression, was:

[1] *Cardiphonia*, p. 50
[2] See, for example, Lord David Cecil, *The Stricken Deer*, pp. 143 f.

Found by one who had Himself
Been hurt by the archers.

At first, under Newton's direction, he employed himself in visiting the poor and in teaching in the Sunday School. Then came the shock of the sudden death of his brother John at Cambridge in 1770, which brought about another breakdown. For a time, although his faith seems to have been shaken, he kept up his outward activities; but a third attack in 1773 after his abortive engagement to Mrs. Unwin drove him completely out of his senses. He felt that he was damned, and even attempted to hang himself, as he had tried to do during his first attack. Worse than Judas, he was outside the means of grace; and after Newton had left and Scott was curate at Olney he never attended religious worship, nor would he join in prayers offered up in his presence. Looking back on this time in 1793, he wrote his poem to Mrs. Unwin—one of the most pathetic ever penned—beginning:

> The twentieth year is well-nigh past,
> Since first our sky was overcast;
> Ah would that this might be the last!
> My Mary!

Southey has blamed Newton for interfering, after he had left Olney, with the lives of both Cowper and Mrs. Unwin.[1] But such a criticism fails to take account of Newton's method of corresponding on religious matters with innumerable spiritual clients. How could he and those to whom he was attached cease to write to one another, especially on the things which they held to be the most important of all?

Newton's successor as curate of Olney was the Rev. Thomas Scott. If Scott's career lacks the romantic flavour which marked that of his predecessor, it has many interesting features, though on a different plane. He was born in February, 1747, at Bratoft in Lincolnshire, where his father was a grazier with a small farm. He seems to have been a man in comfortable circumstances, and his sister married the famous landscape gardener, "Capability" Brown. Scott, after being taught by his mother, went to a school at Burgh, where he began Latin. But soon he was moved, first to Bennington, where the incumbent took

[1] *Life of Cowper*, ii, p. 255

pupils, and then to Scorton in Yorkshire, where the headmaster was the Rev. John Noble. Here he seems to have remained for five years without ever returning home. When he left in 1762 he was apprenticed to a surgeon at Alford, but subsequently was called back to help with the family farm. There, in spite of constant distaste, he worked for nine years, during which he read widely and voraciously, though the necessary books were hard to come by. He was thus, like Newton, largely self-educated, which perhaps explains his somewhat overweening confidence in his own intellectual powers.[1]

Such religious influences as affected him in his youth were evidently of no definite kind; but at the age of sixteen he underwent a crisis before making his first communion, not unlike that which faced Charles Simeon. This crisis recurred with each successive communion, but in the intervals he seems to have paid little attention to religion. Coming across a Socinian commentary on the Bible belonging to his father, he immediately accepted its teaching, and, at a single stroke, both allayed the fears which from time to time had alarmed him, and also flattered his intellectual pride. He became deeply interested in religious questions, and this, combined with a desire to escape from work on the farm, led him to seek ordination. The unorthodoxy of his views and the scanty achievements of his religious life seem not to have troubled him. As he acknowledged in later life, he was then "nearly a Socinian and Pelagian, and wholly an Arminian . . . in a church whose doctrines are diametrically opposed to all three".[2] That he had some difficulty in fulfilling his desires is not altogether surprising; but at length, on September 20, 1772, he was ordained deacon by the Bishop of Lincoln and placed in charge of the parishes of Stoke Goldington and Weston Underwood near Olney.[3]

Scott naturally had no very high standard of ministerial duty, but his methods were suddenly and sharply challenged by the example of Newton. He had already made a point of going to hear him preach, but that had only aroused his con-

[1] Cf. Hazlitt on William Cobbett in *The Spirit of the Age*: "He is a self-taught man, and has the faults as well as the excellences of that class of persons . . . For want of knowing what has been discovered before him, he has not certain general landmarks to refer to or a general standard of thought to apply to individual cases. He relies on his own acuteness and the immediate evidence, without being acquainted with the comparative anatomy or philosophical structure of opinion"

[2] *Works*, i, pp. 13 f.

[3] At one time he lived in a house at Weston which was later occupied by Cowper

tempt; now this despised Evangelical was to stir him to a complete dissatisfaction with himself and his ways. In January, 1774, Newton attended the death-bed of one of Scott's parishioners whom the latter had neglected. It was true that he had never actually been sent for, but none the less his conscience was stricken. This impression was deepened by reading Bishop Burnet's picture of clerical life, and also by Law's *Serious Call*. In May, 1775, he had the chance of preferment, but his awakened conscience made him refuse it; he dared not again subscribe to the Thirty-nine Articles.[1]

Scott's contempt for Newton extended to all "Methodists" and he had warned his flock against such folk. Even in his state of spiritual anxiety he made no attempt to obtain Newton's help; in fact, he tried to draw him into a controversy, in which he promised himself an easy victory. But Newton refused to respond. About this time he read Clarke *On the Scripture Doctrine of the Trinity*, a work of Arian tendency, and found that his Socinian notions were shaken by it.[2] His further progress towards orthodoxy owed little to Evangelical writers —though he read Hervey's *Theron and Aspasio* and Venn on *Zachariah*—but much to the older Anglican divines, such as Hooker *On Justification*, Bishop Hall's *Contemplation* (which had also helped Whitefield) and Bishop Beveridge's writings. At last he worked out a position for himself which differed but little from that of Evangelicalism in its mildly Calvinistic form. One thing which helped him greatly was a fresh study of the Scriptures, which before he had read mainly with a view to gaining knowledge of the original languages.[3]

The suggestion that Scott should follow him came from Newton, with whom Scott was now on intimate terms. But the latter, from his knowledge of the parish and congregation—he had frequently preached there—was unwilling to accept. At length, having been told that Moses Browne was in failing health and that on his death he himself would receive the living, he consented. But he was never happy there and admitted his unpopularity and the smallness of the congregations.[4] Cowper reported to Newton (it must have been on hearsay, for he himself did not attend divine worship) that "Mr. Scott would be admired, were he not so apt to be angry with his congregation. Warmth of temper, indulged in to a degree that may be called scolding, defeats the end of preaching." This letter was written

[1] *Works*, i, pp. 27 f. [2] *Op. cit.*, i, pp. 40 f.
[3] *Op. cit.*, i, p. 29 [4] *Life*, p. 215

on March 29, 1784, and in the following year Scott accepted a chaplaincy at the Lock Hospital.

Moses Browne died shortly afterwards and the new vicar, a Mr. Bean, decided to reside in the parish. Of him Scott wrote that he "was very useful there, and very acceptable to my friends and favourers."[1] Southey said that Bean had "more ability than Mr. Scott, more discretion than Mr. Newton, and was not inferior in poetry to either",[2] a judgment that it is not altogether easy to accept.

In Oxfordshire, there was little Evangelical influence. John Gambold had been rector of Stanton Harcourt, but resigned his living in order to become a bishop with the Moravians. The only signs of life were in Oxford itself. There, as at Cambridge, a good deal of co-operation took place between town and gown in matters of religion. The members of the Holy Club had sought an outlet for their new found desire to serve their fellow men by working in the city; and so it continued. Early in 1739 Kinchin wrote to Whitefield telling him that large numbers of gownsmen were attending the meetings of the societies.[3] Such intercourse with the city would later have serious consequences. The great centre of Evangelicalism in this early period was St. Mary Magdalene, where the Rev. Joseph Jane, tutor of Christ Church, was vicar. He was the son of another Joseph Jane who had been curate in charge of Truro until 1746 and died in the following year. But the revival which affected Oxford in 1761 was the work mainly of his curates Jones and Haweis. The latter was a man of some ability. He was born at Redruth, the son of a solicitor, on January 1, 1733, and educated at Truro Grammar School, where Foote the actor was a schoolfellow. He then went up to Christ Church, moving later to Magdalen Hall. Having proceeded so far as to take an LL.B. he decided to study medicine, and went to Edinburgh where he duly qualified. But he had come under the influence of Walker of Truro and finally took orders. His preaching at Oxford attracted so much notice, especially among undergraduates, that the church was placed out of bounds, and the proctors used to come in during the service to see if any of them were present.[4] A further measure was taken in 1762 by Bishop Hume, who withdrew Haweis's licence. Haweis rather unwisely then appealed to Archbishop Secker, who naturally refused to interfere between a diocesan and one of his clergy. Haweis obtained a chaplaincy

[1] *Life*, p. 223
[2] *Life of Cowper*, ii, p. 291
[3] Wesley, *Journal*, ii, p. 145
[4] Sidney, *Life of Richard Hill*, p. 127

at the Lock Hospital, and later became rector of Aldwinckle, Northampton. Bishop Hume showed further animus against St. Mary Magdalene and the teaching given there, for when Talbot applied for a curacy he refused to license him. Talbot, who had influential friends, proposed to take up the matter in public; but in the end nothing was done about it.[1]

Simeon paid a visit to Oxford in 1783, preaching at Carfax Church. The people were at first suspicious of him, as being a "Methodist", but crowded to hear him in the evening.[2]

[1] *Op. cit.*, pp. 82 ff.   [2] Carus, pp. 56 f.

CHAPTER 15

THE EASTERN COUNTIES

IN the sixteenth and seventeenth centuries the Eastern counties had been a great stronghold of Puritanism, but though not without centres of light (no one can forget Berridge at Everton) their response to the revival was unexpectedly slow.

In Essex, William Unwin, the son of the Rev. Morley Unwin of Huntingdon and the friend of Cowper, after being curate-in-charge of Comberton held the joint livings of Stock Harvard with Ramsden from 1769 to 1786. He had been at Christ's College, Cambridge, where he had won the Chancellor's medal. It was Unwin who had given Doddridge's *Rise and Progress of Religion* to one of Wilberforce's fellow-travellers in 1784, the reading of which was a turning-point in Wilberforce's life. He and his wife were intimate friends of the latter, who shortly before Unwin's death paid them a visit, in April, 1786, of which he records: "My heart opens involuntarily to Unwin and his wife."[1] Mrs. Unwin continued to be a friend of the Wilberforces, as Henry Martyn records meeting her at their house on January 26, 1804.

At Ovington, the rector from 1764 to 1803 was the Rev. George Downing, a popular preacher who at one time was chaplain to Lord Dartmouth. Charles Wesley describes him as "humble, loving, zealous":[2] whilst John preached at Ovington on January 13, 1765 (and then at Titbury) spending the evening at Downing's house.[3]

Another Essex Evangelical incumbent was Robert Storry, vicar of St. Peter's, Colchester. Storry was a Yorkshireman and had been prepared for the ministry by Joseph Milner. He was ordained in 1774 to Horsingham in the North Riding, and in the following year went as curate to Adam at Winteringham, where he lived for six years in the rectory. He married Romaine's daughter. The living he owed to the appointment of Mrs. Wilberforce, the aunt of William and sister of John Thornton. His successful attempts to attract Methodists to his church earned for him the strong condemnation of John Wesley,

---

[1] *Life*, i, p. 110   [2] *Journal*, ii, p. 260   [3] *Journal*, v, p. 105

who, in a sermon on October 11, 1790, described them as "sheep-stealing".

In Suffolk, there was a new opening for preaching at Lakenheath, the scene of an earlier and short-lived revival.[1] Wesley, on the invitation of the people, went there in December, 1757, and again a year later.[2] He also spoke of the opportunity to Madan, who was then in the neighbourhood, and some of the villagers, having heard Madan preach, asked him to go there. The vicar allowed him the use of the church and even consulted him about engaging an Evangelical curate. William Ley (or Lee), who had been a Methodist itinerant before his ordination,[3] went there in consequence, but did not long remain, as the vicar dismissed him. On September 7, 1767, whilst the matter was still in suspense, Berridge wrote him a letter of encouragement. As Wesley had preached at Lakenheath on the previous February 26[4] the breach must have come about suddenly. The work then developed on Methodist lines, but again there was an absence of the spirit of perseverance, for Wesley, on going there in November, 1773, "found the Society . . . entirely vanished away." His visit brought about a temporary revival, but he warned the people that unless they kept together he would not again come to them.[5] Presumably they failed to do so for there is no mention of any further visit in his journal.

Another lamp was lighted when the Rev. John Hallward was presented to the living of Assington and Milden by his Oxford friend, the Rev. Philip Gurdon, who was squire of Assington. He had previously been curate at St. Giles', Reading, and for four years vicar of Shawbury. Hallward had gone up to Worcester College, Oxford, in July, 1766 (he is described in the registers as "gent."), at the age of sixteen, and was elected to a fellowship nine years later. He was already an Evangelical and attended the meetings at the house of Mrs. Durbridge. He lived until 1826, remaining at Assington until the end.[6]

The only other trace of Evangelical leanings in the county that I have come across is at Lowestoft, where one of the curates was on friendly terms with a Methodist class-leader.[7]

Into Norfolk, Evangelicalism seems to have made but a

---

[1] See p. 118   [2] *Journal*, iv, p. 295
[3] Wesley in his will left him a set of his writings
[4] *Journal*, v, p. 196   [5] *Op. cit.*, vi, p. 5
[6] See memoir by J. Bickersteth under the title of *Mortality Swallowed up in Life*
[7] L. F. Church, *Early Methodist People*, p. 12

tardy entry. The Methodists were strong in Norwich, though the society there was subject to constant vicissitudes. On January 18, 1761, Wesley was accompanied by a number of them to the cathedral.[1] Three miles from the city Whitefield met on April 11, 1767, a "clergyman of the establishment who promises well";[2] but we hear no more about him. Madan did much itinerating round both Norwich and Thetford in the early days of the movement; but this again does not seem to have helped in the spread of Evangelicalism. Towards the end of our period, however, things began to look up and a number of Evangelical clergymen obtained livings in the county. In 1783 John Venn became vicar of Little Dunham, where he remained until his move to Clapham nine years later. His appointment to Little Dunham has some interesting features. It was made by a retired Indian civilian named Parry, who had just become squire of the village. Finding the existing incumbent very defective and inefficient, he bought him out, and having been greatly impressed by Venn's preaching presented him to the vacant living.[3] Venn, incidentally, was the first rector to reside in the parish for seventy-five years. Another Evangelical clergyman was Dr. Cookson,[4] a friend of Wilberforce, who was appointed to Forncett by his college (St. John's, Cambridge) in 1788. He found conditions rather adverse, and when Wilberforce paid him a visit on October 9, 1791, he records that Cookson "lamented the deadness of his parish, though he seemed to be truly bent on his important work."[5] The Huntingdonians already had a tabernacle there.

By this time the opposition to Evangelical and Methodist views was gradually relaxing, in Norfolk as elsewhere; and when Wesley opened the meeting-house at Lynn he was the guest of the Rev. E. Edwards, the vicar, an intimate friend of Simeon, and he addressed a meeting attended by all the clergymen in the town, "except one who was lame". He then went on to Diss, where the incumbent was willing to allow him the use of his church but did not know whether the new bishop, Horne, would approve. The bishop happened to be in the neighbourhood and on being consulted made no objection.[6]

The beginnings of Evangelicalism in Lincolnshire have

[1] *Journal*, iv, p. 431   [2] *Letters*, iii, p. 344   [3] *Venn Family Annals*, p. 125

[4] Cookson was a Cumbrian by birth and the uncle of the poet Wordsworth. He had been preceptor to the sons of George III, and was later presented to a canonry at Windsor (1792–1820).

[5] *Life*, i, p. 315   [6] *Journal*, viii, pp. 107 f.

THE EASTERN COUNTIES

already been noticed in connexion with Adam of Winteringham. At Glentworth, a parish between Winteringham and Lincoln, his friend and ally, William Bassett, was vicar from 1729 until his death in 1765. In 1751 he was made archdeacon of Stowe, a very early instance of an Evangelical receiving higher preferment. Walker of Truro, on his visit to Adam in 1757, went on to see Bassett, who was also consulted by Henry Venn on the wisdom of publishing *The Complete Duty of Man*. This little group of Evangelicals in North Lincolnshire was in close touch with their fellows across the Humber, though stormy weather often interrupted their intercourse.

At Grimsby, Wesley preached on June 30, 1788, and the day following, the Rev. Lindsey Haldenby, the vicar, reading the prayers.[1]

In the north-west of the county, and not far from the Yorkshire border, lay Epworth, the birthplace of Wesley. After many years' absence he went there in June, 1742, but the curate refusing to allow him the use of the pulpit he addressed a large crowd from his father's tombstone.[2] The curate seems to have had a special animus against Wesley, constantly denouncing him from the pulpit, and even forbidding him the sacrament.[3] This deprivation, however, was ended by the rector, Mr. Hay, who in July, 1748, gave Wesley "the comfort of receiving the Lord's Supper" in the church of his youth.[4] From 1757 to 1784 Sir William Anderson was the non-resident rector. On his death his son, Sir Charles Anderson, succeeded to both baronetcy and living.[5] The curate from 1762 until 1808 was the Rev. Joshua Gibson. He was an earnest man, but as bitterly opposed to the Methodists as his predecessor. The result was that, in spite of the pleas of Wesley, many left the church.[6] By the express orders of the rector, Wesley was able to preach in Epworth church on June 25, 1780.[7] Two years later there was a sudden, though short-lived, revival in Epworth and its neighbourhood. Wesley again visited his old home, "which I still love beyond most places in the world", in June, 1784, but found six years later that there was scarce a shadow of the former zeal and activity.[8]

When Wesley's father had been rector of Epworth he had held with it the parish of Wroot, which lies to the south-west. The living was given to John Whitelamb (a man of humble birth who had been educated by the Wesleys and was John's

---

[1] *Journal*, vii, pp. 410 f.   [2] *Op. cit.*, iii, pp. 18 f.   [3] *Op. cit.*, iii, p. 61
[4] *Op. cit.*, iii, p. 360   [5] *Op. cit.*, vi, p. 287   [6] *Op. cit.*, vii, p. 414
[7] *Op. cit.*, vi, p. 287   [8] *Op. cit.*, vi, pp. 352 f., 520; viii, p. 78

pupil at Oxford, and had returned as curate to Wroot) on his marriage in January, 1734, with Mary Wesley. Unfortunately, she died in childbirth in the following November. Wesley preached there on June 13, 1742.[1] He also preached at Owston, a few miles south-east of Epworth, on June 20, 1784, and again two years later. He had paid previous visits to the parish, but before 1784 had not been allowed the use of the pulpit.[2]

In the centre of the county and round Lincoln itself no impression seems to have been made, though on April 18, 1745, Wesley had an interview at his request with Mr. Clarke, the minister of Barkwith, near Wragby. Further to the east there was much activity around Spilsby. R. C. Brackenbury, the squire of Raithby, a Cambridge man who had had thoughts of taking orders, came under Wesley's influence, and did much preaching for the Methodists, for whom he built a chapel in the village. Wesley preached in the church on July 3, 1788.[3] But these activities were Methodist rather than Evangelical. In the same neighbourhood, however, there was an incumbent who was a definite Evangelical, the Rev. William Tyler. Tyler was the son of poor parents, and after being trained at Trevecca became a Dissenting preacher in Wales. Later he went to Hull, where Joseph Milner became interested in him. Milner helped him in his studies, and then had him sent up to Magdalene College, Cambridge, in 1778. Four years later he was ordained to a curacy at Partney, a few miles north of Spilsby, but was dismissed by his rector for holding prayer-meetings. In 1786, however, he was presented to the neighbouring living of Bratoft.

Near Sleaford there was another Evangelical, the Rev. John Pugh, vicar of Rauceby and rector of Cranwell, to the west of the town, from 1771 to 1799. Pugh was an Oxford man, and gave a title to Richard Cecil in September, 1776. He seems to have been drawn towards the Methodists rather late in life, for Wesley preached for him in July, 1781, and he attended the Conferences in that and the following years.[4] Pugh had old-fashioned ideas about the powers of the parish priest, and was a very strict disciplinarian—offenders being made to do public penance in the church dressed in a white sheet. There must have been few parishes where such methods survived, even in the late eighteenth century—though William Gilpin began his ministry at Boldre by compelling a farmer guilty

---

[1] *Op. cit.*, iii, p. 24   [2] *Op. cit.*, vi, p. 521; vii, p. 17
[3] *Op. cit.*, vi, pp. 115, 242; vii, p. 412   [4] *Op. cit.*, vi, pp. 327 f.

of adultery to do public penance.¹ Some eight miles to the north of Sleaford the rector of the parishes of Bloxholme and Digby, the Rev. Henry Peckwell, D.D., subscribed to Middleton's *Biographia Evangelica* in 1779, and was later active in the Evangelical cause in London.

Not far away there was a group of Evangelicals near Grantham. Syston Park, the seat of the Thorold family, lay a few miles to the north of the town. Sir John Thorold, the seventh baronet, was a friend of Lady Huntingdon,² and one of the first members of the society in Fetter Lane. He died in 1748, and his successor, another Sir John (high sheriff of Lincolnshire in 1751), took a deep interest in the movement. He had succeeded to Wesley's fellowship at Lincoln College,³ and kept up a correspondence with him. At Belton, near Syston, the work was hindered by quarrels with the Huntingdonian preachers.⁴ A little further to the east was Welby, whose rector, the Rev. William Dodwell, strongly sympathized with Wesley's work, allowing him the use of his pulpit on July 8, 1781, and attending the Conferences of 1781 and 1782. When he died in 1824, after holding the living for nearly half a century, he left £10,000 to the Wesleyan Methodist Missionary Society and a similar sum to the British and Foreign Bible Society.⁵

In the south of the county I have failed to find traces of Evangelicalism, though the Methodists of the marshland were accustomed to attend services at Whitgift and the chapel of ease at Swinfleet.⁶

We come now to the most outstanding figure in the movement as it developed in the Eastern counties, John Berridge, known as Berridge of Everton. He entered it rather late in the day, otherwise he would have deserved a place among the pioneers.⁷

Berridge⁸ was born on March 1, 1716, at Kingston in Nottinghamshire. His father, like the father of Thomas Scott, with

¹ Pugh was described by one of his successors as "a spiritual light on Rauceby Hill in a time of ecclesiastical supineness" (Trollope, *Hist. of Sleaford*)
² *Countess of Huntingdon*, i, p. 77 ³ *Journal*, i, p. 140
⁴ *Op. cit.*, vi, p. 287 ⁵ *Op. cit.*, vi, p. 328
⁶ Church, *Early Methodist People*, pp. 4 f.

⁷ His remains, with a memoir, were published in 1838 by the Rev. Richard Whittingham, vicar of Potton, who had been his curate. For an interesting account of Berridge, see Smyth, *Simeon*, etc., pp. 149 ff.

⁸ The family name of Bishop Beveridge was often spelt Berridge (see Nicholls, *Hist. and Antiquities of the County of Leicester*, III, pt. i, p. 77). There may have been a connexion between them

s

whose early career that of Berridge has some affinity, was a farmer and grazier, though probably of higher standing and wealth. Berridge, until he was fourteen, was educated at Nottingham, where he lived with an aunt. From the first he seems to have been a steady and serious boy, and religious impressions came to him quite early from a schoolfellow with whom he used to read the Bible. When he went back to help on the farm at Kingston he showed such little aptitude that his father decided to send him to the university. Accordingly he entered Clare Hall, Cambridge, in October, 1734, being then in his nineteenth year, and so older than the average undergraduate of those days. Here he gave himself up to the delights of study, working, it is said, sometimes as much as fifteen hours a day; and in 1742 was elected to a fellowship. His studious ways, which brought him a reputation for learning, did not, however, make him a recluse; on the contrary, he was regarded as a witty and amusing companion. One of his favourite books was Samuel Butler's *Hudibras*, which he knew almost by heart, and he had a certain kinship of soul with the famous satirist. But, if he found time amidst his life of intense study for social intercourse, the due observances of religion had been neglected, and, as a consequence, the spiritual side of his nature had suffered; although now in orders, for some ten years he hardly ever found either time or inclination for prayer. This may have been in part the effect, in part the cause, of a drift towards Socinianism. Suddenly, like Newman in regard to Liberalism, he realized the goal towards which he was tending—that of complete unbelief, and in 1749 determined to find some definite spiritual exercise for his clerical calling. He accordingly undertook the curacy of Stapleford, which he combined with his duties in college. His devotion to his new office was so intense that it drew upon him the suspicion of being a Methodist; but, in looking back in later life, he felt that he had failed to preach the full Gospel. This comes out in a remark of Wesley's on July 18, 1759: "We met Mr. B. at Stapleford, five miles from Cambridge. His heart was particularly set on this people, because he was Curate here for five or six years; but never preached a Gospel sermon among them till this evening."[1]

In 1755 Berridge was presented by his college to the living of Everton with Tetworth, which lies partly in Bedfordshire, partly in Huntingdonshire. Here, as at Stapleford, he found

[1] *Journal*, iv, p. 338

THE EASTERN COUNTIES 275

that his labours seemed to produce no fruit, and towards the end of 1757 began to suspect that his failure must be due to some shortcoming in himself. A close study of the Scriptures then convinced him that the doctrine of Justification by Faith, which hitherto he had considered not only foolish, but even harmful, was true, and that, for the future, he must rely not on "works", but on "faith" alone. At once he destroyed all his old sermons and began preaching in an entirely new manner, often extempore. The effect was almost startling, and hearers began to flock to the church from all sides. We have his own account of what took place in a letter to a certain Mr. Daw which Madan sent on to Wesley on April 29, 1758:

> God has been pleased to bless and prosper my labours, in a very extraordinary manner, for these last three months. Since I preached the real Gospel of Christ, seven people in my own parish have now received the Gospel in the appointed way of repentance towards God, and faith towards our Lord Jesus Christ. Nine or ten from Potton are in a very hopeful way, two at Gamlinghay, and two at Eaton. There is now such a storm arising that I know not how it will end, or when.[1]

News of what was going on at Everton soon spread, and in June of the same year John Walsh went over from Bedford to report. He had a ready welcome from Berridge, who expressed his desire to meet Wesley. Wesley accordingly went to Everton in November.[2] Lady Huntingdon, too, had become interested, and she, for her part, sent Romaine and Madan to investigate. At first they were a little doubtful, but at length gave a very favourable report, in consequence of which she herself, with some of her chaplains, paid a visit to Everton. It lasted three days, during which no less than nine sermons were delivered. On her return the good lady carried back Berridge with her "with a view to his spiritual improvement". He preached in London a number of times and also gave expositions in private houses.[3] This was the beginning of regular visits, usually lasting three months, during which Lady Huntingdon, until Berridge got a curate, provided *locums* for his parish.

[1] *Arminian Magazine*, 1797, pp. 612 f. [2] *Op. cit.*, 1780, pp. 104 f.
[3] *Countess of Huntingdon*, i, pp. 399 f.

Berridge began itinerating almost at once, for all around were empty churches and parsons who apparently cared little for the souls committed to them. Many came to Everton, and Berridge felt that he had a message which he could not withhold from them. In May, 1759, he took a further step and began to preach in the open air, standing on a table in a farmyard to do so.

Berridge was not long in finding, rather unexpectedly, an ally from among the neighbouring clergy, the Rev. William Hicks, rector of Wrestlingworth. Hicks, like his fellows, had at first been very hostile to Berridge and his intrusive activities, as well as to the views by which they professed to be inspired; but on August 1, 1758, he suddenly became convinced of his sinful state and six weeks later he found peace. It was on September 17 that, as he told Wesley, he first preached the Gospel; on which Wesley has the note: "from this time he was accounted a fool and madman".[1]

In many ways Berridge and Grimshaw were much alike, though the eccentricities of the latter were outdone by the vicar of Everton; they were especially alike in the success which attended their itinerations and the wide area which they covered. At one time or another Berridge traversed Bedfordshire, Cambridgeshire, and Huntingdonshire, as well as parts of Hertfordshire, Essex, and Suffolk; though, so far as I know, he never preached in his native county of Nottinghamshire. Often he would ride a hundred miles in a week and preach a dozen times.

We have already noticed that one reason for the opposition to the revival preachers was the occurrence at their meetings of mysterious seizures of a dubious physical nature. People would suddenly drop down as if dead, or break out into wild utterances. In the case of Berridge and the people of his neighbourhood these distressing phenomena, for which there is abundant evidence,[2] seem to have been more common than elsewhere. At first they were taken as manifestations of the work of the Spirit, but after a time a reaction set in. After visiting Everton on January 3, 1762, Wesley wrote that people "were in danger of running from east to west. Instead of thinking . . . that none can possibly have true faith, but those that have trances or visions, they were now ready to think, that whoever had anything of this kind, had no faith".[3] How far such

---

[1] *Journal*, iv, p. 335   [2] See especially, *op. cit.*, iv, pp. 317 ff., 359
[3] *Op. cit.*, iv, p. 483

seizures were a species of hysteria and how far the result of conviction of sin it is difficult to say. Perhaps Bishop Ryle summed it up most satisfactorily when he wrote: "The whole subject, like demoniacal possession, is a very deep and mysterious one, and there we must be content to leave it."[1]

Itineration and the added responsibilities which it brought became a serious financial embarrassment to Berridge, in spite of the possession of private means. He had to provide lay evangelists to help him, and, as many if not most of them were poor as well as uneducated, he had not only to supervise their work, but also to maintain them. Romaine wrote in January, 1766: "Yesterday I dined with Mr. Berridge. He was making great complaints of his debts, contracted by his keeping out of his own living, two preachers and their horses, and several local preachers, and for the rent of several barns, in which they preach. He sees that it is wrong to run in debt and will be more careful."[2] In meeting these expenses he was helped by a number of friends (Romaine's letter quoted above is an appeal for assistance for him), especially by the ever generous John Thornton, members of whose family lived in the parish.

Berridge also suffered from the common accusations that he invaded other men's parishes, and that by crowding his own church with strangers he prevented the parishioners from enjoying their rights. So he had to appear before the bishop to explain his conduct. At first he met with a very cold reception, and was told that unless he amended his ways he would probably find himself in Huntingdon gaol. Eventually, however, the bishop, no doubt impressed by Berridge's sincerity, took up a more kindly attitude, and assured him that he was his friend, but that the Church's rules must be observed. He added that it was impossible for one man to preach the Gospel to every creature. To this Berridge replied that if the clergy would only preach the Gospel to their own people there would be no need for him to undertake the task. So they parted; leaving things much as they were before, but Berridge in some jeopardy.

Deliverance came to him from an unexpected quarter; and the way in which it was achieved throws an interesting light on the ecclesiastical world and its methods. Berridge in adopting Methodist views had lost the friendship of a certain fellow of Clare, but when the latter heard that he might be turned

[1] *Christian Leaders of the Last Century*, p. 229 [2] *Works*, pp. 710 f.

out of his living he wrote to Mr. Pitt,[1] whom they had both known at Cambridge, asking for his help. Pitt then approached a certain nobleman to whom the bishop had been indebted for his promotion, and he in turn called on the bishop and addressed him as follows: "My lord, I am informed that you have a very honest fellow named Berridge in your diocese, and that he has been ill-treated by a litigious neighbour. I hear he has accused him to your lordship, and wishes to turn him out of his living. You would oblige me, my lord, if you would take no notice of this person, and not suffer the honest man to be interrupted." The bishop, for his part, was greatly astonished at this new move, and could not imagine how it had come about; but in view of past obligations, and perhaps hoping for more favours, he at once gave way; or, as Berridge put it (the above account is based largely on his own words), "was obliged to bow compliance". Henceforth there was nothing to be feared from his diocesan, and Berridge was free to go his own way.

When he first went to Everton, Berridge kept in close touch with Cambridge and had much influence over some of the undergraduates, such as Rowland Hill and Pentycross. His itinerating trips also led him into the neighbourhood. He even continued to appear in the university pulpit, though not for long. On Sunday, November 25, 1759, his sermon provoked a number of seizures, which must have seriously offended the authorities. He told Wesley afterwards that "one person cried out aloud, but was silent in a few moments. Several dropped down, but made no noise; and the whole congregation, young and old, behaved with seriousness."[2] In June, 1782, he made a new link, riding over with John Venn to meet Charles Simeon.[3] The coming of Henry Venn to Yelling late in 1771 must have brought new encouragement to him, and a friend, who, if not capable of exercising control, could yet give him sound advice.

The immense labours which Berridge undertook might suggest that he was a man of robust health, Ryle even says "He seems to have possessed one of those iron constitutions which nothing but old age can quite break down."[4] This, however, was far from the case. As early as July 17, 1759, he

---

[1] Berridge states that it was the elder Pitt. This is impossible, for he was at Trinity, Oxford, and that long before Berridge went to Clare. It was Thomas Pitt, Lord Camelford (Clare, 1754–58)

[2] Wesley, *Journal*, iv, p. 360

[3] Carus, *Memoirs of the Life of Charles Simeon*, p. 24 n.

[4] *Christian Leaders of the Last Century*, p. 233

said to Wesley, "I am so weak I must leave off field-preaching."[1] However, he persevered, though he did no outside work between 1768 and 1773. As he grew older his health rapidly deteriorated and he began to suffer from delusions. He thought that his body was made of glass, or that it had become of monstrous size.[2] When Henry Venn paid him a visit in the winter of 1791 he found Berridge in a very low state: "His sight is very dim, his ears can scarcely hear, and his faculties are fast decaying, so that, if he continues any time he may outlive the use of them."[3]

Berridge lived for a little more than a year longer, dying in January, 1793, after a few days' illness, in his seventy-seventh year. Vast crowds came to the funeral service when the sermon was preached by Simeon on the text 2 Timothy 4: 7 f. Venn should have been the preacher but was too ill to be present. Over his grave in the churchyard at Everton is an epitaph, composed by himself, and its quaint language gives a good example of the man's nature:

HERE LIE THE EARTHLY REMAINS OF
JOHN BERRIDGE
LATE VICAR OF EVERTON,
AND AN ITINERANT SERVANT OF JESUS CHRIST,
WHO LOVED HIS MASTER AND HIS WORK,
AND AFTER RUNNING ON HIS ERRANDS MANY YEARS
WAS CALLED UP TO WAIT ON HIM ABOVE.

READER
Art thou born again?
No salvation without a new birth!
I was born in sin, February 1716.
Remained ignorant of my fallen state till 1730.
Lived proudly on faith and works for salvation till 1754.
Was admitted to Everton vicarage, 1755.
Fled to Jesus alone for refuge, 1756.
Fell asleep in Christ, January 22, 1793.

In the above account of Berridge much use has been made of records preserved by Wesley. The relations between the two men were very close, and the correspondence which they carried

---

[1] Wesley, *Journal*, iv, p. 337
[2] Brown, *Recollections of the Conversation Parties of the Rev. Charles Simeon*, pp. 202 f.
[3] *Life*, p. 493

on reveals their different characteristics and throws valuable light on the circumstances surrounding the early days of the Evangelical Movement. Both men were very candid in writing to one another, but their outspokenness and different points of view led to no diminution of their friendship. Here are some extracts. Wesley wrote from Dublin in April, 1760:

> It seems to me, that, of all the persons I ever knew, save one, you are the *hardest to be convinced*. I have occasionally spoken to you on many heads; some of a speculative, others of a practical nature; but I do not know that you were ever convinced of one ... and did not vary a hair's breadth. ... Does not this imply the *thinking* very *highly of yourself*? Does it not imply something of *self* sufficiency ... It was not so with my brother and me, when we were first employed in this great work. ... We were glad to be taught by any man. And this, although we were really alone in the work; for there were none that had gone before us therein. ... Whereas *you* have the advantage which we had not; you tread a beaten path. ... Yet it seems you *choose* to stand alone; what was necessity with *us*, is choice with *you*. You like to be unconnected with any, thereby tacitly condemning all.[1]

Berridge took this in good part and invited Wesley to come again to Everton, and added: "Perhaps a little disagreement, in non-essentials, may be designed as one part of our trial, for the exercise of our candour and patience."[2] At a later date (January, 1768) he wrote: "I see no reason why we should keep at a distance, whilst we continue servants of the same Master. ... I am weary of all disputes, and desire to know nothing but Jesus. ... When I saw you in town, I gave you an invitation to Everton; and I now repeat it, offering you very kindly the use of my house and church."

The relations between Berridge and Wesley call for the notice of a rather obscure incident during the Calvinist controversy. A poem appeared in *The Gospel Magazine* entitled "The Serpent and the Fox, or an interview between Old Nick and Old John", over the signature "Ausculator". After many objectionable attacks on Wesley it concluded:

[1] *Letters*, iv, pp. 91 f. [2] *Methodist Magazine*, 1797, p. 305

The Priest with a simpering face
Shook his hair-locks, and paused for a space;
Then sat down to forge lies with his usual grimace.

As the same periodical had already printed a number of similar effusions from Berridge signed "Old Everton", Southey concluded that this very scurrilous attack was also from his pen.[1] Canon Smyth, however, thinks this exceedingly improbable, as Berridge "plainly deplored the controversy and would have been the last man deliberately to inflame it."[2] This is, of course, a weighty opinion, but a doubt must remain. Berridge in the end did take part in the controversy, and used expressions which he later regretted. Moreover the verses are exactly in his somewhat unfortunate literary vein, and he was seldom restrained by considerations of good taste from allowing it expression. It seems to me that the idea underlying the poem may suddenly have occurred to him and was so attractive to his puckish nature that he immediately put it into writing without realizing its full implications or the harm that it might do.

Berridge was an extraordinary character,[3] and his frequent indiscretions were due to his strong sense of the ridiculous; he could not help putting things in a ludicrous way. He once wrote to John Thornton that he was "born with a fool's cap on his head", to which he got the sensible reply: "Pray, my dear sir, is it not high time it was pulled off?" But this he could not do and, it may be suspected, had no real desire for such a limitation. On the other hand, to condemn him, as Southey does, as "buffoon as well as a fanatic", is seriously to misunderstand him.[4]

The quaint remarks and unpremeditated sallies which Berridge introduced into his sermons must have been very effective among rustic audiences, and perhaps this confirmed his natural propensity; like Grimshaw, he did not mind making

[1] *Life of Wesley*, ii, pp. 601 f. Overton, *The Evangelical Revival*, p. 62, attributes the poem to Berridge and is severe in his denunciation, but as he makes the erroneous statement that it was signed "Old Everton" his conclusion is based on a false premise

[2] *Simeon and Church Order*, p. 186

[3] Cf. Bishop Ryle, *op. cit.*, p. 236: "Never, probably, did the grace of God dwell in a vessel of such singularly tempered clay"

[4] Wesley, writing to Lady Huntingdon on March 10, 1759, described him as "one of the most sensible men of all whom it pleased God to employ in reviving Primitive Christianity" (quoted Tyerman, *Wesley*, ii, p. 324). Perhaps further experience changed his opinion

a fool of himself so long as his message went home. But the effect of such eccentricities, when relayed in college common rooms and among the clergy, not to mention the educated laity, must have been damaging to his reputation. His letters also are full of queer conceits which give them a certain piquancy, though they often offend against good taste. So Berridge was regarded by other Evangelicals with mixed feelings; Housman, for example, "loved and respected the sterling worth of [his] character as thoroughly as he disliked his evangelical excesses."[1]

The foibles and eccentricities of any man are liable to receive undue attention and to overset his more admirable qualities. So it has been with Berridge, and we must not allow ourselves to ignore the finer side of his nature. He was a man of real humbleness of mind, constant in self-denial and self-discipline, abundantly kind, and entirely devoted to the service of his Master. In spite of all his quaintness, he had a considerable fund of shrewdness and good sense in practical matters, and often gave helpful advice to his friends and followers. The sympathetic student of his life and work will not find it hard to concur with Overton, that it is "far more easy to laugh at and criticize the foibles of the good man than to imitate his devotedness . . . and the moral courage which enabled him to exchange the dignified position and learned leisure of a University don for the harassing life and despised position of a Methodist preacher —for so the Vicar of Everton would have been termed in his own day".[2]

In Bedfordshire, to which we now turn, much successful itinerating was done by Berridge and his assistants; his parish lay partly in that county, and his curate and biographer, the Rev. Richard Whittingham, was afterwards vicar of Potton. As early as 1739, however, doctrines similar to those of the Methodists and Evangelicals had been preached by the Rev. Jacob Rogers, curate of St. Paul's, Bedford. Meeting with disapproval, he spent his time itinerating in Leicestershire and Nottinghamshire, and also helped Ingham in Yorkshire. Rogers was an unstable and over-enthusiastic character, and, after joining the Baptists, finally threw in his lot with the Moravians. These latter had started work in Bedford in 1741, promising not to proselytize among Church people or even to hold meetings at the time of divine service. But they soon forgot their promise and in 1750 began building a chapel.

Wesley preached a sermon at St. Paul's on March 10, 1758,

[1] *Life of Housman*, p. xxv   [2] In Abbey and Overton, ii, pp. 178 f.

before the judge, taking as his text Romans 14: 10. William Cole, the high sheriff, was so impressed by it that he requested that it might be published.[1] The Cole family became ardent supporters of the Methodist Movement and built a meeting-house at Luton, where, in the absence of Dr. Prior, the non-resident vicar, they occupied his house. Wesley preached in Luton church on January 16, 1772, at the invitation of the curate, the Rev. Coriolanus Coplestone.[2]

In Cambridgeshire, too, there had been much successful itinerating by Berridge and his friends. This had been largely directed by the Rev. Robert Robinson, minister of the Baptist chapel in St. Andrew's Street. More direct Evangelical influence was exerted by a number of dons who took curacies near Cambridge. Berridge, it will be remembered, had had a curacy at Stapleford from 1749 to 1756. Henry Venn, before he became a declared Evangelical, had a curacy at Barton, and though he was there for six months only, his care, especially for the poor of the parish, made a lasting impression. At Comberton, William Unwin had been curate to the Rev. Richard Oakley, the non-resident rector; he was followed by the Rev. William Bennett, fellow and tutor of Emmanuel. Bennett was one of the small group formed by Rowland Hill, and by his preaching he brought back many Methodists to the Church. In 1790 he became Bishop of Cork and Ross. One of the most effective of these curate-dons was Thomas Robinson, fellow of Trinity (later to be affectionately known as Robinson of Leicester). For about two years he held the curacy of Wicham and Witchford, near Ely, where he drew immense congregations including undergraduates from Cambridge, and among them Joseph Milner. But when he adopted the novel practice of hymn-singing he was dismissed by the incumbent. Robinson's great friend Dr. Jobson, was curate of Doddington for thirty years before being appointed to the living of Wisbech.[3]

Cambridge itself was the scene of much Evangelical activity, in which, as in times more recent, the undergraduate members of the university took a prominent part. The desire, on the part of pious young men, to spend their three short years of residence in an attempt to convert the town, instead of using them to acquire a little much needed knowledge is a constant matter of concern to their pastors and masters. But there is

[1] *Journal*, iv, p. 254   [2] *Op. cit.*, v, p. 443

[3] Simeon preached in many villages round Cambridge, including Haddenham and Wilburton; see Carus, p. 60

nothing new about it. So Rowland Hill and his allies not only itinerated in the surrounding villages, but also held meetings in the town. Co-operation between town and gown in their case did not, as at Oxford, involve them in clashes with the university authorities (though in some cases it made it difficult for them to obtain testimonials); it did, however, on occasion expose them to mob violence[1] and the contempt of their fellows.

Evangelicalism in Cambridge, however, did not depend solely on such necessarily sporadic efforts; there were a number of parishes in the town where the Gospel was openly proclaimed. Simeon on December 20, 1784, told Wesley that he knew three such:[2] probably meaning his own Holy Trinity, St. Edward's, of which Christopher Atkinson was vicar, and St. Sepulchre's (the Round Church), whose incumbent was H. W. Coulthurst.[3] Before giving an account of the part which Simeon was already playing as a parish priest, a little may be said of other Evangelical clergymen. Christopher Atkinson was the brother of Miles Atkinson of Leeds, and had been fifth wrangler. He was at the time tutor of Trinity Hall; but seems to have been rather a colourless and unimpressive person, though full of kindness and affection, and had no great success as a preacher.[4] Coulthurst was a man of a different stamp and an energetic and far-seeing parish priest, who was not afraid to make experiments. It was he who initiated the custom of holding evening services in church, a practice which savoured of Methodism.[5] Henry Venn, whom he visited with Simeon in October, 1784, wrote: "he improves every time I see him." He was also a brilliant scholar, having been second wrangler to Isaac Milner in 1775. At this time he was fellow and tutor of Sidney Sussex, but a few years later obtained a wider field for his practical abilities on being appointed vicar of Halifax in 1790. Milner himself held St. Botolph's, from October, 1778, but his college duties and ill-health prevented his giving it much attention personally, though he retained it until his appointment to the deanery of Carlisle in 1791.

We come now to the man who did more than any other for the cause of Evangelicalism in both the university and town—

[1] Sidney, *Life of Rowland Hill*, p. 26 [2] Wesley, *Journal*, vii, pp. 39 f.
[3] Moule, *Charles Simeon*, p. 102, thought that the third parish was St. Giles'
[4] Returning from a holiday, during which Simeon had been in charge of the church, he was greeted by the clerk: "Oh, Sir, I am so glad to see you are come; now we shall have some room" (Moule, *op. cit.*, p. 29)
[5] This was on Sunday, July 13, 1783. Simeon followed his lead on the Sunday following: Carus, pp. 44 n.; 88

Charles Simeon.[1] He had often said to himself as he passed Holy Trinity: "How should I rejoice if God were to give me that church; then might I preach the Gospel there and be a herald for Him in the University." Quite unexpectedly the opportunity came his way. The incumbent died, and the living was in the gift of the bishop, who was a friend of his father. At his own request, Simeon, who had been only a few months in orders and had not yet taken his degree, was appointed in the autumn of 1782. It was, of course, a piece of gross favouritism; yet this appointment was the beginning of a ministry, lasting fifty-four years, which was perhaps as fruitful and significant as any in the long history of the Church of England. There is no shadow of doubt that Simeon was inspired by the highest of motives in making his request for the living; but they were neither understood nor appreciated by the congregation, who had their own ideas as to a new vicar, for, like many a congregation since, they wanted the curate. So Simeon entered on his incumbency with an immense weight of prejudice against him, and it was long before he overcame the opposition and distrust of his people. A weaker man would have been worn out by the methods they employed and by the obloquy brought upon him by the dispute. But, strong in the belief that he was doing the will of God, he held on his way, comforted by the thought that another Simon had once borne the cross for Jesus. In the end his devotion and the power of his preaching won their way; but it was a long and a bitter way.

Before leaving the subject of Evangelicalism in Cambridge, something may be said concerning the Rev. Robert Robinson, to whom reference has already been made in connexion with itinerating in the neighbourhood. Robinson was born at Swaffham in Norfolk, and when quite a youth began to preach in the Tabernacle at Norwich, where huge congregations came to hear him. Becoming a Baptist, he was given, when only twenty-four, the charge of the chapel in St. Andrew's Street, Cambridge, where the same success followed his very fervid preaching. But Robinson seems, like other eloquent orators, to have been lacking in stability, both in character and in opinions, and after a time he was attracted by Unitarianism. It was, in fact, while on a visit to Dr. Priestley at Birmingham, in 1790, that he died.[2]

[1] For an account of his early life and his work in the university, see below pp. 363 ff.

[2] His successor was the well-known Baptist preacher Robert Hall

Huntingdonshire, like the other counties within reach of Everton, had seen a good deal of itinerating by Berridge and his helpers, and there was, for so small a county, a good deal of progress. Here and there Evangelical parishes can be pointed to, some in isolation, others grouped together. On the border near Bedford, John King, a schoolfellow of Cowper, was rector of Pertenhall from 1752 to 1800. He was among those to whom Wesley wrote in April, 1764, and was approved by him.[1] At Stukeley and Offord, not far from Huntingdon, the Gospel was being preached by the Rev. — Brock in 1784.[2] Huntingdon itself, although the Unwins, and Cowper with them, had lived there for a time, does not seem to have been much affected by the revival. Wesley preached in a room there on December 3, 1782, when two clergymen who were present had a serious conversation with him; but two years later, on making inquiries, he found that they were no longer sympathetic.[3] In Godmanchester, Huntingdon's twin neighbour, there are signs of much activity, especially by Henry Venn. Wesley notes on November 25, 1774, that "A large barn was ready in which Mr. Berridge and Mr. Venn used to preach".[4] In August of that year Berridge had written to Mr. John Thornton: "I have been recruiting for Mr. Venn at Godmanchester, a very populous and wicked town near Huntingdon." The visits of Methodist preachers were greatly resented by Venn, who, in 1789, complained that Wesley himself was "ever indefatigable in suggesting prejudices against me".[5] But in this case, at least, Wesley was hardly to blame. The barn had been erected by Mrs. Webster, a convert of Berridge; but being distrustful of Calvinism in even a mild form, she refused to let Venn continue using it. Hearing that Wesley was to preach at Bedford, she went over to listen to him, and, being satisfied with his teaching, offered him the use of the barn.[6]

At St. Neots, the Methodists, much to Wesley's indignation, had left the Church. Here, on December 3, 1776, he had a friendly conversation with Venn.[7] In November, 1782, John Venn was in temporary charge of the living, and the people petitioned the non-resident rector to appoint him permanently, but this he refused to do.[8]

Henry Venn had come to Yelling in 1771, and from it exer-

[1] *Letters*, v, p. 112
[2] *Memoirs of Mr. Coxe Feary*, pp. 16 f.
[3] *Journal*, vi, p. 379; vii, p. 36
[4] *Op. cit.*, vi, p. 52
[5] *Venn Family Annals*, p. 93
[6] *Journal*, vi, p. 52 n. 1
[7] *Op. cit.*, vi, pp. 90, 133
[8] *Life of Henry Venn*, pp. 351, 356 f.

cised a great and beneficent influence, not only in the neighbourhood, but even more in Cambridge, which was distant only about a dozen miles, and thus within easy riding distance,[1] though the bad state of the roads in winter sometimes made the journey difficult. From the first he met with suspicion and hostility from the local clergy, for he had the unusual habit of preaching twice on Sunday, and of holding meetings during the week in the rectory, and was in other ways very active in the performance of his parochial duties. Such energy, exposing as it did their own deficiencies, was not at all to their liking.

As Venn got older his not very robust health began to curtail his activities, and the state of the parish declined. In 1782 he wrote: "My small parish is very much altered for the worse, within these few years. Three farmers whose families were hopeful hearers, are removed, and a fourth is upon the point of removing. They have been succeeded by men of a very profane spirit: scarcely ever will they come to church."[2] Things, however, improved after 1791, when Venn had the help of a very energetic curate, the Rev. Maurice Evans, "who was the means of exciting many to a serious concern for their salvation, who had heard Mr. Venn's preaching without effect, or had relapsed into indifference, after having been once awakened".[3] Robinson of Leicester, who took Venn as his model, records a fine instance of Christian humility on his part in this connexion. His family, jealous of the curate's success where their father had failed, were inclined to belittle him, but Venn rebuked them, quoting John 3: 30, and had himself carried to church to hear him.[4]

Venn, like so many of the other Evangelical leaders, carried on an immense correspondence, and paid frequent visits to other parts, sometimes to preach, sometimes for the sake of his health. He left Yelling, shortly before his death, which occurred on June 24, 1797, and went to live with his son at Clapham.

Although Venn, during his time at Yelling, and especially in its earlier part before his health gave way, did much useful service to the cause of Evangelicalism, his best work had been done at Huddersfield. In character he was much more attractive than some of the other Evangelical leaders, for though he was a convinced Calvinist, he avoided any undue austerity of manner or life. He was a man of a very wide culture, and not

---
[1] Simeon on more than one occasion walked over: see Carus, pp. 24, 82
[2] *Life*, p. 351   [3] *Op. cit.*, p. 520
[4] Vaughan, *Robinson of Leicester*, pp. 252 f.

without a touch of humour; but his dignified bearing sometimes made him a little unapproachable to those who did not perceive the underlying kindliness of his heart. Perhaps the best summing up is that of Sir James Stephen:

> He was one of the most eminent examples of one of the most uncommon of human excellences—the possession of perfect and uninterrupted mental health. The congruity of his intellectual powers was not marred by any discord in his affections, nor did either reason or passion ever abdicate or usurp in his mind the separate provinces over which they were respectively commissioned to reign. . . . Keeping [a] single end continually in view, he made all the resources within his reach at all times tributary to it.[1]

Another Evangelical, if such he may be called, in the county was of a very different type from Venn—the Rev. Thomas Hartley, rector of Winwick, about ten miles north-west of Huntingdon. Whitefield described him as one who preached the Gospel, and he was on terms of intimacy with James Hervey, who spoke of him as his "good friend and pious brother". An able preacher and a very active parish priest, he allowed himself to be over-influenced by various mystical writers, and wrote a book in their defence which aroused the dissatisfaction of Wesley.[2] It is noteworthy that he was not one of the recipients of Wesley's circular sent out in April, 1764. Long before this, Hervey had also become alarmed over his friend's eccentric ideas;[3] whilst Hartley, for his part, criticized the teaching of *Theron and Aspasio* on imputed righteousness, and tried to prevent its publication. Hartley had first been attracted to the mystics through William Law, but his admiration for them became excessive, and after a time he abandoned active work and declared that he was called to a life of contemplation. Amongst his writings was a treatise on the Millennium under the title of *Paradise Restored*; he also translated several of the works of Swedenborg.

In Hertfordshire, all that I have been able to discover of Evangelical activity is comprised in two stray references in letters from Berridge to Newton. In 1780 he wrote: "Mr. Peers,

---

[1] *Essays in Eccles. Biog.*, ii, pp. 107 f.   [2] *Journal*, v, p. 46
[3] See his letter of September 3, 1753, to Lady Fanny Shirley

the Rector of Ickleford, near Hitchin, is newly enlightened to preach Jesus. . . . Sixteen years ago I preached in one of his neighbouring barns, and am now invited to preach in his church. He has driven the Squire and his family from the church, which is a mighty good symptom."[1] Another letter of September 17, 1782, speaks of "A gospel curate . . . sprung up at Royston";[2] who is presumably the "Mr. Waltham" commended by Venn after a visit in December, 1782.[3]

[1] *Works*, p. 413. Peers, who took his degree from Merton College, Oxford, held a number of other livings
[2] *Op. cit.*, p. 418   [3] *Life*, p. 344

CHAPTER 16

THE MIDLANDS

For a survey of the progress of Evangelicalism in the Midlands, Northamptonshire is a convenient starting-point. Northampton itself was a great stronghold of Dissent, with Doddridge as its high priest and father. In the north of the county William Law lived at King's Cliffe, but in complete retirement, and, outside his own small circle, exercised no influence save by his writings. James Hervey, as we have seen, was curate and rector of Weston Favell from 1743 to 1758.

Northampton was only ten miles from Olney, and was naturally not unaffected by its proximity. Matthew Powley worked for a time in the county after his ordination, and, already known to Newton, was introduced by him to the Unwins, whose daughter he married. Some six miles south-west of Olney lay the parish of Aldwinckle, where Dr. Haweis came in 1764, and soon attracted immense congregations. He had great musical gifts, and the singing of the choir so impressed Simeon that he consulted Haweis about improving that at Holy Trinity, Cambridge.[1] He died at Bath on February 11, 1782, and was buried in the Abbey Church.[2]

Moving to the west, we come to another notable centre at Creaton, eight miles from Northampton, and near the Warwickshire border. Its beautiful situation, combined with the spiritual blessings it enjoyed, drew from Newton, on a visit to the parish, the words of Psalm 84: "How amiable are Thy tabernacles". The first to introduce Evangelical teaching was Abraham Maddox (or Maddocks).

Maddox was born in Long Acre in 1713, and, like Madan, had been a lawyer. He was not ordained until 1757. His first curacy was with Hervey, at whose death-bed he was present, and whose successor he had hoped to be. After a short time at Weldon, where his teaching met with opposition, he accepted a curacy at Kettering. There he remained until June, 1770, but had to leave owing to various scandals being put into circulation against him. His real offence, however, was the doctrine which

[1] Moule, *Charles Simeon*, p. 199

[2] A list of his writings is given in Boase and Courtney, *Bibl. Cornub.*, pp. 215 ff.

he taught, and also the large congregations which came to hear him.[1] In 1773 he went to Guilsborough, to which the curacy of Creaton was attached. When he arrived at Creaton the congregation numbered only twenty; but it soon increased so rapidly that a gallery was built; even that could not contain all those who wished to hear, and many stood outside to listen as best they could. Maddox died on July 17, 1785, and his funeral sermon was preached by Thomas Scott, who excelled in such exercises. A congregation, estimated at 2,500, was present, and Scott delivered his oration in the graveyard.[2]

By the influence of Simeon, his successor was Thomas Jones, and it was through his efforts that this small Northamptonshire village became well known in Evangelical circles. Jones[3] was born near Aberystwyth in 1752, the son of a small farmer, but his mother had come from Cumberland. In his youth he was greatly affected by the preaching of Daniel Rowlands, the famous vicar of Llangeitho. After receiving a good education at school he was ordained in 1774. He held a number of curacies in Wales and the neighbouring parts of England before going to Creaton, where he remained until 1833.

The large congregation which Maddox had collected remained true to Jones, in fact its numbers increased. As Creaton was the only centre of Evangelical teaching in the neighbourhood, people came in from many miles around. No other accommodation being available, Jones lived in an inn, called Highgate House, and there, in spite of criticisms, he remained. He worked hard in the parish and took thought for the bodily, as well as the spiritual, needs of his flock, setting up clothing-clubs and introducing other social services. In his early years he used to visit members of the congregation who lived in other parishes, but on the advice of a clerical friend he gave this up as an "irregularity". Although strict in his Churchmanship he was on friendly terms with Dissenters. During his time Creaton became noted for its yearly gathering of Evangelical clergymen, when there was much preaching. The gatherings came to an end owing to the disapproval of Bishop Madan of Peterborough.

At an early period of the movement Martin Madan, the brother of the future bishop,[4] in conjunction with Talbot, vicar

[1] Henry Venn, however, says that he had no success before going to Creaton (*Life*, p. 400)
[2] *Life of Scott*, p. 174
[3] See J. Owen, *Memoir of the Rev. Thomas Jones*, for a fuller account of his life
[4] Spencer Madan did not become bishop until 1794

of Kineton, had done some itinerating in the county.[1] Hervey, whom they visited, described them as "men baptized with the Holy Ghost and with fire, fervent in spirit, and setting their faces like a flint."[2]

Kineton, a poor living, lies across the Warwickshire border, about eight miles from Stratford-on-Avon. Whilst Talbot was there he rebuilt the church. He was a man of means and well connected, as his father was a major-general and his grandfather had been Bishop of Durham; he had also an uncle who was Lord Chancellor. Talbot was educated at Exeter College, Oxford, where one of his contemporaries was Walker of Truro, and proceeded to LL.D. Like other early Evangelicals, he was at one time drawn to the Moravians, but the influence of Romaine kept him loyal to the Church. Talbot has been described as "a ready and pathetic speaker",[3] and he drew large congregations to his church. He was, also, a devoted parish priest, and ever anxious to try out new methods of reaching and influencing his flock; for this purpose he paid a visit to Walker to study his system and to obtain his advice.[4] He left Kineton for St. Giles', Reading, for no other reason than a desire to find a sphere of greater usefulness. A later vicar of Kineton, the Rev. John Harmer, combined it with the living of Butler's Marston. He had preached both for Lady Huntingdon and Wesley.[5] At Loxley, not far away, the vicar, the Rev. Samuel Cooper, was sympathetic to the movement.

In Warwick, not much progress was made. Newton once accepted a temporary charge there, and before going happened to read Acts 18: 10 (Fear not, Paul, for I have many people in this city). On which he has the somewhat caustic comment: "I soon afterwards was disappointed in finding that Paul was not John, and that Corinth was not Warwick."[6]

The early years of the Evangelical movement coincided with the growth of what came to be known as the Black Country, when the countryside was being invaded by coal-fields and iron foundries and its rustic solitude broken into by the whirr of wheels and the noise of engines. The capital of this new district was Birmingham, and it was not long before it received visits from Wesley. Lady Huntingdon, too, was active there and

---

[1] Madan seems to have kept up his link with the county, for in the autumn of 1771 Venn arranged to meet him at Northampton (*Venn Family Annals*, p. 89).

[2] *Countess of Huntingdon*, i, p. 431   [3] *Op. cit.*, ii, p. 396
[4] *Life of Walker*, pp. 479 ff.   [5] Wesley, *Letters*, vi, p. 105 n.
[6] Cecil, *Memoirs of Newton*, p. 76

bought an old play-house which she turned into a preaching hall in charge of the Rev. John Bradford who had had a curacy in Berkshire. In 1774, a new church, St. Mary's, the gift of a Miss Wayman, was consecrated. Its first incumbent was the Rev. John Riland, who had been curate to Venn at Huddersfield and would later move to the family living of Sutton Coldfield, which he held from 1790 to 1822. Venn paid a visit to Birmingham in October, 1783, and wrote: "Mr. Riland, in labours of love, in visiting the sick, in giving largely to the needy, in love to the Saviour, and in humility, has no superior. I suppose he walks five or six miles every day in visiting his people."[1] Soon after going to St. Mary's, Riland enlisted the services of a band of laymen to help in visiting the parishioners; among them the father of Josiah Pratt.[2] Riland was followed by his curate, the Rev. Edward Burn, an Irishman who after being trained at Trevecca went for a few terms to St. Edmund Hall. He remained until his death in 1837. Whilst still curate he had impressed Wesley by his preaching, which was described as excellent.[3]

In Wednesbury, which though not far from Birmingham is in Staffordshire, the Methodists had been very active from the start, and had provoked fierce riots which Wesley described under October 20, 1743[4]. Here, on March 21, 1752, he met Mr. ———, vicar of ———, on whom he commented: "since he has known the pardoning love of God he has been swiftly going on from faith to faith, and growing not in knowledge only, but in love."[5]

The vicar of Wednesbury until 1782 was the Rev. Edward Best, who also held the living of Bilston. Wesley's only recorded visit to the latter place was on March 21, 1770, when he preached in a private house.[6]

Bromwich Heath had been a wild and desolate region, but a road across it had been constructed to carry coal from Wednesbury to Birmingham; in 1752 this was improved so that it could be used by coaches. A remnant of these days still exists at West Bromwich, for the museum was formerly Oak House, a half-timbered mansion with a courtyard. The vicar of West Bromwich was Edward Stillingfleet who was also chaplain to Lord Dartmouth, whose seat, Sandwell, lay in the neighbourhood.[7] Stillingfleet, who, like Wesley, had been a fellow of

---

[1] *Life*, p. 376 [2] *Life of Josiah Pratt*, p. 2 [3] *Journal*, vii, p. 149
[4] *Op. cit.*, iii, pp. 98 ff. [5] *Op. cit.*, iv, p. 13 [6] *Op. cit.*, v, p. 357
[7] Lord Dartmouth offered the living to Romaine, who refused it: see *Countess of Huntingdon*, i, p. 380

Lincoln College, Oxford, was the son of James Stillingfleet of Hotham. William Jesse was curate, and later vicar. Another parish into which Evangelical views made an entry was Darlaston, where Wesley was allowed to preach and take the prayers on July 10, 1782, and again on March 28, 1787, when Horne, the curate of Madeley, read the prayers.[1] The vicar, the Rev. Titus Neve, was non-resident. At Wolverhampton, the Rev. Benjamin Clement, who was the headmaster of the Grammar School, and also vicar of St. John's, was in sympathy with the movement. He had previously been at Dudley, which though it is near to Birmingham is actually in Worcestershire.

In that county there is little trace of definitely Evangelical influence, though there were a few places which gave Wesley a hearing. He preached at St. Andrew's, Worcester, on April 22, 1781, and again on March 21, 1784. The vicar, the Rev. W. Wormington, on the latter occasion said that he was welcome to use the pulpit whenever he was in the city.[2] Earlier still there had been some response to visits from Glascott, Venn, and others; but as they were not allowed to preach in the church Lady Huntingdon built a chapel in Bridport Street, which was opened in 1773. At Kidderminster, the Rev. Mr. Fawcett was favourable to Evangelical views:[3] and Sellon at Breedon used to exchange pulpits with Fletcher.

One place where Methodism, if not Evangelicalism, had an early start was Bengeworth, near Evesham. This was the home of the Seward family whose members were divided in their religious allegiance, which led to much quarrelling among them.[4] William had been converted by Charles Wesley,[5] but later became attached to Whitefield, with whom he went to America in 1739 and for whose use he provided a sloop. William Seward was fatally wounded by a stone thrown by someone in a mob at Hay, and died on October 27, 1740, the first Methodist martyr. His death caused considerable financial embarrassment to Whitefield, who had anticipated further gifts from him. Benjamin was a great supporter of the Wesleys; Henry married a Baptist and had no love for Methodists of any colour; the same is true of Thomas "a pleasure- and preferment-seeking Anglican clergyman".[6]

[1] *Journal*, vi, p. 361; vii, pp. 253 f.   [2] *Op. cit.*, vi, p. 486
[3] See a letter of April 29, 1758, in Gillies's *Hist. Collections*, p. 532
[4] See Charles Wesley, *Journal*, i, pp. 195 ff.
[5] Jackson, *Life of Charles Wesley*, i, p. 187
[6] Wesley, *Journal*, ii, pp. 395 f.

Bengeworth was not a separate parish until 1872, being part of Evesham;[1] Wesley preached in the church there on March 16, 1768, at the request of the Rev. Edward Davies. Five years earlier John Hallward had gone to him as a pupil and was by him induced "to attend to the things of my everlasting peace". Later Bengeworth chapel was in the charge of a Mr. Beale, who lived in the Sewards' old home, and with whom Wesley frequently stopped; the last occasion was on March 17, 1786.[2]

In Shropshire a number of the clergy allowed Rowland Hill to use their pulpits.[3] The Hills lived at Hodnet, where Reginald Heber would one day occupy the living. Evangelical doctrines in the parish do not seem to have been introduced without opposition, for Miss Jane Hill wrote to her brother in 1764: "Mr. Fletcher has preached . . . and given great offence. I hope his labour was not wholly vain, though I have not heard of any good being done."[4] The curate from 1757 to 1776 was the Rev. Mr. Dicken, but it was only during the last five years that "he preached the glorious gospel of Christ."[5] Rowland often preached in the chapel of ease at Weston.

The living of Shawbury, seven miles north-east of Shrewsbury, was in the gift of the Hills and so enjoyed a succession of Evangelical vicars. John Hallward, who before his ordination had preached "prematurely" at Hodnet, with Richard Hill's encouragement,[6] was vicar from 1775 to 1779. He was followed by the Rev. John Mayor, a close friend and constant correspondent of Thomas Scott, who remained there until his death in 1806. Earlier still, James Stillingfleet had been vicar (1767-75), and during his time Henry Venn preached in the parish and found much stirring there.

In Shrewsbury, St. Alkmund's became a great centre of Evangelical influence after the arrival in 1774 of the Rev. Richard de Courcy. De Courcy was an Irish Methodist and had been educated at Trinity College, Dublin. He was at first a follower of Wesley, who thought highly of him, but gradually withdrew from him on account of his Arminianism, and

---

[1] Charles Wesley heads a letter of August 8, 1739, "Bengeworth and Evesham" (*Journal*, i, p. 160).

[2] *Journal*, v, pp. 161, 306, 486; vi, p. 146. Wesley's references to Bengeworth are a little confusing, as he refers to the "rector" (vi, p. 182), and among those who received his circular is — Cooper, who is described as "vicar of Bengeworth" (v, 63 n.). It was the same Cooper who read prayers when Wesley preached in the church on March 18, 1784 (vi, p. 486).

[3] Sidney, *Life of Rowland Hill*, p. 136

[4] Sidney, *Life of Richard Hill*, p. 67   [5] *Op. cit.*, p. 96   [6] *Op. cit.*, p. 100

passed into the circle of Lady Huntingdon, for whom he did much preaching at the Tottenham Court Road chapel and elsewhere. But from her, also, he began to withdraw in 1770. De Courcy attracted immense crowds by his preaching, not only from the town but from the surrounding countryside. Romaine, through the influence of Richard Hill, preached at St. Chad's early in 1770; but he so annoyed Dr. Adams, the incumbent (1731–75), that on reaching the vestry after the service, he turned to him and said: "Sir, my congregation is not used to such doctrine, and I hope I will never hear such again." Later he preached a sermon to denounce Romaine's "errors", to which, after it was printed, Richard Hill was not slow to reply.[1] Another vicar, the Rev. Thomas Stedman (1783–1826), was a correspondent of Sir James Stonhouse.[2]

The outstanding name in Shropshire, and indeed, so far as holiness of life is concerned, in the whole revival, was Fletcher of Madeley.[3] The career of this modern saint of God is of great interest, not only as an example of devoted service and holiness of life, but as throwing incidental light on the social and ecclesiastical conditions of the times.

Fletcher was born at Nyon in Switzerland in 1729, and his original name was Jean Guillaume de la Fléchière. On coming to England, this he anglicized into John William Fletcher, as he found that his friends had difficulty in pronouncing and spelling it. His education he had received at Geneva, where he was a diligent and successful student and acquired a comprehensive knowledge of both theology and philosophy. Fletcher had been intended for the Calvinist ministry, but his gentle soul was revolted by the doctrine of Election, and so he withdrew. In order to earn his living he then took up teaching, and though he had but a slight knowledge of English it was to England that he decided to go. His first eighteen months he spent at a school, where he managed to make himself proficient in the language, and then became tutor to the children of Thomas Hill of Tern Hall near Shrewsbury.[4]

The Methodist Movement was then in full swing, and Fletcher was soon drawn into it. The occasion of his first hearing about

[1] *Op. cit.*, pp. 156 ff.
[2] Their letters were afterwards published: see *Countess of Huntingdon*, i, p. 136
[3] See, further, Tyerman, *Wesley's Designated Successor*, and Lives by F. W. Macdonald and J. Maratt
[4] It was later called Attingham House, and stands at the meeting place of the Tern and Severn

it was almost accidental. Mrs. Hill, struck by his religious earnestness, remarked in fun: "I shall wonder if our tutor does not turn Methodist by and by." "Methodist, Madam," he replied; "pray what is that?" He was told that the Methodists were people who did nothing but pray. "Then," said he, "by the help of God I will find them out."

Having discovered a faith which satisfied his intellectual as well as his spiritual needs, Fletcher's mind turned again to the thought of ordination. But the difficulties seemed insuperable. He was not yet a naturalized Englishman; he had no English degree, and no title. None the less, on March 6, 1757, he was ordained deacon by the Bishop of Hereford, and, on the 15th of the same month, priest, by Bishop Egerton of Bangor in the Chapel Royal of St. James.

Fletcher still retained his post with the Hills; but his views prevented his obtaining many preaching engagements in the neighbourhood, and Mr. Hill warned him, in view of his own political interests, that he must not antagonize the clergy.[1] He did, however, when in London, preach for Lady Huntingdon, and even paid a visit to Everton. On arriving he gave no name, but said that he had come to ask for Berridge's advice and instruction. Berridge, recognizing from his accent that he was a foreigner, inquired where he came from, and, on being told that he was a Swiss, asked if he knew anything of his young fellow-countryman, John Fletcher, about whose preaching and manner of life he had had very impressive accounts from the Wesleys. Fletcher replied that he knew him intimately, and that, if the Wesleys knew him as well, they would not speak so highly of him. "You surprise me in speaking so coldly of a fellow-countryman," Berridge then said, "in whose praise they are so warm." "I have the best reason for speaking of him as I do," replied Fletcher, "for I am John Fletcher."

When his services were no longer required, Mr. Hill offered him the valuable living of Dunham in Cheshire, a small parish in a fine sporting country.[2] But Fletcher refused it; there was too much money and too little work. It was then arranged that Dunham should be given to Mr. Chambers, the vicar of Madeley, and that Fletcher should have Madeley. When Wesley heard that Fletcher was thinking of taking a parish he vainly tried to dissuade him, as he thought that it was not his calling.

[1] He was also enabled to help Richard Hill (*Life of Richard Hill*, pp. 23 f.)

[2] Archbishop Moore complained in 1789 of the practice of thus providing for Swiss tutors. See Sykes, p. 171

Madeley lies in the valley of the Severn, and Wesley, when he was there in July, 1764, thought it "an exceedingly pleasant village encompassed by trees and hills";[1] but already industrialism was coming in to change its character, for in the parish were the famous smelting works of the Darbys at Coalbrook Dale. The population was about 2,000, and Fletcher described them for the most part as "stupid heathens, who seem past all curiosity, as well as all sense of godliness". Here he would labour for the rest of his life—with a long interruption through ill-health from 1776 to 1781—and here he found fame, unexpected and undesired, yet none the less real. Although the surroundings must have been utterly uncongenial to one of his sensitive, delicate nature, refusing all offers of preferment, he insisted on remaining. Colliers, iron workers, and small farmers, coarse and illiterate—for of such, though there were a few resident gentlefolk, his flock mainly consisted—could little appreciate his intellectual and spiritual gifts, and from the first resented his efforts to raise them from the rough and brutal life to which they were accustomed. The fact that he was not an Englishman by birth (he never lost his foreign accent) must also have told against him. But by every means in his power, and even by excessive physical exertions, he tried to draw them to the observance and practice of religion. When they excused themselves from coming to church because they did not wake up in time he went round with a bell every Sunday at 5 a.m., not omitting even the most distant parts of the parish. Devotion such as this at last began to tell, and the congregation grew, until it more than filled the church.

Like other Evangelical clergymen, Fletcher did not think that the provision of Sunday services exhausted his duty, and in addition he held meetings in the outlying parts of his parish, as well as classes for instruction. He also, as Grimshaw had done, tracked down the young people engaged in wanton pleasures and shamed them into better courses. But fierce opposition soon broke out. Some of the farmers refused to pay their tithes; a neighbouring squire threatened to give him a public thrashing; and the colliers arranged a bull-baiting in which the vicar was to take the part of the bull.

Such intense and ceaseless labours began to tell on a constitution which had never been robust, and in 1776 he was gravely ill with consumption. He made a partial recovery which Wesley suggested might be hastened by a preaching tour in

[1] *Journal*, v, p. 87

Cornwall. This his medical man refused to sanction; though he did go as far as Norfolk in November, 1776.[1] In the following July Wesley speaks of him as restored to life in response to many prayers, and a few months later as "almost miraculously recovering from his consumption".[2] But a long rest and a change of climate were demanded, and late in 1777 he went to the south of France, moving thence to his native Switzerland. This treatment proved successful, and he was able to return in the summer of 1781, and even to preach at the Conference. Then at the close of the year he made a delayed though exceedingly happy marriage. His bride was Miss Mary Bosanquet, of Cross Hall, Batley, and they were united there on November 11, only returning to Madeley on January 2, 1782. Fletcher had been in love with her for a quarter of a century, but because she was a rich woman tried to banish her from his mind. By the time of their marriage she had spent most of her fortune in works of charity, so that barrier was removed. In his funeral sermon on Fletcher, Wesley declared that she was the only woman in England worthy of her husband. Her tender and judicious care undoubtedly prolonged Fletcher's life; though after his death she herself had a breakdown, and was so ill in 1787 that Wesley could speak of her as "swiftly growing in grace and ripening for a better world". However, she made a surprising recovery, and by March, 1789, was better than she had been for many years.[3] She used to hold meetings in a tithe barn near the vicarage, which some of the clergy attended. After her husband's death she was allowed to remain on at the vicarage and to continue her ministry; Henry Martyn found her there in August, 1802, and in fact she survived until August 9, 1815.[4]

Fletcher died in 1785 from a fever caught when visiting a parishioner. His last thoughts were with his flock, and as he lay dying he was heard to murmur, "O my poor! what will become of them?" His successor was the son of the patron, Mr. Kenerson; and the Rev. Melville Horne became curate, being ordained on that title in 1786. Melville Horne had been a Methodist itinerant preacher, and his appointment was due to Wesley.[5] His name still appeared in the Wolverhampton

---

[1] *Op. cit.*, vi, pp. 119, 131   [2] *Op. cit.*, vi, pp. 167, 176
[3] *Op. cit.*, vii, p. 480
[4] See the moving description with extracts from her diaries in L. F. Church, *More about the Early Methodist People*, pp. 141 ff.
[5] *Letters*, vii, p. 294

circuit as a "supernumerary" preacher. Later he was one of the founders of the London Missionary Society, and went out to Sierra Leone as a chaplain (1792-94).

Wesley had hoped that Fletcher would succeed him as the leader of the Methodist Movement, but he himself outlived his younger friend, and wrote an account of his selfless life. In the funeral sermon, to which reference has already been made, he gave a noble and merited testimony to his character: "In fourscore years I have known many exemplary men, holy in heart and life, but one equal to him I have not known, one so inwardly and outwardly devoted to God." When Voltaire was confronted with the argument that Jesus Christ must be divine on account of the beauty and holiness of His life, he replied that the life of Fletcher, admittedly a man, was equally admirable. (How this would have horrified Fletcher himself!) These are striking testimonies, and well deserved, for among all the saints no name has a finer fragrance than that of Fletcher of Madeley.

Fletcher was one of the few Evangelical clergymen who kept in close and sympathetic touch with Wesley, and this from the time of his ordination to the close of his life. Not long before his death he suggested that Madeley should become the centre of a Methodist circuit with himself as a supernumerary preacher. His kitchen was in regular use by Methodist preachers. The notion that he should follow Wesley as the leader of the movement seems to have occurred to the latter in 1773. It seemed to Wesley, who was becoming concerned as to what would happen after his death, that the nomination of a successor would prevent confusion. The obvious successor was his brother Charles (he, too, died before John); but he was too strict in his Churchmanship for the bulk of the Methodists; and, after his marriage, did little itinerating and so lost touch with many in the movement. But Fletcher utterly refused to fall in with the plan, though he promised that if he outlived Wesley he would co-operate with Charles to keep the Methodists together.[1]

In the counties of Nottingham and Leicester good progress was reported by Whitefield on November 11, 1739;[2] but little seems to have come of it. Jacob Rogers did some itinerating in the neighbourhood; Wesley preached in a room at Nottingham on June 11, 1741; and Charles established a society there two years later.[3] But nothing definitely Evangelical emerged.

[1] Wesley, *Letters*, vi, pp. 10 ff.; and Moore, *Life of Wesley*, ii, p. 353
[2] *Letters*, i, p. 92   [3] *Journal*, ii, p. 464 n. 2

In Leicestershire, things were much more flourishing, probably owing to Lady Huntingdon having her seat at Castle Donnington. Even so, developments were a little tardy, for Newton wrote in March, 1775: "I am going (if the Lord please) into L. This was lately . . . a dark place . . . and much of it is so still; but the Lord has visited three of the principal towns with Gospel-light."[1]

Markfield, less than ten miles from Leicester, had Ellis as its vicar, a friend of Lady Huntingdon's and very sympathetic to the revival movement. Wesley paid him a visit on June 9, 1741, and on May 2, 1745, preached in the church.[2] Charles preached there in October, 1743, and "was much comforted with my brother Ellis and his increasing little flock".[3] In June, 1746, Lady Huntingdon presented her chaplain, the Rev. George Baddelley, D.D., to the living; but as she was anxious to find a curate to take charge he was evidently to be non-resident.[4] In 1777, Robert Cecil was for a short time in charge of the parish and also of Thornton-with-Bagworth, which he was to hold until Mr. Abbot, the son of the late vicar, was able to succeed. He brought the knowledge of the truth to Abbot and his sister.

There were a number of other parishes scattered up and down the county where Evangelicalism was fostered. In 1750, Lady Huntingdon had vainly tried to get the living of Ashby-de-la-Zouch for Hervey; later on it was held by Walter Sellon, before his return to Breedon as rector. Belton, near Loughborough, had James Glazebrook for vicar. The vicar of Melton Mowbray, the Rev. Dr. Ford, had in early life been bitterly opposed to Methodism, and even filled his pockets with stones to pelt the preachers. But a change came over him, and on June 11, 1775, Wesley received from him "an affectionate letter".[5] In August, 1789, he tried to arrange a visit, but this could not be fitted in.[6]

Wesley paid repeated visits to Leicester from June, 1741, onwards, but does not seem to have been allowed the use of any church. He said of the town that he always felt much

---

[1] *Cardiphonia*, p. 313

[2] *Journal*, ii, p. 462; iii, p. 176. He paid many later visits

[3] *Journal*, i, p. 337

[4] *Countess of Huntingdon*, i, p. 73. R. Housman was in charge (1788-90) and, "though an unpromising sphere of exertion", he had much success (*Life* pp. xxxvii, lxxxiv)

[5] *Journal*, vi, p. 69; *Letters*, vi, p. 228   [6] *Journal*, vii, p. 524

liberty in preaching, but saw little fruit.[1] Leicester, however, was soon to become a great stronghold of Evangelicalism under Thomas Robinson, vicar of St. Mary's, from 1778 to 1813. Robert Hall, the famous Baptist preacher, who had first-hand knowledge of his work, declared that "the revolution which Baxter accomplished at Kidderminster, Robinson effected at Leicester".[2]

Robinson, who was the son of a hosier at Wakefield, was born there in 1749, and after attending the local grammar school, went up in October, 1768, as a sizar to Trinity College, Cambridge. He had at first no very deep religious convictions, but they steadily grew, and the reading of Hervey's *Theron and Aspasio* made him an Evangelical. After a brilliant academic career he became a fellow in 1772, and was offered full-time work in the college, but he felt that his vocation was pastoral. We have already noticed his activities in the Cambridge neighbourhood; and soon he took a curacy at St. Martin's, Leicester (now the cathedral) combined with the afternoon lectureship at St. Mary's. Through the influence of Lord Dartmouth he became vicar of the latter in 1778, being presented by the Lord Chancellor. Up to this time he had taken pupils, among whom was the elder Benjamin Jowett[3] and John Venn, after his unfortunate failure with Milner at Hull.[4]

The teaching of the new vicar was by no means acceptable to many of his congregation, who were old-fashioned Church people; some migrated to other churches, but others remained to stir up trouble in the parish. To offset this, many Dissenters returned to the Church. One cause of disagreement was, as at Witcham, the introduction of hymn-singing. Opposition, however, was gradually overcome and crowds flocked to his preaching, so that new galleries had to be constructed to provide for the ever-increasing body of worshippers. His preaching was marked by a stern gravity; "he stood as the messenger of heaven, and, unmoved by the presence of proud objectors or captious hearers, proclaimed, 'Thus saith the Lord.' "[5]

Robinson's influence was not confined to his work in church, nor even to the visiting of his people, in whose homes he was a ready and welcome guest with none of the sternness which he showed in the pulpit; he was also prominent in every scheme,

---

[1] *Op. cit.*, vi, p. 413
[2] *Character of Thomas Robinson*, p. 9. For a full account, see E. T. Vaughan, *Some Account of the Rev. Thomas Robinson*
[3] *Life of Benjamin Jowett*, i, p. 11   [4] *Venn Family Annals*, pp. 114, 116
[5] Vaughan, *op. cit.*, p. 231

whether secular or spiritual, for bettering the lives of his fellow townsmen. Nor did these activities exhaust his energies. He wrote a number of books, of which *The Christian System* and *Scripture Characters* were once very popular. He had also close friendships with other Evangelical leaders, especially with Henry Venn and Thomas Scott. Among his curates were Robert Housman, who came to him from Langton, near Market Harborough (*Life*, pp. xxxvi f.); and Thomas Lloyd, Simeon's convert, whom he called the "first-fruits of Achaia".

In Derbyshire, the movement had made an early start, for William Greaves, vicar of Ockbrook six miles south of Derby (1734–65) invited Wesley to preach for him on June 10 and 11, 1741.[1] The most active centre, however, was at Hayfield, where John Baddiley was the incumbent. Wesley, who described him as "a sort of second Grimshaw", first heard about him from John Bennet, who wrote from Chinley on October 22, 1748: "The minister of Hayfield . . . is lately converted, and preaches the pure gospel of Jesus Christ. The town is up in arms against him already, breathing out slaughter. Notwithstanding he is as bold as a lion." Baddiley, having weighed the orthodoxy of Wesley's first volume of sermons, "by the standard of Primitive Christianity",[2] expressed his warm approval of them. Soon afterwards he lost his daughter, "a most promising child", and Wesley buried her on April 10, 1755.[3] On October 23, 1756, Charles Wesley preached at Hayfield, during the temporary absence of the vicar, to a house full of parishioners, and on the next day (Sunday) met classes which Baddiley had formed. He also took the services and preached, being conscious of great blessing. He made the comment, "Why does God always accompany the word with double blessing when preached in a church?"[4]

But though Baddiley was willing to copy part of the Methodist organization, forming societies and employing lay assistants, he was strict in his Churchmanship, and very much opposed to allowing too great power to the Methodist preachers, to whom he applied Numbers 11:7 "Ye take too much upon you, ye sons of Levi." He also condemned any thought of separating from the Church, writing to Wesley in June, 1755: "I query much, if, upon dissenting from the Established Church, the divisions and subdivisions of the Methodists among themselves would not exceed those of the anabaptists in Germany."[5]

[1] *Journal*, ii, pp. 463 f.   [2] *Op. cit.*, iv, p. 110 n. 3   [3] *Op. cit.*, iv, p. 111
[4] *Journal*, ii, pp. 132 f. He misspells it Hatfield.
[5] *Methodist Magazine*, 1779, p. 430

A prophecy which was soon fulfilled, though the divisions are now happily healed. Baddiley gradually withdrew from Wesley, but received the circular of April, 1764; he died soon afterwards. Wesley wrote of him on March 23, 1765: "He did run well, till one offence after another swallowed him up."[1]

Another Derbyshire clergyman who received the circular was Walter Sellon, curate of Breedon. Originally a baker, he had been a master at Kingswood School; was then taken up by Lady Huntingdon, and entered Holy Orders.[2] After being vicar of Ashby-de-la-Zouch he returned to Breedon as rector. In spite of his debt to Lady Huntingdon, he took an active part on the side of Wesley in the Calvinist dispute.

In Derby, progress at first was slow, though various of Lady Huntingdon's chaplains itinerated in the neighbourhood. In August, 1765, however, there came a welcome change, for Romaine wrote to Mrs. Medhurst: "We had a most refreshing time—Fifteen pulpits were open—Showers of grace came down—Sinners in great numbers awakened, and believers comforted."[3] He preached there for a whole week, "at the great church and at St. Werburgh's", although there was much opposition from the mayor and churchwardens, and what he calls the "Arian party". Romaine also preached several times at Ashbourne, Driffield, and Belper.

At Ilkeston, Wesley preached in a large and crowded church on July 6, 1786; the vicar, the Rev. George Allen, reading the prayers "with great earnestness and propriety".[4]

Wesley preached on May 24, 1783, at Buxton,[5] which was already developing into a spa, and when Wilberforce paid his first visit there, on the advice of Dr. Hey in September, 1789, he found the church accommodation very inadequate.[6]

Evangelicalism in Cheshire during our period seems to have been confined to two towns, Nantwich and Macclesfield. At Nantwich the rector, the Rev. John Smith, was an Oxford man, the son of Matthew Smith who had been a member of the Holy Club. His contribution seems to have been mainly of a mildly literary nature. He wrote a reply to Madan entitled *Polygamy Indefensible*, and in 1775 *A Vindication of the Freedom of Pastoral Advice or a Review of the Obligations which the Ministers of the Gospel are under plainly to declare the Truth to their Hearers.*

At Macclesfield the somewhat eccentric David Simpson carried

---

[1] *Journal*, v, p. 109 [2] Southey, *Life of Wesley*, ii, p. 373 [3] *Works*, p. 706
[4] *Journal*, vii, p. 186 [5] *Op. cit.*, vi, pp. 412 f. [6] *Life*, i, pp. 244, 317

on a more aggressive work, and his ministry, which lasted from 1775 to 1799, was not unfruitful.[1]

Simpson was the son of a respectable Yorkshire farmer who, though he made no great religious professions, had family prayers. Going up to St. John's College, Cambridge, he became an associate of Rowland Hill, and was also influenced by Berridge, who urged him to preach wherever the opportunity presented itself and to ignore the consequences. On being ordained, Simpson went as curate to William Unwin, and then moved on to Macclesfield, where he had the unusual experience of being violently ejected from the pulpit by his rector. But he had a strong supporter in Charles Roe, the brother of the late rector,[2] and the founder of the silk trade in the town. Roe had made a vow that if his business prospered he would build a church by way of a thank-offering, and he now determined to carry out his promise and to install Simpson as the first incumbent. The church was built in 1775, and Simpson duly appointed. His labours met with great success, and when Wesley visited the parish on Good Friday and Easter Sunday, 1782, there were 1,300 and 800 communicants.[3] One feature of the new church was a magnificent organ, "one of the finest toned I have ever heard", said Wesley.[4] In spite of his success, Simpson was full of all kinds of scruples, and was only prevented by death from giving up his orders. His curate, the Rev. B. B. Collins, had already left to become an unattached clergyman, and to help Wesley. Collins was also a member of St. John's College, Cambridge, and had previously held a curacy in Somerset, but had been dismissed; whereupon he took to itinerating, but helped Berridge in 1779. He was still only a deacon, but Bishop Porteous of Chester at length priested him[5] in October, 1781, and he joined Simpson.

[1] There are two memoirs of Simpson: by Edward Parsons, prefixed to *A Plea for the Deity of Jesus*; and by J. B. Williams, prefixed to *A Plea for Religion and the Sacred Writings*; also a recent study, A. L. Hunt, *David Simpson and the Evangelical Revival*

[2] He had refused to allow Wesley to preach in the church, but did not oppose him (*Journal*, iv, p. 310 n.)

[3] *Op. cit.*, vi, p. 346   [4] *Op. cit.*, vii, p. 152

[5] He had thought of joining the Presbyterians: see Wesley, *Letters*, vii, p. 29

CHAPTER 17

THE NORTH

In the extreme North, where the whole district was responsive to Methodism, there are few signs of Evangelical influences. Wesley, quite early on (it is said that he was inspired by Lady Huntingdon), had seen the strategic importance of Newcastle as a centre for reaching the nearby counties.[1] The work was eminently successful, and in 1767, the first year for which statistics are available, the Newcastle circuit had 1,837 members, a total that was only exceeded in Yorkshire, London, and Lancashire. The churches in Newcastle were not altogether unsympathetic, for on March 10, 1745, Wesley wrote: "We had a useful sermon at All Saints in the morning, and another at our own church in the afternoon. I was much refreshed by both, and united in love with the two preachers and to the clergy in general."[2]

There were, however, a few Evangelical parishes. At Monk Wearmouth (associated with the Venerable Bede) the vicar, the Rev. Thomas Godday, often invited Wesley to preach for him.[3] He lived next to the meeting-house, and had a private entrance by which he could attend the gatherings there. Wesley delivered a charity sermon on June 13, 1790, in aid of the Sunday School "which has already cleared the streets of all the children that used to play there on a Sunday from morning to evening".[4] At Sunderland, also, was the Rev. John Hampson, an ex-Methodist preacher, who in 1785, after a quarrel with Wesley, went to Oxford, was ordained, and came there as curate. He was appointed to the living in 1798. In spite of the earlier misunderstanding he allowed Wesley to use the church on June 1, 1788, when he drew crowded congregations morning and evening.[5]

Hartlepool was the birthplace of Romaine, and he paid visits to it from time to time. Wesley wrote in July, 1757, that he

[1] See H. Pollard, *John Wesley in Northumberland*

[2] *Journal*, iii, p. 166. By "our own church" Wesley meant that of the parish in which the meeting-house was situated

[3] *Op. cit.*, iv, p. 461; v, pp. 166 f., 226. Romaine was also a frequent preacher there (*Works*, p. 659)

[4] *Op. cit.*, viii, p. 71   [5] *Op. cit.*, vii, p. 394

had started a revival there; but as there was no one to follow it up, the people soon relapsed.¹ Later, Romaine's sister married Mr. Heslup, the vicar, and more solid work was done. He wrote to her on November 19, 1768, rejoicing over news of "poor sinners converted, and of believers settled and established"; and again on June 16, 1773: "My thoughts run often about poor Hartlepool. I believe the Lord has a people among you, and I wish he may honour Mr. Heslup, by making him useful to gather them in." Romaine's sister died on July 26, 1793, and he wrote to the bereaved husband exhorting him to exalt Christ by his living and preaching, "that Northumbrian (sic) sinners may hear and live".²

Wickham (or Whickham) had a number of visits from John Wesley in the early days of the movement,³ and Charles was even more active there. On October 31, 1746, the curate and another clergyman expressed their appreciation of the work he was doing, and on December 14 he had a long conversation with them. Five days later he found that they had been forbidden by the bishop to have any more dealings with him.⁴

In Westmorland the only Evangelical seems to have been Thomas Hervey, incumbent of Underbarrow (1766–1806); and in Cumberland, where John Farrer at Stanwix was an isolated beacon, the position was much the same. A number of clergymen, however, attended a meeting at Whitehaven to hear an address by Wesley.⁵ Earlier there had been a welcome for Evangelical preachers at Bootle, both Romaine and De Courcy being allowed to appear in the church. But there was also much disgust on the part of some, and on one occasion when Romaine was about to enter the pulpit he found that the door would not open. Suspecting malice he told the clerk to give out a long psalm, and by the use of a hammer and pincers as noiselessly as possible managed to unfasten it. But it was not long before the church was denied to Evangelicals.⁶

At Carlisle, as in other cathedral cities, the new views were kept out as long as possible. Even as late as July, 1797, and so outside our period, Milner wrote that the Methodists and Dissenters were but feeble folk and carried no weight, and that Evangelicals ought to make openings for themselves.⁷

Moving south into Yorkshire, we come upon a land changing

---

¹ *Op. cit.*, iv, p. 222   ² *Works*, pp. 682, 688, 690
³ *Journal*, iii, pp. 52, 235; iv, p. 28   ⁴ *Journal*, i, pp. 354, 387 f., 433, 436 f.
⁵ *Journal*, v, p. 453   ⁶ Haweis, *Life of Romaine*, pp. 105 f.
⁷ *Life of Dean Milner*, p. 130

its character, especially in the lower districts, as industry drove out agriculture. Once the secluded valleys and open moors had been the scene of the activity, both spiritual and material, of Cistercian monks, who not only had fostered religion but also introduced sheep farming on a big scale. They thus provided the means of beginning the wool trade whose development coincided with the rise of another religious movement.

But the cloth trade in its early stages did not abandon traditional ways. There were few factories, and many of the weavers still lived in cottages, combining their work with the cultivation of field and garden. The towns were but collecting centres, and even as such had few facilities; cloth for sale was hung on the walls of the churchyard at Huddersfield until Sir John Ramsden, in 1768, built the Cloth Hall. Some villages gradually grew into towns, extending their limits up the sides of the surrounding hills; but many remained, for the time, much as they had been. The moors were still wild and desolate, and the few roads were little better than pony tracks; in consequence, the villagers were, through their isolation, as wild and lawless as the bleak and barren country in which they lived. There were but a handful of towns of any size. Hull, indeed, was already a thriving seaport; and York, as in Roman times, a military station; it also had its famous minster.

The whole countryside was ripe for evangelizing and showed itself ready to respond to new religious ideas when once they were proclaimed. It was, perhaps, a little too open to such forces, for divers eccentric movements soon found a ready welcome. Ingham and his followers had been early at work there, then the Moravians stepped in; and, later still, the Sandemanians. It was, however, the Methodists who chiefly throve, and in 1767 they had six circuits in the county and a membership of 6,393, almost exactly a quarter of the total at that date for the whole of the United Kingdom and Ireland.

The rapid spread of Methodism naturally aroused opposition, and in 1753 a sermon was preached in Batley parish church "occasioned by the Enthusiasts of that place", by the Rev. E. Haslam, incumbent of Honley. But intolerance was not all on one side, and some parishes which early accepted Evangelical views showed little consideration for those who differed from them. In March, 1779, the Rev. John Murgatroyd, master of Slaithwaite school, went to deliver a sermon at Marsden, where the living was vacant, and some of the parishioners hoped that he would be appointed. When he arrived, however, he found that the churchwardens and the "Methodistical" party had locked the door and would give him no opportunity, either then or on subsequent occasions when he made the attempt, to preach there.¹ The men of Marsden were a rough crowd, and a later incumbent, the Rev. Abraham Horsfall, "a man of great piety", was treated so harshly that he had to resign.² It is pleasant to record that Mr. Murgatroyd, in spite of his experiences at Marsden, afterwards gave up his "prejudice against the Gospel", and even helped the Rev. Thomas Wilson at Slaithwaite.³

Evangelicalism flourished mainly in the south of the county and aroused little interest among the clergy elsewhere; though the Rev. J. Bottomley of Scarborough was in touch with Venn, who wrote to him in February, 1779.⁴ To the north-west, Wensley, where Wesley preached on October 30, 1743, had a sympathetic rector in "good old Mr. Clayton" who also had charge of Redmire in the same dale where Wesley also preached.⁵ Mr. Clayton, however, was advanced in years and died in July, 1746, after holding the living forty years. Wesley was with him just before his end.⁶

Further to the south, the parish of Clapham lies beneath the shelter of Ingleborough. The vicar, the Rev. C. C. Graves, was a friend of Ingham and preached the Gospel, though he had to endure much opposition from the Moravians.⁷

One strong centre of Evangelicalism there was in the north, Helmsley, where Richard Conyers carried out his faithful ministry. By a happy coincidence it was at Rievaulx Abbey which lies in the parish that the first Cistercian settlement had been made in 1131.⁸

Richard Conyers had taken his LL.D. at Cambridge where he was at Jesus College at the same time as Henry Venn. The two men were friends, and Venn was a trifle "peeved", that Conyers should have surpassed him. When he went to Helmsley he found conditions very backward; but he set himself resolutely to amend them, starting schools, where he taught elementary mathematics. He also introduced singing and catechizing in church. The parish was very large, in some places ten miles

---

¹ See extracts from his diary printed by Canon Hulbert, *Annals of Almondbury*, p. 427

² *Op. cit.*, p. 417   ³ *Op. cit.*, pp. 476 f.   ⁴ *Venn Family Annals*, p. 93

⁵ *Journal*, iii, pp. 109, 140   ⁶ *Op. cit.*, iii, p. 249   ⁷ *Op. cit.*, iii, p. 40

⁸ The monastic chronicler describes it as situated in a deep narrow valley, a place of horror and desolation (*in loco horroris et vastae solitudinis*)

across, but Conyers made it his business to visit every part of it. He was thus a model clergyman even before his "conversion", for as yet he knew nothing of "the gospel plan of salvation"; his views, indeed, inclined towards Socinianism.

His awakening was sudden. Having read Ephesians 3: 8 in church as part of the lesson for the day, he realized that the phrase "the unsearchable riches of Christ" meant nothing to him, and was plunged into despair. Light came to him on Christmas Day, 1758, from two verses, Hebrews 9: 20: "Without shedding of blood there is no remission", and John 1: 7: "The blood of Jesus Christ his son cleanseth us from all sin." He became so excited that he rushed about the house crying, "I have found him, I have found him." On the following Sunday he announced to the congregation the change in his life and outlook. Like Walker at Truro, though not for exactly the same reasons, his announcement lost him the friendship of many, and he was regarded with some contempt. In order to promote the instruction and guidance of his people, Conyers divided them up into bands, men and women, and married and unmarried, being kept separate. He also introduced a kind of Angelus, ringing the church bell and telling the field labourers to stop their work and say a prayer when they heard it. His new views soon spread beyond his parish, for preaching a sermon at the visitation of the Archbishop of York, the latter warned him that if he preached such stuff to his congregation he would drive them mad.

Lord Dartmouth, in a letter to Richard Hill, speaks of Venn having made a tour of the north and paid a visit to Helmsley, where the company and conversation of Conyers had delighted him; he also gave a wonderful account of his "uncommon zeal and extraordinary love to the people who have been converted under him."[1] Conyers was equally happy at the meeting with his old friend, "as he had never before received under his roof a Preacher of his dear Crucified Lord".[2] Among his converts was George Cussons, who afterwards became a noted Methodist leader in that part of Yorkshire, and when later he moved to Scarborough he still kept up a correspondence with his old rector.[3]

Wesley, having heard of Conyers's activities, wrote to him in July, 1759, and for a time they were close friends; but the

---

[1] Sidney, *Life of Richard Hill*, pp. 90 f.
[2] *Life of Henry Venn*, p. 93. The visit took place in September, 1762
[3] L. F. Church, *Early Methodist People*, pp. 226 ff.

rise of the Calvinist dispute brought about some coldness between them. Wesley went to Helmsley on April 17, 1764, but found the rector away, and sadly wrote: "By the books lying in the window and on the table, I easily perceived how he came to be so cold now, who was so warm a year ago. Not one of ours, either verse or prose, was to be seen, but several of another kind."[1]

Conyers occasionally preached for Lady Huntingdon, but he did not care to leave his parish, or indeed to appear in any but his own pulpit. John Thornton paid him a visit in 1765 which was the herald of a close connexion between the two men, for in the same year Thornton's widowed sister, Mrs. Knipe, was married to Conyers. But the union was short-lived as she died almost immediately. Thornton thereupon presented his bereaved brother-in-law to the living of St. Paul's, Deptford. The news that he was to leave Helmsley so distressed the people that they declared that they would lie across the road so that his carriage could not pass. He actually left at midnight in order to avoid the painfulness of taking leave. Berridge strongly disapproved of the move, writing to Thornton: "It has been a matter of surprise to me, how Dr. Conyers could accept of Deptford living, and how Mr. Thornton could present him to it. Has not lucre led him to Deptford, and has not a family connexion ruled your private judgment?" This seems an uncharitable comment on the affair; for Conyers was worthy of any position, and the sudden death of his wife may have been the real cause for the move. It was certainly unfortunate for Helmsley, since his successor proved "more of the wolf than the sheep-dog, and devastated rather than kept the fold."[2]

One who seemed destined to do great work for Evangelicalism was William Jesse, vicar of Hutton, near Malton. He was one of those who received the circular of April, 1764, and had helped Lady Huntingdon at Oathall in Sussex and elsewhere. Venn wrote in 1771 "he is a very excellent man and seems appointed to evangelize the wolds the inhabitants of which are dark almost as Indians".[3] There is, however, no evidence that this forecast was ever fulfilled, even in part.

In the general change of opinion and growth of tolerance which marked the closing years of our period Wesley was allowed to preach in a number of places in this neighbourhood. On May 1, 1780, the vicar of Pateley Bridge, ten miles south-west of Ripon, offered the use of his pulpit and an overflowing

[1] *Journal*, v, pp. 58 f.   [2] *Countess of Huntingdon*, i, p. 374   [3] *Life*, p. 170

congregation assembled.¹ Then on the following June 4 the same thing happened at Staveley, five miles north of Knaresborough, where "Mr. Hartley read the prayers". This, however, was due to no sudden impulse, for Hartley was an Evangelical and had even invited Richard Burdsall, a lay preacher, to address his people in the school house.²

Moving eastwards to the coast we find that Evangelical teaching first made headway at Hull under Joseph Milner. Joseph Milner,³ the elder brother of the more famous Isaac, was born at Leeds in 1744, the son of a poor weaver, and owed much to the energetic efforts of his mother who brought him to the notice of the Atkinsons. By them he was helped in his education, going first to Leeds Grammar School, and then, through Dr. Moore the headmaster and other friends, proceeding to St. Catharine's Hall, Cambridge, where his career fully justified their confidence, for he showed himself a competent classical and mathematical scholar, winning the Chancellor's medal in 1766. Returning to Yorkshire, he opened a private school, and was subsequently appointed headmaster of Hull Grammar School and lecturer at the parish church by the Mayor and Corporation. His election was due in part to "the splendour of his character", in part to the influence "of powerful friends in Leeds".

Milner was greatly admired for his learning, and also for his preaching which Wilberforce in 1796 described as "very practical and good".⁴ Twenty-five years earlier Henry Venn had written: "I was transported by hearing Mr. Milner. In my judgment, he is much the ablest minister that I ever heard open his mouth for Christ."⁵ Venn sent his son to Milner's school, but found his progress so slow that he withdrew him after six months;⁶ Milner was perhaps too much absorbed in his *Church History* to give proper attention to his pupils.

How Milner came to adopt Evangelical views is not quite clear. He himself said that it was owing to reading Hooker *On Justification*, but he seems to have been greatly helped by students from Trevecca who came to Hull to assist Edward Riddell, a pious Dissenter. The latter wrote to Lady Huntingdon that among those affected by them was a Mr. Milner, the headmaster of the Grammar School and lecturer at the

---

¹ *Journal*, vi, p. 275   ² *Op. cit.*, vi, p. 282

³ There is a life of Joseph by his brother Isaac, and a memoir by his life-long friend, James Stillingfleet

⁴ *Life*, ii, p. 156   ⁵ *Life*, p. 171   ⁶ *Venn Family Annals*, p. 113

principal church. "He is constant in his attendance on the ministry of your Ladyship's students." Milner himself wrote to Lady Huntingdon that he had reason to bless this visit.[1] The two statements, however, are capable of reconciliation; for it is extremely improbable that unless Milner had already been "awakened" he would not have deigned to hear such unusual advocates of the Gospel.

Milner's adoption of "Methodistical" views cost him the friendship and support of many of his previous admirers who no longer came to hear him, save when he preached the annual sermon as mayor's chaplain. But their places were soon taken by the poor and ignorant. When the living of Holy Trinity, called the High Church, came vacant in 1797, Milner, who had been lecturer there for many years, was appointed by eleven votes out of thirteen. Unfortunately, on his journey to York for his institution, he caught cold and died shortly afterwards. His election was due to Wilberforce, who had been his pupil, and canvassed the mayor and corporation on his behalf.[2] From 1784 to 1797 the vicar had been the Rev. Thomas Clark, a brother-in-law of Wilberforce, who described him as "a Christian of the true breed; quiet, silent, unobtrusive."[3] Wesley, who preached for him on June 18, 1786, and again on June 22, 1788, also held him in high regard, calling him "a friendly, sensible man, and, I believe, truly fearing God. And such, by the peculiar Providence of God, are all three stated Ministers in Hull".[4]

Hull showed great favour to the Evangelicals, and just after the close of our period Dr. Croft wrote: "The town of Hull affords one unfortunate instance of their success, for all the churches there are occupied by these pretended favourites of heaven."[5] In 1771 the Rev. John King, a former pupil of Milner, became vicar of St. Mary's. He was followed by the Rev. John Barker (1782–1816), a fervent admirer of Walker's sermons, some of which he had printed.[6] At a later date the living was occupied by the Rev. John Scott (1816–34), the son and biographer of Thomas Scott, who was also vicar of North Ferriby. Thomas Dykes was curate of Collingham in 1787, before building St. John's, which was opened for service in 1792.

At Hotham a few miles from the Humber, described by

[1] *Countess of Huntingdon*, i, pp. 303 f.   [2] *Life of Wilberforce*, ii, p. 288
[3] *Op. cit.*, ii, p. 226   [4] *Journal*, vii, pp. 170 f., 405
[5] *Thoughts concerning the Methodists and the Established Church*, p. 29
[6] Sidney, *Life of Walker*, p. 561

Wesley as "one of the pleasantest places I have seen",[1] the Rev. James Stillingfleet had been rector since 1772. He came of a clerical family, being the grandson of the famous Bishop of Worcester,[2] and his son Edward became fellow of Lincoln, whilst his nephew and namesake was involved in the St. Edmund Hall case. Stillingfleet was at Queen's College, Oxford, and before coming to Hotham had been curate in charge of Brierley in the parish of Bradford. His great contribution to the movement was the establishment of a clerical society to which Thomas Adam (then seventy-one) used to come from across the Humber; and amongst other members were William Richardson of York and Joseph Milner. The latter made much use of Stillingfleet's considerable library when writing his *Church History*. But he was also a devoted parish priest and by 1784 his activities were already arousing wide notice.[3] Wilberforce, not yet an Evangelical, remarked to Isaac Milner that he was a good man, but inclined to carry things too far. "Not a bit!" replied his friend.[4]

The introduction of Methodism into York was the outcome of a somewhat unusual and not a little amusing incident. Wesley, after preaching at the meeting-house on Peasholm Green, went to St. Saviour's church, still wearing his robes. The rector, the Rev. Mr. Cordeaux, seeing a clergyman present sent the sexton to invite him to preach, and Wesley at once complied. His sermon, based on the gospel for the day, met with the rector's approval. Afterwards he asked the clerk if he knew who the stranger was, and to his alarm was told: "Sir, he is the vagabond Wesley, against whom you warned us." Realizing that difficulties might arise, he went to the archbishop, informed him of what had taken place, and received the reply that he had done quite right.[5] When Wesley again visited York he preached at St. Saviour's on the morning of May 7, 1786, and in the afternoon at St. Margaret's, in both cases to vast congregations.[6]

There had, however, been Methodist activity much earlier. On June 7, 1755, a Mr. Williamson invited Wesley to preach

[1] *Journal*, vii, p. 406

[2] The author of *Origines Britannicæ*. Pepys said he was "the ablest young man to preach the gospel since the days of the apostles"

[3] Stillingfleet was a ripe scholar, and he and his wife had great social gifts and were much given to hospitality

[4] *Life of Wilberforce*, i, p. 75

[5] *Methodist Magazine*, 1827, p. 458; and Wesley, *Journal*, v, pp. 176 f.

[6] *Op. cit.*, vi, p. 160

for him, but one of the residentiaries warned him that it would be worse for him if he did, and so Wesley, in spite of Williamson's willingness to run the risk, declined.[1] Just over a year later Charles Wesley preached for him on October 3, 1756, and later communicated at the Minster, where the celebrant was Mr. B——, "one who had known the Methodists from their rise in Oxford, and was no enemy to them."[2]

The great Evangelical figure at York was the Rev. William Richardson, for fifty years vicar of St. Michael's, Belfreys. Richardson was born at St. Bees in February, 1745. Although he had no degree he was ordained in 1768. It was when he was curate at Kirby Moorside that he became an Evangelical. He was appointed to St. Michael's in 1771, combining with it the post of vicar-choral at York Minster. His fine presence and admirable voice, together with his musical gifts, gave him great influence, although he met with much opposition at first in his parish. This he soon lived down. Richardson was a keen though sympathetic observer of his fellow men and their ways, and not least of his brother clergy. He had many friends, including Thomas Adam, to whom he recommended Storry when he was in need of a curate, and Joseph Milner, whose sermons he edited. He was a devoted Churchman, and would hear of no criticisms of either Church doctrines or the Prayer Book, always replying: "My faith is exactly that of the Church of England; as far as I know, her doctrines are mine. Her forms of worship are preferred by me before any devotional service I ever heard or saw."[3]

We come now to the West Riding, where there were probably more Evangelical parishes than in any part of England. The beginnings of the movement in this area have already been considered in connexion with Grimshaw of Haworth, and with this parish the further account may conveniently start.

When Grimshaw died in 1763 he was succeeded by the Rev. John Richardson, a native of Crosby in Westmorland, who had been curate to Venn at Huddersfield. He remained there until his death in 1791. Cadogan described him as "a person of an excellent spirit, whose views of divine truth were remarkably clear and evangelical, and whose unaffected piety and exemplary conduct continued to be an ornament to the church of God, and a blessing to that parish".[4] When Wesley visited

---
[1] *Op. cit.*, iv, p. 120   [2] *Op. cit.*, ii, p. 120
[3] Quoted Pearson, *Life of William Hey*, p. 151
[4] In Romaine's *Works*, p. 12

Haworth on August 3, 1766, he found a congregation larger even than in Grimshaw's days; but on July 1, 1770, there is rather a different story: "Being much concerned for the poor parishioners of Haworth, who hear and hear, and are no more affected than stones, I spoke to them in the most cutting manner I could." In spite of these reproaches, the congregations, when he went there on July 5, 1772, were so great that a pulpit in the churchyard had to be extemporized. But Wesley's dissatisfaction continued, and he declared on April 28, 1776, that few of them were yet awakened. This constant denunciation may have annoyed and hurt Richardson, for he refused to allow Wesley to use the pulpit on April 23, 1780, so he went on to Bingley. However, he duly preached on April 23, 1786, and in the same month in 1788 and 1790.[1] He also continued his visits to Bingley, where his friend the Rev. Richard Hartley was vicar. On a visit on July 18, 1784, he had much praise for the newly opened Sunday school.[2]

At Keighley the rector, Mr. Knowlton, had been on friendly terms with Grimshaw, and showed sympathy with the Methodists; his wife, indeed, was a member of a Methodist society, and they ran the only Sunday school in the town. Wesley, however, on his numerous visits does not appear to have preached in the church.

Wesley preached in the churchyard at Baildon, five miles north of Bradford, on July 27, 1766, as the congregation was too large for the church, but he does not appear to have been asked again.[3] At Horsforth, east of Baildon, he preached in the church on May 3, 1786, "with a remarkable blessing".[4]

At Bradford, which even as late as 1794 was a small town with grass growing in the streets, Wesley preached on August 23, 1748, "when none behaved indecently but the curate".[5] Bradford was later to have the benefit of the noble ministry of John Crosse, the famous blind clergyman. Crosse was the son of a Middlesex magistrate, and had been converted through Alexander Coates, a poor Scottish boy with an amazing gift for languages, and, for a time, one of Wesley's preachers. He was educated at St. Edmund Hall, Oxford, and before becoming vicar of Bradford had had curacies at Stone Cross and Todmorden, as well as being in charge of Whitechapel, near Birstall, for ten years. He was there a close friend of Miss

---

[1] *Journal*, v, pp. 180, 374, 475; vi, pp. 103, 274; vii, pp. 157, 381; viii, p. 60
[2] *Op. cit.*, vii, p. 3   [3] *Op. cit.*, v, p. 178
[4] *Op. cit.*, vii, p. 159   [5] *Op. cit.*, iii, p. 369

Bosanquet, who later married Fletcher. The advowson of the living was purchased by his father, but led in this case to the great advantage of the parish. Crosse immediately established class meetings on the Methodist model, and by his preaching attracted such great crowds that the church, large as it was, could not contain them, and additional galleries had to be added from time to time. Wesley, on visiting the parish on April 23, 1786, wrote: "Surely the people of this town are highly favoured, having both a vicar and a curate who preach the truth."[1] Crosse held the living until his death in 1816. The Crosse Theological Scholarship at Cambridge was endowed in his memory.

At Eccleshall, the curate preached the Gospel so effectively that the Methodists from Sheffield used to go out to hear him. But developments here were cut short by his death in August, 1759.[2]

Leeds was a great Methodist centre, and the frequent scene of the annual Conference. In the early days of the movement it received much attention from the leaders. When Charles Wesley went there on May 5, 1743, he was invited to help in administering the sacrament at the parish church, but, for some reason unspecified, he "dreaded their favour more than the stones of Sheffield".[3] Whitefield, accompanied by Grimshaw and Ingham, addressed vast crowds at Leeds in 1750;[4] repeating his visit in September, 1762, this time with Madan and Venn, whom he left there.[5] In spite of Charles Wesley's doubts, the vicars continued to be friendly, and John often preached and helped in the sacrament when the Conference was held there. On August 2, 1789, with the assistance of three other clergymen, he administered it to more than 1,500 communicants.[6]

The most notable Evangelical in Leeds was the Rev. Miles Atkinson. His father, the Rev. Christopher Atkinson, had been a member of the Holy Club and was vicar of Thorp-Arch and of Walton near Boston Spa, from 1749 to 1774. Miles Atkinson was lecturer at Leeds Parish Church (1769), vicar of St. Paul's (1793), as well as vicar of Kippax.[7] His *Practical Sermons* in two volumes enjoyed considerable repute.

[1] *Op. cit.*, vii, p. 157   [2] *Op. cit.*, iv, p. 343
[3] *Op. cit.*, i, p. 313   [4] *Countess of Huntingdon*, i, p. 156
[5] *Letters*, iii, p. 280   [6] *Journal*, vii, p. 524

[7] He was born on September 28, 1741, and educated at Peterhouse, Cambridge. He had a school at Drighlington from 1764 to 1770. He died in February, 1811

Leeds was also notable for its laymen, such as the Milners and Jowetts, but, above all, for the sons of Richard and Mary Hey. Richard Hey was a drysalter and his wife the daughter of a Leeds surgeon, Jacob Simpson. One of the sons, John, was a Cambridge don; another, Samuel, a country clergyman. It is the third son, William,[1] who made the greatest name for himself, both in the movement and in the world at large, not to mention in his native city, of which he was mayor. He was born on September 3, 1736, and when only eighteen became a Methodist, though retaining a strong attachment for the Church. When, however, the movement began to drift away, he left it. This did not mean that he severed all intercourse with Wesley; on the contrary, he entertained him on his visits to Leeds.[2] William Hey was a man of very varied gifts; not only was he a skilled physician, a Fellow of the Royal Society, and the medical adviser of Wilberforce, but he was an accomplished musician, and an avaricious reader, who made it his pleasure to introduce the works of the great writers to young men. In spite of his large practice, he seldom failed to attend church twice each Sunday, and for a time even taught in the Sunday school.

Amongst Hey's closest friends and allies was Miles Atkinson, already mentioned as connected with the parish church and with Kippax. This latter place had early welcomed the Gospel message. Wesley preached there on July 24, 1761, when Romaine read the prayers and Venn was also present.[3] Roger Bentley was the vicar and amongst those who received the circular of April, 1764. At the end of 1770 the living became vacant, and a Mr. S—— was appointed. This gave great alarm to those who had Methodist sympathies, of whom the chief was Mrs. Medhurst, a niece of Lady Huntingdon, and she consulted Romaine, who knew the parish well through his yearly visits. They prayed about the matter, and Romaine approached Lord C—— S——.[4] In the end other provision was found for Mr. S——, and the Rev. Edward Buckley, a keen Evangelical, was presented to Kippax. "If ever there was an answer to prayer, this is" was the comment of Romaine.[5] Soon after

[1] See Pearson, *Life of William Hey*. Canon Smyth took him as an example of family religion (*Simeon and Church Order*, pp. 21, 23)
[2] *Journal*, vi, p. 444; vii, pp. 5, 159   [3] *Op. cit.*, iv, p. 472
[4] This is probably Baron Smythe, the friend of Henry Venn. From January 20, 1770, to January 23, 1771, the great seal was in commission, and he was one of the commissioners. He was not, of course, Lord Chancellor, as Romaine seems to have thought
[5] See the correspondence in Romaine, *Works*, pp. 731 ff.

THE NORTH

Buckley's arrival he had a visit from his friend, Rowland Hill, who was the instrument of many conversions.[1]

At Rawdon, ten miles from Leeds, Mr. Stone was the incumbent, and Wesley, after preaching for him on May 6, 1788 described him as "a truly pious and active man".[2]

An old friend of the Wesley family, Henry Crook, was vicar of Hunslet. Charles Wesley when he preached there found souls awakened by his faithful ministry, and when some of the Methodists questioned whether he was really a "converted" man, he commented: "I cannot doubt his having known the pangs of the new birth. Our brethren question it because he does not use all their phrases, and cannot follow all their violent counsels."[3] Two sermons which Crook delivered in Leeds Parish Church aroused much controversy, for not only did he claim that salvation by faith was taught in the Bible, but also in the Prayer Book and the Articles. Wesley took his services on July 30, 1769, as he was "out of order". This is the last time that he mentions preaching at Hunslet.[4] It was Crook who is said to have overcome the scruples of John Newton about taking orders in the Church; he is even said to have offered him a title.

Halifax, in the eighteenth century, was a very important living, for the parish covered an immense area, and the vicar had twelve chapels of ease in his patronage, including Haworth. The post, from 1731 to 1776, was held by Dr. Leigh, who was also prebendary of York Minster. Wesley, preaching at Halifax on June 2, 1742, found him "a candid inquirer after truth". He again preached there on May 2, 1747, "to a civil, senseless, congregation". Wesley visited Halifax several times in the succeeding years, and remained on friendly terms with Dr. Leigh, but does not record preaching in the church again until April 17, 1774, when he describes it as the largest in the county after York Minster, "yet it could not contain the congregation".[5] He afterwards dined with the vicar, then near the close of his long ministry. The interruption may have been caused by Dr. Leigh's contact with an unfavourable sample of Methodism in Thomas Meyrick, who was his curate. Meyrick was a Cornishman by birth and something of a poet, and had been trained for the law. He joined the Methodists, but was expelled, and

---

[1] Sidney, *Life of Rowland Hill*, p. 54   [2] *Journal*, vii, p. 385
[3] *Journal*, ii, pp. 117, 121 ff.   [4] *Journal*, v, p. 330
[5] *Op. cit.*, iii, pp. 16, 293; vi, p. 15

later took orders. His death in 1770 was brought about by excessive drinking.

In later years Halifax had notable Evangelical vicars, including H. W. Coulthurst, who came there from Cambridge in 1790, and Samuel Knight (from 1817), Adam's last curate at Winteringham, who had the distinction of taking the chair at the meeting at Rauceby on September 30, 1795, which was a step towards the formation of the Church Missionary Society.[1]

At Sowerby, four miles from Halifax, the church stands "on the brow of a high and steep mountain". Mr. Ogden, the curate, after afternoon service, used to attend the Methodist meeting-house. Wesley preached there on April 29, 1788, and at Honley on the next day, the curate reading the service.[2] The Rev. Edward Haslam, the vicar, who had been a stout opponent of Methodism, had died in the previous January.

Elland, about five miles south-east of Halifax, gave its name to the well-known clerical society. Here Burnett was vicar. He had taken his M.A. at Aberdeen and then entered Christ Church, Oxford. Wishing to be ordained, he had difficulties in finding a bishop to accept him, but was eventually given a title at Padstow. Whilst there he came under the influence of Walker of Truro. Later he became curate to Venn at Huddersfield, but suffered from ill-health.[3] He was then appointed to Elland by the vicar of Halifax, where he spent large sums in works of charity. He died in July, 1793, at the age of fifty-eight.

Dewsbury, which Wesley described as "one of the pleasantest towns in England",[4] had given an early welcome to the revival preachers. Charles Wesley, going there on October 10, 1746, commended the minister who, instead of condemning the Methodists unheard, had examined some of them and thereupon expressed "his approbation of the work, and rejoiced that sinners were converted unto God".[5] The name of the vicar was Robson, who had also been affected by John, but later he relapsed, and on his death-bed ordered that no Methodists were to come near him. His curate, who had expressed similar sentiments, died shortly afterwards, which created an immense impression, as Wesley records when he preached there on April 10, 1752.[6] From 1777 to 1806 the living was held by the Rev. Matthew Powley, who owed his appointment to the influence of Lord Dartmouth. He had been at Queen's College, Oxford,

---

[1] Carus, *Memoirs of Simeon*, p. 107
[2] *Journal*, vii, p. 382
[3] Sidney, *Life of Walker*, p. 511
[4] *Journal*, v, p. 81
[5] *Journal*, i, p. 432
[6] *Journal*, iv, p. 17

where his Evangelical views had stood in the way of his obtaining any office in his college. As already recorded, he married Miss Unwin, and was a correspondent of Cowper. He came to Dewsbury from Slaithwaite. The Methodists offered much opposition to his work, upon which Venn sympathized with him in a letter of January 9, 1779;[1] but his own attitude may have been the cause, for he had refused Wesley the use of his pulpit on August 9, 1778, "because it would give offence".[2]

At Birstall, five miles north-west of Dewsbury, Wesley was astonished when he attended morning service on July 29, 1781, by the clerk's announcing that he was to preach in the afternoon. He was, however, only too glad to use the opportunity.[3] Birstall had been the scene of great Methodist activity, and had often been visited by him. Whitechapel was in the parish, though it did not become a separate living (Cleckheaton) until 1837. Eastwood, however, is described as vicar[4] (as was Crosse); probably he was curate in charge only.

Wesley preached in Wakefield Church on April 12, 1752, where the vicar was the Rev. Benjamin Wilson. He seems to have been surprised by the opportunity. "Who would have expected to see me preach in Wakefield church, to so attentive a congregation, a few years ago?"[5] But although he paid regular visits to the town, there is no further record of his again enjoying the privilege.

The death of Grimshaw in 1763 had removed the first great evangelist of the West Riding; but a few years before there had come to Huddersfield one who was to be in some measure his successor, Henry Venn.[6]

Venn's origins were far different from those of Grimshaw, or indeed of most of the first generation of Evangelicals, though very similar to those of the Wesleys. He came of a family with long clerical traditions, and his father, Richard Venn, had ended his days as rector of St. Antholin's. Henry was born on March 2, 1725, and after attending various schools went in June, 1742, to St. John's College, Cambridge, from which he speedily moved to Jesus College. Although the Venns are closely associated with Cambridge—to-day one of them is President of Queens' College —Richard Venn had been the first to go there. As a west country

---

[1] *Venn Family Annals*, p. 93   [2] *Journal*, vi, p. 207   [3] *Op. cit.*, vi, p. 329
[4] *Op. cit.*, v, p. 63 n. He had been a master at Kingswood
[5] *Op. cit.*, iv, p. 18
[6] See *Life*, by his son and grandson; and, for the family, *Venn Family Annals*, by John Venn

family they had been accustomed for generations to go to Exeter College, Oxford. Venn, who had been ordained by Bishop Gibson of London in 1747, was in 1749 elected to a fellowship at Queens'. He remained at Cambridge for more than two years longer, combining his college duties with clerical work in the neighbourhood, before taking a curacy with the Rev. Adam Langley, who had the livings of St. Matthew, Friday Street, and of West Horsley in Surrey. Venn's chief work was the care of West Horsley, where he had leisure for reading, though diligent and successful as a parish priest. It was at this time that he began to discover the limitations of William Law, and took that further step which brought him to a knowledge of the Gospel. In 1754 he went as curate to Clapham, combining it with work in city churches. He became closely attached to Wesley, too closely, thought Walker, until about 1758 he was "brought to believe for himself".[1] In the following year he was offered the living of Huddersfield through the good offices of Lord Dartmouth, although unknown to Sir John Ramsden, the patron. As the living was worth only about £100 a year and he had a growing family, he hesitated long before accepting.[2]

On his journey to Huddersfield he had a chance meeting with Wesley on August 7, for they put up at the same inn at Stevenage.[3] Arriving at his new parish, he found it already growing from a small village to a town.[4] The parish, moreover, covered a wide area, with some 1,400 families living in it.[5] This added greatly to his work, for he had to spend much time riding about the countryside on visits to outlying farms and hamlets. The religious state of the people was deplorable, and Wesley, on a visit to Huddersfield in October, 1757, two years before Venn's coming, said of them: "A wilder people I never saw in England. The men, women, and children filled the streets as we rode along, and appeared just ready to devour us. They were, however, tolerably quiet while I preached; only a few pieces of dirt were thrown; and the bellman came in the middle of the sermon, but was stopped by the gentlemen of the town."[6]

[1] Sidney, *Life of Walker*, p. 435

[2] In *Countess of Huntingdon*, i, p. 276, it is stated that "urged on by the necessities of his family, he accepted the large and valuable living of Huddersfield". A good specimen of the inaccuracy of this work!

[3] Wesley, *Journal*, iv, p. 348

[4] Bishop Ryle, carried away by his imagination, speaks of "a huge, dark, manufacturing town" and of Venn as "the first evangelist of the modern slum" (*Christian Leaders*, pp. 276 ff.).

[5] *Life*, p. 79   [6] *Journal*, iv, p. 210

Venn immediately started weekday services in the various hamlets; but his main efforts were in the town and the services on Sunday. Large crowds, many of them from a distance, soon flocked to hear his preaching; but he was also careful that the rest of the service should be given full attention; and he would often preface it with a short and solemn address reminding the congregation where they were and what they were about to do. One of his great anxieties was that his flock should have a thorough and intelligent knowledge of the Prayer Book, and on two occasions he delivered courses of sermons explaining it. He was also attentive to catechizing in church.

We have already noticed the disagreement which arose with Wesley owing to the visits of Methodist preachers to the parish.[1] But it did not long persist, and Wesley preached in the church on Saturday, July 7, 1764, at very short notice; none the less, the building was "pretty well filled".[2]

Meanwhile, the activities of Venn and of his neighbour, Furly, at Slaithwaite, were arousing the hostility of the clergy whose people went away to hear them. The Rev. Edward Rishton, vicar of Almondbury, the mother church of Huddersfield, was especially active against them. He had a special grievance, for a Methodist meeting was being held in a private house in his parish, led amongst others by Ambrose Moss, a disciple of Venn. He consulted the Archbishop of York as to means of stopping the "deceivers", and was told to avoid controversy and to rely on simple and earnest teaching.[3]

Whilst at Huddersfield, Venn frequently preached for Lady Huntingdon at her various centres, writing on October 28, 1769, "my talent seems to be for Conversion and for Itinerancy". It might have been well if he had spared himself more, for his intense labours began to affect his health. The loss of his beloved wife in 1767[4] also helped to depress him, not to mention financial difficulties due to the smallness of the stipend.[5] It must therefore have been a welcome relief when he was offered the living of Yelland in 1771. He went there in no cheerful spirit, saying: "Nothing would have prevailed on me to leave Huddersfield if my lungs had not received an irreparable injury. . . . Looking upon my dissolution as at no great distance, I go to Yelland as a dying man."

[1] See pp. 191 f. [2] *Journal*, v, p. 82
[3] Hulbert, *Annals of Almondbury*, pp. 119 f.
[4] His curate Riland lived in the vicarage, whose wife looked after Venn and his family
[5] He was helped by Lord Dartmouth and John Thornton

The new vicar unfortunately was no sympathizer with Evangelical views, and the people, not without encouragement from Venn, built Highfield chapel, and appointed as preacher William Moorhouse, who had been a keen follower of Venn, walking over from his home some dozen miles away to hear him. He continued in his post until his death in 1823. As it happened, Venn's successor died in 1773, and the vicar then appointed was satisfactory to him. But by this time Highfield chapel had become a "vested interest" and its congregation unwilling to return to the Church. Venn deeply regretted his hasty action, which had been opposed by Riland. The latter told the people: "Stick to the Church and pray for the conversion of your minister; and if you don't approve of his preaching, remember you have the Gospel in the prayers."

About four miles to the south-west of Huddersfield lay the parish of Slaithwaite, which, after the death in 1760 of the Rev. Joseph Thorns, a scholar and a sporting parson of the old type, had a succession of Evangelical vicars. The first of them was the Rev. Samuel Furly, who in his early days was a disciple of Wesley and one of the most constant of his correspondents. He had been at Queens' College when Venn was a fellow there, and it was he who recommended William Law's *Serious Call* to the latter. After his ordination he had curacies at Lakenheath and Kippax, among others, and was appointed to Slaithwaite by Venn. By this time he had drifted away from Wesley, and come within the orbit of Lady Huntingdon, who paid a visit to his new parish. He has been described as "a faithful and zealous preacher of the everlasting Gospel; rather a Boanerges than a Barnabas".[1] His stay at Slaithwaite lasted only about six years, when he was appointed to Roche in Cornwall. The next vicar was the Rev. Matthew Powley, who remained ten years before going to Dewsbury in 1777. The most famous of the vicars of Slaithwaite, however, was the Rev. Thomas Wilson. Wilson was ordained, rather older than the average and without any academic qualifications, by Archbishop Drummond. He came as curate to Powley, through whose influence he succeeded to the living. He has been described as "A Yorkshireman of plain energetic character and eloquence",[2] and by his labours he gained for himself the title of the apostle of the valley. During his incumbency the congregations so increased that he rebuilt the church on a new

---

[1] *Countess of Huntingdon*, ii, p. 3
[2] Hulbert, *Annals of Almondbury*, p. 420

site and on a very large scale; he also built a new vicarage.[1] There he died in 1809.

The extent to which toleration of Methodist views had spread in Yorkshire can be seen from a tour made by Wesley in 1780. On April 19, after some hesitation, he was allowed to preach a funeral sermon at Otley; on the 23rd, after being refused at Haworth, he preached morning and evening at Bingley; and on the 26th at Heptonstall, seven miles south of Haworth. He then went on to Todmorden, where he was allowed the use of the church.[2] When he next went to Todmorden on April 24, 1788, he "found uncommon liberty among the poor mountaineers".[3] Wesley had often visited the town before (though he had not been allowed the use of the church), and when he saw it on April 25, 1755, he was much impressed by the beauty of the scenery.

> One can hardly conceive anything more delightful than the vale through which we rode from hence. The river ran through the green meadows on the right: the fruitful hills and woods rose on either hand. Yet here and there a rock hung over, the little holes of which put me in mind of those beautiful lines:
>
> Te, Domine, intonsi montes, te saxa loquentur
> Summa Deum, dum montis amat juga pendulus hircus,
> Saxorumque colit latebrosa cuniculus antra![4]

Todmorden lies on the borders of Yorkshire and Lancashire, and for postal purposes is counted to the latter county. There, as in Yorkshire, the dark clouds of industrialism were already coming down on the fells and moors, the latter broken up by deep valleys which sheltered the chimneys of the new cotton mills.

In spite of these similarities, Evangelicalism made but little impression in Lancashire during our period; though the Methodists had considerable success, especially in the growing port of Liverpool and in Manchester. There were, however, reasons which may account for the tardy extension of the revival among Churchpeople. Lancashire, as in the past, was very conservative

---

[1] *Op. cit.*, pp. 258, 416   [2] *Journal*, vi, pp. 274 f.   [3] *Op. cit.*, vii, p. 380

[4] *Op. cit.*, iv, p. 113. The lines are from a paraphrase of Psalm 104 by Wesley's friend, Dr. John Burton

in both politics and religion. Many influential families survived who still clung to the "old religion", as Roman Catholicism was called, and the Jacobites were eagerly welcomed when they reached Manchester in 1745.

The Methodists were active in Manchester from the start. Wesley preached there on June 3, 1733,[1] actually before Methodism, strictly speaking, had arisen; and more definite traces are to be found in a letter written by Whitefield to a Mrs. G——, in which he says: "I rejoice to hear that the seed sown . . . begins to spring up." On the following June 8 he preached at Manchester to immense crowds.[2] He made a point of impressing on the Methodists the need for loyalty to their own societies and also for attending church.[3] There was need for such insistence, for numbers of Methodists allowed themselves to be seduced from their allegiance by the Baptists and others.

At the Collegiate Church, the predominant tone was High Church, but of a fine quality. Wesley records on Good Friday, 1752: "I went to the old church, where Mr. Clayton read prayers, I think the most distinctly, solemnly, and gracefully of any man I ever heard. And the behaviour of the whole congregation was solemn and serious in every part of the service."[4] But even in Manchester other influences had already been at work, for early in the century Lady Anne Bland, daughter of Sir Edward Mosley of Hulme Hall, and a leader of fashionable life in the town, being a Whig and a Presbyterian by upbringing, so disliked the services at the parish church that for a time she attended the famous Cross Street Unitarian chapel which had been built by her father. In 1708 she and her friends obtained permission from Parliament to build a new church the foundation stone of which she laid on May 18, 1709. It was consecrated as St. Ann's on July 17, 1712. When the Young Pretender entered Manchester there was some trepidation among its worshippers, especially as the rector, the Rev. Joseph Hoole, the translator of Tasso, had denounced the Jacobites. He died on November 27, two days before the entry, and when the funeral procession was leaving the church some Jacobite officers were seen approaching. They quietly joined the procession and took their part in the burial service. Among the worshippers at St. Ann's was John Byrom, who lived at Kersal Cell, and in the churchyard is the tomb of Thomas

---

[1] *Journal*, i, p. 466 n.   [2] *Letters*, ii, pp. 331, 355
[3] Charles Wesley, *Journal*, ii, pp. 133 f.   [4] *Journal*, iv, p. 14

Deacon,[1] "the greatest of sinners and the most unworthy of primitive bishops". Deacon was the Non-juror who influenced Clayton, and had he lived a little longer (he died in 1753) might have found a more congenial resting place, as the High Churchmen also built their own church, St. John's, Deansgate, where the Rev. John Clowes, a pupil of Clayton, was the first rector.[2]

Another new church, dedicated to St. James, was built in 1788 by the Rev. Cornelius Bayley, the Evangelical leader. He was born at Ashe in Shropshire and educated at the grammar school there before going to Trinity College, Cambridge. After teaching at Kingswood he went as curate to Fletcher. Bayley was a man of considerable learning, especially in Hebrew (of which he compiled a grammar), and took his D.D. He was much interested in Sunday Schools, and in August, 1784, published an *Address to the Public on Sunday Schools* which attracted much attention. The Methodists, it is said, were in the habit, after holding their own services, of going to St. James's for the sermon and the Lord's Supper. Wesley records that on May 18, 1783, he celebrated there when between 1,300 and 1,400 communicants took part.[3] The Methodists even considered asking Bayley to officiate in their new chapel.[4] He remained at St. James's until his death in 1812.

Other Evangelicals in Manchester were the Rev. John Johnson, a Trevecca student, at St. George's, and the Rev. Edward Smyth, curate at St. Clement's and St. Luke's.

In Salford there is not much to record. While Clayton was still friendly with Wesley, the latter several times preached for him and administered the sacrament at Salford chapel (now Sacred Trinity).[5] At a later time the Rev. Moses Cheek, a former Methodist preacher, was vicar.

The most prominent sympathizer with the movement in Lancashire in early days was the Rev. John Milner, who until his death in 1777 was vicar of Chipping, ten miles from Preston. He was a friend of both Wesley and Ingham and did some itinerating in Yorkshire. Like other Evangelical incumbents he met with ill-feeling from his clerical neighbours, but in spite of this he collected a number of them to meet Wesley at

---

[1] Deacon had been out in the 1715 rebellion, and fled to Manchester to escape notice. He studied medicine there

[2] He had been at Trinity College, Cambridge, and later became notorious for his advocacy of Swedenborgianism. He translated some of the works of Swedenborg

[3] *Journal*, vi, p. 411   [4] Wesley, *Letters*, vii, p. 246

[5] *Journal*, i, pp. 445 f.; iii, p. 295

Ribchester on April 11, 1751.¹ This was Wesley's first visit to Chipping, which thenceforth became "one of his favourite haunts". These visits aroused opposition and Milner had to appear before his bishop after Wesley had preached on June 7, 1752. When he again tried to preach on April 8, 1753, he was prevented by force. There is no record of any further preaching, so the opposition must have prevailed. Trouble with his people and with the clergy of the locality may have preyed on Milner's mind for he became subject to a nervous disorder.²

Liverpool, which Wesley described as "one of the neatest best-built towns I have seen in England",³ was often visited by him. He regularly attended the churches in the town, but was never asked to preach in any of them; but he expressed his pleasure at some of the sermons he heard. On May 6, 1759, after going to St. Nicholas and to St. Thomas, he commented: "It was as if both sermons had been made for me. I pity those who can find no good at church."⁴ But Liverpool, although a prosperous Methodist centre (Pitt Street chapel was opened in 1754), seems to have been untouched by Evangelicalism.

Warrington was first visited by Wesley on April 14, 1755, and frequently afterwards. Here was a well-known academy (1757-86) opened by the Rev. John Seddon, a dissenting minister.⁵ All the students went to hear Wesley preach on March 30, 1772.⁶ His first recorded preaching in the church is on Easter Day (March 26), 1780, and he was allowed to do so again on Good Friday (April 9), 1784, and Easter Day (April 16), 1786.⁷ In 1779 a rather remarkable man had come to the town. This was James Glazebrook, a collier and stone-getter at Madeley, and Fletcher's first convert there. Fletcher educated him and he was among the earliest students at Trevecca. Later he was employed as an itinerant by Lady Huntingdon, but wishing to have a settled cure, by her influence and that of Fletcher, he was ordained in December, 1771, to the curacy of Smisby in Derbyshire, but left before the end of the year. In consequence, he had difficulty in obtaining priest's orders, and it was not until 1777 that Dr. Hurd, Bishop of Worcester, granted them. When he came to Warrington in charge of St. James's (Latchford) the church had not

---

¹ *Op. cit.*, iii, p. 521   ² *Op. cit.*, iv, pp. 31, 59, 92, 332
³ *Op. cit.*, iv, p. 111   ⁴ *Op. cit.*, iv, p. 312; cf. also p. 203
⁵ Of some four hundred students at the academy thirteen took orders in the Church
⁶ *Op. cit.*, iv, p. 11   ⁷ *Op. cit.*, vi, pp. 269 f., 494; vii, p. 155

yet been consecrated. After a time he was presented to the vicarage of Belton in Leicestershire, but at the request of Bishop Cleaver retained the charge of the chapel at Warringon.

Lancaster would have to wait for any real introduction of Evangelicalism until the coming in 1795 of Robert Housman,[1] who is deservedly known as its evangelist. This remarkable man, already mentioned in connexion with Langton, Markfield and Leicester, was born on February 25, 1759, near Lancaster, on an estate which had been in his family for over three centuries. He was educated at Lancaster Grammar School and then apprenticed to a surgeon. Quite suddenly he felt the call to devote himself to the service of the ministry, and, in spite of parental opposition, persisted in his design. He went up to St. John's College, Cambridge, in October, 1780; and in order to save money he "hitch-hiked" the long journey of some two hundred miles.[2] His career was sufficiently successful to give hopes of a fellowship, but this was denied to him on account of his religious views. He was ordained in 1781, before taking his degree. At this time, although sincerely religious, he had not yet come to realize the true meaning of the Gospel: "Of the Cross", he said, "I knew nothing but the name". Fuller knowledge came to him through Simeon, who also brought him into touch with Henry Venn. Housman began work in Lancaster by helping at St. John's chapel on Sundays for some months in 1785 and 1786, but his preaching aroused great offence; some of the congregation made a point of walking out during the sermon, and the few whom he influenced were advised to attend an Independent chapel, as there only was the Gospel being preached in the town. There was thus until 1795 no suggestion of the great work which would later be accomplished. At the end of our period Lancaster was practically untouched so far as Evangelicalism was concerned.

[1] See *Life and Remains of the Rev. R. Housman*
[2] His various means of transport are described in a long letter to his parents (*op. cit.*, pp. xi ff.)

CHAPTER 18

THE WEST

In our survey of this very diverse area we begin with Gloucestershire. The only really active Evangelical clergyman in the county (apart from Bristol) seems to have been the Rev. Samuel Johnson, curate of Cirencester, who used to take part in itinerating tours with Chapman of Bradford-on-Avon and his curate, the Rev. James Brown. He was dismissed in 1776 owing to his views and "irregularities".

Cheltenham, which in later years would be a great Evangelical centre, did not in our period show signs of its future eminence in this respect; nor did it approve of the visits of Wesley, who on March 16, 1768, records that the rector and the Anabaptist minister were equally anxious to silence him, though in vain.[1] For a time the rector allowed the Rev. George Downing, chaplain to Lord Dartmouth, to preach in his church; but he withdrew his permission on account of the large congregations which flocked to hear him. Madan, Venn, and Walker, also preached in the church.[2] In March, 1770, Lady Huntingdon, accompanied by Romaine, paid a visit to the town and the latter, having been refused permission to preach in the church, availed himself of a large schoolroom which had previously been used for the same purpose by Madan, Talbot, and others. She also sent a number of Trevecca students who succeeded in gathering a small following, but one of them turned Baptist and took the people with him. She abandoned Cheltenham in 1782.[3]

Gloucester was, of course, the home of Whitefield, and he preached his first sermon there in June, 1736, in St. Mary Crypt, where he had been baptized. After the sermon a complaint was made to the bishop that he had driven fifteen persons mad.[4] He often preached in Gloucester, and in December, 1741, was able to use the pulpit of St. John the Baptist's, "by a particular providence", for the living was vacant and the churchwardens took the opportunity of asking him.[5] The Rev. Thomas Stock, curate of this church, later helped Robert Raikes in his Sunday school work. Charles Wesley visited

[1] *Journal*, v, p. 520 [2] *Countess of Huntingdon*, i, pp. 428 f., 431
[3] *Op. cit.*, i, pp. 388, 438 [4] *Letters*, i, pp. 18 f. [5] *Op. cit.*, i, p. 346

Gloucester in August, 1739, and at a crowded meeting of the society three clergymen were present. He asked one of them for the use of his pulpit, but "the Minister (one of the better disposed) sent back a civil message, that he would be glad to drink a glass of wine with me, but durst not lend me his pulpit for fifty guineas".[1] Lady Huntingdon's chaplains, however, seem to have occasionally preached in some of the churches. Wesley paid his first regular visit to the city on October 10, 1766, but does not seem to have been there often. Probably Methodism made little progress in this cathedral city, and it was not until 1787 that a meeting-house was built, by which time prejudice was dying down.[2]

In some of the villages there had been opportunities for preaching in the churches. John Wesley was allowed to do so at Pitchcombe on March 14, 1780;[3] but much earlier Charles had gained the confidence of the Rev. — Morgan, rector of Westcote near Stow-on-the-Wold, and greatly affected him and his wife by his sermons. This was in March, 1740.[4] The vicar of Chipping Campden from 1743 to 1791 was the Rev. William Weston, fellow of St. John's College, Cambridge, and author of *Dissertation on the Wonders of Antiquity*, which met with the approval of Wesley. Weston acquiesced in Wesley's wish to preach in his church, but later changed his mind.[5]

Some six miles north of Chipping Campden was the parish of Quinton,[6] whose vicar, the Rev. Samuel Taylor, had early come under Methodist influences. He was born in 1711, the son of the Rev. Abdias Taylor, of St. John's, Worcester, and went up to Merton College, Oxford. Before going to Quinton, which he held from 1738 to 1772, he had been in charge of St. Clement's, Worcester. Charles Wesley took the services and preached on May 19, 1743, probably in the absence of the vicar, for he comments: "Mrs. Taylor was fully convinced of unbelief."[7] John on the following October 19 found "a thin, dull congregation".[8] He does not appear to have preached there again until March 15, 1772.[9]

Five miles west of Quinton and near the Worcester border lay Pebworth, where the Eden family at Broadmaster were on friendly terms with Wesley.[10] Mr. Martin, the squire, however,

[1] *Journal*, i, p. 163   [2] *Journal*, vii, pp. 251, 308   [3] *Op. cit.*, vi, p. 269
[4] *Journal*, i, pp. 204 f.   [5] *Journal*, vi, p. 99; vii, pp. 371 f.
[6] Not to be confused with Quinton, near Birmingham, where there was flourishing Methodist work
[7] *Journal*, i, p. 307   [8] *Journal*, ii, pp. 397 f.   [9] *Op. cit.*, v, p. 448
[10] *Letters*, vii, p. 52; *Journal*, v, p. 251

felt very differently towards him, and when he was announced to preach on March 18, 1768, intervened to prevent it.[1] However, Wesley was able to use the church on March 24, 1776, "the vicar was no weathercock" and on a number of later occasions. He apparently did not spare the squire in his sermons, for he remarks, after preaching on March 17, 1780: "perhaps a last warning to the great man of the parish, Mr. Martin".[2]

Turning south we come to Stinchcombe, near Dursley. The vicar, the Rev. John Andrews, was an Oxford man, having taken his LL.B. from St. Mary's Hall. He paid a visit to America and received the living on his return. Andrews preached for Lady Huntingdon at Bath, but on instituting him to his living Bishop Warburton exacted a promise that he would never again preach outside the parish.[3] Andrews was among the recipients of Wesley's circular of April, 1764.

At Kingswood[4] near Wotton-under-Edge, Wesley took the services and preached on September 5, 1753, at the invitation of Mr. Baylis, the vicar; and again on April 1, 1755, when the congregation was greatly affected, and, as he was later informed, "many of them were much changed, at least in their outward behaviour".[5] After this no further visit is recorded.

When Joseph Jane left Oxford he went to Iron Acton, where already some sympathy with the movement had been shown, for Wesley preached there on May 7, 1744.[6] On his death, Jane left a sum of £4,000 to be disposed of for some religious purpose, preferably for sending out missionaries.[7] This led to two meetings at Rauceby which were the forerunners of the meeting of the Eclectic Society which established the Church Missionary Society.

So we arrive at Bristol, a city of no great area, but thickly populated and very dirty. Pope gave a very unfavourable description of it after a visit in 1735; the only feature for which he had a good word was "the square", that is, Queen Square, so named from Anne who gave the city a charter. "The city is very unpleasant, and no civilized company in it. . . . The streets are as crowded as London, but the best image I can give you of it is, 'tis as if Wapping and Southwark were ten times as big, or all their people ran into London." By this time there

---

[1] *Op. cit.*, v, p. 521 [2] *Op. cit.*, vi, pp. 99, 161, 182, 225, 269, 306, 486
[3] *Countess of Huntingdon*, i, pp. 480 f.
[4] Not to be confused with Kingswood in Bristol itself
[5] *Journal*, iv, pp. 81, 108 [6] *Op. cit.*, iii, p. 134
[7] Carus, *Memoirs of Simeon*, p. 107

were many houses on Redcliff Hill, but both Redcliff and Temple Meads were still open country. The old bridge, with its narrow street of overhanging houses, had been demolished, as had the city gates. At this time Bristol was next to London the most important town in England, but it would soon be outstripped by the growing industrial centres of the North and Midlands. Clifton was already becoming noted for its waters; Bishop Butler went there during his last illness in 1752 before going on to Bath. Wesley preached at the parish church on May 13 and 20, 1739. On the latter occasion the sight of so many rich and apparently careless people moved him deeply. "I was earnestly desirous that some of them might 'enter into the kingdom of heaven'."[1] Lady Huntingdon went to the Hot Wells in March, 1751, after a severe illness. She wrote that "Mr. Hartley, (vicar of Winwick) hath preached several times in the churches with great acceptance."[2]

Bristol has been called "the cradle of Methodism", and the title is an apt one, for it was here that field-preaching was first begun, and here that the first meeting-house was built in the Horse-fair. It was at Bristol, too, that the first steps were taken which led to the separation from the Church. In the early days of the movement Whitefield had been very prominent, but he was gradually ousted by the Wesleys, and when Charles Wesley abandoned itinerating shortly after his marriage he resided there.

Evangelical views seem to have spread rapidly in Bristol and its neighbourhood, which was not always the case in strong Methodist centres, and on March 25, 1756, Walker mentions a group of eight young clergymen who formed a club for mutual encouragement in evangelizing. But though full of zeal they were too much infected with "mysticism, Moravianism, and Methodism".[3] On March 16, 1764, Wesley met "several serious clergymen there".[4]

One very early Evangelical was the Rev. Richard Hart, curate in charge, and from 1759 vicar of St. George's. This was the church built to provide for the needs of the miners of Kingswood, towards which Bishop Butler subscribed £400, besides obtaining donations from his friends. Hart was a Gloucestershire man whose family was well known and honoured in

---

[1] *Journal*, ii, pp. 198, 201. The vicar, the Rev. John Hodges, died on May 21, after sending for Wesley (p. 185).
[2] *Countess of Huntingdon*, i, p. 172 [3] Sidney, *Life of Walker*, p. 188
[4] *Journal*, v, p. 47

Bristol. He was educated at Christ Church, Oxford, were Jane was tutor, and before going to St. George's had served a curacy at Warminster. He remained in the living until his death in 1808. Another Evangelical was the Rev. John Gibbs (1704–44), vicar of St. Mary Redcliffe, who was friendly with Wesley, but, after promising the use of his church, later withdrew his permission.[1] At All Saints was the Rev. Josiah Tucker, who had been Butler's domestic chaplain. He did not entirely approve of Methodism, but carried on a friendly correspondence with Wesley. The latter thought well of his preaching.[2] Tucker was afterwards rector of St. Stephen's and ultimately Dean of Gloucester; he was a great favourite of Hannah More and his letters to her exhibit a strain of genuine Evangelical piety.[3]

One of the great centres of Evangelical influence was Temple Church. It had not been so from the first, for Thomas Becher (1739–44) had refused Charles Wesley the sacrament.[4] The next three vicars were Thomas Jones (1744–55), John Price (1755–66) and Alexander Catcott, the son of Alexander Catcott, headmaster of the Grammar School and rector of St. Stephen's, who wrote a treatise on the Deluge.[5] Then came Joseph Easterbrook (1779–91), a genuine if somewhat eccentric Evangelical.

Easterbrook was the son of a Bristol bell-man and had been educated at Kingswood. He taught for a brief spell at Trevecca, was then ordained, and received the appointment to Temple church from the Corporation. Wesley preached there soon after Easterbrook's arrival and commented: "The congregation here is remarkably well behaved; indeed so are the parishioners in general; and no wonder, since they have had such a succession of rectors, as few parishes in England have had." On September 24, 1786, he speaks of "the indefatigible pains which he [Easterbrook] takes with rich and poor"; and, on September 18, 1790, when both of them were near the end of their lives, he described him as "a pattern to all Bristol, and indeed to all England".[6] Easterbrook died in January, 1791, being scarcely forty years of age. His influence was a little diminished, though perhaps

---

[1] *Op. cit.*, ii, p. 179 d.; *Letters*, i, pp. 297 f.   [2] *Journal*, ii, pp. 181, 341

[3] See R. L. Schuyler, *Josiah Tucker*

[4] The grounds of the refusal were that he was not resident in the parish. When Charles protested the constables were asked to remove him. He had previously heard a "miserable sermon . . . recommending religion as the most likely means to raise a fortune" (*Journal*, i, p. 246)

[5] Wesley mistakenly says that the father also held the living of Temple (*Journal*, vi, pp. 305 f.)

[6] *Op. cit.*, vi, p. 305; vii, p. 211; viii, p. 96

interest in him was increased at least with the vulgar, by his performing exorcisms, in which he was aided by Methodist preachers.[1]

Another strong Evangelical centre was the small parish of St. Werburgh's. Walker wrote in 1755 to the Rev. Richard Symes who was rector: "I greatly rejoice that God has introduced into your large city the purity of the Gospel doctrines by your means in a regular way."[2] St. Werburgh's was the first church in Bristol in which Wesley preached,[3] probably in March, 1739, during the incumbency of Romney Penrose, Symes's predecessor. The outstanding name at St. Werburgh's, however, is that of James Rouquet, curate from 1768 to 1776. Rouquet was the son of French Protestant refugees, and whilst a boy, had heard Whitefield, who exercised a strong influence over him. He later went up to St. John's College, Oxford, where Charles Wesley, on a visit, came across him and testified that he was "not ashamed to confess Christ before men".[4] From his first curacy he was dismissed for over-zealous conduct, including preaching from house to house and in Bristol gaol. Soon afterwards he was given the living of West Harptree by the Lord Chancellor, and ordained priest by Dr. Wills, Bishop of Bath and Wells. By the latter he was very kindly treated, in spite of complaints made to him concerning Rouquet's views; and he invited him to preach an ordination sermon, which provoked still more protests but left the bishop unmoved. Rouquet gave up his living in order to become curate at St. Werburgh's, an office which he combined with a lectureship at St. Nicholas and the chaplaincy of St. Peter's Hospital. It was at St. Werburgh's, and by his invitation, that Rowland Hill preached his first sermon after being ordained. This was on June 8, 1773. Rouquet was not only Evangelical in religion, but also very radical in politics, a further offence to the rich Bristol merchants. By the poor, however, he was held in veneration, and when he died they flocked out of the slums in their thousands to accompany the body of their friend to his grave. He died on November 16, 1776, being then only forty-six; and the last words, thrice repeated, which he uttered were, "I want to go home".[5]

Another remarkable man among the Bristol Evangelicals was James Stonhouse. Stonhouse was born on July 9, 1716, and

[1] *Op. cit.*, vii, p. 362   [2] Letter in *The Christian Guardian*, 1804, p. 274
[3] *Journal*, vi, pp. 140 f.   [4] *Journal*, ii, p. 15 (August 20, 1748)
[5] Sidney, *Life of Rowland Hill*, p. 125

educated at Winchester and St. John's College, Oxford, where he came under Deist influence, and ended by becoming an infidel and an opponent of revealed religion. He settled in Northampton, and the joint efforts of Doddridge and Hervey, whose physician he was, brought him back to the faith. At the age of forty-seven he gave up his practice and took orders. In 1763 he became lecturer at All Saints, Bristol, and remained there until 1782, when he was appointed to St. James's. He died on December 8, 1795, and was buried in the chapel at Hot Wells where an epitaph composed by Hannah More perpetuates his memory. Three years before he had succeeded a distant kinsman in a baronetcy belonging to his family, but the estates passed to his niece, Baroness Rivers. During the last years of his life he had to endure much suffering, and when Wilberforce visited him in the summer of 1789 he described him as "under many bodily tortures, but patient and cheerful".[1]

Wesley preached on March 23, 1777, at St. Ewen's (now joined to Christ Church), but "not upon justification by faith", which he did not think "a profitable subject to an unawakened congregation".[2] The vicar was Romney Penrose, son of the clergyman of the same name who had been at St. Werburgh's.

The Evangelical cause in Bristol, and elsewhere, owed much to a layman, James Ireland, a wealthy sugar-refiner. He gave large sums to help poor clergy and also to train ordinands. Ireland was a regular correspondent of Romaine, and also a sympathetic and generous friend to Fletcher of Madeley, accompanying the latter to the south of France and caring for him during his illness in 1777.[3]

The name most widely known of all those who served the cause of Evangelicalism in Bristol and its neighbourhood, however, was that of Hannah More.[4] This remarkable woman was born on February 2, 1745, at Stapleton, near Bristol. Her father, a schoolmaster, had been brought up as a Presbyterian, but had later become a Churchman and a violent Tory. About 1772 she went up to London, and quickly became well known in the set which centred round Dr. Johnson. Her friendship with Garrick came about in an almost casual manner. The great actor had seen a letter of hers on his representation of King

---

[1] *Life of Wilberforce*, i, p. 243 [2] *Journal*, vi, p. 141

[3] Wesley, *Journal*, vi, p. 176

[4] See, further, W. Roberts, *Memoirs of the Life and Correspondence of Mrs. Hannah More*, which contains numerous letters and extracts from her journals, and M. G. Jones, *Hannah More*

Lear, and was so much impressed by it that he made her acquaintance and introduced her to his circle. Ultimately she went to live with him and his German (Roman Catholic) wife, and after Garrick's death continued to live with his widow. Hannah More was also taken up by Elizabeth Montagu and the "blue stockings". All were impressed by her simplicity and enthusiasm, as well as by her wit and liveliness.[1] She was often consulted by fashionable ladies on religious matters, many of whom were dissatisfied with the kind of life they were leading, though few were prepared to abandon it.

She published her *Thoughts on the Manners of the Great*, anonymously; but from modesty rather than from apprehension of any consequences to herself. It had an enormous vogue, and the authorship soon became an open secret, and did not in the least diminish her popularity. The book, though critical, contained no extravagant reproaches, but was a tactful and sensible exposure of many customs and habits whose evils were not realized by those who indulged in them.

Hannah More came only gradually to adopt Evangelical views and was never strictly "orthodox" according to the straitest school of the party. Having herself lived in the world, she knew its good as well as its bad side, and so had greater sympathy for it than those whose knowledge was purely external and often based on hearsay alone. This gave her much influence on society people, for it was realized that her criticisms were not inspired by envy or jealousy, and that they were put forward with a genuine desire to help. This is true also of her criticisms of some of the clergy of the day; as she herself said: "Surely an earnest wish to turn their attention to objects calculated to promote their true dignity is not the office of an enemy. So to expose the weakness of the land, as to suggest the necessity of internal improvement, and to point out the means of effectual defence is not *treachery*, but *patriotism*."[2] It would be difficult to exaggerate the value of the contribution she made to the growth of religion, and not least to its Evangelical form. Her writings, especially, with their freshness and originality, their insight into character and motive, were immensely popular, and spreading into every level of society did

---

[1] Roberts took upon him to soften down some expressions found in her letters. In a note to her god-daughter, for instance, she spoke of Sir Thomas Acland as "the recreant Knight of Devonshire". This he changed into "the excellent and estimable Sir Thomas Acland", a stilted phrase she herself would never have used

[2] *Strictures on Education*, p. 10

not a little to break down prejudice and to provide a sympathetic atmosphere.

But Hannah More was not content to restrict her efforts to writing alone; she wished to exhibit religion in actual practice. In spite of her great popularity in the fashionable world, and her love of literary society, she had always longed for quiet and peace; and so in 1780 she built a house at Cowslip Green, some ten miles from Bristol on the Exeter road—"my little thatched hermitage", she called it—and there she remained until 1802, when she moved to a larger and more convenient house at Barley Wood near by.

She and her sister Martha immediately began work among the neglected people on the Mendips. This district is in Somerset, and so provides a convenient transition to that county. At the time, it was in a very degraded and even lawless state, and no constable would venture into some of the villages. The two ladies were warned that their lives would be in danger if they undertook work there. They began by opening schools in 1789, at first in a very small way, but gradually penetrating much of the district. Before opening a school or working in a parish they were careful to obtain the approval of the incumbent, which as a rule was gladly given. Some of the clergy, however, were annoyed by activities which drew attention to their own neglect; and one of them, in later days, the Rev. William Shaw, rector of Chelvey, wrote an abusive account of her and her writings under the *nom de plume* of Archibald Mac Sarcasm. The farmers, too, were opposed to educating the children of agricultural labourers, considering that this would unfit them for their proper work. But in spite of all danger and opposition they persisted in their good work, encouraged and supported by men like William Wilberforce, and they succeeded in civilizing the neighbourhood.

Hannah More had another link with Somerset, for her sisters had a house at Bath where she frequently stayed. Bath, in the eighteenth century, was not only the Queen of the West, but also the cultural centre of England to which everybody who was anybody made a habit of resorting. As the means of communication improved it was possible to reach it from most of the south, and even from further afield, with what in those days was regarded as comparative ease. Thus after the lapse of centuries it regained its ancient reputation, for Acqua Regis, as the Romans called it, had been the focus of fashionable society in their day. So great was the throng of visitors that many new houses had to be built, and these in a style more in keeping with the ideas of solid splendour and comfort which then prevailed. The chief architects were John Wood and his son. The Royal Crescent was begun in 1767, and Lansdown Crescent twenty years later; and so it continued to expand until the close of the century. Bath received a further stimulus as a centre of social life when the Prince of Wales (later George II) set up his court there. On a visit in 1777, Walter Scott, a precocious child of six, noted the "river Avon winding round [the Parade] and the lowing of cattle from the opposite hills". A more sophisticated description of the city is to be found in *Humphrey Clinker*, where Lydia Melford speaks of its walks and ponds, its parterres of flowers, and a coffee-house set apart for the ladies, to which young girls were not admitted since the conversation dealt with "politics, scandal, philosophy, and other subjects above our capacity".

Life at Bath was intensely artificial, with a veneer of good breeding and elaborate courtesy which barely concealed, and often disguised, those elementary passions which flourish in such an environment. A fantastic delicacy prevailed which strained out the gnat and swallowed the camel. Pleasure and diversion, and above all gambling, were the chief occupations of those who thronged its streets and buildings; and, indeed, there was little else to occupy them, apart from indulgence in dubious intrigues. So Lord Chesterfield found it; confessing that but for the comfort of returning health he would be disposed to hang himself from sheer boredom. Well might Charles Wesley describe it in 1741, on his first attempt to proclaim the Gospel in this vanity fair, as Satan's headquarters and "that Sodom of our land".[1]

There were, of course, other spas in England, but Bath had no comparable rival. Much of its early success was due to Beau Nash. Nash was the son of a glass manufacturer, and was born at Carmarthen on October 18, 1674. Going up to Jesus College, Oxford, he was soon expelled for his wild life. It was in 1705 that he was appointed master of ceremonies at Bath, and at once laid down a series of most strict rules of etiquette which were meekly accepted by those who frequented the spa. For long his rule was unchallenged; but after a time there was a reaction, and he found himself deserted by his former friends, and fell into extreme poverty. But when he died in 1761 the

---

[1] *Journal*, i, p. 286

city gave him a magnificent funeral; as well it might do for one to whom it owed so much.

There had, however, been an earlier challenge to his authority. On June 5, 1739, Nash publicly asked John Wesley by what right he preached in Bath, and why he was frightening people out of their wits. Wesley was not the man to be overawed by a fashionable upstart, and refused to be browbeaten. Nash thereupon exclaimed, "I desire to know what this people comes here for?" Before Wesley could reply, an old woman in the congregation burst out: "Sir, leave him to me. . . . You, Mr. Nash, take care of your body. We take care of our souls; and for food of our souls we come here." Nash then retired in confusion.[1]

Wesley had early realized the possibilities of Bath as a centre for evangelizing, and preached there for the first time on April 10, 1739. Some of "the great and rich" attended his preaching on January 24, 1743, but Methodism seems to have made but little appeal.[2] As late as 1758 its meetings were held in a crowded room, though plans were being made to build a chapel. The foundation-stone of the chapel in New King Street was laid on December 16, 1777, and it was opened in the following March. Wesley describes it as "about half as large as that at London and nearly upon the same model".[3] One reason for the slow spread of Methodism in its Wesleyan form was no doubt the superior attractions of Lady Huntingdon's chapel. On September 28, 1765, Wesley records: "I preached in Bath: but had only the poor to hear, there being service at the same time, in Lady Huntingdon's chapel. So I was just in my element."[4]

Lady Huntingdon had first gone to Bath in 1739, when her husband took the cure; but it was not until 1765 that she bought land, and established her chapel. Whitefield who preached at the opening described it as "extremely plain, yet equally grand".[5] Wesley preached there on August 25, 1766, which occasioned some surprise, and also celebrated the sacrament and preached on October 5.[6] The chapel was attended by many of the nobility and the wealthy. Beau Nash was on one occasion persuaded to hear Whitefield, but was so quizzed by

---

[1] *Journal*, ii, pp. 211 ff. [2] *Op. cit.*, ii, p. 177; iii, p. 65
[3] *Op. cit.*, iv, p. 285; vi, pp. 177, 224 [4] *Op. cit.*, v, pp. 148 f.
[5] *Letters*, iii, p. 332. He preached in the morning; the evening preacher was Townsend, rector of Pewsey
[6] *Journal*, v, pp. 183, 188

his friends that he never repeated the experiment. Nash has been described as "a monument of irreligion, folly and vice";[1] but this judgment comes from a prejudiced pen. As we have already seen, he kept a letter from Hervey, which he would hardly have done if it had not found some response in him. Nash seems to have regarded religion, or at least attendance at public worship, as becoming to fashionable people. There were daily services at Bath Abbey when such were unusual, and Nash may have supported them, for these were also established at Tunbridge Wells, where he was called in to regulate the life of the spa.

Apart from the preaching of Lady Huntingdon's chaplains, until she severed her link with the Church, Evangelicalism, as distinct from Methodism, was practically unknown in Bath during our period.

One famous preaching house in Bath, the Argyle chapel, had been begun in 1785 by a small group who were dissatisfied with the religious provisions of the city. It was not, however, until the coming of William Jay[2] that its reputation was established.

In the rest of the county there were a number of Evangelical parishes, though these were not of much consequence. At Kingston, a populous place at the foot of the Quantocks four miles north of Taunton, James Brown, who had been curate of Bradford-on-Avon, was vicar. He owed his conversion to a meeting with Joseph Williams, a dissenter to whom he was introduced by his vicar. Williams said to him: "Sir, how does your soul prosper?" Although he gave only a perfunctory reply to this very unexpected greeting, it affected him deeply, and he later sought out Williams to his great spiritual benefit. Brown, who was one of Lady Huntingdon's preachers, has been described as "an elegant scholar and a warm-hearted and generous friend".[3] It was he who gave Rowland Hill a title for ordination. Brown also held the living of Portishead, near Bristol. In February, 1778, his daughter, Anne, was married to the Rev. Sir Harry Trelawney, whose eccentric career has been noticed elsewhere.

Wesley preached at Wellington on September 10, 1775. He found William Jesse ill in bed, and but for his arrival no service would have been possible. On September 2, 1785, Wesley opened a meeting-house there.[4] To the east lies Ilminster, where the

---
[1] *Countess of Huntingdon*, i, p. 445
[2] Sheridan regarded Jay as one of the greatest orators he had ever heard
[3] *Countess of Huntingdon*, ii, p. 11   [4] *Journal*, vi, p. 78; vii, p. 111

vicar was Thomas Eden, a son of Wesley's friend, Henry Eden of Broadmaston, near Evesham. Some eight miles further east is South Petherton, where Coke was curate from 1772 to 1777. He owed his dismissal to the adoption of Methodist practices,[1] so evidently there was little scope for Evangelical expansion in the parish.

In the Mendip district, in addition to the work of Hannah More and her sister, there were a few parishes in which some Evangelical teaching had penetrated, though not very deeply. At Clutton, Wesley was allowed to preach, and read the service on September 14, 1780;[2] at Blagdon, Toplady was vicar for a short time, being succeeded in 1766 by the Rev. John Langhorne, a minor poet and translator of Plutarch, but not an Evangelical.[3] Midsomer Norton was more promising, for Wesley preached and took the service there on September 13, 1776; the rector cheerfully granting the use of his church and himself going into the congregation. Wesley again preached there on September 24, 1778, and on September 30, 1785, when the curate, Mr. Sims, took the service in an admirable way.[4] At Frome, Richard Wilson was an old friend of Romaine,[5] but I have found no trace of Evangelical activity in the parish.

In Wiltshire, there had been a great awakening in May, 1741, led by a layman, but frowned on by the clergy.[6] Even earlier Charles Wesley had worked in the county. On October 14, 1739, he was invited to preach at Bradford-on-Avon, by Chapman, the vicar. The visit, however, was abortive, for at the last minute Chapman refused to allow him the use of his pulpit; "he feared his church would be pulled down; he feared the Bishop would be displeased".[7] But Chapman later came out as a strong and determined Evangelical, and at least two of his curates followed in his steps; James Brown, afterwards vicar of Kingston, and Edward Spencer, rector of Winkfield. The preaching of the latter was condemned as Methodistical and complaints were made to Bishop Hume of Salisbury. Lady Huntingdon vainly tried to get him to join her connexion.[8] Things flourished at Bradford, and Whitefield records preaching in the church in May, 1769, describing it as "a blessed day".[9]

Another notable Evangelical centre was Pewsey, near

---

[1] *Op. cit.*, vi, p. 120   [2] *Op. cit.*, vi, p. 294
[3] He made a proposal of marriage to Hannah More, which she refused
[4] *Op. cit.*, vi, pp. 129, 211; vii, p. 117
[5] *Works*, p. 574. Wilson died in August, 1785
[6] Whitefield, *Letters*, i, p. 266   [7] *Journal*, i, p. 189
[8] *Countess of Huntingdon*, i, p. 266   [9] *Letters*, iii, p. 386

Marlborough. Wesley preached there on October 2, 1764, in spite of the efforts of some of the neighbouring gentry to get the churchwardens to forbid him the use of the pulpit.[1] In 1767 the living was presented to Townsend. Joseph Townsend was the son of a London alderman and was educated at Clare Hall, Cambridge; where, like Berridge, he obtained a fellowship. Later he studied medicine under Dr. Cullen at Edinburgh, where Haweis, who later married his sister, was a fellow student. After his ordination he was much employed by Lady Huntingdon, especially in Scotland. He was a great friend of Newton, who described him as "a ready, lively, humble man"; whilst Venn, who records that he had three young men living with him whom he was preparing for orders, says: "That dear minister has a single eye and a warm heart."[2] Townsend had some literary ability, and after a visit to France and Spain in 1786 published an account of his travels. He was also the author of a number of theological works, including a vindication of the accuracy of the Pentateuch. He lived on until 1817, having been twice married, first to a Miss Nankivell of Truro, and after her death to Lady Clarke.

The influence of the revival teaching seems to have been very slow in affecting Devizes, and Rowland Hill claimed that a sermon of his on the evening of May 5, 1771, was "the first gospel sermon ever preached there".[3] Near to Devizes were the parishes of Little and Great Cheverall, of which Sir James Stonhouse was the non-resident rector. The parishes were in the charge of a Mr. Root, who in 1786-87 sought Wesley's advice about obtaining an assistant.[4]

The only other parishes in Wiltshire where I have been able to trace any Evangelical sympathies were Highworth, near Swindon, where Venn preached in 1775 "to a large congregation"; and Steeple Aston, where Samuel Hey, the younger brother of William, was rector. He was a friend of Robinson of Leicester and officiated at his marriage.[5]

In the South-west the great diocese of Exeter covered the two counties of Devon and Cornwall. Things here were made difficult by the attitude of Bishop Lavington (1747-62); but even before his time the position had not been too promising, at least at first. Whitefield in May, 1743, spoke of a contemplated visit to Exeter and Cornwall, adding: "That is dry ground. I love to range such places." He duly went to Exeter

---

[1] *Journal*, v, p. 98 [2] *Life*, p. 120 [3] Sidney, *Life of Rowland Hill*, p. 56
[4] *Letters*, vii, pp. 311, 368 [5] Vaughan, *Life of Robinson*, p. 74

in August when a number of the clergy "with which this city abounds" went to hear him; but some left before he had finished his sermon.[1] Charles Wesley was also there in the same month, and addressed a large meeting, "mostly gentlemen and ladies, with some Clergy. . . . God gave me favour in their eyes. . . . Many followed me to my inn, to take leave, and wished me good luck in the name of the Lord."[2]

The quarrel between Lavington and the Methodists, owing to an inaccurate version of his primary charge being circulated, has already received notice.[3] The Bishop's prejudice against anything which savoured of Methodism was shown when he refused to accept the testimonials of Dr. Haweis, signed by Walker, Penrose, and Mitchell, as he considered that no reliance could be placed on anyone who preached faith without works. Wesley paid a visit to Exeter cathedral on August 29, 1762, and records that "we had a useful sermon, and the whole service was performed with great seriousness and decency". He attended Holy Communion, at which Bishop Lavington, then near the end of his days, was also present. "I was well pleased to partake of the Lord's Supper with my old opponent."[4]

Methodism flourished much more in Cornwall than in Devon. In 1767 there were 2,160 members, divided into two circuits, East and West, of which the latter claimed three-quarters. Devon had but 413.

It was at Bideford that the men of Devon had their first opportunity of hearing the revival teaching, when Hervey went there as curate. Whitefield on a visit in November, 1743, wrote: "Dear Mr. H——y, one of our first Methodists at Oxford . . . laid the blessed foundation"; and in March, 1750, he spoke of Bideford as having "perhaps one of the best little flocks in England".[5]

Not far from Bideford were the parishes of Ashford and Yarncombe, where Thomas Bliss was rector. He was a native of Oxford, where his father was Professor of Astronomy. As an undergraduate he had been offended by the preaching of Romaine, but succumbed to that of Haweis. Leaving Oxford in 1760 he went for a time to Grimshaw until his appointment to his Devon livings. Toplady described him as "the amiable, the excellent, the zealous, the heavenly-minded", and as "a pattern for believers, and particularly ministers of Jesus".[6] Bliss was a

---

[1] *Letters*, ii, pp. 21, 37   [2] *Journal*, i, p. 333   [3] See pp. 185 f.
[4] *Journal*, iv, pp. 526 f.   [5] *Letters*, ii, pp. 44, 341
[6] *Countess of Huntingdon*, i, p. 391

man of studious habits; but unfortunately suffered from bodily handicaps, being lame, and also afflicted by some kind of nervous complaint to cure which he took large quantities of opium. Death when it came in 1802 was a great relief to him.

Another Evangelical incumbent was Hill, at Tawstock, who applied his large income to religious and charitable purposes. He had been influenced by Thomson of St. Gennys and lived to an advanced age, dying in 1800. Another Devon Evangelical who also reached a great age was Cradock Glascott, vicar of Hatherleigh from 1781 to 1831. He had been chaplain to Lady Huntingdon, and on his appointment the bishop would only institute him on condition that he took an oath not to leave his parish. This he fulfilled, and during his whole incumbency is said never to have missed a Sunday service. Glascott was a friend of Berridge who described him as "a very acceptable person to myself and my flock. Not a dozing face, with a hoarse doctrinal throat; but a right sharp countenance with a clear gospel pipe". He also wrote to Lady Huntingdon in March, 1770: "Before I parted with honest Glascott, I cautioned him much against petticoat snares. He had burnt his wings already; surely he will not imitate a foolish gnat, and hover again over the candle."[1]

At Cornwood the vicar was Thomas Vivian, who had been converted by Wesley's writings. He was born at Kenwyn in 1720 and educated at Truro Grammar School and Exeter College, Oxford. In 1746 he became curate in charge of Truro, thus anticipating his friend Walker, and then went to Redruth. Here his teaching gave much offence, and he was dismissed; but was thereupon presented to Cornwood through the influence of his wife, a daughter of John Hussey, town clerk of Truro. Here amongst other activities he had "classes" for his parishioners on Methodist lines. Vivian wrote a number of works which met with considerable approval. He died in 1793.

In Plymouth, both Wesley and Whitefield found that Dock (i.e. Devonport) was most responsive to Methodist teaching. In February, 1749, the latter speaks of a "truly converted neighbouring clergyman, who has invited me to preach in his church". In September, 1765, he writes: "Mr. Middleton sends me word, that he is blessed at Plymouth, and especially at Dock, and that Kingsbridge christians are lively."[2] The most notable figure in the town as an Evangelical, however, was Robert Hawker, curate, and then vicar, of Charles; where he

[1] *Works*, p. 508   [2] *Letters*, ii, pp. 231, 330

ministered from 1778 to 1828. Hawker was the grandfather of the famous Hawker of Morwenstow, a man of very different views. He himself was an extreme Calvinist and wrote voluminously to expound its doctrines; he also exercised a vigorous discipline over his flock. In spite of his strictness, Hawker was a simple, lovable man, and charitable almost to excess. He was a pioneer in introducing Sunday Schools into the neighbourhood and is said to have compiled the first children's hymn-book.

I have left to the last the most famous of Devon Evangelicals, Augustus Montague Toplady.[1] He was born at Farnham in November, 1740, the only son of Major Richard Toplady who died shortly after at the siege of Cartagena. His maternal uncle was rector of St. Paul's, Deptford. Little is known of his early life, about which he was uncommunicative; but it was spent with his mother at Exeter. Going to Westminster school he showed considerable promise, but instead of proceeding to an English university he went to Trinity College, Dublin. Before this he had already been influenced by Methodism through hearing when only sixteen an address by an itinerant preacher in a barn at Codymain. On this he commented later: "Strange that I, who had so long sat under the means of grace in England, should be brought nigh to God in an obscure part of Ireland, amidst a handful of God's people met together in a barn, and under the ministry of one who could hardly spell his name." During his time at Dublin he corresponded with Wesley, but his "Arminian prejudices", as he called them in later days, were soon thrown aside through studying Dr. Manton's sermons.

Toplady was ordained in 1762, and soon afterwards was presented to Blagdon in Somerset. Four years later he moved to the small parish of Venn-Ottery with Hardford, near Sidmouth; but after two years he exchanged it for Broadhembury, near Honiton, a village lying at the foot of the western slope of the hills dividing Somerset and Devon. He was already suffering from lung trouble and the long hours which he spent in his study did not improve his health. Often he would read into the small hours of the morning in the attempt to quench his "inextinguishable" thirst for knowledge. The moist climate of Devon also affected him, and after vainly trying to get a living in the Midlands, in 1775, he went up to London on medical advice, and there rented the French chapel in Orange street, near Leicester Fields. He also preached in Lady Huntingdon's chapels and for various Evangelical clergymen. But his health

[1] See, further, *The Works of A. M. Toplady, with a Memoir* (6 volumes)

was so seriously undermined that he lived only until August 11, 1778, dying at the age of thirty-eight. After his death a rumour was circulated that he died in despair and blasphemy, and Richard Hill wrote to Wesley accusing him of being its author. The latter contemptuously ignored Hill's letter, a fate which it deserved. Toplady, so far as his health allowed, was a diligent parish priest and beloved by his flock. Although reserved, in personal intercourse he had none of that bitterness which showed itself in his controversial writings.

We now cross the Tamar into Cornwall, where, as we have noted, Methodism was especially strong. But though the people heard gladly they seem to have been backward in their offers of hospitality. On one occasion Wesley remarked to John Nelson: "Brother Nelson, we ought to be thankful that there are plenty of blackberries, for this is the best country I ever saw for getting a stomach, but the worst that ever I saw for getting food. Do the people think we can live by preaching?"[1]

Some account of the early days of Evangelicalism in Cornwall has already been given in connexion with Walker, and before going on to a more general survey it will be well to deal with the sequel to that work. Unfortunately, Walker's death coincided with a change in the living, and the new rector, the Rev. Charles Pye (1761–1803), who was of no very definite type, but opposed to any form of Methodism, chose to become resident. He declared that his pulpit so stank of Calvinism that it could not be purged in a century. It is not surprising, therefore, that those who had hung on Walker's lips found the new conditions very difficult. Wesley hoped that some of them would now join the Methodists, but in this he was disappointed. "They still look on us as rank heretics and will have no fellowship with us", he wrote on September 4, 1766.[2] Many no doubt drifted away into indifference; but at last a number determined to establish their own place of worship where they could still enjoy the services of the Church, but combined with more acceptable teaching. They met in a building which had formerly been used as a cockpit, and as the years went by gradually drifted away from the Church until they became a Congregational chapel.

Walker, however, had not been the first to introduce Evangelicalism into Cornwall. There was an even earlier group in the north-eastern corner which was in touch with Bideford and Hervey's work there. Whitefield wrote from Bideford in

[1] Southey, *Life of Wesley*, ii, pp. 52 f. [2] *Journal*, v, p. 185

November, 1743: "The Rev. J—— N——,[1] rector of St. Gennis (sic), Cornwall, is here. . . . Here also is another clergyman of about eighty years of age, but not above one year old in the school of the knowledge of Christ. He lately preached three times and rode forty miles in a day." Whitefield then paid a visit to St. Gennys, where there was a great "outpouring of God's blessed spirit". When he came again in 1750 he found "an unthought and unexpectedly wide door is opened".[2]

George Thomson,[3] vicar of St. Gennys, was a man of good family and ample private means. He had gone up to Exeter College, Oxford, where he was in residence from 1716 to 1719. After being ordained he served a curacy at Jacobstow, but, finding the duties of his office burdensome (like Walker, he was a man of a gay and social disposition), he took a naval chaplaincy. In 1732 he was presented to St. Gennys by Mr. Eliot, who was a kinsman, and almost immediately rebuilt the vicarage, but did little for the spiritual welfare of his parishioners. From his state of carelessness he was suddenly aroused by a dream, twice repeated, in which he was told that on a certain date he would appear before the judgment seat of Christ to give an account of his life and ministry. On awaking he sent for some of the more serious of his flock and told them what had happened, at the same time begging for their prayers. He then shut himself up and made an earnest study of the Scriptures, and prayed that he might be forgiven for his previous neglect. Light and peace came to him after two weeks. The day specified in the dream came round, and he spent it in prayer with some of his friends. It passed, and nothing happened. Next day he collected the congregation and publicly gave an account of his experience, and of the change in his life. This took place in 1735, and was entirely unconnected with any Methodist influence. When Hervey began to preach similar doctrines at Bideford he speedily got into communication with him, and, when Hervey left, made himself responsible for the care of his converts. Hervey wrote to them telling them that they would receive a monthly visit, and rejoicing that one who had "the unction of the Holy One, and knows the truth as it is in Jesus" was able to teach them the way of God more perfectly.

[1] This should be G—— T—— (i.e. George Thomson)

[2] *Letters*, ii, pp. 44 f., 341

[3] On Thomson and the other early leaders, see G. C. B. Davies, *The Early Cornish Evangelicals, 1735-1760*

Thomson was very active in his parish, and in 1745 reported to his bishop that he preached twice each Lord's Day, "and as often on other days when I can get my people together". In the same returns the vicar of Marhamchurch informed the bishop that one family in his parish frequented Thomson's irregular meetings and accompanied him "at his circumforaneous vociferations". The vicar of Treneglos also stated that he had no Dissenters in his parish "unless they may so be called who go by the name of Methodists, a set of people who are chiefly encouraged and abetted and taught by a neighbouring clergyman". In March, 1748, the clergy of the neighbourhood decided to close their pulpits to Thomson, and he was also denounced to the bishop. The latter thereupon requested Thomson to go and see him, and threatened to strip him of his gown. Thomson at once flung it at the bishop's feet, exclaiming: "I can preach the Gospel without a gown."[1]

When Charles Wesley came to Cornwall, Thomson welcomed him and joined in his preaching tours. John did not visit the parish until June 16, 1745, when he preached in the church, which "was moderately filled with serious hearers, but few of them appeared to feel what they heard".[2]

Thomson lived to the advanced age of eighty-one, but became blind in his latter years. It is said that he was secretly a Moravian.[3] He certainly appears to have been troubled in his religious views, for when Wesley visited him on September 3, 1782, "he had many doubts concerning his final state, and rather feared than desired to die, so that my whole business was to comfort him and to increase and confirm his confidence in God".[4]

The old clergyman whom Whitefield met at Bideford was the Rev. John Bennett, curate of Tresmere, near Launceston, and three other parishes. He did not accept Evangelical views until past seventy years of age, and spent the last ten years of his life in fervent evangelizing. His conversion was due to Thomson. When Charles Wesley met him on July 13, 1744, he found that he had known his father.[5] Both Charles and John often preached for him, but a new vicar was appointed in 1752, and after this there is no record of their doing so. Here, as in so many other places, the spread of Evangelical teaching was checked in the Church, and no doubt those who desired it then became Methodists.

[1] The same story is told of Grimshaw (*Countess of Huntingdon*, i, p. 126)
[2] *Journal*, iii, p. 181   [3] *Countess of Huntingdon*, i, p. 126 n.
[4] *Journal*, vi, p. 367   [5] *Journal*, i, p. 369

Another of the same group was the Rev. John Turner, rector of Week St. Mary until his death in 1772. John Wesley preached there on June 18, 1745, to the largest congregation he had seen in that part of Cornwall. Though Wesley visited the parish on October 2, 1757, there is no record of his again preaching there until September 27, 1762.[1]

The vicar of Padstow, the Rev. Thomas Biddulph, was an Evangelical. He married Martha Tregunna, a convert of Walker, and their son, the Rev. T. T. Biddulph, did much good work at Bristol. Burnett served his first curacy at Padstow. Evangelical influences must have been greatly quickened when Walker's lay friend, William Rawlings, moved there in 1770. At nearby Port Isaac, Mr. Buckingham, the curate, severed his connexion with the Methodists for fear of offending the bishop. None the less, he was dismissed, and later joined Wesley as a clerical assistant.

Roche, which lies in a desolate region some five miles southwest of Bodmin, enjoyed the energetic ministrations of Samuel Furly, who came there from Slaithwaite in 1767.[2] He owed the appointment to Lady Huntingdon, who had introduced him to John Thornton in the previous year. His best years were, however, then past, and before his death he became blind.

One village which was prominent in the early days of the revival was St. Agnes, some ten miles from Truro on the north coast. It was part of the parish of Perranzabuloe, of which James Walker was vicar, and had a succession of Evangelical curates in charge. Vowler, of whom Wesley says that he preached and lived the gospel,[3] made a great impression, but died when only a young man on July 30, 1758. His funeral sermon was preached by Walker of Truro. He was followed by Phelps, who likewise received Wesley's commendation;[4] but he too died only three or four years after going to St. Agnes. The most prominent of those who were in charge of the village, however, was Thomas Wills.[5] He was born at Truro on July 26, 1740, and educated there under George Conon, and later came under the influence of Walker, to whom he owed his conversion. Going up to Magdalen Hall, Oxford, he found himself through Dr. Haweis in a circle of godly men. The bishop of

---

[1] *Journal*, iii, p. 181; iv, pp. 240, 531   [2] *Op. cit.*, v, p. 187

[3] He describes him as preaching "two such thundering sermons . . . as I have scarce heard these twenty years" (*Journal*, iv, p. 234; cf. p. 529).

[4] He calls him "a man of humble, loving tender spirit. Between him and the Methodists most of the parish are now awakened" (*op. cit.*, iv, p. 407).

[5] See *Memoirs of the Life of the Rev. Thomas Wills, by a Friend*

Oxford ordained him in 1762, and he received priest's orders from Bishop Lavington two years later. At St. Agnes he laboured with great vigour and was noted for his strongly Calvinist views. Marrying a niece of Lady Huntingdon, he resigned his curacy in order to become one of her chaplains; but before leaving he built a meeting-house. In 1779 he left the Church and was one of the two ex-clergymen who performed the first ordination for Lady Huntingdon's new connexion. However, a quarrel led in 1788 to the severance of relations. Wills died at Boskenna on May 12, 1802, and was buried at Buryan, where a monument was placed in the church.

South of Truro, and near Falmouth, the living of St. Gluvias was held by the Rev. John Penrose, a schoolfellow and friend of Walker, from 1741 until his death in 1776. The epitaph to him in the church was composed by Hannah More, and the local historian says that he "left a reputation of learning, of piety, and of all the virtues which adorn the clergyman".[1] Another friend and ally of Walker's, Thomas Michell, was vicar of Veryan from 1743 until 1783.

At Redruth, John Collins was vicar. On one occasion he rescued Wesley, whom he had known at Oxford, from an unpleasant encounter. The latter heard him preach "an exceedingly useful sermon" on August 12, 1750; and again, on September 14, 1755, he says that "he read prayers admirably well and preached an excellent sermon".[2] Collins's father, also called John, was High Sheriff in 1720. They came of a very old clerical family, and though Collins befriended Wesley, he never asked him to preach in his church. It is uncertain whether he sympathized fully with Evangelical views, for he dismissed Vivian on account of his doctrines.

In the far west, St. Ives was an early centre of Methodism, and there was a good deal of persecution there. Charles Wesley, on a visit on July 20, 1744, says: "Our warm friend the Curate saluted us courteously." There is, however, little trace of any development of Evangelicalism in the town. At Sancreed, in the middle of the Penwith peninsula, the vicar, the Rev. Edward Hobbs, met with the approval of Wesley.[3] He died in 1772.

The record of Evangelicalism in Cornwall makes rather distressing reading. In the early days there were two strong groups, that in the north-east of the county, and that round Walker at Truro; and at this period Evangelicalism was probably more

---

[1] Davies Gilbert, *Parochial Hist. of Cornwall*, ii, p. 104
[2] *Journal*, iii, pp. 191, 489 f.; iv, p. 135   [3] *Journal*, v, p. 286 n.

flourishing in Cornwall than in any part of England. Then it suddenly collapsed. The reasons for this are various. There was episcopal and clerical disapproval, and changes of incumbencies, for, when the Evangelicals died off, they were followed by clerics of a different colour; but most potent of all was the stronger appeal made by the emotional preaching of the Methodists to the temperament of the people, and the aggressive tactics which they adopted. Even in Walker's day, the intrusion of Methodists in Evangelical centres aroused indignation. But when he protested in the case of St. Agnes, Wesley, in spite of his admiration for Vowler, who was then curate there, made an unsatisfactory reply: "I do not know that every one who preaches the truth has wisdom and experience to guide and govern a flock. I do not know whether Mr. Vowler would or could give that flock all the advantages for holiness which they now enjoy."[1] The Methodists regarded even men like Walker as "well-meaning legalists" and had no scruples about attracting their followers. None the less, Wesley had spoken very highly of the work being done by the Evangelical clergy, writing on September 8, 1760: "By these and the Methodists together, the line is now laid, with no considerable intervals, all along the north sea from the eastern point of Cornwall to the Land's End."[2]

[1] Wesley had received complaints about Vowler's defective teaching: see *Letters*, iii, pp. 221 ff.

[2] *Journal*, iv, p. 407

CHAPTER 19

EVANGELICALISM IN THE UNIVERSITIES

THE state of the universities as already described was not such as to suggest that they were likely fields for religious revival. Although some of the greatest of the Non-jurors had been Cambridge men, it was Oxford which became the home of the Jacobites and of those who professed High Church views. Even after 1745 much of the same outlook persisted, though in a harmless and academic form, manifesting itself mainly in a conservative and suspicious attitude to all novelties. As the Oxford Methodists of 1729, who were perfectly orthodox in their views and High Church in their practices, were uniformly derided and abused, and in various colleges meetings were held to discuss means of suppressing them, it is not surprising that when more questionable ways of propagating religion arose they should awaken deep hostility.

At first, young Evangelicals, in view of the Wesley connexion, were sent to Oxford; and there was much activity there, in which Haweis took a leading part. Romaine was also welcomed by those who shared his views, and in June, 1755, Whitefield could write that many in Oxford were awakened to the knowledge of the truth.[1] Lady Huntingdon also knew of prayer meetings among undergraduates.

The great centre of Evangelicalism was the house of a certain Mrs. Durbridge, a woman of humble birth and the widow of one of Whitefield's converts. There Dr. Stillingfleet, fellow of Merton, Mr. Hallward, fellow of Worcester, Mr. Foster, of Queen's, Mr. Pugh, of Hertford, Mr. Gurdon, of Magdalen, and Mr. Clark, of St. John's, used to gather for prayer and mutual help, much as their predecessors had met under the guidance of Wesley a generation before. Amongst those who attended were also a number of undergraduates from St. Edmund Hall, once a nest of Non-jurors, but now destined to become notorious for a very different type of religion.

The meeting, when it became known, aroused considerable excitement in both city and university, and the authorities of St. Edmund Hall showed great concern.[2] Mr. Higson, the tutor,

---
[1] *Letters*, iii, p. 121
[2] See, further, S. L. Ollard, *The Six Students of St. Edmund Hall*; A. D. Godley, *Oxford in the Eighteenth Century*, pp. 269 ff.; and Sidney, *Life of Sir Richard Hill*, pp. 104 ff.

brought the matter to the notice of the Principal, Dr. Dixon; but the latter refused to take it up seriously. Higson then appealed to the Vice-Chancellor, Dr. Durell, this time with complete success, and a committee was set up to make the necessary inquiries.

As a result, seven students of the Hall were denounced. They were Benjamin Kay, Thomas Jones, Thomas Grove, Erasmus Middleton, Joseph Shipman, James Matthews, and Benjamin Blatch. The case against the last-named was soon dropped, for it was found that he was not a Methodist and not a candidate for orders. It was, indeed, suspected that his name had only been included because he had neglected Mr. Higson's lectures. The accused were brought to a public trial in the chapel of the Hall, to which the Vice-Chancellor and his associates went in solemn procession from the University church.

The chief heads of accusation were four: (*a*) Holding the doctrines of Election, Perseverance, and Justification by Faith without Works; (*b*) Consorting with reputed Methodists, such as Mr. Venn, Mr. Newton, and Mr. Fletcher;[1] (*c*) Attending unlawful meetings; and (*d*) Being destitute of scholarship. In addition, Matthews, Jones, and Shipman were accused of having been engaged in trade, and Middleton of acting as a "minister in Holy Orders" at Cheveley in the Salisbury diocese.

The accusation of being deficient in learning was at once put to the test, and the unfortunate men were bidden to translate a long and obscure extract from the University Statutes—a sufficiently arduous ordeal for any nervous young student. Two of them, however, did this quite readily, as well as rendering passages from the Greek New Testament; the rest failed miserably.

During the trial, Dr. Dixon, the Principal of the Hall, stood up manfully for the students and testified to their general good conduct; whilst Dr. Horne, later Bishop of Norwich, suggested that if they were to be expelled for too much religion, the court might be better employed in inquiring into the lives of those who had too little.[2] Point was given to this last remark by the fact that one of the witnesses for the prosecution was another student of the Hall, a certain John Welling, a man of low birth, no learning, and in the habit of expressing sceptical views.[3]

---

[1] Of these, Venn was a Cambridge man; the other two had never been members of any university

[2] Sidney, *Life of Hill*, p. 41

[3] He later sought orders, excusing his infidel views on the grounds that he only gave vent to them when he was drunk! See Hill, *Pietas Oxoniensis*, pp. 22, 79 n.

EVANGELICALISM IN THE UNIVERSITIES 355

Judgment was given on March 11, 1768, and all six undergraduates were expelled from the university, and thanks were expressed to Mr. Higson for bringing the matter to the notice of the authorities. Technically, the verdict was no doubt a correct one; but the whole proceeding throws a lurid and unsavoury light on the condition of the university. Higson seemed to have been especially venomous because the men neglected his lectures, and he may have also had a personal quarrel with the principal. But behind it all was, not so much concern for the intellectual prestige of the university, as antagonism to Methodism and dislike of any weakening of the barriers between city and university such as joint prayer meetings. Emphasis was laid on attendance at illegal conventicles prohibited by the University Statutes and the presence at them of non-university men; one, Hewett, a stay-maker, who offered up extempore prayer, is actually named.

The judgment was condemned by many, both at Oxford and in the country, and the expulsion was not allowed to take place without protests. One result, typical of the times, was the outbreak of a war of pamphlets. Richard Hill, who, breaking the family connexion with St. John's, Cambridge, had been at Magdalen, issued *Pietas Oxoniensis* with a dedication to the Chancellor, the Earl of Lichfield. This was answered by Nowell. Then Hill responded with *Goliath Slain*, and so the controversy continued, with numbers of other contestants rushing in. One effect was to draw wide public notice to the dispute, and there can be no doubt that the reputation of the university suffered in consequence. The *London Chronicle* printed facetious warnings for undergraduates:

> So drink, ye jovial souls, and swear,
> And all shall then go well;
> But oh! take heed of Hymns and Prayer,
> These cry aloud—E-X-P-E-L.[1]

Dr. Johnson's comment on the case is well known, but not perhaps sufficiently so to preclude quotation. It is, in any case, an interesting expression of his point of view, and also of his felicity in finding illustrations. On April 14, 1772, Boswell records:

> I talked of the recent expulsion of six students from the University of Oxford, who were methodists, and

[1] Quoted, *The Clerk of Oxford in Fiction*, p. 312

would not desist from publickly praying and exhorting. JOHNSON: "Sir, that expulsion was extremely just and proper. What have they to do at a University, who are not willing to be taught, but will presume to teach? sir, they were examined, and found to be mighty ignorant fellows." BOSWELL: "But, was it not hard, sir, to expel them, for I am told they were good beings?" JOHNSON: "I believe they might be good beings; but they were not fit to be in the University of Oxford. A cow is a very good animal in the field; but we turn her out of a garden."

Wesley's main interest in the contest seems to have been in the verdict, which with Nowell's reply to Hill, helped to clear the Church from the charge of predestination.[1] None of the accused had had relations with him.

Other colleges then began to take a strong line with undergraduates suspected of Methodism, expelling them or asking them to remove their names from the books. "Thus were disappointed the hopes of those who were desirous of filling the Church with their votaries."[2] Joseph Benson entered St. Edmund Hall in March, 1769, just after the expulsions; but although a man of undoubted scholarship he was refused testimonials by the Hall and in consequence was never ordained.[3] It is strange, in view of his past record, that he was ever admitted. At the end of the century St. Edmund Hall again became an Evangelical centre and so continued for many years.[4]

Before leaving the St. Edmund Hall case it may be interesting to give brief sketches of the lives and careers of the victims. Thomas Jones, who had been a hairdresser and had received much help from Newton at Olney before going up to Oxford, succeeded in being ordained and became curate of Clifton Reynes near Olney. Kay was of good middle-class stock and was a competent scholar, being bible-clerk at the Hall and holding an Ironmongers' Company exhibition. Thomas Grove unsuccessfully petitioned the Archbishop of Canterbury, begging for re-admission to the university, confessing his former irregularities and promising amendment in future. He was a man of fortune, having a house at Woburn. Rowland Hill visited him in 1773, and affirmed that but for his failure to

[1] *Journal*, v, p. 293 [2] Nowell, *An Answer to Pietas Oxoniensis*, p. 1
[3] Macdonald, *Memoirs of Joseph Benson*, p. 21. He was the son of Joseph Benson of Melerby in Cumberland and twenty-one when he went up
[4] See Bateman, *Life of Daniel Wilson*, i, pp. 50 ff., 110 ff.

obtain re-admission he would have devoted himself to the Church from which he had now separated.[1] Matthews had been instructed by Fletcher before going to St. Edmund, and after his expulsion became a student at Trevecca. Erasmus Middleton had received help from Haweis, and after being driven from Oxford succeeded in entering King's College, Cambridge, where he was helped by Fuller, the banker, who was a Dissenter. He was ordained by the Bishop of Down and served curacies with Romaine and Cadogan, and also had lectureships at St. Benet's, Gracechurch Street, and St. Helen's, Bishopgate. He is well known through his *Biographia Evangelica*. Shipman went to Trevecca, where he was supported by Lady Huntingdon, but his family turned against him and tried to persuade him to leave. He was active in itinerating for Lady Huntingdon in Bristol and the West, but his career was cut short through the breaking of a blood vessel. He died in October 1771.[2]

As a result of the persecution in Oxford, Evangelicals naturally turned to Cambridge, which incidentally had owed its early importance to suspicions of Lollardy at Oxford in the fifteenth century. Dr. Inge has stated that Cambridge "has generally produced men rather than movements",[3] though the Cambridge Platonists of the seventeenth century are an exception. Perhaps another exception may be found in the Evangelical Movement in its second phase; for there can be no question of the immense debt which it owed to Cambridge, at first under Isaac Milner, and later under Charles Simeon.

Academic life at Cambridge was, as we have seen, rather better than at Oxford; but even so, judged by later standards, it was of no high quality. Dr. Parr, however, who went up to Emmanuel in 1765, gives a glowing account of its state. "The unreserved conversation of scholars, the disinterested offices of friendship, the use of valuable books, and the example of good men, are endearments by which Cambridge will keep a strong hold upon my esteem, my respect, and my gratitude, to the latest moment of my life."[4] This testimony comes from one who had a passion for learning; but others, or some of them, also seem to have worked hard. Pitt, when at Pembroke from 1773 onwards, besides studying mathematics also read widely in the classics.[5] Wilberforce, slightly his junior, on going up to

[1] Sidney, *Life of Rowland Hill*, p. 85
[2] There is a moving account of his death in Sidney, *Life of Sir Richard Hill*, pp. 522 ff.
[3] *The Platonic Tradition in English Theology*, p. 40
[4] *Works*, ii, p. 566   [5] Stanhope, *Life of Pitt*, i, p. 15

St. John's in 1776 encountered the less worthy side of Cambridge life: "I was introduced, on the very first night of my arrival, to as licentious a set of men as can be well conceived. They drank hard and their conversation was even worse than their lives." The dons discouraged any attempt at study. "Why in the world should a man of your fortune trouble himself with fagging?" they asked. Wilberforce long retained the poor impression which he then formed of the fellows of colleges. On a visit in 1788 he felt that they had: "neither the solidity of judgment possessed by ordinary men of business, nor the refined feelings and elevated principles which become a studious and sequestered life."[1]

In the matter of orthodoxy, Erasmus Middleton, who had studied at both universities and can have had no bias in favour of Oxford, felt that Cambridge fell far behind the sister university.[2] There can be no doubt that Latitudinarianism had long been flourishing on the banks of the Granta. It may be traced back to Edmund Law, a disciple of Locke, who after being at Christ's, was Master of Peterhouse from 1756 to 1788 and also held a professorship. The great influence in Cambridge, however, was that of William Paley. Paley had a fellowship at Christ's after being senior wrangler in 1763, but left in 1775 to become rector of Musgrave in Westmorland and then in 1782 archdeacon of Carlisle. But in spite of his removal Paley continued to exert considerable influence, especially after the publication in 1785 of his *Principles of Moral and Political Philosophy*.[3] It has become the fashion to disparage Paley; but there is no doubt that he was a man of force and independence of mind, even if no great original thinker. He showed his independence by expressing sympathy with the French Revolution, which called forth Dean Milner's comment: "I am exceedingly sorry to find that Mr. Paley is as loose in his politics as in his religion."[4] Paley is often regarded as only interested in the moral aspects of religion; but this is to misjudge him, for in one of his charges he gave a warning against the danger of preaching up morality to the neglect of doctrine, and added: "We are in such haste to fly from enthusiasm and superstition, that we are approaching to an insensibility to all religious influence."[5]

Another leading Latitudinarian was John Hey, the elder

---

[1] *Life*, i, pp. 10 f., 176 f.; cf. also p. 223
[2] *Biographia Evangelica*, iv, p. 510
[3] The better known *Evidences* was not published until 1794
[4] *Life of Wilberforce*, ii, pp. 2 f. [5] *Works*, vii; *Charge*, vii

brother of William, a very capable college tutor and the first Norrisian Professor of Divinity. After taking his degree from St. Catherine's he had been awarded a fellowship at Sidney Sussex, where he became tutor in 1760, an office which he continued to hold until 1779 when he took two small country livings on the borders of Northampton and Buckinghamshire. When at Sidney Sussex his lectures on "Morality" were so celebrated that students from other colleges were allowed to attend them—then an unheard of thing—and among them William Pitt. His divinity lectures later received high praise from Arnold of Rugby, who wrote on November 21, 1834: "I like no book on the Articles altogether, but Hey's Divinity Lectures at Cambridge seem to me the best and fairest of any that I know of."

The Latitudinarianism of Cambridge, however, was more favourable to a religious revival than the rigid orthodoxy of Oxford. There was in Cambridge much more freedom and less regard for tradition; a sign of this can perhaps be seen in the successful agitation among undergraduates which in 1766 led to the substitution of square caps for the round ones, lined with black silk and edged with velvet, previously worn. For a time, however, the atmosphere of Cambridge told against spiritual progress. Even John Cowper confessed on his deathbed to his poet brother that the prevailing unbelief had so penetrated his life that he had lost all heart for his pastoral duties at St. Benet's.[1]

There seems to have been an early interest at Cambridge in the revival movement parallel to that at Oxford, which affected among others, and that most unexpectedly, Horace Walpole who went down from King's in 1739.[2] Two Cambridge men who became Methodists and contributed hymns to the movement were William Hammond, a man of some learning, who later went over to the Moravians, and Robert Seagrave of Clare, the son of a clergyman and himself in orders though he never held any cure. Seagrave wrote in defence of Whitefield and in 1739 began preaching in Lorrimer's Hall, Cripplegate. He died about 1760.[3] The first Methodist at Cambridge was probably William Delamotte, a convert of Ingham and Charles Wesley,[4] who on going up found the atmosphere of the university had a bad effect on his religious life, though later he succeeded in overcoming it.[5]

[1] Moule, *Charles Simeon*, pp. 10 f.
[2] G. Saintsbury, *The Peace of the Augustans*, p. 23, n. 2
[3] Wesley called on a Mr. Seagrave in London on February 27, 1739 (*Journal*, ii, p. 146, d.), who was probably the same man
[4] *Op. cit.*, i, p. 106   [5] Charles Wesley, *Journal*, i, pp. 108, 110, 113 f.

A new phase occurs with the coming of Rowland Hill to St. John's in 1764. He had already come under religious convictions when at Eton, and had there tried to influence his schoolfellows as afterwards he would try to influence his fellow undergraduates. On December 18 he received a note from Berridge, to whom he had been commended, suggesting that they should meet at the mill at Grantchester, where he then was. Hill duly went, and was so much impressed that he spent the Christmas vacation at Everton. This was the first of many visits. He used to say: "many a mile have I rode, many a storm have I faced, many a snow have I gone through, to hear good old Mr. Berridge; for I felt his ministry, when in my troubles at Cambridge, a comfort and blessing to my soul."[1]

Hill gathered round him a circle of like-minded friends, some dozen in all, including David Simpson, also of St. John's, and two Pembroke men who had come up from Christ's Hospital, Thomas Pentycross and Charles de Coetlogon. Apart from High Church practices their procedure was very much like that of the Holy Club at Oxford. They read together the Greek Testament and other books, they visited the gaol, and, in addition, did much preaching both in the town and in neighbouring parts. As a result they brought down upon them a good deal of criticism, and even those members of the university who claimed to be religious held sternly aloof from them. On one occasion Robinson met Hill in the street and much to the surprise of his companion greeted him publicly.[2]

Small religious coteries in universities have generally but a short life; even the Holy Club would probably not have survived as long as it did if Wesley had not been a resident don; and they tend to die out when the original members go down. So it was with Hill's little circle. By 1771 it had completely disappeared, though Berridge wrote in June of that year to Lady Huntingdon that there were "several serious students at both universities, but I fear they are very prudent and doctrinal, and such would not suit me [as curates]".[3] It was, however, in 1771 that Venn came to Yelling and began to exercise an influence in Cambridge which was of untold good. He was

[1] Sidney, *Life of Rowland Hill*, p. 173
[2] Vaughan, *Life of Robinson of Leicester*, p. 25
[3] *Works*, p. 513. His prejudice against university men continued, for he wrote on December 30, 1788, to John Thornton: "I am not very fond of College youths; they are apt to be lofty and lazy and delicate, and few of them might like to unite with such an offensive character as mine" (*op. cit.*, p. 461)

EVANGELICALISM IN THE UNIVERSITIES 361

much more suited to such an office than Berridge, with his uncouth ways and avowed contempt for the learning in which he had once delighted. Yelling was also some five miles nearer to Cambridge than Everton, an important consideration when all travel had to be done on horseback. Venn quickly got into touch with his old university and wrote on October 9, 1776: "I must not forget to tell you a good piece of news. Another clergyman, a Fellow of Clare Hall, invited me to supper, and I find his heart is all aflame for Christ. He has been four years by himself and sought after wisdom from above, laying aside all other studies."[1]

Prejudice against "Methodists" was still strong in Cambridge, and few colleges would accept their sons. Venn had great difficulty in finding an entry for his own son in 1776; Trinity refused him, but eventually he was accepted by Sidney Sussex.[2] The first college which had shown any disposition to receive Evangelicals was Magdalene,[3] where William Farish was tutor. He even persuaded the college to accept Elland students, but they were tolerated rather than welcomed. Farish had been senior wrangler in 1778, and later became Professor of Chemistry (1784–1813). He was a man of a very ingenious mind, so far as mathematics and mechanics were concerned, but very absent-minded, in fact, the typical "professor" of popular opinion;[4] none the less, he played a leading part in fostering Evangelical views in the university, as also in the town, where he held the living of St. Giles. In thus combining academic and pastoral work he was like other Evangelical dons to whom reference has already been made: Atkinson at Trinity Hall, H. W. Coulthurst[5] at Sidney Sussex, and Simeon at King's.

Another don with Evangelical sympathies was Joseph Jowett, great-uncle of the future Master of Balliol. Jowett was a fellow

[1] *Venn Family Annals*, p. 106. A note refers this to Berridge, which is, of course, quite impossible on chronological grounds. Townsend also is impossible for the same reasons

[2] *Op. cit.*, pp. 114 f.

[3] Magdalene was "the general resort of young men seriously impressed with a sense of religion" (*Memoirs of the Rev. Thos. Dykes*, p. 6). Among the subscribers to Middleton's *Biographia Evangelica* in 1779 was the Rev. Stephen Webster of Magdalene

[4] Towards the end of his life he appeared before a Parliamentary Committee on Railways and expressed the opinion that trains might run as fast as sixty miles an hour. The committee questioned him no further, clearly regarding him as of unsound mind (Moule, *Charles Simeon*, p. 63, n. 1)

[5] He is often referred to as Dr. Coulthurst; but he did not take his D.D. until 1791, the year after going to Halifax

of Trinity Hall and professor of Civil Law; he was also an admirable Latin scholar and a great lover of sacred music. He and Isaac Milner were close allies, and made a habit of spending two hours together twice weekly during term time.

Although there were a number of Evangelical dons they were unable, apart from Farish at Magdalene, to exercise much influence in their various colleges. A great change took place when Isaac Milner became President of Queens' in 1788. Before his election the college had been a notorious centre of Latitudinarianism; but he determined that it should become a centre of Evangelicalism, and set his face firmly against what he called Jacobins and infidels.[1] This was an arduous undertaking, and met with much opposition; but he held on his way with grim Yorkshire resolution, and in the end succeeded in driving out all his opponents, among them the senior tutor, T. F. Palmer, who retired to Scotland, where he became a Unitarian minister. Under Milner's rule Queens', which had been amongst the smallest colleges in the university, grew to be one of the most popular, and a high proportion of its undergraduate members were men reading for orders.

Isaac Milner was the younger brother of Joseph, and it was the latter who, recognizing his outstanding ability, took him from the woollen trade and sent him as a sizar to Queens' in 1770. His career at Cambridge was outstanding; for not only did he become senior wrangler in 1774, but was so far ahead of his nearest rivals that *incomparabilis* was placed after his name in the tripos list. He also gained the First Smith's Prize for mathematics. A fellowship was a natural sequel and this he obtained in January, 1776, a month after his ordination. In spite of his academic successes, Milner was a poor man, and used to walk to and from Leeds, with occasional lifts from wagoners.[2] But his successes had been achieved only at a severe cost, for so greatly had he overworked that his health was permanently affected, and after the autumn of 1775 he never had a single day without suffering,[3] in spite of the devoted skill and attention of Dr. Hey. In 1791 he was made Dean of Carlisle, through the influence of Bishop Pretyman of Lincoln, who had been Pitt's tutor. He was the only Evangelical to obtain high preferment during our period. Milner still retained the Presidency of Queens', and usually resided during term time. In spite of constant ill-health he lived on until 1820.

Milner had immense physical strength, which sickness does

[1] *Life*, p. 243   [2] *Op. cit.*, p. 128   [3] *Op. cit.*, p. 692

not seem to have affected. When on his journey with Wilberforce in 1775, the weight of the carriage was too much for the horses on a frozen road, and it began to run back. Milner was walking behind, and succeeded in stopping it on the very verge of a precipice.[1] It was during this and another journey on the Continent with Wilberforce that the friends read Doddridge's *Rise and Progress of Religion*, and compared its doctrine with the teaching of the Greek New Testament. Their studies had an immense effect on at least one of the friends. Although Milner had decided Evangelical views, he did not, so Wilberforce says, much "affect" them; but a severe fever in April, 1789, which hurried Wilberforce to Cambridge, seems to have deepened them, for the latter wrote that he found him at the end of May, "much weakened—in a very pious frame of mind".[2]

Milner was noted for shrewdness and common sense, which led to his frequently being consulted by others. He hated any kind of unreality or pretension, not least in religion (which may have provoked Wilberforce's remark that he did not much "affect" Evangelical views), and was absolutely straightforward in all his doings, even if a little too decided and determined for those who differed from him. Milner was in many respects a kind of Evangelical Dr. Johnson, gruff and rather unapproachable, but filled with real kindness of heart. He had immense vivacity, and, notwithstanding the rustic manners which he retained to the end, and his broad Yorkshire dialect, very acceptable in social life. John Venn noted that: "even when at Mr. Wilberforce's—who everywhere else led the conversation—he was the centre of attraction".[3]

Such was the man who did so much to lay the foundations of Evangelicalism in Cambridge. But already a younger man was becoming prominent, a man destined to build on those foundations an edifice whose heights were still undreamed of. This was Simeon, whose pastoral labours at Holy Trinity have already been noticed.[4]

Charles Simeon was born at Reading on September 24, 1759, the fourth son of Richard Simeon. On both sides his parents had clerical connexions; his father was the son and grandson of successive vicars of Bucklebury in Berkshire, while his mother, Elizabeth Hutton, was a member of a family which

[1] *Life of Wilberforce*, i, p. 77 [2] *Op. cit.*, i, pp. 75, 223
[3] *Venn Family Annals*, p. 190
[4] For fuller accounts, see Carus, *Memories of the Life of Charles Simeon*; Moule, *Charles Simeon*; and Smyth, *Simeon and Church Order*

provided two archbishops for the Church, one in the reign of Elizabeth and the other in that of George II. His schooldays were spent at Eton, where he was noted chiefly for his physical dexterity and love of horses. Of the influence of religion he knew little or nothing, though he lived a pure life amidst scenes of vice which led him later to say that if he had had a son he would rather see him dead than exposed to a similar experience. He then proceeded, following the normal Etonian progress, to King's College, Cambridge; and there the great crisis of his life suddenly faced him. Soon after going into residence he was informed that in accordance with the college rules he must attend a celebration of the Holy Communion at midterm. For some reason or other he was filled with a sense of utter unworthiness; "Satan himself was as fit to attend as I", he wrote in a private memorandum. He at once began to prepare himself by reading *The Whole Duty of Man*, a High Church manual which was the only religious book of which he knew.[1] He then went on to Bishop Wilson, *On the Lord's Supper*, and from a sentence in it deliverance came to him, and that "conversion" which was to be the starting-point of a life of fervent devotion and selfless service. The sentence ran as follows: "The Jews knew what they did when they transferred their sin to the head of their offering." On the morning of Easter Day (April 4, 1779) a peace came into his soul which never afterwards deserted it. At once he gave himself up to care for others, and to attempt to bring them into the same state of joy and blessing. The college servants, and his family at home, were the immediate and obvious objects of his attention; but he began to yearn for a wider service. In January, 1782, he succeeded as an Etonian to a fellowship at King's, and on that title was ordained at Ely on May 26, although still under the canonical age.

At this time he knew none of the Evangelical leaders, even in the university, and it was not until he began to help Christopher Atkinson at St. Edward's that he found a congenial circle of friends. It was through Atkinson that he got into touch with Henry Venn. His first visit to Yelling, however, made a very unfavourable impression on the young ladies of the household, one of whom records: "When Mr. Simeon paid us his first visit at Yelling, it is impossible to conceive anything more ridiculous than his look and manner were. His

[1] No doubt he had come across it at Eton, where it was one of the books prescribed for Sunday reading

grimaces were beyond anything you can imagine. So, as soon as we were gone, we all got together into the study, and set up an amazing laugh."¹

Wesley met Simeon for the first time at Hinxworth on December 20, 1784, and writes that: "He has spent some time with Mr. Fletcher at Madeley, two kindred souls resembling each other both in fervour of spirit and in the earnestness of their address." He again met Simeon at Hinxworth on October 30, 1787, and the same resemblance struck him once more; he "breathes the very spirit of Mr. Fletcher".²

From his first preaching at Holy Trinity large numbers of undergraduates flocked to hear him, and his power, at least over the younger members of the university, steadily grew. In 1786 Henry Venn wrote: "Mr. Simeon's light shines brighter and brighter. He is highly esteemed and exceedingly despised. O what numbers, if the Lord will, shall come from Cambridge in a few years, to proclaim the glad tidings."³ It was about this time that Simeon preached his first sermon before the university, and though many who went to hear him were full of prejudice, they were profoundly impressed by his earnestness and power.⁴

In order to deepen his influence among the undergraduates and to train those who were contemplating orders, Simeon used to hold conversation classes every Friday in his rooms at King's.⁵ By these and other means he came to hold a position of leadership, but this was nothing to what it afterwards became, and it may be said without any exaggeration that the period from 1791 to his death formed the Simeonite era of the Evangelical Party.⁶ His power, indeed, went far beyond party limits, for Macaulay could write in 1844, looking back to earlier days: "As to Simeon, if you knew what his authority and influence were, and how they extended from Cambridge to the most remote corners of England, you would allow that his real sway in the Church was far greater than that of any primate."⁷

¹ *Venn Family Annals*, p. 119   ² *Journal*, vii, pp. 39, 337 f.
³ Sidney, *Life of Rowland Hill*, pp. 160 f.   ⁴ Carus, pp. 69 f.
⁵ For a description of these meetings, see A. W. Brown, *Recollections of the Conversation Parties of Charles Simeon*

⁶ If Newman had gone up to Cambridge in 1816, as had been contemplated, from his then Evangelical views he would undoubtedly have come under the influence of Simeon. One may speculate on what the outcome would have been for Newman personally and for the Church of England as a whole had he done so

⁷ G. O. Trevelyan, *Life and Letters of Lord Macaulay*, i. pp. 67 f.

CHAPTER 20

EVANGELICAL METHODS

The methods adopted by the Evangelicals were much the same as those of the other groups concerned in the revival; but they were employed with greater respect for Church discipline and order. There was nothing really novel about them, save possibly the Wesleyan "class" system; but older methods were applied with a new effectiveness, and some which had fallen out of use were reintroduced.

In the eighteenth century the most available weapon of both the parish priest and the evangelist was preaching. The elaborate and numerous organizations, characteristic of a modern parish, and the machinery which absorbs so much of the energy of the parson, did not then exist. Personal contacts apart, it was upon the pulpit that he had to rely for affecting his flock. Here, however, we are to consider preaching as primarily a means of conversion, of turning to God those who were alienated from Him or ignorant of His claims upon their lives.

The sermons which have come down to us from the early Evangelicals, as well as those of the Methodists, in their printed form are by no means impressive (they cannot bear comparison with the great Anglican sermons of the previous age), and one wonders why they were so effective. But a printed sermon is one thing, and a sermon as delivered another. "The bows of eloquence are buried with the archers", someone has said; and what is lacking in the printed page is the personality and living force of the preacher. It was this above all else that told on the hearers. Ainger in criticizing Crabbe's sermons complains that they are "plain and formal explanations of a text illustrated by other texts", with no poetic touches, and nothing else by way of illustration. This criticism applies equally to the majority of Evangelical sermons; indeed, few sermons preached in the eighteenth century would, as they stand, be acceptable to a present-day congregation. Taste in this as in other matters has changed immensely.

The most famous preacher of the whole movement was, of course, Whitefield. But Whitefield probably owed more to his extraordinary gifts, gifts which he cultivated with great care, and his remarkable voice and manner, than to the contents of his discourses which lack both literary grace and logical cohesion. None the less he made a striking appeal to some of the most cultivated men of his day—though not to Dr. Johnson, who once remarked: "I never treated Whitefield's ministry with contempt; I believe he did good. But when familiarity and noise claim the praise due to knowledge, art, and elegance, we must beat down such pretensions." Wesley was also critical of his great contemporary, writing on January 28, 1750: "How wise is God in giving different talents to different preachers! Even the little improprieties both of his language and manner were a means of profiting many who would not have been touched by a more correct discourse, or a more calm and regular manner of speaking."[1]

Mark Pattison considered that "The dramatic oratory of Whitefield could not have sustained its power over the same auditors; he had a fresh congregation every Sunday."[2] This is not exactly true; none the less the limited range and scope of Methodist preaching must have eventually proved monotonous to educated hearers. Did Lady Huntingdon, one wonders, ever get "bored" by her preachers? Her function, however, was not that of a hearer, but rather of a theatrical manager who is chiefly concerned with the effect upon the audience. Wesley considered that for a parson to address the same people three times a day was a "vile custom" and forbade his preachers to attempt it.[3]

In fairness to Whitefield it should be said that the printed sermons, from which alone we can form a judgment, were very badly reported, and he himself protested strongly against the publication of mangled versions.[4] In any case, the printing of sermons is a dangerous enterprise; for, as printed, they are little more than mummies, without life or expression, and may do

---

[1] *Journal*, iii, p. 452. Wesley was apt to be critical of other preachers; cf. his comments on Berridge and Hicks, of whom he wrote: "neither of these gentlemen have much eloquence, but seem rather weak in speech, the Lord hereby more clearly showing that this is His own work" (*op. cit.*, iv, p. 321). But later (p. 334) he records an excellent sermon from Hicks. Berridge would have agreed as to the limitations of Hicks's preaching, for he wrote to Newton on September 17, 1782: "Mr. Hicks supplied my church from September last till the following Easter; and fairly drove away half my congregation" (*Works*, p. 418).

[2] *Essays*, ii, p. 20   [3] *Journal*, viii, pp. 92, 109, n. 2

[4] *Letters*, iii, p. 406

serious harm to the reputation of those who delivered them.[1]

The most notable feature of the revival preaching was its simplicity. The early Methodists and Evangelicals did not aim at arousing the admiration of their hearers, but at getting home their message. Men were sinners and in need of a Saviour from their sins, and their object was to tell them about this Saviour. Hence the plainness of language, and even the use of homely illustrations, which they adopted. Some did not scruple to employ vulgar expressions; Grimshaw, according to Newton, chose to deliver his appeals in what he used to term "market language", whilst even the cultivated Hervey did not mind disquieting some of his educated hearers by speaking of "halter", "gallows", and "gibbet", in order to waken them to the real meaning of what he was saying. In adopting this course, the revival preachers were reverting to the practice of the Reformers; in such a way Luther had appealed to the peasants of Germany, and Latimer to the simple folk of our own land. By the avoidance of involved sentences and arguments, no intellectual cross-currents came in to disturb the even flow of their discourses. That this policy was deliberately adopted can be seen from the statement of Wesley in the preface to a volume of his sermons: "I design plain truth for plain people. Therefore, of set purpose, I abstain from all nice and philosophical speculations; from all perplexed and intricate reasonings; and, as far as possible, from even the show of learning, unless in sometimes citing the original Scriptures. . . . Nay, my design is, in some sense, to forget all that ever I read in my life." Such a renunciation would have received the approbation of Milton, perhaps the most erudite of all our poets, who once affirmed that "in matters of religion, he is learnedest who is simplest."

A second characteristic of the preaching was its intense earnestness. The preachers were conscious of having a definite message to deliver, and that which they uttered had an eternal significance for their hearers. This gave their sermons a vital force which distinguished them sharply from the moral essays delivered from the average pulpit in the parish churches. They wished to convince, and a sense of conviction was a primary

[1] Henry Phillpotts, afterwards the famous Bishop of Exeter, in his early days was chaplain to Bishop Barrington of Durham. The latter once asked him to select a dozen of his sermons for publication "which would do him the least discredit". He did so, and the bishop inquired, "Do you think that these will do me credit?" Phillpotts judiciously replied: "I prefer, my lord, to adhere to your lordship's former expression." The sermons were not published

need in the preacher. It is said that Wesley and one of his preachers happened to light upon two women quarrelling near Billingsgate and using language which was more forceful than polite. The preacher suggested that they should move on; but Wesley replied: "Stay, Sammy, stay, and learn how to preach."[1] Some of their efforts to carry conviction descended to what Wesley called "screaming", and he warned them against the practice. "Scream no more at peril of your soul. . . . Speak as earnestly as you can, but do not scream. Speak with all your heart, but with a moderate voice. It was said of our Lord 'He shall not *cry*'. The word properly means he shall not *scream*."[2] There was, indeed, a definite risk that voices might be permanently damaged by such excesses. Whitefield might "love those who thunder out the word";[3] but he was a trained speaker and knew how to use his voice with discretion; others might easily strain it. Henry Venn committed this error and he wrote to his son John in April, 1783, warning him against its dangers.[4]

There was also another danger. Many of the Methodist preachers in attempting to be impressive became ridiculous and grotesque, a fault from which Evangelicals as a rule were free, though Berridge was a frequent offender. When told of this fault he could only reply: "Odd things break out from me as abruptly as croaking from a raven." Such "odd things" were probably in the nature of asides and improvisations, and do not appear in his printed sermon outlines; none the less they helped to support the common opinion that he loved to play the buffoon.

Because of the urgency of their message and the burning zeal which inflamed them the preachers were prepared to deliver the good news anywhere and everywhere, in season and out of season. No place came amiss. If the pulpit of the parish church was closed to them they would mount on a tub or a table, a horse-block or a convenient bench. Wesley even preached on his father's tomb when denied the use of that father's church. Whitefield, although immensely effective in addressing the select assemblies which met in Lady Huntingdon's drawing-room and chapels, was never so happy as when mounted on his "field-throne", with the heavens as a sounding-board. Wesley, on the other hand, embarked on field-preaching against his own

---

[1] Tyerman, *Life of Wesley*, iii, p. 660. Keats also appreciated this aspect of street quarrels, writing in February, 1829: "Though a quarrel in the street is a thing to be hated, the energies displayed in it are fine; the commonest man shows a grace in his quarrel"

[2] *Journal*, vi, p. 72 n.   [3] *Letters*, i, p. 73   [4] *Life*, pp. 364 f.

inclinations, and though he could hold the attention of vast throngs in the open air and regarded such preaching as "the most effectual way of overturning Satan's kingdom", to the end preferred to preach in a church. "What marvel the Devil does not like field-preaching! neither do I; I love a commodious room, a soft cushion, a handsome pulpit: but where is my zeal, if I do not trample all these under foot, in order to save one more soul?"[1]

To-day, preaching in the open air is so much an accepted means of proclaiming the Gospel that it has lost much of its appeal. But it was not so in the eighteenth century, and must then have made a deep impression, especially in isolated country parishes. We can imagine the preacher standing under the shadow of the trees on the village green, and his voice ringing out to those who flocked to see what it all meant. The singing of the hymns must also have been an attractive and novel feature; and no doubt many who never went inside the church, save for baptisms, weddings, and funerals, were much affected.

The preaching was, as we have seen, backed by intense conviction, but, at least for the leaders, it was not exactly spontaneous; much less what can be called extempore. They seem to have achieved a form which they found most effective; and the same sermon, or at least the same text, was used over and over again to different audiences, as can be seen from Wesley's journals. Nor did they despise the use of art. This was especially true of Whitefield, even though he was an orator by the gift of nature, but probably less so of Wesley. Wesley seems to have depended more on the circumstances of the moment and the response of his hearers; though Horace Walpole, who heard him at Bath in October, 1776, described him as: "Wondrous clever, but as evidently an actor as Garrick. He spoke his sermon, but so fast, and with so little accent, that I am sure he has often uttered it, for it was like a lesson."[2] Here one may surmise that it was the unsympathetic "feel" of his audience (the sermon was delivered in Lady Huntingdon's chapel to a polite assembly) that robbed Wesley of his usual force.

The fourfold ideal of Methodist preaching as set forth at the first Conference in 1744 was: "To invite. To convince. To offer Christ. To build up." To carry this out effectively demanded not merely fervour, but also preparation and study. Both Whitefield and Wesley attached great importance to study as a necessary preliminary to preaching; and over and over again

[1] *Journal*, iv, p. 325; cf. v, p. 132   [2] *Letters*, v, p. 16

warnings were issued as to the serious effects which would follow any neglect. In June, 1750, Whitefield wrote: "It has long since been my judgment, that it would be best for many of the present preachers to have a tutor, and retire for a while, and be content with preaching now and then, till they were a little more improved. Otherwise, I fear, many who now make a temporary figure, for want of proper foundation, will run themselves out of breath." Wesley also wrote to one who was neglecting study: "Hence your preaching does not increase; it is just the same as it was seven years ago. It is lively, but not deep; there is little variety; there is no compass of thought. ... Whether you like it or not, read and pray daily.... There is no other way; else you will be a trifler all your days."

The same care in the preparation of their sermons was taken by Evangelical preachers, and those who, for one cause or another, were unable to spare the necessary time did not escape criticism. Jones of Southwark, for example, through pressure of other work, seldom began his preparation before Saturday afternoon or evening, and whilst his earnestness was recognized, his sermons were condemned as rough and unpolished.[1] Some, as they grew older and had much knowledge and experience behind them, tended to give less time to special preparation. Thomas Scott, whose sermons usually lasted an hour, seldom composed them before the day on which they were to be delivered. So, too, Newton in later life gave little time to preparation, and, unfortunately, made no secret of the fact, which Cecil thought most inexpedient. "I have sat in pain when he has spoken unguardedly in this way before young ministers: men, who, with but comparatively slight degrees of his information and experience, would draw encouragement to ascend the pulpit with but little previous study of their subject."[2] Simeon, however, great preacher as he was, and with an unrivalled knowledge of preaching methods, never allowed himself any such latitude, and, though he might have delivered a written sermon many times, gave immense pains to its preparation whenever he used it.

The driving force behind the preachers, as with the first apostles, was personal experience; they testified to what they themselves had known. In the case of the less educated, in spite of all Wesley's efforts, too great a reliance might be placed on such experiences; and, carried away by their own eloquence, they might speak extravagantly. But the great bulk of the

[1] *Life*, p. 231 [2] *Memoirs of John Newton*, p. 69

Methodists, and still more of the Evangelicals, based their preaching on a definite system of belief which they had carefully learned. It was said of the preaching of Jones of Creaton that "the foundation was doctrine, and the superstructure was experience and practice".[1]

If preaching was regarded as the readiest weapon by the promoters of the revival, its limitations were clearly recognized, and not least by Wesley. To him, preaching, unless after-care was available, might be worse than useless. "I am more and more convinced that the Devil himself desires nothing more than this, that the people of any place should be half awakened, and then left to themselves to fall asleep again: therefore, I determine, by the grace of God, not to strike one stroke in any place where I cannot follow the blow."[2] The means adopted by Wesley and a few of the Evangelicals was the establishment of societies.

Such societies had been very popular in the seventeenth and early eighteenth centuries.[3] As early as 1677, Beveridge, then vicar of Ealing, and Dr. Horneck, preacher of the Savoy chapel, had formed what would now be called guilds for young men. Their example was widely copied, and its scope extended; even in the middle of the century many of them were still active.[4] The members met weekly for their mutual encouragement and edification, made their communion at least once a month, and engaged in various religious enterprises, such as visiting gaols, relieving poverty, and promoting the education of poor children. It was these societies which provided a model for both Wesley and the Evangelicals. One of the earliest to be formed as a result of the revival was that at Bideford, of which Hervey was the promoter. Walker of Truro also made use of the system at Truro in 1750. The society at Fetter Lane which was organized in May, 1738, was not, as Whitehead and even Tyerman have stated, a Moravian institution, but simply a society belonging to the Church.[5]

One of the great problems in connexion with these societies was how to exercise adequate supervision. Wesley found that

---

[1] Owen, *Memoir of Jones of Creaton*, p. 81   [2] *Journal*, iii, p. 71

[3] See, further, Wickham Legg, *English Church Life*, etc., pp. 291 ff., with the authorities there given; and especially the contemporary description by Josiah Woodward, *An Account of the Rise and Progress of the Religious Societies in the City of London*

[4] Grimshaw found one at Rochdale when he went there as curate in 1731

[5] See Wesley, *Journal*, i, p. 458; ii, p. 121

without such supervision they would constantly go back, and his journals give a melancholy account of many such declensions. He felt that it was so important a matter that he placed the visiting of the members as amongst the most urgent duties of his preachers. On January 11, 1774, he writes: "I began at the east end of the town to visit the Society from house to house. I know no branch of the pastoral office which is of greater importance than this. But it is so grievous to flesh and blood, that I can prevail on few, even of our Preachers, to undertake it."[1] Another difficulty was that they were likely to get out of hand and to foster conceit and emulation among the leaders. Walker at Truro had some difficulties over this, as had Simeon in Cambridge.[2]

An outstanding feature of Methodist worship was the singing of hymns. The practice, however, was slow in making its way even in Evangelical parishes. English people have always been fond of singing together, and there had been a great and spontaneous outburst of song in the seventeenth century; but it had not affected the Church. By tradition, singing in churches was limited to metrical versions of the psalms. As printing was dear, the members of the congregation did not as a rule possess copies, and so the clerk gave out the psalm, line by line, and they sang it after him. This must have been a somewhat unenlivening process, and not all clerks were skilled at their job. Parson Woodforde notes that on one occasion his clerk's efforts provoked laughter.[3] But this psalm-singing had been a definite factor in the musical education of the English people, for the psalters often contained instructions in the theory of music as well as hints on reading by sight.[4] The older mode had been Sternhold and Hopkins, which Wesley denounced as "miserable, scandalous doggerel", and favourably contrasted the Methodist habit of substituting "psalms and hymns which are both sense and poetry, such as would sooner provoke a critic to turn Christian, than a Christian to turn critic".[5] Some improvement was made when Tate and Brady was substituted; but the older generation disliked even this mild change, and many of them doubtless agreed with the squire in Hannah More's *Florio*, who

[1] *Journal*, vi. p. 9; cf. iv, p. 297; v, pp. 472, 485
[2] Carus, *Memoirs of Life of Simeon*, pp. 141 f.
[3] *The Diary of a Country Parson*, iii, p. 292
[4] On efforts to improve singing in church, see Sykes, pp. 241 f.
[5] *Letters*, iii, p. 227

fear'd 'twould show a falling State,
If Sternhold should give way to Tate:
The Church's downfall he predicted,
Were modern tunes not interdicted.[1]

The entirely novel custom of singing hymns was a much more serious matter, and no doubt it had its dangers, for it might be the occasion of introducing doubtful opinions and of encouraging an emotional and sentimental spirit which was alien to the Prayer Book and to the ethos of the Church[2]. Some disliked hymns on the ground that "all ancient hymns were Popish and all modern hymns were Puritan".[3] Those Evangelicals who ventured to experiment with the new method often found themselves in trouble; Robinson lost his curacy near Ely for this reason, and at Leicester met with much opposition when he introduced hymn-singing.[4] Gradually other Evangelicals took up the practice, and numerous collections were made. The first was that by Madan to which reference has already been made; when it came out in 1760 Cowper and the Unwins used to sing it together at Huntingdon. Others followed, such as those of Conyers of Helmsley (1767), De Courcy (1775), Toplady (1776), Joseph Milner (1780), Cadogan (1785), John Venn (1785), and Cecil (1785).

One great development among Methodists and Evangelicals was an ever-increasing concern for the religious training of the young. This was in line with the general trend of opinion, for children, possibly owing to the influence of Rousseau, were receiving much more consideration than they had formerly done; though it is not always easy to define their exact position in relation to their parents and elders. Watts had made it his aim in the training of children to "steer a middle course between the undue subjection of the Puritans and the licence of the early eighteenth century, when they were made 'familiar companions of their parents almost from the very nursery' ".[5] But this idea of "licence" is not borne out by other evidence; a foreigner who visited England before the middle of the century states that: "Well brought-up children, on rising and going to bed, wish their fathers and mothers 'Good morning' or 'Good evening', and kneeling before them ask for their blessing."[6] So,

---

[1] *Works*, i, p. 62   [2] Moravian hymns were often disgusting and irreverent
[3] Abbey and Overton, ii, p. 51   [4] Vaughan, *Life of Robinson*, pp. 50, 66
[5] Laird, *Philosophical Incursions into Eng. Lit.*, p. 64
[6] De Saussure, *A Foreign View of England in the Reigns of George I and George II*, p. 296

too, Richardson gives a picture of children being strictly subordinated to their elders.[1] The "licence" was evidently much greater towards the close of our period, for Romaine could write in 1789: "The spirit of the times runs strongly against all subordination; even the first commandment with promise, 'Honour thy father and mother', is losing authority daily."[2]

The Evangelicals, as also the Methodists, were exceedingly anxious that their children should share, at the earliest possible moment, in the religious privileges and assurances which they themselves enjoyed. In their anxiety they were apt to commit two serious errors. On the one hand, they were too scrupulous in shielding them from evil influence; and, on the other, they forced the religious side of the child's mind and heart before it was able to understand or appreciate such high matters.

In order to exclude evil influences, the lives of children were subjected to all kinds of restraints; the books they read, the people they met, and the things they were allowed to see, were all carefully supervised. The result was a cloistered virtue unexercised against temptations, which might easily collapse when the protecting care was removed. This over-anxiety seems to betoken a lack of faith, both in the strength of the characters of the children themselves, and also in God's guidance of their lives. But Evangelicals had such a keen perception of the power of sin and the weakness of human nature that they took no risks. It is also to be surmised that this excessive supervision, which was often extended beyond the years of childhood, was due, one hopes unconsciously, to that love of domineering and of managing the lives of others which was characteristic of many of the pious.[3] Such supervision, moreover, was a feature of the schools to which Evangelicals entrusted their growing boys. The establishment at Hammersmith of which a Mr. Elwell was the proprietor was typical. Among its early pupils it numbered Jowett and Cecil, and, beyond our period, Henry Venn Elliott. The biographer of the latter states that "all was suspicion and espionage", and quotes the effect on one of his contemporaries who says: "I was myself so disgusted with religion when I left ... that for many years afterwards I never opened my Bible, and never said my prayers."[4]

This quotation brings us to the second error of the Evangelicals in the treatment of children. They forced religion on

[1] Cf. *Sir Charles Grandison*, IV, letter xxxviii; V, letter xiv [2] *Works*, p. 561
[3] This side as found in a later generation has been caricatured in *The Barretts of Wimpole Street*
[4] Bateman, *Life of H. V. Elliott*, p. 2

their minds, and so led in some cases to a premature development and a spiritual precociousness which often provoked a violent reaction;[1] or it so sickened them of the matter that they were only too glad to have nothing more to do with it.[2] It was in connexion with the spending of Sunday that this evil became most acute. Dr. Johnson had found it "a heavy day"; and, later, Ruskin's feeling towards it must have been typical of many in earlier days. He says: "When I was a child, I lost the pleasure of three-sevenths of my life because of Sunday; for I always had a way of looking forward to things, and a lurid shade was cast over the whole of Friday and Saturday by the horrible sense that Sunday was coming."[3]

The wiser leaders among the Evangelicals were well aware of these dangers, and realized that young minds might have "too much of a good thing". Cecil, in writing *On Family Worship*, expressed the opinion that "The old Dissenters wearied their families"; whilst Thomas Scott was careful to avoid any undue pressing of religion upon his children. The fact that his descendants have supplied clergy, and at least one living bishop, to the Church, is a justification of his policy; though at the end of his life he thought that he might have given them more teaching, especially in learning passages by heart.[4] Henry Venn was also very shrewd in such matters. He himself had derived great spiritual benefit from giving up cricket, of which he was immensely fond, when he was ordained; none the less, he advised parents to exercise care in enforcing upon their children the avoidance of what they regarded as worldly pursuits. He wrote to a lady who consulted him on the matter: "You certainly judge right not to restrain your son from balls, cards, etc., since a mother will never be judged, by a son of his age, capable of determining for him; and perhaps, after your most strict injunctions to have done with such sinful vanities, he would be tempted even to violate your authority."[5]

Wesley's ideas on the way to bring up children were truly horrible. In the school at Kingswood they had to rise at 4 a.m. and to spend an hour in private religious exercises, to join in numerous services, and to fast until 3 p.m. every Friday unless

[1] Here again a modern illustration may be cited in Edmund Gosse's *Father and Son*

[2] Wilberforce quotes the example of the son of a friend who thus reacted, and opines that "he was overdosed with religion and that of an offensive kind, when young" (*Life*, iv, p. 152).

[3] *Fors Clavigera*, XXIV, § 7   [4] *Life*, p. 626

[5] Quoted Ryle, *Christian Leaders*, p. 297

reasons of health made this inadvisable. No play of any kind was allowed. So rigid were the rules that the staff revolted against them, and some parents removed their children.[1]

It is a striking fact that the children of many leading Methodists and Evangelicals proved very unsatisfactory to their parents in later life. John Wesley, of course, had no children; but of Charles's sons none took orders, though some had distinguished careers; Lady Huntingdon's son became an infidel; the son of Ingham was equally disappointing; as was the son of Grimshaw. In later times the descendants of leading Evangelicals would react in various ways, as amongst others the Wilberforces, Macaulays, and Stephens.[2] But we must not forget families like the Venns and the Scotts.

In the training of children in the knowledge and the practice of the Christian faith, Evangelicals made use of the opportunities provided by the services of the Church, and especially of catechizing the young in the presence of the congregation. This means of teaching seems to have been neglected at the time. Walker wrote to the Archbishop of Canterbury telling him of the ignorance of a body of soldiers to whom he was ministering, and attributing it to this cause.[3] He himself made a great use of the method,[4] as did Adam, at the suggestion of Bassett; whilst a number of manuals for the purpose were prepared by Adam, Vivian,[5] and Venn (the latter for those above fourteen).[6]

Meanwhile the child population of the country was steadily increasing owing to improved medical knowledge. Many children were greedily absorbed into the mills and factories, and, in such spare time as they had, were allowed to run wild. This state of affairs aroused the concern of well-meaning people, who began to fear that a race of ignorant savages would grow up, unless steps were taken to educate them. This concern was not entirely new, for charity schools were started in the reign of Queen Anne,[7] with the object of training the children of the poor to

[1] Cf. the remarks of Tyerman, *Wesley*, ii, p. 10

[2] Even so, the Evangelical ferment worked in many of them, although the beliefs on which it was based had been abandoned—its intensity, its selectiveness, its interest in moral questions; cf. N. G. Annan, *Leslie Stephen*

[3] Sidney, *Life of Walker*, pp. 319, 333   [4] *Op. cit.*, pp. 81 ff.

[5] Richardson of York considered that Vivian's exposition was the best that he knew

[6] *Venn Family Annals*, p. 81

[7] See M. G. Jones, *The Charity School Movement*. A volume of sermons preached at an anniversary has been preserved: see Lowther Clarke, *Eighteenth Century Piety*, p. 68

fit them for honest employment as well as to instruct them in the elements of Christianity. They had thus a social as well as a religious aim. The same was also true of Sunday Schools, for they were originally started to give secular as well as religious education; one great object, as in the Mission Field to-day, was to enable the pupils to read the Bible.

The credit for having begun the first Sunday School has been claimed for a number of different people. Buckle in his *History of Civilization* said that it belonged to Lindsay, vicar of Catterick, who established a school, c. 1764. One early pioneer was a young Methodist girl, Hannah Bell of High Wycombe, who began in 1769. Writing to Wesley in the year following, she says: "The children meet twice a week, every Sunday and Monday. They are a wild little company, but seem willing to be instructed. I labour among them, earnestly desiring to promote the interest of the Church of Christ."[1] Then in 1778 David Simpson started something similar at Macclesfield. These were but tentative efforts, and no doubt there were others of which no records remain; the man who really laid the foundations was Robert Raikes, of Gloucester, who began his work in 1780.

Raikes was a wealthy Evangelical layman, whose first charitable efforts were directed to prison reform. Later he came to recognize that the neglect of the children was often the real cause of the growth of crime. Helped by the Rev. Thomas Stock, curate of St. John the Baptist's, he engaged four respectable women to instruct any children they were able to collect, in reading and in the catechism. The school was open from 10 a.m. until noon, and from 1 p.m. until evensong (held in the afternoon), to which they were taken. But this did not end their busy day, for they then returned to school to learn the catechism until 5.30, after which they were dismissed to their homes, being warned not to loiter or behave in a noisy manner. The curate regularly visited the school to examine the children and to enforce discipline, a necessary task with such a turbulent crew, some of whom were so wild that they had to be "hobbled" with logs of wood. But they responded remarkably to the care and affection of Raikes and his helpers, and it is said that in his regular attendance at the daily services in the cathedral he was often accompanied by a small mob of ragamuffins.

In 1783 Raikes published an account of his experiment in

[1] Quoted Wesley, *Journal*, v, p. 104 n.

the *Gloucester Journal*, which was copied by some of the London papers and reprinted by Wesley in the *Arminian Magazine* for 1785. Thus wide attention was aroused and various similar schools were opened up and down the country. Fletcher opened six schools at Madeley, and Thomas Wilson one at Slaithwaite. Their example was speedily followed by Cornelius Bayley at Manchester, and by Miles Atkinson and Dr. Hey at Leeds.[1] The movement seems to have spread rapidly in Yorkshire, and Romaine after a visit in 1784 reported that:

> They have been chiefly used in the manufacturing parts, where there are great numbers of the manufacturers' children employed, as soon as they can do anything at all, all the week, but let loose to mischief and wickedness on the Lord's day. It was with a view to prevent this, and also to instruct them in the way of salvation, for their sakes, and for their parents, and for the public, that several persons, laity as well as clergy, tried to get them together, to teach them to read, write and learn the catechism. The Lord God has marvellously favoured the plan. He has inclined vast numbers of children to come; the parents in general are thankful; and the schoolmasters and mistresses have given great satisfaction.[2]

About the same time Wesley records a visit to Bingley, where he found a school run on interdenominational lines with 240 children meeting every Sunday, under several masters and superintended by the curate. He adds: "I find these schools springing up wherever I go."[3] The movement, indeed, seems to have been widespread, especially among Evangelicals. Cowper wrote to Newton on September 24, 1785, that Thomas Scott was thinking of starting a school, and that Jones at Clifton Reynes had already done so; and also that Mr. Unwin "has been thinking of nothing else day and night for a fortnight".

Among the churches which started Sunday schools was Bath Abbey, and an interesting description of it is contained in a letter received by Maria Holroyd dated August 4, 1787. "I daresay you have heard of Sunday Schools. It is but lately we have

---

[1] Hey, in spite of his exceedingly busy professional life, took an active part in giving instruction: see Pearson, *Life of Hey*, p. 189

[2] *Works*, p. 536   [3] *Journal*, vii, p. 3

had the institution here, and at first it went slowly; but by joining it to a School of Industry, they now crowd all to the other which is a necessary step to that of industry." Special services were held in the evening attended by the children, to the number of nine hundred, who behaved in a perfectly orderly manner, and already were able to join in the worship and to kneel and rise at the proper times. "Reflect how very extraordinary this circumstance alone! When you recollect that most of them were taken out of the streets, untaught and actually almost savage, cursing and swearing, and fighting . . . all day, and many without a home at night."[1]

An effort on an even more ambitious scale was launched at York in 1786, when Richardson formed a Church of England Sunday School Society with Edward Stillingfleet as secretary. It began with ten schools, and over five hundred children attended on the opening Sunday.

One who took a leading part in establishing such schools was the famous Mrs. Trimmer, who wrote a book on how to conduct them with the title *The Œconomy of Charity*. This was published in 1786, and in November of that year she paid a visit to the Queen with a view to starting a Sunday School at Windsor.[2]

Sunday schools did not yet possess buildings of their own, nor were Church day schools yet available. They often met in a cottage which might be let to the parish clerk or some other suitable person on condition that it should be used for the purpose. In some cases the teachers were paid at the rate of a shilling a week. The running of these schools was sometimes costly, especially when handiwork was taught, and they had to depend on the financial support of the pious, which, in view of the usefulness of the cause, was seldom lacking.

It was not everybody, however, who looked upon Sunday Schools with favour. They were a novelty, and as such open to suspicion. Some of the clergy even showed violent antagonism. Nor were the parents quite happy about them, for the idea grew up that they were part of a scheme for transporting children to the colonies, where they would be sold as slaves. Further suspicion was aroused when radical philanthropists copied the method. In his charge for 1800, Bishop Horsley went so far as to declare that "sedition and atheism were the real objects of some of these institutions"; and though this could

[1] *The Girlhood of Maria Holroyd*, p. 17
[2] Lowther Clarke, *Christian Piety*, etc., pp. 119-121

not apply to those conducted by the Evangelicals, prejudice was raised against them. Rowland Hill, who had introduced Sunday Schools into London, preached a sermon in reply to the bishop in which he sketched out the origin, design and real utility of the method.[1] One ecclesiastic, apart from the Evangelicals, who showed his foresight in welcoming and fostering Sunday Schools was Archdeacon Paley.

[1] Sidney, *Life of Rowland Hill*, p. 439

CHAPTER 21

EVANGELICAL DOCTRINES

THE doctrines held by the Evangelicals, as by the early Methodists, were those of the Church of England as contained in the Articles, Prayer Book, and Homilies. Many of the beliefs upon which special emphasis was laid in their preaching were continually being proclaimed in the collects—such as the fallen state of mankind, the need for redemption in Christ Jesus, the work of the Holy Spirit, and man's dependence on God's grace, both "preventive" and following. Whitefield, in his preaching, for example, appealed first of all to Scripture, and then cited the Articles and the collects by way of illustration. But if such doctrines were constantly being brought to the notice of churchgoers, they made little impression. Bishop Warburton has said: "At length the great Gospel-principles of Faith . . . came to be held by many as Fanatical. . . . Morality was advanced so high, and Faith frittered into nonsense, that a new Definition of our religion, (namely that it was only this *republication* of the law of nature) in opposition to its Founders, and unknown to its early Followers, was grown to be the *fashionable tenet* of the times."[1] Grimshaw used to say that if the Articles and Homilies had not been forgotten or neglected, "Methodism would never have appeared".

Where the Evangelicals differed from the common run of Churchmen was in the emphasis they laid on certain doctrines, reviving them and bringing out their true meaning. This also applied to the Methodists, one of whom openly proclaimed that "Methodism is Church of Englandism felt".[2] That was the secret. Though they might hold a very definite creed, it was to them no dry doctrinal system, but represented something which they had verified in their own lives. This difference between the Evangelical preachers and the ordinary clergymen was pointed out long ago by Sir James Stephen, who defined "an orthodox clergyman as one who held in dull and barren formality the very same doctrines which the Evangelical clergyman held in cordial and prolific vitality; or by saying that they

[1] *The Doctrine of Grace*, pp. 316 ff.
[2] L. F. Church, *The Early Methodist People*, p. 97

EVANGELICAL DOCTRINES

differed from each other as solemn triflers differ from the profoundly serious".[1]

The theology of the Evangelicals was in general simple and direct save when dissensions broke out over such mysteries as Predestination and Election, and was intended not to satisfy man's intellectual curiosity, but to save his soul and enable him to live a life worthy of his profession. They were, in other words, much more interested in the practical application of the Gospel than in constructing an elaborate doctrinal system. None the less, they valued orthodox beliefs because they were convinced that in them lay the only sure road to right conduct; for if a man errs concerning the things of God he cannot become a partaker in the divine mind. But orthodoxy was not to be an end in itself, for a barren orthodoxy must lead to spiritual sterility. Dogmas are simply crystallized experience, and to make them effective they must again be liquified and the original experience recaptured. Christianity, as Newton once said, "is not a system of doctrine, but a new creature".

Because they valued orthodox beliefs as the only sure foundation for conduct many Evangelical leaders encouraged their followers, as they advanced in knowledge and experience, to study doctrinal matters. Romaine, for example, expressed the opinion that:

> It is much to be lamented that believers in general take so little pains to get a clear knowledge of the doctrine of the ever-blessed Trinity, for want of which their faith is unsettled, and they are liable to many errors both in judgment and practice. I would therefore most earnestly recommend it to all that are weak in faith to be diligent in hearing and reading what in Scripture is revealed concerning the Trinity in unity, looking up always for the inward teaching of the Holy Spirit; and I would direct them to a form of sound words in the Common Prayer Book for Trinity Sunday, which contains the shortest and best account of the subject I ever saw.[2]

The doctrine of the Trinity was a difficulty to many quite sound Evangelicals, though on purely intellectual grounds.

[1] *Essays in Ecclesiastical Biography*, ii, p. 155
[2] *The Life of Faith* (*Works*, p. 160)

Newton only held it because he was convinced that unless Jesus was divine He was no sufficient Saviour.

> Till God in human flesh I see,
>   My thoughts no comfort find;
> The holy, just, and sacred Three
>   Are terrors to my mind.
>
> But if Immanuel's face appear,
>   My hope, my joy begins;
> His name forbids my slavish fear,
>   His grace removes my sins.[1]

Thus the Trinity was approached through the Incarnation.

Although the Methodists for the most part accepted the doctrines of the Church, it was not a point on which they insisted. This is clearly stated by Wesley, who affirmed that no doctrinal beliefs of any kind were to be demanded from adherents: "but a desire to save their souls. . . . The Methodists alone do not insist on your holding this or that opinion, but they think and let think. Neither do they impose any particular mode of worship, but you may continue to worship in your former manner, be it what it may".[2] Such was not the case with the Evangelicals; to be an Evangelical, the doctrines of the Church must be accepted and its forms of worship observed.

On two other points the Evangelicals differed from the followers of Wesley. With very few exceptions they were Calvinists; and they rejected his doctrine of Christian Perfection. In this latter regard they were at one with many Methodists, who were only induced to preach it by Wesley's insistence. Wesley wrote to Charles from Edinburgh in May, 1768: "I am at my wit's end with regard to two things—the Church, and Christian perfection. Unless both you and I stand in the gap in good earnest, the Methodists will drop them both."[3] As late as August 14, 1776, he found that in Devonshire the preachers either "did not speak of it at all (the peculiar doctrine committed to our trust) or they spoke of it only in general terms".[4] There is something almost pathetic in the way in which Wesley clung to this doctrine;[5] for he himself had never experienced it, and many of those who claimed to have done so later confessed that they had been mistaken—this was true even of Miss Bosanquet, a saint if ever there was one—and of the hundreds

---

[1] See *Cardiphonia*, pp. 232 ff.   [2] *Journal*, vii, p. 389   [3] *Works*, xii, p. 126
[4] *Journal*, vi, p. 120   [5] Tyerman, *Life of Wesley*, ii, p. 598

of his followers in London he had to write: "I doubt whether twenty of them are now as holy and as happy as they were."[1] Yet for thirty years he insisted on preaching it; and he did so because he believed that it was the teaching of the Scriptures.

For the Evangelicals, as for Wesley, the Bible was the supreme test of any doctrine, as it is indeed for the Church of England, for the sixth of the Thirty-nine Articles runs as follows: "Holy Scripture containeth all things necessary to salvation: so that whatsoever is not read therein, nor may be proved thereby, is not to be required of any man, that it should be believed thereby as an article of the Faith, or be thought requisite or necessary to salvation."

The authority of the Scriptures was to be accepted unconditionally, and, as Calvin said, "ought not to be made subject to demonstration and reason"; at the same time it was guaranteed by experience, for, again to quote Calvin, "the certainty which it getteth among us is attained by the witness of the Holy Ghost".[2] The Evangelicals believed in what is called Verbal Inspiration, a theory which has never received the authority of the Church, and, in practice, this meant the Authorized Version, a very imperfect translation in some passages of the original.[3]

The belief that a document is verbally inspired may reduce it to a kind of legal code, single texts of which may be appealed to by way of proof. But such a method fails to take account of that logical inconsistency which characterizes all passionate and intense expressions of religious truth, expressions which are often impatient of intellectual refinements. This was true of St. Paul, who at one moment "offers us a picture of all humanity doomed to suffer the punishment of divine wrath, at another the picture of all humanity redeemed by God's love in Christ."[4]

There were Evangelical leaders who recognized the danger of this appeal to single texts; Walker warned his followers against quoting them apart from their contexts,[5] and Newton pointed out that "Detached texts or sentences may seem to countenance what by no means will accord with the general tenour of the *whole*".[6]

[1] *Works*, xii, pp. 350, 375   [2] *Institutes*, Bk. I, chap. vii
[3] Perhaps the most misleading instances are in connexion with "conversion", which the Greek makes to be the work of man, but the A.V. (like the Vulgate before it) perverts into something done in him (e.g. Matt. 13: 15, 18: 3; Mark 4: 12; Luke 22: 32; Acts 3: 19)
[4] Quick, *The Doctrines of the Creed*, p. 115   [5] *Fifty-two Sermons*, i, p. xii
[6] Quoted Moule, *Charles Simeon*, p. 43

Although the Evangelicals professed belief in the full inspiration and authority of the Bible, by the use of allegorical interpretation they often twisted its plain meaning to conform with their teaching. So it had been with the Reformers who, as Schweitzer has said, read their "own ideas into Paul, in order to receive them back again clothed with Apostolic authority";[1] and so it had been from the earliest days of Christianity. Here again the danger did not pass unobserved. Simeon declared that his endeavour was to bring out of Scripture what was there and not to thrust in what he thought might be there;[2] while Newton protested against the absurd lengths to which allegorical methods might be pressed. "I remember to have heard a preacher who discovered a type of Christ crucified in Absalom hanging by the hair. . . . I think there is no part of Old Testament history from which I could not . . . draw observations that might be suitable to the pulpit, and profitable to His people: so I might perhaps from Livy and Tacitus."[3]

The acceptance of the indisputable authority of the Bible gave to the Evangelicals a firm basis for their beliefs and preaching, and certainly saved them from all uncertainty. Some of the more learned, however, might suffer from momentary perplexity. Henry Martyn, for example, was filled by "terrifying doubts" because references to "infernal possession" are limited to the gospels;[4] but such experiences were rare or concealed, and what Romaine wrote of the Bible in 1783 would have met with general acceptance: "Ever take it up as the oracles of God—the infallible standard of truth. The abiding persuasion of this will save you a deal of trouble and will bring you vast profit."

Taking the Bible as their guide, the Evangelicals believed that the whole world lay in darkness,[5] even that part of it which was professedly Christian; and that man was a fallen creature, totally depraved and corrupt, who would surely perish unless he accepted Christ as his Saviour. "By means of the fall, the soul of every man by nature is altogether dross and base metal", wrote Walker;[6] and Romaine held that "The corruption of our nature by the fall, and our recovery through Jesus Christ, are the two leading truths of the Christian religion".[7]

[1] *Paul and His Interpreters*, p. 2 [2] Quoted Moule, *op. cit.*, p. 97
[3] *Cardiphonia*, p. 419 [4] *Journal*, February 9, 1803
[5] Wesley was not quite so drastic, and even approved the saying of an ancient philosopher that every man possesses some kind of divine inspiration, *Nemo sine afflatu divino fuit* (*Works*, ix, p. 201)
[6] *Christ the Purifier*, p. 23 [7] *Works*, p. 153

Holding such views, the primary duty of the messengers of the Gospel was to convict men of their sinful state and to warn them of the dangers in which they were involved. This gave urgency and drive to their task, in which they invited every Christian to take his part. In this at least they did good service, for it has ever been a weakness in the Church to regard all such matters as the business of the clergy alone.

This aspect of the Evangelical scheme of salvation has been widely criticized as, in the words of F. D. Maurice, making "the sinful man, and not the God of all grace, the foundation of Christian theology". But it has been defended, perhaps a little unexpectedly, by T. H. Green, the philosopher, who wrote: "The common doctrine, which connects the sense of sin with the confidence of salvation, has often been denounced by theologians; but it seems to have its root in the truest feelings which bind earth to heaven . . . our very imperfections may win us to that childlike dependence on God which is only another aspect of the assurance of salvation."[1]

In the opinion of most Evangelicals the turning to God and the acceptance of Christ as Saviour must be a definite act at a particular moment of time. Conversion, in other words, must be instantaneous. The means of this conversion was faith, and for a definition of faith they could turn to the Homily of the Church, where it is said to be: "A sure trust and confidence which a man hath in God, that, through the merits of Christ his sins are forgiven and he is reconciled to the favour of God."

The weakness of this belief is that it fails to take account of the different types of humanity—what Francis Newman called the "once-born" and the "twice-born". There are souls which seem to develop naturally, like plants and flowers, ever growing in the knowledge of the things of God; there are others, especially those who have fallen into grievous sin, who experience a sudden crisis. The idea of conversion thus held tends to exalt the experience of certain individuals into a universal law. None the less, it has its beneficial side, for it was a challenge, facing men with the claims of God upon their lives, which might well transform a merely conventional acceptance of Christianity into a real and living faith. Many of the Evangelical clergy who underwent this experience had led blameless and active lives; but they found that their "conversion" gave them an inward peace and assurance which hitherto had been lacking,

[1] *Works*, iii, p. 25

bringing a greatly increased effectiveness to their work and a sharper edge to their preaching.[1]

Another danger connected with conversion, more particularly for those who accepted the teaching of Calvin, was the notion that those who had once been converted could never perish, however unworthy their subsequent lives might be. This, of course, was not the teaching of Wesley, who looked upon salvation as "not merely the deliverance from hell, but a present deliverance from sin, a restoration of the soul to its primitive health, a recovery of the Divine Nature".[2]

The method of bringing men to a decision was to confront them with the Last Judgment, when, unless they had repented, they would be consigned to the flames of a material hell. Such warnings, conveyed by some fanatical and enthusiastic preacher, must have made a most vivid impression on ignorant souls, all too conscious of their unfitness for the Divine scrutiny. Like their forefathers in the Middle Ages, they were still capable of being terrorized by such a threat; but the better educated and more fashionable were, for the most part, quite immune to such warnings, as Edward Young put it in his *Love of Fame*, written in 1757:

> Since *Sundays* have no balls, the welldress'd *belle*
> Shines in the pew, but smiles to hear of *Hell*.

The impression made on the vulgar was also apt to be fleeting, and most of them would doubtless have agreed with the innkeeper in *Joseph Andrews* when he exclaimed: "What signifies talking about matters so far off?"

The extent to which pious and learned Christians thought upon a material hell is almost unbelievable. There was little exaggeration in Shelley's taunt that:

> Churchmen damn themselves to see
> God's sweet love in burning coals.[3]

On March 6, 1804, Henry Martyn recorded in his journal: "Looked at iron foundry in Wall's Lane: the fierce fire raised many solemn ideas of God's power, and of hell." There were, it may be, some who saw things differently, and Zachary

---

[1] Berridge of Everton and Conyers of Helmsley are obvious examples
[2] *Further Appeal to Men of Reason and Religion*, p. 3
[3] *Peter Bell the Third*, III, xvii

Macaulay was gravely displeased when his small son, seeing a flaming chimney from his nursery window, asked if that was hell.[1] But perhaps his displeasure was caused by the unconscious irreverence of the future historian.

The satisfaction which God accepts for sin is not the repentance of the sinner, as the parable of the Prodigal Son seems to teach, but the offering of the Son of Man on the cross. His blood there shed was a complete atonement for the sins of those who took refuge in Him. It might seem that had Jesus given no teaching at all, but simply died, the Gospel in all its fullness could have been preached. Judged by this standard, Jesus Himself did not preach the Gospel. This apparently was the opinion of Luther, who in the preface to 1 Peter claimed that the Pauline epistles were "more a Gospel than Matthew, Mark and Luke. For these do not set down much more than the story of the works and miracles of Christ; but the grace which we receive through Christ, no one so boldly extols as St. Paul." The Evangelical belief is clearly stated by Simeon, who declared that Christ "in his death 'became a curse for us, that he might deliver us from the curse' to which we were doomed. Thus he did not merely die in our stead, 'the just for the unjust', as a common victim in the place of the offender, but he fully discharged our debt in every particular; so that neither law nor justice can demand anything further at our hands".[2] Thus the Atonement, rather than the Incarnation, was all-important. This is, of course, good Calvinist teaching, for Calvinism "makes the fall of man the central point of its divinity; it treats the incarnation, and all the facts which manifest the Son of God to men, as merely growing out of this, and necessary in consequence of it".[3] Later still, Benjamin Jowett questions whether it was possible, by this doctrine, "so to teach Christ as not to cast a shadow on the holiness and truth of God".[4]

Man received salvation through faith alone; no good works, however meritorious, were of any avail, and man had no righteousness of his own to plead. The sinner who recognized this was in a better position than his respectable neighbour who trusted in his upright conduct. This had been the teaching of Luther; but not all Evangelicals agreed with his doctrine of justification by faith alone in the form which he had taught

---

[1] G. O. Trevelyan, *Life of Macaulay*, i, p. 40

[2] *Horae Homileticæ*, xi, p. 591

[3] F. D. Maurice, *The Kingdom of Christ*, ii, p. 288 (Everyman Library)

[4] "Essay on the Atonement", in *Epistles of St. Paul*

it. Cecil is quite outspoken in the matter: "The Popish error of human merit in justification drove Luther on the other side into the most unwarrantable and unscriptural statements of the doctrine."[1] Walker before him had been equally critical, suspecting that justification by faith tended to set up faith itself as a "work". "Doth faith justify? I answer, No; it is the obedience of Christ which justifies."[2] Saving faith was, for him, a gradual process. It began when a man realized his need for forgiveness and reconciliation; this was followed by the acceptance of the promises of Scripture; and later came the sense of full assurance.[3]

Many whose experiences have been recorded only came to a saving faith after prolonged periods of searching the Scripture and agony in prayer. In such cases "faith" was indeed a work; and that of a most laborious and exacting kind. Conviction came to others as by a sudden illumination. It was these last who moved Liddon to say that justification by faith was really justification by excited feelings.[4]

Conversion, however, was but the beginning of the Christian life, and salvation to be complete must include the power to overcome sin. That is to say that justification must be followed by sanctification. This was the work of the Holy Spirit in the heart of the believer. Wesley held that the two processes ought not to be separated, and that all who were justified received the Holy Spirit; but Fletcher divided them.[5]

Since salvation had to be accepted by each individual for himself, Evangelicalism tended to exalt private judgment at the expense of authority. At the same time it must not be forgotten that the acceptance of any authority itself involves an act of private judgment. This emphasis on the individual undoubtedly gave strength to Evangelicalism; but it was not without its drawbacks, and was a departure from the main stream of Anglican tradition. Gladstone, writing towards the close of his life, said of Newman that he was "never an instructed English Churchman.... He was trained (as I was) in the Evangelical School, which is beyond all others—beyond, for example, the English Nonconformists or Scotch Presbyterians—the school of private judgment."[6]

---

[1] Quoted Abbey and Overton, ii, p. 208
[2] *Nine Sermons on the Covenant of Grace*, p. 30
[3] *Fifty-two Sermons*, i, pp. 88 f.
[4] Johnston, *Life and Letters of H. P. Liddon*, p. 216
[5] Wesley, *Letters*, v, p. 228   [6] *Letters on Church and Religion*, i, p. 406

EVANGELICAL DOCTRINES

If, however, the Evangelicals exalted private judgment they were entirely loyal to the Church. They were in no sense "Low Churchmen" in our period, though in the following century, after the rise of the Oxford Movement, they allied themselves with Low Churchmen (with whom they were soon confounded) in opposing what they regarded as the Romanizing tendencies of that movement. In our period, however, they held firmly to a middle course. This was insisted upon by Simeon who "neither verged towards the great error of over-magnifying the ecclesiastical polity of the Church and placing it in the stead of Christ and Salvation, nor towards the opposite mistake of undervaluing the Sacraments and the authority of an Apostolic Episcopacy."[1]

With the Church they recognized only Episcopal ordination, though admitting the admirable work done by Dissenters in their limited sphere. They might hold the priesthood of all believers and the right and privilege of the believer to direct approach to God without human mediators, yet they also recognized the specialization of function by which certain ways of approach, such as Holy Communion, were in the hands of duly appointed ministers.

As Churchmen they had a deep love for the Book of Common Prayer with its dignified and sober spirit; though some, Hervey among them, felt that it had a deadening effect upon the congregation. The more ardent revivalists might despise those who used mere forms, and delight in excitements in their worship, and also unduly exalt preaching above worship; but this was not so with the vast majority of Evangelicals. A typical Evangelical of a later generation could write: "I have always gone to church expecting to derive greater benefits from the prayers than the sermon." The same writer records his feelings after a visit to Jay's chapel at Bath: "I returned from the *élite* of Dissent thankful to God for His mercy in assigning my place in our Church, and thankful above all for the Liturgy."[2] Simeon held similar views as to the value of the Prayer Book, and they were not shaken, but rather confirmed, by frequent attendances at Presbyterian places of worship when in Scotland. He wrote: "I have on my return to the use of our Liturgy . . . felt it an inestimable privilege that we possess a form of sound words, so adapted in every respect to the wants and desires of all who would worship God in spirit and truth. If *all* men could

[1] Carus, *Memoirs, etc., of Simeon*, p. 845
[2] Bateman, *Life of Henry Venn Elliott*, pp. 38, 141

pray at *all* times as *some* men can *sometimes*, then indeed we might prefer extemporare to pre-composed prayer."[1]

Both John and Charles Wesley held the sacraments in high regard, and so long as they lived encouraged their followers to attend Holy Communion. This sometimes proved embarrassing, or at least surprising, to the clergy. On October 13, 1739, an incumbent in Bristol was definitely annoyed by the numbers Charles brought to Holy Communion; whilst, on October 31, 1756, when the Manchester Methodists attended the "old church", their presence (some fourscore of them) necessitated reconsecration of the elements.[2] John Wesley published two manuals for Holy Communion, one based on the *Imitatio Christi* of Thomas à Kempis, and the other on the writings of Daniel Brevint (1616–95); whilst his hymns for the Communion, and even more those of Charles, are a permanent legacy to all Christian believers. They "knew that Evangelism could only be grounded on worship, and that the central act of Christian worship is at the Table of the Lord".[3]

This emphasis on the value of the sacraments was maintained and developed by the Evangelicals. Wilberforce, to quote a layman, held that: "The Lord's Supper is the rite by which our Saviour Himself commanded His disciples to keep Him in remembrance, and the Sacrament of Baptism shadows out our souls being washed and purified by the Blood of Christ."[4] But, for them, the Holy Communion was no bare commemoration feast, as is clearly stated by Romaine: "What is their attendance upon the Lord's supper? Is it not the communion of the blood of Christ, and the communion of the body of Christ, a real partaking by faith of His broken body, and of His precious bloodshedding, and of all the benefits of His passion?"[5] So too Walker in his *Short Instruction for the Lord's Supper* said: "what is signified, received, and assured in and by the sacraments, is Christ in all his benefits." He went on to point out that the "feeding upon Christ's body" is spiritual and not corporeal, the latter being "an absurd popish invention, not less unprofitable than it is abominable and superstitious". Since

---

[1] Quoted Moule, *Charles Simeon*, p. 166. Macaulay after a visit to Edinburgh expressed a similar opinion: "though Guthrie is a man of considerable powers, his prayers were a prodigious distance from those of our liturgy" (G. O. Trevelyan, *Life of Macaulay*, ii, p. 325)

[2] Charles Wesley, *Journal*, i, p. 189; ii, p. 138

[3] J. E. Rattenbury, *The Eucharistic Hymns of J. and C. Wesley*, p. 8

[4] Quoted G. W. E. Russell, *Short Hist. of the Evang. Movement*, p. 12

[5] *Works*, p. 194 (from *The Life of Faith*)

EVANGELICAL DOCTRINES 393

the body and blood are received by faith, only those who are already joined to the Lord partake in its benefits. Hence, there was no belief in any mechanical effect to be derived from the sacrament, nor undue anxiety to induce believers to attend Holy Communion until they were ready to receive it. This is also brought out by Walker who wrote:

> It is plain no one can be numbered among the faithful till he be converted, yet none but the faithful are actually within the covenant, nor consequently qualified to receive the seal of the covenant. . . . Nevertheless, in the first awakening, people will be pressing for it, and if admitted will surely be resting upon it, and so greatly hurt and hindered by it. As far as I have seen, a year after will be full soon; by which time, unless they have been remarkably diligent and had uncommon opportunities, they will scarcely have attained to so much advancement in faith, and in knowledge of Christ, themselves, their work, and their enemies, as to be capable of receiving this seal of the covenant with suitable discernment.[1]

The sacrament of Baptism was also highly valued by Evangelicals; but they were by no means agreed as to its significance, especially in regard to the question of "baptismal regeneration".[2] This doctrine had been accepted by Wesley, who held that "it is certain that our Church supposes that all who are baptized in their infancy are at the same time born again", and in his *Treatise on Baptism* (1756) he states his position very clearly: "By Baptism we, who were 'by nature children of wrath', are made children of God. And this regeneration, which our Church in so many places ascribes to Baptism, is more than barely being admitted into the Church, though commonly connected therewith." From the opinion of Wilberforce quoted above, it might seem that he held the view that Baptism had a merely symbolical value. This is certainly an unjustified inference, for on one occasion he strenuously upheld baptismal regeneration against Daniel Wilson and J. W. Cunningham. "His ground was that we are told that no man can see God

[1] Sidney, *Life of Walker*, pp. 40 f.
[2] Dean Church, *The Oxford Movement*, p. 263, considered that "the negations and vagueness of the Evangelical party had gravely endangered" the place of Baptism "in the living system of the English Church"

without a change of heart. We believe that infants do see God, and therefore he did not doubt that their hearts are changed at Baptism."[1] Later, the famous Evangelical preacher, Henry Melvill, stoutly maintained that "the Church of England does hold and does teach Baptismal Regeneration", and that the fact would never have been disputed "had not men been anxious to remain in her communion, and yet make her formularies square with their own private notions".

Differences of opinion over the doctrine among Evangelicals seem to have arisen through confusing regeneration and conversion, that is, by supposing that it denied the need for any spiritual change in those who had been baptized. This was to transfer to "regeneration" some features of the Calvinist idea of predestination and the indefectibility of divine grace. Simeon, preaching before the University of Cambridge, tried to make the matter more clear when he said:

> We must distinguish between a change of state and a change of nature. Baptism is a change of state: for by it we become entitled to all the blessings of the new covenant; but it is not a change of nature. A change of nature may be communicated at the time the ordinance is administered; but the ordinance itself does not communicate it.[2]

Though the Evangelicals were loyal Churchmen and though their doctrines were those of the Church, they tended to emphasize certain aspects of the Church's dogmatic system and to neglect others. In this there was a double danger. On the one hand, if too great prominence is given to isolated fragments of the truth they may lose their essential character; and, on the other, the balance of the faith may be disturbed. The Evangelical scheme of salvation, although purporting to be based on Scripture, was in reality derived from part of it only, and that not perfectly understood. It was "Pauline", and even so not a complete "Paulinism". What Dean Inge has said of the Reformers applies equally to the Evangelicals of our period, if not to their modern successors.

> The Paulinism of the Reformation is not a true interpretation of St. Paul's religion. The Apostle of the Gentiles is far

---

[1] Quoted G. W. E. Russell, *op. cit.*, p. 14
[2] Quoted Moule, *op. cit.*, pp. 102 f.

EVANGELICAL DOCTRINES

better understood now than in the days when an elaborate theology of a forensic type was built upon the epistle to the Romans. The Christ-mysticism which is the heart of his personal faith is seen to be far more important for an understanding of his Christianity than his arguments about justification by faith and vicarious atonement.[1]

The real weakness in the Evangelical doctrinal system was that it was too much concerned with the needs of the individual and neglected the wider needs of the community as a whole. That the needs of the individual are a primary concern of the Christian preacher and advocate is not to be denied, but they are not everything. In this defect, however, especially as it applies to the doctrine of the Atonement,[2] they were in line with their contemporaries who had not grasped its wider application; in fact it was not until the late nineteenth century, with the rise of the *Lux Mundi* group and the teaching of P. T. Forsyth, that this came about.[3]

Another defect sometimes alleged against the Evangelical scheme was that it laid too much stress on the prophetical aspects of the Church's life, to the neglect of the priestly; a feature which led Archbishop Benson to write: "They are happy in the Court of Israel and in the Court of the Women. They have never seen the Court of the Priests."[4]

[1] *The Platonic Tradition in English Religious Thought*, p. 30

[2] This inadequate idea of the Atonement was due to the contemporary neglect of Greek theology and the consequent over-emphasis upon the transcendence of God to the forgetfulness of His immanence

[3] See Elliott-Binns, *The Development of English Theology in the Later Nineteenth Century*, pp. 100 f.

[4] *Life*, ii, p. 12

CHAPTER 22

THE LITERATURE OF THE MOVEMENT

It cannot be said that the Evangelical Movement, apart from Cowper, and in a lesser degree, Hannah More, made much contribution to general literature.[1] The movement, though not without men of learning, did not attract many scholars, and those who joined it wrote for practical effect. Even the hymns were primarily intended to be sung and not read, and so were hardly "poems" in the narrower sense. The writings of the Evangelicals are therefore to be valued, not as literature, but as "documents" which reveal the thoughts and ideals which inspired their authors.

If, however, the movement made little direct contribution to literature, indirectly it proved of much service. In the first place it greatly encouraged the habit of reading, since those who were induced to study the Bible would not make it their sole means of mental sustenance; and, secondly, through the Sunday Schools it vastly increased the number who were capable of reading. In other ways also it had an effect upon literature, for it helped to set up new standards of decency and propriety, to which writers had in a measure to conform. In this it may have unduly restrained artistic development, and banished from literature some of the most important aspects of life. Furthermore, by stimulating the emotions, and attaching greater value to them, it prepared the way for the Romantic revival. One feature of that revival was a new interest in the individual, a finding

> Once more in man an object of delight,
> Of pure intelligence and love.

Such interest in the individual and an enhanced estimate of his value, may well have been stimulated by the religious movements of the times.

The Romantic revival, on its literary side, was chiefly to be manifested in poetry. In the first half of the century poetry had

---

[1] Dean Milner and Dr. Hey made scientific contributions to learned journals; Madan translated from the classics; and Townsend published an account of his travels in France and Spain. But these, all told, did not amount to very much

been merely a decoration attached to life, not an attempt to transform it. In accordance with the predominant modes of thought it had been mainly of a satirical, moral, or didactic nature, with little in it to stir the emotions or the imagination. Conventional themes were often eked out by a turgid and declamatory style. But gradually a change came about, and a more healthy and less artificial tone prevailed. Of this change Cowper, above all, in showing that nature can be a source of pure and simple joy, was the real herald.

The emphasis which the Evangelicals placed on human depravity and original sin showed that man was at war with his environment, and not, as the prevailing tone of the earlier part of the century suggested, finding in it a means to his own pleasure and profit. This, too, is a mark of Romanticism in all ages, for as a present-day writer has said, it "implies a belief that humanity, by virtue of the development of the autonomous mind, is in a constant state of conflict with the external universe".[1] Furthermore, the importance placed by Evangelicalism on religious experience as a means of knowing God, gave a new value to "intuition" as against reason in the pursuit of knowledge of every kind. This, too, was in line with the Romantics, for Keats had written in November, 1817: "I have never yet been able to perceive how anything can be known for truth by consecutive reasoning." For him, truth was beauty, and beauty truth.

Too much importance, however, must not be attached to any contribution which the Evangelicals may have made; for that movement was itself part of a general reaction against rationalism and classicalism; and if it coincided with this reaction and gave it added power, it can scarcely be said to have originated it. It is best seen as the religious aspect of a general tendency operating at different levels of life and experience.

Another factor which led to an increased interest in and demand for literature, and especially for fiction of a new type, was the growth of the middle classes, classes from which the Evangelicals drew most of their converts. Centres of culture were established in various provincial towns, among them Birmingham, Bristol, Norwich and Manchester; and the members of these circles were not content with the older literature and the dominance of Dr. Johnson; they had interests of their own for which provision had to be made. Among them was religion. "The Pope school had omitted religious considerations, and

[1] Alexander Comfort, *The Novel in Our Time*

treated religion as a system of abstract philosophy. The new class of readers wanted something more congenial to the teaching of their favourite ministers and chapels."[1]

What, it may be asked, was the attitude of Evangelicals to general literature? To such a question no simple answer can be found, for it varied enormously according to the education and taste of the individual. Many of the more humble found that the Bible supplied all their needs; and it was one of the great achievements of the revival that it restored the Bible to a worthy place in the life and literature of the land. But the movement also attracted, especially from among the clergy, many who were eager students of the classics, a predilection which they did not abandon when they enrolled themselves in the Evangelical ranks. Henry Venn, for instance, was able to coach his son for Cambridge.[2] He had also a wide knowledge of French literature such as was not common among the clergy of his day. When Madan was driven from the Lock chapel, owing to his advocacy of a species of incipient Mormonism, he found consolation in translating Juvenal and Persius. In some cases, however, there was a definite feeling of repulsion and a regret that so much effort had been devoted to the acquisition of classical learning. Berridge, who had spent fifteen hours a day in an insatiable pursuit of knowledge, could write: "I now lament the many years I spent in Cambridge in learning useless lumber—that wisdom of the world which is foolishness with God."[3] William Law, no Evangelical of course, in later life deprecated indulgence in learning by the clergy, regarding it as a waste of energies "which ought to have been given to the care of souls and the worship of God".[4]

Many Evangelicals, who would gladly have kept up their reading of the classics, found either that their interest in them gradually faded, as in the case of Newton, who when he began to study for ordination gave one morning in the week to them until he found that he had more pressing interests;[5] or simply through lack of time. Romaine wrote on January 18, 1763: "I cannot spare a moment for my Homer or Virgil, my favourite Tully or Demosthenes. Adieu for ever all the classics."[6] But for such deprivation they found abundant consolation, as can be seen in a letter which Hervey wrote on November 1, 1746:

---

[1] Leslie Stephen, *Ford Lectures*, p. 153   [2] *Venn Family Annals*, p. 113
[3] *Works*, p. 468
[4] Stephen Hobhouse, *Selected Mystical Writings of Law*, p. 269
[5] *Authentic Narrative*, p. 76   [6] *Works*, p. 693; cf. also pp. 534, 547

THE LITERATURE OF THE MOVEMENT 399

> Away, my Homer! I have no more need of being entertained by you, since Job and the prophets furnish me with images much more magnificent, and lessons infinitely more important. Away, my Horace! Nor shall I suffer any loss by your absence, while the sweet singer of Israel tunes his lyre, and charms me with the finest flights of fancy, and inspires me with the noblest strains of devotion. And even my prime favourite, my Virgil, may withdraw; since, in Isaiah, I enjoy all his majesty of sentiment, all his correctness of judgment, all his propriety of diction.

Hervey, however, did not entirely eschew general literature, for he wrote to his sister on October 12, 1742:

> I once thought, I should make less use of the *Spectator* than you; but now, I believe, the reverse of this is true; for we read one or more of these elegant and instructive papers every morning at breakfast, and they are served up with our tea, according to their original design. We reckon our repast imperfect without a little of Mr. Addison's or Mr. Steele's company.

Many, like Hervey, found in literature a useful and necessary relaxation from the strain of life. Dean Milner would often recite passages from Shakespeare and Milton, and had a great admiration for Pope, and also for Cowper.[1] Henry Venn, as we saw above, found *Clarissa Harlow* irresistible. We may suppose also that the cultivated layman, when he became an Evangelical, did not entirely abandon his interest in the classics (if he had it already) or in general literature. This was certainly true of Wilberforce, who was a constant reader of the classics (so far as his scanty leisure allowed); whilst even the stern Zachary Macaulay was not without literary interests, for his son recalls "a translation of some Spanish comedies—one of the few bright specks in our very sullen library at Clapham".[2]

We come now to the main purpose of this chapter, a survey of the literature produced by the Evangelicals. This literature has an added value since much of it may be regarded as representative; for Evangelicals were in the habit of submitting their

[1] *Life*, p. 719   [2] *Life of Lord Macaulay*, ii, p. 281

writings to one another and of inviting friendly criticism. This is important, for, as we have remarked, their productions have value as "documents", by means of which we can enter into the very atmosphere in which they lived, and thus may read their minds.

But the value of their writings is by no means exhausted by this service; they have distinct merit in the class to which they belong, and Lecky considered that they had never obtained the recognition in literary history which they deserve. Regarded as pure literature, apart from the purpose for which they were written, they may not reach a very high standard—Saintsbury dismissed their prose as very inferior—but they may still be read with profit, even if much of the language used is now obsolete and many of their ideas would be differently expressed. Taken as a whole, they reveal a body of men possessed of a quiet and humble spirit, men who were anxious to devote such talents as they possessed to the glory of God and the abiding welfare of their fellow men. No thought of literary fame ever beguiled them from the strait and narrow path which they followed, for they were no

> tiptoe mortals triumphing to write
> Upon a perishable page,

but men upon whom had been laid a burden of responsibility; and it was to the fulfilling of their high office that all their powers, whether literary or otherwise, were selflessly devoted.

Our survey may most conveniently be divided up under seven heads: (*a*) Sermons; (*b*) Devotional and Instructional works; (*c*) Biblical writings; (*d*) Controversial works; (*e*) Biographies and Journals; (*f*) History; and (*g*) Poetry and Hymns.

(*a*) SERMONS

Sermons may well be considered first, for they constitute the most numerous as well as the most enlightening literary products of the movement. Volumes of sermons were, in any case, popular reading, and Boswell considered a library "very imperfect if it has not a numerous collection of sermons". Later taste would change as "history tacitly replaced religion as the school of public morals",[1] and "standard works" took the place of sermons on the shelves of a gentleman's library.

The relation of spoken and printed sermons has already

[1] C. V. Wedgwood, *Velvet Studies*, p. 155

received consideration; but if the burning utterances of a Whitefield lose much when confined within the covers of a volume, many sermons were couched in a much more literary form, and were doubtless intended for publication. Evangelical preachers made a habit of thus giving to their discourses a wider and more enduring audience[1] (often printing them at the request of their congregations), and it was considered a pious office to publish selections from the sermons of deceased clergymen, generally accompanied by a suitable memoir. Such volumes are, indeed, so numerous that even to enumerate them would be tedious. This being so, we may confine our attention to the sermons of Walker of Truro, one of the greatest of Evangelical preachers and well representative of the rest.

In 1763, two years after Walker's death, there appeared *Fifty-two Sermons on the Baptismal Covenant, the Creed, and the Ten Commandments*, with a memoir by James Stillingfleet. This was followed in 1765 by *Sermons on the Church Catechism*. The favourite collection, however, was that entitled *The Christian: being a Course of Practical Sermons*, with a preface by Adam of Winteringham. It ran through many editions (that of 1825 had an introductory essay by Simeon), the twelfth and last appearing as late as 1879. This popularity was well deserved, for in *The Christian* we have Evangelical preaching at its best. It is pervaded by a positive tone, and there is an absence of those continual denunciations, often degenerating into mere scolding, which marred many sermons. The building up of the faithful is emphasized and there is no attempt unduly to stir the emotions. The language is Scriptural, and the Bible is constantly appealed to, but not apart from reason. In one sermon Walker says: "I trust you have heard nothing which is not as consistent with reason as it is with scripture."[2] The sermons reveal clearly Walker's attitude and method, and make it all the more tragic that his comparatively early death should have robbed the movement of one who would have exercised great influence on its fruitful development.

(b) DEVOTIONAL AND INSTRUCTIONAL WORKS

Here again space forbids the consideration of many writings, and we must confine ourselves to Adam, Romaine, and Henry Venn; though, in addition, some notice will be taken of Hervey

---

[1] Newton published a volume of sermons before he was ordained to prove his fitness for orders. Later he published his *Olney Sermons*

[2] *The Christian*, p. 41

and of Hannah More, who successfully adapted the literary forms of the day to the promulgation of Evangelical truth.

One of the most popular and abiding productions in this class was a series of extracts from the diary of Thomas Adam published posthumously under the title of *Private Thoughts on Religion*. This small volume not only appealed to Evangelicals but also attracted the attention of many who were of a very different outlook, such as Coleridge, and, most unexpectedly, J. S. Mill.[1] Although its general tone is a little morbid and introspective, this is relieved by a number of epigrams; such as "Hell is truth seen too late", "Heaven is wherever God is: in my heart if I desire it", "I see the devil's hook, and yet cannot help nibbling at his bait", and, "It is much easier to join oneself to a sect than to God". Adam himself published his *Lectures on the Catechism* in 1753, which also had wide popularity.

Romaine's chief contribution was his trilogy, *The Life of Faith* (1763), *The Walk of Faith* (1771), and *The Triumph of Faith* (1795). These were published in 1824 in a single work prefixed by a memoir. These volumes are characterized by a profundity and depth which recalls the Puritan divines of a previous age, whose general point of view they share, as also their style and language.

One of the most popular handbooks which appeared during our period was Henry Venn's *The Complete Duty of Man* (1761). This work was designed to displace for Evangelicals the well-known manual *The Whole Duty of Man*. This latter manual was first printed in 1657, and had a great vogue after the Restoration, ranking next to the Bible and the Prayer Book.[2] The Holy Club at Oxford had distributed it along with these, and Wesley included it in his Christian Library. Other Methodist and Evangelical leaders thought much less highly of it; Whitefield was especially vehement in its condemnation, saying that "Its author knew no more of Christianity than Mahomet"; whilst, for Cowper, it was "a repository of self-righteousness and pharisaical lumber". Berridge, for once, was more moderate, admitting that it was "sent abroad with good intent", but adding that "it had failed of its purpose, as all such teaching will. Morality has not thriven since its publication; and never can thrive, unless founded wholly upon grace."[3]

[1] Dr. Chalmers and Bishop Heber also thought very highly of it

[2] Fielding included it with the Bible and Thomas à Kempis in the books read by Joseph Andrews (Bk. I, chap. iii)

[3] *The Christian World Unmasked*, p. 335

Venn's volume, although it became popular with Evangelicals, failed to displace the earlier work. This was probably due to its lack of literary grace and charm. Venn seems deliberately to have adopted what was regarded as an appropriate style in his day for such a manual, and as a result it is dull and prosaic. His grandson John Venn remarked that "we look in vain for any trace of the attractive characteristics which we know to have been so prominent in his personal intercourse". None the less, *The Complete Duty of Man*, if rather dull and not very profound, has a distinct value, especially for the practical life of the Christian, for Venn had an abundant store of experience in dealing with souls upon which he could draw.

We come now to two writers, Hervey and Hannah More, who endeavoured to spread Evangelical ideas by means of current literary forms. Hervey[1] when quite a young man produced *Meditations among the Tombs* (1746), included in which were his "Reflections on a Flower Garden". This volume, at least to a modern reader who is unacquainted with the prevailing taste in genteel circles, is a most extraordinary piece of work, and suggests a caricature rather than a serious writing.[2] What are we to think of passages such as that commenting on the death of an infant: "What did the little hasty sojourner find so forbidding and disgustful in our upper world to occasion its precipitate flight?"; or that on a young lady: "Instead of the sweet and winning aspect, that wore perpetually an attractive smile, grins horribly a naked skull"; or the passage in the "Reflections" in which he condemns those whose laziness keeps them in bed: "Abundance of ruddy streaks tinge the fleeces of the firmament, till at length the dappled aspect of the east is lost in one ardent and boundless blush. Is it the surmise of imagination, or do the skies really redden with shame to see so many supinely stretched on their downy pillows?"

The volume proved amazingly popular and ran through some twenty editions within a few years. Encouraged by its success, Hervey embarked on his best known work, *Theron and Aspasio*, which appeared in 1755. It consists of three long volumes (they run to over 1,300 pages) and takes the form of a series of dialogues and letters on religion between two fictitious persons. "To soften the asperities of argument", Hervey introduced

[1] For a recent and judicious study of Hervey as a writer, see W. E. M. Brown, *The Polished Shaft*, pp. 3–59

[2] Dr. Johnson wrote a parody, *Meditation on a Pudding*. Boswell seems to have been not a little shocked by it

numerous descriptions of scenery (the work would have been much shortened and improved by their omission in whole or in part), of such a fulsome and luxuriant character that they provoke a smile. He can even speak of a scene where "cauliflowers sheltered their fair complexions under a green umbrella, and daisies were gay with the smile of youth, and fair as the virgin snows"! But, as with his earlier volume, the polite world gave *Theron and Aspasio* an appreciative welcome; and it is said that the learned Dr. Parr as a young man took it as a model of style. The success of Hervey's writings and their large circulation made many imitate him, especially in the pulpit—so common was this that Newton warned young men preparing for the ministry against the habit.

Thus the writings of Hervey gave Evangelical views no little prestige and introduced them into circles which would have scorned the homely productions of less eloquent and less cultivated writers. But with the change of taste his influence among the better educated began to wane; only, however, to find new life among humbler folk, a most surprising development in view of his elaborate style; and in Scotland, where Robert Burns read them in his youth, they had an immense circulation. Coleridge, indeed, took the Meditations as an example of the way in which the vulgar were led astray by "counterfeits".

Hannah More adopted a less luxuriant style, and made her appeal in a far different manner; she chose the medium of religious fiction and of tracts for general circulation.[1] Most of the tracts, however, belong to a later period and were called forth by the spread of revolutionary ideas and the popularity of the writings of Thomas Paine. Her *Village Politics*, written under the pseudonym of "Will Chips", did not appear until 1792. There followed a series of *Cheap Repository Tracts* which sold 2,000,000 copies in a single year, whilst one of her best known stories, *The Shepherd of Salisbury Plain*, was translated into many European languages.

Her tales have a strongly dramatic flavour and exhibit great insight into character and motive; and even now arouse and retain the interest of the reader, though he may find the long pious discourses (so typical of the times) a little tedious. Her figures are real human beings, and not mere personifications of certain virtues and vices; whilst the background of their lives

---

[1] The method was not entirely new: cf. Thomas Fuller, *Holy and Profane Studies*

reveals homely facts and circumstances such as would be familiar to those for whom she wrote. Her style, moreover, though perhaps a little too closely modelled on that of Dr. Johnson, is far superior to that of other moral writers of her times; for, unlike so many religious authors, she succeeded in carrying into her writings that charm and lightness of touch which distinguished her conversation. Hannah More had a genius for setting forth commonplace good sense and piety with freshness and animation.

(c) BIBLICAL SCHOLARSHIP

To theological studies as a whole the Evangelicals made but a meagre contribution. They were content to stand in the old paths and would have regarded any indulgence in novel speculations as a profitless or even a dangerous undertaking. Hence their theological writings were confined to exposition on conservative lines. One exception to this may be perhaps found in the interest which many of them took in the original language of the Old Testament; though as this was a help to exposition and understanding it hardly counts as such. Wesley had taken up Hebrew at Oxford and taught it to Hervey and others; whilst Romaine, possibly under Hutchinsonian influence, had given much attention to the subject and produced a revised edition of the *Hebrew Lexicon and Concordance* of Marius de Calasio.[1] Cornelius Bayley also compiled a Hebrew Grammar. Other Evangelicals who had a knowledge of Hebrew, even if they did not write upon it, included Newton, Scott, Burnett, and Haweis.

Townsend defended the accuracy of the Pentateuch, but the Biblical writings of the Evangelicals were in general confined to exposition. Romaine preached courses of sermons on *Psalm CVII* and on *The Song of Songs*; and Venn on *The Prophecy of Zachariah* (father of John the Baptist). The best known of Evangelical expositors, however, was Thomas Scott, whose commentary had an immense and abiding influence. It was begun on January 2, 1788, and completed by June 2, 1792. The commentary appeared in weekly parts, and as Scott had therefore to work under continual pressure, and had little access to libraries, it consists mainly of his own thoughts on the various passages, with a frequent use of the method of explaining one part of the Bible by reference to the rest. The fact that Scott

---

[1] Romaine retained his love of Hebrew to the end, and his last work, published in 1795, was *A Short Hebrew Grammar*

had neither the time nor the opportunity to consult what had been written by others gave to his commentary a certain originality and consistency which is sometimes lacking in similar works produced under more favourable conditions. His comments are often fresh and always sensible; for he had no patience with allegorical and fanciful interpretations, holding that "every passage of scripture has its literal and distinct meaning, which it is the first duty of a commentator to explain, and speaking generally the *spiritual meaning* is no other than this *real* meaning with its fair legitimate application to ourselves".[1] Daniel Wilson, who yearly read the Bible with the aid of Scott, after forty years experience gave it as his opinion that "he surpasses all other commentators by far, with the single exception of the incomparable John Calvin".[2] Up to his death, about 12,000 copies were sold in England, and more than twice as many in America, the proceeds amounting to some £200,000. Of this immense sum the only benefit the author obtained was payment at the rate of a guinea a number, and even this poor recompense he did not always receive.[3]

(*d*) CONTROVERSIAL WORKS

Of these, perhaps the less said the better; so far, that is, as such writings, as in the Calvinist controversy, were launched by one section of the movement against the other. The need to review them is still further lessened by the fact that such writings were a mere rehashing of well-worn argument and made no contribution whatsoever to learning.

It is a little surprising that the Evangelicals produced no works in defence of the Christian faith; though Romaine, before he became identified with the movement, had replied to Warburton's *Divine Legation*. This urgent task they left to others; so Horsley had to deal with the Unitarianism of Priestley, and Paley with the arguments of Hume.

(*e*) BIOGRAPHIES, JOURNALS AND LETTERS

Since the Evangelicals took a deep interest in spiritual experiences, their own and those of others like-minded, it is natural to expect that they would produce numerous writings in which these were set forth, and not least in an autobiographical form—and such is the case. For the historian, these writings are of inestimable value, for they cover not only the

---

[1] *Life of Scott*, p. 636 [2] Bateman, *Life of Daniel Wilson*, ii, p. 145
[3] *Life of Scott*, pp. 269 ff.

thoughts and meditations of their authors, but also the manner in which their beliefs were applied in practical life. Moreover, they supply much information concerning the rise and development of the movement.

If poets are to be judged by their writings alone—a doctrine which Tennyson held so firmly that he once said that if he had the sole copy of an autobiography of Horace he would burn it[1] —this is not the case with men of action whose writings, if they exist, we value on other than literary grounds. But acts and events, although their effects persist, may themselves be forgotten in the absence of definite records. These in the case of the Evangelicals are fortunately abundant—to the great benefit of the historian.

Mention has already been made of the fashion of prefixing memoirs to collections of sermons and other "remains", as they were somewhat quaintly designated, of deceased clergymen. These are as a rule of no great length or merit, though they served the purpose of informing the readers of the main events in the preacher's life and ministry. As such they were adequate; but they scarcely rank as contributions to literature. Many of them are referred to in the various parts of this volume and in the index; to enumerate them here would be a wearisome and unprofitable task, and would turn the section into a species of inventory. There were, in addition, more considerable biographies (here Edwin Sidney was very active, giving us lives of Walker, Richard Hill, and Rowland Hill), as well as accounts of their lives written by the men themselves and also their private journals and correspondence.

A number of Evangelical leaders published autobiographies during their lifetime. Two of such writings, however, stand out from the rest—Newton's *Authentic Narrative* and Scott's *Force of Truth*, both of which deal with the early careers only of their respective authors.

Newton's autobiography has a place, albeit only a small one, in the history of English literature, for not only was it used by Wordsworth in an early draft of *The Excursion*, but also gave ideas to Coleridge for his *Ancient Mariner*.[2] It is certainly an exciting and vivid narrative, and I cannot help thinking that Lord David Cecil does it less than justice when he writes: "It is a fusty, forbidding little book, and more than half of it is pious platitude; but it enshrines within its stilted sentences one of the most fantastic fairy tales that was ever the true story of a

---

[1] *Memoir*, ii, p. 484   [2] See Bernard Martin, *John Newton*

human being."[1] Much more apt was Wesley's estimate when he wrote on August 16, 1769: "To-day I gave a second reading to that lively book, Mr. Newton's 'Account of his own Experiences' ".[2]

If Scott's *Force of Truth* is devoid of exciting incidents it is of equal, if not superior, value, recording as it does with complete candour the story of the author's religious opinions. It was first published in 1778 and went into many later editions in which there was some revision and enlargement, but no substantial alteration. It many ways it recalls Newman's *Apologia*, with which it is not unworthy to be compared, even in style.[3] Like the *Apologia* it records the progress of a mind towards the adoption of views which it had once sternly rejected, and that progress, as in the case of Newman, was a long and gradual one. Both record the various stages of the journey, and also indicate the books which influenced them. Overton called it "one of the most striking treatises ever published by the Evangelical school", adding: "we cannot go quite so far as to say, with Bishop Wilson, that it is equal to the *Confessions of Augustine*".[4] In this Overton is in error, for Daniel Wilson, in his funeral sermon on Scott, distinctly said that it could *not* "be equated" with the *Confessions*.[5] *The Force of Truth*, it may be noticed, was the means of saving Henry Kirk White from the toils of Deism.[6]

Although Scott made public his own experiences, he held that the posthumous revelation of the private thoughts of religious leaders, as contained in their journals and letters, was a task which demanded great circumspection; considering that the memory of many good men had been gravely injured by the indiscreet publication of such material.[7]

Another Evangelical leader went even further than Scott, for Romaine resisted all attempts to persuade him to record his spiritual experiences. His biographer, Cadogan, says of him: "Great as is the loss of the survivors, it is much to the honour of the deceased, that though he had the pen of a ready writer, he employed it not upon himself, but upon his God and Saviour."[8] The same reticence is to be found in such of his

[1] *The Stricken Deer*, p. 111   [2] *Journal*, v, p. 332
[3] The style owed something to the revision of Cowper (*Life of Scott*, p. 127)
[4] In Abbey and Overton, ii, p. 201   [5] *Life of Scott*, p. 581
[6] *Op. cit.*, p. 635
[7] One may compare the harm done in the early days of the Oxford Movement by the publication of Hurrell Froude's *Remains*
[8] Romaine, *Works*, p. 1

letters as were published after his death. They are full of religious ideas and teaching, but contain few personal references, except when writing to members of his family.

The keeping of journals in which the daily progress or decline of the writer was meticulously recorded was a habit common among Evangelicals. It was, indeed, regarded as part of their spiritual discipline. Wesley had set the example; but his journals, which he published at regular intervals, are much more concerned with outward events than with his own private feelings. Whitefield followed the same course, and even the humblest Methodist preacher indulged in the practice.[1] Simeon was here an exception among Evangelicals, for although he started a journal on February 18, 1780, and wrote, "I shall think my religion very much cooled when I remit it", he did not long continue the practice, and confessed later that he had little "taste for Diaries".[2]

Such journals often make melancholy reading, and account not a little, it might seem, for the popular belief that religion is a dull and oppressive pursuit. The weary efforts to unravel "the subtle filaments" of which motives are woven, the anxious inquiries, the over-scrupulous self-questioning, the petty faults exposed and lamented—all these are calculated to disgust the healthy-minded. The effect on those who kept such journals is difficult to assess. In some it may have encouraged an unwholesome introspection; but we must not judge the minds of the writers by this evidence alone. Henry Martyn's journals, for example, suggest that his entire outlook was clouded by melancholy reflections, but according to the testimony of contemporaries he himself was of a most cheerful disposition.

Included in the various biographies, and sometimes inserted in journals, were numerous letters. Separate volumes of letters have also been collected and published, as in the case of Wesley and Whitefield. Newton during his lifetime issued several volumes of his own letters, including *Cardiphonia* (1780). Like some of the other leaders, and indeed more perhaps than any of them, he made a great use of correspondence as a means of spiritual direction, being convinced that he had a special gift for such an employment—"It is the Lord's will that I should do most by my letters."[3] But not all felt they had this special gift; and Simeon, just as he found himself unable to persevere in the keeping of a spiritual diary, also found it an impossible

---

[1] Good use of the material thus provided has been made by L. F. Church in his two volumes on *The Early Methodist People*

[2] Carus, pp. 18, 20   [3] Bull, *John Newton of Olney*, p. 323

task. "As for sitting down to write a religious letter, it is what I cannot do, and what I do not very much admire, unless there be some particular occasion that calls for it."[1]

One work stands apart and forms a transition to the next section: that is the *Biographia Evangelica* of Erasmus Middleton. This very comprehensive compilation was published in four volumes between 1779 and 1786. The writer makes a very wide sweep, and beginning with Wycliffe, includes such unexpected "Evangelicals" as George Herbert, John Smith the Cambridge Platonist, Archbishops Ussher and Leighton, and Bishops Beveridge and Hopkins. Covering as it does so vast a field, Middleton's work is naturally of unequal value, and contains many inaccuracies in points of detail, but as a whole it is well calculated to serve the author's purpose, which was to counteract infidelity and irreligion, on the one hand, and popery and "other heretical Tenets" on the other.

(*f*) CHURCH HISTORY

The outstanding achievement in this field of literature (although the greater part of it falls outside our period) was Joseph Milner's *History of the Church of Christ*, of which he had written three volumes, bringing the record down to the third century, before his death in 1797. His brother Isaac, who incidentally had read the manuscript of the earlier part and corrected its style, added a further two volumes.

Milner's undertaking had been suggested by Newton's *Review of Ecclesiastical History* (1769), and he had already crossed swords with Gibbon in 1781.[2] His intent was to demonstrate, as against the claims of the Roman Church, that "from the days of Peter and Paul there had been an unbroken succession of Christian teachers and of Christian societies, among whom the eternal fire of gospel truth had burnt pure and undefiled by the errors which were abjured in the sixteenth century by the half of Christendom".[3] There is much to be said for Milner's

[1] Carus, *op. cit.*, p. 357
[2] Gibbon's comment is characteristic. "From his grammar school at Kingston-on-Hull, Mr. Joseph Milner pronounces an anathema against all rational religion. *His* faith is a divine taste, a spiritual inspiration; *his* church is a mystic and invisible body; the *natural* Christians, such as Mr. Locke, who believe and interpret the Scriptures, are, in his judgment, no better than profane infidels" (*Memoirs*, edited by G. Birkbeck Hill, p. 319)
[3] Thomas Arnold thought of adopting a similar method as a counterblast to the *Tracts for the Times*: see his letter to Archbishop Whately of May 4, 1836. In the secular sphere something of the kind had occurred to Shelley, who thought to "produce a systematical history of what appear to me to be the genuine elements in human society" (Preface to *Prometheus Unbound*)

thesis, even if he interpreted it rather narrowly; for, after all, the supreme interest of Church History lies not in the development of organization, the elaboration of dogma and its ritual expression, the struggle of Papacy and Empire, or even in the conflict with heretical views, but in the lives of the saints in whom the power of the Gospel was so finely demonstrated.[1] Milner, in his choice of examples, showed a generous and comprehensive spirit. An instance of this is his high commendation of St. Cyprian, with whose ecclesiastical views he can have had but little sympathy. Here the remarks of Overton may be recalled: "Strong Protestant as Milner was, he showed a generous appreciation of the real good which existed in the Church of Rome: a most unusual liberality in theologians of the eighteenth century—High Church as well as Low . . . and he owns that 'our ancestors were undoubtedly indebted, under God, to the Roman See' (ii, p. 441)".[2]

Milner's work provoked many sarcastic comments from better equipped historians. For some reason or other Macaulay had a special animus against him, and his marginal notes on the History are almost scurrilous; one of them, and that a mild sample, runs as follows: "My quarrel with you is that you are ridiculously credulous; that you wrest everything to your own purpose in defiance of all the rules of sound construction; that you are profoundly ignorant of your subject; that your information is second-hand, and that your style is nauseous."[3] Dean Milman, if more restrained, is equally critical: "Milner's History of the Church enjoys an extensive popularity with a considerable class of readers, who are content to accept fervent piety and an accordance with their own religious views, instead of the profound original research, the various erudition, and dispassionate judgment which more rational Christians consider indispensable to an historian."

These are harsh criticisms—but, it must be confessed, not altogether undeserved; for Milner, though possessed of considerable abilities and knowledge, undertook a task far beyond his resources. So vast a scheme could hardly have been carried out by a single scholar unless he had constant access to libraries and was in a position to devote the whole of his time to its accomplishment. This was, of course, quite out of the question

---

[1] Cf. Inge, *The Platonic Tradition*, etc., p. 111: "The true apostolic succession [is] in the lives of the saints. . . . But the record of Christian institutionalism is one of the darkest chapters of history"
[2] In Abbey and Overton, ii, pp. 212 f.
[3] Quoted G. O. Trevelyan, *Life of Macaulay*, ii, p. 284

for a busy schoolmaster and parish priest living in an isolated part of the country.¹

Perhaps the most important outcome of Milner's labours was a revival of interest in the Fathers of the Church, who in the eighteenth century were not only neglected, but even despised. When Watson, later to be Bishop of Llandaff, became Regius Professor of Divinity at Cambridge, having hitherto given no special attention to the subject, he began a course of study to fit himself for his office. This he limited to the Bible; being, in his own words, "much unconcerned about the opinions of councils, fathers, churches, bishops, and other men as little inspired as myself". To this neglect of the Fathers there was, however, at least one exception: Wesley, whose interest had been aroused by Clayton, the son of a Manchester bookseller, frequently read them.

As is well known, it was through reading Milner that Newman first came across extracts from the Fathers: "I read Joseph Milner's *Church History* and was nothing short of enamoured of the long extracts from St. Augustine and the other Fathers which I found there";² and in his translation of Fleury's *Histoire Ecclésiastique* he pays Milner a further tribute, declaring that "in consideration of the love he bore the Fathers in an age when few voices were raised even in apology for them, he is ever to be mentioned in kindness and honour".³

(g) POETRY AND HYMNS

The poems and hymns of the Methodists and Evangelicals were not, as is normally the case, produced by an intense and almost irresistible desire for self-expression on the part of their authors; but, as with the remainder of their literary effusions, were intended to promote the good of others. In such a process there is a danger, haunting all religious verse, that there may be "a kind of dilution, either of the poetry or of the saintliness".⁴ The latter danger was certainly avoided; but this can hardly be said, in many instances, of the former.

The first Evangelical poet to deserve notice is Moses Browne, the largely non-resident vicar of Olney. For many years he was a frequent contributor to the *Gentleman's Magazine*, and also published a series of collected poems under the title of *Sunday Thoughts*. The first volume appeared in 1750, the fourth in

---

¹ For a more sympathetic estimate, see Abbey and Overton, ii, pp. 209 ff.
² *Apologia*, p. 7   ³ *Op. cit.*, i, p. iv
⁴ Charles Morgan, *Liberties of the Mind*, p. 245

1781. Whilst chaplain to the Duke of Somerset, Browne wrote a poem on "Percy Hill", the seat of his patron. Browne was only a moderate poet, and his Christian feeling was superior to his literary ability. To the former we have the testimony of Hervey, who ranked him as "no novice in the sacred school"; as to the latter, we can only judge for ourselves. Browne, however, might not have agreed, for it is said that he aspired to become poet laureate.

Cowper, our next Evangelical poet, though he lived at Olney, was not there in Browne's time. He was, of course, a writer of a far different calibre, and is almost unique among English poets, in that, though he never enjoyed undue popularity, his recognition has been constant and unaffected by waves of fashion. Cowper's most striking achievement was to bring back poetry from the town to the country. Pastoral poetry before his day was a highly artificial product, far removed from the realities of rural life. Cowper, by his simplicity and genuine love of nature, transformed it into something new, and revealed, even to quite ordinary readers, the charms of the world around them. It was not, however, until he was nearly fifty that he found his vocation. He began by co-operating with Newton in the Olney Hymns, published in 1779. Then in 1782 his first volume of poems appeared, and achieved a definite if modest success. This encouraged him to persevere; and three years later he produced *The Task*, the best and most typical of his writings, which showed a distinct advance both in powers of thought and originality of composition. In 1784, in spite of the attempts of Newton to dissuade him, he began a translation of Homer which finally appeared in 1791. This was by no means a success; for he chose a most unsuitable metre, and had, moreover, not the kind of temperament suited to the endeavour. He had written to William Unwin in 1781: "It is but seldom . . . never except for my amusement, that I translate, because I find it disagreeable to work by another's pattern." Perhaps he had turned to translation as a mild and unexciting occupation, better fitted to his mental state than original verse. Later he attempted an edition of Milton, a task beyond his powers and knowledge, as he himself soon realized; and his failure no doubt increased the cloud of depression which hung about him until his death in 1800.

Hannah More, our next poet, was of a very different temperament and of much more restricted abilities. It may even be said of her that she was a skilled versifier rather than a genuine poet; certainly it was not to be her lot to "cancel the great Apollo's salic law" by proving that women could write poetry equal to that of men. Some of her poems, indeed, are really essays in verse, and might with advantage have appeared as prose.

Before her arrival in London in 1772 she had already written a pastoral play, *A Search after Happiness* (1762, second edition 1773), and she followed it up with *The Inflexible Captive* (1774). Her play *Percy* was performed by Garrick at Covent Garden in December, 1777, the actor contributing a prologue and epilogue. It was afterwards translated into German and performed in Vienna. At a later revival Mrs. Siddons took the part of the heroine; but by this time Hannah More had decided that theatre-going was a questionable habit, and she herself did not attend the performance.[1] Two years after the first production of *Percy* her drama *The Fatal Falsehood* appeared, but Garrick was now dead, and she may have felt the loss of his advice. At any rate, the new play had but a dubious reception. She then turned her talents in another direction, and in 1782 published a series of *Sacred Dramas* which quickly went through no less than nineteen editions. Two of her best known poems, *The Bas-Bleu* and *Florio*, appeared in 1786. But more and more her mind was becoming exercised over moral and social questions, and over the ability of religion to cope with them, and so in 1788 she wrote *Thoughts on the Importance of Manners* and a poem on the Slave Trade. Her other poems are in the style of the day, and quite up to the common standard. They are pleasant and easy flowing verses, the product of a cultivated and well-stored mind, and the benevolent and Christian spirit which breathes through them adds to their charm. So popular did they become that some were set to popular tunes; just as a century later Salvation Army lasses would sing their hymns to those then current.

The greatest contribution to English religious poetry made by the Methodists and Evangelicals was through their hymns.[2] Though hymns are written in verse it is rare for a good hymn to be a good poem; and many of the most popular hymns, if the

[1] She had hoped by her dramas to improve the general taste. Later she came to the conclusion that it would have been better to have avoided any contact with the theatre. In including the dramas in a collected edition of her works in 1800, she felt that a formal apology was necessary.

[2] See, further, Julian, *Dictionary of Hymnology*; Frere, Introd. to the *Historical Edition of Hymns Ancient and Modern*, Abbey and Overton, ii, pp. 267 ff.; Henry Bett, *Hymns of Methodism* (revised ed., 1945); and Laird, *Philosophical Incursions into English Literature*, pp. 52 ff.

lines are disregarded, would make excellent prose. On the other hand, those which possess the greatest merit as poems are less adapted to being sung by a congregation.

The eighteenth century, Professor Laird has said, was "the greatest English century of hymn-writing, the evangelistic counterpoise to the sedate urbanity of the Age of Reason".[1] But hymn writing was not entirely new, and in modern times it may be said to have begun in England with George Herbert (1593–1632). His hymns, however, were not intended for congregational use, though some, including "Let all the world in every corner sing" and "Teach me my God and King", proved eminently suited to the purpose, and are still popular. But the hymns of Herbert and others, such as Henry Vaughan, were not the models taken by the eighteenth century writers—they would have to wait for John Keble's *Christian Year* for the succession to be continued.

Credit for introducing the new type of hymn must be given to the Dissenters, and in the first half of the century they produced some of the finest hymns in the language. Here Isaac Watts and Philip Doddridge were pre-eminent. Some of Watts's compositions reach a very high literary level; "O God our help" is among the greatest hymns ever written; while "There is a land of pure delight" and "Jesus shall reign" are not far behind it. But Watts succumbed to that common failing of hymn-writers, he produced too much; there was also in him a streak of something vulgar which now and then emerges, and so he can descend to such doggerel as:

> "Go preach my gospel", saith the Lord,
> "Bid the whole earth my grace receive."
> He shall be saved that trusts my word,
> He shall be damned that won't believe.

Doddridge was almost equally prolific; we possess 374 of his hymns, and if he never quite reached the standard of Watts's best efforts, neither did he fall into his depths. They have a much more uniform merit, and in general are marked by sobriety, common sense and a subdued joyfulness. But he seems to have had but a poor ear for melody and some good verses are spoiled by loose lines. The fact that he composed many of his hymns as illustrations of his sermons may have hampered his muse. It would not be unjust, I think, to say that the majority

[1] Laird, *op. cit.*, p. 52

of hymn-writers suffered from a similar limitation, for, to meet the taste of their contemporaries, they had to endeavour to bring in as much of Scriptural imagery and wording as possible. Among Doddridge's best known contributions are "My God and is thy table spread", "Hark the glad sound", and "Ye servants of the Lord".

It was, however, owing to the Methodists that hymn-singing became a regular feature of public worship; and, though their pioneer efforts were at first unwelcome to others, their lead has been followed by almost every Christian denomination, for even the Roman Church does not disavow their use. The editor of John Wesley's journals[1] claims that it was he, and not Charles, who was the first to give the lead in this matter. But, even if this be granted, John never showed such literary grace or achieved such popularity as were reserved for his younger brother. Of the latter, Overton has said: "That gift of sacred song which he possessed in a remarkable, almost an unparalleled, degree, not only gave light and sweetness to the worship of . . . vast congregations . . . but supplied to a great extent the place of a liturgy and a creed. More people expressed their hopes, their fears, and their beliefs, in the language of Charles Wesley's hymns than in that of John Wesley's sermons."[2] Other Methodist hymn-writers include Oliver, the converted shoe-maker, who wrote "The God of Abraham praise", and Edward Perronet, the author of "All hail the power of Jesu's name".

The Evangelicals, as we have seen, were a little cautious in making use of the new method; but in time they also adopted it, and hymn-writers of considerable merit arose among them. One of the earliest was Toplady; but his hymns, with few exceptions, are of a poor quality, especially when judged by literary standards, though he was capable of rising to nobler heights as in "Christ whose glory fills the skies", whilst in "Rock of ages" he produced one of the most admirable of all such compositions.

The best known Evangelical collection of original hymns is, of course, the *Olney Hymns* of Newton and Cowper. Newton was responsible, among others, for "Approach my soul the mercy seat", "How sweet the name of Jesus sounds", and "Glorious things of Thee are spoken"; whilst from Cowper there came such well-known hymns as "Hark my soul, it is the Lord", "There is a fountain filled with blood", "Oh for a closer walk

---

[1] *Op. cit.*, i, p. 243   [2] *The Evangelical Revival*, p. 34

with God", and "God moves in a mysterious way". One defect of this otherwise excellent collection is its apparent disregard of the Church's calendar. In Book II, entitled "Seasons", there is nothing for Advent, Epiphany, Lent, Good Friday, Eastertide or Whitsuntide, and for Christmas Day only three hymns are provided. The most important season, to judge by the thirty hymns allocated to it, is New Year; on the other hand, seasons unknown to the Church, such as Saturday Evening and The Close of the Year, find ample provision.[1]

Another Evangelical hymn-writer was Berridge, who during a long and tedious illness composed a large number of what he called "Zion's Songs". In apologizing for them, his biographer remarks that they "may not in general please some fastidious readers".[2] This is certainly the case, for the hymns are but sorry effusions, and it might have been thought that Berridge's classical training, even though he had put it behind him, would have made him conscious of their defects. But Berridge had an unbounded confidence in his literary taste, and even ventured to alter some of Charles Wesley's hymns, to the great indignation of his brother. "How vilely", John Wesley wrote, "he has murdered that hymn! weakening the sense, as well as *marring the poetry*."[3]

Before leaving the subject of hymns, something may well be added about one of the best known of them, "Christians awake". The writer was John Byrom, a friend of Clayton and an acquaintance of Charles Wesley. Though Byrom was no "Methodist" he was not without sympathy for the movement, so long as it avoided his great bugbear, Calvinism. He intended the hymn for a Christmas carol for a small daughter, and the organist at the Old Church at Manchester, lighting on the manuscript set it to music and trained the choir to sing it. So on Christmas Eve 1750 they went out to Kersal Cell, Byrom's home, and sang it after dark to the surprise and immense gratification of the author.

[1] Overton, *op. cit.*, p. 150   [2] *Works*, vii, p. 342
[3] *Methodist Magazine*, 1780, p. 499

CHAPTER 23

THE EVANGELICAL ACHIEVEMENT

To make an exact assessment of what the Evangelicals achieved is hardly possible; much of it was by way of influence, and no statistics (such as the Methodists compiled) are available. A further difficulty is the close connexion between the two movements in the early days, for much of the Evangelical honey (one need think only of Walker at Truro and Venn at Huddersfield) went into the Methodist hive. Both had a double task to perform; on the one hand, the evangelization of those untouched by any form of religion, and, on the other, the awakening of dead souls from a merely formal and delusive acceptance of Christianity and the convincing of some just persons of the need for repentance. The latter task, since the Methodists gradually became a separate denomination, was mainly undertaken by the Evangelicals. In this they had much success, restoring that "vital glow" which had been lacking, and making men and women realize that religion did not consist merely in the performance of certain outward acts, but was fundamentally a personal relationship with God through Jesus Christ.

Testimony to their success has been given by not a few, and among them Mr. Gladstone and Mark Pattison, both of whom may be regarded as unprejudiced witnesses. The former, looking back on the religious tradition in which he had been brought up, wrote in 1895: "The Evangelical clergy were the heralds of a real and profound revival, the revival of spiritual life. Every Christian under their scheme had personal dealings with his God and Saviour. The inner life was again acknowledged as a reality, and substituted for that bare, bald compromise between the seen and the unseen world which reduced the share of the 'far more exceeding and eternal' almost to *nil*."[1] The latter emphasized the effect of the Evangelicals on the Church as a whole, writing in 1860: "However decayed may be the Evangelical party as a party, it cannot be denied that its influence, both on our religious ideas and on our Church life, has penetrated far beyond those party limits."[2] The fact that so much of the

[1] *Letters on Church and Religion*, i, pp. 7 f. Sir James Stephen affirmed that any impartial inquirer must be convinced that "the first generation of the clergy designated as 'Evangelical', were the second founders of the Church of England" (*Essays in Eccles. Biog.*, ii, p. 109)
[2] *Essays*, ii, p. 3

Evangelical contribution has been absorbed into the general life of the Church tends to forgetfulness and ignorance of what the movement really did. This is not only ingratitude, but definite loss; for though some may despise its leaders as old fashioned and their message as outmoded there are still many lessons to be learned from them.

Their influence showed itself in a variety of ways. To them above all others may be attributed that improvement in the standard of clerical duty which followed the rise of the movement. Thomas Grenville (1750–1842) said: "I have seen no change in my long life equal to the change in the habits and manners of the clergy."[1] There is no denying that the example of zeal and devotion shown by the Evangelicals in their parishes had the effect of shaming many of their brethren, much as they may at first have resented it, into emulating them.[2]

As the movement spread, its influence came to be exercised also on the laity, especially among the growing middle classes. On the upper classes it worked more slowly; but before the close of our period its effects could be seen in a new interest in religion, and even in questions of theology, which was so common as to be a source of embarrassment to survivors from an older generation. "When in the decline of his life, Mr. Luttrell took a tour of country houses, he told his friends on his return that he had found himself quite put out by the theological talk that prevailed in every house he had visited—except in that perfect gentleman's, the Bishop of ——'s, where the subject never occurred."[3] This was perhaps only a superficial and transient phase, but, so far as it went, not without significance.

Among the lower classes the work was done very largely by the Methodists, and their efforts found a ready and extensive welcome. It has, indeed, often been affirmed that the Methodists saved England from horrors similar to those of the French Revolution. This is a superficial judgment, and ignores other equally important factors. Conditions in this island were very different from those in France, and the grievances which led to the French Revolution were much graver; in any case violent outbreaks are alien to the character of Englishmen as a whole. Nor was there in England that gulf between the classes which

[1] Quoted G. J. Davies, *Papers on Preaching*, p. 8
[2] It was the devotion of Newton which first aroused Thomas Scott to his own deficiencies
[3] Lord Houghton, *Monographs*, p. 285 (quoted by Charles Smyth in *Cambridge Hist. Journal*, vii, p. 169)

was one cause of the French outbreak; in fact, the "insolence" of the upper classes was far greater in the years which followed the Napoleonic wars than ever before. At the same time it must be recognized that the movement did much to give a sober spirit to numerous Englishmen of the lower classes, who might otherwise have been the prey of agitators. When the French Revolution broke out there were but 80,000 Methodists in the country, although the number influenced by them was many times greater. Such inconsiderable numbers could hardly have had a decisive effect.

The influence of the Evangelicals, and of those who co-operated with them in the revival, was not limited to the care of their souls. There was a continually growing awareness of the bodily needs of the poor and oppressed. Already the agitation against slavery was on its way, and if credit for this must be shared with the Quakers and other Dissenters, it was Wilberforce with his political influence who was mainly responsible for bringing the evil to an end.[1]

In their private charities the Evangelicals were immensely generous, especially the wealthy laymen who were drawn into the movement, of whom John Thornton was a pioneer. Here, again, although they did much to support religious enterprises and to provide for needy clergymen, their efforts were not limited to such outlets. Thornton in his charities asked only one question: "May the miseries of man, in any measure, be removed or alleviated?" To Newton he granted £200 a year, and more if necessary, for the purpose of keeping open house and helping the poor.[2] The charity of the pious has often been condemned as doing more harm than good; but the cautious business men who lavished their riches in the early days of the movement did so with entire discrimination and only after careful inquiries. But charity, on however large a scale, could only deal with symptoms, and the Evangelicals, and the Church at large, have often been blamed for limiting their efforts to such means of alleviation without attempting any inquiry into the causes which produced social abuses and sufferings. This accusation, based on the application of modern standards, is both unjust and unreasonable. Factory conditions, for example, arose only gradually, and that after the rise of the movement, and the question of what we call social reform had not yet risen above

[1] It must also be remembered that the abolition of slavery itself, as distinct from the trade in slaves, which did not occur until 1833, was largely the work of another Evangelical, Thomas Fowell Buxton
[2] Cecil, *Memoirs of Newton*, pp. 43 f.

the horizon. Moreover, the whole spirit of the age was utterly against any kind of interference in the lives of the citizens, even if it were thought to be beneficial. Such measures would have been regarded as an infringement of the liberties of which Englishmen were so proud.

If the Evangelicals were not in advance of their age in being aware of the need for working out some kind of social philosophy, so in other similar matters they accepted the conventions of their day; unless, indeed, they involved obvious evils, such as those so courageously exposed by Hannah More in *Thoughts on the Manners of the Great*. There is no reason to suppose, for example, that domestic servants in Evangelical households enjoyed greater privileges or better conditions than others; though their presence at family prayers showed that there was concern for their highest welfare. So, too, those employed in businesses owned by Evangelicals had to endure the prevailing long hours and harsh conditions. Evangelical employers were themselves a hardy lot, and having in their young days undergone the same experiences had no sympathy with any who might complain about them. Daniel Wilson, a little after our period, describes his own experiences in the establishment of his uncle, a silk manufacturer and merchant. The latter was a truly god-fearing man and upright in all his dealings, yet his employees were expected to work from 6 a.m. to 8 p.m. in summer and from 7 a.m. to 8 p.m. in winter.[1] It may be added that he himself observed the same hours.

Mr. Gladstone has said that one reason for the tepid interest which some Evangelicals took in the abolition of the slave trade was their "Toryism".[2] This, too, must be borne in mind. The Evangelicals, like other Churchmen, had a very conservative outlook in politics, and attempts to interfere with social conditions were regarded by many of them as endangering national stability and even as flying in the face of the divine ordinances. In the country districts the clergy were the natural allies and agents of the landowning classes. None the less there were Churchmen who were becoming aware of the need for action and improvement on the widest possible scale. Soon after his appointment to Durham, Bishop Barrington formed a Society for the Bettering of the Condition of the Poor in which he had the co-operation of Addington, the Speaker, Wilberforce, Henry Hoare, Henry Thornton, all of them Evangelicals, as well as others prominent in Church and State.

[1] Bateman, *Life of Daniel Wilson*, i, pp. 4 f.   [2] *Op. cit.*, ii, p. 333

The early Evangelicals have often been accused of being much more concerned over the sufferings of coloured people than over those of their fellow countrymen. Such an accusation cannot be maintained by anyone who has real knowledge of their efforts. Wilberforce, in spite of his weak health and immense labours on behalf of the slaves, was anxious to promote measures to improve the conditions in prisons and factories, to provide for elementary education and to prevent cruelty to children and animals. It was he who suggested to Hannah More her devoted and surely socially beneficial activities in the Mendips. He was well aware that criticisms were being made of the efforts of himself and his helpers, and wrote in 1807: "We should specially guard against appearing to have a world of our own, and to have little sympathy with the sufferings of our countrymen."[1] Nor must the bold line taken by Richard Hill in the House of Commons be forgotten. One of his novel ideas was that revenue might be raised by the taxation of luxuries and places of amusement. In this, no doubt, he had a double motive; the desire to make those pay who could best afford it, and the wish to discourage institutions and habits which he regarded as detrimental to the moral and spiritual life of the nation.[2]

In their very valuable and otherwise fair-minded study, *The Town Labourer*,[3] the Hammonds blame the Evangelicals for caring only for the souls of men, whilst doing nothing to remedy their earthly conditions; and, also, for supporting the government in its repressive measures against those who tried, by agitation and combination, to improve the lot of the workers. As to the latter point, it must be remembered that in the desperate condition of contemporary affairs it was not easy for the government (nor for Evangelicals) to discriminate nicely between those who were genuinely working for reform and those who were out to overthrow the established state of society. This point of view is perhaps better understood to-day than when the Hammonds wrote a generation ago, for we are all too well aware of the ease with which unscrupulous agitators make use of legitimate grievances.

The accusation of caring only for the souls of men is quite unjust in view of Evangelical efforts to remedy evil social conditions. They never underrated the importance of these. Moreover, we must again try to see things as they saw them. They were convinced that the fate of the soul was of infinitely

[1] *Life*, iv, p. 307 [2] Sidney, *Life of Sir Richard Hill*, pp. 355 ff.
[3] *Op. cit.*, pp. 221 ff.

more consequence than that of the body, and acted accordingly. And is there not much to be said for their conviction? Experience has surely taught us that improved social conditions, necessary and admirable though they may be, add little to the happiness and contentment of mankind. Has not their chief effect been to bolster up the idea that material comfort and physical ease and security are the sole objects of human existence? It is not by such conceptions that great characters are hammered out or a nation truly elevated. "A man's life consists not in the things that he possesseth" (Luke 12: 15).

Let us now turn to a consideration of some of the causes which, humanly speaking, account for the spread of the Evangelical movement. Dean Inge once made the profound if slightly cynical remark that: "A religion succeeds, not because it is true, but because it suits its worshippers."[1] This aphorism is, of course, not to be pressed too far; but it undoubtedly reveals one reason for the success of the revival movement in general. It ministered to the needs, often unrealized and certainly unexpressed, of countless men and women in the eighteenth century.

Those whose characters were broken and shattered by sinful indulgence, and whose sense even of self-respect had vanished away, must have found in the new teaching, especially as presented to them by preachers of unshakeable conviction, a way of escape from their burdens and the hope of a fuller life. The joy and happiness which radiated from the faces of the men and women who sought them out might, they were assured, be theirs also. Moreover, the very fact that they were sought after, that there were some who really cared for them and were supremely anxious to promote their highest welfare, must have helped to restore self-respect. They could not be entirely valueless if others showed such interest in them.

It was this intense hunger for souls and care for the salvation of individuals on the part of the promoters and agents of the movement which gave strength to their endeavours. The zeal and energy they exhibited have been exceeded by no other body of Christians, save perhaps those who first proclaimed the Gospel tidings. They lost no opportunity of seeking to bring others to share in the joy and assurance which they had experienced, and this not only by the public preaching of the word, but also in private intercourse. In this latter endeavour Wilberforce was outstanding. In spite of his exceedingly busy

[1] *Platonic Tradition*, etc., p. 14

life and the attention which he paid to the great problems of the day, he constantly schemed to bring his friends and acquaintances to the saving knowledge of Christ.[1] Wilberforce himself had first been attracted to the Evangelicals by reason of their intense earnestness. Here were men and women who realized the momentous nature of the struggle in which they were engaged and the seriousness of the issues at stake. Earnestness was, indeed, a noteworthy feature in all the great Evangelicals, and not least in Henry Martyn. His portrait used to hang over the fireplace in Simeon's dining-room, and the latter would often bring it to the notice of his friends and say: "There, see that blessed man! No one looks at me as he does; he never takes his eyes off me, and seems always to be saying, 'Be serious —be in earnest—don't trifle'. Then, smiling at the picture and gently bowing, he would add, 'And I won't trifle—I won't trifle!' "[2]

Behind this hunger for souls and this earnestness lay a complete trust in God the Holy Spirit, not only as the guide of the Church as a body, but as an enabling force in every believer who sought His aid and counsel. With it went the devout recognition of the right of every Christian to a direct access to God without the intervention of any mediators, either human or semi-divine. In all things they were intensely individualistic.

In this emphasis on the rights and the responsibilities of the individual the Evangelicals were in accord with the Church of England, for by the first question in the catechism the attention of the child is pointed to these very things. It was also a healthy reaction from the religious atmosphere of the times; for the Deists had left a legacy by which the transcendence of God and His greatness and power had become unduly prominent.

The Evangelical belief that a conscious "conversion", a definite acceptance of Christ, was necessary, was another outcome of the individualistic emphasis of the movement. Men and women had to make a decision, to commit themselves to a cause, often openly and in public. This gave strength and solidity to the movement, though it might lead to egotism in the converts. To safeguard them against this danger there was a constant insistence on the duty of sharing their privileges

---

[1] For an interesting account of his methods, see R. Coupland, *William Wilberforce*, pp. 236 f.

[2] Moule, *Charles Simeon*, p. 140

with others. They were saved in order to serve. In most cases such urging was scarcely necessary. The converts realized that they had been drawn away from a narrowly selfish outlook into a wider world; they who had been aliens in a strange country were now sons of God and inheritors of His kingdom. It has been said that "past sins lie like iron upon man's fettered soul"; for them the fetters had been broken, and they had entered into a wonderful experience of serenity and relief, and so, rising from languor and despair, they gladly gave themselves to the freeing of others.

But converts, in the absence of adequate supervision and care, were liable to relapse. So they were gathered into "societies", and, with the Methodists, "classes", where they could receive that spiritual direction and companionship which are so essential for the novice in the Christian life. The whole history of the revival shows the immense importance of such small groups, not for this purpose only, but also for propagating the faith. It is the "cell" method so effectively used by the Communists. By this means religion became a real and absorbing interest in lives which had lacked motive, and almost every moment of their scanty leisure became filled with religious exercises. Living as they did under the eyes of their fellows, and bursting with the new powers which had come into their lives, they were a standing witness to the truths of the Gospel. It was this practical testimony which perhaps more than anything else promoted the growth of the movement among the masses. The hopeless and downtrodden could not fail to be immensely impressed by the change in the lives of their neighbours, who, though living under the same conditions of hardship and strain, were yet able to surmount them and emerge into an atmosphere of continual joy and happiness.[1] Why should not they enjoy a like experience? Even among the higher ranks of society the witness was not ineffective; for there, too, many who had been content to drift along with a merely conventional religion must have been stimulated by the very different faith which animated the Evangelicals. And so ideals which they had abandoned in despair as impossible of attainment were quickened into new life, and the conviction borne upon them that Christianity was no mere Utopian dream, but something capable of realization.[2]

[1] Cf. Hannah More's *Shepherd of Salisbury Plain*, which is based on actual experience

[2] Cf. Matthew Arnold's tribute to his father in "Rugby Chapel"

One department of life where this witness was supremely potent was that of the family. Not only could it be a means of bringing the children to God; but it was also, as in the Mission Field to-day, among the strongest evidences for the value and possibility of the Christian way of life. Wesley continually urged its importance among his followers, calling family religion "the grand *desideratum* among the Methodists"; but the response did not satisfy him, and on April 21, 1776, he complained that it was "still much wanting among us".[1] It was among the Evangelicals that it acquired a fuller representation,[2] and especially in the homes of the clergy. The Methodist preachers, as itinerants, could not furnish such good examples; it was one of the sacrifices they willingly made for the sake of preaching the Gospel. Moreover, the social class from which the Evangelicals were mainly drawn had already traditions of family life, and with them, on economic grounds alone, it could more readily be maintained. In spite of their strictness, and what seems to a later age their lack of consideration for the children, Evangelical homes were frequently the centres of great happiness,[3] as they were undoubtedly effective training grounds for a very high type of character. The strength of the Church of England has ever been shown in its ability to produce, not a few notable saints—though, thank God, the saints of the Anglican communion will compare with those of any other branch of the Church—but good citizens, good fathers and mothers, good husbands and wives.[4]

The mention of strictness in the home brings us to another source of Evangelical strength—the disciplined lives which so many were enabled to lead. Their striving after holiness was no vague, haphazard endeavour, but controlled by system and method. The rules they adopted might not always be those of the Church; but they were carefully planned, often in consultation with others, and in their journals strict note was made of success or failure in observing them.

This disciplined life involved in practice separation from the "world" and all worldly concerns; though not, it may be pointed out, from business and money-making. Liddon, who had been brought up as an Evangelical and later rejected the Evangelical scheme, could none the less pay tribute to the

---

[1] *Journal*, v, p. 193; vi, p. 102
[2] Cf. Smyth, *Charles Simeon and Church Order*, Chap. i
[3] A delightful picture of an Evangelical home will be found in G. W. E. Russell, *Short Hist. of the Evangelical Movement*, Chap. viii
[4] Cf. *Frederick Temple*, ii, p. 567

value of this aspect of it: "As I get older, I feel less and less sympathy for that singular misrepresentation of the real mind of St. Paul and St. John which, by a strange abuse of language, is called 'Evangelicalism'. But whatever is to be said of the 'Evangelical' theology, the strength of the Movement in its early days lay in its renunciation of the world."[1]

The disciplined life, however, had also its positive side; and, above all, it involved setting apart times for prayer and Bible-reading. Prayer played a prominent part in the lives of the Evangelicals and gave them strength for their unending labours. It was also a means for spiritual advance and an instrument for turning other souls to God. Well might Hervey say on his death-bed: "If I had my life to live again, I would spend more of it on my knees."[2]

On the subject of Bible-reading, more needs to be said. By long tradition, the religion of Englishmen has been grounded upon the Bible, and J. R. Green has claimed that the great moral improvement in the English nation which followed the days of Elizabeth was due to this cause.[3] It was also a useful antidote to Popery. During the early eighteenth century the custom seems to have waned, though it was not entirely neglected. Law's John the Shepherd may be an imaginary character, but he was doubtless typical of many humble readers. He and his wife still kept up the habit, and when "Madam the squire's wife one day brought them 'a huge expounding book upon the New Testament' they returned it to her, considering it a waste of time to read more than the 'words of Christ and His apostles . . . just as they left them'". But, for many, though the Bible was held in great and almost superstitious respect (no other book might be placed upon it), and though it was a cherished ornament of many a cottage parlour, the matter ended there. It was not read. Even this scanty reverence was sometimes lacking; the only Bible found by Hannah More in the parish of Cheddar was being used to prop a flower-pot. Among the educated also the reading of the Bible seems to have been abandoned by many. When Sir Joshua Reynolds exhibited his well-known painting, "The Infant Samuel", he was shocked by the number of people who asked who it was supposed to represent.

With the spread of Evangelicalism and Methodism, however,

---

[1] Johnston, *Life of H. P. Liddon*, p. 282
[2] Quoted Bateman, *Life of Daniel Wilson*, i, p. 41
[3] *Short History of the English People*, Chap. viii

there went a renewed turning to the Bible; and so highly was it regarded that some clergymen even forbade the reading of other literature. When Wesley criticized Berridge for taking up this attitude, the latter defended himself by saying that those who read other books generally neglect the Bible.[1] Whitefield was also against such restrictions, and wrote on October 3, 1748: "The dependence upon Christ's immediate teachings, without making use of books and proper means of instruction, you may assure yourself is a terrible temptation. It is the very quintessence of enthusiasm, and will lay you open to a thousand delusions."[2] As we saw above, there was need for such a warning, as many, even among the clergy, were apt to reduce the Bible to a mere legal code of quotable texts, or else to read into it notions of their own. But as the great majority of readers used the Bible for their spiritual nourishment and as something in which they themselves had a vital interest,[3] perhaps no great harm was done. The Bible undoubtedly provided both a unique standard by which conduct could be tested and an ideal of holiness which must have inspired many with the desire to realize it in their own lives.

A movement attracts adherents in part by the loftiness of its declared aims, in part by the motives which it advances as inspiring them; but above all by the character and personality of its leaders. The task of the latter is to manifest the ideals for which the whole movement stands already in process of realization; otherwise its principles, however pure and lofty, will savour of the merely academic. The Evangelical Movement was fortunate in its early leaders. It is true that there was among them no outstanding genius; but there were saints in plenty, men who were notable, not for originality or depth of thought, but for strength and variety of character; men who promoted the objects of the movement more by the nobility of their example than by the novelty of their teaching. In spite of wide differences in temperament, habits of mind, and upbringing, they were one and all characterized by purity and devotion, by vigour and zeal—a zeal, perhaps not always tempered by discretion—and by an intense desire for the salvation of their fellow men. Everything they did sprang from a single centre, and this gave them a solidity and significance

---

[1] Wesley, *Letters*, iv, p. 93 [2] *Letters*, ii, p. 189

[3] Newton said that the Bible was to be read "not as an attorny (*sic*) may read a will, merely to know the sense, but as the heir reads it, as a description and proof of his interest" (*Cardiphonia*, p. 83)

THE EVANGELICAL ACHIEVEMENT 429

for which their natural qualities afford no sufficient explanation. They were intense and effective in proportion to their narrowness. Such concentration is a mark of all reformers in either Church or State.[1] But there is also another explanation. Knowing only too well their weaknesses and acknowledging their failures, they depended utterly upon God. So close was their walk with Him that they sought His help and guidance in even the smallest details of life. They were, for the most part, men of strong and determined character, like Wesley himself, though none of them possessed that organizing ability which enabled him to lay such secure foundations for Methodism. On the whole, they were compelling rather than attractive; and there is little about them of that romantic aura which would surround Keble and Newman a century later.

In the leaders of the Evangelical movement, as in those of the primitive Church, an immense variety of gifts was to be found; "he gave some apostles; and some, prophets; and some, evangelists; and some, pastors and teachers" (Eph. 4: 11). Here we have the twofold work of the Church; evangelizing those outside and building up the faithful. Among the Methodists, Whitefield was the type of the evangelist, one who was never happy unless he was bringing the message of salvation to those who lay in ignorance and sin; in Wesley there was an admirable combination of both types. The Evangelicals, too, had their evangelists—men like Grimshaw and Berridge; they had also their pastors and teachers, men like Walker and Simeon; and in Venn and others, those who served in both capacities. Just as they varied in function, so did they in temperament and in the different social levels from which they were drawn. Many of them, like the Venns, came of clerical families; some were even descended from dignitaries of the Church, such as Talbot, Walker, and the Stillingfleets. Others came from very humble folk: like the Milners; whilst Scott and Berridge were both the sons of graziers. In this there was a remarkable contrast with the Oxford Movement, whose early leaders were almost entirely the product of a similar environment, and, with a few exceptions, members of a single university. But when we come to consider the temperaments of the leaders of the two movements, the contrast is not so striking; for it must not be forgotten that among the Tractarians wild and eccentric spirits were not

[1] Cf. William James, *Varieties of Religious Experience*, p. 339: "Political reformers accomplish their successive tasks in the history of nations by being blind for the time to other causes"

lacking, men who had "too much sail and too little ballast".[1] The Evangelical Movement certainly attracted a large number to whom this would apply. Some were eccentric in their methods, like Grimshaw and Berridge; some in their views, such as Madan and Hartley, Easterbrook of Bristol, and Thomas Pentycross. But such characters are often the most immediately effective, for, as it has been said: "The bulk of what are called entirely 'healthy' people add nothing to the sum of human achievement." None the less, the real seeds of future usefulness were not to be found in the activities of the eccentrics, beneficial and devoted though these might be, but in the wise statesmanship of a Simeon, in the heroic self-sacrifice, unavailing as it seemed, of a Henry Martyn, and in the energy and driving-power of a Wilberforce and the founders of the great societies.

Many of the Evangelical leaders, and here again they had an example in Wesley, tended to be dictatorial. This was, in part, the result of their conviction that they were guided and inspired by the Holy Spirit; in part, the result of the veneration then paid to religious leaders, who frequently aroused that popularity and admiration which to-day are mainly reserved for those who minister to our pleasures—the film-star, the "crooner", the professional athlete—though the eighteenth century had also its idols in the world of drama and sport.

One of the strangest phenomena revealed by a study of Church history is the way in which ecclesiastical tyranny may arise and be tolerated in parties within the Church and sects outside it, who unite in denouncing the domination of the priesthood. Such "tyranny" is in reality more dangerous and more objectionable than that of any priests, for it is personal and not official. The power of the priesthood is curbed and modified by tradition and usage; that of the "minister" has no such limitations. In the Methodist Movement autocracy was personified in Wesley,[2] and the self-acquired authority which

[1] See the letter of Cornish, quoted Isaac Williams, *Autobiography*, pp. 96 f.

[2] Wesley had keen eyes to detect this fault in others, and in reading through his journal it is difficult not to smile at his naïveté. On August 19, 1749, he wrote of Martin Luther: "Doubtless he was a man highly favoured of God, and a blessed instrument in His hand. But oh, what a pity that he had no faithful friend—none that would, at all hazards, rebuke him plainly and sharply for his . . . bitter zeal for opinions, so greatly obstructive of the work of God" (*op. cit.*, iii, p. 409). In another entry for December 24 of the same year he attributes the fall from grace of one of his preachers to "growing wise in his own eyes, he saw this and the other person wrong, and was almost continually offended" (*op. cit.*, iii, pp. 449 f.)

he wielded was greater than that of any bishop. Among the Evangelicals the right to criticize others and to demand their obedience, which some of the leaders assumed, did not pass without observation and comment. Wilberforce speaks of "the excesses of our dear ——s! There is a self-conceit operating through the medium of religious doctrines. If even knowledge puffeth up, how much more self-sufficiency."[1] But such an attitude was uncommon, and the great majority of the rank and file gladly accepted the "tyranny" of their leaders. The prestige which these enjoyed was in large measure dependent on their reputation as preachers. Such prestige is a very dangerous thing, and very apt, save in the most saintly and humble, to lead to undue conceit. Popular preachers are accustomed to the awed silence with which congregations hang upon their words, and it is difficult for them to escape that corroding egotism which lies in wait for the successful orator in every age. That not all Evangelical preachers were able to avoid this snare is evident from an entry in Henry Martyn's journal for February 2, 1803: "I find that in whatever manner the most holy ministers speak of their success, I am very apt to be disgusted at the prominent character of the instrument."

There is, however, much to be said, if not by way of excuse, at least in explanation of the dictatorial attitude adopted by the Evangelicals and other religious leaders. Most of them had undergone profound spiritual experiences, and as a result had become conscious of great blessings which they desired to share with others. The mistake they made was in insisting that these others should conform to their own mould; being unaware that such experiences can never be fully transferred, and in so far as they are transmitted tend to impose unnatural limitations on the recipient. For such experiences, even though themselves inspired by earlier, and especially Biblical models, must be intensely personal, and, therefore, unique. At the same time it is required in advocates of religion that they should testify to the things that they themselves have seen and known; their utterances, if they are to carry full weight, must be marked by conviction and utter confidence; the preachers must be "out and out", and, as a consequence, ignore all qualifications in their pulpit teaching. This is the spirit which the average churchgoer expects and appreciates, even though it may not commend itself to scholars. "A middling doctor is a poor thing", said Owen Whistler in *The Virginian*, "and so is a

[1] *Life*, iv, p. 268

middling lawyer; but save me from a middling man of God." Furthermore, with the growth of lay influence in the movement and the accession of some whose ideas of the relation of minister and people had been derived from those current among Dissenters, the clergy had at times to stand up for their rights. When, for example, some of the board of the Lock Hospital wished to dictate to Thomas Scott the kind of sermons he should preach in order to attract larger congregations, he told them that though they had the power to change him *for* another preacher, they had none to change him *into* another preacher.[1]

The study of the past, unless it is to degenerate into antiquarianism, ought to be pursed with the object of learning lessons of value for the present. This being so, we must consider not only the achievement of the Evangelicals, but also the weaknesses and limitations which the story of the movement reveals. Some of these were discerned by the more clearsighted leaders at the time; others have emerged in the course of its development; whilst others again, not so obvious, are only now apparent through the development of psychology and the deeper study of history. To point out these defects is therefore a necessary and profitable task; but it must be entered into in a constructive and not a critical spirit; in a spirit, moreover, which recognizes with sincere thankfulness the positive qualities of the movement and is humbly grateful for the immense achievements which added to its glory.

Most of the defects in the movement were in reality due to the exaggeration of the very virtues which made it so effective. The intense concern for the individual, for example, tended to a neglect of the community aspects of the faith; the desire for holiness of life, to excessive rigorism and the undue narrowing of interests; the value attached to the Bible, to the ignoring of the history of the Church in later days; and too great an emphasis on the part which the emotions play in the religious life to a neglect of reason. Let us now look at these defects in more detail.

The intense concentration on the individual which characterized the movement had two dangers. It might lead to the depreciation of the corporate side of religion, and it might also lead to self-centredness. In the early days, anxiety to gain converts often involved "disorder", the ignoring of the Church's discipline and organization; but, as Evangelicals began to be

[1] *Life*, p. 236

THE EVANGELICAL ACHIEVEMENT

distinguished from Methodists, this danger diminished, and by the end of our period had practically disappeared. Moule says of Simeon that, though, like the earlier leaders, he was "always in quest ... of individual conversions, [he] was led both by his situation and his reflections to a more distinct sense than most had felt of the claims of corporate and national religious life".[1]

The second danger was a too great preoccupation with their own spiritual state, leading to that egotism which may so easily accompany it.[2] The Methodist rule that anyone, whatever his views, might join their societies, so long as he had a real desire to save his soul, helped to foster this spirit, as did the tone of many of the most popular hymns, such as:

> Jesu, lover of my soul,
> Let me to Thy Bosom fly.

It had been forgotten that Christ, for St. Paul, was the spouse of the Church, not of the individual. The same rather unhealthy emphasis had been characteristic of some of the medieval mystics.

Concentration of any kind must involve limitation, and an exaggerated attention to the spiritual life of the individual often means forgetfulness that man is a body as well as a soul, and that all parts of his complex being must be provided for in any complete religious system. Alexander Knox, in a sympathetic letter to Hannah More, laid his finger on this defect, pointing out that with the Evangelicals there was "too little attention to anything except the salvation of the individual, an anxious self-seeking which might be of an exalted kind, and fruitful of works of righteousness, but which falls short of a higher standard not incapable of being attained".[3] In other words, the Evangelicals made too great a division between the natural and the spiritual, and failed to see man in organic relation to the whole of his environment. They forgot, and others with them, that:

> In this twofold sphere, the twofold man
> Holds firmly to the natural, to reach
> The spiritual beyond it.[4]

---

[1] *Charles Simeon*, p. 260; and cf. Smyth, *Simeon and Church Order*

[2] Cf. Clutton Brock, *What is the Kingdom of Heaven?*, p. 65: "Often the converted are possessed by an unpleasant egotism"

[3] Quoted Abbey and Overton, ii, p. 233

[4] E. B. Browning, *Aurora Leigh*, vii

The ultimate source of this inadequate conception of the extent of religion was a defective idea of God and of the true meaning of existence. For our Lord, at least as depicted in the Synoptic gospels, God was the God of nature, as well as the God of grace, and life was a single whole. But the Evangelical conviction that the Church and the world were strongly antagonistic made them utterly distrustful of many of the higher forms of human usefulness and activity, and tended, as Principal Tulloch has written, to make them conceive of Christianity "rather as something superadded to the highest life of humanity, than as a perfect development of that life".[1] This, of course, did not apply to all Evangelicals; one need but mention Wilberforce, Cowper, Hannah More and Richard Cecil, to disprove the charge; but it was true of the movement as a whole. Even with those who had no vivid consciousness of the antagonism of the Church and the world, an intense preoccupation with the saving of souls led them, if not to avoid, at least to ignore, whole realms of human activity of the highest and most beneficial character—art, scholarship and learning—leaving the mind, as Thomas Arnold has somewhere said: "a fallow field for all unsightly weeds to flourish in". As a result they failed to make any deep impression on the higher intellects of the nation. This was inevitable, for, as one who sympathized with their views in later times, has written: "No form of creed will ever recommend itself to a myriad-minded race, which does not acknowledge that every taste, faculty, and power of human nature is capable of being exercised to the glory of God."[2]

But here again the Evangelicals did not stand alone. The tendency on the part of the intensely religious to undervalue activities which have no direct bearing on the state of the soul can be found in all ages of the Church; and later it was characteristic of Dr. Pusey. This was realized by one who left the Church of England for that of Rome. He felt that Pusey was not fully Catholic because he seemed incapable of taking interest in anything that was not directly, technically, religious, or that was not explicitly connected with religion.[3]

The narrowness of the Evangelical appeal was recognized by some of its leaders; perhaps not so much by its ignoring of such outside interests as in its habit of restricting its teaching to a

---

[1] *Movements of Religious Thought*, etc., p. 13
[2] Quoted Sichell, *Life of Canon Ainger*, p. 83
[3] *Letters of Von Hügel*, p. 254

selection only of the truths of religion. Newton once wrote: "Some, accounted evangelical teachers, have too much confined themselves to a few leading and favourite topics . . . when it is constantly so, the auditories are deprived of much edification and pleasure, which they might receive from a more judicious and comprehensive plan."[1]

Thus the Evangelicals as a whole, carried away by the urgency of the task of saving souls at any cost, lacked that poise which enables men to see life steadily and to see it whole, and shut themselves off from much that gives dignity and grace to man's earthly existence, much that is capable of elevating his heart and mind. But let those blame them whose love for their Master and concern for the spiritual welfare of others can match the all-consuming zeal which distinguished them.

In view of this it is not surprising to find Evangelicals deficient in any appreciation of art and the æsthetic side of life. Some went further, and, with the Puritans, looked upon beauty as the snare of the evil one, a siren voice luring them from the strait path of righteousness. Wesley himself, though in other ways a man of high culture and sensitive to beauty in nature, shared in this view, and had a distinct aversion for the subjects portrayed in the great masters. On visiting a famous collection at Seaton Delaval on May 19, 1764, he wrote that he had seen "such pictures as an honest heathen would be ashamed to receive under his roof, unless he designed his wife and daughters should be common prostitutes. And this is the high fashion! What an abundant proof of the taste of the present age!"[2] To fear the beautiful, however, is the mark of a morbid and unenlightened mind; for there is a "spirit of beauty in the universe which communicates with the faculty of beauty in man".[3]

The lack of an æsthetic sense showed itself in the bareness of the worship in Evangelical churches; though not in them alone, since all parties regarded elaborate and ornamental services as savouring of Popery.[4] But the Evangelicals would still persist in this course when others had abandoned it, and, in Ruskin's view, would actually take pride in degrading their

---

[1] *Cardiphonia*, p. 231 [2] *Journal*, v, pp. 69 f.

[3] Gore, *Belief in God*, p. 54. Henry Martyn's experience was probably unusual, for he could write: "Since I have known God in a saving manner, painting, poetry, and music, have had charms unknown to me before" (quoted Sargent, *Life of H. Martyn*, p. 53)

[4] So the Church in the early empire, in avoiding the "sensuousness" of paganism, fostered an æsthetic of ugliness

worship: "The group calling themselves Evangelical ought no longer to render their religion an offence to men of the world by associating it only with the most vulgar forms of art. It is not necessary that they should admit either music or painting into religious service; but, if they admit either the one or the other, let it not be bad music nor bad painting."[1] They did not seem to realize that the church, God's house, should be at least as dignified and as beautiful as the houses of His worshippers, and that everything done in it should be performed with due care and reverence. The lack of æsthetic taste may have prevented the Evangelicals from appealing to certain temperaments; but, if so, it saved them from the opposite extreme by which such temperaments exaggerate the ritual and æsthetic side of religion, until religion itself becomes little more than a species of fine art.

When, however, all this has been admitted, there is another aspect that must not be forgotten. If the Evangelicals had no appreciation of art, and even feared many forms of beauty, they certainly achieved lives of admirable loveliness; and the saints, too, as Walter Pater recognized, have their place in the house beautiful.

The bareness of Evangelical worship and carelessness over its conduct, at least on the ceremonial side, were very largely due to the unconscious idea that its real object was not the glory of God, but the edification of His people. One may even suspect that some of the more earnest of the Evangelical clergy fell into the Puritan habit of "preaching" the prayers, as though they were addressed, not to God, but to the congregation. In this connexion something may be said about the accusation brought against them that they unduly exalted preaching at the expense of all else. That they exalted it cannot be denied; but they also recognized its limitations; Berridge, for example, wrote to John Thornton on February 22, 1779; "Perhaps this is an age of much hearing, than much praying. The old puritan spirit of devotion is not kindling and breathing among us."[2] Nor did they belittle Holy Communion;[3] on the contrary, it may be said that they were largely responsible for restoring the practice of more frequent communions. In any case, the emphasis on preaching was no new thing; it was characteristic of the religion of the day, as can be seen from the interior arrangement of most churches, where architecturally the altar

---

[1] *Modern Painters*, Pt. IV, Chap. iv, § 23   [2] *Works*, p. 405
[3] See Smyth, *Simeon and Church Order*, p. 228, with the references there given

is often overshadowed or even completely concealed by the pulpit.[1]

Had their worship possessed a deeper sense of awe it might have done something to correct that lack of reverence and reticence in the things of the spirit, which Evangelicals, though not to the same degree, shared with the Methodists. Here again a defect arose from a virtue. Evangelicals were urged to testify to their experiences and to use every opportunity of turning ordinary conversation in a religious direction. This habit frequently led to the dragging down of sacred subjects to a common level, if not to hypocrisy. Much harm was done in this way by vulgar advocates, both to themselves and to the cause they thought to serve. John Thornton, writing to Simeon in November, 1782, warned him against "noisy professors; they are far more to be dreaded than the worldly-minded".[2] Their ignorant zeal could not fail to grate upon more sensitive souls, whose religious feelings, if not so demonstrative, were just as real and deep.

> Why should gentle hearts and true
> Bare to the rude world's withering view
> Their treasure of delight?[3]

After all, there is a time and a place for everything.

This desire to pour out spiritual experiences, which seemed so blatant to more sober-minded Christians, arose in part from that over-emphasis on the emotional side of religion which characterizes all "revival" movements. It was, perhaps, an unconscious attempt to feel once again that high rapture which had marked conversion. But if the turning to God had been accompanied by exalted feelings, such a level could not long be maintained, and the endeavour to prolong it only led to severe tension and constant disappointment. If one may be allowed the comparison, it is like a man and woman falling in love. This begins at an intense emotional level which cannot persist indefinitely—it is too exhausting, too unsuited to everyday life—and no healthy or permanent relationship can be

---

[1] Wickham Legg, *English Church Life*, etc., pp. 148 f., who cites St. Augustine, *Contra Epist. Manichaei*, viii (Migne Patr. Latin., XLII, col. 79), where it is said that the Manichees dressed up a pulpit in the middle of the church and then worshipped before it

[2] Quoted Moule, *op. cit.*, p. 40

[3] Keble's hymn for Lent, IV, from which this is an extract, was written as a protest against the unreserved pouring forth of religious experiences which was still common in his day. Cf. also his review of "The Life of Sir Walter Scott" (*Occasional Papers and Reviews*, p. 17)

maintained at such heights. So is it in the life of the soul. Real progress is achieved, not by trying to live at an impossibly high emotional level,[1] but by joyfully accepting the seemingly dull and commonplace as part of the soul's training, and even times when the face of God seems to be hidden.

The undesirability of attempts to work up the feelings was recognized by the wiser leaders, for they knew that such efforts are enervating and dangerous;[2] it was "the depth and not the tumult of the soul" that really counted. The real test of love to God lay in obedience and a worthy life. Cecil reports that Newton once said: "Don't tell me of your feelings. A traveller would be glad of fine weather, but, if he be a man of business, he will go on."[3] Some even suspected their own reactions to emotional appeals. So Henry Martyn could write in his journal for June 24, 1804: "At times during the service, had a joyful sense of the divine presence, but as it was chiefly during the hymns, I think these affections suspicious."

None the less, there was a tendency to confuse "spiritual" religion with emotional religion, and to regard those who did not readily reveal their deepest feelings as deficient in experience. Evangelicals did not realize that an "intellectual" religion may be just as spiritual as an emotional one; so much depends on the individual temperament. Here again a secular parallel is enlightening. The appeal of music for some people is almost purely sensuous; they delight in the sound and the response it evokes in their feelings; to others, who are capable of an even profounder experience, enjoyment is largely intellectual, and they can find delight in the mere study of a musical score.

Over-emphasis on the emotions may easily lead to a distrust of reason and to a conception of faith, not only as justifying, but as the only way of enlightenment. This had been Wesley's attitude even before the formation of the Holy Club at Oxford. On November 22, 1725, he wrote that "saving faith (including practice) is an assent to what God has revealed because He has revealed it, and not because the truth of it may be evinced by reason."[4] Reason alone, it cannot be denied, is incapable

---

[1] The Methodist notion that "religion of the heart" was "a continuation of rapturous impressions" was condemned by Walker (Sidney, *Life of Walker*, p. 156)

[2] Cf. W. James, *Varieties of Religious Experience*, p. 340: "Spiritual excitement takes pathological forms whenever other interests are too few and the intellect too narrow"

[3] *Memoirs of Newton*, p. 78   [4] *Letters*, i, p. 25

of arriving at spiritual truth; it must take account of religious experience. But such experience in turn must be tested at the bar of reason, and to ignore its claims may produce unfortunate consequences. This, according to a Liberal Evangelical of our own day, was the weakness of the older Evangelicals, who "were apt to interpret . . . experience in somewhat narrow terms; emphasizing the feelings rather than the reason, indeed often neglecting the reason altogether, and in the extreme wing of the party laying claim to an infallible knowledge of the working of the divine Spirit within the heart".[1]

Here again the wiser among the leaders saw the danger of any depreciation of reason. That was the case with Walker; whilst Simeon said that his sermons were to be regarded "not as the effects of enthusiasm, but as the rational dictates of a heart impressed with a sense both of the value of the soul and the importance of eternity."[2]

There is a sense in which it would be true to call the Evangelical movement an unintellectual movement; but it would be a grave error to look upon its leaders as mere "unlearned fanatics". Many of them had been fellows of their colleges, and others, but for their known views, would have attained the same distinction; Isaac Milner had had *incomparabilis* attached to his name in the Mathematical tripos; whilst Henry Martyn was also an outstanding mathematician. But even when reason, and learning with it, were recognized, they were given but a subordinate place, and many Evangelicals would, I suppose, have agreed with Wesley's estimate, written in 1763: "What I believe concerning learning is this: that it is highly expedient for a guide to souls, but not absolutely necessary. What I believe to be absolutely necessary is, a faith unfeigned, the love of God and our neighbour, a burning zeal for the advancement of Christ's kingdom, with a heart and life wholly devoted to God."[3] There were, of course, some who despised learning and even regarded it as evil. When Berridge heard that Whitefield's orphan house in Georgia had been burnt down in 1773, he took it as a sign of the divine displeasure that it had been "perverted" into "a lumber-house for human learning".[4] But Berridge was no typical Evangelical in his attitude to learning, or to many other things.

The need for learning was recognized by the leaders of the

---

[1] V. F. Storr, *The Development of English Theology*, etc., pp. 322 f.
[2] Quoted Moule, *op. cit.*, p. 47   [3] *Works*, xiv, p. 329
[4] Wesley also regretted the change (*Letters*, v, pp. 183 f.; vi, p. 41)

movement, inasmuch as they insisted that ordinands should give full attention to the intellectual side of their training. Cecil is especially outspoken in this matter. "What then should a young minister or candidate for the ministry do? His office says, 'Go to your books: Go to retirement: Go to prayer.' 'No,' says the enthusiast, 'Go to preach. Go to be a witness.' A witness of what? He don't know."[1] Simeon made a point of warning young men at the university that they must devote themselves to their proper studies, even though these were "secular"; and the reading of the Bible itself did not excuse neglect.[2] Had more of the early Evangelicals taken as strong a line as Simeon, the movement might have been preserved from that defective sense of history which was one of its limitations and the cause of the alienation of some of its adherents. This was one of the reasons why Newman repudiated Evangelicalism; it seemed to him to base its whole idea of Christianity on the Bible alone, and to ignore the subsequent history of the Church.[3]

Another weakness arose from the notion that since the whole Bible was inspired, the Old Testament had equal value with the New. This led to an outlook which was too definitely Hebraic, an outlook which was shared even by those Evangelicals who had had a classical training and delighted to continue their studies so far as time allowed. In this they were at one with the Puritans, whom they also followed in their avoidance of worldly pleasures, even some that were entirely innocent. Pleasure, indeed, was hardly suited to dwellers in a lost world. There are in Christianity two distinct elements which may be called "world renouncing" and "world penetrating". The Evangelicals over-emphasized the former; to-day the emphasis is all on the latter. In this matter a study of the Evangelicals can help to redress the balance, for both are necessary to the development of the highest and most healthy spiritual life, whether of the individual or of the community. The world cannot entirely be avoided by the Christian, but he may strive in part to redeem it. Those who attempt to cut themselves

---

[1] *Works*, i, p. 166

[2] Carus, *op. cit.*, p. 843; Brown, *Recollections of the Conversation Parties of Simeon*, pp. 193 f.

[3] It was this defect which drove Harold Browne from their ranks. Having read the fathers of the Primitive Church, he found Evangelicalism defective. Christianity "was to them a Divine revelation of God's will, retold in each generation for the heirs of salvation; not the steady growth of the Church, the great family of God in Christ" (Kitchen, *Bishop Harold Browne*, pp. 48, 50)

off from it miss a valuable school of training, and may lose sympathy with their fellow men.

Puritanism, and Evangelicalism in so far as it had the same outlook, suffers from two grave errors: it tends to make life too simple, and in its practice it is too negative. Life is a very complex matter and conduct cannot easily be divided up into exact categories of right and wrong. In theory we can imagine good and evil as distinct entities, just as we can imagine a straight line or a pure colour; but in real life good and evil are never found in a pure state. Therein lies our tragedy, and also our hope.[1] But an older generation did not recognize this, and thought that direct and infallible answers were possible on all ethical questions. Were they not provided for in the divine Law? Morality, for them, was a fixed and rigid affair, and their applications of the moral law were often cruel and arbitrary; for Puritanism is not content to adopt such views for itself, it ever seeks to enforce them upon others. But restrictions imposed by moralists often provoke strong reactions, and modern psychology has taught us the dangers of repressions. It may be that Cowper, for example, suffered in this way; for, as Chesterton has quaintly put it: "He was damned by John Calvin, he was almost saved by John Gilpin". The community, as well as the individual, may also react (as in the days of the Restoration) against a manner of life which is repellent and only accepted unwillingly.

The other grave defect in Puritanism was that it was too negative, seeming to regard the avoidance of evil as more important than the doing of good. This is, of course, the easier line to pursue; for certain things can be marked off as evil and therefore to be avoided; but the positive following of good is a more difficult matter. Milton, not perhaps so good a Puritan as is sometimes supposed, had recognized this failing, and in the *Areopagitica* had declared: "a dram of well-doing should be preferred before many times as much the forcible hindrance of evil doing."

We must not, however, suppose that all Evangelicals went as far as the Puritans, or that they regarded life with such undue severity. Cecil saw clearly the defects of Puritanism, and wrote: "The Puritans treated man as though he had nothing of the animal about him. There was among them a total excision of

[1] Contrasts can readily be found between crude melodrama and the works of the great dramatists. In Shakespeare, it is the unselfish ambition of Lady Macbeth which leads her to commit crime; and it is the loving daughter who wrecks the heart of Lear. Cf. W. Temple, *Mens Creatrix*, pp. 137 ff.

all amusement and recreation. Everything was effort, everything was severe."[1] Life thus became unduly strained and tense, for the Puritans had not learned, again to quote Milton, that:

> mild Heav'n
> ... disapproves that care, though wise in show,
> That with superfluous burden loads the day
> And, when God sends a cheerful hour, refrains.[2]

Not a few Evangelicals were redeemed from a too portentous gravity by a strong sense of humour. This may be illustrated by a story told of Jones of Creaton. On one occasion he was approached by a man who had often imposed on his predecessor. The man announced himself, with smug hypocrisy, as "a poor pilgrim travelling to Mount Sion". Jones at once replied "I wish you a pleasant journey", and then left him.[3]

Certain amusements were condemned as definitely worldly, and if the list seems to us unduly comprehensive we have to remember the very different state of society in which the early Evangelicals lived. Even Henry Martyn pressed a clerical friend to give up cards, plays, dances, and worldly company.[4] There was no objection, however, to drinking wine, for the evils of intemperance did not then seem to have been realized, and wine was the usual accompaniment of a meal.[5]

Most of the Evangelical leaders condemned card playing and sometimes expressed their disapproval of a common practice in somewhat unusual ways. When Romaine was asked to join in a game and the cards were produced, he said, "Let us ask the blessing of God." His hostess in her surprise exclaimed: "I never heard of such a thing before a game of cards." Romaine then said: "Ought we to engage in anything on which we cannot ask God's blessing?"—and the cards were removed. On another occasion a lady in his congregation told him that she was willing to follow all that he required except to give up cards; she could not be happy without them. "Then, madam," replied Romaine, "cards are your God, and they must save you."[6]

Perhaps the most burdensome of all the Evangelical restrictions was in regard to the keeping of Sunday, which they

---

[1] Quoted Overton, *The Evangelical Revival*, pp. 78 f. [2] *To Cyriac Skinner*
[3] Owen, *Memoir of Jones of Creaton*, p. 337
[4] *Journal* for September 2, 1804
[5] Cf. *op. cit.* for January 18, 1805; Wesley, *Journal*, iii, p. 450; *Life of Wilberforce*, iv, p. 322
[6] Ryle, *Christian Leaders*, etc., p. 170

equated with the Jewish sabbath. Only the most necessary work was to be performed on it, and a farmer who took advantage of a fine Sunday to gather in the harvest was regarded as well-nigh lost.[1] Romaine's father went so far as to forbid any of his family to go out on Sunday, except to church, and the whole day was devoted to the reading of the Bible and "other devout exercises at home".[2] But even on the question of the observance of Sunday there were Evangelicals who took a broader view, and, whilst recognizing the extreme importance of the custom, were willing on occasion to use it for labour in a good cause. This was the case with Wilberforce, and his diary contains entries such as the following: "Spent Sunday as a working day—did not go to church—Slave Trade. Gave up Sunday to slave business—did business and so ended the sabbath. I hope it was a grief to me the whole time to turn it from its true purposes." He also objected to the use of the word sabbath for Sunday, though this had been his own practice. "I don't like to call it the sabbath, as I do not consider it in the light in which it is viewed by many religious men."[3] But those who showed a tendency to "profane" the sabbath were liable to stern criticism. Even clergymen who drove to church, often a necessary proceeding in the case of the elderly or sickly, did not escape. Rowland Hill once found on his desk a note saying that the prayers of the congregation were desired for him "that he will not go riding about in his carriage on a Sunday". He read it out and then added: "If the writer of this piece of impertinence is in the congregation and will go into the vestry after service, and let me put a saddle on his back, I will ride him home instead of going in my carriage."[4] On a like occasion Henry Venn Elliott, to whom a carriage was a necessity, quoted in his defence the practice of the Shunammite woman who had her ass saddled on the sabbath (2 Kings 4: 23 f.).

Some of the clergy were also censured for card-playing. Adam, as a young man, had been exceedingly fond of it, but gave it up in order not to offend weaker souls. Towards the end of his life, however, he reverted to the practice as a means of relaxation; but again abandoned it as some scandal was aroused. Isaac Milner, though he never felt that card playing, except for

---

[1] Cranmer in his visitation articles had told the clergy to teach their people that they would grievously offend God if they did *not* work on Sunday in harvest time
[2] Cadogan in *Works of Romaine*, p. 2
[3] *Life*, i, pp. 289 f.; v, p. 143   [4] Sidney, *Life of Rowland Hill*, p. 120

money, was an evil, also gave it up for a similar reason. But he still kept a pack for tricks. An old friend finding it on his table remonstrated with him, whereupon the dean rather caustically replied: "While you live never be afraid of bugbears."[1]

This over-censorious spirit was unfortunately only too common among Evangelicals. Newton observed that it was especially prevalent among young converts who "can hardly bear with any who do not discover the same earnestness as themselves".[2] Criticism was not limited to what were regarded as worldly habits; it was also extended to preaching. Berridge was far too fond of condemning others as no true "gospel labourers".[3] The habit was often discouraging to young clergymen. When Simeon preached for Riland at St. Mary's, Birmingham, in August, 1783, the latter "did not say one word of commendation of the sermon but found fault with it on account of tautology, and want of richness in the application".[4]

This tendency to criticize others and to think them in error was a natural sequel of Evangelical "individualism" and confidence in divine guidance. Others who differed from them must be deluded. Here also Newton has some wise remarks: "A man, truly illuminated, will no more despise others, than Bartimeus, after his own eyes were opened, would take a stick, and beat every blind man he met." And again: "Do you reflect that another Christian may be doing God's work, though his mode of doing it may not meet your taste, any more than your taste meets his?"[5]

One motive for this critical spirit was undoubtedly the conviction, largely unconscious, that the powers of evil were so strong that constant vigilance was necessary in reviewing their own lives and those of others. No risks could be taken, for even an angel of light might prove to be an emissary of the prince of darkness. Such criticism, often dignified by the term "speaking the truth in love", caused much pain to those who, often quite unjustly, were subjected to it. Even men and women of advanced spirituality and kindly nature could indulge in it. A daughter-in-law of the Thorntons once exclaimed bitterly: "If there were a spot upon the glorious sun himself the Thorntons would notice it."[6] Henry Martyn, who suffered much from the

---

[1] *Life of Dean Milner*, p. 54   [2] *Cardiphonia*, p. 12
[3] *Countess of Huntingdon*, ii, pp. 422 ff.
[4] See his letter to Henry Venn in Carus, *op. cit.*, p. 55
[5] Cecil, *Memoirs of Newton*, pp. 78, 92
[6] Quoted E. M. Forster, *Abinger Harvest*, p. 242. Mr. Forster, it may be remarked, was the great-grandchild of Henry Thornton

well-meant but often tactless criticisms of his elders, wrote in his journal for March 22, 1805: "Why do I look for my happiness even to the saints? They are able to wound the feelings of their brethren even as others."

Such were some of the defects and limitations which impeded the progress of the Evangelical movement, and again I would emphasize that they are exposed in no spirit of hostile criticism, but as faults to be avoided by their successors, and, indeed, by Christians of every allegiance. I have also been at pains to point out that they were, in large measure, discerned by the wiser leaders of the movement at the time. That in spite of them Evangelicals achieved so much in extending the Kingdom of God and revivifying the Church is a strong testimony to their inherent strength and effectiveness. Truly God was with them.

CHAPTER 24

THE POSITION AT 1789

By 1789 the fruits of the Evangelical Movement were already being garnered, though so far the harvest was not large. In our period its efforts had been chiefly experimental and unco-ordinated, as, indeed, was fitting in an age which was predominantly one of pioneering; but now a change was becoming apparent, the Evangelicals were being shaped into a definite party within the Church, even though such unity as they possessed was still rather one of spiritual sympathy and co-operation than of outward organization. This inner bond, however, was no bad preliminary to something more tangible; it was, indeed, valued as a necessary preparation. "There is", as Romaine said, "a union which sanctifies all others",[1] and he and some like-minded clerics were accustomed to spend an hour every Friday in prayer for one another.[2]

If the Evangelicals were making tentative efforts at unity, they were also becoming clearly distinguishable from the Methodists. The Calvinist controversy had shown that they were unwilling to accept Wesley as their leader, whilst the secession of Lady Huntingdon and her followers had cut them off from the other branch of Methodism. Henceforth they would stand more firmly on their own feet. This was all to the good, for it freed them from influences which, though professing to be loyal to the Church, were really alien to its ethos. The whole movement gained in balance, sobriety, and reverence by the withdrawal of these turbulent elements, and was, moreover, in a stronger position to appeal to those Churchmen who, though in sympathy with their teaching, or much of it, were loathe to identify themselves with anything which savoured of Methodism and its devices.

Henceforth little is heard of Evangelicals itinerating in other men's parishes, though the desire to act as wandering evangelists seems to have persisted in the hearts of some who contemplated ordination. These were sternly discouraged, but as late as March, 1798, Cecil wrote to Daniel Wilson, who had asked his advice about taking orders:

[1] *Works*, p. 534   [2] *Op. cit.*, pp. 15 ff.

I love consistency. If you think you have a general call to evangelize and to go about proclaiming the glad tidings of salvation, then you cannot conscientiously enter the Established Church. Now I don't call Mr. Whitefield or Mr. Berridge inconsistent characters. They entered the Church in the simplicity of their hearts; God afterwards called them to another line. . . . But to promise regularity while at the same time a man intends to be irregular, cannot be done with a good conscience.[1]

It has to be remembered that even after the split many Methodists retained a connexion with the Church, and frequently attended its worship and made regular communions. Some still observed the rule of not holding meetings during the time of divine service. The replies to Bishop Barrington's questions on his primary visitation in 1792 show that the clergy carefully distinguished between Methodists and Dissenters.

The Evangelicals, however, were not anxious to keep up any link with Methodism, which, especially after the death of Wesley, became definitely a form of Dissent, and as such was to be avoided; the sons of Isaac must not frequent the tabernacles of Ishmael. Even Henry Martyn took this view and notes in his journal for September 2, 1804: "Mr. Andrews, a Methodist, begged me to preach at their chapel, which I refused, of course." There was, also, a distinct tendency to minimize the connexion which had existed in earlier days,[2] and especially to apologize for indulgence by some Evangelical clergy in irregular practices. There is a striking passage in the *Life of Henry Venn*, which had been prepared by his son, John Venn, and was edited by his grandson, Henry Venn junior. The former says:

> Induced by the hope of doing good, my father, in certain instances preached in unconsecrated places. But having acknowledged this, it becomes my pleasing duty to state that he was no advocate for irregularity in others; that when he afterwards considered it in its different bearings and connexions he lamented that he had given way to it, and restrained several other persons from such acts by the most cogent arguments.

[1] Bateman, *Life of Daniel Wilson*, i, pp. 40 f.   [2] See above p. 134

Another illustration may be found in connexion with Joseph Milner's *Essay on Methodism*, included by William Richardson in a posthumous collection of his works. Richardson disliked the title, thinking that it might connect those "who act in an orderly way, with the proper Methodists. What was then termed Methodism, is now called Evangelicalism". In a later edition, after consultation with Dean Milner, "the vile term Methodism" was expunged, and "Evangelical Religion" substituted.[1]

Some of the dislike of being associated with Methodists may have had a social origin, especially when Evangelicalism began to spread among the upper and middle classes. This possibly is one reason for Hannah More's vigorous protest against having had dealings with Dissenters. She wrote to the Bishop of Bath and Wells in 1801:

> As to connexion with conventicles of any kind, I never had any. Had I been irregular, should I not have gone sometimes, during my winter residence at Bath, to Lady Huntingdon's chapel, a place of great occasional resort? Should I never have gone to some of Whitefield's or Wesley's tabernacles, in London where I have spent a long spring for thirty years? Should I not have strayed now and then into some Methodist meeting in the country? Yet not one of these things have I ever done.[2]

To Hannah More some of the credit is due (as to Hervey at an earlier date) for the favourable attitude of some of the better educated towards Evangelicalism, but in this Cowper was the chief agent. "The bitterest enemy of Evangelicalism who read Cowper's poems could not deny that here at least was one man, a scholar and a gentleman, with a refined and cultured mind and a brilliant wit, who was not only favourably disposed to the obnoxious doctrines, but held them to be the very life and soul of Christianity."[3] But purely literary influences alone cannot account for the growth of the movement among the upper and middle classes. It might remove prejudice and prepare the way; but, to gain adherents, personal work was necessary. This, I think, was provided largely by the increasing

---

[1] *Life of Dean Milner*, p. 373
[2] Quoted Russell, *Short Hist. of the Evangel. Movement*, p. 45
[3] Abbey and Overton, ii, p. 200

body of influential laymen who had become Evangelicals, and the part which they were taking in the movement.

In this work, Wilberforce, as we have already seen, was very prominent, he felt that as a layman he had opportunities denied to the clergy. To spread the Gospel among the higher classes of the nation "was a work which could hardly be committed to the hands of any ecclesiastic; while it required for its proper execution the full devotion of rank, influence, and talents of the highest order".[1] In Wilberforce these qualities were found in an ever-increasing degree; so great, indeed, did his fame become, both here and on the Continent, that Victor Hugo could write to John Morley in April, 1866, "that the England he loved was the England of Shakespeare, of Newton, and of Wilberforce."[2] But that was still in the future, and in our period there were other laymen who probably did more for the movement than even Wilberforce, and his later reputation and the vast scale upon which he worked must not be allowed to obscure their achievements.

Notable among these earlier laymen were the Earl of Dartmouth; Ireland, the wealthy Bristol shipowner; William Hey, the devout physician; Richard Hill, and Robert Raikes, the Sunday School pioneer. The outstanding name, however, is that of John Thornton (1720–90). Thornton was a director of the Russia company and one of the wealthiest men of his day and his charities were magnificent. "Few have ever done more to feed the hungry, clothe the naked, and help all that suffer adversity."[3] He used his commercial connexions for the circulation of the Bible and other Christian works, and even had them printed at his expense.[4] But perhaps his main contribution to the party lay in his statesmanship; a quality in which the clerical leaders were somewhat lacking. Thornton applied his keen mind, which was used to dealing with affairs on a vast and comprehensive scale, to some of the problems which faced the party. He it was who inaugurated the policy, usually associated with the name of Simeon, of buying up advowsons so that there should be a continuity of Evangelical teaching in parishes where a change of incumbent might grievously affect it. His will, proved in 1790, appointed a body of clerical trustees, including John Venn, to fill vacancies as they arose.

Henry Thornton (1760–1815) followed closely in the steps of his father. Incidentally, it was his purchase in 1792 of Battersea

[1] *Life of Wilberforce*, i, p. 130
[2] Morley, *Recollections*, i, p. 74
[3] *Life of Henry Venn*, p. 482
[4] Cecil, *Memoir of Newton*, p. 333

Rise from one of the Lubbocks which provided the nucleus for the Clapham "sect". For years he spent but a small proportion of his income on himself, having decided that his ample fortune "ought never to be increased by accumulation, nor diminished by sumptiousness"; and devoted the rest to the encouragement of good works.

There were many other laymen who are known to have given active support to the movement whose names are no longer remembered, but whose influence had weight at the time. Among them were Eli Bates, the author of *A Chinese Fragment: containing an Enquiry into the Present State of Religion in England* (1786);[1] and John Jowett (1743-1800), a brother of Professor Jowett and great-uncle of Benjamin. Jowett was a native of Leeds, and came under the influence of Dr. Hey, with whom he used to walk over to Huddersfield to hear Venn. Later he moved to London, where he established a highly successful business. He was one of the founders of the Church Missionary Society, and his daughter, Elizabeth, married Josiah Pratt. His youngest son William, fellow of St. John's College, Cambridge, who ended his days as rector of Clapham, where he succeeded John Venn, was the first Cambridge graduate to volunteer for the Church Missionary Society.

The accession of these wealthy laymen was a great asset to the movement; but it had its dangers. Thomas Scott lamented the growth of luxurious habits among some of them, and especially their elaborate dinners (for which in the next generation the Clapham sect would also be criticized). At one dinner a prominent cleric exclaimed: "If we proceed thus, we shall soon get the gout numbered among the privileges of the gospel!" Scott could not take the matter so light-heartedly, and his outspoken comments led to a cessation of invitations to such feasts.[2] Even among the Methodists the growth of riches was presenting problems, and Wesley wrote in the *Arminian Magazine* for 1789: "Do not you seek happiness in dress, furniture, pictures, gardens; or anything else which pleases the eye? Do not you grow soft and delicate? unable to bear cold, heat, the wind or the rain, as you did when you were poor? Are you not increasing in goods, laying up treasures on earth; instead of restoring to God, in the poor, not so much or so much, but all that you can spare?"

[1] Pearson, *Life of Hey*, ii, pp. 27 ff. He anticipated the device of Lowes Dickinson's *Letters from a Chinese Official*
[2] *Life*, pp. 243 f.

THE POSITION AT 1789

Although certain fields of notable Evangelical activity were not fully occupied before 1789, there were already signs of interest in them. Such was the question of slavery. This was potentially abolished with the coming of Jesus into the world; and St. Paul unconsciously foretold the manner of its abolition, not of necessity but willingly, in his letter to Philemon; but it took seventeen centuries for Christians to realize that it was fundamentally inconsistent with their faith. Even among the leaders of the revival movement, this inconsistency was only realized gradually. Whitefield bought a number of slaves in 1751 to work the land attached to his Orphan House in Georgia (hoping that they might be instructed in the Christian faith), and was quite convinced of his right to make use of them. "As for the lawfulness of keeping slaves, I have no doubt, since I hear of some that were bought with Abraham's money, and some that were born in his house."[1] Hervey, in return for Whitefield's hospitality when in London, gave him £30 to buy a slave; adding, "may the Lord Jesus Christ give you, or rather take for Himself, the precious soul of the poor slave".[2] Wesley, however, recognized the evils of the slave trade, calling it on February 12, 1772, "that execrable sum of all villanies. . . . I read of nothing like it in the heathen world, whether ancient or modern; and it infinitely exceeds, in every instance of barbarity, whatever Christian slaves suffer in Mahometan countries".[3] His indignation had been aroused by reading a Quaker exposure of the system; and it was the Quakers who took a prominent part in the agitation against it. But without the influence and activities of Wilberforce it would hardly have been abolished as early as 1807. Although the agitation against the slave trade had been going on for many years it was not until 1775, when a commission was appointed to inquire into it, that any government action was taken. This was perhaps intended to quieten the agitators; but Granville Sharpe and the Quakers did not let the matter drop, and petitions were presented to Parliament and much literature was circulated. A further stimulus was given when Thomas Clarkson of St. John's College, Cambridge, was drawn into the agitation. It was not, however, until 1787 that Wilberforce's interest became acute. This arose from the suggestion of William Pitt, as he himself has recorded. "Pitt recommended me to undertake its conduct, as a subject suited to my character and

[1] *Works*, ii, p. 404   [2] Tyerman, *Oxford Methodists*, p. 277
[3] *Journal*, v, p. 446

talents. At length, I well remember, after a conversation in the open air at the root of an old tree at Holwood, just above the vale of Keston, I resolved to give notice on a fit occasion in the House of Commons of my intention to bring the subject forward."[1]

About the same time another cause to which Christians had been strangely blind began to attract attention, that of preaching the Gospel to all races of mankind. It is true that as early as 1701 the Society for the Propagation of the Gospel had been founded (it was this society which sent out the Wesleys and others to Georgia), but its activities had been but small; and in 1777 Watson, the future bishop, refused to support it on the grounds that it was more anxious to proselytize Dissenters than to convert the heathen. Eleven years later he gave it as his opinion that Christianity would be propagated more by science and commerce than by direct missionary activities. He little foresaw that science would one day discredit all religions for many educated heathen or that commerce would exploit the heathen for its own ends and so discredit Christianity. In any case, the annual income of the S.P.G. from subscribers was only about £500. The Society for Promoting Christian Knowledge also sent a few Lutherans to South India. Apart from the Church of England there had been Danish missions in India for seventy years; and the Moravians had begun work in Greenland, Labrador, and elsewhere; whilst the Methodists were active among the negroes in the West Indies. The Methodists were also concerned about India, but without any action being taken. Wesley records on February 14, 1784: "I desired all our Preachers to meet, and consider thoroughly the proposal of sending Missionaries to the East Indies. After the matter had been fully considered, we were unanimous in our judgment, that we have no call thither yet, no invitation, no providential opening of any kind."[2]

The Evangelicals were also turning their thoughts in the same direction, though it was not until 1799 that the Church Missionary Society was founded. It arose largely through what was known as the Eclectic Society.[3] This society had been founded in 1783 for religious discussions. It had only four members to begin with: Newton, Cecil, Henry Foster, and the layman, Eli Bates; but others were soon added to their number, including some from the country, of whom Simeon was one.

[1] *Life*, i, pp. 150 f.   [2] *Journal*, vi, p. 476
[3] See, further, Hole, *Early Hist. of the C.M.S.*, pp. 16 ff.

There was also a move to establish societies for work at home as well as overseas. The Society for Promoting Christian Knowledge had been founded in 1698; but, like its sister, the Society for the Propagation of the Gospel, had not shown any great enterprise. In 1777 a society was established to circulate the Bible among the men in His Majesty's forces; it received such meagre support, however, that it soon fell into debt.[1] These rather tentative efforts did not seem to hold out much promise, but the years which followed, in spite of the outbreak of the Napoleonic Wars, would witness an amazing development in the formation of organizations for such purposes.[2] In the meantime they showed that men's minds were being turned in the right direction, and when founded would do much to unite those who sympathized with the doctrines of the revival; the Evangelicals, in particular, would owe an immense debt to the C.M.S. as a unifying force.

We have already, in Chapters 13 to 19 above, taken notice of the spread of Evangelical views in various parts of the country and in the universities. They show that, though general, it was of different intensity in different areas; whilst at the universities Evangelicalism, discouraged at Oxford, was establishing itself in Cambridge. Equally varied were the effects upon it of the spread of Methodism. In some districts where Methodism was strong, such as Yorkshire and Bristol, it also flourished; in others, such as Newcastle and London, its progress was but slow and uncertain; whilst in Cornwall it had lost the advantage of an early start. Conventional Churchmanship was strongly entrenched in the cathedral cities, and they were immune to the effects of the revival; this was true even of Carlisle, where Milner was Dean. So, too, the spas, which would become notable centres of Evangelicalism, had made little response; the golden age of Bath, Tunbridge Wells, and Cheltenham still lay in the future.

In London, after facing much discouragement, the movement was at last making headway. Henry Venn, writing in 1783, expressed himself as delighted with the number and quality of the Evangelical clergy there, mentioning among others, "the admirable talents and evangelical preaching of Dr. Peckwell".[3] In the growing towns also the movement was making way. Venn, commenting on this, had written in 1774: "When I set out, twenty-four years ago, I knew but of Truro

[1] Romaine, *Works*, p. 25
[2] See my *Religion in the Victorian Era*, pp. 36 ff., 375 ff. [3] *Life*, pp. 361 f.

and Bradford in Wiltshire where the Gospel was preached in towns."[1]

By 1789 the position had improved still further, with the work of Robinson at Leicester, Cadogan at Reading, not to mention the various Yorkshire towns. There was, indeed, a new readiness to hear the message. Jones of Creaton wrote, in May, 1787, of the neighbouring counties of Northamptonshire and Leicestershire, "wherever an open door is made for the gospel ... the churches are crowded ... gospel ministers are increasing".[2] In addition, there was a much more sympathetic attitude on the part of those who were not ready to identify themselves fully with the party. This held out great promise for future growth.

But if the number of Evangelical clergymen was steadily increasing, and the breakdown of prejudice was opening more and more pulpits to them, there was no sign of the party's possessing influence in the Church at large. Save for Dean Milner and Archdeacon Bassett, no Evangelical clergyman had received high preferment. This neglect in the case of Walker had aroused the indignation of Hervey, who wrote: "What a reproach it is to our men in power, nay to the nation itself, that so valuable a person should at this time of life be no more than a country curate. But he, good man, disregards the things of this world."[3] A reputation for holding Evangelical views might even stand in the way of advancement. Cadogan, it is said, was for this reason passed over when a canonry was vacant at Westminster.[4] Newton once humorously remarked to a friend, that if the devil "had the disposal of preferments, since he knows the effect of them, you and I should soon be dignitaries."[5]

The Evangelicals certainly did not suffer from that all too frequent clerical complaint, obsession with the thought of preferment. They realized that such things were not for them; and many, as with the early Tractarians, deliberately avoided opportunities which came their way. This was the case with Thomas Adam when his former tutor became Archbishop of York. Fletcher also refused to avail himself of the favourable notice taken by George III of his pamphlets on the American War of Independence—and when the Lord Chancellor inquired, at the royal command, if he could serve him in any way, he replied: "I want nothing but more grace."

---

[1] *Op. cit.*, p. 209   [2] Owen, *Memoir of Jones of Creaton*, p. 104
[3] Quoted Sidney, *Life of Walker*, p. 557   [4] Cecil, *Memoirs of Cadogan*, p. lx
[5] Cecil, *Memoirs of Newton*, p. 80

THE POSITION AT 1789 455

If, however, those in authority were chary in promoting Evangelicals, there was a growing recognition of the good work that they were doing; they were even held up to the rest of the clergy as examples, especially of the effects of preaching the full Gospel. Bishop Horsley in his charge of 1790 said that if the people were "nourished with the sincere milk of the word, by their proper pastors, they would refuse a drink of doubtful quality mingled by a stranger. In a word, our churches would be thronged; while the moralizing Unitarian would be left to read his dull weekly lecture to the walls of his deserted conventicle; and the Field-Preacher would bellow unregarded to the wilderness."

This lack of influence no doubt saved the party in its early days from ecclesiastical politicians who might have been tempted to substitute carefully devised schemes for trust in spiritual power to advance their cause. None the less, if Evangelicals were to take their rightful place in the counsels of the Church, wise statesmanship would be necessary. This it had lacked; for its leaders had no policy beyond the conversion and care of individuals, and showed no capacity for estimating the needs of the complicated and varying situations in which the party found itself, much less of providing remedies for them. One great weakness was the absence of unity; the only unity they seemed to value was one of spiritual fellowship. Wesley had dismissed them as "a rope of sand"; and though this harsh judgment was aroused by their refusal to accept him as their leader, it had an element of truth in it. But it was not the whole truth, for in several centres there had been attempts to gather Evangelicals together; Walker had done it at Truro; there was the little group in South Yorkshire; and the Elland Society in the West Riding, not to mention the Eclectic Society. Walker, indeed, had in October, 1759, suggested, in a letter to Adam, that a resolution should be drawn up for Evangelical clergy to sign, professing their loyalty to the Church and its discipline and repudiating all irregularities. This might have been a first step to fuller organization. Adam, however, and Bassett with him, disliked the idea; it seemed to them to have the nature of a challenge and might cause clamour.[1]

One obvious reason for the lack of Evangelical unity was the absence of a single leader to whom they could look for guidance and direction. Here we have an interesting parallel to what took place in the sixteenth century. Protestants on the

[1] Sidney, *Life of Walker*, pp. 495 ff.

Continent might call themselves Lutherans or Calvinists, but the Anglican Reformation was the work of men who remained within the Church, and no single one of them was sufficiently outstanding to give his name to the movement, had such a step ever been contemplated. So in the revival movement of the eighteenth century there were those who looked up to Wesley or the Countess of Huntingdon as their leader; but loyal Churchmen refused to avow themselves as the disciples of any human master.

If an untimely death had not robbed the movement of the services of Walker he might very well have filled the role, but this is no necessary conclusion. G. O. Trevelyan regarded Newton as the founder of the Evangelicals as a party.[1] This is scarcely a sound judgment; none the less, Newton, after his arrival in London, formed a valuable centre, and he was in close touch with the growing body of laymen who were bringing new strength and direction to the movement. Henry Venn at Yelling was also from his retirement exercising a quiet but pervasive influence, especially through his contacts with the young men who were going forth from Cambridge to serve the cause. But it was at Cambridge itself that the man arose who would bring to Evangelicalism the mind of a statesman and the organizing ability which had previously been wanting. To Simeon, above all others, it was due that in the days to come Evangelicalism achieved greater unity and a more definite purpose; and so was in a position to meet the opportunities and the responsibilities which the coming years would provide.

Our period closes on the eve of the French Revolution. That outbreak, once its real nature was understood and the promise of its earlier days had been falsified, came as a profound shock to Englishmen (we see the extent of this shock in Wordsworth and Coleridge), and turned the thoughts of many of them into more serious channels. It was, to quote the Hammonds, "a warning against irreligion and the frivolous life. The red skies of Paris sobered the English Sunday and filled the English churches".[2] The outrages which accompanied its progress seemed to demonstrate the folly of trusting in things which could so easily be destroyed, and to establish the Evangelical and Christian doctrine of the fallen state of man. It now came to be easier to accept belief in the devil and in his power in the world. Thus the need for God and of some kind of religion

[1] *Life of Macaulay*, i, p. 9 [2] *The Town Labourer*, p. 235

became manifest to many who were beginning to take life seriously.

There were also other factors at work in the same direction. The influence of Voltaire and those who agreed with him had fostered a spirit of pessimism and unbelief. Men felt that they were involved in an existence which had no meaning and no hope. This generated a profound dissatisfaction and a consequent reaction which, in the spheres of literature and art, found expression in the Romantic movement. Many who became conscious of the futility of ideas which they had once eagerly embraced remained sceptical, for the time, and unwilling to commit themselves to more satisfying teaching. The shock of the French Revolution forced some of them to a point when decision became absolutely necessary.

It was the Evangelical Movement which, above all other forms of religion, reaped the main benefits of the newly-born seriousness, since it, more than its rivals, seemed to promise to meet the needs which had become so urgent. Similar teaching might, it need scarcely be emphasized, be found among the Methodists and other Dissenting sects; but many Dissenters had expressed their sympathy with the views of the revolutionaries, and the struggle with France which followed had called forth a new sense of loyalty in the nation; and that loyalty took the form of an increased attachment to the national Church. The various developments which had marked the Evangelical Movement during its early period had prepared it for this very emergency; the pioneering epoch was now past; unity within the party was growing, its aims and objects were more clearly seen; and so it was ready, under the guidance of God, to undertake the task of ministering to the newly-awakened longing for the things of the spirit. It was, indeed, about to enter upon a second spring.

INDEX

ABDY, WM., 241
Abingdon, 254
Adam, Thos., 131f., 159ff., 314f., 377, 402, 443, 454f.
Addison, 39, 79, 96
Aldwinckle, 290
Allegorical Interpretation, 386, 406
Almondbury, 323
America, 28f., 32f., 118, 126, 222f.
Andrews, John, 332
Anne, Queen, 23f., 100, 332
Antinomianism, 119, 144, 147, 178, 199f.
Apologetics, 14, 61, 66, 95, 406
Architecture, 82f.; see Houses.
Aristocracy, 18, 38, 40ff., 137ff., 337, 420
Arnold, Thos., 359, 410, 425, 434
Art, 21, 81ff., 195, 244f., 435f.
Articles, The Thirty-nine, 121, 170f., 203, 382, 385
Ashby-de-la-Zouch, 301, 304
Ashford, 344
Assington, 269
Aston Sandford, 255
Atkinson, Christopher, Sr., 317
do., do., Jr., 284, 364
do., Miles, 178, 317f., 379
Atonement, The, 113, 122f., 126, 136, 389, 395
Augustine, St., 116, 408, 412, 437

BADDILEY, JOHN, 313f.
Baildon, 316
Banstead, 163f.
Baptism, 393f.
Barrington, Bishop, 368, 421, 447
Barton, 283
Bassett, Archdeacon, 271, 377, 455
Bateman, R. T., 237f.
Bates, Eli, 450, 452
Bath, 144, 221, 231, 338ff., 379f., 391
Bathing, Sea, 18, 49
Batley, 299, 308
Baxter, Rd., 121, 216, 302
Bayley, Cornelius, 327, 379, 405
Bedford, 282f., 286
do., Chapel, 244f.
Belton (Leics.), 301
do. (Lincs.), 273
Bengeworth, 294f.
Bennett, Bishop, 283
Bennett, John, 349
Benson, Joseph, 177, 356
do., Bishop, 187
Bentley, Rd., 64, 105, 186
do., Roger, 318
Berridge, John, 131, 203, 205, 253f., 269, 273ff., 286, 288f., 297, 311, 360, 436; and Lady Huntingdon, 137, 177, 231, 246, 345; and J. Wesley, 279f.; Writings, 205, 280f., 417
Best, Edward, 293
Beveridge, Bishop, 129f., 265, 273, 410
Bexley, 249

Bible, The, 60, 113, 170, 173, 205, 385f., 398f., 427f., 440
Biddulph, Thos., 350
Bideford, 144, 344, 347f., 372
Bilston, 293
Bingley, 316, 379
Birmingham, 83, 199, 292f., 397
Birstall, 321
Bishops, The, 33, 100ff., 173f., 182, 223; and Methodism, 186ff., 219f., 225, 270, 307
Blackburne, Archdeacon, 171
Blackstone, 87, 108
Blagdon, 342
Blake, John, 247
Bliss, Thos., 344f.
Böhler, Peter, 119f.
Bolingbroke, Viscount, 87, 138f., 189
Bosanquet, Mary (Mrs. Fletcher), 299, 316f., 384
Boswell, Jas., 68, 73, 78, 400, 403
Bottomley, J., 309
Brackenbury, R. C., 214, 272
Bradford, 316f.
do., John, 293
do.-on-Avon, 234, 342
Bratoft, 263, 272
Breedon, 294, 301, 304
Brighton, 131, 137, 251f.
Bristol, 34, 125f., 185, 192, 229, 332ff., 350, 357, 392, 397
Broadhembury, 346
Brodbelt, G. C., 255
Broughton, Thos., 128, 237
Brown, "Capability," 83f., 263
do., Jas., 330, 341f.
Browne, Moses, 256f., 265f., 412f.
Buckley, Edward, 318f.
Bunyan, John, 98, 120f.
Burke, Edmund, 55, 73, 78, 171, 177
Burn, Edward, 293
Burnet, Bishop, 102, 265
Burnett, Geo., 178, 320
Bute, Lord, 27f.
Butler, Bishop, 26, 45, 58f., 85, 92, 94f., 101, 109ff., 115, 184f., 333
do., Samuel, 274
Buxton, 304
Byrom, John, 122, 128, 326, 417

CADOGAN, W. B., 240, 252f., 315, 454
Calvin, 385, 406, 441
Calvinism, 135, 197, 286, 296, 346f., 351, 388f., 394, 417; and the Church of England, 203, 356
Calvinist Controversy, The, 196ff., 280f.
Camberwell, 240
Cambridge, 232, 283ff.
do., Platonists, 184, 357, 410
do., University, 62, 64f., 171, 180, 357ff.
Card-playing, 50, 442ff.
Carlisle, 307, 453
Caroline of Anspach, Queen, 25, 97, 139
Catechizing, 157, 239, 323, 377

INDEX

Catlett, Mary (Mrs. Newton), 241, 258ff.
Cavendish, Henry, 57
Cecil, Rd., 244f., 257, 272, 301, 376, 390, 440ff., 446f., 452
Cennick, J., 120, 185, 229
Chapman, —., 330, 342
Chelsea, 240
Cheltenham, 86, 330
Chesham Bois, 255
Chesterfield, Lord, 43, 339
Children, 54f., 377, 426; Religious care for, 374ff. See also Catechizing, Sunday Schools.
Chipping, 327f.
do. Campden, 331
Christian Perfection, 198, 215, 384
Church Missionary Society, The, 164, 244, 320, 450, 452f.
Church Services, 106f., 151, 326, 435
Churches, New, 82f., 108f., 172, 305, 326f.
do., State of, 102, 109
Cirencester, 330
Clapham, 240, 246, 287, 450
Clark, Thos., 313
Clarke, Thos., 246, 255f.
Class Distinctions, 38, 65, 126, 141f.
Clayton, John, 128, 326f., 412
Clement, Benj., 294
Clergy, State of, 101ff., 174ff., 189, 337, 419; Social Position of, 102, 139, 174; Training of, 65f., 176ff., 440
ical Secessions, 113, 180ff., 195, 218, 230, 362
do. Societies, 157, 314, 455. See Elland Society.
Clerkenwell, 217f.
Clifton, 333
do., Raynes, 265
Clutton, 342
Coke, Dr., 223, 342
Colchester, 268f.
Coleridge, 121, 402, 404, 407
Collingtree, 143, 146
Collins, B. B., 209, 305
do., John, 351
Comberton, 268, 289
Communication, Means of, 13, 34f., 173, 287, 293, 308, 338
Communion, Holy, 101, 106, 227f., 364, 391ff., 436
Complete Duty of Man, The, 161, 271, 402f.
Congleton, 204
Congreve, 35, 49, 79
Conon, Geo., 133, 155ff., 350
Continental Influences, 21, 40f., 50, 83
Conversion, 16, 128, 190, 237, 310, 319, 385, 387f., 394, 424f.
Convocation, 99, 186
Conyers, Rd., 186, 240, 309ff.
Cookson, Dr., 270
Copleston, Bishop, 94
Cornwall, 155, 344f., 347ff.
Cornwood, 345
Coulthurst, H. W., 284, 320, 361
Cowper, Wm., 68f., 255f., 261ff., 441; Writings, 73, 397, 413; quoted, 67, 81, 105, 139f., 175, 181, 213, 256, 402

Crabbe, 31, 36, 51, 78, 105, 175ff.
Creaton, 290f.
Crime, 51f., 378
Crook, Hy., 319
Crosse, John, 230, 316f.
Cruelty, 48, 52, 422
Cudworth, Wm., 146f.

DARNEY, WM., 118, 150
Dartmouth, The Earl of, 38, 139f., 161, 217, 260f., 268, 293, 302, 310, 322, 330
Davies, Edward, 295
Deacon, Thos., 128, 326f.
De Coetlogon, Chas., 243f., 253, 360
De Courcy, Rd., 295f., 307
Defoe, 34, 74
Deism, 11, 91ff., 171, 336, 408, 424
Delamotte, Wm., 359
Deptford, 226, 240, 346
Derby, 222, 304
Devizes, 343
Dewsbury, 320
Dickinson, Peard, 209, 251
Disraeli quoted, 28, 36
Diss, 270
Dissenters, 66, 88, 91, 96, 179, 188, 193, 210f., 217, 228, 290, 391, 448
Dissenting Academies, 62, 66, 110f., 179, 328
Doddridge, Philip, 66, 111, 146, 193, 290, 415f.
Dodwell, Wm., 273
Downing, Geo., 268, 330
Drama, 49f., 79ff., 414, 441
Dress, 13, 21, 39f.
Drummond, Archbishop, 186, 324
Drunkenness, 46, 51, 55, 149, 320, 354, 358
Duelling, 50f.
Dummer, 127, 252
Dunham, Little, 270
Durbridge, Mrs., 269, 353
Dyer, Geo., 246

EARTHQUAKES, 90, 236f.
Easterbrook, Jos., 177, 192, 334f.
Eccleshall, 317
Eclectic Society, 332, 452
Eden, Thos., 342
Education, 13, 69ff., 338. See Dissenting Academies, Schools, Universities.
do., of Girls, 43f., 69
Edwards, E., 270
Eighteenth Century, 15ff., 23, 32, 53f., 59
Elland, 320
do. Society, 178, 255f., 361
Elliott, Hy. Venn, 375, 391, 443
Ellis, —., 301
Emotions, Appeal to the, 13, 56, 215, 374, 390, 437f.
Enthusiasm, 20f., 183ff.
Epworth, 271
Eton College, 66, 67f., 360, 364
Evangelical, The Term, 132
Evangelicals, Doctrines, 196f., 382ff.; Growth, 234ff., 247, 333, 448f., 453f.;

INDEX

Evangelicals—*continued.*
  Leaders, 15f., 168f., 244, 287, 409, 428ff., 439; and Learning, 56, 396, 398ff.; and Social Evils, 291, 302f., 335, 420ff.; and Methodists, 131ff., 149f., 158, 160, 169, 190f., 208ff., 332, 384, 447ff.; Lack of Unity, 169, 198, 208ff., 446, 453, 455
Evans, Maurice, 287
Evanson, Edward, 180f.
Everton, 274ff.
Evesham, 295
Exeter, 188, 343f., 346
Eyre, John, 252

FAITH, JUSTIFICATION BY, 143f., 196, 200, 274, 389f.
Fakenham, 221
Family Life, 46, 53, 376f., 426
Farish, Wm., 361
Fathers, Study of the, 412, 440
Feathers' Tavern, 171, 180
Field Preaching, 126, 164, 220f., 369f.
Fielding, Hy., 67, 70, 75, 77, 102f., 388
Fletcher, J. W., 200f., 203, 205, 207, 209f., 214, 294, 296ff., 327, 336, 454
Foote, Samuel, 195, 266
Forncett, 270
Foster, Hy., 167, 245f., 353, 452
Fox, Chas. Jas., 31, 50
French Protestants, 118, 236, 346
do. Revolution, 17, 31, 41, 358, 419f., 456f.
Furly, Samuel, 209f., 251, 323f., 350

GAINSBOROUGH, THOS., 38, 82
Gambling, 50, 339. See Card-playing.
Gambold, John, 124, 266
Gardens, 83f.
Garrick, David, 21, 79, 336f., 414
George I, 23ff., 50
do. II, 25f., 50, 101, 139, 339
do. III, 26ff., 80, 142, 179, 270, 454
Gibbon, Edward, 19, 31, 32, 40, 55, 60, 63f., 67, 95, 410
Gibbs, John, 334
Gibson, Bishop, 116, 186, 322
do., Joshua, 271
Gladstone, W. E., 28, 94, 390, 418, 421
Glascott, Cradock, 294, 345
Glazebrook, Jas., 173f., 214, 301, 328f.
Glentworth, 271
Gloucester, 330f., 378
Godday, Thos., 306
Godmanchester, 286
Goethe, 76, 94, 237
Goldsmith, Oliver, 36, 76, 79, 89, 108, 175
Goode, Wm., 163, 167
Gordon, Lord George, 30f., 182, 232
Grafton, The Duke of, 27, 181
Graves, C. C., 309
Gray, Thos., 27, 40, 62, 64, 66f., 76, 78, 83
Greaves, Wm., 303
Grimsby, 271
Grimshaw, Wm., 109, 118, 148ff., 315ff., 344
Grove, Thos., 354, 356f.
Gurdon, Philip, 253, 269, 353

HALIFAX, 160, 284, 319f.
Hall, Robt., 285, 302
do., Westley, 199
Hallward, John, 252f., 269, 295, 353
Hammond, Wm., 359
Hampson, John, 306
Harmer, John, 255, 292
Harris, Howell, 65, 118, 178
Hart, Rd., 333f.
Hartlepool, 42, 47, 162, 306f.
Hartley, J., 312
do., Rd., 316
do., Thos., 288, 333
Hastings, Lady Elizabeth, 68, 70
do., Lady Margaret, 126, 135
Hatherleigh, 345
Haweis, Thos., 186, 217, 218f., 257, 266, 290, 343f.
Hawker, Robt., 345f.
Hawkstone, 230
Haworth, 150ff., 315f.
Hayes, 248f.
Hayfield, 303
Hazlitt, Wm., 73, 180, 264
Hebrew, Study of, 63, 163, 405
Hell, 152, 388f., 402
Helmsley, 309f.
Herbert, Geo., 106, 410, 415
Herring, Archbishop, 103, 237
Hervey, Jas., 143ff., 159, 190, 215, 288, 290, 348, 451; Writings, 147f., 398ff., 403f. See *Theron and Aspasio.*
do., Thos., 307
Hey, John, 180, 318, 358f.
do., Samuel, 318, 343
do., Wm., 59, 178, 226, 318, 379, 396, 450
Hicks, Wm., 276, 367
High Wycombe, 255, 378
Highworth, 343
Hill, Brian, 170
do., Sir Rd., 129, 168, 203, 232, 243, 347, 355, 422
do., Rowland, 129, 141, 168, 194, 204f., 230ff., 295, 319, 335, 341, 343, 356f., 381, 443; and Cambridge, 231, 253, 284, 360f.
do., Thos., 296f.
Hinxworth, 34, 207, 365
History, Interest in, 60f., 400
Hoadley, Bishop, 99, 163
Hogarth, 80, 82, 195
Honley, 320
Hooker quoted, 18, 32, 92, 105, 133, 197, 212, 265, 312
Hopkins, Bishop, 129f., 410
Horne, Bishop, 237, 270, 354
do., Melville, 294, 299f.
Horsley, Bishop, 180, 380, 406, 455
Hospitals, 54
Hotham, 313f.
Housman, Robt., 282, 301f., 303, 329
Houses, 13, 37, 42, 82f., 339
Huddersfield, 191f., 261, 308, 321ff.
Hull, 308, 312f.
Human Depravity, 206, 386, 397, 456
Hume, Bishop, 186, 266f., 342
do., David, 58, 60, 88, 92, 194
Hunslet, 319

INDEX

Huntingdon, 286
do., Countess of, 43, 119, 136ff., 177, 181, 187f., 201ff., 216ff., 231f., 249f., 253ff., 275, 292f., 301, 304, 312f., 323, 330, 333, 340ff.
Hurd, Bishop, 105, 173, 186
Hutchinsonians, 63, 112, 163
Hutton, Archbishop, 159
Hymns, 81, 254, 283, 302, 359, 373, 414ff., 433, 438

INDIVIDUAL, INTEREST IN THE, 37, 58, 390, 395f., 424f., 432ff.
Industrial Revolution, The, 36f., 292, 298, 307f., 325
Ingham, Benjamin, 124, 126f., 166, 308, 317
Ilkeston, 304
Ilminster, 341f.
Ireland, Jas., 336, 449
Iron Acton, 332
Islington, 239
Itinerancy, 118, 123, 125, 152, 191, 212ff., 276f., 323, 330, 446f.

JACOBITES, THE, 24, 63, 115, 185, 326, 353
Jane, Joseph, 266, 332
Jay, Wm., 341, 391
Jenks, Benjamin, 116, 144
Jesse, Wm. (Hutton), 311
do., Wm. (West Bromwich), 294
Johnson, Samuel, 330
do., (Dr.) Samuel, 18, 39, 41, 52, 61, 62f., 65, 68, 73, 77, 172, 174, 175f., 355f., 367, 376, 403
Jones, Thos. (Clifton Reynes), 255, 354, 356
do., do. (Creaton), 176, 188, 291, 372, 442, 454
do., do. (Southwark), 239f.
Journals, 407ff., 426
Jowett, Benjamin, 302
do., do. (Balliol), 206, 361, 389
do., Hy., 205f.
do., John, 59, 450
do., Jos., 361f.
do., Wm., 450
Junius, Letters of, 29, 73, 181
Justices of the Peace, 28, 41f., 193f.

KANT, 19f., 170
Keats, 369, 397
Keble, John, 99, 121, 161, 415, 437
Keighley, 150, 316
Kenwyn, 157, 345
Kettering, 290f.
Kinchin, Chas., 127, 143, 190, 252, 266
Kineton, 292
King, John, 286
Kingston (Notts), 273f.
do. (Somerset), 231, 341
Kingswood (Bristol), 123, 126, 333
do. School, 304, 334, 376f.
do. (near Wotton), 332

Kippax, 317f.
Knight, Samuel, 160, 320
Knox, Alexander, 433

LAITY, WORK OF, 293, 387, 432, 448ff.
Lakenheath, 118, 269
Lancashire, 325ff.
Lanlivery, 154
Lardner, 111, 179
Latitudinarianism, 91, 101, 358f., 362
Lavington, Bishop, 185f., 343f.
Law, Wm., 79, 93, 103, 109, 121ff., 133, 290. See *Serious Call*.
Lawson, John, 427
Lectureships, 164, 246
Leeds, 159, 317f.
Leicester, 301ff.
Leigh, Dr., 319f.
Letter-writing, 73, 409f.
Lewes, 245, 252
Ley, Wm., 269
Lindsay, Theophilus, 181, 378
Literature, 77ff., 396ff.
Liverpool, 259, 328
Lock Hospital Chapel, 241ff., 432
Locke, John, 20, 56ff., 93, 410
London, 28, 31, 34, 46, 51f., 96, 108f., 144, 164ff., 172, 197, 235ff., 261, 453f.
Long Acre Chapel, 236, 245f.
Lower Classes, 13, 18, 40, 46f., 70, 89, 419ff.
Lowth, Bishop, 63, 188, 223
Luther, 119, 122, 368, 389f., 430
Luton, 283
Lynn (King's), 204, 270

MACAULAY, LORD, 76, 89, 219, 234, 365, 389, 392, 411
do., Zachary, 389, 399
Macclesfield, 304f., 378
Madan, Bishop, 291
do., Martin, 81, 199, 241ff., 269, 275, 291, 304
Maddox, Abraham, 290f.
Madeley, 296ff.
Manchester, 34, 100f., 172, 326f., 392, 397, 417
Manning, Chas., 248
Markfield, 301
Marsden, 308f.
Martyn, Hy., 123, 158, 215, 386, 388, 409, 424, 444f.
Matthews, Jas., 354, 357
Maurice, F. D., 11, 197, 387, 389
Mayor, John, 295
Meeting Houses, 152, 190, 211, 221, 225, 227, 307, 333, 351
Melton Mowbray, 301
Mendips, The, 156, 338, 342
Methodism, 130f., 297; Beginnings, 123f., 333; Growth, 33, 172, 306, 308, 326, 344; Separation, 219ff., 303
Meyrick, Thos., 319f.
Middle Classes, 44ff., 53, 72f., 214, 397f.
Middleton, Erasmus, 130, 182, 240, 354, 357f., 361, 410
Midsomer Norton, 342

462 INDEX

Mill, J. S., 94, 402
Millennium, The, 89, 249, 288
Milner, Isaac, 62, 65, 158, 284, 362f., 399, 443f.
do., John, 327f.
do., Joseph, 272, 283, 312ff., 410ff., 448
Milton, 43, 74, 368, 399, 441f.
Mobs, 30f., 91, 152, 183, 193f., 284, 293f. See Riots.
Monk Wearmouth, 306
Montagu, Lady Mary Wortley, 43, 73f.
Moravians, 118ff., 126, 127, 239, 252, 266, 282, 308f., 333, 359, 452
Morden College, 246, 257
More, Hannah, 156, 243, 334, 336ff., 342, 448; Writings, 337, 404f., 413f.; quoted, 21, 40, 45, 50, 69, 174, 235, 373f.
Murgatroyd, John, 308f.
Music, 80f., 242, 290, 373, 436, 438. See Oratorios.
Mysticism, 93, 121, 129, 288, 333, 433

NANTWICH, 304
Nash, Beau, 144, 339ff.
Nelson, Robt., 90
Newcastle, 47, 306
do., Duke of, 101
Newman, Cardinal, 99, 100, 118, 130, 365, 390, 408, 412, 429
Newton, Sir Isaac, 57, 64, 449
do., John, 38, 151, 182, 213, 240, 257ff., 290, 292, 301, 371, 384ff., 435, 438, 444, 452, 454, 456; Writings, 140, 407ff.
Non-jurors, The, 12, 90, 353
Non-residence, 105f., 174f., 270
North, Lord, 27, 29ff., 179
Northampton, 66, 290, 292, 336
Norwich, 221, 270, 397
Nottingham, 300
Novels, 74ff.
Nowell, Dr., 203, 311

OATHILL, 137, 311
Ogden, —., 320
Olney, 210f., 256ff., 290
do., Hymns, 413, 416f.
Oratorios, 81, 242
Orthodox, The, 89ff., 382f.
Ovington, 268
Oxford, 266f.
do., Methodists, 123ff., 353, 360
do., Movement, 16, 123f., 391, 408, 429f., 454
do., University, 62ff., 166, 353ff.

PADSTOW, 320, 350
Paley, Wm., Archdeacon, 358, 381, 406
Parr, Dr., 357, 404
Pateley Bridge, 311f.
Pater, Walter, 436
Patronage, 65, 97, 101
Pattison, Mark, 59, 61, 95, 367, 418
Pattrick, Geo., 246f.
Pebworth, 331f.

Peckwell, Dr., 273, 453
Penrose, John, 351
do., Romney, 336
Pentycross, Thos., 253f., 360
Perronet, Chas., 251
do., Edward, 251, 416
do., Vincent, 250f.
Pewsey, 342f.
Piers, Hy., 249f.
Pitt, Wm., Earl of Chatham, 26f., 29, 278
do., Wm., 30ff., 95, 357, 359, 451f.
do., Thos., 278
Philanthropy, 56f., 111
Philosophy, 56f., 170, 194
Pluralism, 105f.
Plymouth, 29, 345f.
do. Dock, 194, 345f.
Poetry, 77f., 396f., 412ff.
Pope, Alexander, 41, 77f., 83, 107, 139, 332, 397f., 399
Population, 34, 100, 235
Porson, 66, 171
Portishead, 341
Potter, Archbishop, 119, 142, 187f.
Potton, 275, 282
Powley, Matthew, 243, 290, 320f., 324
Prayer Book, 218, 226, 228, 315, 323, 391f.
do. Meetings, 211f., 352
Preachers, Lay, 14, 208, 212, 221f., 303f., 373
Preaching, 82, 136, 146, 151, 238, 265, 302, 366ff., 431, 436f. See Sermons.
do., French, 108
Preferment, 104f., 161, 176, 454
Priestley, Jos., 58, 110, 179f., 285
Prison Reform, 54, 378, 422
Private Judgment, 91, 390
Proprietory Chapels, 241
Pugh, John, 272f.
Puritans, The, 43, 98, 113, 120f., 212, 215f., 265, 430f., 441f.; Exclusion of, 12, 98
Pusey, Dr., 99, 434

QUAKERS, THE, 111f., 171, 222, 420, 451
Quinton, 331

RAIKES, ROBT., 378f.
Raithby, 272
Ramsden, Sir John, 308, 322
Rauceby, 245, 272, 320
Rawdon, 319
Rawlings, Wm., 158
Reason, Appeal to, 20, 57ff., 170, 397, 401, 438f.
Redruth, 266, 351
Religion, Natural, 91ff., 382
Reynolds, Sir Joshua, 38, 53, 82, 427
Richardson, John, 315f.
do., Samuel, 42, 44, 55, 72ff., 77, 86, 105, 148, 375
do., Wm., 210, 315, 380, 448
Riland, John, 243, 293, 323f., 444
Riots, 30f., 47, 182, 231, 236, 293
Robinson, Robt., 283, 285
do., Thos., 283, 287, 302f., 343, 360

INDEX 463

Rochdale, 149, 372
Roche, 350
Rogers, Jacob, 282
Romaine, Wm., 59, 130, 137, 145, 161ff., 200, 211, 236f., 251f., 268, 275, 296, 304, 306f., 318f., 398, 408, 442, 446; Writings, 163, 168, 386; quoted, 114, 197, 277, 375, 379, 383, 386
Roman Catholicism, 85, 114f., 182, 185f., 195, 219, 228, 326, 410f., 435
Romantic Movement, 78, 396f., 457
Rouquet, Jas., 335
Rousseau, 94, 374
Routh, Martin, 99
Rowlands, Daniel, 118, 291
Royston, 289
Rural Life, 14, 35ff., 41, 53, 104, 173, 260f.
Ruskin, 12, 72, 81, 376, 435f.
Ryland, John, 146

SACRAMENTS, 228f., 392ff.
St. Agnes, 350, 352
St. Edmund Hall Case, 353ff.
St. Gennys, 348f.
St. Gluvias, 351
St. Ives, 351
St. Neots, 286
Salford, 128, 327
Salters' Hall Conference, 113f.
Sancreed, 351
Sandemanians, 126f., 308
Scarborough, 49, 309f.
Scepticism, 58, 60, 85ff., 170ff., 354, 457
Schools, Charity, 71
do., Grammar, 63, 70, 312
do., Private, 68f., 70, 375
do., Public, 66ff., 364
Science, Natural, 57f., 62, 64, 180, 396, 452
Scott, Thos., 59f., 122f., 131, 148, 211f., 230, 244, 254f., 263ff., 291, 376, 450; Writings, 405f., 408
do., Sir Walter, 55, 76f., 339
Seagrave, Robt., 359
Secker, Archbishop, 102, 110, 131, 187, 266
Seizures, 12f., 183, 276ff.
Sellon, Walter, 203, 294, 301, 304
Serious Call to a Devout and Holy Life, A, 121ff., 159, 265
Sermons, 107f., 156f., 176, 234, 242, 366ff., 371, 400f., 439
Servants, Domestic, 39, 44, 86, 88, 105, 421
Seward Family, 294
Shaftesbury, Lord, 72, 87f., 258
Shawbury, 295
Sheffield, 317
Shelley, 235, 388, 410
Sheridan, 79f., 341
Sherlock, Bishop, 237
Shipman, Jos., 354, 357
Shirley, Lady Fanny, 144ff., 148, 288
do., Walter, 200f., 203, 216
Shoreditch, 246
Shoreham, 86, 250f.
Shrewsbury, 295f.
Sidney, Edwin, 158, 169, 407

Simeon, Chas., 147, 156f., 207, 212, 267, 278, 283f., 290, 329, 363ff., 391f., 409f., 424, 433, 439f., 444, 456
Simpson, David, 304f., 360, 378
do., John, 127
Slaithwaite, 308f., 323f., 379
Slavery, 259, 414, 420ff., 451ff.
Smith, John, 304
Smollett, 49, 75, 77, 103, 194, 339
Smyth, Edward, 221
Societies, Religious, 144, 157, 191f., 372f., 425
Society for Promoting Christian Knowledge, 71, 128, 452f.
do. for the Propagation of the Gospel, 452f.
do. for the Reformation of Manners, 53f.
Southey, 67, 110, 263, 266, 281
Southwark, 232, 239f., 241
Sowerby, 320
Spectator, The, 53, 73, 108f., 399
Spencer, Edward, 342
Spilsby, 272
Spitalfields, 118, 235, 238
Stanwix, 307
Stapleford, 274
Staveley, 312
Steele, Rd., 43, 75, 87, 106f.
Stephen, Sir Jas., 134, 288, 382f., 418
Sterne, 40, 56, 75ff., 105, 132
Stillingfleet, Bishop, 223, 314
do., Edward, 293f., 314, 380
do., Jas. (Hotham), 294f., 314, 401
do., do. (Oxford), 353
Stinchcombe, 332
Stock Harward, 268
Stock, Thos., 331, 378
Stonehouse, Geo., 239
Stonhouse, Sir Jas., 132, 296, 335f., 343
Storry, Robt., 160, 192, 268f., 315
Study, Need for, 178, 192, 268f., 315
Sunday Observance, 88, 150f., 376, 443
do. Schools, 255, 306, 327, 378ff.
Sunderland, 306
Superstition, 89f., 150
Surrey Chapel, 230, 232f.
Swedenborg, 288, 327
Swift, Dean, 21, 73, 102, 108
Symes, Rd., 335

TALBOT, WM., 132, 252, 267, 292
Talland, 154
Tawstock, 345
Taylor, Samuel, 331
do., Wm., 217f.
Thackeray, 26, 139, 241
Theatres, 78ff., 195, 414, 442. See Drama.
Theron and Aspasio, 144f., 147f., 265, 288, 302, 403f.
Thomson, Geo., 144, 345, 348f.
Thornton, Hy., 13, 244, 444, 449f.
do., John, 160, 217, 240, 246, 277, 281, 311, 420, 437, 449
Thorold Family, 273
Tillotson, Archbishop, 79, 90ff., 121
Tiverton, 86
Todmorden, 149, 316, 325

INDEX

Toplady, A. M., 133, 203ff., 344, 346ff., 416
Towns, 34ff., 45, 308, 322; Religion in, 99f., 173, 453f.
Townsend, Jos., 215, 340, 343, 361, 396, 405
Trade, Growth of, 38f., 44f.; Contempt for, 39, 174, 354
Trelawney, Sir Harry, 195, 341
Tresmere, 349
Trevecca College, 136f., 177f., 200, 218, 253f., 272, 293, 312f., 330, 357
Trimmer, Mrs., 380
Trowbridge, 175
Truro, 154ff., 266, 345, 347, 372
Tucker, Dean, 189, 334
Tunbridge Wells, 249f., 341
Turner, John, 350
Tyler, Wm., 272

UNDERBARROW, 307
Unitarianism, 112ff., 171, 179ff., 285, 310, 326
Universities, 61ff., 353ff. See Cambridge, Oxford.
Unwin, Mary (Mrs.), 263
do., Wm., 268, 283, 305, 413
Uxbridge, 248f.

VENN, EDWARD, 172
do., Hy., 74f., 81, 122, 128, 131, 136ff., 153, 178, 191f., 205, 209f., 215, 230, 243, 252, 261, 278f., 286ff., 309f., 315, 321ff., 343, 360f., 364f., 376; quoted, 146, 254, 284, 311, 453f.; Writings, 402f., 405. See *The Complete Duty of Man*.
do., John, 131, 270, 278, 286, 302, 363
do., Rd., 189f., 238f., 321
Verbal Inspiration, 385f.
Vivian, Thos., 133f., 345, 377
Voltaire, 45, 94, 300, 457
Vowler, J., 350, 352

WAKEFIELD, 321
Walker, Samuel, 132, 154ff., 166, 191, 211, 320, 333, 335, 347, 350ff., 377, 385f., 390ff., 400, 454, 456
Wallingford, 253f.
Walpole, Horace, 25, 26f., 35, 46, 50, 51, 73, 76, 88, 121, 139, 236, 359, 370
do., Sir Robt., 23, 25ff.
Warburton, Bishop, 50, 92, 111, 115, 120, 186, 332, 382
Warrington, 328f.
Warwick, 292
Watson, Bishop, 62, 87, 98
Watts, Isaac, 110, 146, 257, 415
Wednesbury, 204, 293
Week St. Mary, 350
Welby, 273
Wellington (Somerset), 341
Wensley, 309
Wesley, Chas., 125, 200, 239, 248f., 252, 294, 315, 317, 330f., 317, 330f., 339, 344, 392; Churchmanship, 125, 153, 192, 221,
225, 300, 303; Hymns, 237, 239, 392, 416f.; quoted, 24 and *passim*
do., John, quoted or referred to, 24, 28, 29f., and *passim*; Churchmanship, 129, 217, 227ff.; and Lady Huntingdon, 136, 138, 201; and Whitefield, 125, 198f., 201
do., Martha, 199
do., Mary, 272
do., Samuel, 113, 213
do., do., junior, 213
do., Susanna, 113, 129
West Bromwich, 293f.
West Harptree, 335
Westcote, 331
Westminster School, 63, 67f., 346
Weston Favell, 143ff.
do. Underwood, 264
do., Wm., 331
Whiston, Wm., 89, 101, 115
White, Gilbert, 176
Whitechapel (Yorks), 316, 321
Whitefield, Geo., 90, 119f., 122, 125f., 135ff., 144, 187, 190, 193, 195, 198f., 245, 294, 326, 330, 343f., 450; Preaching, 125, 138f., 366f.; Churchmanship, 217, 382
Whitehaven, 307
Whitelambe, John, 271
Whittingham, Rd., 282
Whole Duty of Man, The, 364, 402
Wickham, 307
Wilberforce, Wm., 13, 45, 68f., 70, 90, 176, 178, 181, 211, 243f., 246, 268, 270, 304, 312ff., 336, 338, 357f., 363, 393f., 399, 422ff., 431, 449, 451f.
Wilkes, John, 28
Williams, Thos., 255
Wills, Bishop, 335
do., Thos., 141, 217f., 243, 254, 350f.
Wilson, Benjamin, 321
do., Bishop, 119, 364
do., Daniel, 94, 161, 393f., 408, 448
do., Thos., 309, 324f., 379
Winchester, 252
Winteringham, 159ff., 268
Winwick, 288
Wisbech, 283
Wolverhampton, 294
Women, Position of, 43f., 50, 134f., 222
do. Preachers, 221f.
Woodd, Basil, 246
Woodforde, Parson, 80, 174, 373
Woolston, Thos., 88
Worcester, 294, 331
Wordsworth, Wm., 37, 78, 270, 407
Wotton, 128
Wrestlingworth, 34, 276
Wroot, 271

YELLING, 286, 323, 360f.
York, 103, 308, 314f., 319
Yorkshire, 48, 307ff.
Young, Edward, 78, 388

ZINZENDORF, COUNT, 118ff.

www.ingramcontent.com/pod-product-compliance
Lightning Source LLC
Chambersburg PA
CBHW071223290426
44108CB00013B/1267